Praise for *Ma Chère Maman – Mon Cher Enfant*

Lucien Durosoir is not nearly as well-known as a composer in the English-speaking world as he should be. In the lyricism and sheer beauty of his music, he can remind the listener of Edward Elgar. But unlike Elgar, Durosoir was young enough to serve in the trenches of the Great War. Like millions of his comrades, he was also a prolific letter writer. The letters between him and his mother, Louise, are elegantly translated and wonderfully presented here. They represent a rich tapestry of the grim circumstances in and out of the trenches of the Great War. They also highlight strategies of survival, physical and emotional, but also romantic. Elizabeth Schoonmaker Auld has done us a great service by making these letters available. They can only increase our admiration for this great composer and exemplary survivor of this horrible conflict.

Leonard V. Smith, Frederick B. Artz Professor of History, Oberlin College

This highly readable, idiomatic translation of the Durosoir letter collection provides an important first-person perspective of life at the front, the perspective of a mature, well-educated man whose talent placed him in an unusual position. We see the evolving relationship between a mother and son, the optimism turned to frustration as the war drags on. The letters tell a story, day to day, that is comic, poignant, insightful.

Joseph T. Acquisto, Professor of French, University of Vermont

Lucien Durosoir's extended correspondence with his mother reveals his exceptional courage and leadership as a soldier, as well as his ingenuity in finding ways to make music amidst the deprivations of war. Via his vivid descriptive writing, and Elizabeth Auld's superb translation, we experience the immediacy of war through the eyes (and ears) of a mature and artistic spirit.

Linda Laurent, Professor Emerita of Music, Central Connecticut State University

A Blackwater Press book

First published in Great Britain and the United States of America by Blackwater Press, LLC

Copyright © Elizabeth Schoonmaker Auld, 2022

Printed and bound in Canada by Imprimerie Gauvin

Library of Congress Control Number: 2022941238

ISBN 978-1-7357747-7-0 (paperback)

Cover design by Eilidh Muldoon

Blackwater Press
120 Capitol Street
Charleston, WV 25301
United States

www.blackwaterpress.com

Find this book's gallery at:
blackwaterpress.com/durosoir

FSC
www.fsc.org

MIX
Paper
FSC® C100212

Ma Chère Maman – Mon Cher Enfant

The letters of Lucien and Louise Durosoir, 1914-1919

Edited and translated by
ELIZABETH SCHOONMAKER AULD

Contents

To Luc

Foreword

My father was 57 years old when I was born, and I was only 19 when he died—not much time really but enough to get to know him. I knew my grandmother only by her reputation. As a boy, I was always curious, and asked a lot of questions and so, in that short time, I learned much about him and his life, but there was more to discover.

The Great War was distant to me as a young boy living through the Nazi occupation. Still, my child's brain was aware of something big, unusual, and very difficult in my father's past. When I was young, a farmworker used to come to work in our garden. The only subject that he and my father had in common was their wartime experience. As different as they were, that topic brought them together. I was fascinated by the stories they told. Sometimes I dug around in a little chest containing pictures from that time. When I asked my father about them, he scolded me: those were not to be discussed, they were private. One day, his friend Henri Magne came to visit, and I heard him say to my father, "You have all your letters, why don't you publish them?" My father replied, "I have no desire to open that correspondence, to relive that period."

Those words followed me, unconsciously, throughout my life and, at times, I felt a deep need to know what was in the letters. Eventually, many years later, something finally pushed me to open the closets and look into the boxes within. There I found my father's wartime letters along with his music scores, his mother's letters, and many other documents and pieces of correspondence. I turned first, avidly, to my father's letters. Astounded by how rich they were, I resolved to transcribe them in their entirety, resulting in some nine hundred densely typed pages. In 2005, I published selections from Lucien Durosoir's letters, adding the notebooks of his wartime companion Maurice Maréchal.[1]

---

[1] Luc Durosoir, *Deux Musiciens dans la Grande Guerre* (Paris: Editions Tallandier: 2005).

Then there was my grandmother, Louise, and her letters. She wrote more letters, more often, and her letters were always long. They remained untranscribed until my dear friend and editor of this volume urged me to get to work on them. I had thought them uninteresting, repetitive, filled-with lists and complaints. To my delight, I discovered my grandmother to be quite a remarkable person—strong, clever, intelligent. Though not young and not in particularly good health—she suffered from a form of rheumatism and frequent colds that went into her lungs—her real pain was not physical. She suffered enormously during the war, differently from her son, but no less painfully. Lonely, separated from her only child, worried, filled with uncertainty, she was left alone to deal with their finances and manage the household. And, unlike Lucien, she was not surrounded by friends.

The conversations that Lucien and Louise had through their letters were their mutual source of sanity and, in a sense, a way for them to survive. Reading them allowed me the rare privilege of knowing the two of them, sometimes quite intimately.

My father loved to write—he wrote well and easily. His style is elegant, varied, powerful, and filled with metaphor—all abundantly evident in his letters. He might well have chosen to write about the war years as a way of freeing himself from the trauma, from the way his view of life was changed by his experiences. But he didn't...at least not in words.

That desire to write, the need to write, meshed with his growing desire to compose music. In his musical creations, my father, whose career as a violinist was stolen by the war, found a way to prove to himself that, at age 41, he wasn't finished. One might expect that, without the war, my father would have been a different composer, one more in line with the end of French romanticism. But living through the war, in the midst of such unimaginable violence, altered him. Moreover, the many hours he spent discussing music with the composer André Caplet during the war helped form his own idea of what his music might be like.

I believe that their conversations, their discussions at the front, in the pigeon loft at Suippes, made my father the composer we know. He used to say that his music would not be understood by his contemporaries; I believe he truly composed for himself, to say what he had to say, and that he had no interest in having others hear it, misunderstand it, or criticize it.

The next step then, after the letters, was his music. With the invaluable help of my wife, Georgie, together we explored and edited the scores. They are now all published and all forty of his works have been recorded. His story, in his unique musical language, is finally being heard.

I have finished everything I needed to do. The publication of his music doesn't contradict his wishes. He never said that he didn't want his music played, just that it was too soon to bring it to life during his lifetime. In the course of nearly twenty years, I have brought out of nothing a story dear to my heart. I take great satisfaction in the successful completion of my work.

The publication of this book, bringing the story of Lucien and Louise Durosoir to a new audience, gives me great pride. It is something I never even dreamed of.

Luc Durosoir
Bélus, May 2021

Introduction

I first heard about Lucien Durosoir from his son, Luc, over dinner in Paris some fifteen years ago. Luc's enthusiasm for his father's experiences and work was contagious. When a selection of his letters appeared in French in 2005, I had trouble putting the book down.

My suggestion to Luc of an English translation was welcomed eagerly; the French publisher agreed. I began to translate the original volume. The project took a new shape when I learned that the family also possessed his mother's letters.

The result is a book that resembles very little the one I originally translated. It includes many more of Lucien's letters and a large selection of those written by Louise. Lucien's letters had all been transcribed, but Louise's existed only in their original handwritten form. The transcription of the thousands of pages— she wrote more often and her letters were always long—was an enormous task. Louise saved all the letters Lucien wrote and, in March 1915, Lucien started sending his mother's letters back to her to be saved. The entirety of the letters, originals and transcriptions, are now filed, page by page, in binders in the Durosoir family archive.

Lucien made every effort to write to his mother at least daily. The letters are written on both sides of paper that is about six inches by nine inches, in careful, small script. Louise wrote even more often, frequently using the sides and top of the sheet to finish what she wanted to say. Usually two pages long, with no paragraphs to save space, the sudden changes of topic sometimes shock as they jump from the everyday to the tragic. The letters replaced the face-to-face conversations these two had always had.

A brief biography of Lucien and Louise will serve as a useful backdrop to what follows. Lucien Durosoir was born December 5, 1878, to Louise Marie Durosoir and Léon Durosoir. Louise was the daughter and only child of successful vegetable growers and merchants living in St. Mandé and Vincennes, suburbs on the eastern edge of Paris. Léon too was an only child, born into a distinguished family that included many military officers, including one who served under Napoleon. Léon chose not to pursue a military career but, instead, worked in business. After their marriage, the Durosoirs lived in Boulogne, on the opposite side of Paris. In 1890, Léon died from pneumonia after saving the lives of two children from drowning in an icy lake in the Bois de Boulogne. Louise and young Lucien were left dependent on Léon's wealthy stepfather. A lover of art and music, Louise made sure to expose her son to all that Paris had to offer.

After a concert by the famous violin virtuoso Pablo de Sarasate, a young Lucien declared he would be a violinist. He studied privately from age 8 to 16 when he was accepted to the Conservatoire Supérieur in Paris, only to be expelled six months later.

Lucien began his career in 1898 as first violin in the Orchestre Colonne.[2] Between 1899 and 1901, Lucien studied violin in Frankfurt. For the next fourteen years, Lucien played concerts throughout France and Europe— including appearances in Berlin, Vienna, Moscow, Munich, Leipzig, Budapest, Dresden, Geneva, and Prague. He is best remembered for giving the premier performances to a new audience of a number of great works. In 1901, he gave the Paris premier of Richard Strauss's Violin Concerto in D minor and, in 1903, of the Brahms Violin Concerto in D Major. In 1910, Lucien played the Viennese première of Fauré's Sonata in A Major for Violin and Piano. Critics in Vienna referred to him as "the violin virtuoso Mr. Lucien Durosoir"and praised his interpretations:

> In this program, which included the Sonata in A minor for solo violin by J. S. Bach, concertos by Viotti, and Saint-Saëns, the artist proved that he is not only a virtuoso of phenomenal qualities, but also an accomplished musician. In his playing of Bach's Sonata, whose grandiose difficulties seem to disappear under his bow, Mr. Durosoir presents himself as a serious musician who, with his noble, spirited playing, relays the beauty of Bach's music to the listeners.[3]

By 1914, he and his mother regularly divided their time between their primary residences in Brittany and Vincennes. Louise inherited a considerable fortune from her parents which included a number of rental properties, in Vincennes, Paris, and Boulogne. The income from the properties and interest from investments allowed them to live comfortably and gave Lucien the freedom to pursue his career without worrying about making money to live on. Lucien served as an ordinary, second-class soldier, moving from the rear to the trenches, to stretcher bearer, to musician, to secretary, to pigeon keeper. He never was far

[2] The Orchestre Colonne was founded in 1873 by Edouard Colonne.
[3] Der Morgen Wiener Mondagblatt, 1909-1910, Durosoir family archives.

from his violin. Where it took him and what he did with it form the backbone of his war story and the letters.

Lucien returned home early in 1919. In addition to working to regain his violin technique, he began composing. His dream of a career in the United States ended when his frail mother sustained an accident which rendered her an invalid. In 1926 he settled with his mother in Bélus, a small town in southwest France. Between 1919 and 1935 he composed approximately 30 pieces of chamber music, and by 1950 a total of 41 works. These timeless works are only now beginning to receive the respect and attention they deserve.

Louise died in 1934. The following year, Lucien married Hortense Catcharry, a young woman from Bélus. Their son, Luc, was born in 1936, and daughter Solange in 1937. During the Nazi occupation their house served, for a time, as an infirmary for German soldiers. Lucien hid his violin, his music, and his fluency in German. After 1945, the end of World War Two, he returned to composing. His last piece was written in 1950.

He died in 1955, on his 77th birthday.

Editorial Treatment

It was impossible to present the letters in their entirety: they are too long, there are too many, they are often repetitive. I have eliminated many, and made significant cuts to others, with a goal of maintaining the continuity of the story. The letters are always dated, maintaining the date formats used by each person: for Lucien, numeric dates, for Louise, the name of the month and often the day of the week. They both wrote daily as often as possible; the absence of a date does not mean there was no letter that day. I have left numbers as they were: sometimes spelled out, sometimes numerical. Passages cut are indicated by [...]. I have inserted paragraph breaks for ease and better flow. Louise starts every letter with *mon cher enfant*: my dear child. Her letters, which begin in March 1915, usually end with the expression *je t'embrasse*, which equates to closing by saying "love," and often she wishes him good health. Lucien starts his letters with *ma chère Maman, ma petite Maman, ma petite minou*; my dear mother, my dear little mother, or my dear little kitten. Almost all of these expressions have been cut.

How to present the two sets of letters in a fashion that maintained the conversational aspect without confusing the reader presented a challenge. I have opted, when possible, to place Louise's letter after the one just received from Lucien. This inevitably leads to some confusion in who knew what when. For this, I apologize and rely on you, the reader, to understand.

Throughout, the reader will find reference to home leave. Soldiers were granted about a week of leave on a regular schedule, officially three or four times a year; this explains the reference to "my turn," or the third or the fourth turn. The leave gave Lucien time to see his mother and friends. One would like to have had a microphone on the wall to capture their discussions; Lucien was free to talk about things he couldn't describe in his letters. We have only the letters after each home leave as clues to their conversations.

This translation aims to keep as much of the flavor of the French as possible. I use regularly a number of French terms, italicized, which are defined in the

Glossary. Exceptionally, Lucien headed his letters with a location, indicating his position or status. These headings are kept; they are original to the letters.

The letters speak often about pictures, or illustrations. I strongly urge the reader to consult this book's gallery on the Blackwater website (blackwaterpress. com/durosoir) to benefit from the wonderful trove of pictures from the Durosoir archive. In addition to the pictures, the gallery presents essays that speak to Lucien's career as a violinist and to his compositions, as well as an essay about the post war years by his wife. These materials will enrich your understanding of Lucien Durosoir and merit your attention.

Each year is preceded by a brief historical note, written to put the letters for that year in context. These sections do not pretend to be a history of the war. They represent my personal choices from the events of that year.

This has been a work of passion and love. I am now part of the Durosoir family: Lucien and Louise are more familiar to me than my own grandparents. It has also been an unexpected education in more ways than I can enumerate here. There are a great many first-person descriptions of the horrors of the First World War. This book paints a broader story while capturing the enormous folly of war. It is in that spirit that I present it.

Elizabeth Schoonmaker Auld
Paris, 2022

Louise and Lucien, circa 1895

Lucien: composer and soldier

1914

The assassination of Archduke Franz Ferdinand on June 28, 1914, the event that unleashed World War I, was the final straw in the unrest building up in eastern Europe. Power struggles and alliances in that unstable part of Europe led to a situation in the summer of 1914 which saw Germany allied with the Austro-Hungarians and France and England allied with Russia.

Before the crisis at the end of June, General Helmuth von Moltke, Chief of the German General Staff, had written: "If only things would finally boil over—we are ready; the sooner the better."[4] The Franco-Prussian war, the last time France faced Germany, in 1870-71, had resulted in the loss of Alsace and Lorraine to Germany and a serious blow to French morale. While Germany used the following years to build up military and industrial might and prepare for another attempt at domination of Europe, France focused on strengthening her defenses. This included improving logistics, especially railways for troop deployment.[5]

The weeks following the assassination in Sarajevo saw the two sides maneuvering, preparing for war, trying to prevent it, and waiting for the Austrians to decide what they wanted to do. Finally, Austria declared war on Serbia on July 28; on August 1 Germany mobilized its troops and declared war on Russia; France issued a general mobilization order on August 2; that night Germany moved troops into Luxembourg in preparation for an entry into Belgium; Germany declared war on France on August 3; Great Britain was at war by midnight on August 4.

All this was happening while Lucien Durosoir and his mother were quietly enjoying the tiny seaside town of Port Lazo, in Brittany, planning for a fall concert season. It is unlikely, however, that they were unaware of what was happening.

---

[4] H. von Moltke; cited in Peter Hart, *The Great War: A Combat History of the First World War*, (Oxford: Oxford University Press, 2013), 25-26.

[5] Hart, *The Great War*, 13-15.

Newspapers reached everyone. In the end, war proved to be unavoidable, and Lucien Durosoir found himself in a cattle car on his way to the unknown.

At the start of the war, because of his age, Lucien was part of a reserve unit (territorial) and was thus spared the bloody first part of the war.[6] His time was spent in training exercises, forced marches, supply duties and, when he could find an instrument, playing in church and for the local people. He arrived at the front, entering the trenches with soldiers ten to fifteen years younger than he, in November 1914.

While Lucien and his fellow territorials, posted near Cherbourg,[7] were getting in shape by doing long marches, watching the coastline, and becoming increasingly bored, the story was very different in the area between France and Germany. Both the German and French armies started out planning on a war of movement, attacks and counterattacks, each army hoping to take whatever territory would make for a swift victory. The British needed time to build an army and get their forces in place in France; this meant that the French were alone in holding off Germany.

One of the greatest, perhaps the greatest, battle of the war, the Battle of the Marne, exemplifies French determination and was a strategic triumph.[8] General Joffre's order of the day is telling:

> We are about to engage in a battle on which the fate of our country depends and it is important to remind all ranks that the moment has passed for looking to the rear; all our efforts must be directed to attacking and driving back the enemy. Troops that can advance no farther must, at any price, hold on to the ground they have conquered and die on the spot rather than give way. Under the circumstances which face us, no act of weakness can be tolerated.[9]

In that battle and others during this war of movement, the French lost some of their best officers and soldiers.[10]

This last period of the war of movement, sometimes called the Race to the Sea, consisted of attempts by both sides to outflank each other on the north and break through the enemy line. The fighting centered around the Belgian

---

[6] The *Armée territoriale* was created in 1872 as a military reserve, made up of men from age 34 to 49, deemed too old and no longer well enough trained to join an active regiment. Over time, they all were moved to the fighting units. Lucien was officially a *territorial* until the end of the war, but he moved to the fighting line in November 1914.

[7] Important port city at the tip of the Cotentin Peninsula, in Normandy (Département de la Manche).

[8] Hart, *The Great War*, 87.

[9] General Joseph Jacques Césaire Joffre, Commander in Chief of French forces from 1914 to 1916, cited in Hart, *The Great War*, 66. He was affectionately called *grand-père* by the soldiers.

[10] A. J. P. Taylor, *The First World War, An Illustrated History*, (New York: Penguin Books, 1966) 25.

city of Ypres. The British and French held off the Germans and the trenches reached across Europe to the North Sea.[11] A young French marine described the experience thus:

> The German artillery is quite remarkable. The fire of the heavy guns is admirably precise and well regulated. The other day, I saw six shell craters in a 30-meter diameter circle; and these shells came from more than 7,000 meters away. But however accurate their fire, a trench gives shelter untouchable by artillery. Well dug-in infantry can only be dislodged by infantry, and properly by enemy bayonets. [...] our trenches are really just holes in the ground, sited at random where men get precarious rest on slippery clay, covered with a thin bed of straw.[12]

Trench warfare, to last four long years, had begun. With the establishment of the front from Switzerland to the North Sea, the war of trenches became the pattern, "a war of deadlock and prolonged battering which seemed as if it might go on indefinitely."[13] Men were left to survive or not, fighting in battles to win ground that was quickly taken back by the enemy. They were forced to endure the boredom, fear, filth and extreme temperatures of living in what were essentially ditches. No one asked what the war was about. Taylor argues that there was no clear aim to the war other than for the Germans to win, and the Allies to not lose.[14]

[11] Hart, *The Great War*, 77.
[12] Hart, *The Great War*, 78.
[13] Taylor, *The First World War*, 47.
[14] Taylor, *The First World War*, 67.

The Letters

8/4/1914.

Dear Maman, I arrived in Caen Tuesday about 9 a.m. after a long and uncomfortable trip. Unbelievable enthusiasm everywhere, no news yet other than that Belgium's neutrality has been violated and Germany has declared war on Belgium.[15] They will find themselves all alone against Europe. Based on what they are telling us, our regiment, the 23rd territorial, leaves tomorrow, Wednesday, at 6 a.m. for Cherbourg. We will be spread out all along the coast to prevent any possible landings. Excuse my handwriting, I'm writing on the door of an armoire. […]

8/5/1914.

[…] Gonneville. […] We left Caen Wednesday morning; reveille at 2 a.m. (rather early!). We slept in a teachers' training school, a magnificent building with a lovely park. Departure for Cherbourg in cattle cars. Along the way, one fellow developed DTs; it took six men to hold this crazy fellow down, you can imagine how much fun that was! Off the train in Cherbourg, 18 more kilometers to get to this little village where we will be protecting defensive installations and gasoline supplies for the submarines. Will we be staying here? No one knows anything: if things continue as they are right now, we will not be of much use here.

It seems the Germans also invaded Holland: they now have against them Belgium, Holland, and England. According to official information, the English landed 100,000 men in Dunkirk, Boulogne, and Le Havre. In the Balkans there are the Russians. Japan is calling up its navy and may send men. It's all too much, they are done for, that is everyone's opinion. More news: the Mediterranean fleet sank the *Panthère* and the *Breslau*.[16] No news from the ground, it's all about the mobilization. Thirty-thousand men will leave from Caen and 28,000 from Falaise—now that's an army! […] We are sleeping on the floor and eating dry bread, at least so far. […]

---

[15] Alfred von Schlieffen (1833-1913). The Germans invaded Belgium in the first days of August, following the Schlieffen plan. Schlieffen planned for Germany to use Belgium as a funnel into France; the short frontier between France and Germany was heavily fortified on both sides. Taylor, *The First World War,* 20-21.

[16] This has to be false news. The two German battlecruisers that were in the Mediterranean were the larger *Goeben* and smaller *Breslau*. The two ships tried to interfere with French troop convoys from North Africa to Marseille. Through a series of missteps by the British and French, they escaped and made it back through the Dardanelles. Hart, *La Grande Guerre,* 168.

It's been raining continuously since last night and the countryside around us is becoming a swamp. […] They are making us do maneuvers, jumping over and climbing walls; this is not to the taste of many of the reservists who are out of condition for such exercise. I did well to have done Swedish gymnastics.

One of my friends, M. Balembois, is assistant director at the Louvre,[17] and another, M. Dumont, a finisher for Christofle, two really good fellows. The supply corps is certainly not trying to spoil us; fortunately, in this region with its wonderful farms, it's not rare to find farmers with 30 cows. We have excellent butter, milk, and cream. Exportations have been suspended so butter costs 10 sous a pound and eggs 26 sous a dozen.

The official news is very good for us: it appears that Berlin sent home the English ambassador. Hearing that, England immediately attacked the German fleet which, they say, is in really bad shape. Switzerland, invaded also, is coming on line.[18] Our troops came back from Alsace after really tough fighting. There is general enthusiasm and we are mostly complaining about being so far away from the action. The opinion of the officers is that the Germans will not hold out long under these conditions. […]

8/8/1914.

We made a hard 20-kilometer march to Cap Lévy, along a route between Barfleur and Cherbourg. We were right next to the sea, we could breathe the sea air, but sadly we could not go in the water, although we rather needed to. Today I gave my laundry to the owner of a restaurant where we've eaten occasionally; I'll have it back tomorrow. It was unbelievably filthy. […]

The country here is quite pretty and we are starting to get used to our new life. […]

8/9/1914.

[…] The past two days we've been guarding the roads night and day, no one can pass without a document signed by the mayor that affirms his identity. It's

[17] The Louvre was a department store across from the palace and museum. Department stores flourished in nineteenth-century Paris, starting with the Bon Marché, the Louvre, Au Printemps, and La Samaritaine. Alfred Fierro, *Histoire de Paris illustrée* (Le Pérégrinateur: Toulouse, 2010) 140.

[18] Again, false news: Switzerland was never invaded, and maintained its neutrality throughout the war. Louise also writes about this in January 1917. There were no reporters at the front to send the truth back to the newspapers. The military had every interest in telling the soldiers how well things were going, to keep up morale. Volumes have been written about propaganda from the front, in this and more recent wars, notably the Vietnam conflict.

rather funny to see how scared the people are when they hear "halt" and find themselves at the end of a bayonet.

This is essentially a milk producing area. Usually the milk is collected by companies from Cherbourg who turn it into butter and cheese and distribute it, especially to England. At this time, all traffic is suspended; as a result, butter is very cheap, from 10 to 15 sous a pound. And what butter it is!

As far as news, you may already know of the crushing defeat of the Germans at the gates of Liège which they have not yet been able to capture. The German request for a 24-hour truce will, I think, get cannon fire in response. [...]

8/10/1914.

[...] Yesterday, Sunday afternoon, we took a walk to a spot 3 kilometers from Gonneville where there is a magnificent property by the name of *La Filature* (because there used to be a spinning factory, now abandoned). Mme Lelong, the owner of the café where we take some meals to supplement our rations, gave us a suitcase which belonged to the two sons of the house who left a few days ago for the border. We were greeted in the most gracious way. We visited the lovely wooded property, took a walk along a large lake where the owners cultivate trout. We even got to take six as a sample, which we ate that evening. [...]

The victory of the English navy might hasten our departure; I don't know what there would be to do here. Seventeen German ships sunk and 7 for the English. According to that same news report we have entered Mulhouse and Alsace is celebrating. The Belgians have been totally admirable; the Germans have 25,000 dead. The Germans expected to cut across Belgium as easily as a knife cuts through butter. They were much mistaken as in many other things, and now the French army is in Belgium. We'll make a serious push toward Cologne along the Rhine valley, take Alsace from the other side and make the Germans decamp even faster. They seem to be in a bad position and I don't think this will last long. The German army doesn't seem to have, this time, either the enthusiasm or the confidence. Here the situation is the opposite: we are almost disappointed at our inaction, although guarding gasoline supplies is necessary. We did shoot at some suspicious guys during the night. [...]

8/11/1914.

[...] There are, in Cherbourg and the surrounding area, over 80,000 men under the command of General Marion. [...] Yesterday we walked 20 kilometers; really painful in this heat. Up to now, I'm lucky to have no problems with my feet, they are quickly getting tougher, but the shoes I brought are about done for. The soles are fine but the uppers are falling apart. Fortunately, I chose a totally new pair of *brodequins* rather than some leisure shoes. [...]

It's now official that French troops are in Colmar and the Germans are on the run, especially faced with the bayonet. I hope it won't be long before I see Port Lazo again. The most painful part here is the near complete lack of hygiene. We look a bit like drunken bums. But one gets used to everything [...]

8/13/1914.

[...] We are organizing a concert Saturday at the chateau of Mme de Chivrey, for the benefit of the Red Cross. I will probably go to Cherbourg today, by car, to get some instruments.

I hope you are eating as you should and finding what you need. As for us, we are not doing too badly. Aside from potatoes there are no vegetables, the meat is of good quality. It is 24 sous for a nice piece.[19] [...] We march daily more and more; that is training us to tolerate the fatigue of military life. Lots of us are catching colds, getting dysentery, etc. So far, I am untouched by all this despite terrible sleeping conditions: we sleep in a stable on a rather thin bed of straw, basically on hard ground. I have not taken my clothes off since leaving home, I'd be too cold at night. [...]

8/14/1914.

[...] Life here is rather monotonous and most of the soldiers are bored. We have a concert scheduled for Saturday August 15. Yesterday, I was in Cherbourg with several buddies to get the things we need. Mme Magne,[20] owner of a music and piano store, loaned me a violin, a real dud worth 40 francs and with which I obviously am managing as well as possible. [...] Yesterday I practiced about an hour. My hand, which has gotten stiff because of not playing, is bothering me a bit. [...] The piano for the concert, provided by Mme Chivrey, is *une vraie casserole.*[21] The wife of the army doctor intends to be our accompanist; that will certainly be laughable for I've heard her play! [...] Cherbourg, as a town, is dirty, but the beach is lovely, and the town seems well supplied. [...]

8/15/1914.

[...] We had a terrible storm last night. In fact, for the past several days it's been exceedingly hot. Yesterday I was again in Cherbourg to look for music for

---

[19] Lucien was preoccupied with the cost of food up to the end of the war. Soldiers were not responsible for their own food or lodging, but Lucien and his friends wanted, and found, better food and better lodging.

[20] Mme Magne was the mother of Henri, who became an inseparable companion of Lucien's during the war. Pianos Magne continues to be a leading source of the best pianos and of piano maintenance, with locations in Paris and Versailles.

[21] A piece of junk, the picturesque French term *casserole* is a cooking pot.

some songs for our concert. In such heat, the air was foul, as Cherbourg is a very dirty town. I prefer Gonneville where the air is pure and pleasant.

The news from the east is becoming more precise, there are clashes all along the front and things seem to not be going well for the Germans. Generalissimo Joffre, our supreme commander, is very capable if you listen to the officers. Let's hope so. [...] I don't think this war will last more than three months. [...]

8/17/1914.

[...] Our concert was a great success, despite the rain that messed up the end. At the last minute, Hass, the pianist of the *Concerts Touche* accompanied everything.[22] He's in the 4th company; we also have a tenor from the Opera, Nansen,[23] with a really lovely voice. [...] In the morning we played for High Mass; I played the Delage prelude and the Bach *aria*,[24] Nansen sang Franck's *Panis Angelicus* accompanied by violin,[25] a really lovely service. The pastor was moved to tears, he had never heard anything like that at Gonneville. The Red Cross took in more than 200 francs. The concert took place in the main court-yard of the Château de Chivrey. The marquise presided, surrounded by her 5 daughters and two sons; we lunched with the officers and that evening we all were at the priest's where we had a sumptuous meal with plenty of champagne. I had the impression I'd returned, a bit, to civilization. [...]

Today I'm going to Cherbourg to take back the instruments we were loaned; it will be a welcome distraction [...]

8/18/1914.

I just this instant received your two letters and the chamomiles you sent. Thank you for all the shipments you propose, but they will surely never get to me, or if they do, it will be with a great delay. And I don't need anything. In terms of food, I'm in a really good location. I thank you very much. Our weather is also very hot but here it is quite breezy. We have a lot more wind than in Brittany; we are very close to the seacoast. Aside from a few minor sunburns, my health is excellent and I am managing the little fatigues of being a soldier quite easily. From now on, I will send my letters without stamps but I don't believe they will go faster.[26] All the services are terribly disorganized and will certainly work bet-

---

[22] Firmin Touche, violinist, who formed a string quartet before the war.

[23] Georges-Louis Nansen (1878-?).

[24] Maurice Delage (1879-1961); Johann Sebastian Bach (1685-1750). It is impossible to know what aria he referred to, but Louise would have understood.

[25] César Franck (1822-1890), *Panis Angelicus*, FWV 61b, Op. 12, for tenor, cello, harp, organ.

[26] Louise occasionally sent him postage stamps; a letter with a stamp could reach its destination in about 24 hours. When near a post office, Lucien used one, or bought one, to make sure the letter arrived quickly.

ter in a bit. […] I was not able to buy a pair of folding scissors. We were picked up at the train station and taken directly to the barracks, given uniforms and we couldn't leave until time to depart for Cherbourg. But don't worry. A friend has a pair and, should I need them, he'll let me use them. I also was not able to buy glasses, but, rest easy, I rarely use my *pince-nez*. […]

I don't drink the water; I drink cider and in the evening a bit of red wine. The wine in Normandy is good but they are selling it for 1,5 francs a bottle. I am with good friends and managing my money with great care. […]

8/19/1914.

We leave tomorrow morning for Tourlaville, that means we are getting closer to Cherbourg. Our section, at least, will be billeted in the Château de Tourlaville, a famous place and apparently very beautiful. […] We are going to organize another concert for next Sunday at the chateau, […] again for the benefit of the Red Cross and we hope to distinguish ourselves. The assistant prefect of Cherbourg, the admirals, the general command, colonels, etc., ladies of the Red Cross, and all the town elite will be there. Tourlaville is linked to Cherbourg by a tramway. […] I am going to Cherbourg tomorrow for instruments. I am going to try to find a better instrument than the last time, it wouldn't stay in tune. We will also have to rent a piano so our music is respectable. […]

8/21/1914.

[…] Here we are, moved and settled in on a farm about a kilometer from any other inhabitants. Fortunately, the farm is a big one, we can get milk, butter, cream, eggs, and even pork, cider and wine. That is to say, we are pretty lucky. […]

There can be no doubt, the Germans have prepared for themselves a dreadful fate; they asked for it. Yesterday, during our move, we walked about 12 kilometers with our packs in the afternoon after having done the same in the morning. A good number of the guys gave up. I was tired, but I didn't have even a scratch on my feet. My pack weighs 22 kilos. […]

8/23/1914.

[…] Thank you for all your good advice. I pay careful attention to my health and so far I am just fine. My feet are doing well and I easily bear the fatigue and boredom of this job. I'm surrounded by good friends and, if we happen to end up in battle, we will stick together. […] We are quite nicely settled on the farm; the farmers are good people. How long is this life going to last, that's what we don't know! [...] It's only been three days that I've been receiving your letters. There is a delay of at least a week. [...]

8/24/1914.

[...] Our comrades are now engaged in battles everywhere and a good number of families will soon be facing difficult times. Let's not think about that and remember that our duty is obvious, that we represent justice and liberty. We continue our training and will soon be prepared to set out on foot, in case they happen to call on the territorials.

Second letter, same day.

The concert was very successful, and the Cools pieces,[27] even without accompaniment, worked well. I played on a real dud but I wasn't too rusty. I also played for Mass on the 15th and 16th, both times for the Red Cross. They took in almost 200 francs—the *curé* was thrilled. I dined that night at the presbytery with the officers. We had hoped to organize an even larger concert at the Chateau de Tourlaville, but the commanding officer did not give his permission. [...]

8/25/1914.

We leave tomorrow the 26th for Octeville, 1 kilometer from Cherbourg: this move is probably the last. [...]

8/26/1914.

Octeville. We are now settled in Octeville, near Cherbourg. We had to walk 12 kilometers in pouring rain. Fortunately, the weather in the afternoon was lovely, which helped us dry our clothes. According to public rumors, we will likely be here for a month, but I don't believe it; two battalions are now grouped together and we might leave any minute. It is now official that our machine gunners have left for Reims. [...] The news we received today is much better. What is more, our regiment, now very well trained, is trembling with impatience, we ask for nothing more than to get going. [...]

8/27/1914.

To answer your letter of August 19, I can tell you that we were received by Mlle... at the *filature* in the most gracious way. That young woman has three older brothers in the east. She stayed with her ailing mother and a younger 17-year-old brother. The reception was the sort one sees from distinguished,

---

[27] Eugene Cools (1877-1936).

educated people. The trout were superb and they took great pleasure in offering them to us. [...]

I got my shoes repaired and they will last as long as necessary. In place of what they call *chaussures de repos*,[28] I chose a pair of *brodequins* and am very pleased; in a month I will get a good pair of new shoes that will last for months. They fit me well because I tried them on carefully. I didn't get any allowance but I don't really care. I spend little money, at most 4 francs a day, and as a result, unless something unforeseen arises, I will not need money until October 15 [...] Postscript: in Octeville we sleep at the national stud farm in horse stalls, fortunately we have plenty of straw. [...]

8/28/1914.

[...] I'm writing this in a field where they brought us today to try to clean up. At the bottom of this field runs the Divette, a pretty little river where we have been able to soak our feet and take a good bath. That has done us a world of good. According to the official news from our officers, we are doing an admirable job of holding off the Germans who are hitting us with incredible force. According to Lieutenant Perrin who just came by to talk to me, the German losses are huge compared with ours. [...]

8/29/1914

[...] The weather has turned very lovely and warm, which we much prefer. Two regiments from Cherbourg have left and we already are hearing that we will be maintaining the garrison there. They are now treating us as though we were in the barracks, so it would be just as well for us to be there; at least it would be more comfortable. You must smile at the talk of being comfortable in the barracks, but remember that for a month we have been sleeping on straw, in stables or basements. At this moment, we are in the Octeville horse farm and a dozen men sleep in the stall of one stallion, that is flattering for the stallion! We've not lost our sense of humor—we've thought about decorating the stalls.

The Russians are moving quickly to save us the risk of a winter campaign. As we wait, we maintain our faith in the virtue of right and freedom. [...]

8/30/1914.

[...] The region of Cherbourg is remarkably pretty, and I would hope we can come back later to visit. I've been gone a whole month and the Germans, despite their enormous efforts, have barely managed to make a dent in the departments of the Nord. A bit of patience and we will be victorious. We do not know any-

---

[28] Shoes for rest, leisure shoes.

thing about our future destination, most of the troops in Cherbourg have already left; we await confidently the result of this combat between giants, but oh, how much grief and ruin! What savages these brutes are! [...]

9/1/1914.

[...] I just received your letter from August 24. You tell me to do some counterpoint, but you have no idea of what we are doing, the set-up we have! We don't even have a table; I am writing this sitting cross-legged on some straw. It is, sadly, impossible to get any work done. [...]

At the wish of our colonel, we will be organizing a musical Mass in Octeville next Sunday. I saw Noël, the tenor from the Opéra, and we will go to Cherbourg tomorrow to get music and instruments. That will exempt me from the rest of the week, and what is more, I will meet the colonel. It appears he likes music and, if we stay here, it may be possible to organize something. I am delighted to get my fingers back on a violin, even a bad one. [...]

9/3/1914.

[...] I am going to try to work a bit on counterpoint, a mix of 4-part and embellished. Could you be so good as to send me one or two small sheets of music paper? I don't have the time to work on a fugue, it requires too much time and concentration. Rather I can do a bit of counterpoint when I have a free half-hour, that will be enough to keep my pen active. Thank you for the rose you sent; the fragrance filled the letter. [...]

You shouldn't worry too much about the German advance in the Aisne and along the Oise, we are all sure they will not only be stopped but wiped out, as they have ventured too far. [...]

9/4/1914.

[...] I bought a wool sweater which I put on when I got back from marching, it is warm and light. I paid 8 francs 50 for it. As for my beard, rest easy, I didn't keep it for the concert; I looked too awful to appear in public. I had it shaved off in Cherbourg and since then I get a shave every week. [...]

9/5/1914.

[...] This Sunday we play at the 10 a.m. High Mass in the church in Octeville. I am playing the Bach *aria*, the Svendsen *Romance*,[29] and the accompaniment of Franck's *Panis Angelicus*. Hass, the pianist from the *Concerts Touche*, will play the

---

[29] Johan Svendsen (1840-1911), Violin Romance in G major, Op. 26.

organ. I was able to get the parts in Cherbourg. Noël, the tenor from the Opéra, will sing the *Panis* and Niedermeyer's *Pater Noster*.[30] There will be a lot of people at the Mass—all the military people plus, certainly, all the civilians from Octeville and a few hundred people from Cherbourg, as the priest in Octeville has put up posters. [...]

Many people in Paris are frightened by precautions being taken and the departure of the government.[31] You should certainly not be afraid as the most recent news is good and the Germans may pay dearly for their audacity. It appears that 100,000 Russians have landed in Ostende and Anvers. [...]

9/7/1914.

I write every day, this time in answer to your August 31st letter where you accuse me of neglecting you. I never let a day pass without writing to you. [...] The wife of a buddy bought him a camera. I think he may be a professional photographer. He took some pictures of our group. He's supposed to give me postal cards with the pictures and I'll send some to you.

Yesterday we played in the Octeville church with great success, and the colonel was very pleased. The countess of... who came from Cherbourg to hear us is going to arrange for us to play next Sunday at the Church of the Trinity in Cherbourg. We'll see what comes of that. [...]

9/8/1914.

Today I had a one-day leave as compensation for Sunday. I took advantage of it to go to Urville, then to Grèville, about 15 kilometers from Cherbourg in the direction of the cape of la Hague. I had lunch in a small hotel: before lunch, I got to take a wonderful swim which got me really clean. I was able to take care of my fingernails. Urville and Gréville are very green but I prefer our Breton beaches. To get to Urville, there is a tramway which only charges us 0.90 francs. This is the best day since I got here. What a joy—cool, clean water! In Cherbourg, it's dirty and muddy. [...]

9/9/1914.

I just received 4 letters from the 3rd to 5th of September. I don't know why you aren't receiving my letters as I have always sent them regularly. True, for a week now we have had a lot to do. There have been many troop transports from Cherbourg, either by boat or by train. On the other hand, many refugees are arriving

---

[30] Louis Niedermeyer (1802-1861).

[31] The French government moved to Bordeaux on September 2, 1914, fearing a German advance toward the capital. They returned in December of the same year.

from the Département du Nord, and Cherbourg has been, literally, invaded. This is no reason to panic, the occupation of the northeast part of France was a carefully planned strategy. First, we wanted to avoid total destruction of Belgium, which has done us a great service. Second the Germans are about where we want them, that is on the plains of Champagne, there where the Huns long ago suffered the shock of defeat. Based on what we are told, the Germans have 800,000 to 900,000 men, totally exhausted, lacking sleep because they are constantly under attack; now they are faced with a huge number of forces. They'll be totally crushed. It's odd that they didn't foresee the trap. Once again pride is blind. They hoped to find us soft and divided; they found exactly the opposite. Have confidence, in a few days things will appear very different. […]

Second letter, same day.

[…] Thank you for sending the pears. They were good and in good condition. Don't send any more for now; that makes you spend money and I find here as many pears as I could want. […] Don't send me any more socks or anything else; my pack is overloaded. […]

Based on today's news, the Germans seem to have been beaten, this should not last much longer. We waited on purpose to fight on the plains of Champagne: the poor local people! There won't be much wine this year. If only the Germans haven't burned the vines! But let's not dwell any longer on all this sad news, let's look to the end and hope it will be soon. As to Paris, there is certainly no danger at present. […]

9/10/1914.

This morning it was rainy and we had no training or maneuvers because the ground quickly became a swamp. […] I seem to be among the hardiest of us. About 40 percent of the men are from Normandy and they don't stop complaining; it gets on my nerves. […]

9/11/1914.

The weather is much less hot and when it's not raining, quite nice. We spend our time on maneuvers which after a while become tiresome. […]

9/12/1914.

[…] I'll send you a picture as soon as I can. As I explained, one of my comrades who has a lovely camera took several group pictures with me in them. He should give us postcards of them. He sent the film to his wife in Caen, but the whole process is not fast as most photographers are at this time under the flag and the products for developing photos are not easily replaced. [...]

The weather's turned a bit cooler over the past few days; they've given us blankets for the night so sleeping conditions have improved a bit.

At this point, according to the latest news, there is a raging battle pitting 4 million men against each other; it may be, in my opinion, the biggest clash in all of history. We have all the best reasons to be hopeful. Today I'm on watch, and I'm writing on a table and sitting on a chair; it seems strange since for some time now I've not seen any furniture at all. [...]

9/14/1914.

[...] I received today your letters of 10 and 11 September. I am astonished that you are not receiving my letters as I write absolutely every day. [...] I never go to Octeville; it is 2 kilometers from here and we are terribly tired at night after marching 25 to 30 kilometers That is why I've not bought any postal cards of Octeville. I will try to get some, however, to please you.

My food is simple, grilled mutton chops and frites, or veal and frites, that is the daily menu; occasionally some green beans, rarely any cheese, and a pear as there are a lot of pears this year. The mutton is particularly good. [...] All the wells are dried up and we walk about 800 meters to get water. [...]

You see how crushed the Germans are, it seems to be the final defeat, too bad for them. What patience Joffre had to draw them into this trap. They have pulled out of Champagne and left over 100,000 prisoners. [...]

9/15/1914.

You make fun of me in your letter of September 11 because of the sweater I bought. You seem to think I'm not taking precautions. You are much mistaken: I pay very close attention to myself, totally normal in such circumstances. As to cotton undershorts they are useless as I never wear them and my sack only holds so much. As it is, it weighs 34 kilos. I guarantee you that, were you to weigh it, you would be horrified; human strength has its limits.

The Mass came off very well, the quest for money for the Red Cross brought in more than 400 francs, which is wonderful. The church was packed. The entire army command was there. I played the Svendsen *Romance* and the Bach *aria* on a violin that, although better than the first, was still nothing great.

I am not letting my beard grow, as it is so difficult for us to wash that I'd soon be totally filthy. I shave with a comrade's razor. You could send mine, the one marked "Émile," the brush, shaving cream and soap. No use sending the strop. [...]

I think you must know the news which is extremely good. In a little bit of time the Germans will be completely defeated and out of France. [...]

9/16/1914.

[...] We've done a lot of marching in the past few days, 50 kilometers in two days; tomorrow we do 35 kilometers with a cold meal in the field. [...] Imagine, all this will end much more quickly than we thought two weeks ago. [...]

9/17/1914.

Today the weather is dreadful; for several days the weather's been getting worse. That doesn't keep us from continuing our marches and drills. You will be reassured to know that I am quite toughened up and it's odd how easily one can stand all sorts of fatigue and bad weather as long as his will stays strong. [...]

Something very nice happened to our group. As I told you, we were sleeping in a stallion's stall. Some of the horses belonging to the owner of the stable were sickened because of their poor living conditions. Since these animals are worth a lot of money, he asked the colonel for 3 stalls for his animals. As chance would have it, we were in one of those stalls and we are now housed in a little room that stores tools and saddles. It's over a basement and we are well protected against wind and humidity. We've made a lot of people jealous.

I'm doing a bit of counterpoint, but only a little, writing on the inside of envelopes as in the example I'm sending you or whatever else I can find. I've asked you to send me some music paper: a hard notebook is inconvenient. I couldn't put it in my pack. I found no music paper of any sort in Cherbourg. [...]

9/18/1914.

I'm working on counterpoint as much as I can. My mind is a bit numb; I've become numbed by physical fatigue and this military profession, which I'd never engaged in with as much fervor as now. I have no musical ideas and I really have to struggle to do counterpoint. I am completely healthy. I am however rather sobered: many of my buddies have the blues, they drink too much and certainly smoke a lot, more than they should. Time is beginning to seem long, and yet it's still a long way from being over. [...]

9/21/1914.

I'm sending postcards from around here: Octeville, Landemer, it's very pretty. Our firing ground is in this area. Last Sunday I was in Urville, a pretty beach 15 kilometers from Cherbourg. [...] One is a picture of the Château de Tourlaville; we were in a farm nearby. [...]

9/22/1914.

[…] Next Sunday. the colonel has asked us to organize another Mass to benefit the Red Cross. Today I'm going into town to get a violin. I have the address of an amateur. He may have a better instrument than those I've played up to now. I'm going to take advantage of less marching for a few days to practice. Yesterday I wrote to ask you to have a sweater knit for me, if possible, because it will be much warmer than the store-bought ones. During night watch, I'll put one over the other, under my *capote*. […]

9/24/1914.

[…] We now have, in our company, a clarinetist from chez Colonne named Vandoren. At the Mass on Sunday, we are going to play Thomé's *L'Andante religioso* and the Largo from Bach's Concerto for Two Violins.[32] He will play the second violin part on the clarinet. Here is how my life goes: up at 5 a.m., if not 4:30, gulp down a cup of coffee that is more like hot water, which manages to warm me up; sometimes swallow a roll when the merchant from Octeville gets to us, which doesn't happen every day. At 10 a.m. I eat at an inn located at the entry to the horse farm; this inn is far from luxurious, there are never any vegetables except potatoes. At 5 p.m. in the evening, same thing. Since being here, our mess has been awful, that's why I have to go to the inn to eat. The inn is filled with 50 very noisy soldiers, it's impossible to write there. That's why I am writing with a marking pencil here, stretched out on the straw because we have nothing like a table or a chair. I have done a little bit of counterpoint in these conditions. I'm sending you two picture postcards. The group of 3 men has me in the middle, Balembois on my right, and on my left the big one is Dumont who is very clever and handy. In the regiment, they refer to the three of us as *les trois démerdards*.[33] In the other group is our lieutenant, Lieutenant Perrin, professor of applied physics at the Sorbonne, famous in his field and a delightful man, a charming storyteller. […]

9/25/1914.

[…] I found a lady in Cherbourg, Mme Sauvegrain, who loaned me a violin—a Tyrolien, Stainer model,[34] in good condition and with reasonably good sound. It's the best instrument I've had here so far. She was really lovely—it was her husband's violin. He was a great lover of music, a sailor; he has been dead for ten years. […]

---

[32] Francis Thomé (1850-1909); J. S. Bach, Concerto for Two Violins in D minor, BWV 1043.

[33] Lucien wrote *les trois démerdards*. It describes someone who can always find a way around the rules, or always get out of a sticky situation.

[34] Jacob Stainer (1617-1683).

From what we see, the war may well last beyond January. There are only two things that can quickly stop Germany: first, not enough money (and they have certainly taken steps to prevent this), second, not enough horses, which is a real possibility. Information here says that more than half of the German cavalry has been destroyed. There are about 5 million horses in Germany that could be used but they can't bring in more because of the blockade. That source of weakness will only get worse. [...]

9/28/1914.

I received your letters from September 23 and 24 and am happy to learn that my letters are being delivered more regularly. Yesterday we played for Mass in Octeville for a huge public, 300 people outside the church—a great success. I played a violin that wasn't bad at all and it's the first time that my sound could be enjoyed. The effect was enormous; the colonel was very pleased. This will certainly have some repercussions—maybe one day we will play in Cherbourg. [...]

Most Sundays I've gone to Urville to spend a nice day, with the swim the most important part. I've had my hair cut twice; we have an excellent Parisian barber. [...]

9/29/1914.

[...] I'm writing today on guard duty after a beautiful, but somewhat chilly night. We are doing a great deal of marching at night, which is especially tiring.

A lot of wounded men are arriving in Cherbourg—three thousand in just two days. All the hospitals are filling up, and they are making changes to the barracks to receive the wounded. We talk a lot with them on Sundays, bring them fruit and cakes. Almost all have wounds to their limbs. I expect that they are sending the less seriously wounded here. I saw one who had both hands and his cheek hit by the same bullet. By a stroke of luck, no bones were hit and his injury will not amount to much.

They have also announced that 5000 German prisoners will be arriving. We are preparing a camp near Urville to house them. I don't know whether we will have to guard them, that would be just another task like all the others. The 70th which was in Cherbourg has been sent to the battlefield to bury the dead. That is certainly a gruesome task, let's hope that we won't have to do it. [...]

Second letter, same day.

[...] I just this minute received your two letters from September 26. I thought I had given you all possible explanations. I will describe our life here again. We wake up at 5 a.m. and at about 6 a.m. we leave for some maneuvers, usually walking. Between 5 and 6, I drink a glass of black coffee our company provides (we call it juice). When a person selling rolls comes, I buy two for three sous. That is breakfast. We get back about 10 or 10:30 and it is lunchtime. At the entrance to the horse farm is an inn where, in normal times, the stable workers drink. I go there as soon as I get back from our march for a modest meal, generally a mutton chop with mashed or fried potatoes, cheese and fruit, a liter of cider or a can of beer as wine is very expensive and awful. I also have a coffee. For each meal, I spend between 1,25 and 1,50, never more. In the evening, between 5 and 7 I have a meal just like that one. The people who run this inn are not very interested in business so they never vary the menu. In the afternoon, from 1 to 5, we do more exercises or a march. Twice a week we have two extra marches, at night, one from 8 p.m. to 1 am, the second from 2 a.m. to 7 a.m. As you can imagine, that is really enough! We now are marching at least 140 kilometers a week, an average of 25 kilometers a day.

I know, dear mother, that you feel the weight of solitude, but, my dear *mimi*, I'm not having much fun here, believe me. This will be a huge sacrifice if the war continues into spring, which we have to be prepared for. Thinking of our fellow soldiers who are on the front line gives us courage and strength. I don't know that we are going to be here much longer; rumors are that some territorials have already been sent into action; that doesn't seem strange given the huge losses we are having. They would not have been sent just to give the troops who have been fighting these past two months a break. We will see. If the slightest order to move arrives, I will write immediately and, if possible, every day. You have to be resolute and strong. As the injured we saw at Cherbourg said, there is rarely time to write. Many regiments had 20 hours out of 24 of marching, it's awful; and you haven't seen their clothes which were brand-new at the beginning. One would say that they've been living under a bridge for the past year, they are in such bad shape. […]

For the Spassky there is no time to waste;[35] I think it was supposed to pay 2 schillings, that is two francs fifty at the beginning of October. You should write to Chenel around October 15. I don't know whether he will pay given the suspension in rents for families of mobilized soldiers. That is reasonable, but if businesses continue to function, like our place in Boulogne (if it's not closed) or the Foyer du Soldat, which has some resemblance to a business, in my opinion the rent should be paid.[36] […]

The Urville beach is beautiful, typical of Normandy beaches, that is, beautiful sand, very few pebbles, and an expanse of at least 6 kilometers. I went swimming three times during my three visits to Urville. The waves are strong, a bit

---

[35] Lucien and Louise had money placed in a number of investment funds, among them Spassky and Columbia, as well as the Bank of France.

[36] The *Foyer du Soldat* was one of their rental properties, a sort of dormitory for soldiers.

like Saint-Pair and even stronger—we are not far from the famous Blanchard narrows. The beach, thus, is rather dangerous. [...]

10/1/1914.

[...] For two days now I've not received a letter, the service is still not very good. [...] The health of my friends is still fine, but cases of typhoid fever are starting to be seen in the area, so we are extra cautious about hygiene. I don't drink the water and will eat no more fresh lettuce or fruits. They are planning to vaccinate us against typhoid fever next week. We were just vaccinated against smallpox. The vaccination worked; I had a bit of fever for two days and a slightly swollen arm. [...]

10/2/1914.

[...] Today marks two months since my departure from Port Lazo. Let us hope, let us continue to hope, that we will be freed by January 1. The most recent news seems astounding: General van Kluck's army is said to have suffered a huge defeat, with 100,000 prisoners; this would be the prelude to the German's overall retreat.[37] There is also a rumor that General Joffre has been, or will be, named *Maréchal de France*. This would be the right title for this cold, calculating, and scientific man who will have freed our land.

I am sending in this letter an article from the *Petit Parisien* which shows a practical way to make a sweater and also an excellent way to make a garment with paper lining to provide protection when it's cold. [...] You could also knit some sort of mittens or cuffs. And send me, please, some tissue paper for the WC. [...]

10/3/1914.

[...] Recently I bought an excellent fleece-lined vest, it's light and warm. I have to explain this purchase by saying that I haven't been given a jacket, I have just the sweater I bought and my *capote*. The weather is getting chillier. I bought this vest with the captain's permission for 17,50 francs. He said I will be reimbursed after the war if there is any money. I'm not counting on it; I've not yet been paid anything for my shoes. [...]

10/5/1914.

[...] Today, at 3 p.m., we leave Octeville. When I say "we" leave, it is only the classes 1899, 1898, and 1897, all together about 1200 men. I'm in the class 1898.[38] We go by detachments of about 200 men to Caen, Falaise, Evreux,

---

[37] Alexandre von Kluck (1846-1934), general and leader of the 1st German Army in 1914.
[38] Class refers to the year of the soldier's military service.

Lisieux, Bernay, Rouen and Le Havre. I don't yet know in which city I will end up. [...] Based on what they tell us, we are going to serve at regimental garrisons in these cities to permit the active and reserve active forces to join the front. We have to expect that one of these days they will start using us also. From a certain point of view, at least right now, we will have better living conditions as we'll be in barracks, not in the open air. [...]

There is extraordinary hustle and bustle everywhere so I'm writing in haste today. A good number of our non-commissioned officers are coming with us. As for the officers, we don't yet know. So, dear Maman, au revoir. It is possible that I will not have any news from you for several days because of this move. I hope you will continue to receive my letters.

On October 6, Lucien and his regiment left the Cherbourg area for Le Havre, a distance of about 220 kilometers, where they were attached to the garrison of the 129th Infantry Regiment.

10/6/1914. 8 a.m.

I'm taking advantage of a rest period to write a brief note. I am part of 150 from our regiment going to Le Havre. We have no idea what we will be doing there, even the officers don't know. I received the sweater you sent just 20 minutes before we left: it is absolutely wonderful and will be a great help. The one I have is nothing in comparison. You must have paid a lot for it. [...]

10/7/1914.

Le Havre. We are in the Kléber barracks. [...] It took 22 hours to get here. [...]

10/8/1914.

[...] We are housed here temporarily. I don't yet know what they are going to do with us. [...] We are not miserable; our lodgings are certainly better here. We receive daily a good number of new recruits from the 1914 class who are being sent back to the infantry from the cavalry because there are not enough horses. [...]

I am still with my friends, that is Dumont, Balembois, and Corporals Vincent, Barthe, and Dufour. A lot of troops, about 25,000, have been sent from Le Havre toward Dunkirk and Ostende. We have a lot of Englishmen here; it's their principal center for restocking food. We watch their maneuvers, it's very funny, they are jolly-well dressed with a lot of very practical details. Unlike us, they are also very well fed, with tea and jam in the morning, etc. [...]

10/9/1914.

[...] Le Havre, which I'm getting to know, is a beautiful, large city, where life is definitely more expensive than in Cherbourg. It has the feel of a wealthy city. There are many small restaurants, in general not very good. A policeman who is also a soldier in the 129th told me about La Petite Tonne, the restaurant I'm going to this evening. The food there is good, well prepared, with good ingredients and reasonable prices. For 1,75 francs one eats very well. Indeed, all elegance is missing, we have neither tablecloth nor napkins. We are fortunately used to that as we've done without for a long time now. Sleeping conditions in the barracks are reduced to their most simple form: a straw mattress without much straw. Not even a blanket, the ones belonging to the regiment are given to the new recruits and the others are sent to the front. [...]

10/11/1914.

[...] You should see the wounded, even the slightly wounded; they are all of them pale and thin, a result of exhaustion as well as their wounds. The Alan boys are all at the front.[39] As for Jean, he will certainly find the change very dif-ficult—they don't treat you with kid gloves. He will be leaving for the front soon as the 1914 class will be mobilized after the 15th of this month. That means they consider them to have had enough training, given that in these circumstances, knowing how to shoot and do long marches are the only two requirements. [...].

10/12/1914.

[...] I didn't receive a letter today. There doesn't seem to be much order at this regimental station. They don't distribute the mail; we have to go ask for it and we can never get hold of the sergeant in charge of mail. Almost all the soldiers staying here, whether active duty or reserves, are from Le Havre. Their principal preoccupation is to get over the wall to go home. It's quite amusing in the morn-ing to watch everyone trying to leave. As far as work goes, it's almost impossible. In the barracks, it's noisy and chaotic. Basically, it's not much fun, at my age, to take up barrack life again. In our prior encampment, near Cherbourg, we were much freer, we didn't have this feeling of confinement. [...]

---

[39] A family close to the Durosoirs. Two of the five sons survived the war.

10/13/1914.

[...] We moved our rooms to under the eaves. In a few days, the Belgian high command will come to stay in the rooms we were in, because the Belgian king arrives today in Le Havre where he and the queen will be living from now on. That is because of the fall of Anvers.[...]

An important number of French troops left today for Dunkirk. From that regiment, 300 men are going to the front. According to a friend, whose brother is part of the staff headquarters of Le Havre, 350,000 men from all over France are heading to join the Belgians and the English to create havoc for the Germans. The operations, although slow, are excellent, plus the Russians are advancing rapidly. [...]

10/14/1914.

[...] You asked what army corps I belong to. It's the 3rd. I don't know the division or the names of the generals, no one knows anything. The only thing to know is that I belong to the 129th regiment, 25th supply company. If I am sent to the front and cannot tell you the name of the place, which is forbidden by the military authority, you should write to this address, the regiment garrison—it forwards letters. Don't expect too much, as the soldiers at the front, despite their good intentions, cannot write very often. A good number of our group have relatives, brothers, etc. from whom they have had no word in over a month. [...]

10/16/1914.

[...] When we leave for the front, the army but also private citizens give us a great many things (blankets, gloves, socks, shirts, underwear, chocolate, tobacco and more); the main problem is figuring out a practical way to carry it all. [...]

10/18/1914.

[...] Last week, 350 men left, including two of our comrades. This week we expect 600 more to leave. I don't believe that I and my friends will be part of that group, but afterwards I really do believe it will be our turn. [...]

When we leave, we will probably not go directly to the front—there is a specific way of doing things. Thus the 250 who left last week, including Corporal Dufour, a great friend of the 23rd, music engraver at Costallat, went to Achères near Paris. There, at a central garrison, they examine the men and make note of what class they belong to. They stay there at least a week, then are sent to a regional base located very close to the front, from which the regiments draw replacements according to their needs. As a result, those who leave, say October

15, only get to the front three weeks later. Since I don't think I'll be leaving this week, I don't expect to be at the front before the 15th or 20th of November. [...]

10/19/1914.

[...] I was very happy to get this pretty card from Port Lazo: it gave me much pleasure as I left a piece of my heart there. How wonderful and calm that place is! I remember the vacation unfortunately interrupted. What a joy to see our house again. Rest assured that all these difficulties make me more mature and help me appreciate the happiness of home and the peaceful life. [...]

If you don't receive any news for a long time, you should go to the city hall where we live, i.e., Vincennes. There they give you a list, such and such regiment, company, killed or missing. When they say "missing" there is always hope, one could have been injured or taken prisoner, which makes it impossible to provide more information. These are painful topics, but we need to talk about these things. Don't worry, if I go into combat, I have no intention of being left there! The number of persons killed in our unit is quite low: five percent of the active men, but we aren't there yet. [...]

10/20/1914.

[...] For the past 2 days, we have done nothing. They were changing the uniform of the men who left this morning. They've replaced the red kepi with a blue one and they now put blue combat pants over the red ones. All that makes it less easy to see us; from a distance blue mixes in with the ground whereas red can be seen a kilometer away. To get this uniform changed, we had to really have bullets fired at us. For years now it's been impossible to change the color of the pants. My thoughts on this don't matter much, but those in charge were certainly negligent about this. [...]

10/22/1914.

[...] You announce your departure for November 5; that is fine. But I think you need a pass; at this time no one in France can travel without that document. Check to see whether you need to go to the town hall or the police station to get it. [...]

Mme Mauhavel's letter did not astonish me;[40] she has kept her tobacco store open. I don't know whether she can refuse completely to pay a reduced rent. M. Colas can help you with that.[41] [...]

---

[40] Mme Mauhavel ran a tobacco store and café in one of the Durosoir's buildings in Boulogne. She paid no rent throughout the war because her husband was serving at the front.
[41] M. Colas was their notary and lawyer.

Dumont has left us. They were asking for metal workers for a factory in St. Denis and, since he could do the work they needed, he left. Balembois and I miss him a lot. [...]

10/24/1914.

[...] Today I received packages with the mittens, a pair of socks, some paper, and some flannel which I will use to make a belt. The one I brought with me is totally worn out and I'll throw it away. I will cut the flannel into two pieces and sew them together and I will have a fine belt. [...]

You ask about Vandoren. He was at the garrison in Caen; because of a misinterpretation of orders, those men were sent to the battle of the Marne. Vandoren quickly fell ill and was evacuated to Cherbourg. That is where I met him. He played with me in the last music Mass in Octeville. He is charming and I miss him; he stayed behind with his friends. He is of the class of 1892, thus much older than me. In the group picture you have, he is the one behind me. [...]

10/25/1914.

[...] I received a nice note from M. Lambert; his son-in-law has been sent to the infantry in Dreux. Maybe he will be able to return to the aviation unit. M. Lambert regrets being no longer young; he would take the greatest pleasure in fighting the Germans. [...]

10/26/1914.

[...] I've received no letters today, nor yesterday. From what you say, you receive mine regularly. That is sadly not true for me. I receive 3 or 4 at once, then none for 2 or 3 days. We can't complain because, at the front, they receive almost nothing. [...]

Two days ago we moved from our rooms under the eaves to one on the third floor, which had been occupied by the English who have just left. [...]

I don't know whether you've written to M. Martin in Cumières. I think often of them; I fear that poor Cumières has suffered much destruction. They must have had a very hard time, though not as bad as in the area around Reims which has been ravaged. [...]

10/27/1914.

[...] I don't know whether you have any news from M. and Mme Geoffroy: they must be very worried about their son—what an ordeal! I have to say that, in general, the artillery has been much less tested compared with the infantry.

La reine des batailles has been hit very hard.[42] Most of the class of 1914 went into the infantry [...]

10/28/1914.

[...] You give me the news of the Alan sons. The oldest is a prisoner so his fate is determined. I can understand that Clément is very unhappy to have to stay in Africa given all his experience. As for Jean, this is surely very hard for him. I understand he wants to chase after the Germans after all the evil and destruction they've done to us. We all have a degree of rage in our hearts.

In your letter of the 25th you speak of the notary in Vincennes and of M. Laville's offer.[43] Of course we must accept, reserving the right to make changes in the future. You can be sure he reads the newspapers and knows his rights; he could have paid nothing at all. [...]

Tomorrow, 800 men are leaving. We've not yet been chosen so there is a very good chance we'll not leave. If the opposite happens, I will do everything possible to send you word, however brief. [...]

10/29/1914.

[...] You mention train tickets; the ones you have are not any good now, they were only for the trip from Paris to Brittany. You will need to buy a new ticket to travel back to Vincennes. You mention also coal: I'm not surprised that in Vincennes they are no longer selling coal. There is sure to be a shortage. You will get some coke as soon as you can. It doesn't make much difference. There is still a bit of coal in the basement, enough for at least 10 days. [...]

10/30/1914.

[...] As for the charges you need to pay, wait for the tax collector's bill. Once you have it, go see the notary and tell him that none of your tenants are paying rent, that your investments are not paying either, that you cannot pay right now or you will have nothing to live on. You have no business and your son is in the army so he is not earning a penny. After the war, when we have some money, we will pay in arrears. That is the argument to use. [...]

I suggest that you buy some kerosene for your stove as you may not be able to find much coke. There is still a bit of wood in the basement. [...]

---

[42] The queen of the battle forces.
[43] M. Laville was a tenant who must have made an offer to pay part of the rent.

11/1/1914.

[...] I just received this minute your October 29 letter. Surely, war is the most terrible of scourges, but we must accept it. We can do nothing about it. In the present situation we are fighting for our country, our liberty, and our love for the human condition. The announced departure will take place at 10 o'clock in the morning [...]

I will take only one pair of shoes, those I am wearing. When we leave, we will be given a magnificent pair of new English boots. There are 500,000 pairs in Le Havre for our use. We cannot even think of putting a pair in our bag as, with everything we are taking—linens, cans of food, blankets, jacket, mess tin, camping equipment, toiletry items—the weight of the bag is unbelievable. [...]

My dear Maman, you give me advice with lots of touching details, you can't begin to think I could follow them. You obviously have no idea of our living conditions. [...] We have to carry as little as possible, become tough, simple, and hardy, that is the rule we need to follow. When I say "hardy," I don't mean just able to fight fatigue, but also the climate, the cold, the rain: we are managing very well. It's rather curious how human nature adapts to these living conditions, so very different from what we've known. I leave for a winter campaign without the slightest apprehension. [...]

11/2/1914.

[...] I received today your package with the flannel belt, the straw insoles, and paper, but I don't need any of that; it will just be a nuisance. When you get back to Vincennes, I will ask for three flannel shirts [...] and my steel watch—it's annoying not to know what time it is. But for the love of God, do not send anything I don't ask for. [...]

11/4/1914.

Le Havre. [...] I was not able to write yesterday: we had an exercise that took all day. I left at 7 a.m. and only got back to the barracks around 7 p.m. I was rather tired because we ran a good part of the day. [...] I hope you had a good trip, without too much effort. [...]

Second letter, same day.

[...] I was a bit distracted by thoughts of Port Lazo when the major came to visit all the units left here. The visit was just a formality; the major is new and he wanted to get an idea about the state of the troops. They just announced firmly that the class of 1914 will soon leave for the front lines. Young Alan will certainly leave if he hasn't already left. When you are back in Vincennes, you can find out more about that.

Dear Maman, I have a feeling that we will be leaving soon; we have to remember that we've been here a month. The weather is still lovely and not cold; I am still in excellent health, and I look wonderfully healthy. We've been lucky to spend this time at the seacoast. [...]

11/5/1914.

[...] Tomorrow we have another exercise that will take all day, with a cold meal on the field—at least 30 kilometers. Fortunately, we have splendid weather. [...] Excuse me for not writing more but I must go to bed; we leave at 6 a.m. [...]

11/6/1914.

[...] I'm again writing a short note: we left this morning at 7 and returned at 5:30. [...] Time to clean up and it is already 6 p.m. and I am in a restaurant where I am writing.

For a week now, our training has been intense: I think that is an indication of our impending departure. But we haven't heard talk of anything. [...]

I had to interrupt myself as they brought my dinner, which consists of tapioca with milk, some melon, veal and carrots, a pear, and a can of beer. All that for 1,40 francs in a restaurant run by an English foundation similar to the Salvation Army. The restaurant is good, very clean, and very inexpensive. It's a charitable foundation for the English soldiers who are crossing the channel by the thousands, but French soldiers are most welcome. [...]

11/8/1914.

[...] Responding to your letter of the third, I would say that one shouldn't be concerned about Turkey; they have asked for suicide. Sure, Germany pushed them into an adventure which will cost them dearly, and furthermore, it's two months too late. Russia is completely ready and not at all troubled to put 300,000 to 400,000 men on Turkey's back; what is more, the Balkans will join the party in order to get a piece of the cake [...]

In your letter of the 4th you talk about how long the war will last. This war will be shorter than one might have thought a while ago. The Germans show signs of exhaustion, while the English are building up their forces astonishingly. You can't imagine what is landing in Le Havre: Englishmen with their pageantry and their little skirts over their nervous legs, Canadians with rich fur coats, it's a real invasion! According to what the English tell us, they will have 1 million men at the front. [...] The Germans will soon be worn out by the crushing forces that encircle them. I'm looking wonderful, it's probably due to living a life in the open air. I certainly won't be among those unable to fight, [...]

11/9/1914.

[...] I note that your trip was hard and tiring. It's a bit of a repetition of what I went through when I left for Caen; it took 29 hours and I had to pass through Alençon. [...]

So many thoughts about whether, yes or no, we will return to Port Lazo, so much will happen before next summer and for the moment we have other preoccupations. [...] You must be happy to get back to a good bed; as for me, I can't even remember what that is. Since I left, I've not yet slept in a bed with sheets, mattress, etc., though that doesn't keep me from sleeping well. I am sure that when the time comes to sleep in a nice comfortable bed, sleep will abandon me as it will seem so strange! [...]

Tomorrow will make 5 weeks that I've been in Le Havre and we are not yet preparing to leave; they are taking the class of 1914. When we left Cherbourg, everyone believed we would be under fire soon. What's even more strange, we heard officially yesterday that the rest of the 23rd left for the department of the Nord to reinforce a territorial division. That shows just how much all this is due to chance. He who thinks he won't be going into the battle finds himself the first there and vice versa. That is why I don't think it is worth trying to go right or left in this military system. [...]

This morning I was vaccinated against typhoid fever—an injection in the shoulder. I think that there will be a second in a few days. The result is a bit of fever and dizziness, so they are keeping us quiet. With the bad weather, the number of cases of typhoid will multiply, so I'm happy to have been vaccinated. [...]

11/11/1914.

[...] I eat almost every evening in the English restaurant. [...] A lot of the English go up to the 2nd floor where there is a piano, where, with a chaplain, they sing hymns. That is [...] not much like a French restaurant, but no matter, I'm doing fine. [...]

11/12/1914.

[...] We had a minute of anxiety today: it is again a matter of a departure and this morning, I and my friends were chosen to be next. They needed 65 men in addition to the new recruits. But they just told us that the number is down to 35. As a result, we still are not leaving, all these endless rumors of departures are really quite unnerving. This will be the 13th departure from the 129th, 13,000 men in all. There must be huge numbers of active forces at the front. We will probably leave for the battle in December. [...]

11/13/1914.

Just this minute, I was told that I leave tonight or tomorrow morning to join, I believe, the 129th near Reims. [...] I am leaving in excellent health and am very well trained. I will surely get out of this [...] I'll write every day I can. [...]

11/14/1914.

[...] We are stopping about an hour here and I can't tell you in what direction we are going, it's forbidden. I will pass by the home of the Cunaults.[44] [...]

11/15/1914.

[...] We arrived last night at 6:30 p.m. after a trip of 24 hours near the town you know about. In the dark of night, we covered some 10 kilometers through wide-open fields to get to the farm where we are posted. Our principal enemies here will be the dampness and the mud which we sink into up to our ankles. Fortunately, I have two excellent pair of socks. [...]

The corps I am part of is mostly resting now; we will be taking watch in the trenches about 600-700 meters from the enemy. We spend two days in the trenches, then come back to our quarters for three days. For the past 20 days the 129th has had a dozen injuries, no one killed; that will help you see that the risk at this point is not that great. [...] We move at night and, up to now, I've not found the cannon firing frightening; in fact, it's quite majestic, this deep voice which dominates all the noises of the clear, calm night, as the heavy artillery continues through the night. I thank you for the little binoculars which are excellent and certainly very useful. [...]

11/16/1914.

[...] This is the address you should write to from now on: 3rd company, 3rd section, 129th infantry regiment. [...] Since last night, I'm in the trenches. Fortunately, my buddies Balembois, Dehuysser, etc. are with me, not in the same squadron but at least in the same section. A section is made up of 4 squadrons. We've been in the trenches since yesterday. Here's how they are arranged: there are 3 lines of trenches, one behind the other, about 500 meters apart, at different angles. We spend 6 days in the trenches: two days in the last line where we are right now, a type of bunker where things are not too bad and there is not

---

[44] Georges Cunault (1856-1941), French luthier and good friend of Lucien's. Lucien left Le Havre on the 13th, he was in Villemonble ("in front of Cunault's home") when he wrote this letter, and the next day they were near Reims. It was an immediate baptism of fire. The French offensives in Champagne continued until March 1915. From now on, Lucien was careful not to directly disclose much information about where he was. As often as possible, he used references to people, places, things that Louise would have recognized.

too much to fear; two days in the second line, a real trench in the earth with out-posts, etc.; and, finally, two days in the first trench which is barely 400 meters from the German lines with outposts about 200 meters from them, in which 3 or 4 of us are together. These outposts are obviously the most dangerous places and we have to be very alert.

Here is what the Germans often do: they creep out of their trenches one by one and crawl as near as 50 meters from our lines. They group together behind any sort of obstacle; once all together, they attack one trench. Thus, the watch-men must have their eyes peeled and be alert and warn their comrades. [...] We have orders not to shoot to prevent revealing to the German artillery the loca-tion of our trenches; otherwise they would bomb us. According to the orders we have, we are not trying to advance, only to keep the Germans from advancing; the big work is done elsewhere, so we are not in much danger. We just need to be very careful and not show ourselves. Shells whistle over our heads; we have gotten used to it. [...]

11/19/1914.

[...] This is my third day in the trenches and, for the past 2 days, the damp weather we had been having has turned to intense cold: 6 degrees below zero. This is the bitter cold you know well from the time in Chalons. The cold weather has made the nights very hard although we are very well covered; so, you see, it's the start of the winter campaign, let's hope it won't be very long. The Germans appear to be running out of steam. Yesterday, we were in the third line. We were far enough from the front and settled in at 5 p.m. at the end of the day because we can't use any light which could serve as target for the artillery. There, in the semi-darkness, we had a café-concert, everyone taking a turn with his little song. The entire event was just plain fun. The roar of the shells served a bit as a *basse obstinée*,[45] which added to the effect.

Today we are in the first line and in the outposts. We hear whistling of bul-lets, as though surrounded by bumble bees, while a terrible artillery duel rages at some distance from us. We are seated in the bottom of our deep trenches, and all this is happening over our heads, so we are in no danger. If it weren't for the cold, we would be totally fine. I sculpted a quite comfortable chair out of the clay. [...]

---

[45] Ground bass, basso ostinato, or continuo refers to the bass part of music of the late seventeenth through the late eighteenth centuries. Played by a keyboard instrument and either bass viol or cello, it provides the basis for the upper voices and the improvisation inherent in the style and period. In his letters, Lucien refers to this as *basse continue* or *basse obstinée*.

[…] The little pair of binoculars you sent will be of the greatest use. Thanks to them, these past days in the outpost, I clearly spotted the Prussians who were crawling on their stomachs under some trees. I told the lieutenant and we hit them with a salvo of gun fire that made them quickly turn around. Where did you buy them? How much did you pay for this little item, cute and practical and for which I thank you from the bottom of my heart? Their value to me has no price. […]

I make sure to have my canteen full of rum or some other alcoholic beverage; with the weather we are having it is indispensable. For the past 4 days, the temperatures have been 10 to 12 degrees below zero and life out in the open in that temperature is rather awful; one does however get a bit used to it. Still, you have to experience a night in the trenches, barely moving, to understand. Yesterday, I saw Balembois in tears because of the cold. I am lucky to be a bit overweight, I feel it less. […]

I buy sausage, chocolate, cheese, jam from the locals; in the outposts much of the time we don't get enough to eat. It all depends on what is happening: as much as they want to bring the food, under the bullets and shells, it's not very easy. […] I don't need a razor or anything, I'm going to let my beard grow, it's much simpler: decorum is of little interest to us, we all look like thieves. […] If you can send my travel blanket, I'd prefer it. It won't be any heavier than the one I have, and will be much warmer. Also send a long warm scarf for my nose. Now that I've experienced a bit of fighting, I can say that the general situation here doesn't frighten me. We don't pay much attention to the bullets; we only watch for the shells and we easily hear them coming. They whistle in the air and, after a while, we learn to predict where they will land. Fortunately, here, the artillery doesn't shoot much at us; they are trying to destroy the opposing artillery and the shells pass 100 meters over our heads. It's just another sort of music, we get used to it rather quickly […]

[…] You are worried about our sleeping conditions—they are pretty basic. Because of the cold that has settled in these past days, we spend only 4 days in the trenches; the first two, we sleep on straw, or in barns that have been bombed and thus are open to the elements; the next two days we are in the trenches completely outdoors—it's really very hard, but one gets used to it. For the two days of rest afterward, we return to the rear to sleep, either in the cellars of a chateau, very large and solid and where it is warm, or on a farm where the winds make themselves at home. Fortunately, this life in the open air makes us hardy and I'm very healthy, not the hint of a cold […]

[…] When we want to watch the enemy, we have observation posts that are well hidden, but they don't show themselves any more than we do. At night, ears are more useful than eyes; the slightest noise can be heard at several hundred meters. We are heading to the farm of the *marais*,[46] so called because it neighbors a swamp where right now wild ducks have gathered. This farm, however, shows signs of the war and is certainly not going to be the last word in comfort for us. […] I thank you for sending the compass. I had thought about it for some time and finally bought one in Le Havre. But no matter, I'll give that one to a buddy. In my squad there is a printer from Rouen, Monsieur Rolland,[47] a delightful man, a good musician brought up in the cathedral choir school and, even with his profession, fills the post of organist. Really a charming man, a great friend. […]

[…] Yesterday I received your two letters of the 18th and 19th. I couldn't answer them right away because, with my buddies, I worked all day with a pick and shovel, something new for me, to make what they call a *sape*, that is a covered passageway leading to a trench which is about 300 meters from the Germans. I am writing right in the midst of shooting and shelling, buried deep in a trench—there's not much to fear.

The weather is bitter cold, down to 12 degrees below zero. Yesterday, it snowed all day. […] I have some oil cloth I bought on purpose in Le Havre, but it is very heavy. During the week, I manage to fill my canteen with rum or other liquor, thanks to a nurse who travels through this region and runs errands. I've never drunk so much alcohol. But in these glacial temperatures, at night, it's absolutely essential. We've found a way to construct a little alcohol stove and we make grogs, which do us a lot of good. We will for a long time remember this terrible life which reveals the character and inner resources of each of us. […]

[…] Yesterday we got out of the trenches after four days there, two in the front line, the farthest forward stronghold. All day long there was heavy firing and my friends and I spent a good part of the day in the bomb shelters, underground shelters where one is relatively safe from the explosions. Today I'm on watch in a little area about 2 kilometers from our encampment. The entire squadron occu-

---

[46] Swamp.

[47] Lucien Durosoir and Georges Rolland spent a year together in the trenches. Their friendship continued after the war; at his organist friend's death from a brain tumor in 1945, Lucien dedicated *Trois Préludes*, a piece for organ, to him.

pies a pretty little house in regrettably sad condition: walls and furniture all torn apart. You would have to see it to believe it. We lit the stove in the kitchen and made quite a good dinner: rice with chocolate, steak, a meal that is an exception to our usual fare. […] You could send me a small bottle of glycerin, as my hands are getting ruined by the cold and working with the earth. […]

11/28/1914.

[…] Due to the weather, we are only spending 4 days in the trenches. During the 2 days of rest, however, we do a lot of chores. Here's what our days in the trenches are like: in the morning and for lunch, we have canned food—sardines, tuna, jam, gruyère, and bread. In the evening, only after the sun is set, the cook brings soup, beef, and coffee; but since the kitchen is a good distance from the trenches, the food is pretty cold. The hardest part of being in the trenches is not the danger, nor the whistling shells—all of that we manage to not care a bit about—but staying immobile and quiet, no matter what the weather. […] Fortunately for us, the Russians are moving in giant steps and the Kaiser will soon need to face them;[48] in a month the Russians have a good chance to be in Berlin. […]

11/29/1914.

[…] Today we are moving to a new series of trenches. The weather has gotten a lot milder, unfortunately it has become rainy and that's no fun. In the trenches, we barely have room to lie down or sleep. Mostly we need to stay armed and ready; the watch could give an alert at any time and we have to be prepared, rifle in hand, to respond instantly. It is far from comfortable, but when the weather isn't too bad it's bearable. It's all the bad weather that makes the trenches really hard.

In your letter of the 24th, you are curious about the length of this war and say you are getting close to losing courage. You must not, dear Maman. I don't believe right now that this war will last very long. We are fighting back and, if we are not advancing, it is to prevent sacrificing human lives. Countless numbers of Russians are advancing rapidly and Guillaume will have to send almost all his forces against the Russians if he doesn't want to see Berlin invaded in the near future. He may have already waited too long. He will automatically pull his large force out of our country and that's the moment when, without great danger, we will move forward. I hope that, before February, decisive events will have taken place and changed the picture. We need to have patience and tolerate our misery with courage. Think of our great grandparents who did so much and went through so much. […]

---

[48] Kaiser Wilhelm II.

11/30/1914.

[…] Today I received a package containing a balaclava for my face, a pair of socks and some chocolate […] Please, don't send any more; I have everything I need and more. I don't think I'll use all the socks I have throughout the whole war. You know, once a week, the city of Le Havre sends a huge package for each company in the 129th. This is Le Havre's regiment, made up almost entirely of men from there. This package, which is then raffled off, contains a lot of things, wool clothes, socks, balaclavas, tobacco, pipes, chocolate, candy, really a whole lot of nice, useful things. […] We are expecting a German attack—we have received reinforcements and are on alert every night. […]

12/1/1914.

[…] I am writing this to you seated comfortably in my clay seat, my mediocre blanket over my legs, completely covered by the oilcloth which keeps me nice and warm, so I am just fine. The shells whistle quite frequently over our heads, but not that many in the past few days. The Germans rarely reply to our cannon shots and we get the impression that they are busy moving on, leaving in front of us just a curtain of troops. The news is getting better. […] You could send me by train a small package of food. Wrap it in rags and label it "warm clothes." I would love some sugar as it is absolutely impossible to get any here. […]

12/2/1914.

[…] I'm going to introduce you to some of my new buddies. One of them, Rolland, is from Rouen, where he is head of an important print shop. He is a good musician and holds the post of organist in a church in Rouen. He's a nice, intelligent man, 32 years old. The other one, Vessot, had a food business in Soissons: his house was completely destroyed by the Germans. He is completely ruined and his wife is a refugee in Paris, staying with family. He's a former sales-man at the Bon Marché, a very friendly guy, easy to get along with. The three of us are almost never apart. The rest of the squad is made up of peasants, very brave, but with whom we don't feel much connection. Balembois is in a neigh-boring squad, about 10 meters away from us, which means that we see each other every day and we are often a group of four; we visit each other in the trenches and share grogs. […]

12/3/1914.

[…] Today I received four packages. […] My friends Rolland and Vessot also get food packages. As we three do the cooking together, it's very practical and adds to the basic supplies we get here. Sending me two or three packages a month will be enough, every 10 days, maybe the 1st, the 10th, and the 20th of the month: that way we don't risk having too much arrive at once. Put in fewer cookies and more solid items: canned goods, meat or rabbit pâté for instance; with this bad weather we need more substantial food. [...] From time to time, you could send a delicacy, it makes us feel as if we are back in the civilized world when we eat it. I am drinking little, two cups of coffee a day, that's all; I never drink water. In the past few days, in Saint-Thierry, we were able to get four bottles of dry champagne, from a poor woman whose two children had just been killed by a shell. She was preparing to leave here. They were her last bottles and she cried as she sold them to us. I hadn't drunk any wine for two weeks; it really did us good. There is nothing of that sort to be found around here any longer and our company provides a quarter-bottle of red wine a week, red wine that can only be called rot-gut. With some effort, we can buy alcohol (and it is pretty mediocre) for 4 francs a liter. [...] We do miss having an occasional glass of Bordeaux, especially when we are out of the trenches. But we will make up for this later. This morning marked four months since I left. Let us hope that it won't take as many for me to come back. Today we started 48 hours on reserve and are lodged in champagne cellars 12 meters underground, completely sheltered from the shelling. Put some candles in your next shipment—it is impossible to get any lamps—and also a box of matches. I thank you for sending me all these packages, opened with childish glee. [...]

12/4/1914.

[...] The company still gives us food when we are in the front lines, two cans of sardines and one of tuna for 14 men. As you can see, there's little abundance or variety. When you send foodstuffs on a fixed date, you'd do well to send them by train. A box of 3 to 5 kilos would certainly be less expensive than the post. It passes through Le Havre and takes two or three days longer, but that doesn't matter for canned goods, hard sausage, or jam. [...] I'm always talking about food and you must think that I'm becoming very materialistic. But we are so badly, and filthily, fed that food other than that which the company so stingily furnishes is greatly welcome and around here it is becoming impossible to find anything. And they sell for 3 francs for what usually costs 0,75. [...]

12/5/1914.

[...] I received your letter of December 1; here we are starting the fifth month of the war and very clever would be the person who could predict anything right now. [...] In the newspapers, they say we are well fed and we have a quarter liter of wine every day, rum, fresh meat. I don't know in what regiment that is the case, but it's certainly not ours. We have about that much wine a week and, during that same amount of time, what amounts to two small glasses of eau-de-vie. What is more, at least one day out of two, we eat frozen meat which is not very good. There are very few potatoes and very little rice; as for coffee or tea, we get some twice a day but it is pretty awful, nothing like in the civilian world, and very badly prepared. In this regiment I've noticed that the food is prepared by men who have no talent for cooking, nor much in general for anything else in the military world. The result is disgusting cuisine.

I read that story in *Le Petit Parisien*, what nerve! And *Le Matin* and their stories of comfortable trenches![49] I don't know what their correspondents saw, maybe a special trench for our leaders. Reality for us is not like that, and neither our trenches nor our food leave anything to envy. Right now is not the time to place blame, but I can't wait for afterward: lots of stories will be told that will not honor some people!

I thank you for sending the stove, but I have to repeat, don't send me anything except what I ask for. You listen to your heart and you send something; you don't take into consideration our situation. You aren't thinking of the day when I have to move forward; I will have to throw away half of what is in my pack, or risk exhaustion on the trip, as a donkey couldn't manage to carry all of it. I beg you, from now on, send only what I ask for. […] I received the sleeping bag which will be very useful; to use it, I need to be able to take my shoes off and, unfortunately, I've not been able to do that for two weeks! […]

12/6/1914.

[…] Rolland, Vessot, and Balembois organized today a small celebration for my birthday and my 36 years. Rolland managed somehow to get a chicken and eating roast chicken seemed to us a great plan. We also managed to find an apple that was exquisite and very tasty. Rolland, a true Norman, really appreciated it. This morning they gave me two chrysanthemums wrapped in white paper, and that's how I spent my birthday. Naturally, I received your bottle of rum, the metal ball which will prove useful, and the diaper pins. You can send me some mint and chamomile—we will certainly make some good herbal tea. You are spending an enormous sum just to send the packages. You should pay attention, as the war could last longer than we predict. […]

---

[49] "The rear was at the origin and never really stopped being the place where the soldiers were brainwashed. […] The newspapers […] made one believe in a front line of concrete, well organized everywhere, with comfortable and even pleasant trenches." Jacques Meyer, *Les Soldats de la Grande Guerre* (Paris: Hachette, 1966), 218. *Bourrage de crâne*, literally stuffing the skull, is the French expression for brainwashing.

12/7/1914.

[…] We were just subjected to a serious bombing, about 25 shells fell on us in the space of ten minutes and the last hit barely 15 meters from us. We are all covered in dirt. Our company is known as the "bring good luck company" of the regiment because we've had only one person wounded in a month and half. My very clever friend Vessot managed, with enormous difficulty, to find three eggs which we ate fried and we then made an excellent coffee, very different from the usual. We put the coffee in boiling water and, after it boils again, we filter it through very fine, very clean, batiste underwear. We end up with a delicious Turkish coffee. […]

Rolling around in the mud as we are doing, we barely look human. Our rifles are all rusty and covered with mud. Only one thing is important—that the mechanism work, so we are careful to remove any dirt that would affect how they function. Vessot, Rolland and I make meals together with what we receive. Rolland especially receives wonderful things that his wife and mother-in-law, both excellent cooks, send him. They make terrines and pâté. For Christmas he will receive a pâté de foie gras and we will be able to create the most presentable meals. We changed lieutenants about 10 days ago and the new one, an "excellent military man," doesn't bother himself with what we eat and the food is much worse since he's been in command of the company. You mention sardines. They give us one can of 10 sardines for 7 men and one can of tuna also for 7 men, that's not very much. They've never given us any jam. […] We exist under a constant bombardment, we get used to it and it doesn't keep us from laughing and, some nights, having café-concert parties. The shells that explode, near and farther away, serve as the applause. If you could see us, you would not be as tormented as you certainly are. The bad weather is far more annoying than the firing from the enemy. We always come out fine, we have so many resources on our side! […]

12/9/1914.

As I told you, I never drink water, just a bit of wine when they agree to give us some. Otherwise, I drink daily only two glasses of mediocre coffee. For the past 2 days, with the coffee I received, we make excellent coffee after lunch. You could send me more. […]

I used my sleeping bag for the first time last night because we are at rest. I have to be at rest to use it because I have to be able to take my shoes off: it's like sleeping in sheets. […] We are leaving tonight for Berry-au-Bac, where the battle is raging right now. […] I would prefer to march and fight than to be dying from cold in the trenches with shells falling on our heads; we don't even see a pointed helmet! […]

12/12/1914.

[...] I couldn't write yesterday [...] We left the farm of the *marais* where we had a 24-hour rest on Wednesday at 9 p.m. We arrived at 3 a.m. in Prouilly and left at 12:30 on Thursday, arrived at 5 p.m. at Retheuil, left at 8 p.m. and finally, at 1:30 a.m., arrived in the woods near Craonne. I don't know whether we are now in the valley of the Aisne. We covered more than 40 kilometers with all our gear, it was exhausting, and a good number of soldiers stopped along the way to be picked up by vehicles. We are lodged in underground structures dug by the engineers; we have chimneys and we make a wood fire. One could easily get used to this life in caves. It's rather interesting to see how we are installed here: in the blink of an eye the regiment disappeared underground. Our job is changing: the trenches here, in old quarries, are very comfortable. We are now at rest for 6 or 7 days, after which we will spend 6 days each in trenches of the first and second lines. [...]

Second letter, same day.

[...] We are dug in here at the edge of a forest and are now in the department of the Aisne. Our service goes as follows: a week of rest which we are now doing, a week in the second line, and a week in the front line. When we have finished all that we will be in the new year and will have spent Christmas in the trenches. We are quite near Craonne, but we have no way to get extra food; there is nothing for 10 kilometers behind us and we need a pass from the general to cross the lines. What is more, a canal serves as the boundary of the two departments. German artillery watches the bridge over the canal constantly; we can only cross at night. [...] The area we are in was the scene of violent fighting—the poor farms and villages in ruin are testimony. Right now, all is calm. For the most part, we are happy to have changed location; I was beginning to get bored at Saint-Thierry where we were stuck in dreadful mud. [...]

12/13/1914.

[...] I will send a careful little note to Mme Duez to help her understand that our life is not always rosy, [50] but that we accept it so our wives and children, or old women like her, can enjoy what they have in peace. If you could see the devastation that is everywhere in this part of the country, with not a house left standing, you couldn't help but find egotistical the thoughts of a good number of people who, warm and sheltered, "don't give a damn," to use a military expression. Those who sleep in their beds cannot imagine what it is like to spend hours stuck in this clay, at night, in the wind and rain, constantly searching the

---

[50] Mme Duez was a wealthy widow in Boulogne: a friend of the family and very important to Lucien and Louise during the war.

horizon, listening for the slightest sound, or to try to sleep in mud and shit, hearing the sudden sharp sound of a passing shell cutting through the air, or the humming of bullets around you on these lonely nights. We think of those we have left there. The wooden crosses all around us are too numerous to count. We also think of those who don't recognize all the sacrifices being made for them, so they can be at ease. I am sure that after the war I will not be very kindly disposed toward those who talk the way you describe, making jokes of our suffering about which they really know nothing. My health remains excellent, I've never been so strong, and I think I can say, without boasting, that I am often the source of consolation, by my gaiety, for my less strong friends around me who don't have my endurance. I adapt quickly to all circumstances and never complain. Let's hope that these ordeals don't continue too long; a good number of the guys are losing courage, largely because of the separation from their families. [...]

12/15/1914.

[...] I couldn't write yesterday, the 14th, as we spent the whole day building underground shelters so we didn't have to sleep under the stars. By nightfall, we were exhausted. [...]

12/17/1914.

[...] Here we are in the second line trenches, some say for six days, others for four, but it really doesn't matter. We are in the woods; there are a lot of trees in this part of the Aisne. We are housed in underground *gourbis* that have some similarities to burrows. Fortunately, the weather is good and not terribly cold. The machine gun shelling goes on continuously here, but the cannon thunders less than at Saint-Thierry [...] where we were. Here we are not far from the Craonne plateau. The countryside is completely wooded; if you buy the map Taride #3, which is for the northeast, you will be able to follow our movement. I'll give you the indications you need. Obviously, the Germans mine the trenches before leaving them so, when we find an empty trench, we don't enter. The engineers inspect it and most often we dig a new one just in front. It would be too easy for us to get blown up. We've made that mistake, and now don't let ourselves be duped! [...]

If you send me another small package, think about putting in a few candles; there are absolutely none to be found around here. The nearest habitable area is more than 15 kilometers away. Ventelay is fairly close, but not a single house is left standing and naturally there are no people left. The nights are long and they have the nerve to give us two candles a week for a squadron of 15 men. Suffice to say that we are condemned to darkness. [...]

I think a lot about my violins, now silent. My hands are not too badly damaged, but my fingers are quite stiff. If that's all that happens, it will be nothing. Up to now I've not had any diarrhea; many others have and it makes one quite ill. The WCs in the trenches consist simply of a passageway leading to a wider area where we relieve ourselves and, like cats, cover it up with dirt. It's primitive. [...]

12/18/1914.

[...] We have not a single drop of alcohol to burn and we can't have any more, so we no longer have anything to warm us. You could send me something another buddy has and which works quite well, they call it a *réchaud du soldat*, it's a can wrapped in a tricolor ribbon which holds solidified alcohol. Two little pieces of iron support the mess tin and it works extremely well: the alcohol is lit with a match. Once extinguished, the alcohol solidifies again. No danger and no odor. By sending me one now and then some of this solidified alcohol, we will have what we need to cook. It's not heavy and very small. Try to find that for me, it must be sold in a lot of places. My old cooker doesn't work and sending liquid alcohol is impossible. You could also send me those nightlights that burn without oil. [...] They would be more practical and less expensive than candles. [...]

12/19/1914.

[...] Yesterday we were subjected to a terrible shelling and spent our time lying flat like moles. The weather is magnificent, but much too warm which brings rain. The river Aisne is rising and the front-line trenches are flooded. There are 10 centimeters of water in them and teams of men are kept busy emptying out the water, all very interesting. [...] We build a grid of wood on stilts to keep our feet out of the water. [...]

They only send packages on from Le Havre when they have enough to make a load: that explains the delay of some packages. [...] They use a typical military expression: "I don't give a damn." That's the philosophy and ends any argument. Here, we know nothing about what's happening. If you can, from time to time, send a copy of *Le Matin* or another paper or even *L'Information*, that would make me very happy. [...] The rumor is that there will be important news from Austria, and also that President Wilson has proposed mediation to the Allies. I don't know what truth there may be in all these rumors, but that doesn't stop the trading of gun and cannon battles with the Germans. The woods we are in are full of squirrels, wonderfully charming animals, but totally frightened, not only by our presence, but by all the noise of the artillery. [...]

12/20/1914.

[...] There is still a persistent rumor that we will very shortly be leaving for Alsace. I will not mind moving, as we are in a very wooded region, very humid, and dangerous because of the terrain: it is easy to be surprised. The weather is still very mild, too mild, unfortunately, as it rains almost every night and the Aisne rises, threatening us with big floods, which would certainly not make us very happy. That's why I'd prefer Alsace where we will surely find snow, but also colder weather which I would prefer. I like cold more than dampness, as rain doesn't keep us from being cold also. The water here is absolutely awful, filled with German corpses. We have to go several kilometers for water, even for cooking. No need to tell you that I don't ever drink the water. I only drink coffee: we make it with what you send me whenever possible, that is, every time we can make a fire. We have to make sure not to signal our location to the Germans or they start shelling us. [...] The life we are leading for the moment is somewhat stupefying: barely a few hours of daylight, and little to no light for the long nights. I try to lighten things for my comrades who are very sad about the situation, especially with the holidays coming. We have to be philosophical and to maintain our good French gaiety. I try to do that, and I continue in excellent health. [...]

12/21/1914.

[...] In our situation right now, luck determines everything: shells explode without interruption and we are often amazed by what makes the difference between being hit or not being hit by a shell. Given the frightening number of projectiles fired (yesterday afternoon more than 300) the proportion of people hurt is very small, but therein lies the question of luck! [...]

12/22/1914.

[...] My friends Rolland and Vessot both received packages: gingerbread, candied chestnuts, figs, soft caramels, all for Christmas. I'm giving you the list so you see how much fun it is to unwrap all these bundles. We received today the packages sent by the city of Le Havre; I got mittens, a lovely hand-knitted nose-warmer, and a pencil. I also got some English soap. One other time I received a flannel belt and woolen gloves. It is not worth your sending all those things as we receive enough, regularly, to replace the worn-out ones. [...] You probably read in the paper that they are going to give each of us a package to celebrate the New Year. Apparently, we will have one bottle of champagne for four of us. They would do better not to waste money on that extravagance and give relatively drinkable wine a bit more often. Our wine, as well as the announced gifts, is pilfered before reaching us! Others serve themselves before we can. [...]

12/23/1914.

[…] We will leave tonight for Ventelay, ten or so kilometers from here, for about six days of rest. Where we are is simply too dangerous and the cannon fire so terrible that the men's nerves are frazzled! That's why they will replace us. I am in very good health and in excellent spirits as my cheerfulness can't be changed; I am not one who gets depressed. […]

12/25/1914.

[…] I was not able to write yesterday. We were relieved from our position on the 23rd at 9:00 in the evening and we headed for Ventelay for our rest. We were on the way when, about 11 p.m., there was a violent German attack. We turned back quickly to support our comrades. When we got there, the Germans had fortunately been repelled; the result of all that was that we arrived at our rest spot in the morning of the 24th after having run and marched all night. Thus, quite exhausted, I stayed in bed a good part of the 24th. I went to midnight Mass, said by the military chaplain in a little old barn. It was like the stable in Bethlehem, as there were indeed animals. They had placed a pine tree and a few candles in the middle of the altar; it was absolutely touching to see this ceremony in a barn half fallen down. The chaplain gave a timely homily, simple and very moving. I will certainly never again see a midnight Mass like that. […] This Christmas Eve was celebrated with Julien Balembois, Rolland, and Vessot and reminded us of better times. So here we are in Ventelay, a rather large village, for about six days; then, back to our woods and our holes. […]

12/27/1914.

[…] I was not able to write yesterday and here is why: during our famous relief night, the commander noticed that there were a significant number of laggards. In our defense we had marched and run part of the night. But he must have gotten the idea that we were not fast enough! The life we are leading in the trenches, stuck in one place, certainly does make us stiff. So, Saturday, he decided to limber us up and ordered a 28-kilometer march—that was tough. We left in the morning, ate lunch on the way and only got home in the evening. I was tired and it was also too late to write to you. […]

We've been in Ventelay for two days: we can, for an exorbitant price, procure some wine, 30 sous a liter. That seems good to us and we take advantage of it, obviously without abusing it. […] Two days ago, in report, they read a speech by General Joffre, telling us that the enemy, broken by the battle of the Marne, the Aisne and the Yser, was weakened and that we were going to take the offensive along the entire line, rather than the defensive which we've done up to now, and that he was calling on us to throw the Germans out of France. We ask nothing more; it is obviously hard for us to be in danger of being killed, stupidly, without even having seen a Prussian. I made the acquaintance of the chaplain of the regiment. I told him I was a violinist and, at the next opportunity, if he can get hold of an instrument for me, he will surely call on me to play; he's an older man and really very good, friendly, as well as a staunch patriot. He told me that he would come visit me in the trenches. [...]

12/31/1914.

[...] I was again not able to write yesterday. We left Ventelay on the 29ᵗʰ at 7 p.m. and arrived at our lines near La Ville-aux-Bois about 11 p.m. Our lines are far to the left of our previous location and, what is more, we are totally in the front line; never have we been so close to the Germans. We are in a sort of trench shack with two trees embedded in it. Don't forget that we are still in the woods, and the trenches of the *Boches* are about 30 meters in front of us.[51] As a result, out of a squadron of 16 men, there are always 8 who have their rifles in their hands; we change places every hour in order to rest. All this continues day and night. We are firing non-stop to prevent the Germans from surfacing. The Germans also have observers who shoot at us, it's a crackling that doesn't end. Their artillery can't fire on us; if a shell exploded in our trench, the shrapnel could just as easily hurt the Germans. They are therefore obliged to aim farther back at the second and third lines. For the moment, the shells are only passing over our heads, but what a barrage! The result is considerable nervous fatigue.

I am one of the best watchmen in the squadron, given my character and my age (I am the oldest) so when they need someone for a long and patient watch, especially at night, the leaders generally choose me. They quickly figure out their men and their characters. I was therefore rather tired yesterday and, despite wanting to, I couldn't write. Add to that the fact that we have done a lot of cleaning and improving of our new shelter and you have my explanation for my silence of yesterday. [...] You can't imagine the mental fatigue caused by our positions; one moment of inattention could be fatal. Many men are depressed, including, unfortunately, my friend Rolland. [...] However, here we are on the eve of a new year. It begins for us under dreadful conditions; let's hope that it will quickly bring greater happiness which would be to go home safe and healthy. I wish you, thus, dear Maman, good health, and fervently hope to see us together soon. [...]

---

[51] The expression *boche* is a pejorative term for a German.

1915

None of the combatants, neither England, France, nor Germany expected there still to be war in 1915: Germany's entire strategy was based on a quick victory. Instead, they found themselves caught in a war on two fronts. The two enemies—France and Russia—were fully mobilized while Great Britain's strength, not just her navy, was slowly growing.[52]

As for the French (and British), they could not let the Germans stay within sixty miles of Paris and control much of northeast France, with its coal and iron reserves. Starting in December 1914 and well into 1915, the French launched a series of major offensives. What resulted was what Leonard Smith calls "nibbling," both sides taking a bit of territory which they then lost to the other.[53] French casualties on the Champagne front in February and March totaled over 40,000.[54] Not yet ready to learn, starting on March 30, Joffre undertook another spring offensive that gained nothing significant and cost the French another sixty-five thousand men.

The relatively green British forces undertook the Battle of Neuve Chapelle, on March 10. Their story was not much different. Then came the Second Battle of Ypres where, on April 22, the Germans released some one hundred and sixty-eight tons of chlorine. The ensuing battle, involving French troops from North Africa along with Canadians, and British, did not die down until May 31. British casualties numbered 60,000.[55] The year continued in the same vein; no one gained much except more experience in building better defenses and killing more of the enemy.

---

[52] Hart, *The Great War,* 78.

[53] Leonard V. Smith, *Between Mutiny and Obedience, The Cast of the French Fifth Infantry Division During World War I* (Princeton: Princeton University Press, 1994) 99.

[54] Hart, *The Great War,* 129.

[55] Hart, *The Great War,* 144.

From April to June, Lucien participated in two important battles. His descriptions and reactions are frightening and enlightening. Throughout the war, he had amazing good luck, escaping death in a variety of ways. These two battles, especially the second, saw him directly in the line of fire with all his *poilu* comrades.

The first of these was the Battle of Neuville-St. Vaast. The village of Neuville-St. Vaast was the best approach to a sector of high ground, the Vimy Ridge. The town was heavily fortified with artillery, mortars, mines, machine guns and had underground shelters to protect the enemy.[56] Three weeks of fighting, beginning on May 9, brought the 39th DI to the outskirts of the village.[57] When the 5th DI arrived, on May 26, it was obvious that frontal assault was the only way to capture the village.[58] After finally taking the village, on June 9, the French had suffered about two thousand casualties to conquer less than one square kilometer of ground.[59]

The second battle, the last in which Lucien was actively engaged in fighting, was part of the Artois Offensive. The French preceded the attack with six days of artillery barrage, switching targets to try to confuse the Germans. Each barrage seemed stronger than the previous, but it was never enough. The territory gained was nothing compared with the casualties. See Lucien's letter of 6/25/1915.

Lucien's letters, missing for July and August, resume in September as the French military leaders were gearing up for yet another offensive, this one to be wider in scale and involving more of the French and British units. General Joffre wanted continued offensives in various places to prevent the Germans from concentrating their forces to break through. General Foch,[60] more reasoned or realistic, favored restrained, well-planned attacks. General Pétain,[61] at the time junior but increasingly respected, believed the war was one of attrition where the last man standing would be victor; as such, he advocated defensive strategies that would conserve manpower.[62] Begun on September 24, the great Artois and Champagne Offensives met with small successes at great cost of life, but the German defenses were so well established and deep that Joffre suspended the offensive on September 30.

Corporal Henri Laporte's description of moving from camp to the trenches paints a picture applicable to all of these advances:

> The Champagne battlefields had a strange appearance! Moist soil, chalky, white and grey. A little vegetation at the camp exit—some

---

[56] Smith, *Between Mutiny and Obedience*, 108.
[57] Infantry Division
[58] Smith, *Between Mutiny and Obedience*, 109.
[59] Smith, *Between Mutiny and Obedience*, 110.
[60] Ferdinand Foch, 1870-1929, served as Supreme Allied Commander from March 26, 1918, to the end of the war.
[61] Philippe Pétain (1856-1951), led the French troops to victory at Verdun.
[62] Hart, *The Great War*, 148.

clumps of meagre trees—followed by the great sad and desolate plain, like a vast cemetery for the living. After an hour's march in the open, we advanced in single file through communication trenches filled with water and white mud, freezing cold and glutinous. Ever since we set off it rained non-stop, like melted snow. After marching for 3 long hours, we at last reached the trenches, but what a pitiable state of utter filth! The rain never stopped falling. We occupied the front lines and found the Germans were about 100 metres from us. Apart from surprise attacks, it was no longer a war of bombs and grenades; the artillery was the real threat. The sector, for the moment, was relatively quiet. The temperature was totally freezing, the rain had stopped but what mud! We were covered from head to foot! That evening, my half-section was not on duty. When night fell, we divided into ten two-man dugouts about 2 metres deep underneath the parapet. We were obliged to bail out the water that flooded our shelters, to a depth of about 50 centimeters, water seeping through the chalk walls. We used a canvas bucket and made a chain, passing it back to throw the water behind the parapet. After half an hour of this toil, we wrapped ourselves in our soaking wet blankets, heads resting against the walls—luckily our helmets protected us from some of the damp. We tried to get some sleep, but the cold made it impossible. Moreover, the water seeped in and soon forced us to repeat the operation, a few shells bursting from time to time reminding us of the reality of our position.[63]

The French generals claimed modest success from this campaign. The French attacked in Champagne on 25 September, but it was ultimately not to their advantage as the Germans had a second line ready.[64]

This time the French suffered 3600 casualties: thirty-four infantry officers killed, sixty-three wounded and three missing; from the NCOs and common soldiers 971 were killed with 2091 wounded and 578 missing. This bloodshed did not result in securing much more territory; essentially a strip of land just over one kilometer wide and 300 to 700 meters deep, less than half a square kilometer for 3600 casualties.[65]

By the end of 1915, on the Western Front, 730,000 French soldiers had been killed, and casualties numbered over a million.[66]

Lucien became a stretcher bearer in June 1915, sparing him living in the trenches for days on end. As a stretcher bearer, however, he had to reach the wounded and carry them back over near impossible terrain. Although the main

[63] Henri Laporte, cited in Hart, *The Great War*, 152.
[64] Taylor, *The First World War*, 97.
[65] Smith, *Between Mutiny and Obedience*, 110.
[66] Hart, *The Great War*, 154.

offensive was over, the nibbling continued throughout the year. It was obvious that the allies would not "nibble" their way to the German border any time soon.

For Lucien, the pivotal event of the latter part of 1915 was the request, from General Mangin,[67] that he form a string quartet. His violin had gotten him out of the trenches; now it was to provide him astonishing opportunities and freedom.

---

[67] Charles Mangin (1866-1925), general of Lucien's unit for the first half of the war and again at the end, known for his bravery and the demands he placed on his men. A great music lover, he was the force behind the formation of the chamber music ensemble and the grouping of the musicians (Durosoir, Maurice Maréchal, André Caplet and others) together. *Deux Musiciens*, 75.

The Letters

[…] I just this minute received your letters from December 25 and 26. […] I am very interested in *L'Information*, send me that paper as often as possible. They have a sense of the practical realities lacking in many other daily papers, which read more like novels. […] We spent Christmas day at rest on a farm near Ventelay. We went back on service the 29th for about 12 days. Christmas was just between us, with a lovely menu: foie gras, omelet with lard, gingerbread, all bought at great price by our very clever friend Vessot. He moves around from café to café and is very good at getting around people and finding things when others find nothing. […]

We are in a real swamp, in muck up to our necks, filthy as pigs and it's impossible to find water for shaving. As to cooking, we have to go about 3 kilometers along passages called *sapes*, where we sink in mud up to our knees. Last night, the Germans sent us terrible New Year wishes. I had watch from 11 p.m. to 1 a.m., so I saw 1915 come in. At 10 minutes to midnight, a flare suddenly shot up, lasting 50 seconds. After that, we heard a terrible whistling, a sound I know well, and three shells exploded 20 meters on my right and 10 meters behind in the trench. The force of the explosion left me lying on the ground. I was hit by clods of earth, and then I again heard a whistling. I threw myself into the shelter holes and again three shells exploded in the same places. Suddenly everyone was on their feet; we wondered whether this was going to continue. Two more flares were sent up, but we could not see anything. Then they launched several more shots farther to the right. We all told ourselves that this was not our moment. We were calm and serious. We realize in such situations that we hold on by a thread and the shallowest of men end up with serious thoughts. All things considered, what a magnificent education is this terrible ordeal! Aside from critical times such as this, we face danger with a smile on our faces. It would be a serious error to think we are sad. […]

We managed to get a bottle of champagne for four of us, and some ham, apples and nuts. We drank the champagne last night. Indeed, we shouldn't have expected it to be very good! In the next package of 5 or 6 kilos you could put a bottle of 1904: this would be for my name day, although I will receive it much later. That will bring back old memories. It is easy to mail in a straw case. Certainly, the army could give us a better quality, but they choose it to please ordinary men and give the illusion of a bit of luxury in the trenches. The last saucisson d'Arles you sent was especially delicious; the little cans of liver pâté gave me much pleasure, it's very good and very practical and we never get anything like it. We get sardines from time to time, we have had our fill of them, the more because they are not of particularly good quality. [...]

1/2/1915.

[...] I just received your letter from December 24 and only that one. Right now, there is a big delay in the distribution of letters; clearly packages take precedence over letters. [...] We have, alas, rain night and day and are bogged down in mud. Fortunately, the type of shelter we are in has a wood floor, which protects us from the wet ground. The roof is less good and water filters through. That's when I am happy to have my two meters of oil cloth. We can't think of fixing the roof. The moment we raise our head, we are a target, and these swine are good shots. It's the same thing when we try to remove the bodies of men and horses that are filling the river; we are the object of such an intense barrage that we have to give up. We have to come to terms with the situation and live in the muck. It's interesting to see how easily the human carcass adapts to such deplorable living conditions. Still, we are all healthy and illnesses are rare. As for me personally, I have gotten thinner, but I have much more endurance and I have yet to catch my first cold. Basically, man was made to live a free and uncivilized life and not to shut himself up in cities where he becomes anemic. [...]

1/3/1915.

[...] Today I received your letter from December 23 in which you tell me about packages I've long since received. [...] I received this morning two letters from Madame Duez. She likes to send cards. It makes my hair stand on end to get cards like this, stupid and ridiculous, but well intentioned. [...] For sure, it may be good for man to have a strong religious faith in the broad sense of the word. I however consider it a weakness of the spirit to carry blessed medals and other objects that serve more or less as fetishes. One should try to avoid that childish, petty belief. I easily excuse ordinary people who believe in that, but I am broad-minded enough not to rely on such things. The high ideal I believe in at this moment is sufficient in itself. Certainly, my fate is in the hands of God. All it takes is a shell to resolve the question, but wearing a medallion of some kind can do nothing, that would be too simple. Leave that illusion to those whom it consoles; they find strength in it, but as for me, I don't need that kind of strength, I find it in myself.[68] [...]

---

[68] Lucien's comments are totally in line with what his son says about him: "My father was not, strictly speaking, religious, but he nourished a belief in the soul. [...] He was certainly not anticlerical; he found men of religion interesting, people with whom one could have discussions." in Lionel Pons, "Entretien avec Luc Durosoir," in *Un Compositeur né Romantique,* Éd. Lionel Pons, (Albi: Éditions Multilingues Fraction. Albi), 270.

So, as I told you, I will be on service until about January 10. Tomorrow night, the 4th, we move back to the second line. I hope you are not too tormented. I am doing admirably well and here it is two months that I am unhurt. We have to hope that continues. Don't be sad, please, it would trouble me a lot to think that your courage is weakening while mine is not. [...]

1/4/1915.

[...] Today I've received your letters from December 25, 29 and 30. [...] We are right now in a trench just in front of a village called La Ville-aux-Bois. This village, where the Germans occupy the houses and admirably constructed observation posts from which they shoot at us, is about 80 meters away. We also fire on the houses. As you can see, we are not far from Craonne and Berry-au-Bac. [...]

1/5/1915.

[...] I received today your letter of December 28. [...] I see from your letter that you think I am worn out with fatigue, don't believe any of it. I am taking all of this with a strength that astonishes my comrades; they didn't believe my career would have made me so strong. On the other hand, I see guys from the country, who should really be able to deal with the fatigue better than me, constantly complaining.

True, as you know, I do well on little sleep and am not a big eater. Here, we have to manage with little food, little drink, and little sleep. For many of my comrades those are important things, so they see the dark side everywhere; although I don't see things as rosy, I look at the bright side of things, that is to say, always the comic side which, fortunately, isn't hard to find. Many poor guys believed that this war would last three months and now that they know it will last at least as long as it already has, they let themselves get discouraged. Had someone told me that I would spend 8 to 10 months sleeping on straw or just the ground, never seeing a bed, I'd have been astonished. Thank you for burning a candle for me, but it does not make me happy to see you relying on things like that rather than finding within yourself and your belief in life the strength needed for this ordeal. Have confidence, dear Maman, have confidence! [...]

1/6/1915.

[...] What a mix of emotions today! For days now, we had the feeling the Germans were working on passages in our direction. Especially at night we heard the sounds of pick-axes. We made the officers from the Engineer Corps come and, after meticulous examination, they declared that the entire trench was mined and that we needed to move out as quickly as possible. The area had become really very dangerous, so close to 3 a.m. this morning they gave the order to pack up and be ready to leave in 15 minutes. That's what we did, but what a show as we moved out with our packs in the very middle of the night, without any light, silently to not attract attention. Finally, we broke camp without any damage and we settled down, outdoors, a kilometer to the left. Absolutely everyone has worked since morning with spade and pick-axe in order to make a trench and to be a bit sheltered at night. We just barely had enough time. Yesterday we were heavily shelled, and it was time that we left that dangerous place. Fortunately, the weather is very nice today, sunny and no rain. My hands are covered with dirt, so my paper is not very clean. I received today by registered mail your portrait. I was very happy to get it.

Sailors from Brest and Lorient, who had just installed the revolving cannon they brought with them, visited us in our foxholes yesterday. We chatted a bit about Brittany. One of them was from Locquémeau. He talked a lot about his area as well as about Longuivy where his parents and his wife live. He showed me numerous quite lovely postal cards. My thoughts once again transported me there, to that lovely country which, fortunately, isn't seeing the horrors that exist here. I have already heard that we will not go to Ventelay for rest this time, but to a wooded area in the rear where there are quite comfortable foxholes, so they say. Well, we will see. […]

1/7/1915.

[…] Today I received your letter from December 28 and at the same time the package from December 18 with rillettes, head cheese, figs, plums and a bottle of wine, and at the same time a package with pâté and ham that kept well. I figured they were for my feast day, and I thank you very much.

For the past 48 hours things have heated up in our region: the opposing artilleries send back and forth very violent attacks. Fortunately, we come out of them more or less unhurt, although this is a fairly dangerous type of shooting. Along with that, for 24 hours, we have had a terrible storm, rain and wind, the ugliest weather one can imagine. So, on Sunday, we will welcome our 6 days of rest with the greatest pleasure; we are living in terrible mud and getting cleaned up will be more than a luxury. […]

1/8/1915.

[…] I just received your letters from December 27, 30, 31 and January 1, 2 and 3 […] and at the same time three packages, I don't have time to open them this morning as I need to leave for duty. The duty I'll be doing is cleaning the *sape*. The *sapes* are passageways that serve all the trenches and all the foxholes. Right now, we sink 30 to 40 centimeters deep in mud. We are forced to throw down pieces of wood to walk on, otherwise we would get stuck and it would be totally impossible to leave in a hurry should it be necessary. The engineers bring us what are called *rondin*,[69] and teams of men, of which I am part this morning, place them in the *sapes*. The work warms us up. In my case, I am not easily cold: I generally have warm feet, the straw soles are excellent. As for my socks, they are in good condition and don't get wet.

I leave this service Sunday evening January 10th, about 6 p.m. We will be in Ventelay by 10 p.m. for 6 days of rest. This time we will not have it stolen from us. It will take us at least 48 hours to get clean! We will take showers which the military authority is obliged to organize. We are too dirty! And I will change underwear; I'll take advantage of the six days to get the ones I take off washed. I haven't mentioned my little binoculars, as I can't write a journal every day—I've neither the time nor a place to do it—but the binoculars serve me often. Having shown myself to be patient, tenacious, and not much inclined to fall asleep, I am on watch frequently Others are less fortunate and fall asleep at night, standing up, with the Germans 50 meters away. I already told you where I am. The houses that are 60 meters from us and from which the Germans are shooting at us are in a town called La Ville-aux-Bois, a town completely destroyed by shells. […] You will find it on your map, not far from Pontavert.

On the 2nd, 3rd, and 4th of January we were attacked furiously, the shells really rained down, etc. They were pushed back and our losses were nearly nothing, except we mostly did not sleep. […] If people were to see us on parade in Paris in our current condition, they would have immediately an idea of the kind of life we are leading. But, in the dirt and mud, our spirit shines and our morale is excellent, that's the most important. As to the filth, we have to accept our lot and stick our hands in shit when necessary. […]

1/9/1915.

[…] I didn't receive any letter today; on the other hand, I received 4 packages; with the 3 yesterday, that makes seven. People in the company are starting to think that everything is for me. Yesterday there was a delicious plum cake, figs, coffee, butter, a bit of gingerbread, some raisins, and a newspaper. Today there are two goat cheeses, 3 oranges, 4 apples, 5 candles, a box of matches, a pair of insoles, laces, two cans of mackerel, butter, coffee, a strainer, some emery paper and *L'Information*. […]

We have had a rough time with the Germans and their damned bombing. In the past 48 hours, their firing has practically stopped; the French artillery has poured so much on them that they must have wiped them out or forced them

---

[69] Logs

to pull back. We are a bit calmer but, between the 3rd and 7th of January, all the voices of hell were shouting, we will remember that. [...]

1/10/1915.

[...] I received just now your letter from January 4. [...] We must not exaggerate, Maman, I am tired but not suffering. I don't call having cold feet or sloshing about in mud suffering. For sure, it is painful to stand guard attentively, at night, in quite horrible weather, but for someone like me, blessed with totally robust health, this is not suffering, just exhausting. I am always in good spirits, whether it's raining, freezing, or windy; that is clearly the product of my good health. As to the bombing and shooting, it's not very much fun, but truly one gets accustomed, fairly easily, to the psychological and physical effect of these harrowing explosions. The shells have to explode right next to you for you to begin to be afraid. Certainly, being on watch (and especially staying alert) is difficult, but with good humor and good health, the time passes fairly quickly. Let's hope that all this will not continue inordinately long. Funny thing, we get used to living with feet in water, or at least always wet, and I swear to you that we are not any colder for that. The straw soles you send me are really excellent and keep my feet nice and warm. We are leaving this evening for 6 days of rest. [...] Rubber boots would get stuck in the mud and thus would be useless; at times our feet pull out of our lace-up boots. Dear Maman, be strong. [...]

1/12/1915.

[...] Here we are at Ventelay; I couldn't write yesterday, the 11th; it's always the same story; our relief, given our location, was very difficult. It started at 9 o'clock at night on the 10th and it was 4 o'clock in the morning when we arrived, exhausted, in Ventelay. We had the bad luck to make the entire trek in a wind and rain storm. Yesterday, I didn't get up until noon, took time to clean up a bit, and mail time had long since passed. [...]

We had supper last night with a good-natured farm wife. We had a good cabbage soup, cold pork, a hard-boiled egg, sautéed potatoes, and jam. It had been a long time since we'd had such a meal. It totally revived us. [...]

1/14/1915.

[...] Today we had what is known as a presentation of arms meaning that our division general decorated 4 officers, one battalion of the 129th with the flag, and one battalion of the 148th with the flag of the music regiment. Everyone was gathered in a large field on the outskirts of Ventelay. The setting was not lacking in grandeur; it was impressive, especially with the terrible rumbling of the cannons in the distance, creating a *basse obstinée* to the music. The sight of all those men in uniforms, with their tanned, determined faces, is a far cry from that of the soldiers in the towns. It all added a dreadful tone of solemnity to the review. I am happy to have seen it. Our division general, General Mangin, seems an energetic fellow; I like him. He doesn't seem stupid, far from it. [...]

1/15/1915.

[...] I received today your letters from 8 and 9 January. [...] I note that you went to Boulogne for our business. I completely agree with Master Colas: as long as Mme Mauhavel is working, there is no reason she should pay absolutely nothing. It's different if she asks for a reduction in the rent; you will discuss that with her and Master Colas, but it is unacceptable for her to pay nothing. You should also think about Mme Boissard: is her shop closed? I would be very surprised if she is renting no furnished rooms, given the number of soldiers in Vincennes. She has certainly rented some rooms; in that case, she has no reason not to pay some rent. [...]

Our trenches are just about 50 meters in front of La Ville-aux-Bois. In the past few two days, the French artillery has basically destroyed La Ville-aux-Bois with a violent attack because the Germans were mowing us down very easily, their position looked down on us. The big difficulty was that, because we were so close to the town, the explosions of the French shells could reach us also; we stayed as far down as possible during the shelling. [...]

Pontavert is 3 kilometers behind our trenches, we are about 6 kilometers to the left of Craonne and 8 or 10 to the right of Berry-au-Bac. There is a lot of activity here right now. [...]

Thank you for the violets you sent. [...] We have to resume our service Saturday night the 16th, but we won't be in the front line; we just spent 12 days there so we will surely be in the second line, possibly the third. The position will be much less hard and won't require our constant attention. We enjoy our rest time with great pleasure and take advantage of the time to get really clean; however, the showers don't work yet, we are just in the process of getting them organized. [...]

1/16/1915.

[...] I received this morning your letters from January 10, 11, and 12 and a package. [...] Today about 4 p.m. we will leave for the trenches; we will be in the 3rd line very near where the colonel is located. [...]

For sure many people were not prepared for a war that lasts this long, and they are disillusioned. [...]

[…] We arrived last night about 9 p.m. at our third-line stations, after a very tiring trip in the midst of an inextricable mass of vehicles. One army corps, whose number I don't want to say, set off two days ago from near us; it is heading toward Soissons to face the violent German attack which forced us to pull back a bit. The result is that all the roads are blocked by an unimaginable number of vehicles of all sorts. The engineers have enormous trucks loaded with boats because this area is flooded. Our station in third line is named *le bois du colonel,*[70] as it's where the colonel has his residence. The place is almost free of danger. A few shells reach us, but we are in anti-shell *gourbis,* solid and well made. […]

About 18 days ago, we were given a list of the territorials in the 129th. There are only 20 of us in the company. The garrisons now have a lot of young men who, recovered from their illness or their wounds, could certainly replace us, and we could be sent back to the territorial regiments. It's within the range of possibility. But we'll see, as the time goes on […]

[…] I send in haste these few lines. I took watch yesterday and am only just back, having spent about 12 hours; I have hardly the time to write, I scratch out this note so as not to leave you a day without news. […]

[…] I received today two packages, one with butter, a goat cheese and two lemons, the other with a can of herring, 6 packages of chocolate and 2 copies of *L'Information.* […]

I could only write a brief word yesterday. Our squadron was on watch and it was a very hard watch that lasted 12 hours out of 24, that is there was no real way to rest. We kept watch in the middle of a true storm of wind, hail, snow, etc. For two days now it's been rather cold; I don't know whether the weather is going to return to really cold. […]

We have a review by the colonel at 4 p.m.; we will then leave to take up another position for 3 days, then we will return for 3 days to where we are now, and then we go elsewhere for 3 days, which makes 12 days. We will be relieved of service on January 28. […]

Of course, I've retained a fond memory of Port Lazo; the tragic circumstances which forced me to leave adds to it, such that the memory in my heart is more profound. I still have the postcards you sent from there, and quite often, when I

---

[70] Colonel's woods.

have some free time, I let myself be distracted by studying the majestic formation of the cliffs. [...]

1/20/1915.

[...] Today I received your letter of 14 January. [...] You suggest that I put on layers of underwear and flannel vests to stay warmer; unfortunately, that is not very practical. It makes me feel so stuffed that it is hard to move and it is essential that we be able to move rapidly. [...]

Yesterday, we changed sector. We have arrived in a part of the woods that we've not yet occupied and where we are relatively calm, with quite good huts without much water. Right now, in the trenches, there is as much as 70 centimeters of water; we pump it out, but it always comes back. [...] We are going to the *bois du colonel* for 3 days; after that we'll have 6 days of rest safe from danger. Since being here, I've let my beard grow, I'm beginning to look like a sapper; my beard is very heavy, I look completely savage. [...]

1/21/1915.

[...] Today I received your letters from January 15 and 16. [...] There was, over by Soissons, a tremendous attack, according to what they have told us. In addition to a corps of the army of Von Kluck, there was a division of the Hunsingen army and we had only 3 brigades to face these forces, in other words, 18,000 men facing 62,000. Naturally there were more forces in the rear. They tell us that the Germans lost more than 10,000 men in this whole affair and we have already gained back some of the lost ground. The troops fighting over there fired to their last cartridge and their last shell; those troops couldn't be resupplied because of the flooding. You have no idea to what extent the entire countryside is under water and the resupply teams must have terrible worries. [...]

1/22/1915.

[...] I received your letters from January 17 and 18, and a package. [...] You mention my oilcloth. It is still in good condition; it has served me well in many ways. [...] I put it over me when I'm on watch; I make it into a cape with a diaper pin, you might call it a "macfarlane." When I go to bed, I put it over my covers; it's very warm, and if it rains in the *gourbi*, which happens frequently, I don't get wet. When the ground is damp, I put it under me. So, you see, it serves in many ways. [...]

I am happy to learn that Mme Boissard is paying you, that is proof of good will. I had mentioned selling some Columbia in case you needed money, but with the money that is coming in, that should not be necessary. I really don't want to sell Columbia which, along with the Spassky, will over time give us rewards. In my opinion, the war should not cost us too much. As long as I come home healthy and in one piece, we won't have much to complain about.

I will be out of the trenches January 28. This past night we had a terrible wind and rain storm. Our *gourbi* is very open. It is raining in, and that's why this letter is all wet. Yesterday I would have written outdoors, but right now shells are exploding 15 meters above us, thus we are staying in the shelter. You can rest easy with regard to alcohol, I only consume it when I need it. I don't like drunkards and there are many around us, that's no exaggeration. During rests, half the company is blotto, which I find disgraceful. The good fortune of having escaped danger doesn't justify this behavior in which, sadly, some officers share. [...]

1/24/1915.

[...] I received your letters from 19 and 20 January. [...] I couldn't write yesterday as I was chosen for a pioneer's duty, a chore that lasted until 5 p.m. During the entire day, I worked with pick and shovel, and obviously, I couldn't write. [...]

I received yesterday a package with three oranges, and indeed I don't remember what else. I must tell you that at this moment I'm writing in an underground *gourbi*, bent in half as it is not high enough to stand; one candle provides the light. The shelling is horrific, the ground doesn't stop trembling violently. All night long, at Berry-au-Bac, the battle raged. [...]

1/26/1915.

[...] I haven't yet received a letter today, but I received two packages, one with pâté in excellent condition and the other with a cake. Today is Julien's feast day and naturally I invited him to share the pâté (which was excellent) and the cake. [...]

Yesterday, about 2 p.m., we had a terrible attack by the Germans which was repelled. It seems that even around Berry-au-Bac we have made important advances. Started by an artillery duel, the bombardment quickly spread and, from Berry-au-Bac to Soissons, it was soon nothing but a lightning storm of cannon shots, machine guns, etc. I had never yet heard such a noise. We could no longer tell whether the shells were coming or going. We were in the second line and immediately put our packs on our backs to go wherever our presence was needed. The reserves came running from everywhere. It's a strange sight to see thousands of men pop out from everywhere in a place that had been very quiet. The noise was crazy and one has the impression that a formidable steel curtain is stopping the invasion, a great barrier which announces: Stop here! You will have an idea of the noise when I tell you that, behind us, 30 pieces of artillery were firing at least 150 shots a minute, enough to make one deaf, I had to put cotton in my ears. That lasted for two hours, then quieted down and the night was very tranquil. We are worried about the 27th, Guillaume's birthday. [...]

1/27/1915.

[...] Today I received two letters from 21 and 22 January. [...] I've already told you that we leave active duty tomorrow evening, the 28th, and we are going to Ventelay, but unfortunately not to Ventelay itself but to the farm of the Faîtres, a kilometer this side of Ventelay; it will be less easy to find extra things. [...]

I don't believe the 3rd corps will be moved to the rear, as we were told not long ago, but there is still talk of sending the territorials back to their territorial companies. We are about 20 territorials in each company, and the company is composed of 250 men. [...] You tell me you hear cannons: the 75 mm has a very dry detonation, quick and violent; the 105, 155, and 220 have detonations that are dull and deep, but make relatively less noise. In Vincennes they must be testing new cannons or new powders. [...]

1/28/1915.

[...] It's tonight that we leave for rest, we certainly deserve it. For some time now the attacks have been very violent. Last night there was tremendous fighting near Soissons: rockets, three and four at a time, shot into the sky, and the rumble of artillery never stopped. That lasted three hours, from 10 p.m. to 1 a.m. [...]

About a half-hour ago, the adjutant had just barely left his *gourbi*, he was about 10 meters away, when a shell exploded above, collapsing his *gourbi*. What luck for him! Here everything is a matter of luck or good fortune. For several days now we have had snow-like weather, but no snow fell and suddenly last night, about 8 p.m., the winds turned to the east and the cold took hold, fiercely. Eight degrees below zero last night. In any case this weather will be healthier. For our shoes, we get grease twice a week; we grease our shoes with great care, otherwise they will become hard. I have to say that I almost never have cold feet, straw soles are excellent at keeping me warm. [...]

Tonight we will travel 12 kilometers with the greatest pleasure. [...]

1/29/1915.

[...] For sure our last duty in the trenches was unreal: we changed places four times in twelve days. [...] Yesterday, several hours before we were relieved, we were in enormous danger. Here are three dates—31 December, 6 January, and 28 January—on which I escaped miraculously, let's hope that continues. [...] Our region, from Soissons just past Berry-au-Bac, is right now in continuous movement, and there are constant attacks and counterattacks. It's in God's hands. What a shelling! And you should see what one of our shells is like. In La Ville-aux-Bois, I saw a house completely flattened by one of our bombs, it's incredible. [...]

Just today, in Ventelay, I received my shipment from January 4 and the two from the 12th, which I call the big packages. I also received three little ones. Fortunately, I did not have to carry all that. [...]

1/30/1915.

[...] I received today your letters from January 25 and 26. I note that you worry a lot about me; that serves no purpose and can't change anything. Our last four days on active duty were very difficult, with constant attacks by the Germans. They were stopped with great losses; our artillery showers them with a violence you cannot imagine. Our company has been very lucky; in three days we only had two wounded, neither seriously. [...]

1/31/1915.

[...] I received your letters from January 27 and 28. [...] We leave tonight for another encampment, quite near here but which brings us closer to Craonne. I can't say more; yesterday they read us a memo stating that it is forbidden to speak of or to name the area we are in. Many letters will be opened and disciplinary action will be taken against those who are caught. Thus I can't say more. I believe that there will be one of these days an attack against Craonne. There are a lot of troops concentrated there. [...]

2/1/1915.

[...] We made the short trip, about 4 kilometers, during a wind and snow storm. Fortunately, it didn't last; today is not as cold, almost thawing. We found here some good people who made us lunch, partly with what we brought with us. Today we ate potatoes in their skins with our butter, it was very delicious, the more so because for some time we've been deprived of this sort of food. There is not an abundance of vegetables. It's always meat, frozen meat from Chili, Australia, and Argentina, the meat in itself is good; but eating it constantly produces a type of itchy rash which the doctors aren't familiar with. At this moment, many men are suffering from it. It's the absence of fresh vegetables. The doctors don't want to evacuate those who have this condition; they tell them to eat green vegetables, it's a bit ironic. [...]

2/2/1915.

[...] There can be no doubt, in a few months the Germans will be worn out, as the allies are maintaining the blockade rigorously. We need to have a lot of patience and resignation, qualities which are much harder to have than brief outbursts of bravery. It is quite dreadful to stay stoically in the trenches and put up with the terrible weather and shelling. [...]

2/4/1915.

[...] Today I received your letter of January 29. Time passes very slowly for us all, but fortunately we understand that this time, which is quiet for us, wears down the German forces considerably. All the enemy attacks are pushed back with frightful losses. The bodies of the *Boches* lie in piles. On the other hand, if we take the offensive, it will hardly be before the middle of March; we need to be pretty sure of the weather. As for our officers (I don't mean the superiors, whom I don't know, but the junior officers about whom we can make judgments) they are, alas, very ordinary people, quite vulgar and inclined to be drunkards. One has to remember that ours is a regiment of men from Normandy and that this vice is quite common. The 3rd corps, has, I believe, since the beginning, and especially at the beginning, given proof of incompetence—poor commanders and soldiers who performed badly under fire. You could send me a bit of that ointment which Ligneul prescribes for cracked fingertips, in these conditions they are becoming quite painful. [...]

2/5/1915.

[...] If we didn't have any personal resources, we would be really quite unhappy. The area we are in at the moment is not, in itself, dangerous, but we cannot use any fire. The smoke can be seen from very far away. As a result we don't cook at all and for the 36 hours that we've been here, they brought us only one plate of meat with a few rare potatoes. My buddies are literally dying of hunger. In this respect, we are certainly very poorly organized. [...] Fortunate are those, like our little group, who have some provisions of their own. [...]

2/6/1915.

[...] Over the past 3 days, our company has received 100 sheepskins: they will distribute them soon. But it's stupid, that should have been done on December 1. Now that the real cold is past, we are burdened with them needlessly. What is more, the skins are filled with fleas and lice, and once the wool has absorbed the rain, it's dreadfully heavy. For my part, I don't want one. I never had frozen feet.

I just need to not tighten my legs, nor my feet and to do a bit of Swedish gymnastics. The Germans' boots are certainly better than ours. […]

The artillery is making a lot of noise. Obviously, ours is dominating and wiping out, more and more, the German artillery. Our new 105 caliber guns, batteries of which arrive every day, are demolishing all the German batteries. According to the artillerymen, it is a remarkable piece of equipment, just as good as the 75; the range is 14 kilometers instead of 6, and the shell weighs 16.5 kilograms rather than 8. Nothing can stand up to this projectile, it is alarming to hear it go off. The shell of the 155 caliber weighs 47 kilos and has a range of 18 kilometers. We have two of them covering 200 meters. They are "Charlotte" and "Catherine;" when they fire the earth shakes three kilometers around. […]

2/8/1915.

[…] I was unable to write yesterday despite my efforts; I was on watch in a fairly dangerous area which required extra vigilance. It is when we are at rest, no longer bolstered by nervous energy, that we are aware of our fatigue. […]

I realized, this winter, how little I am inclined to be cold, how tough I was in all respects when compared to my companions. […] I often thought about Maman Marie,[71] and how she barely ever warmed herself. […]

2/9/1915.

[…] For two days we have had horrifying artillery duels and we all have the feeling the German guns are being destroyed one after the other. Last night there was a lot of commotion, fighting along the entire line from Berry to Craonne—a terrible racket. Being on reserve, we had our packs ready to take us wherever we were needed. It was just an alert; we soon went back into our *gourbis*. We leave for the front line tonight and will go for rest the night of the 15th. […]

2/10/1915.

[…] General Mangin came to our trenches yesterday; our commanding officer was aware of this visit which was a surprise for us. Just that morning we got a very generous water ration, something we had waited a long time for. The only purpose was to keep the men from complaining, should the general happen to question any of them; that's just what happened. But rather than picking a timid dope, he just happened to pick someone with intelligence, who told him that we never got any wine, or almost never, never any eau-de-vie, and described the ridiculous distribution that morning. The general got angry and said that every

---

[71] Maman Marie was Louise's mother, Charlotte. Papa Marie, Louise's father, was named Jean-Baptiste Marie. Louise and Lucien lived with Louise's parents until their deaths.

day we were supposed to have some wine and some rum and that we deserved it. In short, there was excitement and a ruckus all along the line! The officers went a bit wild; the complaint was justified and I think that the result will be a fairer distribution more often. There is no doubt that there is pilfering and food is taken from the rations we would most like to have.

We have, obviously, changed location and are now in the front lines. We have four hours of guard duty each night, and two hours each day. At night for two hours, in front of the trenches, we set up what they call listening posts; we have to listen carefully, and be vigilant to an extreme. Naturally those on guard duty in the trenches are counting on us—50 meters in front of them—to warn them should we see or think we see something unusual. We will go on rest the night of the 15th, and will be in either Ventelay or Concevreux for Mardi Gras. We will try, if we can find what we need, to make crêpes and even, according to what Rolland says, apple crêpes: he says they are exquisite. [...]

2/12/1915.

[...] You could send me some sugar as we use a lot. I will also need candles. I use them up quickly; the company never gives us any and we are mostly lodged in underground *gourbis*. After 5:30 we need to light them, we can't always be in the dark, it's depressing. Rolland and Vessot also receive candles, but even among the three of us, we barely manage. [...] You make me laugh when you tell me not to shake the hand of those who have itches from insects; those who don't have them, like me, are the exception. Dear Maman, here everyone is covered with lice, fleas, crabs, etc.; we march through all imaginable dung heaps, and we can't wash even a little, there is no water. I take care of myself, and avoid the worst, but one can't be delicate. [...]

2/14/1915.

[...] I will answer all your questions. We were supposed to go off duty the night of the 15th, but the battalion at rest had been vaccinated against typhoid and there were quite a few who got sick. Their rest had to be prolonged. As a result, we will not leave for rest until the night of the 17th, at least that is what we are hearing. You are right that our officers and sub-officers are not superior people: they are, in general, quite vulgar, and many of our men would do better in their place. It is definitely true for me. Had I thought I would be part of a war, I could easily have been a reserve lieutenant. What is done is done, we can't go back. You believe, rightly, that this terrible life with no distractions of any sort seems burdensome for a number of officers accustomed to a fortunate and easy life. [...]

2/16/1915.

[...] There must be some truth in the rumors about the territorials and their return to the corps in the rear, but we can't let that go to our heads, and I will not believe it until I see it in writing. So far, I don't believe any of it and urge you to do the same. When they have us at the front, they don't let us go—you don't leave here unless wounded or dead. At the garrison, it's different. When some-one with little conscience knows how to handle things and plays up to superiors, sometimes he can find a way to get himself settled in a really calm place—I've seen it happen. I would be ashamed to do the same. Later, in person, I will be able to tell you a lot of stories; here I never know that my letters are not being read.

The sheepskins arrived too late—as with much else an example of disorder and waste. Some officers, rather than distributing the sleeping bags intended for the men, cover their *gourbis* with them, putting dirt on top, making a watertight roof for them. They couldn't care less about the water that gushes into the *gourbis* of the troops: "let them manage for themselves!" That's the rule here for all of us. But let's leave this topic. [...]

2/17/1915.

[...] You could send me, in a steel box, one or two boxes of matches, as we can't find any here. We leave this evening for C. for rest for four days.[72] Things will be quieter for us than in the trenches, but not as calm as in Ventelay; occa-sionally German shells reach C. We are closer to the lines here, so we can't enjoy complete rest, we are always on edge. Our artillery shelling, for 48 hours, has been horrendous, but the German artillery must be either absent or destroyed, as it responds hardly at all. We have launched more than 500 shells, four to eight at a time. From our slits we see melanite shells falling on the German trenches and the earth flying up as much as 20 meters, it's frightening. It is hard to imagine how many we've fired in two days. We are all convinced that they have pulled back a lot of troops to send to the Russian front where the danger, for them, is growing. It is natural to think that the war will last into July, however a lot of good minds believe that, given the enormous losses they are suffering on the Russian front, we could see the war end sooner than we expect. Let's wish for that without believing in it too much. [...]

2/18/1915.

[...] Finally, we are at rest, we arrived last night about 11 p.m., during a dreadful torrent of wind and rain. We were drenched, we made a good grog

---

[72] Lucien at times used the first letter of names of towns: C for Concevreaux, for example.

when we arrived, which made us feel a lot better. Our relief took place, fortunately, without incident. I say "fortunately" because for three days the bombing had been non-stop, and if the *Boches* had replied at the moment of our relief, we would have been quite upset. [...] We are staying here, in Concevreux, in a house where a good woman is lodging us, she cooks for us, we eat potatoes with skins, carrots which we find delicious. We can bathe and I am going to wash my clothes. [...]

2/20/1915.

[...] Please be so good as to send me some candles; being deprived of light is a great hardship: nothing is possible, not reading or writing—it's sad. I thank you with all my heart for your loving shipments. The ordeal we are undergoing is really very difficult; particularly the length, and the uncertainty we all have as to the end of this damned war. Some days the most courageous are afraid. I watch comrades, especially those with young children; this life weighs on them and becomes, basically, intolerable. I find it very hard to bolster their failing courage. This moral suffering makes our physical suffering harder. Let us hope that the Russians, with their great effort, will squash the Germans and in so doing cut short our ordeal. To think that it will soon be seven months that I've not slept in a bed and haven't gotten undressed! I would not have believed it possible, but it's true! Still, in spite of everything, time passes and has to bring a solution. [...]

2/22/1915.

[...] This morning I received your two letters from the 16th and 17th, [...] a package of candles, and a box of Cadum.[73] You could have sent me a smaller box. I have here enough to treat the rashes of an entire section. Up until now I have been fortunate to not get fleas. I check very often and I have only killed one. On the other hand, I have some rashes around my wrists. The major says it is due to the straw on which we sleep. No matter, some treatments with Cadum will easily take care of it. [...]

2/23/1915.

[...] I hear around me the terrific news that the English-French Navy broke through the Dardanelles. If this is true, it will have a great influence on the war and its length. Italy, France, and England will receive Russian wheat, and what is more, Russian troops will easily be able to land in Marseille. The journey from Sebastopol to Marseille is only 6 days long. You must know that the Russian army easily has a formidable number of men (8 to 10 million). The

---

[73] A French soap created in 1907.

shortage of roads and rail lines allows a maximum of 4 million at the front. That army will be able to plug holes and create new ones, which wears out the *Boches* enormously. If only they could put six or more million men at the front, the Germans couldn't resist for long. But with the Dardanelles in our possession, everything changes. We could, with the help of England, move to Marseille important numbers of Russian forces which could be sent to Alsace, or another point on our front line. This reinforcement would be far from useless and would certainly benefit us. […]

2/24/1915.

[…] The city of Le Havre continues to send packages, though somewhat less frequently than before. I think there are concerts in Vincennes. Lucky are those who think about things like that at a time like this, they have hardly any worries. The Bastide you mention is in fact one of the Leforts. He can't be even thirty years old, he must have been discharged; it's the same with Kretly who, although still active, remains in Rouen where, according to Rolland, he is playing. Recently I see that Boucherit is playing in Paris. There are some strapping men who will not have suffered the harm of the war and that's why I will reply to Mangeot's letter;[74] after the war they should publish the names of those who fought and those who stayed home. […] Here's a draft of the letter for Mangeot:

> Dear sir, Called to the 23rd territorial from Caen, after the 4th of August I was sent to Cherbourg and there, until October 6, I was in several encampments. On October 6, with 100 of my comrades, I was sent to the garrison of the 129th Infantry Regiment in Le Havre, and November 13 sent as reinforcement to my regiment which was at that time near Brimont not far from Reims. Since December 12, I am in the area of Craonne and Berry-au-Bac. These names alone must tell you a lot. After the war, we will have much more time to talk. I have been lucky, up to now, to keep my health and my life, which is a lot given the conditions of our existence. Do I need to tell you that music seems to me a distant dream, and that I envy (although I am not very jealous by nature) those who have not been separated from their instrument? Veuillez agréer, cher monsieur Mangeot.[75]

2/27/1915.

[…] Our friend Dehuysser of the 23rd is still waiting for a Kodak, I hope that I will be able to send you a picture of me and some pictures of the trenches. We

---

[74] André Louis Mangeot (1883-1970), violinist, director of *Monde musical*.
[75] The formal French way of closing a letter, something like "please be assured of my high esteem."

are all much changed, all with beards, tanned faces; we have also gotten thinner. Tomorrow, February 28 we will leave for rest in Concevreux for 4 days; I do not yet know whether we will be vaccinated. It would certainly be wise as the sun is getting hotter and soon everything will stink everywhere. Imagine that, in front of us, between La Ville-aux-Bois and C, there are over 800 German corpses that have been there 3 or 4 months. The crows tear at them. We can't go get them to bury them, we'd be killed. It's not been bad so far but in a little while it will be foul. [...]

2/28/1915.

[...] You are amazing with your talk of a portrait; you imagine that we have nothing to do but go to the photographer, but there is no photographer and I don't know anyone in the battalion who has a camera. Our friend Dehuysser should receive his Kodak, he's waiting for it, but once he has it and has taken our pictures, he will still have to send the plates to Paris to be developed, then they must be returned to him. It will certainly be some time before I can send you my picture. Rest easy, you will have it but you have to be patient. I am sadly surprised by the death of Monsieur T, which you announce at the end of your letter. He's the last person I saw in Port Lazo as I left. He even accompanied me a bit along the way wishing me good luck. How curious it is, I who for months have been exposed to death am still here and he, who basically was in good health, is gone. Life is fleeting, that's what we see here. [...]

3/1/1915.

I am writing very early this morning. I am in Concevreux; we arrived last night about 11 p.m. The weather was dry, cold, with a dreadful wind. I just received your letter from February 26; I've been told I have three packages but they will not be distributed until this afternoon. That means I cannot tell you the contents but based on what you tell me it is probably the three terrines of cod. I am astonished that you didn't receive any letters from February 19 and 20; I write absolutely every day. When I cannot write because of some circumstance over which I have no control, which happens rarely; I let you know in advance. I am shocked that you tell me I don't list the packages I receive; I always do. [...] I always receive the packages you send. It's only the most recent, from February 26, that I've not received yet; they will arrive soon. From now on, you would do well not to send the packages by registered mail. You will save money and time and they don't arrive any faster, just the opposite. I had a long discussion today with the mail clerk and he strongly advises that you not register any packages from now on. I share his opinion. [...]

If you can, from time to time, send me a bit of alcohol for cooking, in sturdy bottles, well padded, that would be good. But absolutely don't forget to send some solid alcohol. I am not very rich right now and I would not like to run out. It's been some time since we could get any charcoal. Everyone steals as much as possible. We quickly grab a sack when we can.

I do not know why the service moves from one sector to another. No one has been able to give me an explanation. Maybe it is the division general who is in charge and decides as he sees fit. Our division general is General Mangin, a very lively man but hard and demanding of his soldiers. He may be the one who writes the rules that pertain to us. Naturally the same officers and non-commissioned officers are always with us and you can imagine they are no happier than the ordinary soldier. When they are at rest, they have beds to sleep in. When I think that it will be almost 7 months since I slept in a bed, the amount of suffering we've endured becomes clear. I can't believe that the high command doesn't think about all that, especially for us territorials. A good many of our class are in garrisons and thus relatively privileged compared with me. We don't ask for much; we would be satisfied with two weeks of rest with good beds and food that comes close to civilian food. [...]

The first letter from Louise. As mentioned, she formatted her letters by writing out the name of the month, unlike Lucien.

Saturday, March 6, 1915.

Mon cher enfant, I received your letter dated Monday March 1. [...] Of course I want a picture of you. You will soon have been in the trenches for 4 months. I would love to see you as you are now. [...] I could even have come see you during your six days of rest in Ventelay. Some wives may have done that. Had I known when your rest period started, I could have arranged to be in Ventelay that day and to stay there for six days. You say there is an infirmary. If there is an infirmary, there are wounded and sick men. The relatives of these injured and sick must come see them. But it was a tall order for me just to learn that your rest would be in Ventelay. I had to drag out of you the name of the place. [...]

When you write you need to tell me right away what is happening; your letters arrive five days after you write them. You are starting to find this trial long. You need to keep up your faith and your great spirit in order to chase away the discouragement and sadness that threaten to overcome you. [...] You are one of the lucky ones to be surrounded by love. How many poor soldiers separated from their families never have, or rarely have, news from their loved ones. [...] I think of you constantly: and I think about all the horrible things, the psychological suffering added to the physical hardship of the trenches. Sometimes I wish I could be doing my part. [...] I would like to know you have been vaccinated so you don't risk typhoid fever. I could send a little bottle of Epsom salts for the miasmas which will spread everywhere with the temperature that is getting hotter every day. Maybe also some phenylated water.[76] I'll think about it. Today I've sent four packages by mail, unregistered:

1ˢᵗ: A can of solid alcohol, not the same brand, this one may be better, and two apples.

2ⁿᵈ: Six lovely apples. Be sure to eat the fruit I send.

3ʳᵈ: A veal and ham pâté.

4ᵗʰ: A cake, six chocolate madeleines, two bars of chocolate, a deep aluminum plate, an aluminum pot with a folding cover. These things will be very useful. You will tell me if you need a knife. You will please list for me the packages you receive so I know none are lost. They are no longer registered. I put the 6 chocolate madeleines and two bars of chocolate in the pot. [...] I sent you two pairs of straw insoles covered with wool.

The water meter for the house at 17 rue Nicolai has been repaired. I received the bill: 3,50. [...] With all the work, plus the travel time for the technician, the real charge was 5,30 but they sent back 1,05 in stamps. It's a very honest business. [...] I also received a bill for 20 F for sewer charges for a different building. Then there are the charges for liability insurance for two properties which means I'll have to pay them. Money keeps disappearing even when I pay attention. How much do you have left? Do you need me to wire some? [...]

3/2/1915.

I received today your letter of February 24 and 4 packages with a can of solid alcohol, 2 apples, 2 cheeses, some butter, some coffee, 3 packages of petits beurres, some packages of cocoa and two issues of *L'Information* from February 24 and 25. Yesterday I received the 3 terrines of cod; we ate that for lunch today, at the home of our good woman who heated them in a bain-marie. It was absolutely delicious. [...] We are enjoying our rest and are quite content; the good woman in whose home we spend our days is very welcoming and very clean. [...] I know that camphor is good against lice. Vessot gave me some, it helps but doesn't stop them. In truth, we need to undress frequently and inspect our underwear. We win the battle by staying clean; there are so many guys who don't care and are unclean out of laziness. [...]

---

[76] Phenol, referred to sometimes as carbolic acid, was useful for sterilizing surgical equipment.

March 7, 1915.

I received last evening at 8 your letter from March 2 in which you tell me you are enjoying your rest and that the good woman who is providing you lodgings is very nice and very clean. All the better that you give her your underthings to wash and mend. Four days are rather short to be sure the clothes are really dry; you must be careful not to wear damp underwear.

I'm delighted that the cod with onions and apples provided a feast. It's my own recipe. It's not very fancy. I thought that apples could replace potatoes which are not always very good reheated. [...]

3/3/1915.

I received today your letter from February 28 and 5 packages. [...] We will leave tomorrow, March 4, for the trenches, where we will stay for only 4 days, then return for 4 days at Concevreux. After that, I do not know what we will be doing. A lot of rumors are going around right now; they say that, after March 7, no more letters or packages will be distributed, everything stopped, as in a full mobilization, because of troop and equipment transport to the front. [...] I got over my cold a while ago; it was no more than a head cold. [...]

3/4/1915.

I received today your letter of the 27th, it arrived after the one from the 28th. [...] During this last departure from Concevreux for the trenches, the weather was quite warm and I arrived almost swimming in sweat. We took up a position in a very dangerous open area that was a swamp. The engineers, in order to protect us, had dammed up a little river and we had, in front of us, veritable lakes: unfortunately, our trenches are half under water. After arriving soaked in sweat and spending the night with my feet in the water, the next day I came down with a cold, but fortunately only that. The magic of our life in the open air meant that, after three days, I no longer had my cold. In the city, under ordinary conditions, I would have been quite ill. Here, with this rustic life, one becomes as tough as nails. [...] The season that is coming will be more dangerous in a number of ways, as the sun is now very hot and the nights are always very cold; we cannot take off our clothes, but sometimes we get very hot. [...]

March 8, 1915

[...] I received a card from Mme Duez inviting me for next Sunday, March 14. I had asked her whether she was free last Sunday, March 7. She wasn't; that very day she was going to a lecture presented by Mme Henri Robert in the *Salle de l'Horticulture*, rue de Grenelle, "French prisoners in Germany." If there was something interesting like that on the 14th, she would like me to reserve places and she'd reimburse me; we could go together to a lecture of some sort and have dinner at Scossa's.[77] The Gare St. Lazare makes her trip back to Boulogne easy. She is clingy, that woman. I don't leave the house; how could I reserve places in advance? I will certainly not go to Paris for that, or even to the post office to use the phone. No, I will tell her that I cannot go to Paris and that a lecture, however interesting, deprives me of the time to write to you and send you what you need. [...]

3/6/1915.

I was not able to write yesterday; I was on 24-hour guard duty that was so busy it didn't leave me any free time. In the past 2 days I received your letters from March 1 and 2 and a large number of packages. [...] As for sending a picture, I need to find the right time to have one taken. Dehuysser still hasn't received his camera and as I told you no one in our company, nor among the nurses that I run into in Concevreux, has one. [...]

I beg you to send me several packages of good quality incense paper in order to combat the dreadful smells of our *gourbis*. We have no fresh straw, everything in the area is old and used up, and our dung heaps stink. The toilet water arrived just in time. Send me also a little steel or aluminum plate; my mess tin is beyond use. I left it outside our *gourbi* and it was hit by some shrapnel from a shell exploding above us. Besides, a plate will be more useful and easier to wash, the bottom of the mess tin is disgusting. [...]

3/7/1915.

I received this morning your letters from March 3 and 4. [...] You ask me why the Germans don't bury their dead; the area where all the bodies lie is between the lines and neither side can venture onto this ground without risking lives; it would require a cease fire of several hours but, unfortunately, they have taken advantage of cease-fires to safely install new batteries; so we don't grant them any longer. [...]

3/8/1915.

I received today your letter from March 5 and no package. We leave this evening for rest and there we will no doubt find letters and packages. We are going to Concevreux for 4 days. There we can rest well; we have a house where we spend our days, take our meals, shave and clean up. It is only to sleep that we have to go back to the cantonment. Yes, they had definitely said that the territo-

---

[77] The Café-Restaurant Scossa, Place Victor Hugo, Paris.

rials would be moved back, but that has been said for so long that I have little by little lost all hope of leaving the front before the very end. […] The important thing is to stay well, I have that luck, so much the better; all I can hope for is to return safe and sound. […] I have to finish this letter quickly as they are calling me for some work, and here, in the colonel's woods, the army comes first, after all! There are chores all day long. Our colonel is a dreamer. He makes us constantly undo and redo things. […]

3/9/1915.

I received just this instant your letter from March 6. You ask insistently for a photo; I understand, but I have to find the way to get one taken. […] You speak of coming to Ventelay or to the front; it is obvious you don't understand anything. No women, not even the officers' wives, can get up to the lines. The only women in this area are those rare residents who have not fled. […] As for naming locations, it is strictly forbidden; if a letter was opened and I was caught, I would spend 2 weeks in prison. That's not at all interesting and for that reason I rarely give you a name of a place. […] I would like some Epsom salts—it smells so dreadful at times! That is why I asked you for *papier d'Arménie*.[78] […]

I don't worry about me catching cold. I have to be in unusual conditions to catch one. Fortunately I'm not about to go back to that damned Plizon. [See letter from March 18.]

March 11 and 12, 1915.

[…] I think you must have received your wine. It was shipped on February 10, that makes a month. I find that quite long and wonder what causes these shipments sent by rail to be so delayed. Today I prepared a new shipment of wine: a bottle of Bordeaux Malescot 1900 and a half-bottle of ordinary wine. The wine is packaged in a long wooden box. It is not wide enough for two bottles. I am very happy that M. Bouchard gives me wooden boxes which are well made and very sturdy. […]

I send you every day a copy of *L'Information*. I often forget to tell you but you just need to pay attention to the papers that wrap the packages I send and set them aside to read. […]

---

[78] *Papier d'Arménie* is still available in little packets. It is a paper impregnated with benzoin resin from Laos. Lucien used it to combat the dreadful odors surrounding him.

3/10/1915.

I received no letters today, but there were 4 packages. [...] I received a letter from Coraboeuf which I'm sending to you.[79] He also sent me three copies of his latest works; I'm sending you those also. He still has his wonderful, fine, and distinctive talent. I find his portraits full of life and distinguished. He is fortunate to be able to work; from what he says, he will appear again in front of the review board. I seriously doubt he will be taken, especially because of his age, 43 or 44 years old. I don't believe they ever send anyone of that age to the front. [...]

Don't send me any more money: I still have 350 francs and that is more than I need. I spend really very little, mostly when at rest, or sometimes in the trenches, when I manage to pay someone else to do a particularly unpleasant chore assigned to me. [...]

March 13, 1915.

I received a letter about my aunt Eugénie Guillot, in Sèvres; she died, at age 72, a few days after her son. The funeral is tomorrow at 1 p.m.; she will be buried in Boulogne. I am very unhappy not to be able to go, but tomorrow I have packages to prepare and send to you. I would have to rush to be at the funeral home in Sèvres before 1 p.m. For the past few days I've had pains in my left arm and shoulder. I think it's not serious but tomorrow, I'd have to leave Vincennes for Sevres early, without a proper lunch, then go to the cemetery in Boulogne, then come home at who knows what hour, I would be exhausted. I truly regret not being able to show this respect for the family, but I think I would pay dearly for the effort. [...]

3/11/1915.

I received your letter of March 7 and three packages. [...] As I told you, we are well off here: since the last time we have finally found an extremely clean house where we spend our days. We take our meals here and obviously we wash up. When I give my underwear to be washed, it comes right back beautifully washed and ironed and always totally dry for our departure. [...] Your cod with potatoes was truly superb, a good idea. The mutton stew was also very good; it's a bit fanciful to send things like that, but they provide a change. What I would like to have, and have used up, is some more foie gras Marie. It is very good, and convenient when one has to eat quickly, in case of an alert or something like that. [...]

I asked for some *papier d'Arménie*, you could also send some Epsom salts because our *gourbis* smell horrible. This stinking mud surrounds us. The nurses throw in

---

[79] Jean Coraboeuf (1870-1947), painter and engraver, friend of the Durosoirs.

bleach but it would take tubfuls to make any difference. The papier d'Arménie will be very helpful. [...]

We leave tomorrow evening March 12 for the trenches. I don't know whether it is for 8 days or 12. We'll be in the sector of La Ville-aux-Bois; we'll have to keep our eyes open. [...]

3/12/1915.

I received today your two letters from March 8 and 9 and 4 packages containing 3 terrines of lentils and sausages and 4 little jars of mint cream. It's a bit crazy to send things like that; you spend a lot of money buying containers like those cute little glasses we have to give to our good woman. [...] Don't trouble yourself so much making little meals to send; it's a bit unreal and makes a lot of packages and expense for not very much. They are making a few comments about the number of packages I receive but you know I don't pay much attention to that. [...]

3/14/1915.

I just received your letter from March 11 and at the same time 7 packages: your beef dish made up one package. The problem with things like that is that they multiply the number of shipments and, darn it, I cannot pretend I am not receiving five or six packages daily. It makes everyone talk. I am on very good terms with the mail clerk so maybe he doesn't want to say anything, but all the men who carry the sacks with packages say quite openly that if everyone received that many, they would never finish their work. Without completely agreeing with them, there is some truth in all that. You send more and more packages for what really do not add up to much—puddings, prepared meals. "Not much" does not mean you don't work to make the dishes; you do it very well, for sure. But what I mean is that the shipments don't really do me much good, don't last long and multiply the number. So try not to send more than 3 shipments a day; you can't avoid sending canned goods. They are the only things that don't take up much space and are nourishing and useful. I tell you all this because, really, people are starting to talk. Although I appreciate the value of your meals, it makes for too many packages. [...]

Thursday, March 18, 1915.

I received this morning your letter of March 14 in which you complain about too many packages (an abundance of good things can't be bad). The 7 packages you received in one day were sent on two different days. It's the post that distributed some of them late. [...] You talk about fresh fruit and jam but you didn't mention the kilo of mirabelles I sent. [...] I send you apples, oranges,

lemons, which are all fresh, not to mention plums, figs, and honey. There is nothing else to be found, and pretty soon it will be very dull as there won't be any
more apples or oranges, and I think jam will become scarce. You say that Vessot
receives little hams. They can't be very big as the weight limit is 1 kilogram […]
So one person receives 4 or 5 packages a day, or 2 or 3, or only once or twice
a week, that is not the concern of the person who distributes them. The postal
administration benefits; if the service were suddenly stopped, I think the government would have trouble. […] I'll pay attention and only send, on average,
three a day as I did today. I put the terrines all in one package, but it's not always
easy. I need special boxes depending on what is being put in the package. […]

3/15/1915.

I received today your letter of March 12 and three packages. […] I also
received *L'Information* from the 11th and 12th. From what I read, there will be
no suspension in the distribution of letters and packages; it was a false German
rumor circulated by I don't know who. […] I am in the trenches for 12 days, that
is, until the evening of the 24th, and we will then be in Concevreux for 6 days. I
heard that we will have two marches during those six days, it is possible but not
yet certain. Our lodging at Concevreux is in the stables of a large farm; there is
not a free bed anywhere in this area, they are all taken by the officers. We spend
our days in the home of a good woman, but we have to leave to sleep in our stable; we are used to it. […]

Friday, March 19, 1915.

I did not receive a letter this morning, but found one when I came home at
5. I went to see M. and Mme Lambert as I told you. […] I am pleased that you
were able to wear the wool socks Mme Lambert knitted: new wool holds the heat
much better than wool that has been washed a number of times. […] I did not
stop to see Mme Armengaud; I would have gotten home too late. I can't make a
fire before I go out, so I have to light a fire after I come home which wastes time;
that is why I am writing so late. […] I do not much like to go out. I find I spend
an inordinate amount of time doing nothing. There are people who are only
happy when they go out. I think they don't like or don't know how to deal with
their interior lives. I will probably go see Mme Armengaud on Tuesday, and the
Cunault's on Thursday (since they don't come visit me). And I need to visit Mme
Duez. I think I told you she has the grippe and asked me to come see her in Boulogne.[80] You could write a short note to her […] a few lines would please her.

---

[80] Old-fashioned word for influenza.

3/16/1915.

I didn't receive any letters today, but I did receive 2 packages. [...] I have the great pleasure of sending you the picture of our group. You will know me immediately, even though my big beard greatly changes my expression; a nurse who knows one of us recently received his camera in Concevreux and took our picture immediately. Here are the people in the group: in the front me and Rolland (a printer in Rouen and amateur organist, a really nice guy, a bit stubborn); in the back are Julien, Corporal Deschamps, and Vessot. Julien is a good friend who has followed me faithfully since August 3. Corporal Deschamps is a friend of Rolland's who changed companies six weeks ago and is charming (he has a doctorate in law and was going to be a notary public in Rouen, but ended up representing the insurance company La Nationale for the Département de la Seine-Inférieure: a very good position). According to Rolland, he earns at least 40,000 francs a year. Vessot is the coffee merchant. It's a good picture of our group. The photo was taken in the Mme Marion's courtyard, at the home where we get our meals in Concevreux. [...]

3/17/1915.

I haven't yet today received a letter, but I did receive 3 packages. [...] We change sectors tomorrow and go to La Ville-aux-Bois, where we were during the terrible weather of January 1. We all have an unforgettable memory of that area. The new moon brought good weather and it is already quite warm, the odors are starting to be not so sweet and I burn some papier d'Arménie with pleasure and sniff my Epsom salts. We are even starting to see mosquitoes. Let's hope we won't be here for the real heat. The *gourbis*, with the heat we have now, are becoming unlivable. It's no longer possible to sleep in those airless holes. Our spirits are improving; spring is here, we are coming out of what seems a dream, a torpor, a long sleep. We almost take pleasure in taking watch at night. Two days ago, I was on watch at a forward post from midnight to 5 a.m. I could hear the sound of the woods and the cries and songs of all sorts of animals who also feel spring coming. There is just a bit of thunder from artillery but nothing like what we have heard; our area is really quite quiet right now. [...]

3/18/1915.

[...] I am very worried about what you say about the pains you have in your hands and arms. You mention them in your letter of March 13, but not at all in the letters from the 14th or 15th. That worries me a bit: you are not sitting in drafts? You could go see Ligneul about it and take a bit of sodium salicylate. As you don't mention them in your later letters, I have to hope it is nothing and that you are better. I also received 3 packages this morning. [...] I understand that you could not go to Boulogne because of your pain and all you have to do. I'm worried about the pain. Tell me more in your next letters.

The menu for the meal with Sargent Leduc was very simple and complete: a rabbit stew caught that morning by one of our friends, a good hunter, then the veal and ham pâté, fried potatoes, an omelet with jam (I made the omelet, beating the egg whites separately), cheese, fruit, coffee. As you can see it was a wonderful lunch, something we rarely have. It was partly to thank him for finding a photographer with a camera. [...]

I mentioned the sacré Plizon when talking about my cold. Here is what I was talking about. It's a position in this sector named for the stream we dammed up. That created, on the plain in front of us, a dreadful flood. Our trenches there are awful, at least half full of water; what is more, as we are easily seen in that location, shells come from the Craonne plateau and sweep across them. In daylight, the position is almost untenable; we have to stay completely stretched out flat on our sheepskins, without raising our heads, otherwise, "Watch out for the bullets!" We pee into old food tins, it's only at night that we can move a bit. This confounded position is occupied by half a company, for 24 hours, alternating. The position overlooks a broad valley and we absolutely must not lose it. We pay heavily for it as there are frequent accidents. That is where I got my cold. I am quite fortunate not to have caught anything worse. That's why I call it the sacré Plizon. That answers your question. [...]

We are moving tonight; we are going to the front lines in La Ville-aux-Bois. We will keep our eyes open as the *Boches* are as close as 27 meters and an average of 50 meters away; we exchange bombs and grenades. [...] Today I received the *L'Information* of the 15th and you can be sure there is not a paper in my packages that isn't read. We have not many distractions and take pleasure in reading a newspaper. Maybe Monsieur Alan has some old books he doesn't much care about; you could send me some from time to time, as I can't work, my mind is numb, but I can always read a bit. [...]

3/19/1915.

I didn't receive a letter today, but I did receive 5 packages. [...] We changed locations last night, we are now in La Ville-aux-Bois. Being on watch here is painful; we are on our feet day and night and the weather has gotten very cold again—sudden downpours and an arctic wind blowing hard. It's the last gasp of winter, and seems even worse because we had some days of spring-like temperatures. The socks Mme Lambert sent are very warm; by changing my straw soles every week, I rarely have cold feet. We all have had cold feet at times this winter, despite the precautions we take. One can't stay in frozen mud for months at a time without some consequences. [...]

Tuesday, March 23, 1915.

[...] I read in the copy of *L'Information* I sent that the Germans are bombing Soissons and Reims. They have hit those two cities and those two cathedrals with a great many shells. Here they are again starting battles in the entire Aisne valley. Be very careful, your trenches are so close to those of the Germans that I am always afraid they will blow them up or somehow burn them. [...]

3/20/1915.

I received your letters from March 16 and 17 as well as three packages. [...] When the weather is nice, i.e., no rain, I prefer 12 days in the trenches because the relief is less frequent. Being relieved in the middle of the night and walking kilometers through muddy *sapes* is not at all fun and quite exhausting. [...] Rolland is still receiving an abundance of provisions; his mother-in-law worked as a *charcutière* and knows how to make very good pâtés of all kinds and has the time to do it. [...] Thank you for the cans of foie gras; pay attention to that sort of food which serves me very well. [...]

I fully expect Mme Mauhavel to profit from the new moratorium: still it's open to debate. Her husband is definitely mobilized but her business is open and she must be earning a certain amount of money from it. We will see what happens. [...]

I received the map from *L'Information*, I will keep it. It will be very interesting in a bit of time to compare it with a later map to see the progress, progress which should now move quickly. [...]

3/21/1915.

I didn't yet receive a letter today; I hope you are well. [...] At night it is freezing cold; we have had 7 or 8 degrees below zero, it's a harsh reminder of winter which we are no longer used to. Fortunately, the days are nicer, even quite hot, which means we are very cold at night and hot during the day. We already hear the birds singing in the woods, the blackbird in the morning and the nightingale at night. Spring will be here soon, today according to the calendar but not the temperature, and already the trees have little green shoots everywhere. It will be hard to stay in the trenches in the nice weather with the heat, after having suffered through the cold. We will have a hard time in the heat and will be dreadfully thirsty. There is still no water, and no one thinks about giving us any. Things are still quiet; however last night, about 6 p.m., there was quite a violent artillery duel. We are so used to this type of show that we don't worry a bit about it; it would have to fall on top of us for us to pay any attention. [...]

Friday, March 26, 1915, 4 p.m.

I received last night at 8:00 your letter dated Sunday March 21, and this morning I didn't receive anything. I will probably have news this evening as this upsurge in activity in the entire Aisne valley is worrying me. The artillery duels, the bombings, the planes…it never stops! You will read in *L'Information* about the Zeppelin raid over Paris Saturday night into Sunday March 21. In Vincennes, that same night, the bugles, the drums, and even sirens alerted us to their arrival or their departure from Paris, at 5:00 in the morning. I got up, got dressed, and went down to the dining room. As it is daylight at 5:30 in the morning now, I didn't go back to bed and got to work by 6 a.m. In the night of Monday into Tuesday, from the 22 to 23rd, same alert at 11 p.m. which lasted until 2:00 in the morning. And during the night of Wednesday into Thursday, from the 24th to the 25th, again the same thing. I don't know whether it will go on like this. I think they want to destroy the factories, but it is sad when people are injured and killed. Last night was quiet because it rained and everything was as dark as inside an oven! […]

3/22/1915.

I received this morning your letter of March 18 and two packages. […] I have no real problem with respect to my packages, no one would really dare complain. There are, nevertheless, malicious rumors. That is not for you to worry about; what you need to do is consolidate packages and find solid, light containers. I'm sure that is not easy. I have to end this letter very quickly. My captain is calling me right now; I'm going with him to be an observer from a haystack until tomorrow morning. We will study the artillery fire and at the same time try to see whether the *Boches* are really working in this area tonight. […]

3/23/1915.

I received today your letters of the 19th and 20th and no package. […] Since I've been here, I've been noticed and had I wanted a promotion, I could have had it, but I always refused. I want to stay in the ranks but that doesn't mean that I let them walk all over me. […] Today you are at the Armengaud's, and Thursday you will be at Cunault's home. That is a lot of moving around this week. You will love his instruments; I really hope to get one of his violins and then for him to make a copy of my Guarnerius. Of course, Cunault and many others are wishing for an end to this war, but we, who have suffered so much and given so much, we would not want all that to be for nothing and, since we are here, we prefer to see the Germans out of France, crushed and completely unable to start another horror like this, at least for a century, so that we can be in peace and spared these nightmares. The Germans don't know how tenacious we are. So, keep your spirits up and above all don't be impatient. These people who have stolen everything, destroyed and ruined everything, tortured and killed women and children, these monsters must be crushed. What joy when our shells are raining on them! But there will still be much to do, we can't hide from that. Oh, we who will have fought this terrible war, will have certainly earned our rest afterwards. What happiness when finally we are home again. I can't think about that, I need to stay strong, and, now that we've gone through almost 8 months of war, tell myself that another year is not that much longer. I am fortunate to be in robust health and to have lived through all the challenges quite well. [...]

Saturday, March 27, 1915, 5:30.

[...] people speak wearily about the war and the Germans are really counting on that to achieve their goals. Sending Zeppelins to Paris is as much, or more, to demoralize and wear down the population as to destroy factories. They resort to anything to have the last word! I know that this ordeal is long and painful, but isn't it a thousand times worse for all you poor soldiers who put up with suffering and deprivation with great stoicism? Why? Because you have the firm hope to chase these Germans, so horribly cruel. As you say: you haven't suffered and worked with such patience to not see a new era of prosperity and calm replace this carnage! [...]

3/25/1915.

I couldn't write yesterday as I again spent the day with a lieutenant from among us as observer from a haystack. Yesterday we bombed La Ville-aux-Bois with our 155s; it was alarming to see entire houses explode with one shot and to see the ground from the German trenches fly up to 20 meters in the air. What is more, toward evening, we launched 12 bombs of cheddite, an English explosive that is quite extraordinary. These bombs contain 2300 kilos of explosive, and we fire them ourselves, a hundred or so meters, with new and quite small weapons; the effect is amazing, the detonation is huge, and the displaced air current knocks a man more than 30 meters away to the ground. The *Boches* weren't laughing! I was watching all that with binoculars, and the lieutenant called constantly to correct the firing based on what we could see. We got out of our haystack just in time; about ten minutes after we left, it went up in flames after a shell fell on it.

I am not surprised that you find me wild looking, no one here takes me for a lamb and all these events have hardened me. I exude strength and energy, I have a lot of courage, nothing frightens me, that's why the lieutenant likes my company during difficult missions. He is well aware that, no matter what happens, I will not abandon him. I am becoming a nasty person and when I see heads and body parts of all these swine flying around, as we did yesterday, you can be sure that I am screaming into the telephone "send more." We arrived at Concevreux at 12:30 last night and are at rest for six days. [...]

3/26/1915.

I didn't receive a letter last night. Here in Concevreux we receive our mail and packages about 7:30 in the evening. [...] We leave tomorrow morning at 4:30 for a 25-kilometer march with a cold meal in open air and will practice setting up tents, etc. We are outraged by the exhaustion they impose on us. It seems reasonable to us that, when we are at rest, they should leave us alone and let us enjoy the calm. Those in charge obviously don't share this opinion, and until they do, they will continue to annoy us.

Today we received wonderful velvet pants to replace our red ones which were covered with a layer of blue cotton. I took a shower in the infirmary and it felt wonderful. I just recently became acquainted with two nurses: Silège, a music critic, and Marcel Hutin, a young pianist. I had hoped to play today at a Mass for those who died this week, but I was not able to find a violin. I had written to Monteux,[81] who is in the ambulance corps at Ventelay (I just learned this), but he sent back a reply that, unfortunately, he did not have a violin. I will have another opportunity. [...]

Friday, April 2, 1915, 3 p.m.

[...] I see in *L'Information* today in the official *communiqué*: "Near the Cholera Farm (north of Berry-au-Bac) we blew up a string of mines while the enemy were working on them and followed the explosion with a shower of 75 mm shells. A German listening post disappeared into the shell hole." [...]

3/28/1915.

I couldn't write yesterday; we left at 4 a.m. and didn't get back until 7:30 p.m. We covered 22 kilometers and had a long (6 hours) pause. The companies on the march took advantage of the long break to get as drunk as possible, which meant that at least 15 percent of the active soldiers were drunk and some dead drunk, so the return was epic. As a result, they are going to make us do drills every day. Tomorrow, Monday, we will make another march which this time will be 30 kilometers. They believe that by keeping us busy and wearing us out, there will be less drinking. It is always the serious guys who pay for the others; it's sad. But what can you expect, you have to believe the evidence: the recruits from Normandy are mostly drunkards. [...]

---

[81] Pierre Monteux (1875-1964).

Now I will answer your letters of March 23, 24 and 25. [...] I note, from what you say, that you find my portrait somber and wild. That is because I've become more of a soldier and much less fearful. My friends, except for Rolland and maybe Balembois, are not gung-ho military types. Rolland is always calm, even in the midst of danger. Balembois is a bit more nervous but the others are scared to death. [...] I won't be able to write tomorrow because of the march we have to do. [...]

3/30/1915.

I reply today to your letters from March 26 and 27. [...] I am very happy that Zeppelins didn't drop anything on Vincennes. But you shouldn't be too frightened—they are not as dangerous as one might believe. Still, you were wise to go down to the ground floor. [...] The airplanes which we see daily are much worse. [...]

I have heard the nightingale singing a number of times already: it's not very easy to write down as it is not a song that repeats. It changes and what characterizes it is the smoothness, I could believe it to be an Amati. The unexpected runs and trills and extraordinary sweetness amaze me and keep me interested. [...] We will probably never attack Craonne; it is impossible to attack the plateau from the front. We would all end up dying here for no purpose. We would have to go around it to get the *Boches* to abandon such a formidable position. We are laying mines in front of us (obviously I can't tell you where) and someday soon we will blow up everything. [...] I went to the Palm Sunday Mass at the church in Concevreux, that's where I got the boxwood I sent. These gatherings where there are only soldiers are very impressive. [...]

4/1/1915.

I didn't receive a letter yesterday before we left Concevreux last night. We have no idea why our departure was delayed by a day, but it doesn't really matter. We took advantage and enjoyed the extra day. The night before had been awful: rain, snow, wind, and it would have been a terrible way to start our 12 days. The weather has gotten nice again. It gets fairly cold at night, things freeze, but the weather is splendid. [...] For several days the cannonade has gotten quite lively; it's like the Germans are furious. But they find out who they are talking to when our artillery responds with energy. The big event here is that the trenches of La Ville-aux-Bois were bombed by the 210 guns and aerial torpedoes. All the works were bombed, but the 5th company which was occupying that area suffered few losses because it quickly moved to bomb-proof shelters and our artillery intervened immediately, firing on the German batteries.

Right now, we are on Hill 87. We are only there at night; early in the morning we pull back into our *gourbis* which are 2 kilometers away, in the woods. This is because, during the day, that area is heavily shelled. The Germans are wasting their munitions because there is no one there except 5 sentinels totally safe in covered bomb shelters. This morning we watched one of our airplanes chase the Germans. It seems that it was Voisin,[82] the famous builder, who undertook the chase. The Germans fired more than 400 shells without touching him. It was impressive watching all those bombs explode in the sky, and the aircraft turn or drop suddenly each time the explosions got close. What sangfroid the men who go up in the planes must have, and what a good example they set for us all! Our hearts shudder at the sight and the anguish is terrible; more than 50,000 men must have been watching the spectacle. [...]

4/2/1915.

I received today your two letters from March 29 and 2 packages with the cauliflower terrines and the sausage. [...] The shipments are always tossed around a lot and naturally the terrines are broken. When I eat what they contain I pick them over very carefully. I also just received the shipment of wine you sent on March 11: it was in very good condition. [...]

I am not becoming a nasty person, but it is certainly true that one's sensitivity becomes blunted; I walk past corpses without paying any attention. That wasn't the case at first; we were moved by all that, but now it doesn't bother us. I often keep watch at night surrounded by corpses without even thinking about it. I don't try to stand out, I never try to put myself first, but the activity is becoming more intense and the officers have had the time to appreciate their men. [...]

4/3/1915.

[...] Today I received your letters from March 30 and 31, along with 4 packages containing 4 cauliflower and sausage terrines which arrived in good condition plus the two empty bidons, a bidon of cooking alcohol, a sponge, a bottle of rum which I gave to the mail officer and which made him very happy. In response to your letter of the 30th I can tell you that it has been very cold for 10 days—at 5-6 below zero it is horribly cold. The days are very sunny and even a bit warm, but since last night it's been raining, rain nonstop. The temperature is milder but it is not very nice, all the more because we were just subjected to a German attack which started at La Ville-aux-Bois, the sector we were in 10 days ago; the company there now was heavily shelled and suffered serious losses. We took part in the defense, with our bayonets fixed believe it or not, that is to say it

---

[82] Gabriel Voisin (1880-1973), aviation pioneer and creator of Europe's first manned, engine-powered, heavier-than-air craft. He also invented the metal hangar.

was a very tough fight. Our company had very few injuries and nothing serious; we got out of a bad situation in good shape. The Germans suffered enormous losses. I am wearing the socks from the Lamberts but you could send me some straw insoles as our feet took a good bath yesterday during the fighting in the pouring rain. I changed to a new set of insoles this morning.

I received a new pair of golden-brown velvet pants which are quite warm. My other two pairs were falling to pieces and no longer very warm. According-ing to very strict orders, only men who have been in the front lines are to wear our light blue *capote*, it's a sign of distinction. My pea coat is still in pretty good shape. I hope to not need it after about May 15. When I am walking, I put it in my sack although it's rather bulky. Later I'll only wear my *capote*. Still, I'll keep my sweater to wear at night: it is extremely warm and of very good quality. […]

In Concevreux there is a new shower installation and Silège comes for us at a time when it is empty and he showers us himself, it's wonderful. We were not able to turn up a violin anywhere in this area. We heard of a major who had one, but the information was not accurate. That means I am unable to play. I am receiving all my packages but often two one day and four the next. Because of the events right now the watch service has doubled in intensity and is truly exhausting. We spend our nights almost totally outdoors; we do not sleep more than two hours. Fortunately, it is not cold now, but there is the rain. I use my lit-tle cape and my oil cloth. […]

Wednesday, April 7, 1915, 3 p.m.

I received this morning at 9 your letter of April 3. […] You charged with a bayonet? The German attack continues? It started the 29th or 30th of March when you were in Concevreux. I read in *L'Information* that German planes flew over the Aisne valley and that Soissons and Reims were bombed. They must have been scouting the area in order to be sure where their bombs would land. […] It's a matter of keeping your eyes open and paying attention: be cautious in all you do. […]

4/4/1915.

I received today your letter from April 1 and 5 packages. […] I am writing today, Easter, to not leave you without news, but I'm on watch for two days with our entire squadron and have to interrupt my letter to go on duty. The weather is awful, absolutely nonstop rain and wind. It's a sad Easter day. […]

Saturday, April 10, 1915, 5:00.

I finally received, this morning, news from you—your letter dated Easter Sunday, April 4. […] I see, in *L'Information*, that Hindenburg is coming to take command of the western front. You will certainly have some intense activity. […] Time is passing, April is melting away, we are almost at the 15th. Patience and perseverance are excellent virtues and seem quite rare, but we need them. it's our tenacity that will wear down the Germans and get rid of them. They are on our soil and have planted themselves here. They themselves will have to pull themselves up. That is, we need some good luck to force them to decamp. Let's hope that day will be soon and that we will finally be freed from this dreadful nightmare. […]

4/6/1915.

Yesterday I received your April 2 letter and today the one from the 3rd. As I told you, I couldn't reply yesterday; for the past two days I've been in the *bois triangulaire*,[83] a position far forward that we have held for just a short time. We are in the midst of the woods without any shelter, only two pieces of corrugated metal which are positioned on tree branches under which those who are not on watch take shelter when it rains. The position requires extreme vigilance and those who are not on duty still keep watch for their own safety. Our region is full of movement. The Cholera Farm is just a bit to our right; it's because of that mine incident that our relief was postponed one day.

We too are preparing a number of mines. Meanwhile, we are starting to launch aerial torpedoes, weighing 58 kilos with a range of 500 to 600 meters— new devices with frightening results which we have only just begun to use. There is a special cannon for them. The purpose is to destroy cement trenches. The Germans, enraged by the Cholera episode tried to attack us at La Ville-aux-Bois. They were pushed back and yesterday, about 5 p.m., they shelled our right horribly. But during the night, we bombed their trenches, launching more than 500 cannon shots and the regiment to our right, whose number I cannot give you, attacked the trench; none of our men fired a single shot, the trench was filled with dead bodies and they took only five prisoners. Those men were raving mad! The explosives we are using are terrifying and beyond comparison with what the *Boches* launch on us. So there, our side has made another advance.

During my next rest at Concevreux I will try, if possible, to find some post-cards of the area to send you. It's a very pretty countryside and the Aisne valley is superb, though I and many others would have preferred to see it another way. Do not worry. I am not spending my money. I pay close attention and it is absolutely not necessary for you to send me more as I still have 305 francs, which is sufficient for all circumstances. It's relatively quite a lot of money and, if I didn't have pockets in my flannel vests, it would be a nuisance. […]

---

[83] Triangular woods, in the Somme.

You do not need to tell me to write to you. Only when it's completely impossible for me do I not do so.. You can tell from my letters that I write every day and you cannot imagine under what conditions I do it; I really have to want to write. Our bitter cold weather has given way to showery weather—a slight chill to the air, a hot sun, and an occasional shower, very disagreeable weather. I stay wrapped in my cape and my oil cloth; this is not the moment to give those up.

4/7/1915.

We just spent a terrible night of watch with dreadful weather, pouring rain, hail, and wind. We looked just like drowned dogs. What is more, about 9 p.m., we made a simulated attack on La Ville-aux-Bois—violent shelling and cannon fire—to draw the attention of the Germans and detain their forces. The real attack was made on Berry-au-Bac. No one slept much last night and our next rest, if this continues, will be very well deserved. [...]

4/8/1915.

Today I received your letter of April 5 and at the same time the two packages promised. I am receiving now your letters and packages at the same time, which was never true before—I always received the letters a little after the packages. [...] We will remember this Easter Sunday and Monday; we were totally drenched. As to writing down the trills of the nightingale, to start with they are totally unusual, not really notes, more a whistling, and then, at night when I hear them, I cannot pay much attention as there are, unfortunately, other things to do and my attention is drawn elsewhere. [...]

Right now, given the activity in our region, we are on edge and don't have a lot of time; plus, it never stops raining. I am writing to you standing up, barely sheltered by a plank, that's why my handwriting is so dreadful. [...] You talk about composing music; once I am home, I will need to work on fugues and counterpoint to get back in practice. That will require at least six months, and I am so eager to get to work that I will work quickly. All the more because I have thought a lot about the fact that it will be maybe a year before I can give any concerts because of mourning and the state of the economy. When that time comes, we will see! But I am eager to get to work, I miss it terribly. [...]

4/9/1915.

I didn't receive a letter today and only one package with a terrine of chocolate pudding. There must be something going on, some disturbance in the system as today there have basically been no letters or packages. Let's hope the service will be back to normal tomorrow. [...] We are settled in on Hill 87 and, as it is being bombed regularly, we have new *gourbis* that are very odd: we go down into a cave and arrive at a tunnel lined with metal, a bit like the métro above which are at least 4 meters of bags and cans filled with earth. It is a completely safe shelter, there is not much to fear from the biggest bombs. On the other hand, we are a bit crowded: there are twenty of us inside, lodged one above the other. The height of the tunnel is 2.2 meters and, one meter off the ground on one side, there are benches covered with sheepskins on which 10 men sleep, and the ten others below them. It's not ideal but we are sheltered from the rain and the shells which can always fall on us.

Cooking and other tasks are more difficult and we are less to ourselves than in the *gourbis* for two or four men, but we manage as best we can. The authorities are starting to build this sort of shelter everywhere, first because the old *gourbis* collapse after the winter and become uninhabitable and because the artillery duels are becoming more and more frequent and more fierce. When I say "duels," I should add that our artillery comes out crushingly superior. For the past five days, in our region, more than 1,000 bombs have been launched daily; it is totally horrifying and we are using a new explosive, much more powerful than melinite. The *Boches* who are taken prisoner are nearly all out of their minds; I wouldn't want to find myself in their trenches when we are bombing them. [...]

4/10/1915.

I received today your letters from April 6th and 7th. [...] The solidified alcohol I receive is used up quickly, even though this latest brand is better than the preceding one. We heat things up usually three times a day. [...] The Cholera that was blown up on our right is not a hamlet but a very large farm. Directly on our left is Craonne and then Hurtebise and Bois-Foulon and then Craonnel. In all our area there is increased activity and I think we are preparing an attack on the Craonne plateau. Once removed from this imposing position, the *Boches* will have to retreat at least 25 kilometers. There is no good position to settle into.[84] [...]

This time I received only two broken terrines out of seven. It's not surprising that they get broken as all the packages are put into a huge sack which the post officer's assistant puts over his shoulder; then he makes his way through the narrow *sapes*. It gets very shaken around and he can hardly do anything differently. I have to pick out the broken pieces very carefully. [...]

We actually prefer Hill 87 to La Ville-aux-Bois, it's not as close to the enemy, but there are some inconveniences, each location has some. Yes, we were involved in a very serious situation at the beginning of the month and we got out of it quite well, it's the *Boches* who had very large losses. As it happens, we

---

[84] This is the area of the Chemin des Dames.

have Von Kluck in front of us, but he has just been wounded; as for Franchet d'Espèrey,[85] we hear very good things. The generals we have now have all been put to the test and we no longer have to fear the miscalculations of the beginning of the war. [...]

The showers do us a world of good, all the more because there is no shortage of vermin in the trenches. L. is not a sickly person. He is a sturdy fellow, and he is being a coward. It is unfortunate that people like that didn't live in the north where all the furniture has been destroyed, homes burned, bodies brutalized, all of that would have changed their opinion. We have among us young boys from the north, 18 to 20 years old, whose mothers and sisters have been mistreated; you should hear what they think of the *Boches*. They have only one thought, as do we all, that is to kill as many as possible. [...] You'd better believe that after the war I will speak harshly; those who risk their lives and come back will have earned that right. [...]

4/11/1915.

I just this instant received your letter from April 8 and 4 packages, the three terrines are in good condition, for once nothing broken. [...] I also received a letter from Bastien which I'm sending to you. The Bois-le-Prêtre is an extremely dangerous spot;[86] there is fighting essentially daily, if not in one place then in another. True, Bois-le-Prêtre has 7 kilometers of front line and is very hilly. They delay letters from there intentionally; they do the same for any front line that is seeing major fighting. It could be strategically important to delay some details; they don't want that information published too soon. [...]

We are very clever, there is no doubt about that, and we improvise rapidly in unimaginable ways but there is no obvious organization. Too often we undo something that has already been done then need to redo it. [...] The weather is awful, still rainy, we have a lot of hail and I do believe it is just as unpleasant as the middle of the winter. The only difference is the nights are less long, the watch is less tiring, and we have hope for nicer days. [...]

4/12/1915.

I received this morning your letter from April 9th and the three packages listed in the letter, that is a can of particularly lovely cherries, a can of duck, the half-pound of chocolate, a quart of butter, a quart of coffee, and 4 packs of cocoa.

We are in the trenches for another day because of our extra day of rest; we will not leave until tomorrow night, April 13, for 6 days in Concevreux, at least

---

[85] General Louis Franchet d'Espèrey (1856-1942), participated in the Battle of the Marne. In 1917 he replaced Foch as commander of the Armies of the North.

[86] The pastor's woods.

that is what we hope. As I told you, we spent Easter and Easter Monday on watch in a terrible storm. We will remember Easter Day 1915. The weather since yesterday seems better. Let's hope that the new moon, an April moon, will bring good weather. [...]

At my next rest, I'm going to send back to you my little alcohol stove which is very heavy and not needed now. [...] I'm not proud of my velvet pants but they are very practical and warm enough. Our new *capote* is sky blue. There were some that were blue-gray but very few and they took them back. Once washed, the color fades and becomes undefinable. What is sure is that at dusk or at night, at 25 meters you see nothing. This is a marked difference from the old one. [...] You can relax; I keep my eyes open, for sure, and as time goes by, we gain a lot of experience. We are used to hearing and interpreting night-time noises, which was not true at the beginning when we were frightened by anything. [...]

Friday April 16, 1915.

[...] In today's *L'Information* I see: "last night, near Berry-au-Bac we took a German trench which the enemy took back during the night. We were immediately able to settle into a different trench nearby." [...]

4/13/1915.

I received today your April 10th letter and the 3 packages you listed, that is: a pound of plums, some sugar, *L'Information*, some herbs (chervil and chives), a bottle of formalin,[87] which will be useful, and 4 madeleines from Vinay. Everything arrived in good condition. Thank you very much. The smoked trout is really very good. My friends, Rolland and Vessot and others like all your food, especially the cod. What was also really excellent was the rice cake with cherries, a great success; the cherries in syrup are equally good, they are fresh and wonderful.

Marshall Hindenburg can come to our front; he will be well received. It is too late now to surprise us—our artillery is formidable and we have a lot of new equipment which is extraordinarily effecting and demoralizing. If he undertakes a fierce offensive, he will succeed only in getting everyone killed. He may well have tried to surprise the Russians who didn't have the benefit of a sufficiently vast rail system. Here in France it's a different story. The Germans have a good network but we too have one in excellent condition which, in many places, has been expanded. That means we can bring forces in astonishing numbers to a place in a matter of hours. That is the stuff of a strong counterattack. Many officers are even pleased to know that Hindenburg is coming. They hope that

---

[87] Formalin is an aqueous solution of formaldehyde. Lucien and his friends used it to preserve their feet from moisture.

he will have the imprudence to attack and manage to kill 500,000 men without much danger to us. [...] At this time, the *Boches* are starting to retreat seriously, in one place and another, always pulling back.

One of these days I will send you containers you can fill with burning alcohol. That way you won't have to buy new ones and for me, it costs very little to send them back. I thank you for sending the shipment of wine: I will probably receive it at the next rest, around May first. It's not worth sending me a big package of provisions, first because it takes a long time to arrive, and then, because of what is happening, we may well be called out on maneuvers and it will be very inconvenient to drag a lot of stuff along during a quick pull-out. Yes, I drank the Malescot and it was really good: those Médocs are exquisite wines and later I will again buy some with great pleasure. There was frost again last night, but the weather is wonderful and the sun very hot. We leave tonight for Concevreux for 6 days. If everything happens normally, we should resume service on April 19th at night, which brings us to the first of May. But there may be something new between now and then. [...]

Monday April 19, 1915, 5:00.

[...] Lunch at Mme Bastien's did not start until 1:00. We ate sardines, saucisson, and butter; roast veal with a mixture of vegetables [...], then potato dumplings, then some salad, Camembert, a rice cake made by Mme Bastien, tea, coffee. For wine, a white Bordeaux which was good and a small glass of a red Bordeaux, an old St. Émilion. With us there was a woman from Rethel, a refugee whose house was burned with everything in it. Mme Bastien met her when she went to Montluçon with her sister and her little son André when she feared the Prussians would enter Paris. This woman has for clothing only what she was wearing, her fur which she brought with her, a bit of lingerie which she had bundled up. She took some cash she had in the house. But since September that is running low. I think she has relatives in Paris, her son is the director of an insurance company but all her identification papers were burned. Situations like that are rather sad. [...]

4/14/1915.

I didn't receive a letter last night upon my arrival in Concevreux—we receive letters and packages in the evening about 8 p.m. Our relief happens later and later; the days are getting longer, and we have to wait until night to move troops. I didn't arrive in Concevreux until 12:15 a.m. At the bridge in Chaudardes, two and a half kilometers from Concevreux, poor Balembois fell into a hole, which happens to us all quite frequently. But this time he was hurt. He leaned on me for the rest of the trip and we moved slowly, which explains our lateness. Today his leg was massaged, but it is swollen and he will not be able to walk for a week. [...]

Today I'm sending you three empty containers so you can send me more cooking alcohol. It's really more economical than solid alcohol, and shuttling the bidons back and forth will cost a lot less. So here we are at rest in Concevreux for six days. Tonight, we take watch from 7 p.m. until 7 p.m. tomorrow night. That keeps us from having to do the first march which takes place in the morning with a departure at 4 a.m. There is always a half-company on watch in Concevreux; the three bridges over the Aisne and the canal are always busy. We are lucky that our turn to take watch falls on a marching day so at least we avoid that. The worst would have been to have to do the march and take watch after we got back. [...]

Today I received a card from M. Lambert: he is very worried about his son-in-law from whom he has had no news for a month or so. It happens that he was fighting in Perthes and the losses there have been severe. Let us hope, for his sake, that he is either a prisoner or may be injured. [...] This morning I took a wonderful shower. By the way, send me a flat piece of soap that will fit in a metal box. Mine is completely used up. The showers use up soap very quickly, but what a good feeling it is to come out of one. You could also send me some candles and matches. [...]

4/15/1915.

I just this instant received your letter from the 11th and the 12th; I also received three packages, one with sugar and three lemons, another with sugar and three oranges, and the third with two cans of foie gras and a small package of Beurres Lu.[88] I'm on watch tonight as I write to you, that is during the night from the 14th to the 15th. We are on watch at the bridge of Concevreux, a bridge over the canal; our guard house is the train station of Concevreux so we are pretty well off here. I didn't want to lie down. The straw in the waiting room is old, it's not much more than dust and certainly full of vermin. I much prefer passing the night on the wooden bench from the Allez brothers, which is one way to remind myself of the good city of Paris. Still, as I don't have much to do, I profit from the time to take care of mail. I am quite at peace; I hear those in the room next to me snoring like organ pipes. [...]

Jean was lucky to find a violin; me, I've not been able to find anything in the entire region. I did see one in a wine merchant's shop in Ventelay but, in addition to being a piece of junk, the price was 30 francs. It was in dreadful condition, not a single string, and the bow had 17 or 18 hairs. There was hardly any

---

[88] A brand of butter cookie.

way to make a sound. Outside of this squeaky fiddle, I've not been able to find anything in the whole area. [...]

We got a new colonel several days ago: it seems he finds us out of shape and wants to make us do a lot of maneuvers during our rest. He is new, he may want to show a lot of zeal, but I doubt strongly that he will succeed. All of us, officer or regular soldier, we are starting to bare our teeth when someone has the pretension to make us work excessively during our rest. We just ask that they let us be, which is natural.

Dear Maman, it is not a sacrifice for me to write to you, far from it but in many places it is very difficult. You should not worry too much if you go without news for several days. If we are moving forward and fighting as you might expect one of these days, you have to realize that it will not only be difficult for me to write but the mail service will suffer greatly. During the early days of the war, when there were huge battles in the North, the relatives of those mobilized waited three weeks to a month without word of their loved ones. I tell you all this so that, if you read in the newspapers of an advance forward and go a bit of time without news, you won't worry. For my part, I will do the impossible to write as often as possible.

We can't think about the consequences of this war; a good many poor people will be hopelessly ruined. [...]. Certainly the harm that catastrophes like this bring about is incalculable, and that's why a good many people believed this war impossible. They believed that the Germans had feelings, they didn't understand the coldness and rapacity of that savage race. Events have opened many eyes and now, in the face of what has happened, one has to accept the inevitable and do all possible to protect this country from a return of these brutes. [...]

4/16/1915.

Yesterday I received your letter of April 13th and at the same time two packages. [...] I received the proof of the portrait Rolland sent as film to Rouen. I sent this proof to Cunault. Rolland expects others soon. As soon as they are in my possession, I'll send one to Coraboeuf and the rest to you. [...] I am sending you three containers so that you can return them full of alcohol for burning.

Yesterday, our company car went to Fismes for resupply. We asked the price of cooking alcohol, they wanted 1,95 a liter, that is exorbitant! Everything in Fismes is extremely expensive; the officers of our sector resupply themselves, or get themselves resupplied there, and these *"messieurs"* with their double appointments (the price of the war is very high) lack for nothing: fish, oysters, chicken are all part of the game. In Fismes a bony chicken goes for 10 to 12 francs and everything else is just as expensive, imagine! [...] You could send me one of my large portraits on paper for Rolland who will be very happy to have it. That will make some publicity for me. Later, with his relatives in Rouen, we could maybe do something there. The march that took place yesterday was very long and my comrades didn't get back until 8:30 p.m. Supposedly there will be another march on Sunday. I am going to put some formalin on my feet, they will toughen up quickly. Formalin is perfect for that; the only inconvenience is that it makes the feet black but fortunately we don't show our feet in a salon. This formalin makes our skin hard as animal's horns, it's strange. [....]

4/17/1915.

I received yesterday your letter of April 14 along with the three packages you mentioned: cooked apricots, sugar, 3 oranges, an apricot clafoutis which was really excellent. It seems to me that it was Mme Tavernier's mother who spoke of that dish, I even seem to remember that we had it at their home. It was very good.

For some days now the packages are arriving in good shape: the bowls with the cold pork were all intact. I know there is a place in Paris where one can take packages to be sent for free, because a sergeant we know, a Parisian, received one recently. But I can just imagine the crowds there. That would not be very pleasant. On the other hand, you could send me packages of wine a bit more frequently that way; they have always arrived perfectly fine. The wine they distribute here is truly awful and they only give the minimum. As for what we buy in Concevreux, it is equally as bad and exorbitantly expensive. Bubbly lemonade sold as Champagne for 4,50 a bottle; so-called Médoc 3 francs; Saint Emilion for 5 francs. Really ridiculous prices, especially in view of what is in the bottles. I prefer drinking coffee. The wine you send me from time to time seems exceptional, it's so different from what we have here. I wonder how it is possible that they can sell such awful stuff in a country where there is so much good wine. There are very few here who know much about wine. I find it amusing when I watch officers and soldiers drinking these liquids and clacking their tongues in a sign of approval. It's very funny. [...]

The tunnels we are building now in all the trenches are certainly good shelters for us. They are buried very deep underground, and above them two meters of bags of dirt, which means that we are quite sure to be safe from really big mortars. The old *gourbis* fell in one after another and, my God, in the case of a bombing, I don't know that I wouldn't have preferred to be in the *sape* as to be in one of those holes with illusory protection and falling debris that could smother you. Le Petit Jean sent me a short word which I'm sending to you. [...] According-ing to him he attacked at night. His brief letter is full of emotion, the poor kid, he's young, I see this in the youngsters who are with us. We have more 18-year-old soldiers than they do; they are brave but in general lack our calm. Tomorrow we go on a march for the whole day and I don't know whether I'll be able to write, I will try. [...]

4/18/1915.

Today I received your letter of April 15. [...] When I get home, I will absolutely apply myself to my studies of technique so rudely interrupted. I will have to work again on counterpoint and a lot on the fugue. I will need a good six months of solid work before turning to the study of composition. I will be able to do it all the more because it will be at least a year before I can perform in public; all that depends on when we come home. But there will be such mourning that one has to foresee a year of almost total pause of concerts. Also, I think it will take me at least 6 months to get back in shape. I will thus have all the leisure I need to spend at least 6 hours a day on technical work. My brain is definitely dulled. [...]

I brought writing material with me and I am writing very quickly, sitting on a pile of stones on the side of the road. We are in Burgundy, 5 kilometers from Ventelay, and not very far from Berry-au-Bac; we can hear the rumble of the cannon. There has been a lot of action for the past few days on our right: Cholera, Berry, etc. [...]

Friday April 23, 1915, noon

[...] I went to the notary in Vincennes. Only M. Laville paid anything, 250 francs. He is always punctual, but I think he is doing this in order to pay only half his rent, and he doesn't pay his common charges. M. Boissard died; he was buried last Sunday April 18, the day I had lunch with Mme Bastien so I was not able to go to the funeral and was quite upset about that. Mme Boissard might have thought there was some bad will on my part. I went to present my excuses on Tuesday. When she saw me, she said: "I will go to the notary," because she thought I was coming about the rent, then she saw she was mistaken. I hope she will pay something. This death came at a bad time for us, just at the end of a lease term. [...]

For Mme Mauhaval, I first wrote to M. Colas to ask him whether she had sent any money. M. Colas is very busy right now and takes a rather long time to answer, so I am going to write to Mme Lefèvre to ask her to discuss this with Mme Mauhaval. I will ask her whether the café is open (it was closed when I went there but with the good weather coming, it seems to me that this establishment should be open). I will also ask Mme Lefèvre to inquire about M. Mauhaval. He was in Alsace, but recent events may have changed that and I need to be informed before I go to Boulogne. [...]

4/19/1915.

I received yesterday your letter of April 16 and two packages. [...] I also received yesterday a package sent by Cunault with a sausage that looks delicious, and a cake from Potin, some little cakes stuffed with gooseberries. I sent him two days ago a picture of our group. I will write to thank him. From what he wrote, he has just left for Burgundy. He has 100 territorials staying there and they have shown no concern for his property and may have drunk his wine. He is going to put a stop to all that. […]

The Germans are moving around with an Austrian 305 caliber gun: these enormous pieces are mounted on trucks and are hitting some of the lines in the rear. The range of these guns is enormous—up to 20 kilometers. Four of their shells fell on Concevreux, two in the fields, one next to Madame Marion's house. By extraordinary luck, we had left just 2 minutes earlier, we were 100 meters away. Another fell on the church square in front of the post office. With exceptional luck, no one was injured, just some material damage. All the windows in Madame Marion's house were broken by the force. These shells are at least a meter in diameter; they dig holes 5 meters in diameter, and when someone goes down into one of them, he disappears. All the area around us has received some of these shells, unfortunately not with the same luck we had. That is yet another hurdle passed. We go back to the trenches tonight for 12 days, that is, until May 1.

Coraboeuf is well aware of our sacrifices and says so. He is very good to us. I am convinced that we would do very well if we bought some of his father's wine, even more so because it was exceptional last year. Mme Duez is what they call *une glue*,[89] and you should avoid as much as possible the hold she wants to have over you. Even more because she is happy to receive but not to give. I know well that many people keep letters; the Armengauds can certainly keep mine, there is nothing compromising in them. What you tell me doesn't make me angry, first because you are a dear little *minou*, and then because you take me for a sweet little child. But I am a ferocious, bearded little child, and mean, and woe to those who try to annoy me!!! War has not made me very kind but, for my little mommy, I will always be a little lamb. […]

4/20/1915.

Last night, before we left, I received your two letters from April 17 as well as the veal pâté and the ham, that's the only package I received. I will surely receive the others tomorrow morning. […] The pâté was excellent. Yes, the Germans did take back their trenches, but since then we've retaken them and, this time, I think it is for good. As for the canvas shelters, they are not badly constructed, but a little small for the number of men they think can fit in them. As for being surprised, there are always soldiers on watch and they quickly sound the alarm; we always sleep with one eye open. The reliefs are not too badly managed. They

---

[89] A clingy person.

are always at night; it is hard to avoid making some noise as much as we try. Our company has never had an accident during a relief and now that we know our sector pretty well the relief happens more quickly.

My alcohol stove is now unusable. It has been banged around so much in our trenches and has been so badly abused that it is not worth the cost of shipment. Boy scout heaters are very handy and the liquid alcohol burns well in them. [...] Here we are on service since last night; if nothing changes we will leave the evening of May 1. A week ago, we got a new colonel who doesn't seem very accommodating. He makes us change sectors every 4 days instead of every 6. The purpose is to reduce fatigue in the difficult places. We are right now in reserve at the command post for 4 days, then 8 days in the front lines *au grand casque*, then *au gros chêne*.[90] It's relatively calm. Today it is very hot and if that continues our tongues will be hanging out after having chattered with cold. I used the formalin you sent but I find it hard to use. I do not know whether what you sent was pure formol; it burns the skin. I added a certain amount of water. It didn't work very well so I decided to use it just as I received it, painting my feet with a brush. Please send more and ask Ligneul for instructions. [...]

Sunday, April 25, 1915.

[...] I sent you several copies of *L'Information*. You will see that the Germans are using poison gas. [...]

4/21/1915.

I didn't receive a letter this morning, but I received the three packages that I expected yesterday. [...] Rolland's feast day is the 23rd, the day after tomorrow—his name is George. Maybe you could put a bottle of champagne 1904 in his honor in your next package. [...] That would please me very much, all the more because all his friends are giving him something. I'd like to give him an excellent bottle to drink. He will really enjoy it as he is very fond of food and loves good things. [...]

Everything is calm in our sector right now; we are the ones sending projectiles of all sizes toward the Germans. They respond very little and feebly. [...] This Aisne valley is very pretty, especially now that the trees are all in flower. It's picturesque and very hilly. [...]

4/22/1915.

I didn't receive a letter this morning. Have you gone two days without writing or is the post delayed because of some sort of incident? I think it's probably the

[90] Literally "the big helmet" and the "big oak tree."

latter because I did receive 3 packages. […] I thank you for all of that. I believe you to be in good health and that your health isn't the reason for the absence of news. Julien received this morning news from our old friend Barthe who was promoted from corporal to sergeant. You remember, he's the one who was wine merchant on the Place de l'Opéra. He was in the class of 1897, he stayed in Le Havre. Just recently he was sent to the camp at Potigny, near Falaise, to train the new group of the classes 1915 and 1916. He is only 7 or 8 months older than I am. We notice, rightly, that bistrot and café owners certainly enjoy a number of favors, in brief they don't want to do their duty. Say what you like, I think equality is an illusion.

Ever since we had the luck to get a new colonel, we are much more bothered; this one is a stickler. We have to continually be fully equipped, not do this or that. Even worse, several times in the past few days two generals have come by, including General Mangin, so we are obliged to do a lot of cleaning up: we scrape the *sapes*, we polish, we brush, we shine, in short all the stupidity of the barracks. This is beginning to really annoy us and seems quite useless in light of what is happening. It's odd how the military is so mean-spirited while things of the greatest urgency are never attended to. The other colonel wasn't very good, but he had one thing going for him, he didn't bother us. […]

We are moving tomorrow night to get to the *grand casque*, it takes about 20 minutes via the *sape*. We are quite safe, few bombs are falling, our sector is calm right now. I expect, dear Maman, to have your news tomorrow as here we receive letters and packages at 7 a.m. I cannot usually answer until the afternoon and the letters go to the postal officer about 5 p.m. The times for receiving and distributing mail are different in different sectors. We will spend 4 days at the *grand casque*, then 4 days at the *gros chêne*, this is the idea of our new colonel. He's the one in charge of details like this. […] Right now, we are hearing a rumor I can't really believe, that General Mangin will be going to Constantinople and taking his division with him. Can you imagine the trip from here to there? I don't believe that impossible tale. There are so many rumors floating about since I've been at the front. […]

4/24/1915.

I'm writing quickly today, I have watch all day; there is no shelter where we are and I don't really have the time to write. I am in good health. Lucien.

4/25/1915.

As I told you yesterday, I received the 4 packages you mentioned in your April 20th letter. […] I am sorry the envelope with my picture was folded. There is a framer in the rue du Midi, next to the pastry shop, to the right as you head toward the Cours de Vincennes. Maybe he could frame it for you. As to the formalin, it's not that I found the bottle small, it's that I wonder about how best to use it, ask Ligneul. Is this formalin pure, should I paint my feet with the formalin as it comes? In short, ask him for directions as I've never used this product. From what others have said it is very effective, it toughens the skin on the feet remarkably.

I make a lot of herbal tea and received the tilleul and chamomile. This morning I received your letters from April 21 and 22 and the three packages of rillettes. [...] You should not be too concerned about the Zeppelins, they aren't really very dangerous; the atmospheric conditions need to be just right for them to accomplish anything, and what is more, there are warnings. [...]

There are some changes in our sector: the 35th territorial left yesterday for an unknown destination. Every so often, we hear the front. This evening we move to the *bois triangulaire*. Yesterday we had a terrible rain and our ground is so completely saturated with water that we have up to 10 centimeters in the *sapes*. Fortunately, the temperatures are mild. There is a new rumor running around: that the entire 3rd corps will go to rest. We'll see whether the outcome of current efforts will justify these lies. I won't believe it until I actually leave. [...]

4/26/1915.

I received this morning your letter from April 23 and 4 packages I've not had time to open. Something has happened that is of prime importance and has everyone in a flurry. That is the official announcement of the departure of the entire 3rd army corps. We leave tomorrow evening, the 27th, for Ventelay where we will assemble and the next day, the 28th, depart for the unknown. Everyone is talking about it and making all sorts of guesses: some say we are going for rest for 3 weeks, others that we are heading in the direction of Verdun; anything is possible. The only sure thing is that we have no idea. There is even talk that we will be transported in buses. [...]

This is a truly momentous event in our lives and something new for us. Let us hope that luck continues to shine on us. Because of this move, it's possible that you will receive my letters somewhat irregularly for a few days, don't worry about it. The weather is again lovely and we will be leaving our woods just as the flowers and greenery are starting to appear, that is, the most enjoyable time. [...] We have to be more prepared for fierce battles; we have to end this. It is all up to God's grace. As soon as I can, I'll give you a new address or a new sector. [...]

4/27/1915.

I received this morning your letter of April 24 and the 4 packages listed in the letter. I also received the shipment of wine from the 17th, that is the Cérans

1900 and a half-bottle of red. Thank you. I've noticed that the 5-kilo packages are taking much less time to arrive.

Speaking about the shells fired here and there, we are used to this concert of all the calibers: the 155 shells which are 90 centimeters tall and weigh 47 kilos and now howitzers of 220, 290, and 350 calibers that send projectiles as high as 150 meters. They are designed to destroy fortifications, not to kill troops. From this perspective, the 75 is much more dangerous; it fires 20 shots a minute and showers a very large area. The huge shells arrive rather slowly and we have to lie down. In general there is not much to fear but the noise is horrendous. It's harder on the nerves than it is dangerous. We get used to it. [...] Our departure is delayed; they now say it will be May 1. But it is official, that is absolutely sure. [...] For 18 hours now we've heard the cannon fire without stop, very far away, in the direction of Arras or Lille, and we know there is a big battle underway. [...]

4/28/1915.

I received this morning your letter of the 25ᵗʰ of April. I didn't know how to use the formalin; no one was able to give me any useful advice. I know that pure formalin burns so I was cautious. It's up to Ligneul to tell me how it should be used. The glycerin soap you bought from him is quite extraordinary. I believe it is the best soap I've ever used. We must remember to buy some later. [...]

I completely understand that you do not go out of your way for Mme Duez, she has never done anything to justify that. I'm not surprised that the postal employees in Vincennes know you and know my name. I am disturbed to make so much work for you and I am very grateful.

Rolland, who loves cider, received two bottles. He brews it himself and so is very sure about what he is drinking. His cider is excellent; I might well buy some from him after the war. [...]

4/29/1915.

I received this morning your letter of April 25. [...] If I told you late about Rolland's feast day, it's because I didn't know about it. Vessot was looking at the calendar and completely by chance, just a few days before, noticed that it was the St. George. I had already received the shipment of wine with the bottle of Cérans and the half-bottle of Ludon, and yesterday I received the bottle of Cérans with the mechanical stopper. Unaccustomed as we are to any respectable wine, we find these delicious. They are providing us with much more wine than they used to; two quarts, that is 1/2 a liter; but they are coarse wines from the south of France, heavy enough to cut with a knife. It would be good to dilute them. Unfortunately, our water is of questionable quality which makes the wine not very nice to drink. As there is nothing else, we are forced to make do. The wine we receive from you seems to us worthy of the palace of the gods. [...]

As I have told you, our new colonel is a pest, is he trying to prove his zeal like someone newly promoted? We don't know, but he annoys us a lot, for tiny infractions he gives 15 days of prison and sends men in front of war councils for nothing at all. It's shameful to watch. We need to be on our toes night and day because he wanders around the sector.

Our departure is again delayed, they told us officially in report. We will thus be relieved as expected the evening of May 1, then we'll see. Rumors have it that we will be concentrated around Dijon to form an army of 500,000 men. Whoever survives will see. While we wait, we let the time pass and try not to worry. For several days it has been very hot. That will obviously not last long as it is not at all normal. I am going to cut off the sleeves of my flannel jacket and I'd ask you, please, to send me within a week two pair of linen undershorts, only two, and one pair of cotton socks. Send me what I tell you and please no more; I'd have to throw them away. [...]

4/30/1915.

Today I received your letter of the April 26th and the 5 packages you mention. [...] The changes for us seem to be on hold, maybe because of the important battle taking place right now in Flanders. In theory we should be relieved tomorrow night and if we end up at rest it will be in Roucy, east of Ventelay and not far from Concevreux. According to the current rumors, it is sure that the army corps will leave this region and certainly without much delay.

The packages sent by train take much less time now. Rolland received one yesterday, with fresh apricots and cherries, jam, and a bottle of cider. That package took 6 days, and that is nothing compared to the time it took a few months ago. The heat is stifling and life in the trenches is close to becoming impossible. [...]

Tomorrow is May 1. When I realize that in 45 days it will be a year since we left for Port Lazo! Time goes by and nothing points to the end of this calamity. The fighting will become more and more violent; with good weather we will certainly start to move. We cannot stay this way for 10 years. For several days we feel the earth tremble constantly and the cannons rumble from an imperceptible distance. It must come from the north and has to be astoundingly loud to reach us. We read in the newspapers that the eastern corps which was moved to the north charged the Germans singing the *Marseillaise*. [...]

5/1/1915.

I didn't receive a letter today but 4 packages with [...] some formalin and a brush. I immediately applied a layer of pure formalin to my feet. It makes the feet stiff at first, but after a half-hour the softness comes back and the skin is tougher. It was essential; after the humidity of the winter, my feet were all soft and mushy. […]

We leave tonight for six days of rest in Roucy. […] We'll be leaving our sector just when everything is becoming splendid—violets, lilies of the valley every-where, and trees are all ready to put out flowers. […] Everyone is still talking about our transfer, saying that "surely they are sending us to the Dardanelles, to Black Russia, to Italy," all sorts of places where we will certainly never go. […]

Sunday, May 2, 1915, 6 p.m.

[…] The lilacs are blooming in the gardens. I'm not sending a bunch as it's too big for a letter. […] It took this unfortunate war for me to learn what color they are: there is one white and one lilac color. The gardeners who usually trim them to keep them from flowering didn't this year so the poor bushes bloomed. […]

Wednesday, May 5, 1915.

[…] The workers at the post office are good with me, but they are not too happy when I bring a large package, like one with lettuce. They do not accept packages over 1 kilo because they will be stopped along the way. Registered packages are frequently weighed in the central station in Paris; not all of them, of course, as that would take much too much time. The larger packages are the ones chosen. The employees say to themselves, rightly: "Ah! There is a large package, it must be over the limit." A lot of small packages weigh more than a kilo but it is mostly the big ones that are noticed. The lettuce I took yesterday, for the second time, still weighed a little more than a kilo. The worker was very nice and agreed to take it, not registered, telling me that it was at my risk. The mailing of these packages is truly comical. […]

5/2/1915.

I received this morning your letters of April 27, 28, and 29, and 5 packages. […] We are now in Roucy, but I had the bad luck to be given guard duty when we arrived. […]

I think I'd better not tell much of what I've seen. Roucy is the seat for the divi-sion, very well supplied. And all the services are staying here, which gives this village the appearance of a lively little city. […]

Thursday May 6, 1915.

[…] M. and Mme Lambert are very worried about their son-in-law. They've had no news for a long time. There has been violent fighting in Perthes and in

Mesnil les Hurlus. I don't understand what you said about Roucy: "I think I'd better not tell much of what I've seen." That's what you write. It's a puzzle for me! [...]

5/3/1915.

I received today your letter from April 30 and, of course, no packages because you stopped sending them with good reason. [...] I received this morning a package from Mme Bastien. It was carefully planned and every little thing demonstrated the wish to be friendly. I will thank her immediately. There was a box of pâte de fruit, a can of sardines, three little cans of pâté from Roquelaure, a bit of sugar, a box of candy, a tube of chocolate cigarettes, 3 little jars of jam, a package of petits beurres and an almond cake. Everything was carefully chosen. [...] As I told you, I have absolutely no need of money and don't want you to send me any; that would oblige me to carry much more than I need. [...]

The pack I carry is extraordinarily heavy and, if I was heading toward the front, I would have to throw out some things. With the ammunition, the weapons, clothes, etc., I'm carrying 45 kilos. I can't hope to be very agile, so I have to lighten the load. [...]

5/4/1915.

Today I am writing in the middle of a field, 5 kilometers from Ventelay. We are on maneuvers. The problem is that we left at 2:30 a.m. and will not get back to Roucy until 9 this evening. [...]

5/5/1915.

I received this morning three packages and a letter from May 1. [...] I am writing again in haste; from this morning to evening we are on work detail because of our upcoming departure. We are filling up the wagons, cleaning all the campsites, all the rifles, basically it's a great hustle and bustle, everyone shouting, swearing. There is no way to find any quiet and I can find only a few moments to write. [...] What a nuisance, they are calling me again, I don't even have time to write. I prefer the trenches to a rest like this! [...]

5/6/1915.

I received today your letters from May 2 and the 6 packages listed in those letters. [...] We all have flashlights; Rolland (who sells them) had them sent during the winter. They are more useful during that season than in the period we are entering. Still, thank you; yours is more practical, it fits in my hand better. But don't send any more batteries for now, it would be useless. As I've told you many times, I have no need of a money order. I still have almost 240 francs and that is enough for any need that might arise. [...]

Tuesday May 11, 1915.

[...] I did a bit of arranging in the garden. There were so many weeds it looked like a meadow. I found a gardener who lives in the washer woman's neighborhood; he's a good gardener although he drinks a bit from time to time. As long as he is sober on the days he comes to work, that's all I ask. I pay him 10 francs and give him some tools. [...] For winter I had him plant onions, leeks, carrots, spinach: the ground is thus cleaned up and being used. I'll be very happy to have all that done. The strawberry plants that were left are all together now and are starting to flower. It was important to get all that work done so I can profit a bit from the garden. The hedge is trimmed, it really needed it. [...]

5/7/1915.

I received yesterday your letter of May 4 and three packages. [...] We still have no news about our impending transfer; in the meantime we leave tonight to take up duty in the trenches. From what they say, we should not be there more than 3 or 4 days, then we will be relieved to go to the rear to join other regiments from our Corps. [...]

5/8/1915.

I received this morning two letters from May 5 and four packages. [...] The little area of Roucy where we were billeted is very simply wonderful: first, there is the chateau of the lords of Roucy, which is magnificent, then there are many vestiges of older buildings, terraced gardens, and all surrounded by woody hills with waterfalls, etc., in short, a beautiful place. The problem for us is that the division is there, which means work of all sorts spoiling our stay. We went back to the trenches yesterday. We are in the area that the 35th territorial occupied before us, to the right of La Ville-aux-Bois, and it is not bad at all in this weather. [...]

5/9/1915.

I received this morning three packages but no letter. [...] The Zeppelins do not pose much threat for Paris. They would have to drop their bombs on ammunition factories, or factories working for the army. That is almost impossible; one would have to know the area very well and the dark makes it very difficult. The result is that the bombs fall anywhere. [...] Our airplanes fly during the day over targets probably already designated and cause quite useful destruction. [...] Yesterday we saw a Voisin shoot down an Aviatik right in front of our lines; it swept down on it like a bird of prey,[91] all the time shooting at him with his machine gun. The Aviatik turned over and fell to the ground; the pilots were certainly killed. [...]

Our woods are absolutely filled with lilies of the valley, and we decorate all our graves with flowers. I am sending you a few stems; you can say that it is a lily of the valley that bloomed under German bullets. The trees are all chopped to pieces. [...]

Wednesday May 12, 1915.

[...] I thank you for the lilies of the valley you picked for me: they gave me great pleasure. Yes, it is a lily of the valley that has bloomed under the German bullets! All the trees will be destroyed. Alas, what ravages for our beautiful country and how do we make these Germans, who are so dug in, leave?

5/10/1915.

I received this morning your letter from May 6 and two letters from the 7th. [...] I am writing at 5 a.m. The mail is distributed at 4:30 a.m. Our night-time duty consists of one group of men from 8 p.m. to midnight, the other from midnight to 4 a.m. [...] In the daytime, from 4 a.m. on, two men from each squadron stand guard for two hours, which makes about 5 hours of watch for each man, and with the nights that means 9 hours of watch out of 24 hours. Add to that the tasks that fall on us from all directions and our day is very busy. So, today, I finished at 4 a.m., my comrades rushed to the *gourbis* to start snoring; me, as the weather is gorgeous, I waited for the mail and that is why I am here, seated on a log, answering you at 5:00 in the morning. [...]

Poor M. and Mme Lambert! [...] I fear for their son-in-law. We have to hope he was taken prisoner but I don't hold out much hope. At Perthes there were just a tiny number of men taken prisoner while a huge number were killed and injured. We lost 40,000 men in two weeks. The Germans left there almost 100,000. These details are little known by the public; Silège, from the Medical Service, told me. [...]

Dear Maman, all your repeated recommendations to be careful make me laugh a bit. It is absolutely impossible to have any sort of regular habits. We are always outdoors in all sorts of weather: rain, wind, cold, we couldn't care less. We are sleeping now on the ground, if necessary on a pile of pebbles. There is no possibility of keeping to a diet. What a slap in the face for the doctors, with all their warnings! Everyone grumbles but is healthy. As to risks, like my comrades, I have become a crafty old monkey, but that is no insurance against a

[91] An Aviatik was a German biplane used for reconnaissance.

bullet or a bomb blast; that is a matter of chance. We laugh at the gas, the precautions we need to take are easy and effective. [...]

I say again that I don't need any money. I have enough to last a long time; if I am ever taken prisoner, which I wouldn't want, I have no plan to be frisked by the enemy and to give him French money. Whenever they can, they take all the clothes off the dead and injured, including jewelry, wedding rings, etc. It is impossible to imagine a more loathsome people, they are vampires. [...]

5/11/1915.

I received this morning your letter from May 8. [...] We were supposed to leave last night for Ventelay, but yesterday, about 1 p.m., the *Boches* started a violent attack directly on our right, and we were part of the defense. The whole thing lasted until 4 a.m.; we fired more than 2,000 shells on them. We are still holding our breath in fear of a counterattack and we obviously won't be relieved tonight. We are awaiting new orders, which they say should be coming soon. [...]

5/12/1915.

I received today 5 packages but no letter. [...] We are now on the alert for the attacks and counterattacks which happen constantly. This all started three days ago. The exact day we were going to leave, the *Boches* made a good move. After a copious amount of shelling, they managed to take, just on our right, about 250 meters of trenches. Their timing was not very good. That night in addition to our troops, there were all those men set to replace us, all of us ready to respond. Franchet d'Espèrey and Mangin ordered a counterattack. It was too much for them; more than 3,000 shells and a terrible amount of rifle fire, then a bayonet assault, and during the night we took back everything. They left more than 800 dead on the battlefield, plus innumerable injured. We had 150 killed and injured. All night long we heard the *Boche* trucks coming to get the injured. Yesterday, to follow up on our advantage, we took more territory, with almost no losses on our side. We expect a counterattack tonight. From time to time, our artillery showers them with a hail of bullets. [...]

General Mangin was in the front lines with the soldiers: he has no fear. He is not like certain officers, the so-called general staff, who hunker down when they hear the whistling of shells.

It is very hot and the lemons are much appreciated; we have water that the nurses give us. They sterilize it with permanganate, which gives it a slightly bitter taste, but we don't worry about it. I am still in good health, a bit feverish as we almost never get any sleep, an hour here and there. We need to be on alert, we grab our rifles at the sound of any shooting. We sleep with it, it's our wife. Warm hugs, Lucien.

5/13/1915.

I received this morning your letters from May 9 and 10. [...] You could send me a Swiss army knife, with all different blades and tools. [...] Be careful when you buy it; they are quite expensive and there are a lot of imitations that are not of much worth. [...]

Second letter, same day.

I'm adding a note to my letter of this morning to ask you to send me some mini-scores. My friends' conversation is very nice, but aside from helping me get to know them, it is a bit provincial and gossipy. Their talk doesn't always interest me, so send me two Beethoven scores (chamber music), the two Brahms (chamber music) and a symphony of Beethoven and of Brahms, all in mini-scores. That will "un-deaden" my brain (if I can use a term like that) and I will send them back to you when I've studied them seriously. The newspapers are stupid and boredom ends up taking over. These will allow me to isolate myself with a useful distraction and commune with the masters. [...]

5/14/1915.

I received this morning your letter from May 11. [...] I am on watch: we can certainly conjugate the verb *être de garde*.[92] The entire unit is armed, and we barely sleep. Those dirty *Boches* are really getting bashed and I hope that shortly there will be great results. [...]

We are not complaining much about our food right now: the government is trying to improve it. For some time now, we get pork and even lamb and plenty of potatoes. Clearly the complaints have done some good. [...]

We are always ready to move on, yet no one is talking about our departure. So, as I said yesterday, I would be very happy to receive some pocket scores which I will return once I've worked on them. It is daylight now from 5:30 a.m. to 8:30 at night; I certainly can't work on composition—first, there is no workspace, no table, no chairs, no benches, and it is very difficult to do any serious work in such conditions. Plus, the mind is not very calm. It's different when it comes to looking at a score: I can come back to where I left off and it's easier to get back to my thoughts. In any case, it will be a useful and pleasant companion, better than listening to guys talking about going home, saying they don't give a damn about

---

[92] To be on guard duty.

the Germans, that they can go ahead and keep the territory they've conquered. Those are the sorts of discussions that surround me. […]

5/15/1915.

I received this morning your letter from May 12 and the two packages listed in the letter […] the pair of undershorts, the pair of socks, and two cotton caps. It is unbelievable the way you insist on sending me more linens than I ask for, now when the military authorities are doing all they can to lighten our sacks. It's as if you take perverse pleasure in making it heavier, and heaven only knows how many times I've told you that I didn't need any more socks or undershorts. […]

I'd have sent you postcards from Concevreux, Ventelay, or Roucy long ago but there have been none now for months and obviously there are things more important than printing more postcards. That is sad, because this countryside is superb. […]

Our departure is official; we leave tonight at midnight unless there is an attack that forces us to stay here. […]

I received a card from poor M. Lambert. His son-in-law was killed in Perthes, he now has the official notification. I will write him today and send the card tomorrow. This is bad luck for his daughter; according to him his son-in-law was 25 years old. The attack at Perthes, the Beauséjour farm, cost us dearly. […] We are leaving here tonight, around midnight or 1 a.m. We have to cover a minimum of 16 kilometers to get to Prouilly; that will be no big deal, especially as the night is cool. […]

Tuesday, May 18, 1915.

I received last night at 8 p.m. your little note adding to your letter of May 12. For sure, not seeing a note of music must be a hardship. What surprises me is that you haven't asked sooner! I always figured you were either too busy or too tormented to find time to study scores! […] I think this music won't encumber you too much. You could have asked for less. But at least it will be a comfort for you and will put you in communication with the masters you love. As you analyze these works, pay attention all the same to what is happening around you. You are not living in a quiet, restful or safe place! I sent you a full sheet of letter paper and a white envelope so you can write me on the way, if by chance you have left. […]

Second letter, same day.

I just received, at 4:30, your letter from Saturday May 15 which announces your departure at midnight if the Germans don't attack to take back the trenches that are now in your possession? It was a true battle that took place during the three days before May 13? What terrible losses! So many dead and wounded to gain such a tiny advantage! This trench war is a terrible thing: to advance 100 meters and often not even be able to keep that, what a way to die! And this could last how long? One could fill a whole volume with exclamation points. But truce to all that. Lamentations don't do any good. To the contrary, we still find strength and courage in hope and we always need to be motivated by great firmness and will. […]

5/16/1915.

I received today your letter from May 13, the 5 packages listed in the letter, and the wine you sent for Rolland's saint day, that is the 1904 champagne and the half of Ludon. We were relieved last night at 1 a.m. […] No one knows in what direction we will be going. There is a fierce battle in the north, between the North Sea and Arras, so it would not be surprising if we were sent in that direction. I hear that the mail will be stopped for a few days at Noisy-le-Sec because of troop movement and also probably so that the public will not get news too quickly. As to this business about the *Grand Chef*,[93] it's laughable, that's the name they have given me. Even the sergeants know me by that name, which some buddies gave me because of the advice I've given and the moral authority I've been able to bring to several difficult situations. […]

Dear Maman, I do not know what fate has in store for me: according to what one can imagine, we will soon be in the middle of the battle. I will fight with energy and sangfroid, increased by six months of slowly acquired experience. Obviously, I can't know what my fate will be, but should I disappear, something we mustn't imagine, think, believe that this sacrifice, which many others have also agreed to, was made to save our country and her children, that is, the future; it's for them that we have endured such suffering. You must, therefore, pay attention to the children, to musicians, take care of young violinists, that will fulfill your days and will be a way to continue my existence. Please excuse me for speaking to you this way, which will no doubt cause you much pain, but we have to confront all eventualities. Let us hope I get out of this. I will do everything I can do to be careful and clever. I do not know whether we will be in the battle, but one can't help but think about it. In spite of all this, I dream of our past life and hope firmly that our interesting life will resume, even better, in the future. Dear Maman, I will write every day, as long as it's possible, if only one line. Do not be afraid when you don't receive a letter, there can be long delays. My dear Maman, I love you with all my heart.

---

[93] Big Chief.

Friday, May 21, 1915.

Naturally, since your letter of Sunday May 16, I've had no news. [...] You may be writing but the mail is held back to keep the public from receiving information. I keep hoping that, one of these days, I will have some letters! I am still sending packages. I think that you, the soldiers, are receiving your letters and packages? In your letters, please think to let me know as it is useless for me to spend and waste money (this is not the time) for you to receive nothing. [...]

On Sunday the 23rd I will go see Mme Tavernier as I promised. First, however, I will write to Mme Duez to thank her again for her rhubarb, then to tell her that I will not go to St. Cloud for dinner (she invited me) on that day. I would get home very late and, with Marguerite coming the next day for housecleaning, it would exhaust me. [...] I will have to go back to Boulogne again one of these days and I can make the detour to see her then.

I wait impatiently for news from you, as I am longing to know where you are, my dear child! I wish you good health and much courage, I know you aren't lacking in courage. As for the rest, it's chance. If you happen to be wounded, try to get bandaged quickly if possible. [...]

Second letter, same day, 6 p.m.

[...] Naturally, in the midst of a rain of projectiles from the weapons and the artillery modern armies have, it is simply luck if one gets out alive. The strength, the sangfroid, and the courage of a man who is fighting in such a hell need to be up to the challenges and his greatness of soul and his feelings rise above everything. All these qualities I know you have and I am sure you will do your duty and use your intelligence and perspicacity as much as possible! As for me, I am and will be courageous. My heart bleeds, despite the strength of will and the virility I have. Aren't you the everything of my affection? But be great and strong, my much-loved son! And you will come back to me ennobled! I am going to tell you again, if you are wounded, try to get bandaged as quickly as possible and get a tetanus shot. [...]

5/18/1915.

I couldn't write yesterday because of the many difficulties of our move. I received this morning only your letters from May 14 and 15. [...]

We haven't gone very far—up to now we are on foot—but we have reached a rail line and will most probably depart sometime today. We are formally forbidden to give the names of towns or the region, as the troop movement at present is extraordinary because of the huge battle in the North. I will probably again pass in front of Cunault's house, as a neighboring train station is a dispatch station and from there we will be sent elsewhere. I am sure we are going into the action. [...]

We have lost about 50 percent of the soldiers who took part in the recent, very violent battles. A considerable portion of those were injured, but nevertheless they are not able to fight. [...] I say again that you may go several days without news, but do not rush to conclusions which may not be true, and wait for the news that I make every effort to send. Be brave and think about what the country is suffering. I repeat, nothing can convey an idea of the devastation in the area of the battles. One has to wonder whether life will bloom again there; if it does, it will be over many graves. The blood of the country is being swallowed up in this abyss. Woe to the *Boches* who, with enormous arrogance, have brought about such extermination. All well-principled people believe the same and are sacrificing their lives. [...]

5/19/1915.

I received this morning your two letters from May 16 and 9 packages, because of the delay in delivery caused by our move. [...]

I note that your Sunday visits to Boulogne yielded no results. We'll just have to wait. Madame Duez was very nice to offer to help; that is the first time I've heard her suggest anything even vaguely important. You should not disdain her offer; the time may come when you need help if no one pays, which is not what I wish for. [...]

5/20/1915.

I received yesterday three packages [...] and no letter. We are still in the same situation, waiting from one moment to another for an order to depart that never comes. They managed to dig up a violin for me from a former merchant now set up as photographer. It's a real dud with steel A and E strings—there is no other source of strings in the area. The bow has almost no hair but, still, I have the essentials. It's not without emotion that I've been playing this so-called instrument, and I'm pleased to find that, although my right arm is a bit stiff, my fingers are not bad at all. In short, I think that a month would be enough to get back in form. I played with Marcel Hutin who is a stretcher bearer. We managed to find the Beethoven sonatas. I played the "Spring" Sonata and the C Minor.[94] The news is spreading that there is a spectacular violinist here and the commander came last night to hear us. I may benefit from this one of these days to join the nurses or the stretcher bearers. I would have better lodging, better food, and with somewhat less work, less exposure to danger. Given my age (I am

[94] Ludwig van Beethoven (1770-1827), Violin Sonata No. 5, Op. 24 and Violin Sonata No. 7, Op. 30, No. 2.

one of the oldest in the regiment) and after six months spent under fire, I may be able to join them along with Hutin, Silège, and the young Loignon, a very bright medical student from Paris who is wild about music. Silège is looking into it and hopes to make it happen soon. Besides, that wouldn't separate me from my friends Rolland, Vessot, and Balembois, only I would no longer have guard duty at night and would sleep at the first-aid station which, for the most part, is pretty well constructed. [...]

5/21/1915.

I received yesterday your letters from May 17 and 18 and 4 packages. [...] At this time we can consider ourselves at rest; we are far enough away from the front that we do not hear the noise of the cannons. If this situation continues, this will be the rest so long announced. [...] We only have 4 hours of drill or theory a day, which is not much.

I am very happy to have a violin, however terrible. Still it is an instrument and, with Hutin, I am playing almost all the Beethoven sonatas, which gives me deep pleasure. It seems to me that I am playing better and more profoundly; it's very strange. Our piano is not in the best condition either, but at least it is playable. Our little reputation is spreading and last night the commander came to hear us; among all the officers, there are actually very few who like serious music. If they didn't exercise a bit of restraint, I'm sure they would ask us to play a waltz. However, we, and the officers with us, are able to face what is coming and still immerse ourselves in music in the midst of a pretty countryside. Let us hope that our wake-up call will not be too sudden or the pill too bitter. [...]

5/23/1915.

I couldn't write yesterday despite all my good intentions. We were piled 40 men to a cattle car: it was very difficult to sit and the jolts were so bad that writing became impossible. I've moved to the town where cousin Louis lives. We left our village at midnight and got out of the cars at about 7 p.m. We are drinking beer right now. That tells you something about the area we are in. For now, we are far from the battle lines, in the rear, but obviously this situation can't last long. [...]

In cousin Louis' town, with this large train station, how extraordinary! There were a lot of people asking us where we came from and our rather savage appearance was a source of curiosity. The region we are in now, although not as beautiful as the Aisne valley, is still quite nice. [...]

There is something I want to talk to you about, which worries me a bit as I don't want to frighten you, but it is so very important that I will do it anyway. You know that, in the war we are fighting, especially now when we come out of the trenches, man-to-man combat is frequent. However, in the *sapes* the rifle and bayonet are not very practical. If you bump into the side of the trench with your gun, you find yourself unarmed and you have to jump on your enemy like a dog. If I am speaking about this, it's because it's what I've seen. We need short weapons; the officers have them but they don't bother to give them to us. Human life is not worth much to some of them. I would like for you to send me a so-called hunting knife, sharp and pointed, with a solid handle and made like this.[95] I don't need it to be luxurious, but made of the best quality steel; the weapon needs to come with a sheath and a hook that I can attach to my belt (this is very important). Secondly, an automatic pistol with six or seven shots: a weapon like that is very flat and easy to put in a pocket, all the cartridges are in one clip, naturally a weapon with a safety catch. You should send it in a soft case, such as deerskin, and 25 bullets. Two such weapons could save my life in many circumstances. I saw it just recently: a sergeant, one of my buddies, completely disarmed, owes his life to his automatic pistol with which he killed three *Boches*, giving him time to run to safety. For both these weapons, they don't need to be luxurious, but of good quality. Don't let this scare you, having those things doesn't mean that I will use them, but I'd much prefer to have them. To buy them, go to a serious arms merchant, Salmon in Paris near Châtelet, where I bought the rifle. Pay close attention, this is very important. [...]

Thursday, May 27, 1915.

[...] I went into Paris to buy your automatic pistol and, when I arrived in front of the store of the arms seller Salmon, I found it shut. Since the mobilization, the shop has been closed. I asked a shoemaker in the little street at the corner to point me to an arms seller in the area. I knew there was one on the rue de Rivoli, and another on the rue de Richelieu, not far from the shops of the Louvre, but this shoemaker encouraged me to go to the gun shop on Saint Etienne, near the Bourse du Commerce, then changed his mind, and suggested I ask for information at the cartridge factory on that same little street. There a young employee told me I would not find an automatic pistol in a gun shop; they are not allowed to sell them. This cartridge factory makes automatic pistols for which the army pays 125 francs each and which it delivers to the army in Vincennes. Then he told me he had for sale a Browning automatic pistol which a lady whose husband had died left with him because she needed money. The pistol was for sale for 60 francs. I bought it and have sent it to you. It has six shots, and a spare clip. In each clip there is one blank in order to check that it is working. This employee

[95] A picture of the original letter, complete with a diagram of what the knife should look like, is available on the Blackwater website.

definitely told me that I would not find an automatic pistol in any gun store. I think I did well to buy this arm and am sending it to you immediately.[96] [...]

5/24/1915.

I haven't yet received any letters or packages. [...] For the past two days we've been camped in an absolutely delightful village. Our farm, the last in the countryside, is next to a huge field with a lot of apple trees; all the trees are in bloom and the country is really superb at this time. When we arrived, we passed through the valley of the Ourcq, the part of France which contains the town where Racine was born, a part of the Île-de-France which I didn't know—the train line that passes through it is not a major line. This part is, as I said, surprisingly beautiful. During the Battle of the Marne, there were fierce battles here, but spring and life have already erased all traces and, if it weren't for all the tombs, one would never know that so many men fought each other here.

We are, thus, at rest in a beautiful area, but this will certainly not last long; we hear the cannon that rumbles dreadfully, non-stop, day and night. It is hard to imagine all the stuff we are dropping on the heads of the *Boches*. I asked you yesterday for two weapons, an automatic pistol, either 6 or 7-caliber, and a dagger or hunting knife with a blade of 20 to 25 centimeters maximum. As I told you, do not buy luxurious ones, but good, solid weapons: they could soon be of enormous benefit to me.

Apparently, in order to sustain an intense effort, a regiment is only on duty for 24 hours. If the 129th were to attack today, tomorrow, as long as the battle makes it possible, a different regiment would take its place after 24 hours. This way, not only do they not totally exhaust everyone in a regiment, but they can ask for a greater effort. Everyone is full of enthusiasm; it's working. We come out of our trenches and the *Boches* start to retreat, this is the beginning of the end. It was depressing to stay in our holes. I am going to shave because of the heat, so send me the razor marked "Émile," my strop, and my shaving paste, but absolutely nothing else except a small round mirror with a little ring to attach it. A beard, in our new situation, is becoming really unbearable. We are drinking dark beer here, it is good and very refreshing, they sell it to us for 0,20 a liter, in normal times it is sold for 0,10. [...]

5/25/1915.

Today like yesterday and the preceding days, I didn't receive any letters or packages. It appears they are holding everything, on purpose, at Noisy-le-Sec, to prevent news getting out right now. [...]

---

[96] During the Nazi occupation, this pistol suffered an odd fate. See this book's gallery.

Last night, new orders arrived and this morning at 10:00 we set off in American motor trucks specially designed to transport troops. It's unbelievable how many trucks there are; one driver said there were more than 50,000. So, in short, we have changed locations and are now in the Artois. Things are really heating up in this sector; the sector we left was like rosewater by comparison. But no matter, what is sure is that we will be in the trenches tomorrow night. At this moment we are in the woods and will sleep under the stars. Fortunately, the temperature is magnificent and it really is not very inconvenient. We arrived covered in dust, as these endless convoys raise clouds of dust that spread for 100 meters, no one's face looks human. Right now, a water work detail is busy bringing us water so we can clean up a bit. The countryside here is very flat; very few trees. We are very far from the grand scenery of the Aisne valley. It will certainly be very hot on these bare plains, however being on watch is easier than in the woods. [...]

I was very well-received in Courlandon, where we were before coming here. The people who housed us, Belgians, were absolutely charming. The violin played a role in all that. I am sending you the husband's card. You could send him a postcard portrait.[97] [...]

5/26/1915.

As usual no letters or packages. Yesterday we arrived about 3:30 and our transports had just deposited us near some woods when, about 5:00, after I finished writing, the order came to go take the second line in an area about 20 kilometers away from where we found ourselves. We set off immediately, but unfortunately the sector was unfamiliar to the officers who hadn't studied it, with the result that we wandered all night long and didn't arrive at our positions until 7 a.m. We had had our backpacks on for 19 hours, our feet were burning, and our bodies were in a state of indescribable fatigue. What is more, we arrived right in the midst of a bombing, which did not make it easy to take up our positions. You know this sector of the Artois. It's here that, for two weeks, we have made big advances. There are a number of sectors, but we are in one of the best known and, if the bell tower still existed, we would have a wonderful vantage point from it. Unfortunately, it is lying on the ground, as are most of the houses around it.

The artillery rages day and night non-stop and rest is completely impossible. There is a continuous thundering in which detonations alternate with explosions. Here the entire regiment is on duty, there is no relief, that is to say that, after a certain length of time, the entire regiment is replaced by another. The 3rd corps has replaced the one that led the attack; that corps had been there for 18 days and the state of exhaustion was frightful. The men had no shirts and

---

[97] Lucien had professional pictures taken and produced in quantity in the form of postcards.

their clothes were in tatters. What would the Parisians say had they seen, as we did, the men coming out of these battles between titans? Our losses were not really very great, few killed and a good number of lightly wounded. By contrast the *Boches* lost huge numbers and they continue to lose lives, as they are counterattacking like madmen; we count the corpses by the thousands in front of our lines. We spray them with gasoline using strong pumps and set them on fire. That's the only way to get rid of them.

I am telling you things that very few of the men tell their loved ones, but I prefer to be honest and share with you the extent of the horror we are going to see. With the heat, our suffering will be intense, as we have nothing to drink. They give us just a quarter of a liter of coffee a day; our kitchens here are 6 kilometers away and we can't go there during the daylight. Send me some more sugar, lemons, tubes of menthol, and a small bottle of coffee essence Trablet, which is good to drink cold with boiled water. [...]

5/26/1915.

Always the same refrain, neither letter nor package, the entire postal service is completely stopped; I don't even know whether our letters are being sent—they take them but don't say anything more. Everyone is unhappy and we don't understand the reasons for such a step. The only plausible reason would be that the artillery is using so much ammunition that all the men and transport vehicles are needed for that; postal service and personal interests are less important than defense. If that is the reason, there is nothing more to be said, but other motives are not justifiable. Just because we are in a particularly dangerous place is not a reason to refuse us all our mail. That takes away any possible distraction and all moral solace, at least for many of us, and I don't think it has a good result. What's more, and this is an observation I've made for a long time now and many facts support it, the high command considers us a bit like cannon fodder. They don't worry much about the essentials, not to mention our well-being. On the other hand, for them nothing is too good or too beautiful, and I think there are some who will never again have such a good life. You only have to look closely at them to understand all you need to know about their sentiments, like the way they lounge in the most beautiful automobiles for which they paid very little.

In short, after the war, they will be asked for answers but that won't bring back to life the poor souls who have been the victims of the ignorance and stupidity of their leaders. So, we bomb, we bomb, and we bomb yet again, it can make one deaf and I've had to put cotton in my ears to stand it. They say we will be in this hell for 16 days. Is there any truth in that, I don't know? Let us hope we don't go all that time without news.

I think we will have to clean out part of the field and village in front of us. By the grace of God! Our artillery is hitting them so hard the task is easier, but those pigs often have very solid little forts, defended by machine guns, and that is what is dangerous. We learned yesterday that Italy has declared war: that was read to us in report as obviously no newspapers are reaching us, and we don't know anything. I am bolstering my buddies, for whom this extraordinary life is terribly depressing, as best I can. [...]

5/28/1915.

Finally, the mail is back, it arrived last night, and this morning I received your letters of the 19, 20, 21 (two), 22, and 23 May as well as a lot of packages. [...] At midnight on the 22nd we set off from Jonchery-sur-Vesles where we had been sent from Courlandon. When we left, no one could tell us our destination; our chief has sealed envelopes and along the way our itinerary is revealed, little by little. There were all sorts of rumors of course. I was thinking to the North because of the intensity of the fighting there and I was not mistaken.

In your letter of the 20th, you speak of the letter Vessot sent you. He sent it because I had told him how much you worried. [...] I had Mme Leken in Ventelay send you my flannel jacket (the least good of them) and two empty containers. I sent the jacket to lighten my pack. Two are enough, I prefer having three shirts. I want you to send what I need and not burden me beyond what I can manage. If the post officer will take the package, I'll send two empty containers. [...]

Try not to displease Mme Duez too much; her offers to help are very nice and, if the war drags on, you may be obliged to accept. I will write a little note thanking her for her lovely offer.

In case of injury we all have a package of bandages in a pocket of our *capote*, to use either by ourselves or with the help of a comrade while waiting for more care. [...]

In answer to your question of the 21st, serum against tetanus is used regularly. Right now, medical care, trains, vehicles, etc. are all very well organized. Naturally, picking up and moving the injured away from the firing line is the most difficult part and takes the longest. [...]

To reply to your letter of the 23rd, this is the first time I've found a violin in Ventelay. They found one for me earlier but it was horrible: no strings, coming apart, and broken, of no use at all. The one from Courlandon was also quite bad but it was possible to play it and that was the essential thing. If Silège, Hutin, and I manage to get together, it wouldn't be as nurses, rather as stretcher bearers. That can't happen until there is a vacancy, but I am hopeful. The nurses and stretcher bearers are all working in my favor; they'd really like to have me with them. [...]

Replying to your letter of the 24th, the knife will serve me well. I realize it is an imitation of a Swiss Army knife but it will do. Send me the weapons I've asked for; they will prove very useful.

I don't need any money; the packages we all receive keep us from having to buy much in terms of food. [...] I still have 220 francs so don't need any more. The weather has been very hot but for the last 36 hours at least it has been surprisingly very cold. Our sector is still the same, that is, we are totally dazed by all the explosions which don't stop, day or night, and end up causing our heads to vibrate. At this time, we are constantly fighting off the *Boche* attacks. Those poor guys are getting themselves killed like flies. One of these days we will manage to push them back another six to ten kilometers, if possible. That doesn't seem like much, but when you consider the defenses they have set up, you think differently. We are north of Arras, that is all I can tell you. This location is mentioned frequently in the *communiqués* these past days. [...]

5/29/1915.

I received this morning your letters from May 25 and 26. [...] I am writing on paper that Corporal Deschamps loaned me, with his name at the top. There is a shortage right now of letter paper. That won't last long: Rolland is a printer and owns a bookstore. He receives some quite frequently and should receive more soon. I am going to write to Mme Duez, Mme Tavernier, and M. Armengaud today; I will use the three blank pages I have left. [...]

Deschamps is the least admirable of our friends; in addition to having a closed mind, he is very provincial and rigidly and excessively religious. Add to that an astounding ego. He thinks only of himself, never about others. We cannot count on him in any circumstance. It's a pity because he is educated, an excellent musician, and plays the piano well. But you can be sure he would never pay to hear someone else play. He is very rich and holds a very good job.[98] Still, he is miserly to the extreme. [...] I judge him severely, but in this life we are leading, the soul is transparent. There is no comparison between him and Rolland or Vessot who, both, are very good companions. [...]

As I told you yesterday, I just need to wait to transfer to the stretcher bearers; there has to be a vacancy. Naturally there are regulations for that like everything else, so many nurses, so many stretcher bearers and no more. The nurses and stretcher bearers always follow the units; their task is also very dangerous because they have to pick up the injured men under fire and the *Boches* take perverse pleasure in shooting at the Red Cross. But, in general, the service is nicer and much of the time less difficult. [...]

---

[98] Deschamps was the director of an insurance company.

You did well to accept Mme Duez's invitation. You shouldn't disdain her too much; some day you may need to turn to her. You could change Marguerite's day or have her come a bit later so as not to be too tired. Nothing obliges you to do anything one day over another. I couldn't take the violin for two reasons: first it belongs to an itinerant photographer based for now in Courlandon, who is doing very, very well financially; then I could not put a violin case on my pack. It is very heavy and realistically I cannot add anything. That much weight could prove fatal in an attack. We have to remember we are not on maneuvers. As stretcher bearer, things would be different; I could put my violin in the nurses' car. That changes everything. For now, we just have to see what happens.

This morning I received the Catalan knife that you sent, for which I thank you. What I asked for will be more practical because of the hilt which keeps the user from hurting himself. As soon as I have that dagger, I will give this knife to Vessot. What made us laugh was the stone you sent with it, which seems to mean that once we've dulled the knife on the bones of the Germans, we can sharpen it. We will definitely kill as many as possible, those pigs, those butchers of women and children. Vessot is not a strong man but he is clever, and more, he is not afraid which is really important in this business. There are so many cowards around us, I can't tolerate that weakness. I have less indulgence than Rolland who claims it is an illness. [...]

We are subjected to constant bombardment, twice during the daytime yesterday, three times last night with shells of all calibers, little ones, big ones, there are some for all tastes. We are in trenches called *les ouvrages blancs* that were taken last week.[99] They have not yet accepted this operation which cost them dearly; they are trying to get revenge by hitting us with at least 50,000 kilos of bullets a day. We cover our ears, that's all we can do, while waiting for them to hit us with something else. [...]

Friday, June 4, 1915.

[...] This morning I went to the knife merchant who showed me a hunting knife which has a guard but the blade closes up. This knife fits into a leather sheath with a copper tip. It has a leather ring to slip on to your belt. The blade is 20 centimeters long. It's a terrible weapon that could disembowel a bear. It cost 21 francs which is a hefty price. [...]

5/30/1915.

I received this morning your two letters from the 26 and 27th of May, as well as three packages with peas, green beans, the automatic pistol, the charger and the brush, and twenty-five cartridges. It's a very nice weapon and will prove

---

[99] White constructions, or works, as in battle works.

very useful. The price you paid, 60 francs, is certainly reasonable given its good condition. I am not surprised that the government has stopped the sale of weapons and is slowly buying them up. They furnish them to the officers who have obsolete revolvers that are more than 30 years old. I am very lucky to have this weapon: it will be very useful in the man-to-man combat which we will be subjected to one of these days. [...] As soon as I receive the dagger, I will give the knife to Vessot. [...] Vessot is also getting an automatic pistol from one of his cousins who collects weapons and has some nice ones. The Taride map number 1 shows you all the regions in the north. [...]

I understand now how you happened to see M. Delours' son. I didn't realize how old he is. So, M. Delours will soon have both his sons in the battle. It was wise of him to get them into the artillery; the infantry is awful, much more exposed to danger, fatigue, and less well cared for. We do not have the same supply system as the artillery, who use their horses and cars and any old excuse to find all they need.

You did well to buy the pistol, dear Maman, and I thank you heartily. [...]

5/31/1915.

Today I received no letter and no packages. [...] Yesterday there was an attack here in which several regiments were involved: one of our battalions participated. A solid bombing like none I've ever heard prepared for the attack. The cannons here thunder non-stop, but usually it's only 5 or 6 bombs at a time. Yesterday, more than 500 were firing without interruption from 1 p.m. to 8 p.m. The noise was beyond anything you can imagine. On the horizon all we could see was smoke and dust; ten shells exploded every second, villages burned; finally, from this attack, we took a number of trenches, the losses in our battalion were not very great. The *Boches* tried to take revenge by hitting back with an all-out shelling, most of it on us. To end this tale, I will say that the cannon thunders all the time and with this incessant banging rest is nearly impossible. What rest for the mind and the nerves it will be when we find the calm of the rear! [...]

6/1/1915.

I received today your letter from May 28. [...] Don't spend money on totally useless things which I receive in quantity. I did not need two jars of glycerin; you just sent me one. [...] I prefer things that go in the mouth which you are neglecting a bit—a can of pâté is a real necessity in the life we are leading right now where we can rarely cook and we find nothing to buy. [...]

The little round mirror you sent is exactly what I needed and I thank you for sending it. It was a good idea to shave; in this area the dust is intense and a good deal of dirt is being thrown in the air. I would be very dirty with a beard.

The cannonade here is horrifying but, so far, the 129th has not done much fighting. All the injured these past few days are victims of absolutely crazy bombing. You cannot imagine the noise, the dust, the nervous energy it produces. We can no longer sleep. We have to move a lot of earth in order to find a little shelter. Every day we take 150 to 200 prisoners: they all look completely defeated and seem happy to get out of such hell. We have the painful impression that we are in a penal colony; we are curled up underground all night long, then come out to dig shelters. Rest is nonexistent. As for the kitchens, they are 6 kilometers behind us and they bring us something to eat once a day around midnight, naturally cold, even the coffee. We have never been more badly fed. Most attention is paid to munitions; that takes up entire trains every day. […] Fortunately, I have my scores, without them I'd be horribly bored. […]

Sunday, June 6, 1915.

[…] I think I am sending more packages than before. It's crazy the amount I am spending, not all for food stuff. I am aware that where you are there is not an abundance of food and that sometimes you have to go without eating. I am doing everything possible to respond to that situation. I send every day an average of 4 packages. […] I read in the *communiqués* that the fighting is still hot north of Arras. Le Labyrinthe, La Sucrerie Souchez,[100] all those names come up all the time and I don't doubt that the bombing is intense. I so much want you to move to another area; the danger where you are is enormous. […]

6/2/1915.

I received today your letter from May 29. […] I thank you for all the packages which I am receiving at this difficult time. A regiment that is part of our brigade had the task last night of taking the last houses still under German control in Neuville-Saint-Vaast. The operation started yesterday afternoon with a big shelling. The regiment went up against enormous forces and at 7 p.m. we were sent to reinforce them. There was only one house still in the hands of the *Boches*, isolated and they'd made it a real fort. In the middle of the street protecting this house was a barricade with machine guns. We took them out last night, but our captain was killed along with many others. The other regiment suffered terribly. So, in short, we are going to attack this last house tonight and it will be a big job. We are very sorry about our captain: he had a lot of faults, including drink, but still he was very brave and cared about the life of his men. He was really well-liked and this is, for us, a real loss.

---

[100] The Labyrinth and the Souchez sugar factory, north of Arras.

As I've told you already, I can't transfer to the stretcher bearers except when they have a vacancy. Right now, they are having a bad time: they don't stop day or night. Our regiment, although not having had too many losses, has still lost about 500 men in the past week—very few killed but many wounded. The nurses and stretcher bearers have a huge task.

I had already seen ruins but nothing compared with Neuville: there is no longer a single stone standing, everything is just a tangle of wood, steel, and lots of objects. It is horrible and we need to keep our eyes open—we can no longer sleep. I don't think we will stay long here as there are limits to one's strength and we are just about at the end. I don't know whether this letter will be sent, but at least that doesn't keep me from writing. […]

6/4/1915.

I'm writing in a hurry today; yesterday I couldn't. We are at Neuville-Saint-Vaast. Nothing can convey what it is like, the ruins are unimaginable. Nothing is left standing, there are a dozen homes to take back on the outskirts. This is a terrible, savage war. Our adjutant was gravely wounded yesterday; as I told you the day before yesterday our captain was killed. Yesterday we had 5 killed and 32 wounded. Our group still is lucky. In conclusion, I'm fine. […]

6/6/1915.

I could not write yesterday; it was a dreadful day and continues today. We are sweeping Neuville-Saint-Vaast; there is not a house left to retake and it is crazy. I think I should be able to write tomorrow or the next day, if I am still standing, which I hope. We will be relieved tonight or tomorrow; our division cannot not keep up this effort […]

6/7/1915.

I can finally write to you. We've been in Neuville-Saint-Vaast for 12 days; when we arrived, the Germans occupied half the village. Now we have taken back all of it and are occupying the German front line trenches around the town. The effort that required on our part defies comprehension. Right now, we are in Maroeuil, a few kilometers to the rear and are quite likely headed for rest. The regiment needs to be reformed because we have lost many men. Our colonel was killed; many companies no longer have any officers. Our captain was killed, our adjutant and a lieutenant wounded, and yet we are the lucky ones. Our company has not suffered much; we had only 6 killed and 31 wounded and have about 200 men left. Many companies only have about 80 men. The regiment lost 1,000 men: killed, wounded, disappeared. Neuville is a horror that goes beyond anything the imagination can conjure up: it is not destroyed, it is flattened, buried. Over 300,000 shells fell on us and the town. Our regiment performed so well that Mangin, the division general shook the hands of many of us. [...]

You cannot possibly imagine what this war is like; I will never forget. We had to move every ruin, behind every stone was a German. There were barricades everywhere with machine guns, all of that under a shower of bomb and grenades and asphyxiating gas. The day before yesterday, Julien threw more than 200 grenades; I fired my rifle many times to protect the grenade throwers. I took down a good many men quite calmly. My rifle, in my hands, was broken by a bomb and all that with shells whistling and exploding constantly, day and night. We went 7 days without sleeping; aerial rockets exploded from time to time making craters 10 meters in diameter and 4 meters deep. Night was lit up by the fires; anything that could burn did. All this fighting was in the middle of a dreadful stench, as there were hundreds of dead bodies on the ground that had been there for more than three weeks. Add to that the moaning and groaning of the wounded. Nothing can tell the story of these scenes of horror.

My pistol served me twice when, each time, I killed a *Boche* at point-blank range. I don't know how it is that I am still alive. I didn't believe I'd ever get out of such a hell. All my friends are safe. A bit of calm will be good for us; we are feverish with lack of sleep and have a burning thirst. We often went without eating or drinking; it was impossible to bring us anything, all that moved was immediately killed. When we were relieved last night, it was under a hail of shells up to the last minute. The *Boches* are extremely angry and they bomb everywhere and everything with a blind vengeance.

On our right, the Labyrinth which they talk about in the *communiqués* was blown away yesterday afternoon. I have to admit that, before I got here, I didn't know what war was like. It is tragic, and horribly spectacular. At night, these fires, this total destruction, the frightening torture of shelling, all that takes on a poignant, indefinable character. The stretcher bearers are totally spent, they can no longer pick up the wounded, they've had to call on old territorials. Silège and Hutin have lost 10 kilos. Right now joining the stretcher bearers is not the right path, their job is nothing like that at La Ville-aux-Bois which was mostly rest. [...]

I could have slept all day, but I really wanted to write to you. Along with everything else, the past few days have been dreadfully hot. We've suffered from thirst, the dust was terrible, and we were sweating horribly with nothing to drink. I now understand suffering from thirst, the tongue stuck to the roof of the mouth, almost unable to talk. [...] Although exhausted, not as much as others, I am very well, I'm praying for calm, and let's hope that we will have it for at least 2 weeks. [...]

6/8/1915.

I received this morning 4 packages [...] and no letter. [...] We are still in Maroeuil and we have no news about moving. [...] We have a new company chief; he seems picky and I think he will frequently make us miss our Captain Senot who left us alone when we were at rest. We will see what this one does; he would do well, given the state of our nerves, to let us be. We are not on active duty and have little interest in petty military details. Men who are constantly risking their lives need not to be bothered with all those little annoyances. It is odd that so many people don't understand this basic truth. [...]

6/9/1915.

I received today your letters from June 4 and 5 and 4 packages. [...] The dagger is a splendid weapon and you can be sure it will serve me well if we should find ourselves embedded in similar fights. It is less dangerous to use than the knife I received. I thank you very much and Vessot asks me to thank you for the knife I've given him. [...]

I am pleased that Mme Boissard and the Foyer du Soldat paid you something. You should keep your eyes on the Spassky; it has gone up a lot recently and might pay something. [...] Let's hope that Mme Mauhavel will also agree to give you something. It makes little sense that her business is open and she doesn't pay something, however little. I think that she is truly abusing the situation and doesn't give me a very good impression of her. We are nearing July and if this continues, she cannot put off her payments forever. You will give my greetings to Mme Muisy and give me news; I suppose you will go see Léontine whom you never mention. How is Fernand? [...]

6/10/1915.

I received last evening your letter from June 6 and 4 packages. [...] I am at rest, here's how we got here: last night, about 3 a.m., we received a sudden order to pick up our packs and we were soon heading towards Arras. After 6 kilometers, we found buses which took us to a village named Le Souich, seven kilometers from Doullens. This village is delightful, buried in greenery and more than 25 kilometers from our lines, that means we don't hear the cannon noise; it is absolute quiet, calm and rest. [...]

Before we left, General Mangin, the division general, made sure to thank us with the Order of the Day for the persistent and incessant attacks our regiment made with bravery, in particular June 3 to 5th, attacks that were in large part responsible for the taking of the rest of the village. [...]

We have a new company commander who will make us miss our good Senot, killed at the deadly barricade which we lost seven times and finally managed to take for good. I do hope that the heroic efforts of so many men will not have been in vain and that we will soon see our enemies clear out. [...]

6/11/1915.

I received last evening your letter of June 7. [...] The gigantic battle continues; yesterday we saw at least 1,000 buses and trucks taking thousands of men to who knows where. Modern transportation is extraordinary; this plethora of vehicles makes a lot possible.

Last night we had a terrible storm followed by a lot of rain which fortunately cooled things down. I have kept, and will probably always keep, a blanket; even in summer it is very helpful. My oilcloth is still in good condition; recently I've not needed it so often. Do not spend money to buy me another, that serves no purpose. On the outside of my pack, I attach three rolls all bundled together: in the first, my blanket and 3 books; in the second, my tent cloth and two books; in the third, my oilcloth and 2 books. I left my sleeping bag a while ago; it was quite worn out and no longer of any use. [...]

6/12/1915.

I received today your letters from June 8 and 9 and the 8 packages listed in them. [...] I don't have much time to write today; we are going 4 kilometers to pass in review by the commanding general of the army who wants to congratulate us on the total capture of Neuville. The 129th was completely responsible for that.

The Labyrinth is a sort of fort 500 meters to the left of Neuville which the 74th took. The fort was admirably organized and they had a dreadful time capturing it. Now that we have passed through that storm, I am very pleased to have participated in an action like that at Neuville which will be part of the annals of the war. You cannot begin to imagine what it was like. I hope I will be able to tell you, in person, the extraordinary and impressive details. We lived through 10 unforgettable days, the last word in horror. During that effort, in addition to the shells which fell by the thousands, it was a matter of who could withstand the lack of sleep, the hunger, and the thirst. In this endurance test, we showed ourselves to be better than our enemies and much cleverer. We killed a great many, with cunning; in this horrible manhunt there is nevertheless something fascinating. [...]

6/13/1915.

I received this morning your letter of June 10. [...] Yesterday we had the review by General Mangin; that meant a lot of fussiness and the waiting was very tiring. In fact, we walked 15 kilometers and waited for 2 to 3 hours on a

huge field in full sun. [...] The military brass doesn't want to, or cannot, understand that we are not here for show and that, when we are not engaged in
actions, they should leave us alone. The ridiculous part of this war is that, away
from the front, they want to order us around like 20-year-old kids at camp. They
pay no attention to our age or the situation. At Neuville, when our captain was
killed, each section chief took the command. Fortunately, in this type of war,
personal cleverness is more important than centralized command. I drank as
little as possible in Neuville, many others drank the water from the wells in the
area which was disgusting, due to the collapse of everything and corpses everywhere. It was, to be sure, a terrible situation not soon to be forgotten. [...] Alas,
it will soon be a year since we left for Port Lazo, how far away that seems! [...]

6/14/1915.

Yesterday I received your letter from the 10th of June. [...] I will not write
much as they are pestering us with things to do. We just finished a 15-kilome-
ter march at a running pace which, is, of course, ridiculous. Our new colonel,
whom we barely know, is very tough, he comes from the infantry. [...] He forgets
that most of us are no longer very young and that we are very tired. [...]

There is no point in your sending me cartridges for my little pistol; I only used
5 out of 50. You understand that I don't use the weapon except in special circumstances, point blank fighting, and I used it with the greatest sangfroid. What
is more, in the midst of these events, I never lost my head and could not have
seen the situation more clearly. [...]

One of my comrades was impressed by the knife I gave Vessot. He asked me
whether I could get one like that for him. He will reimburse me the cost. He
would actually like one a bit larger. Tomorrow I will send a 5-franc bill so you
don't spend your money for this; and I apologize for the inconvenience this
causes. [...]

Wednesday, June 24, 1915.

I received yesterday at 4 p.m. your short note from June 14. When will this carnage end? Are there ten houses left to destroy? How many dead and wounded
will there be? Alas, you need to maintain this advantage. The Germans must
be bringing in huge reinforcements. I don't know where they get all those men.
It seems that, the more who disappear, the more they find. [...] In the official
communiqué of June 8, I read: "In Neuville-Saint-Vaast, we have taken, with very
intense combat, a new group of houses. In the area of the Labyrinth a German
counterattack was repelled." So all the houses you spoke of haven't yet been
taken? That place called the Labyrinth must not be far from Neuville. [...] Yes,
you can well say that this region is not just destroyed, but sent to the bowels of

the earth—how horrible! How can an entire people, a nation, one man, declare war and a war like this that unleashes the most awful of scourges! It is beyond imagination. And when I see the liveliness, the people, in short normal life in the streets of Vincennes, I ask myself whether I am dreaming, and whether you are really there, facing bullets and guns. What an agonizing hallucination. [...]

6/15/1915.

I received last evening your letter of June 11. [...] There is a rumor, which I believe well-founded, that we leave today for Avesnes-le-Comte or thereabouts to take up the positions held by a division that is going to the front. There is every chance in the world that, after about 10 days, that would be about June 25, we will go back to the shooting. We have received reinforcements; our regiment has been rebuilt and there is so much activity in our region it is logical to think that we will soon be sent back to the front. [...]

Do not torment yourself too much; that does no good. No matter what, if my fate is to remain here, then that is what will happen. If the opposite is true, so much the better. [...]

6/16/1915.

I received this morning your letters from June 12 and 13. [...] We are in Fosseux, south of Avesnes-le-Comte, behind Arras. I do not know whether we'll be here very long, for my part I do not think so. There is talk of a general offensive, and if that happens, we will certainly be part of it. There are some corps which are lucky and are enjoying, or have enjoyed, a long rest. Unfortunately, our regiment doesn't appear to share that luck; we have never had any rest. One might have thought that the regiments that participated in an affair like that of Neuville would be sent to the rear for a while. Nothing like it, our rest seems very brief. [...]

In order to become a stretcher bearer, as I've explained, there has to be a vacancy and that hasn't yet happened. My status doesn't give me any rights. I am not listed as musician, I didn't do my military service as a musician, I was part of the regular company. Had I served three years as musician then I would have had a better chance to be among the stretcher bearers from the beginning. [...]

This area is infested with troops, so many that it is impossible to move around. Seeing this spectacle as well as the endless convoys on the roads is stupefying. You, in Paris, cannot imagine, even a little, what goes on in this war. Everything is huge and horrible. [...]

Second letter, same day.

I write again, we just received the order to depart. The destination is not known. We may just be moving to another billeting site, always in the direction of the front. [...] This Artois, which I did not know, is very pretty, very green. It doesn't have the grandeur of the Aisne valley where the scenery is somewhat majestic. In this part of the Artois, the villages are filled with greenery. From a distance the roofs are not visible; one takes them to be little groves of trees. [...]

6/17/1915.

We left Fosseux yesterday and have arrived in a region whose name I don't know. [...] According to rumors, we have moved forward at least 10 kilometers, and, in a burst of energy, we are hoping to break the German lines. We have here 300,000 bayonets, 60,000 cavalry, plus artillery. You see what an enormous effort this is. Our division is to be part of the charge; we will be transported as often as possible in vehicles. We are delighted to be advancing; if we have to fight, we prefer to see the *Boches* pull back. It's a good sign and will shorten this terrible war. It's like in a dream, seeing everything moving at this time. If the *Boches* continue to pull back, we will soon have taken back Douai and Lille which would be very important. Headquarters, with the grand-père,[101] is not far away, we do know that, and it gives us confidence. [...]

6/18/1915.

We were moved last night by auto to a place above Aubigny on the road to Béthune. We are camping in the open air on the lawn of a beautiful chateau. I believe we are the 2nd or 3rd reserve for the corps in action right now. [...]

I totally agree with you about Mme Mauhavel. I feel that, because she is working, she should be able to pay something. The moratorium doesn't mean that one shouldn't pay rent. Her business has not totally stopped. If she continues to show bad faith, I urge you to go explain this to a justice of the peace. Otherwise, we will be dupes of people who don't keep their word. [...]

6/19/1915.

Yesterday I received your two letters from June 15 and 16. [...] I realize that the price of coal, even if not of good quality, has gone up a lot and this winter it will certainly be very expensive. [...]

What is interesting in my group here is that, if one of us were wounded, the others would make every effort to get him out and into the hands of the nurses. Quick removal of the wounded in places like Neuville was totally impossible,

---

[101] General Joffre.

beyond the capacity of men and machines. We would need entire regiments of stretcher bearers and nurses. There are obviously times when there are not enough of them and we, the soldiers, do everything we can. I have bandaged some wounded who waited a long time for the nurses. You keep asking about stretcher bearer, I assure you that, until there is a vacancy, it is impossible for me or anyone else. The rules control the number of stretcher bearers, two for each company. As long as those two still exist, there is nothing to do but wait. [...]

Fatigue and weariness are everywhere, not to mention the misery and the depopulation due to the length of the war. This war with modern machines is such that we cannot make any serious advances, nor can the *Boches*. To advance 3 kilometers, 20,000 men are killed. At this rate, by the time we reach the French border there won't be any army left. This worry, which is very obvious in our leaders, will certainly shorten this nightmare, and it will be a dreadful lesson for humanity. [...]

6/20/1915.

I received last night your letter of June 17. [...] I don't need any underwear. Above all, do not send me anything without my specifically requesting it. You complicate my life when you send those spontaneous gifts. [...] We are moving out at 3 p.m., we do not know where we are going. One might say we are familiar with moving; our suitcase is quickly packed. [...]

6/25/1915.

Finally, we are again out of hell, and what we saw and what we suffered is quite beyond comparison with what has happened since the war began.

Here is how things unfolded. We left Fosseux Saturday. On Sunday they dropped us at Villers-Châtel and immediately led us to Hill 119. This place is called the Cabaret rouge.[102] It's next to Souchez, between there and Mont-Saint-Éloi. At 2 a.m. we were in the front lines, our left was almost up to the sugar refinery at Souchez. Hill 119 was taken by the Moroccan division and at great cost. To understand the situation, you need to know that this place has become the extreme advance point of the front. We were holding this line at the points I've marked. Because of errors, the wings A and C did not advance. The result was that we were surrounded on three sides by Germans; we were under fire from all directions. We had been there since 1 a.m.: at exactly 2 a.m. an unbelievable bombing started on our position, a bombing that lasted 22 hours, until midnight Monday into Tuesday. We were terrified during the entire period, enormous shells, many filled with molten phosphorus, landed twenty a minute

---

[102] The "red cabaret" was a house with a roof and walls of red brick, destroyed in 1915. It is the name of the largest English cemetery from World War I.

for 22 hours. It was petrifying, these shells fell 10 meters in front of us, 5 meters behind, in short surrounded us non-stop. I don't know how we didn't all end up dead.

We suffered huge losses; half our company is wiped out but all my friends in our group are still standing. I was with comrades from the 12th squad, they were all killed around me. I made several dangerous leaps, propelled by blasts that continued without stopping.

While all this bombing was taking place, the Germans were making a movement on our right and managed to cut off the communication trench and set up machine guns in them. For 14 hours, our regiment was completely surrounded. We had no more bombs, our bullets were being used up, and the moment arrived when we expected to be taken prisoner.

Fortunately, the *Zouaves*,[103] alerted to our predicament (improvising—as no one was aware of our situation until very late, which our commanders should be ashamed of), made a fierce attack, got us out and managed to give us more ammunition. The Germans attacked us with everything they had and were beaten back with enormous losses. Our commanders finally evacuated us from this position which we couldn't possibly hold. Finally we managed to pull out, with the 3rd and 4th companies serving as our rear guard and the Germans following our every step and bombing us. We attacked them several times to give us a bit of space. Eventually we managed to get out of that position and reached the second line where the *Zouaves*, well dug in, stopped them completely. We had gone 60 hours without sleeping, without eating and without drinking. I ate two or three cans of pâté without bread, as I didn't have any, but the thirst we suffered, with the battle, the heat, the dust, is unimaginable. When we reached the rear, they had tubs of water waiting for us which we pounced on like animals.

Never will I forget the terrible events I was part of. Needless to say, we are all utterly exhausted, but right now we are in the rear in La Conté where we are resting. We earned it. They are again giving us the "order of the day" for our heroism and tenacity, in particular our company which got itself killed in order to protect the retreat. I never lost my calm and my sangfroid, but very often it seemed my time had come and I thought of you and our past life. I have to say, it was all incredible. I have already gotten over the shock to my nerves, but what horror and what a memory! Based on what they are saying, I expect us to soon be removed from this area which has become, for so many of my poor comrades, a place of terror and torture. I am finishing this letter right now as the mail pick-up is at 10:00. I will continue to write, but I want this one to go immediately. I embrace you tenderly.

---

[103] Troops predominantly from North Africa; they fought valiantly for France.

Second letter, same day.

I am thus continuing my other letter. Needless to say, during this time, I've not received any letters or packages. [...] A good many people can't wait for the end. Many have lost heart, especially after scenes like the one we just got out of. The mind is frightened by the prospect of a second winter campaign. Will people have the strength to stand it if necessary? I doubt it. I see an evolution around me and believe civilians are suffering more than we are. Alas, true, a year ago we were in peace at Port Lazo and we never imagined such a cataclysm. I can assure you that I will soon join the stretcher bearers, my nomination goes through 48 hours from now, I've been told that officially. There are two vacancies. Two were wounded and they need to be replaced. As soon as it is official, I will tell you. Things will be quieter there and I will be in very good company. [...]

For my part, I think it is going to be very difficult to get the Germans to leave our country; we are a bit like two bulls, head-to-head. And neither one can move backwards. When you think about it, we can't wipe out the entire male population of our country, especially the most active. Do you realize that, according to the exact figures we learned from an officer of the high command, a friend of Deschamps, as of now we have 450,000 dead and 650,000 injured—crippled, wooden legs, only one arm, so a wasted human being, mostly unable to work? That makes 1.1 million men destroyed, that is a third of the working age population of the country. Our government must be really worried about this; after all one can't throw the entire human race into the furnace. I think the solution will come another way. [...]

Monday, June 28, 1915.

No news this morning. [...] I am very happy that your buddy Dehuysser is with you; you describe him as a guy with a lot of presence and sangfroid. In such dangerous situations, one needs as many men like that as possible. It is much easier to face danger surrounded by men one can count on. Sadly, in battles like the one at Neuville-Saint-Vaast, the wounded who cannot get up and aren't lucky enough to find some form of help are likely to die for lack of immediate care and evacuation. [...] It's better not to dwell too much on that. We would need an army of stretcher bearers and nurses—obviously impossible! And to think that all this human death and suffering is due to the stubborn, foolish pride of one man. Will he ever find suitable punishment? [...]

Tuesday, June 29, 1915.

I received today at 4 p.m. the continuation of your letter from Friday June 25. I thank you for this correspondence which lets me know you are still alive and have again escaped the terrible danger that surrounded you. Let your friends know how happy I am to know them safe. After being involved in the fight from the end of May to June 6, to have enjoyed something only barely resembling rest until the 20th, and then be thrown right back into the furnace is a frightening nightmare. If you are all still standing, Providence protected you, and you should thank "her" from the bottom of your hearts. If I shed tears at the thought you could disappear, I cried with joy in learning that your being named stretcher bearer was only a matter of hours. Not that I think you will no longer be in danger; the Germans fire at the Red Cross. Exploding shells, gas bombs, aerial torpedoes, etc. do not spare those who collect the wounded. Just the opposite, they have to risk a lot to care for so many unfortunate men, but I am happy to think that you will have some quiet time, better food, and that your poor legs, which must be so very tired, can enjoy a more complete rest. [...]

Wednesday, June 30, 1915.

I received your letter from Sunday June 27th. That letter announces your appointment to the stretcher bearers. This a happy day for me and it is the first time in many months that I feel a bit of joy. [...]

6/26/1915.

I didn't receive a letter today, but I did receive 3 packages. [...] I am confirming what I already said, that, unless something unexpected happens, the decision to make me a stretcher bearer will be published tomorrow or the next day. So [...] I will need many fewer packages; I think you could send me only one a day. That would be absolutely enough, alternating sugar, lemons (but very few), cheese (very useful), small or medium sized cans of food (that would be better now since I won't be sharing with five comrades), hard boiled eggs, cans of fruit. [...]

In the battalion, there are 16 stretcher bearers and 8 nurses. They cook together. They buy what they need to supplement and make good meals. Everyone pays a modest sum weekly for the supplements. The nurse who does the cooking is an excellent chef. [...]

I will almost certainly ask you to send me a violin as soon as my nomination is official, but I'll tell you more and will explain what I want. [...]

6/27/1915.

129th Infantry, Postal Sector 93, Stretcher Bearer 1st Battalion.[104] As of today, I entered the ranks of the stretcher bearers, and this is what you should use for my address. I am going to be able to play music; we have to hope I will not be

---

[104] Lucien indicated a new location or status with a phrase like this.

continually in a hell like recently. The infirmary vehicle will transport my violin, so I want you to send me first my Geneva in the case I always use;[105] second, my Serdet bow and the Tartini copy made by Merciolle; third, 6 E strings, three A strings, two D strings, and three G strings in a metal box. You will rub the G strings with some emery paper. Send as many as you can of the old ones. Fourth, some rosin, an ordinary mute, and a lead mute. Go, see Cunault so he can check the bridge and the seams; I expect it is in good condition. He will package it since he knows how. You will send the package by way of Le Havre, registered mail of course. I hope to have the instrument in two weeks. [...]

The battalion doctor, Monsieur Faget, has been very nice, all thanks to the awful violin from Courlandon. With that old thing I was still able to charm those around me. My violin will not be in danger; it will always be watched by someone. Send also, via Le Havre, the Peters editions of the Beethoven and Mozart sonatas, as well as the Bach sonatas in the Peters editions, the boxed set; I am going to rework them immediately. I am happy and send love. [...]

6/28/1915.

I continue to write. I had to stop my previous letter because the mail was leaving at 10 a.m. [...] My dear Maman, you make me laugh when you say it worries you to see us camping in the open air on the grass. It's very simple: we take our tent cloth, some sticks that we cut, and in the flick of an eye the tent is put up. We are six together in a tent. [...] When it is set up properly, it can rain but nothing penetrates the cloth. Around the tent we dig a deep ditch for the run-off and we are all set. I will say that the life in the open air is very healthy. I've been with the other stretcher bearers in a house for two days and I am literally suffocating. [...]

Lucien's letters for the months of July, August, and early September 1915 did not survive. Louise's letters from that time allow us a glimpse into what Lucien did during these months.

Monday, July 5, 1915.

Yesterday, Sunday, I had a visit from Léontine, Ferdinand, and Suzanne.[106] When you asked me for news of Léontine and Fernand, it was very difficult

---

[105] "The Geneva" refers to a violin made in the eighteenth century by Storioni that Lucien acquired in Geneva. He was surprised as he had believed he was only purchasing the elaborately decorated case.

[106] Cousins from the Durosoir family in Boulogne.

for me to reply. Now that you have endured all this unimaginable suffering, and death has brushed you with its wings several times, your spirit has grown stronger in the face of the evil and horrors you have witnessed. Thus, without fear of diminishing your courage (which would perhaps have been the case a few months ago) I can tell you of the death, on October 10, 1914, of poor Fernand from a bullet wound to his left arm. Complications led to his end. He was apparently well-treated right away in Toul, but was sent back to Chambéry. During the trip, he probably needed his bandage changed. Once at the hospital at Chambéry, he hemorrhaged, two, three times. Shards of bone had pierced the main artery. They opened his arm to take out the pieces of bone. It would have been better to have cut off his arm; they would almost certainly have saved him, but I think there was no surgeon. Tetanus set in and he died in the midst of great suffering. A nun in the hospital, who knew Mme Niot, had talked to Fernand, or taken care of him (I don't really know). She sent a dispatch to Mme Niot to tell his family. Léontine left imediately for Chambéry and after many delays managed to see her son who was near death but still recognized her. That, my poor child, is how Fernand died. I think I did the right thing to not tell you until now. Arriving at this time, this news will not have the same effect as it would have had last October when you were announcing your departure at any moment for the front. So many have disappeared that the pain you might feel is lessened a bit by all you have seen and endured.

It is the same for M. and Mme Lambert's son-in-law. I hadn't told you about it and they agreed they would not speak of it. But M. Lambert couldn't keep quiet for long. His son-in-law died a hero and he felt the need to talk about it, so he told you. [...]

Tuesday, July 6, 1915.

[...] I saw in *L'Information* that artists, painters, designers, engravers are putting their impressions and memories of this awful war on paper and canvas. It seems to me that you, as a musician, would want to create a permanent memory of two places, Neuville and Souchez, where you expected to die. I would be very happy for you to write a simple piece for violin and piano conveying your impressions: a short adagio to start, a movement expressive of the horror of combat and all you heard, with slow parts in places to express the suffering (if you agree), and an adagio or lento to close, a sort of thank you to heaven for protecting you. If I were in your situation, I think that would make my brain work. [...]

Wednesday, July 7, 1915.

[...] Again I suggest that you not only spend time on violin [...] but that the terrible emotions you experienced be fixed forever. The musician only has one way; that is to compose a piece of music that will last forever and give him honor and success. You cannot write a long, serious piece, and that is not what is needed. You should be able to play the piece as soon as possible. […] You should, therefore, write a short piece like *Airs Russes* or *Airs Bohémiens*.[107] With the memories that must haunt your mind, you will certainly come up with the right, expressive phrases; you have only to look into your heart. Your violin and bow will do the rest. Do try to come up with imitative sounds, double-stops, harmonics, etc. Think of an interesting piece but accessible for the public. This will be a bit of you and your military life, which comes and goes in sonorous waves and sad or funereal phrases, depending on your feelings. That is why I have added three large sheets of music paper. […] Even though you are now in the stretcher bearers, I know that danger exists, I'm not deluding myself. And on your side, I ask you to not let yourself fall into a false sense of safety. […]

Thursday July 8, 1915.

[…] Yesterday I sent you some music. You should play Mozart's Sonata #4 in E minor.[108] It's the one you played with Loyonnet for your first chamber music concert. […] Beethoven's Sonata in A (I think)[109] […] which you worked on at Saint Pair, and about which Berlioz speaks with emotion in his memoirs is a sonata to work on. […] Finally, I sent you a pot of honey. It is to be eaten on an empty stomach to refresh your body which must be on fire after all these terrible emotions. […]

Your two bottles of 1904 were sent on July 3, I hope you will receive them. Rue du Bouloi and rue de Palestro, where they ship packages for free, no longer want people to send liquids because of accidents. The bottles break and damage other shipments; when they notice that the packages contain liquids, the shipment stays here. Mme Bastien packed yours very well, in a way that the "glous-glous" can't be heard. […]

Friday, July 9, 1915.

[…] I keep thinking about the piece you could compose in the style of the *Airs Russes*. A free and easy cadence, principal theme, development of the theme

---

[107] Henri Wieniawski (1833-1880), *Airs Russes, Souvenir de Moscou* (1853), Op. 6. Pablo de Sarasate (1844-1908); *Airs Bohémiens*, for violin and orchestra, Op. 20.

[108] Wolfgang Amadeus Mozart (1756-1791), K 304/300c.

[109] The reference to Hector Berlioz (1803-1869) suggests that Louise is referring to Sonata No. 9, Op. 47, "Kreutzer." Berlioz described the sonata as "outrageously unintelligible" in Laura Kelley, "The Kreutzer Sonata: Love, Murder, and the Violin," September 27, 2018, http://chambermusicsociety.org/about/news/the-kreutzer-sonata-love-murder-and-the-violin..

[…], a relatively lively tempo by the return of the theme that expresses your principal emotions (a few notes of the *Marseillaise* in minor might fit in well). […]

Sunday, July 11, 1915.

I didn't write last night as I had hoped. […] I had dinner with Mme Duez. She wanted very much to keep me there longer, which meant that I got home late. I took the métro (there is now a station in Boulogne).[110] It's a fast trip, but in the evening, the tramways in Vincennes only run every half-hour, which means not profiting from the rapid first part of the trip. I read a letter you sent to Mme Duez in which you ask her to be so good as to send some pharmaceutical products for your infirmary. I think it didn't make her angry and that she will send what you asked for. We need to be very tactful with her, […] write some nice long letters (not too long). You now have a good reason to do that, the change in your life is an ideal subject. She likes to have people write her interesting letters. She is not stupid but always fearful that people are more interested in her money than in her. It is understandable. She has been exploited all sorts of ways and people still try to do it. That means that when one has a request to make, it needs to be done frankly and with the understanding that if she has not the means to do it, one is still grateful. […] She was very friendly with me and again offered to help me in terms of money if I needed it. I thanked her and told her that I would probably need it (despite my efforts) if the war lasted through the winter, as it seems about to. […]

Tuesday, July 13, 1915.

I received yesterday afternoon your letter from Wednesday July 7th, and this morning the one from the 8th. I will do what you suggest about Mme Mauhaval. […] I was not able to see her as I had planned last Saturday but, passing by the traffic circle, I saw that her café was open, and likewise, when I took the tramway from Boulogne to Auteuil at 9:30 p.m., I saw that it was still open. Thus, without having to work enormously hard, with the café open during the week and on Sundays, she is adding to the money she makes from her shop. I will wait for the end of this week to go to Boulogne to resolve this issue. At the same time, I will see Madame Duez and raise the question of money; she was the first person to offer me some financial help. I admit I was there to talk to her about that. […]

About the death of poor Fernand, I thought I was doing the right thing in not telling you about it right away because I thought, and still think, that learning this news now would affect you less. I did it because I care too much for you. Why make those who suffer and who give so much for their country reason to

---

[110] Line 1 of the Paris Métro, inaugurated in 1890, ran from the Porte de Vincennes to Porte Maillot and was slowly extended westward, passing through Boulogne.

be sad. Let us leave them ignorant of those already lost in the torment, so that their lives not be upset and their ideal not distracted for an instant by sadness. You have to understand that. The two or three times I went to Boulogne for my business, I never saw anyone except the notary, Mme Lefèvre, Mme Mauhaval, M. Pierron.

Saturday, July 17, 1915.

[…] I learned from Mme Bastien that many soldiers are bringing home to their wives, their mothers, and other relatives rings and pins made from the remains of German bombs. […]

Sunday, July 18, 1915.

[…] You say you will leave the trenches Thursday July 22 and may be able to come home on leave at the end of July or early August. I was thinking about going to Boulogne toward the end of next week, but I will not budge from the house. You might arrive on a day when I am absent. […] There you are in Neuville, in that sector which must bring back so many terrible, sad memories. I read in the *communiqué* of July 17: "North of Arras the cannon barrage continued during the night; it was particularly violent north of Souchez and between Neuville and Roclincourt." After the Souchez offensive of June 22 and 23, the Germans have gotten a foothold there. They want to take Calais at all cost. […]

Thursday, July 22, 1915.

[…] The use of poison gas is abominable; do you have masks to protect you? Those people use all possible ways to reach their goal. […] It is another way to save their ammunition—death by poisoning. […]

Sunday July 25, 1915.

[…] M. and Mme Lambert's son-in-law died from shrapnel that shredded his belly. He must not have suffered; he probably died instantly. One of his comrades who witnessed his death wrote to their daughter. He carried out that sad task as you did. You however had the pain of being present through the agonizing death of that poor young man who, his youth fighting against the final suffering, did not die suddenly—a terrible sight which one never forgets. Were you able to move him out of the battleground to bury him and tell his family where his body was resting? That is one of the things that terrifies me the most, the thought that these unfortunate men have no graves. […]

Monday, July 26, 1915, afternoon.

I received this morning your letter from Wednesday July 21 and am relieved to learn that your wine and your violin arrived. [...]

Thursday, August 5, 1915.

I received last night your letter from Saturday July 31 in which you give me hope that you will not go back to the trenches right away as you expected, rather that you will move farther to the rear near St. Pol (are the Germans bombing that city?) to get more rest for 10 days. So much the better. That may be due to the miserable state of health of your regiment. [...]

Saturday, August 7, 1915.

[...] Mme Duez's name is Louise. Her name day is thus the 25th of August. You will send her a letter opener; that will be better than a ring. I will send you a small tricolor ribbon and you will tie it to the letter opener, along with some wildflowers you pick, all for the day before the 24th of August if possible. [...] For me I would like a paperweight. If this all makes you spend too much, I can send a 20 franc note in a letter. [...]

Sunday, August 8, 1915.

[...] Yesterday I went to Boulogne, first to the notary to see whether Mme Mauhaval had deposited something to the account (she had not). [...] She is someone who knows perfectly well that she has the law on her side and that nothing can force her to pay on her account. She complains a lot about the new law which prohibits giving (selling) drinks to soldiers at any hour of the day. Mme Lefèvre had told me that there was no chance I would get any money from her. [...] Mme Mauhaval told me, in no uncertain words: "In April, if the law demands that I pay, I will. (I will borrow from my parents) etc." It is clear, there is nothing to be done as long as the law gives tenants unlimited protection. [...] We have to hope that M. Mauhaval has luck on his side and comes back safe and sound. I asked Mme Duez for 1000 Francs. Any more and I think I'd have frightened her. This is for 18 months; if necessary, she will renew for 6 months or a year. The interest is 5 percent. [...] I will immediately give her the interest for a year. [...]

Between August 8 and August 17, Lucien spent time at home on leave.

Tuesday, August 17, 1915.

As I write to you, you must be on the train. [...] I hope your regiment stays in the same place for a while and that you can enjoy some calm. You need rest, to recover morally and physically. [...]

Saturday, August 21, 1915.

[...] If they give you a new *capote*, think about saving a fairly large piece of the old one. I can make a small cloth to put on a nightstand. [...] That would be a souvenir of the trenches at Berry-au-Bac and the battles at Neuville-Saint-Vaast and Souchez which you were part of; that *capote* has seen a little bit of everything. [...]

Tuesday, August 24, 1915.

[...] When soldiers practice throwing grenades, aren't the grenades empty? So how did the lieutenant receive a mortal injury to his chest? That is awful! One survives real danger and death finds him while at rest! [...]

Wednesday, August 25, 1915.

I received this morning your letter of Sunday August 22 with the photographs of Neuville, of Hill 119 (Souchez), the trench you were in during those famous battles. They all look the same to me, I will use a magnifying glass to see them better. Too bad your back was turned at the moment the picture was taken. I just have to imagine you there. I am taken by great emotion as I look at these little squares of paper. You were so close to being left there, being killed like your comrades. [...]

Thursday, August 26, 1915.

I received this morning your letter of August 23 and thank you for your name day wishes. Like you, I hope that unforeseen events will put an end, sooner than we think, to this long, unfortunate war. And that we will have the pleasure of seeing each other, you unhurt and me in good health; I am getting older just like all mortals and cannot escape the little weaknesses inherent with a ripe old age. However, all that will be unimportant if only you have the good fortune to stay safe and well and are able to devote yourself to your art as in the past. [...] I will be very happy for you to have 20 more days of rest. That would bring you to the 15th of September. How time goes by! Events seem to be moving more slowly. Imagine, in December as you turn 37, you may still be in uniform. Last year, when your comrades celebrated your birthday, all of you expected this to be over by spring! [...]

Sunday, August 29, 1915.

I received yesterday afternoon your letter from Wednesday August 25. […] I had intended to send you this morning a pâté from the charcutier on the rue du Midi;) you could have given me your opinion on its quality. But last night I had quite a bit of fever, this grippe is at its peak. It would not be wise for me to go out. […]

I suggested you try to join the music regiment as cymbal player. You don't play any instrument used in military music. (This winter, had you thought about it, you could have worked on the clarinet, I think that wouldn't take too long and is not very hard.) […]

Wednesday, September 1, 1915.

I did not receive a letter this morning […] Right now I find the mail delivery very regular. I am better, but I need to be careful. I don't want to go out tomorrow so will not send any packages. Marguerite took the two packages I promised you to the post this morning, […] included is a band of flannel that can work as a belt. This band is not very bulky as it is just ordinary flannel and so quite lightweight. […] I couldn't find anything better in the shop in Vincennes where I looked. It will be good enough for now. For winter I will make sure to find the best flannel. […] At night you should wear the belt. The nights are becoming longer and cooler and, at about 2 or 3 a.m. one becomes quite aware of that fact. You who sleep outdoors, or almost outdoors, need to take the most elementary precautions. […] Last year at this time you were wearing a belt around your kidneys; wool develops a nice warmth around the kidneys and the stomach to avoid colic.

September is here, we are heading toward cool weather, long nights. It is not without sadness that I realize that you will be plunged into seemingly endless dark hours. However, I find it difficult to believe that you will have to fight a complete winter campaign. New events will probably happen and change the face of things. That is to wish for but it will not happen without more sacrifice. Alas, this challenge which has gone on for more than a year is a bad dream. What will be the wake-up? […]

Mme Bastien came to see me yesterday about 2 p.m. Her husband left that morning from Montreuil to take the 7:00 train from the Gare du Nord. She was still very emotional about this departure and was sorry that the evil grippe I'm still suffering from kept me from seeing her husband and participating in the reunion in his honor. He bought a lot of things in Paris, among them a 3-liter wine skin covered with gray-blue cloth. […] Those of us who stupidly went to the Belle Jardiniere to buy a poor little 1-liter bidon could have gone to the Louvre and bought one like it. You would not have had the annoyance of having a bidon that leaked and soiled your clothes, not to mention the quantity of wine that was diminished due to evaporation. If you would like a wine skin like that, when I am feeling better, I will go to the Louvre to find one to send to you.

Did you write to Coraboeuf? Not on Byrrh paper?[111] You shouldn't let your good, distinguished taste be changed in the slightest ways. You can't say "it's war, so I don't give a damn." [...] It is with this cowardly and weak excuse that we played Germany's game and let their cheapness of all sorts change the distinction that characterizes us. [...] We must stay true to ourselves and not let ourselves be pulled into vulgarity. I don't know the surroundings you've lived in for a year; I would be disappointed to see that the faults and weaknesses of your comrades are rubbing off on you. Over time, one grows accustomed and doesn't recognize a lot of things and starts down the slippery slope.

Pierrot is darling! Martel is charming! Maybe you are judging them superficially, by their outside. One needs to observe people sometimes for a long time to truly judge them. As for Hutin, you had written that he was a charming fellow, very nice, and boom! your balloon of enthusiasm burst and you don't speak of him any longer. You shouldn't be in haste to speak about people. [...] Force yourself to observe others, that is a quality one has to practice; make an effort, it is worth it. If you misjudge, you are the dupe.

I don't know why M. Alan is involved with sending addresses to the Violet firm. They don't ask for anything more than to spread publicity and increase their profits (absinthe and other strong alcohols being illegal, the sale of quinquina,[112] Dubonnet and other fortified wines will just increase). I would not be surprised if the Byrrh company sent M. Alan several liters of its wine to thank him for his propaganda. I am pretty sure of that because he reacted so much when I told him what I thought about the wine merchant letter paper; I could see my remark touched him. I didn't insist because it is none of my business and I did not want to upset him. He replied with a very abrupt tone that he didn't care much about sentiment and the paper did not cost anything. [...] I wanted to tell him that the paper I use costs 0,05 centimes for five sheets and for this tiny expenditure I would prefer to use paper with no message. [...]

Thursday September 2, 1915.

I just had a visit from one of your comrades who brought me a letter opener. It was an enormous surprise and I am very happy to have such a lovely, moving souvenir. The name of Neuville-St-Vaast is for you as for me a reminder of terrible days. This object is very nicely made, and the red copper mixed with the yellow copper make a lovely contrast. If you could send one to Coraboeuf, with inscription, I think he would be very happy. You could send one also to Mme

---

[111] Paper with the Byrrh letterhead. Byrrh is a wine-based *apéritif* very popular in the early twentieth century.

[112] A flavored wine, served as an *apéritif*, originally containing quinine.

Bastien. Those are the only two people to whom I would want to send this souvenir, Coraboeuf because he has always been very generous toward you, and Mme Bastien because she sent you two packages and she receives us both into her family, in a simple and friendly way. It would be a thoughtful thank you.

You will send the pen holder to young Bastien. For Coraboeuf, you will also send a ring. He who draws will always have his eyes on it. For the pen holder for his daughter, you will not send it to him. You will send it to me, and I will take it to him. I remind you that you promised a letter-opener to Mme Cunault. I sent you the list of rings with fairly precise measurements. It's up to you to remember to give them to the person making them. Definitely, all those who make these objects will have a lot of work. There will even be, in Paris, an exposition of these objects and the sales will profit the soldiers at the front. *Le Matin* is getting involved. I am sure there will be exploitation and the people buying these souvenirs in Paris will not be at all sure that the material used is really German copper or aluminum. That is why you need to hurry and get these rings and letter openers made. I want to be sure that they are really from metal collected on the battlefield. You realize that, in order not to lose a command, the soldiers at the front who are working these metals and earning some income will not reject the idea of ordering metal from Paris. And they will also raise prices. It will become a nice little business, think "traffic." [...] Think about a pencil holder for yourself, that's all, but do hurry.

The young man who came to the house was dressed in civilian clothes and with his wife. I took them into the dining room to be able to thank them. They only stayed a few minutes; they had visits and shopping to do. [...]

Second letter, same day.

I received last night your letter from Sunday August 27. I also received the curious picture of Neuville on June 1. That, with the one you already sent, make a precious document. [...] On another subject, I was pleased to learn that you played the Bach *Air* and the meditation from *Thaïs* last Sunday and in the afternoon the accompaniment of Franck's *Panis Angelicus* for those men who suffer so much, psychologically and physically. [...] As you play you should sing the melody, you could do it. The Franck *Panis* is so lovely; I understand how it touches the humble. You should write an adagio. I don't understand how that does not become a necessity for you. You could play this adagio in church to console the men. Expressive phrases, you can surely find many. As for an accompaniment, you cannot make me believe that you feel incapable of doing something good. Get going my dear, much beloved child…work, try, I would be so happy. You will say that I am always pushing you. It is natural. Don't see in that my intention to scold; to the contrary, the love I have for you is so limitless that I would see you great, above everyone. [...]

Friday, September 3, 1915.

I received this morning your letter of Tuesday, August 31. I am relieved that you received the quinquina and the rum sent on August 24. I would have inquired at the post, but as the package contained liquids, that could have been a problem and would have made them mistrust me for the future. [...] I spend really too much time on the construction and solidity of these shipments in case something unexpected happens, an accident, a big package falling on a small box. All these packages have to be stuffed into bags; they are squeezed one against the other. [...] I feel much better today and am taking great care, I hope to be completely well in a few days. That will not keep me from getting some aspirin to have in case I need it. [...]

Sunday, September 5, 1915.

I received this morning your two letters from September 1 and 2. [...] I think they are looking for a lot of men for the "aerostation" right now; Balembois was clever to request that because it was a sure way to not end up in the trenches again. I told you that I received the letter opener your friend brought on Thursday. It was a surprise that made me very happy; you had said that it would take some time to find the *ceinture d'obus*.[113] [...] The red copper is thus from a French bullet, flattened, and the yellow copper from a German bullet. One can tell from the handle that the person who made this object is not a professional [...] but it is very lovely just as it is. [...]

I did not go out to mail the letters myself. My grippe is better, but I have a bit of bronchitis. I bought some cod liver oil and have started to take some each morning. I am taking all the precautions, but it takes time. [...]

Tuesday, September 7, 1915.

I received this morning your letter of Saturday, September 4 saying you were going back to the trenches that evening. The weather there must be nice; here in Vincennes since Saturday it is warm and getting hotter. The new moon is next Thursday; let's hope that the temperature will not change and we will have a nice autumn. So there you are underground for 10 days. [...] I would be happy to know you are wearing your flannel wrap. It is not very thick so will probably not last long. Let me know when you need another.

Rolland gave you a pen. I have often thought of sending you one but they are very expensive. Pencils are much easier; you don't need ink which can be a nuisance. [...]

---

[113] A bomb belt: strips of metal that wrapped around bombs. Copper ones were turned into souvenirs.

I wrote to Mme Violet to tell her I accept her price of 10,80 for the 24 copies of the Souchez picture and asked her to make 3 enlargements for us. [...]

Thursday, September 9, 1915.

I received this morning your letter from September 5. [...] Tell me the price you are paying for the rings and other things you are having made. I wouldn't want them to exploit you. I am pleased that Vessot was named stretcher bearer; now he is reunited with you and Rolland. I see in the *communiqués* of *L'Informa-tion* that there is violent cannon fighting north and south of Arras. The artillery seems to be fighting hard everywhere. Are you in the Neuville sector or the Souchez sector? [...] When you were home on leave, I felt you needed to clear your head. You found the leave short. Alas, so did I. [...]

Friday, September 10, 1915.

I received this morning your letter of September 6. [...] You must now be in the front lines. An offensive will certainly take place soon; Joffre's review was an indication. He wanted to assess the physical and moral strength of the men. If the German artillery is not responding much to the French, it's to economize their ammunition for the French offensive, if and when it takes place. [...] Yes, if, like Orpheus, you wanted to charm the ferocious beasts, that is, the Germans, they would all fall at your feet and we could hang them all. That would not use much ammunition. But your violin is resting! You could think about composing a poignant adagio to charm the beasts and soften their ferocity. [...]

Lucien's letters resume.

9/9/1915.

129th Infantry Division, Stretcher bearer 1st Battalion. Just a note today to tell you I am still in good health; this evening we go to the front line (our battalion) but not my company which is in reserve. This morning I was with the auxiliary doctor to check out the sector, that is, the positions we will take up this evening. [...]

Sunday, September 12, 1915.

I received this morning your two letters from September 8 and 9. [...] The postcards that Rolland gave you are quite funny, a bit on the dark side; the faces are quite like beasts. One shudders to think that brutes like that have occupied our country now for a year and wonders when we will be able to get rid of them. They are still using burning liquids in the Argonne; they took a trench with such an inhumane weapon. It is easy to understand why someone whose body is sprayed with fire gives up the trench. [...] We will never be able to make these bloody brutes pay enough for all the harm they are doing. [...]

9/10/1915.

I received yesterday your letter from the 7th and 2 packages. [...] Pierrot is going to make a ring for Marguerite something like the one I gave Cunault. It may not be quite as nice, but no matter. He will also make me a letter-opener. There is no need to send me money; I received the 5-franc bill and will sell the pictures I receive. [...] As for your ring, you can relax, the metal will come from *Boche* rockets. None of that is any real trouble; it just demands a bit of effort. I don't have everyone right at hand, I need to chase after them a bit. [...]

Monday, September 13, 1915.

Having received two letters yesterday, this morning I have no news; I hope you are well and that the heat we are having right now is not bothering you. It's like the middle of July. [...] I often think of M. Martin and all his family and don't dare write for fear of receiving terrible news. It's better, for now, just to keep quiet and hope they are still all alive. When I remember that we were in Cumières in June 1914 to celebrate the Pentecost holiday and how the champagne flowed, I wonder whether the cellars are now empty and whether those poor people who earn their living with the harvest of that famous wine are not now living in misery. I don't know whether the Germans passed through Cumières, maybe not! [...]

I hope that during your next rest period you will compose an adagio or a romance or nocturne for violin, something lasting; you could certainly do that. One doesn't need 20 years of study and experience to write a page of heartfelt music; as for the accompaniment for those lines of melody, at least for something not very long, you could do that very nicely. And that would get you in the habit of composing. One learns by doing, so compose, compose, compose. If I were in your place, I think I would need to translate for my instrument what I was feeling. So take up the pen! You have a pen now, and a nice one.

You could send me the original and that day I would be so happy! You will see, once you get started, you will not be able to stop; the adagio will give way to an allegro or a Paganini-style étude. You can do it; you must. We must spread your name every way possible, and it is creating something like that, much more than concerts, that gives you class, remember Kreissler. For pieces you have arranged or edited, you should have printed the fingerings and liaisons which are part of your musical personality. [...]

9/11/1915.

[...] I hope today to have the time to write more; I am on duty in the country-side and will have less to do than at the central post where we run all the errands for the medical service. We are on duty in the countryside only when something is going on. I received the music you sent and only today looked to see what it was. It will be very useful but you needn't have included the *Marseillaise*. [...]

We transport lots of things from various posts to the central station, always on foot; that is how, yesterday, I spent part of the day wandering all over the place with a carboy of sodium hyposulfite weighing 35 kilos. I carried it on my back like a sack of coal. Our trench life is very physical; we are always on foot. It would be perfect if we didn't have to see and help with such suffering and such horrible injuries. [...]

9/12/1915.

I received yesterday your letters of September 8 and 9. [...] I don't know why you accuse me of not being frank; I don't tell you everything when I don't have time and there are more important things to say. [...]

Yesterday, Rolland and I buried the body of a poor fellow who fell on May 9. He was from the 329th and we went to pick him up in a field about 10 meters from our lines. We had to wait for night and it wasn't easy. This body had been found just a few days earlier. That is a dreadful job, and dangerous. Fortunately, not very frequent.

In general, I pay 1,50 for the rings; yours will cost 5 francs, the one for Coraboeuf at least 3 francs and my pen holders 2,50 each. For the letter-openers, we will see. [...]

We are much better off now in terms of water; they have done some work to improve the situation. Right now they are digging an artesian well in Neuville. [...]

9/13/1915.

[...] I received yesterday your letter of September 10. [...] We will proba-bly be relieved tomorrow night, the 14th, or maybe the 15th. [...] Since 2 a.m. last night we have had much to do—a good number of wounded to patch up. The *Boches*, who attacked our right, were repelled with many losses. We had 15 dead and about 30 wounded, which is not a lot given the size of the attack. In short, we carried 3 dead men whom we buried this morning. That means that we basically didn't get any sleep. In the midst of this sad task, we found, quite by

accident, some all-season strawberries in what is left of the garden of the Château de Neuville. You can just imagine our astonishment and joy; Pierrot and
Rolland and I ate them with relish. Since it was 5 a.m., they were covered with
dew and simply exquisite. In the same garden, however ravaged and dug up, we
also uncovered a rose bush, looking not very good but with a few roses. In the
midst of such devastation and such ruins, that seemed strange, this poetry and
these ruins under an ideally pure sky. We cut the roses. Because of the rarity of
this event, I'm sending you one in a package, so it may arrive in fairly good condition. A rose from Neuville, I know many people who would pay its weight in
gold. [...]

There is a rumor that we will go to rest for a bit, maybe 10 days, and then will
take part in the attack for which there are huge preparations. This attack will be
large scale. It's the definitive effort which, one is hoping, will throw the stinking
beast out of our country. Mangin was telling his officers recently: "from Belfort
to the North Sea, the same day at the same hour." A generalized push forward,
it will be preceded by a huge bombardment, which will make the ones we've
seen nothing but child's play. Everywhere there is a huge amount of artillery and
many new pieces of equipment, and the number of bodies needed to fire them is
unbelievable; it has to be close to 10,000. All the *Boches* will be squashed in their
trenches. I cannot say now anything about the grand preparations being made,
but it appears, based on letters from others, that it is the same all along the front.
That way the attack will be less hard on us; the *Boches*, attacked all along the
front, will not be able to bring large reserves or big guns to any one place. They
will have to hang in there and be wiped out under the terrible fire. Their line will
surely be broken in several places. There will be people left dead on the ground,
but we hope that this effort will be successful. The war would end quickly. [...]

9/14/1915.

I received yesterday your letter from September 11 and a package. [...] Rolland now is also receiving a package every three days. When our work brings us
together, we eat with our friend Vessot. Our service moves us all over the place
and sometimes we don't see each other all day long. [...]

For the past 48 hours our service has been very difficult. One after the other,
we had 15 men killed by aerial bombs and transporting all these bodies at night
along very narrow *sapes* is painfully difficult, much worse than you can imagine.
But it's necessary, as we need to make sure these bodies disappear as much for
the morale of those in the front lines as out of respect for the deceased. These
aerial bombs are dreadful machines, fortunately not very precise and with very
short range. They shatter and destroy the *sapes*. Woe to anyone who happens to
be in one! Their concussion is so strong that the bodies are almost undressed,

their clothes shredded, and the dead left without a mark on them. The blood vessels inside the body explode. So, it is a sad task. [...]

9/15/1915.

I received yesterday your letter of September 12. [...] The *Boches* right now are furious; they are well aware that we are preparing something against them that will be irreversible. Enraged, they are using everything possible, the unimaginable, to fight us. They can try as hard as they want, it will not stop us from sending them home. [...]

Friday, September 17, 1915.

As I received two letters yesterday, I did not have any news this morning. [...] I did my purge last night and it is taking effect today so I will not go to the post to send the packages.[114] [...] I wrote to the shops at the Louvre about the cost of a gourd. A gourd in pigskin covered with sky blue cloth that holds 3 liters costs 14 francs, 75 centimes. I will write to have them send me one fairly soon. I think it will be quite sturdy and certainly convenient. [...]

Saturday, September 18, 1915.

I received no news this morning. Were you relieved on Tuesday? I read in the *communiqués* of September 16 and 17: "in the area near Neuville and Roclincourt and around Arras, our batteries are responding to a violent bombing by the enemy" and "in Artois between Angres and Souchez and south of Arras, our batteries, in response to heavy enemy bombing, have seriously damaged their installations." That means that you had a lot of German bombing on the 14th and 15th. I don't know whether you were still near Neuville. If so, you will have had a number of injured and dead soldiers? Is that why I have no news? [...]

Sunday, September 19, 1915.

I received this morning your two letters from the 14th and 15th. I am very happy as I was getting quite worried. That damned Neuville sector is so perilous that I breathe easier when I know you are not there. [...]

9/16/1915.

I received last evening your letter from September 13. [...] We are leaving tonight for rest. I'm the one who will leave at 6 p.m. to prepare the quarters, that is, find where we will stay, rooms for the doctors, straw for us, etc. In short,

---

[114] A purge involved using natural laxatives to clear the body of noxious elements.

all the details. We are going to where we were a month and a half ago, that is, to Hermaville, at least 20 kilometers from here. We are in the front line which means there are at least 8 kilometers of *sapes* to go through to reach a road. [...]

From what I hear, we will only be at rest for 4 or 5 days; I have trouble believing that. Our regiment is totally exhausted—the intense work for the past 12 days plus the 20 kilometers we have to cover to get to a rest place only to stay 4 days, it seems unreal to me. [...]

I will try to start on something while at rest. But if we are only there 4 or 5 days, I will probably not have time to lay out the plan. I first have to determine the key, then the modulations I want to make, then write the fundamentals, a canvas on which I can write. I'll see what that produces. To do that I need quiet and time. [...]

9/17/1915.

I received last night [...] your letter from September 14. [...] From what they are telling us, we will only be at rest 5 or 6 days. At that point we will be on the eve of extremely important events. In any case, if our regiment makes the attack, we will not be in the trenches more than 6 to 8 days. Once we get to a place which for now I cannot mention, it's absolutely forbidden, we will be replaced by a fresh regiment. We are very lucky to be in the stretcher bearer corps, as we don't have to fight and we run many fewer risks. Truly, everyone is waiting impatiently for this attack. The officers believe it is well prepared and that we are very strong right now in terms of artillery and munitions so they are very optimistic. So much the better, for the love of God, as we could escape another winter campaign. [...]

We will be in Neuville, our first-aid post will be in the middle of the area. Yesterday there was a notice circulated that forbids all pictures without permission of the general, which is to say that officers will be taking pictures. But Rolland still has his camera and, on the sly, he may be able to get a few. [...]

Monday, September 20, 1915.

I received this morning your two letters from Thursday the 16th and Friday the 17th as well as the rose you picked in Neuville and the 6 original postcards Rolland gave you. If you are at rest for only 5 or 6 days [...] you will not have much time to think about your composition. You should have jotted down the melodies and the bass parts when you were at rest for more than 20 days. [...]

9/18/1915.

I received last night your letter from September 15. [...] As for the rings, I ordered 4: for Suzanne, Mme Lambert, M. Lambert, and M. Alan. Yours is ready; I will send it tomorrow. [...] Since September 4, the weather has been exceptional, very dry. For us, that is perfect as we have no desire for it to rain. But the peasants in the area are complaining; they cannot work the land which is as hard as steel. [...]

Yesterday we set up a shower, gift of M. Deutsch de la Meurthe in the 129th, a very practical device. This morning we showered two companies, and, at the end of that ceremony, we took an excellent, long shower. [...]

Tuesday, September 21, 1915.

I received this morning your letter from September 18. [...] And your composition (the adagio), don't forget to think about it also. You mustn't let your brain get lazy. You have to make it work. That is true in everything. The result will be tangible. It will probably not be a work of genius; as long as it comes from the heart, I am convinced you will make it good. To become a blacksmith, one has to strike the anvil; you do nothing. The notes will not put themselves under your pen all by themselves. Get going, my son. [...]

9/19/1915.

Today I was pestered all day long, so am writing at 7 p.m. This morning I played for the 10 a.m. High Mass in Hermaville where we have been stationed before, a very nice church with a very good organ. Accompanied by Rolland, I played the prelude from *Déluge*,[115] Handel's Largo,[116] and Bach's *Air de la Pentecôte*.[117] These different pieces were very effective. Sergeant Lafont, who has quite a lovely tenor voice, sang the *Sanctus* by Beethoven and Stradella's *Pie Jesu*.[118][...] Tomorrow morning, at 8:30, we have a funeral service for the regiment's dead. [...]

I haven't written about Martel,[119] but I am nearly always with him; he cannot manage without either me or Rolland for his religious services. Not to mention the labor we provide to help him bury the dead in the trenches. [...]

Saturday, September 25, 1915, 11:30 a.m.

I didn't receive a letter today but I received two pencil holders and a flower, a daisy I think. Thank you. I will wait for you to explain how to use the pencil holders—I don't think they are pen holders because I don't see how you could put the pen in one. [...] Today's package had apparently been opened because

---

[115] Camille Saint-Saëns (1835-1921), *Le Déluge*, Op. 45.
[116] George Frideric Handel (1685-1759), Largo, "Ombra mai fu," from *Xerxes*, HWV 40.
[117] J. S. Bach, *Pentecost Cantata*, BWV 68.
[118] Beethoven, *Missa Solemnia*, D major, Op. 123; Alessandro Stradella (1643-1682).
[119] The company chaplain.

there was no string. [...] The one I received yesterday, with my ring, had not been opened. [...]

I am quite worried to not have any news from you; I read in the *communiqué* of September 20 "the artillery battle continues in the Artois, especially in the sector of Souchez and Neuville. The enemy launched incendiary bombs on Reims and surroundings; several homes caught fire but the fires were quickly extinguished" and on September 24 "an artillery battle took place all night long near Arras; our batteries wrought serious damage on a number of enemy organization locations." [...]

9/20/1915.

This morning I just finished playing for our memorial service. All the officers from the regiment were there. The service was extremely effective; the Hermaville church has excellent acoustics. [...] The sound was superb. The violin bought in Geneva is now quite good, it has a resonant, mellow tone. The colonel was very pleased. His face when listening to music shows how much he likes it. [...] The *Air de la Pentecôte* is magnificent, with an exceptional freshness and filled with light. What a masterpiece! Same for Handel's Largo, which is very moving. [...]

Monday, September 27, 1915, 2:30 p.m.

I've not received any news since the 23rd when your letters of 19 and 20 September arrived. I see that the offensive took place north of Arras and that the last German trenches in Souchez are in your hands, the same for Neuville. You now control all the Labyrinth. I would really love to be so fortunate as to have a letter confirming all this. If the military authority is letting the newspapers talk about this, the letters that were held back must now be sent to their recipients.

In one of your recent letters you feared that I hadn't received the rose you picked in Neuville. I wrote that it arrived in perfect condition. It was stuck into a bit of raw potato which preserved its freshness. It will, however, be harder to preserve than if it had been pressed between the pages of a book. In its current state, it would turn to dust if touched. I wrapped it in a bit of tissue paper and put in your library. The color is lovely—a dark red with a touch of brightness.

I also told you that I received my ring, which I find to be deliciously delicate. [...]

9/21/1915.

I received last evening your letter of September 18. [...] According to what they are saying, tomorrow night, Wednesday, we will go back to the trenches for the large-scale attack which should take place on Saturday or Sunday. Don't forget that this attack is happening along the entire front from Belfort all the way to the North Sea. [...] Everyone here is very optimistic that this will succeed. We all expect to move forward and could be in Lens quite quickly, then take Lille and Douai without much effort. The artillery has started their bombing and it will increase over the next days. The earth shakes here and we are 20 kilometers away. I would not be surprised if, in Paris, you could hear the noise, it is so incredible. [...] We are quite feverish and would like to be 2 weeks older. [...] My violin will stay in the medical car along with my music; we cannot pretend that the risks will not increase as we advance. [...]

9/22/1915.

I received yesterday your letter from September 19. [...] We leave the Neuville sector this afternoon at 4 p.m. to take up the trenches in front of here. We are expecting the attack to take place Saturday or Sunday, after what will be a frightening preparation by the artillery. We are all setting out with confidence and we are even hoping to not have too many losses because the enemy will be crushed. [...] We are using new bombs, 108 kilos in weight, which are horrifying: they are destined to shatter and destroy the trenches. Men killed by these bombs don't suffer, death is instantaneous. For sure Guillaume, the swine, should not be sleeping very well, but he probably has no conscience. [...]

I sent you two pen holders; they are German bullets collected at Neuville. You pull the bullet from its casing and turn it over. Then you only need to insert a pencil or a pen. [...]

9/24/1915.

I received this morning your letter from September 21 and two packages. [...] We are living right now in the midst of mind-numbing chaos, so intense is the bombing—the ground smokes and shakes everywhere. It has rained a bit these past two days (storms) which has completely soaked the ground. The attack, so we hear, will be tomorrow morning. Thus, tomorrow at the same time all the soldiers from Belfort to the North Sea will surge forward. At least 2 million men will rush the Germans, in the midst of the deafening roar of the artillery. It will be an extraordinary sight. I only have one thing to say, all the officers are very confident. So, God willing, may this large-scale attack be successful! We are experiencing at this moment, in hell, all the agitation of the waiting. You can be sure, I have carefully saved my liquor, which may be only too useful for me. [...]

I ordered the rings in plenty of time, but for some time now the *poilus* have been dreadfully tired by all their work. They don't have the heart to do that sort of thing. I cannot blame them. I sent yours to you, along with the two pen holders. I hope you have received them all. You can well imagine that, for some time now, I have no thoughts of music; I am completely exhausted. We need all our willpower to stay levelheaded and courageous. I am being bothered again. I need to go to the central post for the orders for this night; just like the companies, we will have orders to move out. Everything seems admirably well organized. [...]

Wednesday September 29, 1915.

Still no news. [...] I know nothing of what has happened from the 22th to the 29th. The weather is abominable, a real storm. All night I heard the rain falling steadily. If you are having the same weather, you must be in quite a state. [...]

9/29/1915.

I received yesterday your letter of September 20 and 4 packages. [...] I am right now in Neuville, in a wonderful cave. I am totally exhausted after being relieved yesterday, which was very difficult. I'm going to rest. The bombing has started, and so far, the *Boches* are not responding much. Here, in my cave, I am very safe. [...]

Friday morning October 1, 1915.

I received your letters from Friday September 24 and 29. [...] For sure we need to pursue the Germans nonstop. Can we do it? We have to hope so, but at the cost of how many human lives? You must all be exhausted? And if this goes on for a while, will you be able to give all the effort demanded of you? Your fatigue and misery must go beyond anything one can imagine.

I received this morning the card: "Correspondance des armées de la République" dated September 29. I thank you infinitely my dear and beloved child for these few reassuring lines. You could always add a few words like "I received letters and packages, or I haven't received any letters or packages since..." so I know whether the packages reach you and bring you some comfort. [...]

10/2/1915.

A word in haste, I am still well, though tired. [...] The weather is better but what a time we have just come through! We expect to be relieved any day, it's essential, we are totally exhausted! Let's not hide the facts: in short, in this region, the attack failed. One can't kill so many men to take just three kilometers. At that rate, there are not enough Frenchmen to take back our country. I hope that things will be more successful in Champagne. Much love.

10/4/1915.

Since last evening we are on reserve; we are in Neuville but this part of the sector is calmer. There is much talk about our corps being relieved this evening or tomorrow. It's about time as, morally and physically, our men have had enough. It's been a really long time since I've been this tired. But that's nothing as long as I'm still alive, which many of my fellow soldiers can no longer say. The 3rd Corps received the Order of the Day of the Army, but it suffered severe losses. The infantry lost 80 percent of its active men, sadly a large number of them killed. Our 3rd Company has been sorely tested and had we, Rolland, Vessot, and I, remained with them, chances are good that we would be sleeping our final sleep. For me, I have still been protected; the danger is huge for everyone. Our friend Schratz was fatally wounded. Dandelot was wounded in the arm, not seriously, and has been evacuated. Sergeants Barbite and Lainel were mortally injured. The sights during these days have been terrible. Alas, war is ghastly and the enemy's defensive lines here are very strong. We are just a bit outside of Vimy. The Corps that takes our place will most likely make the attack on Douai. There is still an enormous effort needed to push back the *Boches*, and at the price of so many lives, you cannot even imagine. [...]

I have continued to receive my packages and they have been of enormous help to me. I finished the rum and the ginger which helped a lot. The weather was dreadful, mud like putty and there are 30 to 40 centimeters of that glue in our *sapes*. The general public cannot imagine our suffering. When I receive letters like the one I'm sending you from Madame Duez, it's pitiful! We aren't getting stronger, as she believes. Rather we are being worn down and our suffering this time was especially great. We are fervently hoping to be relieved tonight or tomorrow. A good number of men are in tears, the shock was so violent. I will give you more details when I'm at rest in the rear; here we are just in the 3rd line, all of us ready to go on attack. [...] I'm going to try to sleep a bit, the first time in a week; it's absolutely necessary. [...]

Friday October 8, 1915, 7:00 p.m.

[...] I received today at 4 p.m. your letter from October 4. [...] The German defenses in the north of France must be incredible and I keep asking myself whether we will be able to free our land from their grasp. They've been building these defenses daily for a year; they must never stop digging, cementing, and taking advantage of the lay of the land to make a fortress. To achieve our goals, we will need things like dynamite which can destroy anything. Our scientists and chemists should find a way to wipe out the Germans by whatever means. We can't have any scruples with people like that who want to annihilate us and intend to keep the land they occupy. [...] It is the duty of the military command and war ministry to act in a way that men's lives are protected. If this keeps up, there will not be a single French man left except those over age 50 or under 16. It is horrible.! […]

10/7/1915.

Still in the same sector and in good health. Unfortunately, the weather is terrible. Kisses, Still receiving packages, Lucien.

10/10/1915.

Excuse me for not writing these past days, but when you know more about what we've been doing, you will understand. Only one word now: never since the beginning of this war have I been as tired, as exhausted, as I am right now. We got out of that place of horror at 1 a.m., the night of the 7th to 8th after having taken part in a last attack against the Bois de la Folie. We finally got to Acq about 10 a.m. after a relief that took all our remaining force. That day we didn't even have the strength to eat. The next day, the 9th, we left on foot for Beaudricourt where we are now, and since midnight on the 9th I have slept nonstop. I just got up; it is 2 p.m. I'm going to have a bite to eat and go back to bed. I hope tomorrow to write a long letter where I will give you all the details of our adventure. Dandelot has a leg wound and is in a hospital in Quimper. Schratz, my friend from the 23rd was killed. He only got here June 10, part of reinforcements. He was from a class older than mine. But, we, at least, have once again gotten out of a dreadful situation, thanks to God. […]

I received all your packages, they did me much good, although there often was no time to eat what they contained. […]

Monday October 11, 1915, 2:00 p.m.

[…] I did not receive news this morning and am worried. I read in the *communiqués* that the German counterattacks are violent. […] So, my dear child, I beg you to be very careful. You have been lucky so far to still be in one piece, but this is not finished! Keep your eyes open, and do not let pass any opportunity that could help you. […]

10/11/1915.

Finally, today I am rested and a bit calmer. I will try to answer all your questions. First, I can tell you I've just slept 48 hours straight, that was the most important thing. So, to sum up what we did: the offensive took place on a Saturday, I think it was September 25. We had been in the trenches since Tuesday evening. The attack started at midnight Saturday. The shelling which preceded it was truly frightening. We were supposed to go as far as the road to Lille and the Bois de la Folie. To do that we needed to take out three successive lines of trenches: the *Dent de Scie*; the *Verre à l'Eau*; and the *Tranchée de la Justice*.[120] We learned later that the *Boches* had in the previous two days brought in the troops which had been in Russia and that it was the troop of elites we attacked. We managed to take the first two trenches. [...] At the third, we fell on our faces. The *Boches* had sheltered the active fighters in caves where there wasn't much danger. As soon as the watchmen, who all had telephones with buried wires, gave the alarm, the *Boches* surged out with machine guns and immediately went on attack.

The battle was fought with bombs and even flaming gasoline. Starting Saturday night, the injured arrived in a way that overwhelmed us. In my opinion the offensive was made with many too many men at one time, leading to indescribable confusion in the regiments all mixed together. Briefly, from Saturday night to Wednesday night we never stopped bandaging and, in the midst of dreadful shelling, carrying out the wounded through *sapes* which the constant rain had turned into veritable sinkholes. We sank in up to our knees. You can well imagine how much courage and energy we needed to continue in such conditions, it's indescribable. We transported the injured who couldn't walk to Neuville where there were doctors.

It's truly embarrassing how few doctors came to the front lines. The nurses and stretcher bearers were the ones constantly at the front line. Right now, we are all the same, without enough arms to transport and bandage so many at the same time. There were wounded left in bomb craters for 2 or 3 days before being taken out and we could do nothing about it. We needed, suddenly, 500 people to help us. At night, we wandered over the fields to find the wounded who had dragged themselves between the lines into bomb craters for shelter and I can tell you the bullets whistled. I, with Rolland, Vessot, and the young nurse Loignon, we had a tough job.

On Thursday we were relieved during the night and taken to Écurie, arriving about midnight. It's from there I sent a card. That very night, at 6 p.m., we left to occupy, on the left side of Neuville, the sunken path of the Orchard of la Folie, an old German trench taken by the 36th which the *Boches* shelled nonstop day and night with 210s because they expected we would shelter our reserves there. We, the reserves of the 39th, the 5th, and the 119th, were the ones that continued the attack.

In the end, we stayed there until the 7th, in mud up to our thighs under constant shelling which killed or injured 200 men. That meant that we never stopped our work, day or night, under the ceaseless firing. We had reached the ultimate state of exhaustion; I, for one, didn't have the strength to eat. We could no longer drag ourselves to our relief station.

---

[120] The trenches were the Sawtooth, the Water Glass, and the Trench of Justice.

Finally, at this time, we are at rest, but I don't believe it will be for long. Based on what they are saying, our sector will change a bit. We will be going to Roclincourt near Arras. We have to pass through that city to get there. It's not as bad as Neuville or Souchez, but it is still not truly a sector for rest. We can always hope, but it is sure that our rest won't be long. In this area, we haven't had great results and the losses have been enormous. The musicians at times like this also serve as stretcher bearers. They were not very fortunate; they had 4 killed and 5 wounded, while we had only one wounded. It's a matter of luck. And as far as that goes, my luck seems unique.

I will try, if possible, to get back to music but it's difficult as right now our officers change constantly. We have a new colonel (I got along very well with the former one) and a new commander. We had 28 officers killed or wounded. [...]

Barring an order to the contrary, we will hold a memorial service for our dead and that will be the time for me to meet our new colonel. The morale of our men is quite low after such dreadful trials. Alas, I see no solution to that. I watch our population being swallowed up and disappearing; the insufficient numbers of reinforcements that arrive are garbage. One should have no illusions. Based on what we are seeing, and what I know, the situation can be summed up like this: the soldiers are admirable, they have sacrificed everything while the leaders are, with a few exceptions, incompetent and on their honeymoon. Our elected officials are getting rich on the incredible commissions they receive from government purchases. All this time, the *poilus* are watering the land of France with their blood and their sacrifice may be in vain. That is the sad truth. [...]

October 12, 1915, 10:30 a.m.

[...] I did not receive any news this morning, which makes me think you are not in a billet or you would have written. [...] In the *communiqué* of October 11, I read: "new information confirms that the violent counterattacks launched by the Germans in recent days against the English and French lines near Noos and in the North have led to a serious and costly failure. The principal assault was made by an active force of 3 to 4 divisions which were completely repelled and dispersed. The number of enemy dead on the battlefield is estimated to be 7 to 8 thousand men." If the enemy has lost that many men, one has to assume that the English and French have lost the same number. [...]

Thursday October 14, 1915, 11:30 a.m.

[...] I received this morning your letter of October 11 [...] Since September 23 you have been in the trenches, that makes 15 days on service without a pause. You must no longer be good for anything and I hope you will have some rest in the rear. I don't see Baudricourt on the map, it must be very small. So there you are, once again, out of a terrible ordeal without a scratch, we have to thank God! But I am telling you again to improve your situation if you can, and as quickly as possible—either you join the nurses or the music regiment.

Young Alan had the good luck to be able to join the music regiment. [...] He only works on music. I forgot to tell you that he told his father that he was in Suippes and sleeping in a tent, and that he was just as comfortable as in his bed. [...] That gets him away from the trenches and all the suffering there. Mme Duez believes you've had so much experience that you have come up with all sorts of ways to protect yourselves from bad weather, that you have a crocodile skin on your backs for the rain which you slide off in nice weather. All those good people who have a good bed at night, warm clothes for the winter and light clothes for summer end up thinking that you are immune. They say "they are strong and hardened;" my reply, "or worn out."

I don't know whether you and your comrades can take showers where you are, something that would be very good for you. If not, one has to hope that there is enough water for you to wash yourselves thoroughly. Take advantage of this rest to have your underwear washed and repaired. Your shirts can't be in very good shape. I will not send any winter underwear until you ask for it. When the weather is so damp and warm, I know that you should not wear too much because you sweat a lot. [...]

10/12/1915.

I received yesterday your letters from October 8 and 9 and 3 packages. [...] Recently they have been asking for mechanics, metallurgists, or aviators with a diploma. I can't try for any of those posts. I should not complain about the little advantage I've gotten; many others would like to have it. They are pulling guys younger than 36 out of the automobile corps and other easier jobs for the front lines. They are sending us reinforcements who are 42 years old. It's a shame to see such old guys sent to active-duty regiments. If I can get into the music corps, I will do it. But, as I told you, our officers change constantly. It is hard to count on any serious support in these conditions. If I were ever evacuated for a mild injury, I would lose my place and be sent back into the ranks, that's the rule. That's why I am not hoping to leave though I also would love to have 3 to 4 months to rest in the rear. One starts to hope for a small injury to the leg or the thigh, which gets you quite a long rest. I'd rather not be injured and just continue to endure this misery. Nevertheless, the long duration of this state of affairs is agonizing. [...]

This morning our memorial service didn't take place. In its place we had a review, announced at the last minute, by Mangin. I saw our dear general up close and there are no other words, he looks awful, which doesn't inspire confidence. [...]

10/13/1915.

I am in a great rush. Last night I played at the lodgings of the new colonel, a fan of the violin, and got back at 11:00 this morning. I played for the memorial service and this morning Captain Paquier called me from the brigade, asking me to come play at 1:00. [...] Could you be so kind as to send me several E strings and the A string that is on the Guadagnini,[121] if it's not broken.

Saturday, October 16, 1915, 11 a.m.

[...] I received this morning your letter of October 13 in which you tell me that you played for the new colonel, a violin lover.[122] That news is of the greatest interest to me; if you aren't transferred to the music regiment, after meeting this music lover, I will describe you with an epithet I don't want you to hear for now. [...] True, your service as stretcher bearer is a little improvement over where you were, but your place really is in the *musique*.[123] You will have a bit more time to take care of yourself and to be able to write a piece (obviously short), to put on paper melodic ideas which you can then elaborate and arrange. If you had done that during the long rest you enjoyed in July, you would now have a canvas you had only to embroider. A musician like you should compose. You should find someone to sing Faure's *Crucifixus* with your violin accompaniment.[124] If it had occurred to you to copy the words, you would now have that piece. There is no point in writing an accompaniment if you don't play it. You are unbelievably apathetic. [...]

10/14/1915.

Yesterday I received your letter from the 11th as well as the package with the bottle of gin that arrived in good condition. [...] I will carefully save the alcohol, as I don't know what will happen next and, in difficult conditions, alcohol is of great help. [...]

Those who talk about the war ending in November don't know what they are talking about. I wonder on what they base their conclusion—certainly not on the facts. One has to agree that Germany will have given us a powerful lesson, showing us how to organize and fight a war; all we have done is copy them. It is a miracle that, as organized as they are, they haven't rapidly beaten us. The

---

[121] Giuseppe Guadagnini (1736-1805), maker of Lucien's most valuable violin.

[122] The new colonel, Colonel Valzi, was very important in allowing Lucien and colleagues to work on music.

[123] The *musique* was a regiment that consisted of musicians to play for ceremonies; it was really an army band. Lucien was officially a member, playing cymbals, but he participated very little.

[124] Jean-Baptiste Faure (1830-1914), French operatic baritone and composer. He composed a number of songs, including *Crucifixus*.

praise goes, not to our officers who, for the most part, are incompetent, but to the *poilus* who with intelligence and heroism have sacrificed their lives. The few intelligent officers have to agree. Ordinary French people during this war have been admirable, sacrificing everything, for whom? For leaders, many of whom are filling their pockets while others get themselves killed. [...]

Our preparation for this war was worthless: the officers have ideas from another era, or none at all. When one of them makes an error, he never admits it, he gives speeches and meanwhile the events continue. That explains the medi-ocre results we've seen. Our regiments have frequently gotten farther than their assigned objective, driving into the midst of the *Boches*, but without reinforce-ment, no liaison with the other weapons and most of all, without the leadership of those in charge. So we have to pull back. The result is that lots of courageous fellows have gotten themselves killed, why, and for whom? My fellow soldiers, who are not the imbeciles the officers would believe, ask themselves when all this will end. [...]

Yesterday I played for Colonel Viennot at the brigade. He's serving as brigade general, a friendly and cultured man. That means that, for now, since everyone knows me, I am in a special position. [...] That doesn't stop me, however, from carrying out my service. It's not when they are sending men 42 years of age as reinforcement that I should try to change anything; I am already very privileged. For me to transfer to the brigade as secretary, there would have to be a vacancy which is not the case. If I knew how to drive a car or ride a bicycle, I might have had a chance. Unfortunately, I never learned. At least for the bicycle, it is a bit your fault as you never wanted me to learn. If ever I was to be evacuated, I would then be returned to another regiment as reinforcement, a simple soldier 2nd class. That would put me far from what I have here where I am known as "Durosoir, the violinist, who plays for the colonel and the general." I continue to be careful; that doesn't keep me from watching for opportunities. [...]

10/15/1915.

I received last night your letter of October 12. [...] I played this morning for a memorial service in Sus-Saint-Léger, the area where the 2nd and 3rd battalions are billeted. As for us, we are in Beaudricourt, about 1500 meters away from there. We had already played this service here, and we repeated it at Sus. I no longer have an E string. My violin's last trip in the medical car was quite rough, the humidity was such that my strings are all softened and E strings break like threads. I managed to buy two, in metal, in Doullens while waiting for the ones I asked you for. [...]

I am starting to recover from my fatigue. We hear cannons firing nonstop; the *Boches* are still attacking Souchy and Neuville. [...] With our defenses and artillery, they will have enormous losses and won't gain an inch of ground. [...]

Monday October 18, 1915, 2:30 p.m.

[…] I received this morning your letters from October 14 and 15. […] You talk about a bicycle: you really have to be able to ride a bicycle to be a secretary? You never learned, not because I didn't want you to, but because you spent all your time when young working on the violin. […] You devoted yourself almost entirely to studying it. […] Had you been satisfied to just play in orchestras, you would have found the time to learn to ride a bicycle had you wanted. We both agreed that that type of sport posed certain dangers to a virtuoso violinist; an accident, which happens often, could have been devastating for you. We talked a lot about that and agreed that walking was much better and healthier. […]

10/16/1915.

I received yesterday your letter from October 13. […] Contrary to what they were saying at the beginning, our rest continues; based on what I hear, it will likely continue even longer. That doesn't bother me in the least; we could get completely back in shape. Yesterday I got a new *capote* and a wonderful new vareuse. […] As part of the Red Cross, we can get clothing quite easily, at least right now, because we have provided a hugely important service.

You seem very nervous in your letters; I no longer recognize you. Calm down, please, and don't forget that I am in a situation many others covet. I will try to get into the music regiment but, to tell the truth, I don't see that I'd gain very much. Obviously, it is better when times are normal, but in ordeals like we've just been through, we all face the same fate. You have to remember that I don't play any of those instruments, and the guy with the cymbals is not about to let me have them. Given the contacts I enjoy everywhere, the doctors give me respect others envy and, what is more, they clearly watch out for me. It is hard to ask for more, especially when we see reinforcements arriving with 42-year-olds in them. They look at our situations with envy. Rest assured, if I see a real possibility, I will jump on it with both feet. But, for now I need to be careful, and I'm not eager to change from a one-eyed horse to a blind one. […]

10/17/1915.

Our rest is definitely going to last longer; tonight 20 men from each company are leaving on pass, 10 percent of the active force. […] The colonel left today on leave, but I had a long chat with him yesterday afternoon when I met him at a concert given by the *musique* of the 129th. He said that, if we end up spending the winter here, he wants to form a string quartet. He is a musician, plays the violin, and owns three including a Guadagnini, so he wants me to put together a quartet. I managed to speak to the leader of the *musique*—a young man, new to the regiment. This young man, who is only an assistant, plays flute and also has a first prize in piano from the Lyon Conservatory. He is thus ready to take me in the *musique* as cymbal player. He realizes that I'm friendly with the colonel and the brigadier. Monsieur Maire, our chief doctor, has given his permission for me to change service. I only need to wait for the return of the colonel so he can sign the decision. [...]

Here are my thoughts on how to organize the quartet. Yesterday morning we got a new reinforcement, André Caplet, Prix de Rome, well-known orchestra conductor who directed the opera season for several years in Boston.[125] I had a long conversation with him yesterday and even introduced him to the colonel. He is a sergeant, we'll find him a way, all the more because he is sickly and has one bad eye. He is one of the questionable reinforcements we are receiving now. We must really need men to take people like him. So, in brief, he will play viola in the quartet—certainly it will be interesting to see what kind of musician he is. He seems very timid. For sure he is disoriented finding himself at the front, it's the first time he's been here. The cellist will be Dehuysser and another musician, who apparently plays the violin fairly well, will be second violin. The assistant chief of the *musique* will play piano when we play trios, quartets or quintets; we'll be able to take on all forms of chamber music.

We may be going to serve in the sector of Roclincourt, just in front of Arras. It's a much calmer sector than Neuville and we would do 10 days of trenches and 20 days of rest, which would not be bad if we have to get through winter. The future, since we have to spend it in this damned Artois, is shaping up fairly well. [...]

The music regiment stays way to the rear and never comes as far as the trenches, except to help the stretcher bearers.

October 19, 1915, 11 a.m.

[...] I didn't receive any news this morning. [...] I sent the strings you asked for on the 17th in a box with 6 hard-boiled eggs and a little bottle of vinaigrette.

---

[125] André Caplet (1878-1925), composer and orchestral conductor. Born in Le Havre, Caplet studied piano, then music notation and composition at the Le Havre music school and at the Conservatoire de Paris, which he entered in 1896. He won the Prix de Rome in 1901. In 1907 he met Debussy, whom he greatly admired, and he wrote the orchestration for several of Debussy's compositions: *The Martyre de Saint Sébastien, Children's Corner, La Boîte à joujoux.* Many famous artists interpreted his music: Claire Croiza, Jane Bathori, Philippe Gaubert, Gaston Poulet, Maurice Maréchal, and more. While conductor of the Boston Opera Orchestra, Caplet made an effort to diffuse French music. He returned to France in the spring of 1914 and arrived at the front as a sergeant in September 1915. In May 1916 General Mangin commissioned a heroic march for the 5th Division *(La Marche Héroïque)* He participated actively in the life of the string ensemble created by Lucien Durosoir. In poor health, probably gassed toward the end of the war, he died in 1925. Durosoir, *Deux Musiciens,* 140.

If you had thought to ask for them sooner, you would have them by now. You never change. [...]

In three weeks, you will have been in the trenches for a year; it is now time for others to take that place. I would not have said that a year ago but things do not seem to be moving in a very reassuring direction and those who govern us give little reason to believe they are up to this task. It makes one stop and think. [...]

10/18/1915.

Vessot left on pass last night. [...] He took with him a good-sized piece of my old *capote*. We cut it out of the back which was the part in best shape and the least dirty. He will come see you, along with my old friend from the 23rd, Sergeant Leduc. [...]

The colonel is away on leave. My situation will not be settled until he returns, about 10 days from now. During this time, there are starting to be some conspiracies. In the music regiment, there are older members who are not happy to have me join them. They expect it to make more work for them. Bad musicians are always jealous of good ones, that is why I told you yesterday that we mustn't sell the bearskin until we've killed the bear. Fortunately, I was warned about these intrigues, and he who is aware of what is happening is worth two who aren't. Still, I'd like to see the colonel soon. [...] Rolland and some other comrades who know about this are amused by the struggle which is, in a way, a reflection of what is happening everywhere. For now I will keep all my music; if the colonel's project comes to fruition, I will certainly not have too much. [...]

Beaudricourt is fairly far from the front, about 10 kilometers away from Frévent where we landed when we first arrived in this area and 15 kilometers from Doullens where General Joffre had his headquarters for a time. I think the offensive around us is finished. We hear very little noise from the cannons. This offensive must have been very costly; I calculate at least 100,000 men because our 3rd Corps alone lost 12,000 killed, injured, or disappeared. [...]

Thursday, October 21, 1915, noon.

[...] I received this morning your letter from the 18 October in which you say that your friend Vessot left on leave October 17 and will bring the piece of your *capote*. Thank you very much. I am happy to have a piece of the cloth which saw everything [...] and for me evokes what you suffered in Neuville and Souchez. [...] Vessot let me know last evening that he will come to Vincennes today in the afternoon. I am going to hurry to write so I can eat lunch and be ready to receive your brother-in-arms. [...]

Second letter, same day. 6:30 p.m.

[…] Your friend Vessot and Mme Vessot came about 3 p.m. Vessot gave me the piece of cloth from your *capote*; it is not very big, just barely enough. […] He seemed very happy to be on leave, and he is very grateful to you for all you did to have him transferred to the stretcher bearers. He was very excited to see you and Rolland again. […]

They brought me a few roses and some mimosa, a way of indirectly thanking you. I thanked them and scolded them a bit; those poor people have absolutely nothing. They told me that they had only had their house in Soissons for two months when war broke out; they had a lot of things not yet unpacked. All was taken and destroyed. Vessot said that he is in Paris, Villa Niel, with his parents but he added that it is not the same as being in their own home. […]

10/19/1915.

I received yesterday your letter from October 16. […] As of now, I can consider my change to the *musique* a done deal. […]

I will wait to find a second violinist before asking you to send me the string quartets. […] The first result of my transfer to the music regiment will be almost the end of the packages. As I won't be in the trenches, I have no reason to receive all those provisions. We are always stationed in the rear where we can find anything we want. And the music regiment is even better fed than the stretcher bearers. […]

10/20/1915.

Musician of the 129th. So, you see, by the entry above, that my entry into the music regiment is official. […] Send me from now on only two packages a week, that will be enough. Use up the supplies you have in the house but do not buy more. I received your letter from October 17 yesterday. […]

10/21/1915.

[…] I am now in very good condition and totally rested. Colonel Viennot, our brigade general, is a lovely man who likes music. […] Captain Paquier is his ordinance officer and he also loves music and is of an unusual intelligence. The big event today is that we move out tomorrow morning. We take the train 8 kilometers from here and will be concentrated near Amiens. […] No matter what, it will be hard for any place to be worse than Neuville, or even to equal it. That sector was truly hell and we stayed there 4 and a half months. You may find yourself without any news for a day or two; it all depends on how fast we can accomplish this move. The entire Army Corps has to move; that will take some time. [...]

10/22/1915.

[...] Right now, I have 3 cans of alcohol for burning. It's a bit silly; I'm loaded up like an imbecile. I also do not need so much eau-de-vie. That is good when I'm in the trenches, but otherwise I never drink it. [...] My top strings broke because my violin was exposed to a lot of humidity during the fifteen very rainy days I was in the trenches. In the space of 4 days, I broke 4 strings. [...]

Sunday, October 24, 1915, 7 p.m.

[...] The weather today is dreadful. I don't know whether you have rain, or where you are. I wonder whether your oilcloth is in good condition. I will buy 2 meters of oil cloth as soon as you ask for it. You will have to think about wearing warmer undershirts, and long-sleeve flannel shirts. I should send you two. The ones you have must be in terrible condition. [...] I would like to know that you have new shoes, important in this rainy weather. You were telling me recently that you hoped to receive some boots. [...] I await news from you impatiently; pay attention to your health. With the change of season, anything could happen. [...]

10/23/1915.

[...] Most likely I will not have time to play violin with the music band as accompaniment. [...] I will have to make quite an effort to rehearse with the quartet, and also the trios with the *sous-chef*, plus practicing violin and working on the parts, etc. That is enough to take up the entire day; and what is more, I need to practice the music for cymbals. Being a cymbal player is more difficult than one might think, it requires paying extremely close attention. I admit that I will have work that is fairly interesting, which makes me very happy. For the quartet to be acceptably good will take a lot of effort. [...]

The musicians in the band are in general very young and not very good. They couldn't care less about playing interesting music, what they want is to do nothing. That is not what interests me. My attention is on my relationship with the officers. As for the musicians, for the most part, it is "good morning," "good evening." Mostly I just ignore them, it's simpler that way. As for the colonel, you can well imagine that I have no intention of clashing with him. To his credit, he likes good authors and good music; that is rare enough to be noted. [...]

Despite what I told you, you are still sending me too many packages which make things difficult for me with all this moving around. I think I will not be able to write tomorrow; we will probably spend our day on the train in cattle cars. […]

10/25/1915.

Yesterday morning we left from Aubrometz where we had been camped for two days. […] We've now arrived in Chaussoy where we will camp for we don't know how long. We are apparently not far from Amiens. In any case, there is a good part of the army corps here; we will be taken elsewhere and obviously know nothing about the destination. […]

As always, we traveled in cattle cars and were generally in great spirits: we are very happy to be leaving the Artois. Dehuysser got off the train to attend to a call of nature and was left behind when the train unexpectedly departed. He joined us this morning—a reason for a good laugh. […] People are very friendly in this part of Picardy. True they rarely see troops. We can get everything we need here. Butter is selling for 52 sous a pound. […]

10/26/1915.

[…] For now, two packages a week will suffice, one with cheese, jam, butter, the other with things like sardines or pâté. Occasionally a bit of rum because of the rain, and some burning alcohol once a month. For now our destination is not determined and I cannot yet tell what our life will look like. We have some rehearsals here; there are concerts every afternoon at 4 with rehearsal in the morning and afternoon. I only go to the afternoon rehearsals; in the morning, I shave, write to you, and practice violin. Once we are settled, I will probably rehearse quartets and trios from 11:20 a.m. to 1 p.m.; then rehearse from 2:00 to 3:00 with the band; concert at 4:00, and again chamber music rehearsal from 6:30 to 8:00. That will be a full day. Playing cymbals requires a lot of courage and attention, it's more difficult than one might think. I saw Vessot this morning, just back from leave; he was very pleased by your warm welcome and delighted by his leave. […]

10/27/1915.

[…] We are going to play this afternoon in a neighboring town. It is 5 kilometers from here, but that will be a nice walk as the weather is not too bad. In the morning I work in Beaucousin's room (he is a lieutenant telephone operator). He plays a bit of violin himself and is very nice. The room is quiet and I can work conscientiously. In two weeks, with regular practice, my fingers will be fairly good. […]

Saturday, October 30, 1915, 11 a.m.

[…] I received this morning your letter of October 27. […] You must tell me what your sleeping arrangements are, how you are eating? Can you wash up properly? Do you take showers? Have you started to play chamber music? You must have a few hours of calm; I could send your slippers to keep your feet warm. Or if you do not want to take off your shoes because they will feel cold and damp when you put them back on, I could send paper booties that go over socks (they make all sorts of garments out of paper—vests, shorts). Now that you are out of the trenches, you must be able to take off your shoes at night. Do you need a pair of booties to keep your feet warm? You must answer all these questions and ask for what you need. […]

10/28/1915.

I received yesterday four letters, 2 from the 24th, and one from the 25th and one from the 26th. […] Now let's talk about clothing. My oilcloth is in good shape, so keep the one you bought and send it only when I ask for it. As for underclothes, I'm not going to change yet; I am well covered with a new pair of pants, a vest and new *capote*, all in wool and very warm. I need to pay attention. The band does a lot of walking, we play in neighboring towns and, if my underthings were any warmer, I could not stand it. The weather is not cold enough. I received some new shoes but they are of poor quality and you could send mine. Mail your package from the rue du Bouloi; they arrive with mathematical regularity, in two or three days. When you send underwear, do the same. Once a week, you could send the same way, which costs nothing, a package with two or three cans of food, a bit of sugar, chocolate, some fruit. That package can weigh 3 or 4 kilos, it doesn't matter. To send the package, you have to go into Paris but it will save shipping costs and so is worth it. Only use the regular mail to send me some rum, once a month. […]

For the moment Caplet is still sergeant in a company of the 3rd battalion. When the colonel gets back, he will arrange a way to get him out of that company. […] It will certainly be wonderful to play chamber music, if events give us the latitude. […]

Sunday, October 31, 1915, 11:30 a.m.

[…] Tomorrow I will wrap up your shoes in a box that I will send from Paris, rue du Bouloi and I will be able to see how those packages are received and sent. Monsieur Bouchard says that one needs to stand in line in a courtyard, then climb up a narrow flight of stairs leading to the first floor where they take the packages. […]

I will also try to get some information on the rue de Palestro, behind the Potin toward the Boulevard Sébastapol. One can send packages at no cost from there also. M. Alan sends them to Jean from there. [...]

10/30/1915.

[...] I could not write yesterday; for two days now. I've been overwhelmed. Rehearsal from 8 to 11 in the morning, another at 1:30 and concert at 3:30. Concerts every day and in neighboring towns where other battalions are camped. That means we often walk 10 kilometers to give a concert. What really became overwhelming is that tomorrow is Sunday, Monday is All Saints Day, and Tuesday the Day of the Dead. We have a music Mass each day. The band plays special pieces, and I play two pieces for each service. [...]

Dehuysser left on leave yesterday. He will come see you. [...] You will give him my bow case; that will permit me in the future to send back my bow for re-hairing. Dehuysser entered the music regiment at the end of July. He had been on active duty and is a very good saxophonist. Dehuysser will bring back his cello and play cello in the quartet. [...]

10/31/1915.

I received yesterday your letter from October 30. [...] We are lodged in the outbuildings of the Chateau of Chaussoy, in an attic and on straw, it's not too bad. Here at the front we never see beds like you mention; they are fine for those hiding at home! [...]

11/3/1915.

Two days now that I've not had time to write. Monday, All Saints' Day, I first played at 8:30 in the hall of the chateau for a Mass with about 200 people. Then, at 10:30, I played at the parish church 2 kilometers from there. At 1:30, rehearsal, and at 3:30 concert at Jumel, 5 kilometers away (so 10 kilometers round trip). Back about 6, and at 7:30 I played for the commander. I got to bed about 10:30, totally wiped out! Yesterday, the Day of the Dead, there was a service at Berny, 2.5 kilometers from here. I played there for the 8:30 Mass. During the Mass, an officer from the command of General Hache, leader of the army corps, came to ask me to play at Moreuil, 12 kilometers from us. An automobile from the Corps came to get us at 10:00 and at 11 am I was playing in the church of Moreuil, a superb church, very large, with a great organ. Rolland, who came to accompany me, was delighted. Total success and General Hache sent an officer from his service to compliment us. I played a Bach aria, Handel's Largo, and a Bach chorale. We then had lunch with the general's warrant officers (and dined very well, I must say). We were brought back to Chaussoy about 4 p.m. When I got there, I found Caplet who had come to see the chief of the *musique* and also the colonel who got back last night. We dined together, with the chief of the music regiment, then left to play music at the chateau until 10 p.m. I played the Cools' piece and the first three Beethoven sonatas.

Caplet is a passionate musician and very, very good. He is very easy and accepting. He was happy to be making music as he's been deprived for a long time. He is a close friend of Debussy and Ravel,[126] and I believe that, eventually, there will be something to do with him. He wants to perform the string quartets of both of those composers. I couldn't ask for more. I find him very interesting and friendly. We are here until the 15th of November, at least that's what they tell us. Caplet will have a viola sent and, soon, I will send you the list of the music I need you to send. [...]

Saturday, November 6, 1915, 11:00 a.m.

[...] I put two handkerchiefs in the package sent today. It is more acceptable to have one in your pocket when you go to see the colonel or other officers than pulling out a rag to blow your nose when necessary. [...]

Second letter, same day, 5:30 p.m.

[...] I'm pleased you met Caplet and that he is a good musician. [...] It is easy to talk about shipping from rue du Bouloi, but I will never be able to take all those packages there. I will continue to send them by the post and we'll see. [...]

11/4/1915.

[...] Yesterday I received the money order for 100 francs, for which I thank you, but which I did not need. You should also send me some music. I saw the colonel last evening. During the afternoon, I had been to Ailly to play for the brigade general. So, for now, send the Haydn,[127] Mozart, Schumann,[128] Schubert quartets and Beethoven up to number 10, with parts. Also send the sonatas of Franck,[129] Lekeu,[130] and Fauré,[131] as well as those of Schumann, plus the Beethoven string trios. We will see about trios with piano later. [...] One of these days, I am going to play for General Mangin who, according to Colonel Viennot, likes music.

---

[126] Joseph Maurice Ravel (1875-1937).

[127] Franz Joseph Haydn (1732-1809).

[128] Robert Schumann (1810-1856), Three String Quartets, in F minor, F and A major, Op. 41.

[129] Franck, Sonata for violin and piano in A major, FWV 9.

[130] Guillaume Lekeu (1870-1894), Sonata for violin and piano, V. 64, in G major.

[131] Gabriel Fauré (1845-1924).

11/6/1915.

Yesterday I received your letters from November 3 and 4 and the two packages with my boots and the linoleum insoles. The shoes are magnificent and fit me like gloves. Their only fault is that they are much too nice for what I would have been doing had I stayed in the trenches. Now, when I find myself more often with the officers, they make a wonderful pair of city shoes. [...] My shoes are much nicer than those of the officers. [...]

Last evening, at the home of the colonel, Caplet and I played the Beethoven sonatas in f and C Minor, plus the *Rondo* and *Bohemian Airs*. Overall enthusiasm. [...] Here as well as elsewhere, everyone is jealous of each other. I am not like that, thank heaven. I am much envied. I can't help it if I play the violin too well. I can't play like a pig just to please them. [...]

Monday, November 8, 1915.

[...] I will try to send a package from rue du Bouloi; I will see how long it takes me and if it is easy. I am the first to recognize that I need to save money. However, I'm very afraid of catching a cold. If I go to rue du Bouloi, I will leave in the morning. That means I won't be able to start a fire; I never start one when I am going out, for safety reasons. I realize that, if I had a salamander,[132] it would be very practical as when I got back from running errands, I would not be cold and there would always be regular heat. I have to arrange things otherwise. I hesitate to ask M. Alan to do me the favor of going every week to rue du Bouloi: first, because I don't much like the idea of him knowing my business, and second, because it embarrasses me to have to be so grateful to him. Right now, he has a cold. He only has anthracite powder to heat with; he went to Montmartre to get some clay soil to mix with the coal dust to make balls to put in his little stove. [...]

11/7/1915.

I received last evening your letter from November 5. [...] I thank you for what you send; I can well understand your hesitation about going into Paris in bad weather. I suggested that because it would make only one trip for you, and there are economies to be had on the shipping. But do what you like. [...]

What you could send me is a sleeping bag as mine has been useless for some time now. But not one covered in rubber, rather one in waterproof cloth, with some sort of coating. I've seen some that would be perfect, very lightweight. Pay attention to the weight. [...]

---

[132] A cast iron stove for heat.

Thursday, November 11, 1915.

[...] You mention the rue Radziwill to send free packages, along with the rue de Palestro. The rue du Bouloi is closest to Vincennes. When M. Alan comes on Saturday to bring the eggs, I will ask him whether it would be a bother for him to occasionally take a package to Paris for me. We'll see what he replies. In any case, I'll ask how to get to rue Radziwill. I know I need to save money and one free package a week would save quite a bit. [...]

11/9/1915.

[...] Last evening Caplet and I played at the colonel's and I'm going back there tonight. We are playing the Beethoven sonatas and I play the virtuoso pieces. I also played the *Chaconne*.[133] [...] I am working very hard right now, rehearsals, my own practice, and performance in the evening. [...] I can truthfully say that if I didn't have the consolation of playing interesting music, I would prefer to be back with the stretcher bearers. Our surroundings were excellent; the music regiment is vulgar. What is more, the music we play is vile, the musicians play out of tune like pigs. In short, it would not be very much fun if I weren't here with good musicians and with the hope of soon making music. [...]

Friday, November 12, 1915, 11 a.m.

[...] When I look at the sky at this moment and see the clouds arrive and announce rain, I think of those poor unfortunate soldiers, in the trenches, with their feet and probably part of their legs in mud, then I thank God to have put into your hands an instrument which is permitting you to be away from all that misery. [...]

11/10/1915.

[...] You are wasting your money a bit uselessly in sending me wine; here, at rest, I find all I want for 1 franc a liter. And I do not drink even a half-liter a day. [...] I never told you about having lunch with Rolland and Vessot because it didn't seem very important. They are stationed 100 meters away and for us to have lunch together is totally normal, of no particular import. I do not have that much time to write; I tell you the most important things and omit the little daily details. [...]

---

[133] J. S. Bach, Partita in D minor for solo violin, BWV 1004.

11/11/1915.

I received your two letters from 8 November. [...] I am going to actively work on the rings now that the jewelry makers are back from leave, but it's much harder than you think. Most of those guys make them for their families and when you ask them for one, they don't say "no," but put it off forever. As I obviously don't want to spend 5 francs for each ring, I am obliged to wait. [...]

Dehuysser did not bring back his cello, he did not have a wooden case for it, just one in leather. He is having one made out of wood but it was not finished so he came back without his instrument. I scolded him; he has written to ask you to send his in a package if the case is not ready. That way he will have it in a few days. Caplet also sent for his viola which should arrive soon. You should send me the Beethoven and Schumann trios with piano. When we are in the trenches, Caplet and Sergeant Lemoine (the second violinist) will be there and not able to work on quartets. I can work on the trios with Dehuysser and the assistant director on piano, that way we will not lose time. If the assistant director cannot do it, in the music regiment of the 36th, which is part of our brigade, there is a pianist named Magne, a student of Diemer,[134] who is excellent. He has a lovely touch and wonderful technique. [...]

Saturday, November 13, 1915, 11:30 a.m.

[...] I received yesterday at 4:00 your letter from November 10, it is really nasty, you seem very annoyed. [...] I've asked you in my recent letters what's gotten into you? You seem very distracted, silly. You are probably very busy; everyone wants to benefit from your talent. [...] Now that I've told you all that I think and that I only want what is best for you, you will do what you want. I won't mention it again. [...]

Second letter, same day, 7 p.m.

[...] I received today your letter from November 11. I find that one reasonable and I am starting to hope that your brain has settled down. You must by now have received all the music you asked for. [...] Those packages together must have weighed 18 kilograms: each one was at least 200 grams over the regulation weight of 3 kg. The employees were very nice and still took them. If I had tried to take the music to rue du Bouloi, as you wanted me to, I would have had to rent a donkey to ride with the music in the baskets on each side of the animal. I would have made a sensational entry, me with my packages and my beast. The children would have surrounded me with hoots. Maybe all those hoots would

---

[134] Louis Diemer, professor at the Paris Conservatory.

have changed to ovations when I explained that all those packages were going to a *poilu*. […]

11/12/1915.

I received last night your two letters from November 9 and 3 packages […] Caplet is a fine young man, the soul of an artist, simple and modest. Along with all that, he makes fun of all quirks and ridiculousness in a most comic manner. He is very happy to play music with me and to get away for a bit from the commonness of the conversations of the sentinels; he told me quite openly. […]

11/13/1915.

[…] I got to bed very late last night; I played at the colonel's the Lekeu Sonata,[135] the Franck Sonata, then Bach's G minor,[136] and we spent a long time talking. It was 12:30 a.m. when I got to bed. […] I am playing again tonight at the colonel's: he has invited important people from the town, the mayor, the *curé*. I am now only waiting for the Beethoven trios and the Schumann (with piano). You could send me the Haydn Trio which is quite brilliant and will have great effect. […]

The weather has been terrible for two days, a true storm. Despite the weather, we rehearse in a barn where breezes are quite at home; fortunately, we are used to bad weather. […]

Wednesday, November 17, 1915, 1:30 p.m.

[…] Yesterday I prepared a long box like the ones you have received by train in which I put a bottle of crémant 1904 and a half-bottle of red Ludon. It will ship on the 18th by train so you receive this wine around December 5, the anniversary of your birth. My heart takes no joy in preparing that; I wonder how long this war will last and what will become of us. […]

11/15/1915.

I couldn't write yesterday and this letter will not go out until tomorrow. On Saturday we received a sudden order to change quarters by Sunday morning. So we left Chaussoy Sunday morning, walked for 27 kilometers and arrived in Villers-Bretonneux, a small city with 6,000 residents. It's the first time we've been stationed in such a large city, we've always been in villages or hamlets. This is an industrial city, with a lot of wool and velvet factories. […]

---

[135] Lekeu, Violin sonata in F major.
[136] J. S. Bach, Violin sonata No. 1 in G minor, BWV 1001.

As I have told you, and repeat, you should send only one package a week and I will tell what I need. [...] Send me, please, something called a *bougie Pigeon*.[137] It's an oil lamp in the form of a candle. It is very practical, provides better light than a candle, is less expensive and can replace the flashlight, even outdoors. Just send the candle, I can get the oil I need here. I can put it in one of my steel containers. It is useless, therefore, to send me any candles or batteries for the flashlight. [...]

I was playing for the brigade Saturday when the order to move was called in by the division. Magne, an excellent pianist in the 36th, and I played the Beethoven F minor Sonata, the Franck Sonata, the *Bohemian Airs* by Sarasate—a huge success with everyone. I will certainly be playing a lot in the days to come. Here, in Villers, are stationed not only the brigade but the division, and Mangin is coming back from pass the 17th. Our colonel's name is Valzi, I think he is from Marseilles. [...]

Caplet is still a sergeant in the 9th Company, he's a very nice fellow, I think we like each other mutually. He knew my name, but he didn't expect to find me such a good violinist. [...]

Thursday, November 18, 1915, 11 a.m.

I didn't receive a letter this morning, nor yesterday as I had hoped. I think you are in good health and that you haven't been able to write because of your musical presentation for the colonel or maybe General Mangin. I would really like to know that you have received your sleeping bag because you must not be very warm in your attic. [...]

You should write a short letter to Mme Duez to find out how she is. You mustn't put that task aside. I will write to tell her I'll come see her Saturday November 27; I too have not been in touch in a long time. Naturally I will tell her that you were involved in the September 25 offensive and that I was so terribly worried and preoccupied that I put aside my friends. Don't ignore her; she might think that we don't worry about her except when we need her help. [...]

You don't talk about your job as cymbal player. I wonder what one has to do to get different sounds from the cymbals. [...] Don't they need to play the notes on the page? Explain how that works. When you are playing chamber music, you should pay attention to how you hold the violin. You should tilt the fingerboard under the stand to avoid holding it too much to the left. That helps you see the music easily, so I recommend it. Last night I looked at Baillot's *L'Art du violon* and he says that when one is seated, one should tilt the end of the violin which changes a bit the direction of the bow hair on the string.[138] It becomes too strident with the violin too far to the left. [...]

---

[137] *Bougie* is a candle. *Pigeon* is the maker. Lucien describes it well.

[138] Pierre Baillot, *L'Art du violon. Nouvelle méthode dédiee à ses élèves* (Paris: Imprimerie du Conservatoire de musique, 1834).

Second letter, same day, 6 p.m.

I received this afternoon your long letter dated Monday November 15. So there you are, in Villers-Bretonneux, a city of 6,000 souls. You are moving toward the north and I wonder whether you will be replacing the English. I'd have preferred that you not return to that cold, damp climate. […]

I hope you will receive your sleeping bag; it will come in very handy. You are asking me for a cloth bucket as well as a *bougie Pigeon*. I just sent two boxes of English candles, the battery you asked for, and some new *molletières* you can save for when you play for the officers. […]

11/16/1915.

I don't know what got into you with your letter of November 13. I was in such a bad mood when I wrote my letter. I admit I don't remember it at all. I remember writing about the pâté and the wine. The truth is that you are sending me too many packages. I am bothered by all I receive; I can't manage to eat everything but I can't just pass it around to get rid of it, that would be stupid, I eat much less than when I'm in the trenches. I was probably unhappy because you are always talking about saving money and you are spending it like crazy. This time you sent me two pencils; you sent two just two weeks ago. What do you expect me to do with all these pencils? Just one lasts me three months. I am very careful and don't lose my things. The leather laces are not necessary right now either. I have at least 4 pairs in my pack. […]

11/17/1915.

I received today your letter from November 15. […] Caplet, who usually conducts in Boston and Covent Garden, had a two-year leave from America and had accepted the role of principal orchestra conductor at the Opéra. […] Yesterday for General Mangin, we played the Franck Sonata, the F minor of Beethoven, the *Bohemian Airs* of Sarasate, the Fauré *Berceuse*,[139] the Bach *aria* and a Paganini Caprice. Caplet played the *Death of Isolde* on the piano.[140] We had considerable success.[141]

---

[139] Fauré, Op. 16, for solo violin and piano.

[140] Richard Wagner (1813-1883). *Liebestod* is the final dramatic music from *Tristan und Isolde* (1859).

[141] Mangin wrote to his wife during this period: "This evening the first session of music. At the piano Sergeant Capelet […], prix de Rome […]; on the violin Durosoir, international violinist from Königsberg to Porto […]. I think we will organize a string quartet […] The cello travels with us, at my demand, in its case disguised as a quarter of a cow in a meat sack." Mangin, *Lettres de guerre. 1914-1918.* (Paris: Librairie Arthème Fayard, 1950), 65. Quoted in Durosoir, *Deux Musiciens*, 145.

It is worth getting to know Mangin, his very lively face frequently lights up, one can't deny his intelligence. He invited us back tomorrow at the same time, that is about 5 p.m. We left his place yesterday at 7:15 and by 8:30 we were at the colonel's where we played until 11:00 at night. Tomorrow, at Mangin's, we will play the delightful Haydn Sonata and the "Kreuzer" Sonata,[142] and I'll play some other pieces. Mangin is housed in a wonderful place with, in the living room, a beautiful new Érard.[143] Caplet was in seventh heaven. In the audience, in addition to Mangin, was Colonel Viennot and his officers, our colonel, and the general staff of the division. [...]

It is very good for me to be playing all this music, but that doesn't take the place of working on counterpoint and fugues. The two activities are very different and I am sure that once I am home, I will have to start over with the counterpoint and fugues, it will take several months. But I will work with a new passion, energized by this long period of doing no work. The colonel has ordered the engineers to make me a case for all my music to keep it in good condition. [...]

11/18/1915.

I received today your letter from November 16. [...] You can send me the two Mazurkas of Wieniawski, but not *Moïse*,[144] which is a dreadful piece. I'd also like for you to send me the accompaniments for the Mendelssohn concerto,[145] the Max Bruch G minor and *Symphonie Espagnole*.[146] I have the violin parts for those three works but not the piano parts and the colonel would like to hear these concerti from time to time. Now that I have a good music case, I am sure my music will be safe. [...]

Sergeant Lemoine, the second son of an important coal merchant in Rouen, will play second violin in our future quartet. He came back yesterday from pass and brought with him a beautiful Vuillaume with a lovely sound.[147] We are just waiting for the viola and the cello then can start work; they are on their way so it's just a matter of a day or two. [...]

---

[142] Beethoven, Violin Sonata No. 9, Op. 47 in A major.
[143] An Érard piano. The company was founded by Sébastien Érard (1796-1855).
[144] Nicolo Paganini (1782-1840), Sonata "a Preghiera" (Moses Fantasy) MS 23. Variations for the fourth string based on a theme from *Mosè in Egitto* by Rossini.
[145] Felix Mendelssohn (1809-1847), Violin Concerto in E minor, Op. 64.
[146] Max Bruch (1838-1920). Lucien was the first violinist to play Bruch's Violin Concerto in G minor in France, in 1904. Édouard Lalo (1823-1892).
[147] Vuillaume, an important family of French luthiers.

11/19/1915.

I received just now your letters from November 17 and 18 and no packages. I say that not to criticize, just to state the fact. [...] I'm sending you today my lightweight sweater, two empty bottles, and the rings for Monsieur Alan and Marguerite. I managed to buy them from some comrades; they are not pretty but they are in fact made by *poilus* at the front. Thank you very much for the champagne [...] for my birthday. Certainly, when Rolland, Julien, and Vessot wished me happy birthday last year in Saint-Thierry I never dreamed that a year later I would find myself still in this situation. This hiatus to normal life is truly awful. [...]

Cymbals always play the same note, but there is infinite variation between PPPP to FFF, and it is not easy to play a good crescendo. I've practiced that a bit. The hardest part is placing the stroke of the cymbal at just the right time; it is not always as easy as it looks. [...]

I am going to the colonel's place tonight and we are going to start playing trios. I managed to uncover in the town a fairly decent cello. People have been taken advantage of, so they hide what they have of any value. They are right to do that. I do not know how much longer we will be in Villers-Brettoneux; this little city is far from unpleasant. [...]

Sunday, November 21, 1915, 11:30 a.m.

I received this morning your letter from November 19. [...] In it I found M. Alan's. What he writes is unfortunately true; with a few exceptions, our leaders and politicians are not worth much. They have led us into ruin and shame and they fill their pockets while you are getting killed to keep the Germans from advancing. For sure, the war was unavoidable, but had we been prepared, armed, how much disaster and how many lives could have been spared! After the setback of 1870 and the lesson imposed on us, our leaders are real criminals and we should treat them as such. [...]

I hate receiving some of your letters in which you childishly complain about being in the midst of coarse people, etc., that you would prefer this, or that, when the heavenly instrument you play with great talent allowed you to change your situation and, like Orpheus, charm and attract not those wild beasts but superior officers who can appreciate the emotion of your songs. You have to think of getting out of this cataclysm safe and whole and it is your violin that will accomplish that miracle without any other help. You have given enough proof of your courage and sangfroid that one can see what you are worth. You are ready to prove it again when, unfortunately, circumstances require it; you are musician and stretcher bearer. If you have any sense at all, you will realize that I am not wrong to say this to you. [...]

I could not write yesterday; I was in Amiens, as you will see when you receive the cards I sent from there. Here is why. One of our oldest officers was injured recently when a horse kicked him in the stomach. He was taken to Amiens by car but was dying as he got there. The burial was at Saint-Martin-d'Amiens. The night before last, while we were playing as usual at the colonel's, he asked me and Rolland to come the next day to Amiens to play for the memorial service. I left at 9 a.m. and after playing the aria of Bach and the Handel Largo for the service, Rolland and I spent the day in Amiens. We had a wonderful lunch and visited the cathedral. What a precious work of art, and it's fortunate that the *Boches* didn't have time to damage it. I took the train at 4:15 and was back in Villers by 6. That little trip broke up the monotony of our existence. Today at 5, for the second time, I will go to play for General Mangin. [...]

I received today your two letters from November 20. Yesterday at 5 p.m., at General Mangin's, the pianist Magne and I played the Haydn Trio with Dehuysser,[148] then Corelli's *Folia*,[149] Bruneau's *Romance*, a piece by Cools, the Lacroix *Berceuse*, a Paganini Caprice and the first movement of Wieniawski. I added, as an encore, Fauré's *Berceuse*. A tremendous success! General Mangin had invited a lot of officers, including the general staff assigned to General Hache, the chief of the 3rd Army Corps. I expect one of these days to play for him. We will begin working as a quartet as soon as Caplet's viola arrives, within the next two or three days. We are starting to work seriously as a trio, on Beethoven's first and Schumann's first. [...]

With Magne and Caplet, I will also be presenting the sonatas. We have to play again at Mangin's on Wednesday. I'll play the "Kreutzer" with Magne and the Lekeu Sonata with Caplet. If we have a trio ready, we will also play that. So here we up to our necks in rehearsals. I am very pleased, under these conditions, to be staying with some good people and to have a good bed, it's very nice. A lieutenant took me to Amiens this morning, to meet one of his cousins (a lieutenant in the automobile division). His cousin, a charming young woman who plays the piano very well, wanted to meet me. I just got back this instant, after having traveled at 80 kilometers an hour in the general's car. This lieutenant, so I hear, wants to have me in his division. He says that Mangin is a very open-minded person of whom one can ask anything. [...]

I am still going to try to write to Madame Duez today, but she will have to excuse me a bit; I truly do not have a free minute. Yesterday morning I played

---

[148] Haydn, String quartet No. 38, G major.
[149] Archangelo Corelli (1653-1713), Violin sonata in D minor, Op. 5, No. 12 "La Folia."

for the Military Mass at 9:00 and the Parish Mass at 10 to a considerable crowd. [...]

11/24/1915.

I couldn't write yesterday, no time for it. There was supposed to be a maneuver yesterday that couldn't take place because of the fog; General Mangin took advantage of that to ask us to play the concert scheduled for today. Dehuysser is no longer part of our group, he clearly was not up to the level. Like many people, he bragged about what he could do, and once his back was to the wall, he couldn't follow us. [...] He couldn't easily get through the Beethoven or Schumann trios, which he didn't understand at all. When he didn't bring his cello back from Paris, I was suspicious. Of course, his reason for leaving the group was that it was too tiring to rehearse every evening, all sorts of bad explanations. [...] So we were stuck. [...]

At that point, I met up with Deschamps who is at division headquarters and told him about the problem. He suggests I go see Niverd (from Alençon—you know him); he is driving a postal vehicle. So I found him, talked to him, and in 15 minutes everything was set. He is 38 years old, a cellist (2nd prize from the Conservatory), and very nice and an excellent musician.[150] We agreed to rehearse that very evening. That explains how, on November 22, Saint Cecilia's Day, at 8 p.m. we made our debut at the colonel's dinner, reading the first Beethoven Quartet and the Mozart D minor.[151] Niverd plays with a lovely sound and he is a musician, and more important, he's ready and eager to play in a quartet. That will keep him in the rear, give him more freedom, and allow us to rehearse quite easily. The funniest part is that we made our debut for General Mangin with Beethoven's 1st String Quartet. We will go back tomorrow and play the Schumann 1st.[152] [...]

I made the acquaintance of a number of officers and it is possible that, rather than stay with the military band next time my unit goes to the trenches, I will be sent to the division *en subsistance* to play for Mangin. Nothing unpleasant in that prospect. Niverd will have his instrument sent; the colonel will take charge of the transport. We will soon be well known by the entire army corps; our delicate and precise execution of the music is being noticed. Caplet plays viola very well and is a talented musician with a lot of different colors. It is a pleasure to play with him. Time is passing most agreeably, and profitably. [...]

Quite soon, when we have polished some quartets, we will play for the public. This is all becoming quite interesting. Caplet, who is very funny, says that,

---

[150] Lucien Niverd (1879-1967), Violin sonata in B major.
[151] Beethoven, String quartet No. 1 in F major, Op. 18; Mozart, Quartet No 15 in D minor, K. 421/417b.
[152] Schumann, Quartet No. 1 in A minor, Op. 41, No. 1.

should this war last for another year or two, we will become a stellar quartet and will find ourselves engaged to play after the war. [...]

Monday, November 22, 1915, 11 a.m.

[...] I haven't received any news this morning, but I did receive yesterday a package you sent. The package contained a light sweater which, parenthetically, was very dirty, two empty bottles, and the two rings for Marguerite and M. Alan. I gave Marguerite the one for her, with the serpent. (She begs me to thank you) I will take M. Alan's to him tomorrow morning. I find his very nice, the Cross of Lorraine in copper looks like gold and adds an important touch to the ring. [...]

Tuesday, November 23, 1915, noon.

I didn't receive a letter today. I hope you will be able to send me news soon. [...] I just received the cloth bucket, the crepe paper sleeveless vest, and the *bougie Pigeon*. I won't send these things until you are settled somewhere so they don't have to chase after you. [...] You didn't explain what a *bougie Pigeon* is, whether it had a large base for stability that takes up a lot of room. You mustn't forget that you carry all your gear when you are moving from place to place, so tell me exactly how the *bougie Pigeon* you want is made. I rather think this one is not right. The Louvre must have had this candlestick somewhere in the store for a long time. When I unwrapped it, I noticed it had been cleaned. Had it been new, that is, recent, it would not have needed cleaning. I will send back this one if it is not what you want. I'll wait to hear from you. [...]

When I send the piano accompaniments for the concerti [...] I will send also the Sinding *Romance* which you played on your first concert.[153] A fond memory, it is lovely and you can play it to great effect. M. Tracol has marked the fingerings and marked out the tied notes; it's up to you to judge and play it the way you like best. [...]

11/25/1915.

I received yesterday your letter from November 22. [...] Sergeant Lemoine is a cultured man, a chemist from the Nancy Institute. He has received a very strong education. He is a very good musician, has always played a lot of chamber music, he plays the violin very well. He has studied at least 8 years. He is in his thirties. In the quartet, he is a bit timid, but with experience that will change. He is from Rouen, son of an important coal merchant. Rolland says they are very well off; for me this is an excellent future connection for Rouen. It is not Colonel Vessot who plays violin (he is the brigade colonel) rather it is Colonel

---

[153] Christian Sinding (1856-1941), Romance in E minor, Op. 9.

Valzi who is a passably good amateur. [...] He loves music and is familiar with a lot from having attended many concerts. [...]

Caplet considers me a first-rate artist; we don't praise each other but I can tell from his actions that he holds me in deep esteem. He has several times said how happy he is to have met me. General Mangin must play piano, probably rather badly, but at least he plays. [...]

Monday, November 29, 1915, 11 a.m.

[...] I received this morning your letter from November 25. [...] I am happy that Monsieur Lemoine [...] is an amateur and a person of culture. I'd have been worried had he been a professional; that would have been too much with a professional cellist also. He too would have wanted to show himself outside of the ensemble and play solos. That would have diminished your chances to play alone very often. [...]

I went to see Mme Duez on Saturday. [...] She received me in her bedroom because she didn't want to light her heater. She bought a large amount of coal last winter and none this year. She burns wood in the fireplace in her bedroom, but not much so I got rather cold. I will only visit her in the nice weather. [...]

11/26/1915.

I received yesterday your letter of November 23. I reply immediately to your question about the *bougie Pigeon*. You were right to question what the Louvre sent you; they are trying to sell you a *rossignol*.[154] What I want is a slightly fatter candle, like the ones used in automobiles. No foot, nothing, it's a copper candle that can go in a pocket. If the Louvre doesn't have them, you will find one at the Pigeon store itself. It is really a good idea to go to the trouble; I expect that, this winter, you will save at least 20 francs on candles and batteries. [...]

In the next package you send, on the 30th, you can put the Pigeon candle, the canvas bucket and the paper jacket. I can put a few bulky items in the box for my music. [...]

Last night at Mangin's we played the Haydn Trio and Schumann's 1st String Quartet with great success. We will probably go back on Sunday. We are becoming more and more appreciated. [...] Life goes on calmly and we would gladly stay here to the end of the war, but we are sure to have a wake-up call. [...]

11/27/1915.

I just received your letter of November 25 and two packages, one with music, the other with 8 candles (something totally useless right now since the people

---

[154] *Rossignol* is a nightingale; as rare as a white elephant.

who lodge me provide gaslight), the reglementary cloth bucket (you could have found one smaller, less expensive) and the paper vest which will be of great use. There was also some paper for the toilets. [...] My bed in the house where I am lodged costs me nothing; they have to lodge me and give me light. I only pay a little supplement for what I eat. For 1 franc a day, these good people give me breakfast, lunch and dinner. They eat simply but well and especially a lot of vegetables which makes me very happy. [...]

Wednesday, December 1, 1915, 2 p.m.

I received today your letter from November 27. [...] If I sent you candles, it's from the goodness of my heart. I thought you might need some light to get ready for bed as well as to rehearse. I do not know what time of day you work on chamber music. I do not know whether you are still compelled to practice with the band and if you are still playing the cymbal part. You tell me absolutely nothing. If you had told me sooner that you had a place to sleep that included light, I would probably not have sent the candles. They were to tide you over until I could send the famous *bougie Pigeon*. That is not going to fall out of the sky. [...]

You could have told me sooner that you take your meals most of the time with the people who are housing you, and that you eat a lot of vegetables. [...] You must not be eating all the food I send you if, as you keep repeating, you get your meals from those good people. I do not like the idea that you are giving it away. When you were eating with your comrades, I think they were the ones who ate two-thirds of what I sent to you. You should not make me spend money for others. [...]

11/29/1915.

There is something strange with the mail; I just received all at the same time your letters from 24, 25, 26 and 27 November, and you complain that you are not receiving my letters despite my writing daily. [...] Sergeant Lemoine is an amateur violinist who worked at the Chemistry Institute in Nancy for 3 years; at the same time he took, for pleasure, violin lessons at the Conservatory in that city. He is a quite good violinist, a good musician and has played a lot of chamber music. In short, he is a perfect second violinist for the quartet. [...]

Magne is 25 years old, and right now, professor of piano at the music school in Caen. [...] If the war lasts long enough, I will have become acquainted with all the chamber music I don't yet know; that would be a great, and unexpected benefit, I must admit. Up to now, Mangin has not invited a lot of people: just the superior officers of the 36th and 129th divisions, Colonel Viennot who is the brigade general, and once, I think, General Hache's Chief of Staff. [...]

I don't know why you adopt such a strange tone. I write every day but I cannot describe my life minute by minute with the tiniest details. You think I'm getting up late because I sleep in town. No, I am up at 8:30 a.m., ready for the day. For someone who gets to bed every day about midnight, that is not bad. [...]

11/30/1915.

I just received your three letters, 2 from the 28th and one from the 29th. [...] Caplet, who has had his fill of the people who surround him at the mess-hall [...] was talking about money this morning and said: "during the next rest, why don't we find a place where, for a set price daily, we, the entire quartet, could eat in a musical atmosphere." It's a wonderful idea; to make it possible, we just need to receive, from the state, a fixed amount of between 1,70 and 1,90 a day. That allows soldiers to find meals that suit them. I will take charge of arranging to receive the *franc prêt* and our life will be even nicer.[155] We will be able to talk about our concerts. [...]

The cathedral in Amiens is sublime, filled with all sorts of art works—wooden sculptures and paintings. How fortunate that the *Boches* only stayed in Amiens 10 or 12 days and didn't destroy anything. Otherwise, this magnificent cathedral would have suffered the same fate as the one in Reims. [...]

Niverd is a very nice, simple fellow. In addition to playing cello, he has a music and piano store in Alençon and tunes pianos. He is quite busy with his service in the auto company and is not at all thinking about promoting himself as a cellist. That doesn't stop him from being a good musician and holding his part in the quartet very well. [...]

My friend Pierrot will probably make the ring for Coraboeuf. I will arrange to buy in Amiens a little medal of the child crying. Pierrot will use it to make the bezel of the ring which will be lovely. I would love to have him make a letter opener for me; for that we would have to find a strap from a shell, but one of the old ones which are in copper and easier to work on. The new ones are an alloy and break under the hammer. [...]

12/1/1915.

I just received your letter of November 29 in which you say you are going to work on getting the *bougie Pigeon*. You can send it to me in the next big package, about December 10. Here, I have light and do not use my candles at all. I have at least a dozen. [...] I heard that we will be leaving Villers-Bretonneux about the 10th of the month. I should receive the big package after I get to my new destination rather than here, so you will wait until I tell you to send it.

---

[155] A sum paid to a soldier so he can pay for his own food.

I haven't yet received the shipment of wine that was going through Le Havre. I hope to have my hands on it for December 5, my birthday. I can still see myself last year in Saint-Thierry when Julien, Rolland, and Vessot brought me a bouquet of flowers and we ate a chicken that Vessot had somehow come up with. [...]

Sunday, December 5, 1915, noon.

[...] Today is your birthday. [...] Tell me exactly the days and the time of the rehearsals for the chamber music and solos. [...] All of that is very interesting for me. Here alone, like an owl, holed up in my house I can tell myself: "Lucien is rehearsing at such an such hour," or "Lucien is playing the X Quartet or the Y solo this afternoon at 5." Those thoughts give me great pleasure. [...]

12/2/1915.

I just received your letter of November 30. [...] In fact now we play every evening at Colonel Valzi's, but it is not a performance, rather we are rehearsing there. We prepare what we will play at General Mangin's two or three times a week. On the days when we go to Mangin's at 5:00, we rehearse at 2:30. It's wonderful practice for us, and since we need to play well, we really have to work. [...]

I eat every day with the people who are housing me, except when Caplet (or Rolland, or Sergeant Leduc, or Chauvel) invite me to eat with them. I try to avoid invitations because that wastes my time a bit; there is so much to do I don't want to waste any time at all. The people I am staying with are very careful and their cooking is simple but excellent, a good pot-au-feu, or a stew, lots of vegetables, salad, in short food that reminds me of happier times. I am absolutely fine and would love for this to continue. But alas, the end is near. Wherever I am, I will find the best lodging I can and will not be one of those who suffer. The people who lodge me have a little 4-room house; I sleep in the dining room on a very good folding bed. [...]

12/4/1915.

I received today your letters of December 2 and 3. [...] Tomorrow, Sunday, my birthday, I will eat the foie gras and will drink the wine, probably with Dumant who is very nice, a good friend. [...]

Today the colonel invited the quartet for dinner at 6:30, then we will work on the Mozart Quartet in C which we will play on Sunday at a 5:00 concert at the division.[156] Then, on Monday night, at the request of the colonel, the quartet

---

[156] Mozart, String quartet No. 4, K 157.

will give a concert with the Mozart, the first Beethoven in F, and the first Schumann in A minor. You see the interest this is generating; there will be at least 100 officers. During the two weeks that this circus has lasted, I've not once touched the cymbals. Jacquet had to grudgingly relieve me of that duty. […]

12/5/1915.

I thought I would have time to write again yesterday, but it was absolutely impossible to find a quiet moment to pick up the pen. […]. Caplet received, from Le Havre, a huge viola; it is at least 42 centimeters long. He gets very tired playing it. It's an old French instrument, very beautiful with a wonderful sound. Niverd will soon have his cello, and we will be well set up with instruments. While Caplet and Lemoine are in the trenches, I will try to have myself sent, *en subsistance*, to the division. Magne will do the same. Niverd will always be with the division. That way we can play trios every day, plus, we will stay with Mangin. The sector is quiet so I don't think that will be difficult. Not to mention that the division will be very bored in Méricourt where it is supposed to go and will be happy to have us there.

I hope to have home leave soon, probably around Christmas. I think I will get 8 days rather than 6, and if I can arrange transport independently to get to the train in Amiens, I will have 9 days. […] I will keep you informed. […]

Thursday, December 9, 1915, 11:30 a.m.

I received yesterday at 4:00 your letter from December 5. […] On December 5th you must have had a lot of free time because the concert for General Mangin was canceled. It's really too bad that reception didn't take place; it would have been, for all of you, a sort of dress rehearsal. […] Still I think the concert on December 6 was not only a great accomplishment but a great success. I hope echoes of that will reach me. […]

I was enormously pleased by your announcement of 9 days of leave around Christmas. You will be able to be a bit calm, at home, and we will be able to talk a bit about our business. […]

12/6/1915.

I just received your letters from December 4. […] After the war, there will be much to do, we can talk more about it during my leave. I agree with you, I cannot stop working. In fact, there will be a lot for everyone to do. But I don't believe it will be in France. I'm thinking about America—Canada and the United States. We'll talk again about that. […]

Friday, December 10, 1915, 11 a.m.

[…] If you come home soon […] you will bring back your worn-out underthings […] and you can decide whether you need a third set. That would probably be useful; if you continue to play music, you will feel the need to change clothes when you get back from a reception. Having three sets of underwear is not a luxury. And since you are sleeping in a bed, you should have two shirts so you can change from your daytime shirt when you go to bed; that is healthier and cleaner. If you come, we will buy two shirts in brushed cotton at the Louvre. They should not be too much during a move; you told me yourself that the case for your music is very large and you can use it to hold some underwear during a move. […]

12/7/1915.

I just received your letter from December 5. […] Generally, in the morning I rehearse with Magne the sonatas or the pieces I will play for Mangin; at about 5 p.m. I get together with Caplet and Lemoine in the home of Madame Larmouillat, a person with many connections, who also likes music. She has two salons and an excellent Pleyel.[157] Many military men, officers and soldiers, intellectuals, come to her place. […]

Last night we played our quartets in the conference room of the boys' school. The success was more than we expected. A lot of people, at least 300 people, soldiers, a hundred or so officers, and what is even better, an attentive public who were very interested. Our playing surpassed our expectations and truly, given the short amount of time we've been working, it was not bad at all, very together. […] I am sending the program from that session in the letter. A simple program not to make fun of, rather a great memory. That's why we have all signed the first public program as a souvenir. It will be interesting to look at later. […]

I'm worried about your cold; you should not hesitate to take some aspirin at the beginning of a cold—do not wait. In fact, you should take several, spread out during the day. That way you may be able to avoid it. […]

Friday, December 11, 1915, 11:30 a.m.

[…] I received yesterday afternoon your letter from the 7th in which you share your enormous success! Good for you! I was afraid M. Lemoine would be nervous. True, if he made a few mistakes, they weren't noticed by the audience. And your rich and emotive playing probably carried away your friends. It's not the same for Caplet and Niverd, who are used to playing in public, mostly for Lem-

---

[157] Piano company founded by composer Ignace Pleyel in 1807.

oine. Supported by you three, he made out like pro. It was very successful, that is what is important, and the colonel must be very satisfied with his artists. [...]

12/8/1915.

I just received your letter from December 6. [...] Last night at the colonel's, we read the Svendsen Quartet.[158] None of us like it. It's very sonorous, but very redundant and filled with prosaic formulas that make one weep. It's strange that I could have liked this quartet which is really just honest mediocrity. That shows that, as one gets older, musical tastes get purer and after experiencing beautiful things we can no longer stand the mediocre. Tonight we'll read Smetana,[159] and I hope he will stand up better to the test. [...]

You don't say anything about your health. I hope your cold is better, but do not fear to take one or two aspirin tablets at the first symptoms or even a hint of a cold. You stand a good chance of stopping the illness. [...]

The people in this area are facing great hardship. The spinning mills are no long receiving any wool; very soon, in at most 10 days, all the factories will have to close because they lack the raw material. It is a true catastrophe for these poor people who depend on their salary to pay for what they need to live. [...]

12/9/1915.

Today I received your two letters from December 7. The first thing to tell you is that we are leaving for the trenches on the 11th, that will be Saturday. It is official. You can thus send, when you get this letter, the usual package from the rue de Palestro. The last Camembert was astonishing, one of the best I've ever eaten. [...] I drank my wine with Dumant who invited me to dinner—it was exquisite. The apples arrived in good condition. The package only took 3 days, that is exactly the same as the 1 kilo packages you were sending through the mail. [...]

Today, Thursday, General Mangin has invited General Hache and all his general staff for dinner and after the dinner, at 9:00, there will be a musical evening. [...] I think Mangin, who is charming, has arranged this on purpose and spent some time preparing it. [...] I will play Fauré's *Berceuse*. [...] The quartet will play the first Beethoven and the first Schumann. That is the one we heard played by Joachim: it is splendid. [...]

For our quartet concert, we had a particularly thoughtful audience that was quite moved. [...] As soon as circumstances permit, we will give another one. I don't know whether the chief of the band will exempt me forever. I will do all I can to make sure he does, but I do have to be careful. [...]

[158] Svendsen, Quartet in A minor, Op. 1.
[159] Bedrich Smetana (1824-1884).

I may be able to leave even sooner than I thought, by Christmas and maybe sooner. I will try to keep you posted. We have again entered the bad weather season but it is not like last year. We have not had any rain and for my part I am quite content. [...]

12/10/1915.

I just received your letter from December 8. The regiment is going back to the trenches tomorrow; the music regiment doesn't leave for the new site until the next day. There are at least 22 kilometers to cover to get to the new place. According to the latest rumors, we should be going to the trenches for 40 days. Last night, at 9:00, was the last concert at General Mangin's. We had bad luck: at the last minute General Hache was not able to come so there was only his Chief of Staff and three or four other members of his staff. [...]

Caplet is delighted with all this music. He never expected to come to the front and be part of a quartet under such good conditions. I get along well with him; we have the same ideas and feelings. He knows how to rehearse a group; we recognize in him the orchestra conductor with much experience. [...]

12/11/1915.

Just this instant I received your letter from December 9. The regiment left today. Tomorrow morning at 8 a.m. we will set off for our new billet, about 25 kilometers from here. Tomorrow will therefore be quite hard. [...] I didn't play at the church on November 28 nor December 5. The pastor made it really difficult for Martel to organize military Masses. [...]

I am rather worried that you catch cold so often; you should start drinking cod liver oil regularly. And when you feel the beginning of a cold, immediately take some aspirin. Darn it, the sea air strengthened your lungs but unfortunately you didn't go to the coast last summer. [...]

12/13/1915.

I received last night your letter from December 10. [...] Our new encampment is very close to the *Boche* lines, 3 kilometers, but at the foot of a very steep hill thus out of reach of the enemy artillery fire. There are a lot of people here: in addition to the music regiment and more from our section, there is an engineer base, artillery, territorials, in short, a huge number of military personnel. It was very difficult to find a bed; however, after 3 hours and paying 0.75 a day (which obviously increases my expenses) I found one. [...] A considerable number of beds are reserved for officers with lodging coupons, and, by golly, there is a lot of demand for the few beds left and the locals can charge a lot. I have a fine little room, not a bad bed, and I am right next to the dining room with a stove, so I will not be cold.

My music case is big, obviously, but I have a lot of music so there isn't much space left. I put in my jacket, my sleeping bag, a pair of shoes, and my rucksack with the heaviest cans. It was full and I could not have added anything else. It is just fanciful to talk about nightshirts. All that ignores the practical consideration which says "have as little as possible." I have plenty with two flannel shirts, one on my back and the other being washed. I have it back in two to three days. If you think I change clothes when I get home in the evening, you are thinking of civilian life, not military life. [...]

Thursday, December 16, 1915.

[...] I just received your letters of the 11th and 13th. [...] My cold is going away but it is still there and becoming chronic. Spending several months at the sea-side each year fortifies me, sort of shields me. Last winter, if I didn't get sick, it was thanks to the iodine stored in my lungs. The same is not true this year and despite all my precautions, the weakness becomes clear. Starting today, I will go back to drinking cod liver oil, but it is hard to find as much as one might want. I have half a liter that I bought during my last illness last year. I will use it up and if I need more, it may be difficult to find. [...]

12/15/1915.

I couldn't write yesterday; the colonel asked for me and I was in his *gourbi* in the trenches. He is quite well situated. The trenches here are nothing like the ones we've seen up to now. There are almost no passageways. You get to them almost directly from the road. Unfortunately, we are in a swampy region, the Somme and the Somme Canal. All that is water, always water. And with the rain these recent days, the terrain is totally soaked and, in lots of places, the men are in liquid mud much higher than their knees. It's a terrible situation, and a good number of places in the trenches are almost inaccessible, it takes a long time to get there. Now, with the cold that has set in these past three days, frozen feet are quite common.

The colonel had me come so he could explain why we shouldn't consider a Midnight Mass for the regiment. I will hold one at Cappy, where we are, for those who are there, but very few of the officers or the other men from the regiment will attend. I am hoping to leave on pass the day after Christmas. General Hache has forbidden distractions or any music while the division is in the trenches. I cannot say he is wrong, as it is certainly dreadful to think that guys could be dying of cold while the general is listening to lovely music in front of a good fire. There is something shocking in that. It is likely that the brigade will be relieved in 20 days by the other brigade of the division, so this will be just a small interruption and will we have a long rest afterward. No one can imagine the state of this sector, and what blocks of mud our poor comrades turn into. So much suffering the public knows nothing of! [...]

This afternoon I got to see Caplet and Lemoine who are liaison agents to the 3rd battalion and are in a totally other part of the sector from us. Our sector, which takes something like the form of a fan, is very spread out, more than 12 kilometers of front lines. I found both of them in good health, though deep in mud. We shared a liter of red wine that I had brought and was able to heat up. With the good crackers they had, it made a good five o'clock and I didn't get back until dark; it takes a good two hours to get to where they are. [...]

12/17/1915.

I received yesterday your letter of December 14. [...] A group departed yesterday on their regular leave. It was my turn to leave with them. At the colonel's request, I stayed to organize the Midnight Mass. Caplet and Lemoine are in the trenches and won't be able to come, so I have to arrange a program with me and a singer, with Magne or Rolland on the harmonium. [...]. The music regiment is not rehearsing right now, it is busy all day long, sweeping streets in the morning, filling cars, unloading barges, disinfecting the sheep skins; in short, it is serving everyone. Obviously, they wanted me to be part of all that but I fought it like the devil and spoke with Jacquet (the chief). He was hesitant. He would dearly have liked to see me doing all that sort of work. I told him that, if he didn't excuse me, I would go talk to the colonel. It was settled; I am only working on music. All my comrades are dying of envy. [...]

12/18/1915.

I received today your two letters from December 16. [...] At this moment, thanks to a number of stupid decisions, the future looks very dark; few are those who would try to say when this war will end. A heavy boredom is starting to oppress everyone; having no end in sight is a terrible burden. It's up to God! Here in our billeting site we will celebrate Midnight Mass in the local church. Few officers and soldiers from the 129th will be able to attend; only those who happen to be in the rear with us. I don't even know that the colonel will be there. There is a real fear that the Germans will do something that night. I will play the Andante from Bach's Concerto for Two Violins with Dumant who plays the violin nicely, and then the Andante from the Mendelssohn Concerto. [...]

12/19/1915.

I received today your letters of December 17 and 18. [...] In this little town, it is impossible for me to have a lodging coupon. I have really only one fear—that one day or another the military authority will take our beds for officers. Some engineers are due to arrive soon and I don't really see any place for them to stay. I will do everything I can to stay here where I am well off. As for my timidity, as you call it, it is obvious that you haven't heard me here. Every time we need to ask an officer for something, I'm the one who does it because I manage to speak to my superiors with ease. [...]

12/20/1915.

Today the mail is late and I don't have a letter yet. I gave the colonel this morning the program for Midnight Mass and spoke to him about my leave. I will probably leave on the 26th, in the afternoon and should be home about 7 a.m. in the morning. I will have permission to leave individually, which saves me 24 hours. The colonel did not want to officially give me a week's leave; no one else has had that and there is a lot of jealousy already surrounding me. But I will "cheat" a bit, as the colonel said. [...] I will have 8 full days at home. [...] The first thing I will do is take a nice hot bath then sleep for a few hours in my own bed after traveling all night. [...]

Thursday, December 23, 1915, 5:00 p.m.

[...] I just received your letter of December 20. [...] I am counting on you at 7:00 a.m. on December 27. I will write immediately to Mme Lambert to tell her we cannot come for lunch on the 27th as I had promised but that we can come on the 29th. We will go see Cunault on the 28th and you will bring your violin and your bows, or just your bows. [...] You could also get the new bridge you want. I was thinking that your shoes would surely need a bit of repair. Try to get a new pair as soon as possible. Only one pair in the type of terrain you run around in is not sufficient. [...]

12/21/1915.

Something seems to be terribly messed up with the postal service. I still don't have a letter today and the regiment didn't receive anything, not a letter nor a package. The mail officer claims that the letters and packages must have been sent to a different sector by mistake. With the holiday, there is much more mail. [...]

The weather is abominable, a fine cold rain that doesn't stop and the sector, in such weather, no matter all our efforts, is a total sewer. You should see the faces of the poor guys basically glued in mud. May those who have good beds to sleep in right now remember those who, day and night, are in water and mud! It's sad to admit, but very few people can imagine what sort of suffering they are going through. It's not very glamorous, and requires endurance and patience. Alas, later, many of these unfortunate guys in the trenches will retain bitter memories. I, myself, was very lucky to have gotten through that terrible part without problem. My hardy constitution resisted the bad weather. I am however very happy not to be spending a second winter in the same conditions. […]

12/22/1915.

I still have no letter this morning. […] I still hope to leave on Sunday the 26th and arrive in Vincennes about 7:00 in the morning. […] We are really sad exiles. We drag ourselves through our vagabond existence like gypsies, except for the important fact that they have their homes and their families with them. The rain has started again, with a cold, persistent mist. This is surely the most awful season; it's not really light at 8:00 in the morning. I feel a bit like a dormouse hiding in his hole. It will be really good for me to be able to immerse myself in Vincennes. […]

12/23/1915.

[…] For Christmas Eve, Rolland and Leduc are organizing something. Here we can easily find some goodies. The English, who are in Braz (3 kilometers away from us), have a governmental cooperative which sells cans of fruit for 1,25, magnificent jam for 0,60, plum puddings, in short, all sorts of wonderful things at normal prices. We could wish our government would do something like that rather than letting unscrupulous merchants take advantage of us. […]

12/24/1915.

I received yesterday your letter from December 21. […] It is true that I will pay something for my individual trip—to be exact, 2,75, not counting food. I will probably not eat in the dining car which is not expensive but not very good from what I hear. I will eat in one of the restaurants around the station, for a modest price. You can relax, I will not miss the train. […] I will bring my violin as my case needs some small repairs, and I want Cunault to make a new bridge. I will have the bow, the Tartini copy, repaired as I use it constantly. For now, I am leaving my Serdet for Caplet who asked to borrow it. […]

I am playing tonight the Mendelssohn *Andante*, the Bach *Lento* (with Dumant), the Handel Largo. Our tenor, Lafont, is coming with Rolland and will sing *Le*

Ciel a visité la Terre—the Gounod carol—and, naturally *Minuit Chrétien.*[160] Sunday morning, the 26th, I'll go see the colonel so he can sign my pass; in the afternoon, about 1 p.m., I'll set off. At 2 a.m., in Amiens, I will take the train for Paris and arrive about 6 or 7 on the morning of the 27th. [...]

Lucien came home for leave on December 27, 1915.

---

[160] Adolphe Adams.

1916

For the French, 1916 was defined by the Battle of Verdun. A small city on the Meuse River, Verdun had a long history in the defense of France. Attila the Hun failed to take it in the fifth century; in 843, it became part of the Holy Roman Empire; in 1648 it was awarded to France in the Peace of Westphalia. In 1914, the city was defended by two important, modernized forts: Douaumont and Vaux. When the Germans began bombing, on February 21, Verdun sat behind a forward bulge in the French line. The battle that resulted lasted three hundred and two days, nearly all of 1916, and injured or killed some seventy thousand men.

Lucien wrote about two particularly difficult battles during his time at Verdun: the Bois de la Caillette (April 2-17) and the Douaumont Fort (May 22-24).

About the Bois de la Caillette, Lieutenant Colonel Valzi, commander of the 129th regiment and one of Lucien's superiors, wrote: "Under continuous bombardment night and day, officers and men outdid each other in commitment and endurance." Battalion Commander Pourel continued the praise: "Without weakening and for eight long days, the battalion remained at its post, realizing gains it was able to hold." He added that the machine-gun section that supported the 3rd Battalion "survived eleven long days in placements where trenches no longer existed, under incessant bombardment [...]." Lieutenant Desaubliaux, who led the machine gun section, described the Battle of Verdun as "nothing less than a pure contest of French and German masculinity."[161]

The Douaumont attack was the best-known engagement of the 5th DI. It represented "the dramatic, courageous futility that characterized the Battle of Verdun as a whole."[162] It was without doubt the single bloodiest operation of the 5th DI during the war: 894 men were killed, with 2857 wounded and another

---

[161] All quoted in Smith, *Between Mutiny and Obedience*, 138.
[162] Smith, *Between Mutiny and Obedience*, 143.

1608 missing.[163] The fort had been taken but was held for only twenty-four hours, and was not retaken until the last days of the battle.

Both sides at Verdun fought, literally, for the sake of fighting. There was no prize to be gained or lost, only men to be killed and glory to be won. The conflict at Verdun was particularly intense. At some time during the long months, no less than 115 divisions were crammed in on one side or the other on a front that was rarely more than five miles wide. Many French units were on the brink of mutiny, but they held Verdun.[164]

The 5th DI moved next to the area around the village of Les Éparges, about 15 kilometers south of Verdun, and remained there until February 1917. The goal was to hold the line; the units' resources were not sufficient to launch an offensive which would have invited a more vigorous counterattack by the Germans. The mood of the *poilus*, trapped in the trenches with nothing much to do but contemplate the ever-present danger, the risk of dying for no purpose, changed. Not only were they trapped by their military situation, but they were also literally trapped in mud. Smith quotes Private Legentil, Class of 1916, machine gunner, about moving his machine gun to the front lines:

> The men had to crawl for three hours through a "thick and glutinous bed of mud" to get to the assigned position. Dragging bulky and heavy ammunition proved especially painful: "How will we get there? Good will, human resistance, has its limits. We stop every hundred meters, despite the comments of the liaison agent, who is in a hurry to get us there so he can go take a nap. [...] In fact, once day broke, you had to sit down, and a big devil like Caron [a comrade] had to lie down so as not to be seen from the front. Painful hours, interminable days, without even being able to stand up to take a few steps, not even for bodily functions. Naturally, you relieve yourself the best you can, where you are."[165]

During this time, Lucien was remarkably free to work on music, with great success, although he was occasionally called back to stretcher-bearer duties. His friend Vessot wrote to Louise:

> Lucien is making a name for himself in his new role. He is received by the brigade general, the division general, and even the general of the Army Corps. If this continues, I rather expect to see him become close to our dear grand-père Joffre.[166]

---

[163] Smith, *Between Mutiny and Obedience*, 144.

[164] Taylor, *The First World War*, 123-126.

[165] Unpublished memoir. Cited in Smith, *Between Mutiny and Obedience*, 166.

[166] Letter from Vessot to Louise, November 20, 1915. Durosoir family archives.

On December 13, 1916, General Joffre was replaced as Commander-in-Chief by General Robert Nivelle. Despite the generally low morale of the *poilus* after a seemingly endless war, the appointment of Nivelle appears to have given them some new confidence. In the spring of 1917, a soldier from the 129th RI wrote that "we have confidence in the great spring offensive, which we *must hope* will be decisive, because, with Nivelle, we have an amazing man from the artillery who has proved himself at Verdun and in whom we have confidence."[167]

The events of 1916 showed that this confidence was misplaced.

---

[167] Smith, *Between Mutiny and Obedience*, 171.

The Letters

I arrived yesterday in A. without difficulty. The vehicles I expected were there waiting for me and at 2:30 I was at the barracks. But my room was occupied by a lieutenant in the artillery and there was no question of my taking the second bed in the room. He actually declared it strange that I would even consider it, so I set out to find another room and it was not easy. I finally found a room for myself with a camp bed for 0,50 francs a day. I am pleased to have found it; I can sleep well and am alone. [...] I saw Rolland last night, [...] he is quite bored. I understand him. I'm a bit depressed myself, I'm going to give myself a push and start working. It is raining and the weather is for the dogs, so I am happy to have shelter rather than being in the trenches. [...]

Saturday, January 8, 1916, 10:30.

I still have not received any news from you but I hope to have a letter at 4 p.m., the time I usually receive your correspondence. [...] I found you a bit nervous; the doctor who saw you about your eyes told you the same thing. Avoid drinking too much alcohol and too much wine. Should you be fortunate enough to come home unharmed, you could still have nervous problems. You don't realize this right now and the feverish life you are leading takes away all judgment about this. Be wise therefore and careful in everything, in your conduct as well as what you eat, and don't drink at every occasion. For you soldiers who have just escaped from danger, or who are exhausted or depressed by the misery inherent in your situation, it seems natural to drink glass after glass, because any sort of liquid seems to calm and appease the thirst that most of the time consumes you. But you end up abusing it and it becomes a habit when it should be only an exception. Reason and wisdom have to prevail if you want to keep your health and everything that comes with it. [...]

Sunday, January 9, 1916.

[...] Still no news this morning and as it's Sunday there is no mail at 4 or at 7:30. I'll probably receive your letter tomorrow morning. I hope you will have written a long letter and told me all about your trip, your arrival, what you've been doing since January 5. If so, you deserve my compliments as you are not usually so explicit. One might say you find it repugnant to describe your life and the events around you. However, what is more natural? I take pleasure in telling you all I do and the tiniest incidents of my existence which I think you will find interesting. Maybe not. You have a strange nature—are you doing lots of naughty things to be so mysterious?

I have a grippe that started yesterday, not very serious. But it seems I have taken a subscription to this charming illness this winter. I took an aspirin last night; during the night I had a bit of fever. Maybe it would have been higher had I not taken the aspirin. Today before lunch, I took one, and this evening I will take another. They don't seem to do much good. The fatigue of recent days has a lot to do with this illness. The life we led for a week was exhausting and I got run down. I was all ready for a cold. […]

Monday, January 10, 1916, 11 a.m.

I received this morning the two letters from Thursday January 6, the one from Friday 7th. […] I don't know your friends Caplet and Lemoine so I cannot write to send them my New Year wishes. Please be my interpreter and tell them that I regret not being able to come to where you are, incognito, and to have the pleasure of hearing you. I would have to be able to turn into a bird and come perch on the branch of a tree near where you rehearse. […]

1/7/1916.

Since getting back, I've not yet received one of your letters. I spent yesterday in Chuignes, where Caplet's battalion is at rest right now. Everything has changed. It is not yet certain, but it appears we will stay here at least a month. […]

Yesterday I had lunch and dinner with Caplet and Lemoine, who will be at rest for another three days. We agreed that, during their next rest, I will ask to be transferred to their battalion for the duration of that rest period and we will play quartets. I need to go see Niverd in a few days to discuss this with him. He's been on leave the past two days. They tell me he is expected to bring back his cello. He would come to Méricourt, which is not very far, by bicycle. […]

1/8/1916.

I will probably receive a letter today and maybe my knife. […] I will ask to be sent temporarily to Caplet's battalion as of the 18th, so we can be a quartet for the 8 days of his rest. I don't know whether I will need my package as Caplet and Lemoine are very well fed at their mess; they pay one franc extra. For now I think you shouldn't send me anything. If I need anything between now and then, the English offer me provisions at a very good price. That means I won't need a shipment until the 26th or 27th of January. Much could happen between now and then; I will keep you informed.

Since we've been here, the sector has gotten very active and now it's just about as bad as La Ville-aux-Bois; it was calmer before we got here. We shoot at them and they obviously shoot back. [...] What is striking is the fall in the value of the Deutschemark these past 15 days. If it continues Germany will not be able to continue much longer. They will be bankrupt. [...]

I am sending you two photos that Dumant took. The first is Christmas Eve, during the rehearsal at the church, Rolland facing the harmonium. We were playing the Mendelssohn Andante. The sun was shining on me and you will see the strange deformation caused by the light. We couldn't create another like it if we tried. The second is me in my oilcloth. Dressed like that, I look like an archer from a village during the Middle Ages. All that I would need is the bow and the quiver. [...]

I just saw Martel. He is very tired right now. The sector is quite large; he runs nonstop, right and left, to offer consolation. [...]

1/9/1916.

Yesterday I received your letter from January 6 and this morning the one from the 7th. I've not yet received the package with my knife. [...] Army life is very lazy, but I am eating reasonably, and do not drink much, for which I don't deserve much credit; the wines are quite awful and expensive. As for paying attention to women, please have the goodness to believe that I have very little interest in that sort of thing. Besides, the few examples of womanhood in this area are the final word in ugliness and filth. One would really have to have the desire. I am quite able to restrain myself. As for being influenced by the ideas of others, these uneducated, unmusical good-for-nothings will not have much effect on me. I think it may be just the opposite.

According to what we hear, we will be in this sector a long time without being relieved. They are talking about March and maybe April. That will be horrible for the poor *poilus*; I seriously doubt they can withstand such a hardship. Each battalion now has a week of rest alternating with a week in the trenches. But during the so-called rest, they serve as workers day and night which means they don't get any rest.

Caplet goes back on service tonight and, in a week, during their rest, I think I will go back to working on the quartets with them. Right now Niverd is on leave; as soon as he's back, I will get to work so that everything happens without complication. [...]

Once the regiment has a supply of shoes and pants, I will request some. For the moment, there are none. [...]

Wednesday, January 12, 1916, 2 p.m.

I received this morning your letter from Sunday, January 9. [...] Mme Bastien came to see me yesterday and brought me some flowers. [...] I had nothing in the house, neither cookies nor candy, and since I was unable to go out to buy anything (having too bad a cold) I offered her nothing, not even tea. That was not very polite but I was still too sick to do much of anything. She fully understood. When I am better, I will go see her. You absolutely must ask Pierrot to make a pen holder or a letter opener for her. The gifts she sends you are too significant for you to send only a simple souvenir. [...]

1/10/1916.

I received last night very late your package with 2 bananas, some raisins, and my knife. [...] My writing today is tiny as this is the last sheet of paper I have. [...]

Today I will play at Lieutenant Poumier's. [...] He is a graduate of *l'École Polytechnique*, from a good family, well brought up, and a true music lover. Cloëz,[168] the pianist who is Levy's student, is here. He is a nurse in the 43rd artillery which arrived in our area a few days ago. The lieutenant discovered him; those who love music search out those who play. We will play this afternoon the Franck and "Kreutzer" Sonatas, obviously without rehearsal. [...] Cloëz is an excellent musician, without Magne's facility but a better musician with a good ear. We are playing at the engineers' mess, in a quite lovely house with a piano which, although not great, will have to do. [...] The same young lieutenant from the *École Polytechnique* likes music so much that, when he learned that we would probably resume our quartet rehearsals in a week or so, he asked to come listen to us. You can well imagine that I said yes. [...]

The weather is gray and sad. The men are afraid, rightfully I think, that after such a hard winter, we will be sent back for two months of rest. That would mean that we would be ready, by the beginning of May, to be sent to a bad place for the spring offensive. Will there be one? I don't know. When one looks at the results of the September 25 offensive, one becomes just a bit skeptical. We don't have hundreds of thousands of men to sacrifice to no purpose. The leaders should consider that. [...]

1/11/1916.

Last night I received your letter from January 8. [...] You can rest easy about my drinking; I absolutely do not drink—not even a liter of wine a week, I drink at best a tiny bit of poiré at mealtime,[169] and, as to liquor, I don't drink any,

---

[168] Gustave Cloëz (1890-1970).
[169] A hard cider made of pears.

saving what I have for unpredictable situations. [...] In this war I've learned to make rapid decisions and act on them. You can well imagine that there are moments when there is no room for discussion. As for problems of nerves, now or in the future, I think you can be totally reassured. What the doctor told me doesn't worry me much. I don't have a lot of faith in doctors, and what is more, that doctor was asking me questions about heredity. [...] If you saw me drink a bit of good wine while at home it's because I've been deprived for a long time. It was a luxury. [...]

I played yesterday at noon for the engineers; they had prepared for us a wonderful tea with English cakes they went to Braz for. I played the Franck Sonata, the "Kreutzer," and the *Chaconne*. They truly enjoyed all that; there are few distractions here. Young Lieutenant Pommier (or Poumier, I'm not sure I'm spelling his name correctly) was absolutely blown away. He says that if we played music like that in the trenches, the war would stop right now. [...]

Friday, January 14, 1916, 11 a.m.

[...] The civil or military government should set up canteens (as the English have done) where you could buy what you need at affordable prices. It is shameful that men who are sacrificing everything for their country and from whom so much is asked should be prey to brazen shopkeepers and forced to spend so much money only to obtain, most of the time, dreadful rubbish. But that is the way things are done in France and it will always be the same: bribery, trickery (that occurs with a good many of those who govern us) will always prevail. For the one voice that speaks up in the name of humanity and honesty, a thousand others will do everything to silence it. It is always the little man who pays. We must hope that, after the war, the voters will see clearly and turn out this vile rabble. [...]

1/12/1916.

I received your letter of January 9 yesterday. I'm surprised you haven't yet received any of mine; they seem to take 4 days to arrive. How strange you are with your scolding! I tell you absolutely everything I do, even the tiniest things, and am happy when you do the same. I understand that there is nothing in your life. What bothers me especially is that you again have a cold. I worry that you will wear yourself out and catch pneumonia. If you cough a bit, buy immediately some syrup from Ligneul, and describe your symptoms so he can advise you. You should drink some cod liver oil regularly. As for aspirin tablets, they are excellent. You can take up to 6 in 24 hours, not just one at night which is obviously not enough. You need to take this seriously as colds that don't go away are worrisome. Six to 8 drops of tincture of iodine every morning, in some milk, also strengthens your system. [...]

I take my meals at the mess of the 2nd Company and am well sheltered. Big Robert, the cook, is a good guy, careful and agreeable. [...]

Césarine (Vessot) is now on leave and told me he was going to protest in front of *Le Matin* because that paper says we are fine and have dry feet. More men are leaving on pass tonight, Pierrot among them. He will make your ring, that is settled. As soon as he is back, we will get the gold medal with the crying child. [...]

Saturday, January 15, 1916, 11 a.m.

I received this morning your letter from January 12. [...] I am pleased that you are eating well at the mess of the 2nd company and that the cook, big Robert, is clean, smart, and a good guy. But with all that, you don't tell me anything about the menu, which I've asked about with insistence in my recent letters. That information will come, I hope, but I shouldn't have to ask for it. Yes, I call you "strange" because I have to pull words out of you one by one, and for me, this task is tiring and makes me sad. [...]

1/13/1916.

I received last night your letter from January 10 and am happy that you now have my letters from January 6 and 7. [...] I am no longer feeling depressed. We have resumed our daily routine, but the day after I got back, boy, were my spirits low! It was certainly because of the weather. With the constant rain, the sky so low, the days so short, this is really the saddest moment of the year. And of course, the longer the home leave, the harder the separation. [...]

We are in this sector for what may be a long time. The 1st battalion never moves; this part of the sector is the calmest. The 2nd relieves the 3rd, alternating every week. That is why I will have myself transferred to Caplet's battalion each time it is at rest. That keeps me from having to walk the 10 kilometers between Cappy and Chuignes in the mud. Niverd will have to come every evening by bicycle, also 10 kilometers, and it's hard. He is on leave right now; once I know that he can make that trip, I'll arrange the rest. [...]

The wind is still blowing fiercely; this is truly awful weather. We wish fervently for April, to see the sun a bit. Still, I am much better off than those in the trenches. You didn't mention your cold in your letter of the 10th; please let me know and take care of yourself. [...]

1/14/1916.

I did not receive a letter yesterday and am quite concerned. I hope it is not your cold that prevented you from writing, rather just the mail being delayed.

[...] It is a beautiful day but very cold. The windstorm has given way to ice. That would be all right but, unfortunately, with the mud, we will certainly have a number of cases of frozen feet. When leather gets wet and then dries on feet that are stuck in increasingly cold mud, there is not much to be done.

This morning I went to Lieutenant Poumier's to try to tune the piano which was terribly out of tune. I was quite successful; naturally, my first attempt, it took a long time, almost three hours but it is now tuned reasonably well. [...] From now on I will tune it myself. [...] During this war, we can say I've done all sorts of jobs. But that one, for a musician, is not very difficult. I do not understand why pianists don't tune their instrument. [...]

Monday, January 17, 1916, 2:30 p.m.

I received this morning your two letters from Thursday and Friday, January 13 and 14. I am happy that your ennui has gone away. Such sad weather, so foggy, and these enigmatic events end up a crushing weight! We have to fight against it and hope that we will soon be delivered from this Minotaur. We can give that name to this war as, every day, it devours men, gold, and energy. I am a bit worried about the shanty you've rented and are sleeping in. If you are no longer making a fire, you will start having pains; your bed and mattress are not likely the best in terms of comfort. You are probably not well covered. Since you have a stove (make sure the pipes don't have holes and that the stove is in good condition so you don't asphyxiate yourself!) get any kind of wood wherever you can and warm yourself. [...]

1/15/1916.

Last night I received your two letters from January 11 and 12. We now need to put our name and address in our letters, otherwise there is a good chance the letter will not arrive. Lots of soldiers were not signing their letters so they could say anything they wanted. To stop this, under the threat of the letters not being sent, we need to put our name and address. [...]

If Pierrot could make a letter opener, I would keep it for myself. Unfortunately, it is impossible to find any shell straps in pure copper and the others break under the hammer. You could give Mme Bastien one of my pen holders from Neuville; I have two of them. You think that all I have to do is place an order to have something? At this time, all the men are overworked and worn out with fatigue and the constant tasks they have to do. In these conditions, in the mud where they are located, one can't dream of asking anything more. [...]

You think this is a good time to talk to Mangin or to the colonel about the quartet. At this point, they are quite worried about the condition of the sector. And Mangin just chewed out the colonel. That was quite a scene. I just need to play dead and work quietly in our quartets while Caplet's battalion is at rest. I think my plan is going to work. To try to talk to Mangin about that subject at this time, when all the men are stuck in mud, would be a great way to be sent back to the company. [...] I have no intention of drawing the attention of powerful people who have many other problems to deal with.

As for sobriety, we can't be anything else here in Cappy as there is not much for sale; as for the fairer sex, it is rare and not well represented. [...]

1/16/1916.

Yesterday, I received your letter from January 3. I went again to see Caplet in Moulin to settle the details for our next endeavor. Pourel's battalion, to which both Caplet and Lemoine belong, leaves the trenches tomorrow night, Monday, for 8 days of rest. Tuesday, after lunch, I'll set off for Chuignes, I won't get too tired—a medical vehicle will take me and my stuff to Chuignes. There, I'll eat at the mess hall with the liaison agents and with Caplet and Lemoine, and will share their room in a sort of dormitory with camp beds made by the soldiers. We put our straw mat on the cot and have a very comfortable place to sleep. Of course I take my pack, my blanket, sleeping bag, etc. I think we will rehearse tonight. Doctor Gourcerolles, the doctor for the 3rd battalion, will put his heated room at our disposition every day, all day long.

Today I am going to Méricourt to talk to Niverd and propose my project. I think he is back from his home leave. He was supposed to bring his cello. We would take it to Chuignes and he could come every evening by bicycle. [...] We are celebrating the resumption of our work and a good number of people are also happy about it. [...] I am keeping my house in Cappy; that way it will be there when I get back. [...] I will leave my box of music there, well protected. I'll only take the music I need. I can lock the door and the key is in my pocket, so I'm not worried. [...]

1/17/1916.

I did not receive a letter today. I hope that is not because of your health. I saw Niverd yesterday at Méricourt. I took an ambulance vehicle to Chuignolles. I still had three kilometers to go to get to Méricourt. [...] It is all set; he will come every evening by bicycle and we will be able to resume our quartet studies for a week. He did not bring his cello back with him, rather he shipped it. I don't expect him to have it before Wednesday and he will send it right away to Chuignes. Fortunately, there is an awful cello here which I can take to Chuignes so we can play without delay tomorrow. [...]

I managed to see General Mangin who was at the Château de Méricourt. I gave him, from Coraboeuf, the copy of the portrait of Prince Pontiatowski and his sons. I also took advantage of the time to pay my respects and give him wishes for the New Year. He was very friendly, but, as he said, there is no room right now for music. Later, during our rest, we will get caught up. [...]

I am going to try to see whether it would be possible to have the piano from the engineers' lodgings; that would be very useful for us as there is not one here. I tuned it again this morning, with more success. [...]

Thursday, January 20, 1916, 11:30 a.m.

I received this morning your letter from January 17. [...] Try not to walk too much in the mud; you have only one pair of shoes and they must be damp. Ask for shoes and a pair of pants as soon as possible. [...]

1/18/1916.

I received yesterday your letters of 14 and 15 January. I hope your health is improving. [...] If we need a piano in Chuignes, the engineers will bring theirs; it will not be that difficult to transport. I am leaving today about 1 p.m. for Chuignes in an ambulance vehicle. In addition to my personal effects, I am taking quite a lot of music, my violin, and a cello. The cello, which belongs to a watchmaker, is dreadful but it will allow us to work until Niverd receives his. [...] I saw Lemoine last night. He assures me that the sleeping conditions and the food will be "very comfortable" as the English say. Thus, everything is for the best in the best of worlds, to quote Candide. The perspective of playing in a quartet for 7 or 8 days is nothing but the most pleasant; time will pass quickly.

The army would have done well to set up, in the rear, canteens run by soldiers' widows for example where they could sell necessities, if not at cost, at a very reasonable price. But here there is absolutely no organization and the shopkeepers really take advantage and charge a ransom for their products. Imagine, bad wine costs 0,90 for red and 1,10 for white. It's really excessive. [...] Robert's menus are not very varied and with good reason: steak and fries, or soup and beef, or stew with potatoes or beans or lentils, that's all. But it's good and properly done. [...]

1/19/1916.

I received today your letter from January 16. [...] We are settled in the room of Dr. Gourcerolles who, very nicely, has placed his quarters at our disposition. We had, however, a disagreeable surprise. Instead of seeing Niverd arrive during the evening, we only received a letter telling us that he was obliged to postpone our rendez-vous. The weather was very bad, it was pouring rain, but more important, he has a mild case of rheumatism. That really disappointed us. [...] I passed a very pleasant evening with Caplet and Lemoine with whom

I played chess—a magnificent game I've learned recently from some really talented players. [...]

Sunday, January 23, 1916, noon.

I received this morning your letter from January 20. [...] Monsieur Alan mailed the big package from rue de Palestro yesterday. [...] The package is huge: it must weigh 10 kilos. I was worn out from packing it. I think I'd prefer to pack a trunk; I have to guess the weight of each can and choose a box big enough to hold everything. I do not have a box just the right size for what I am sending easily at hand and it is more difficult than you might think. I had a difficult night from Saturday to Sunday. I'm better now but I need to be very careful. In addition to the grippe, my nerves are shot. All that will get better. I just leave what I am unable to do. [...]

1/20/1916.

I received yesterday your letter of January 17. [...] Niverd did not come yesterday. His illness must be rather serious; we are hoping to see him today. [...]

1/21/1916.

I received yesterday your letter of January 18. [...] Niverd still has not come; that means we have not yet worked on any quartets, which is annoying. [...] I received just now your letter of January 19, much earlier than expected. You ask about our meals; that is an easy question. In the morning hot chocolate, toast with butter and jam, which is very good and very English; at noon, either roast beef or lamb, fries or vegetables; in the evening, soup, stew, salad, cheese, jam. And coffee with every meal. That doesn't count the extra food Caplet and Lemoine frequently supply. We have nothing to complain about. We eat in a room in the town hall: there is a good stove always lit. [...]

1/22/1916.

[...] Caplet and I visited poor Niverd this afternoon. He has an attack of rheumatism in his left hand, one finger is swollen like a sausage. Obviously, he cannot play the cello right now. This is very bad timing as it's thrown all our plans into the air. As he says, we have to hope that by the next rest, that is in about 10 days, he will be completely cured and able to do his part. I will go back to Cappy most likely on Tuesday, where I'll find the engineer officers who, according to Lieutenant Poumier this morning, are bored without me. [...]

Wednesday, January 26, 1916, 11:30 a.m.

[...] You end your letter by telling me to take care of myself; it seems to me that 3 of the members of the quartet are taking very good care of their bodies! Those dear people are not wrong, but I would love for the 1ˢᵗ violin, along with taking care of his body, to pay the most attention to his art and surprise me, one day, by sending me a composition for his instrument (however simple and short it might be). [...]

1/23/1916.

I received yesterday your letter from January 20. [...] Niverd has received his instrument, that we know. It is really bad luck that he was stricken by this unfortunate rheumatism just at the moment we were going to start playing. I have perfected the Bach concerto for two violins. Lemoine is a good musician and upholds his part very nicely. I have not yet had the time to work on Niverd's Sonata; it looks well written and interesting. As soon as there are any shoes to be had, you can be sure I will not wait to ask for a pair. The piano in Cappy has been badly treated and doesn't stay in tune well. Still it is something I can get experience on and that is enough. Pierrot is coming back today or tomorrow and will find your letter. I have the little gold medal that will be used for your ring; Cloëz had to go to Amiens yesterday and brought it back. It will certainly be very pretty. [...]

1/25/1916.

I received yesterday your letter from January 22. You are being hard on Niverd. We went to see him and sadly found him with one finger all swollen, an attack of rheumatism which is bad timing for us. [...] Caplet's battalion was to return to the trenches tonight, but it is staying where it is and will not relieve the other battalion. They tell us we will all be relieved (the entire regiment) about February 5. That means that the 3ʳᵈ battalion will have 11 days of rest. I will stay with Caplet and Lemoine until February 5. In the 274ᵗʰ regiment there is a cellist named Maréchal,[170] who took first prize at the Conservatory. Unfortunately, that regiment is no longer attached to our division and we can't even think of having him transferred. [...]

1/27/1916.

I received yesterday your January 24ᵗʰ letter. Today I've not received any mail; I hope it will come soon. You told me to eat my asparagus points with some eggs, as an omelet. Unfortunately, eggs are very rare here and we can't even hope to

---

[170] Maurice Maréchal (1892-1964).

find some. I will just have to eat my asparagus in a different way, that's all there is to it. [...]

Last evening Caplet, Lemoine and I were at Commander Pourel's place; Lemoine and I played Bach's concerto for two violins, with Caplet accompanying on the viola. Then I played the *Airs Russes* and Beethoven's *Romance in G*,[171] accompanied by Caplet and Lemoine. It sounded quite good. If we could add the cello accompaniment, it would be perfect and better than the piano. As soon as we have the instrument Lieutenant Poumier is arranging for me, we will organize something and Commander Pourel will invite the colonel for the evening. I think he will accept as he's not in a good mood right now. [...]

Monday, January 31, 1916, 2:30 p.m.

I did not receive a letter today; didn't you write on the 28th? [...] You must have seen in the newspapers that a Zeppelin, or a number of them, came to Paris in the nights of Saturday to Sunday, January 29-30 and Sunday to Monday, January 30-31? I don't know whether that will continue, but in Vincennes, about 10 p.m. both nights, the siren sounded an alert. There were a lot of dead and injured. In the past months the Germans must have built a number of them; they must be ahead of us. A few days ago, I saw in *L'Information* that a Zeppelin had dropped bombs on the villages around Épernay. And I had to think that, unfortunately, Paris being not far from Épernay, we would also have a visit from those machines! We don't have enough planes for continuous patrols to keep the Zeppelins away. It seems to me that our civil and military organization is not so great and that we are far from having enough intelligence and energy in those two areas. One has to hope that Germany runs out of money for all this to end. They seem to be regaining strength on our front. I hope very much that we won't launch an offensive to kill thousands of men and that we let them attack us so we can decimate them! Because, of course, I hope we are well enough fortified not to fear a breakthrough. And the generalissimo, let's not even go there! What is he doing? He doesn't visit the different fronts any more. All that is quite strange! I thought the principal role of the generalissimo was to move constantly from one place to another so he could know and predict everything. [...]

1/28/1916.

Today there is emotion everywhere. Battalion Commander Pourel received the alert that we should all pack up and be ready to leave. In the entire sector, for the past 5 to 6 hours, there has been quite a heavy bombing, Apparently the *Boches* were attacked by the English last night and, in revenge, they may shell the entire sector. But in any case, fearing a *Boche* attack, our battalion is armed and

---

[171] Beethoven, Romance in G major for violin and orchestra, Op. 40.

ready: since we are at rest, in case of a *Boche* attack, we are considered reserves
for the rest of the regiment. In case of an attack, we will be sent where the need
is greatest. It is 1:30 and the bombing has quieted down. I think all our anxiety
will be for nothing. We lunched in the basement of our house which we use for
shelter from bombs. [...]

I played last night for the commander the Boccherini Sonata and an étude by
Fiorillo,[172] accompanied by Lemoine and Caplet. [...] I saw Lieutenant Poumier
this morning; he agreed that I would go tomorrow morning to fetch the piano
and take it back on Thursday. We are to organize a bit of a concert Wednesday
evening. I think today's events will not change that. The son of M. Lyon, the
director of the Pleyel piano company, is supposed to come. He is a lieutenant in
the artillery and quite near us. Lieutenant Poumier knows him well—they were
together at *Polytechnique*. Caplet also knows him and his father very well. [...]

I think we are feeling the repercussions of what took place at Neuville where,
so we hear, the Germans received a beating with a capital letter. [...] They must
have lost a huge number of men; they are furious about not winning. [...] Cappy
was hit very hard—I just learned that about two thousand shells fell. There are
some 50 houses demolished, especially around the church. [...]

1/29/1916.

As I told you yesterday, there is no mail today. [...] The entire sector is in turmoil; reinforcements arrive night and day. The cannon is roaring horribly. The
3rd battalion left last night about 9:00 p.m., no news since from them. I stayed
where I was. With all the instruments, my music case and Caplet's, I cannot
move; I have no way to transport all that. We are waiting for battalion vehicles
to move the officers' canteen. When they arrive, I will put all my things in them
and then leave. [...] No one knows anything about what is happening in the sector, just that the cannon roars nonstop. [...] For a so-called quiet sector, emotion
is running high! Relax, I am very careful. [...]

1/30/1916.

I received yesterday your two letters from January 26 and 27. I am still in the
same spot with the secretaries. The cannon is still roaring, reinforcements go
by constantly. There are most awful rumors about the fate of the regiment, but
as it is impossible to find out anything at all, we have to be circumspect. At this
time, also, they must be censoring mail rigorously. For sure, the *Boches* launched
a huge attack on our sector against troops that were quite spread out and, worse,
exhausted by fifty days in the mud and damp. There had been so much talk

---

[172] Luigi Boccherini (1743-1805); Federigo Fiorillo (c. 1755-1823), 36 Études or caprices for
violin, Op. 3.

about our sector being safe and not likely to be attacked. Later I'll be able to talk more freely. [...]

Your reproaches in your last letter were a bit excessive. It's true that after the war many people will have different ideas, so will I. I plan to use my talent for some practical good. [...] I am pleased to know you received the amount of money you mentioned, and also that M. Guyot came to see you. Let's hope it's a sign that he will make a significant payment. For goodness's sake, when those men come to see you, if they talk about the lease, I think you should ask them for 3 years under the same conditions. If they ask for more, you can point out that, without the war, you would never have renewed the lease under those terms, that the rent hasn't changed in 15 years. Everywhere else it has risen significantly. [...]

Here we are at the end of January and nothing allows us to expect to be freed from this nightmare by May. The *Boches* may be hurting financially and economically, but from the military standpoint, they know what they are doing and, as for munitions, they have plenty. Our experience these past days proves that. And the shells they are firing aren't small ones, always 150 or 210-caliber. [...]

February 3, 1916, noon.

I received this morning your letters from January 28 and 30 (I received your letter of the 29th yesterday). [...] The *communiqué* of January 30, 1916, 1:00 p.m. said: "The Germans announced last evening (that is Saturday January 29) an attack on our positions south of the Somme, near Dompierre. The enemy artillery was driven back into the trenches by our barrage and our fire power." If, as I fear, this action was not good for your regiment, all or part of it may have been taken prisoner. Or were there a lot of deaths? All this silence is worrisome. I understand nothing about all this. If the Germans attacked with force that means they were well-informed on what you were capable of. Their espionage service is so well-organized that they must know everything that's happening on our side. It seems to me that we should have the same sort of spies and that the officers in charge should be informed on the enemy's plans. The role of the soldier is passive, he obeys, that's all he can do! The role of the leaders is to make things happen, to question and detect the plans, whatever they are, to show some initiative, some creativity in dangerous situations. Do we have people capable of that? I'm not sure and it's sad. They are saying that the Germans are getting worn out. In any case, they still have munitions. That poor little area of C... which was hit with 2,000 bombs is proof. [...]

As to the matter of taxes, they certainly cannot impose tax on anything other than what I receive. Many people declare nothing or almost nothing, whereas for some, like me, that is the truth. I don't know that we can hold out very long. The question of money is starting to become quite painful. [...]

1/31/1916.

I received late last night your letter from January 28. All my baggage, my music, and Caplet's case were turned over to the battalion vehicle. I had nothing else to do at Chuignes, so I returned to Cappy where there was work to do. I found that area partially destroyed. [...] Right now, the sector is quiet, but the *Boches* are still shelling. I am regularly on service as stretcher bearer but fortunately the work is diminishing. I think the sector will quiet down again. Or at least, if there are attacks, we will no longer be part of them; the regiment is to be relieved shortly. We have lost a good number of men, and what is more, those who went through this siege after fifty-one days in the trenches are truly at the end of their human capacity. So we all are waiting to be relieved imminently. [...] We have to hope not to have to travel very far; the regiment will not have the force.

As you see, fate sidetracks the best projects. For the second time, for a different reason, we were again prevented from making music. [...] Martel had all his vestments burned in the medical vehicle where they were stored. He is devastated. This morning I saw Lemoine and Caplet. The latter is totally unrecognizable after these four days of torment. They charged with their bayonets. We were happy to find each other in good shape. [...]

2/1/1916.

I received yesterday your letter of January 29. [...] We should not have any illusions, the situation in France will be difficult for a long time. [...] As for working on violin, right now I am carrying the wounded which is very tiring. We have had no newspapers for a few days. I heard something about Zeppelins over Paris. In our area, things seem to be calming down and we all believe that the 129th will be relieved any day now. [...]

2/2/1916.

I received yesterday your letter from January 30. Today is quite calm. We continue to have a bit of shelling daily; that is, a hundred or so shells fall on Cappy. We live partly in basements. Lieutenant Poumier's piano is in pieces: it's been tuned for eternity. The military authorities made all remaining civilians leave—a wise move as this area is clearly uninhabitable. We are eating all the pigeons, rabbits, chickens that were left. [...] We have a great deal of work right now; in addition to bringing out the wounded we dig ditches and bury the dead. Mournful work as you can imagine. I find myself reflecting on the gravedigger in Hamlet, all the more as the shells whistling not far from our heads remind us that life is, for many, very short. [...]

Saturday, February 5, 1916, noon.

Last night I received your letter of Wednesday, February 2—it didn't take very long to get to me. Naturally I didn't have a letter this morning, but I hope to receive one this evening. I am worried about all that is happening and would love to know that you are far from that tragic place. It is completely normal for your regiment to be relieved—the men could no longer withstand or repel a new attack if one happened. They probably told you that the new sector, where you've been for almost two months, was quiet so that you wouldn't be afraid and could sleep soundly! However, for the past three weeks at least, the *communiqués* speak daily about that area. I didn't have good feelings about all that and worried that something just like what happened would start. […]

2/3/1916.

No mail today. […] The bombing is decreasing in intensity. The artillery that arrived in our sector recently is so powerful and hitting the *Boches* so hard that they can't think of anything else. So they are paying little attention to C and only launch a volley on our area from time to time. We will not be relieved as expected; rather we are here until the 8th to 10th of February. That means we stay here another week; it's still long but somewhat more bearable. The relief will be for the entire corps. […]

Sunday, February 6, 1916, 11 a.m.

I received last evening your letter from February 3 and this morning the one from the 4th. […] If the entire 3rd Corps is relieved, that means another corps has to come take its place. […] So you are stuck and have to wait. I would so like to know you are out of that area where you have done more than enough. I am constantly worried; the days cannot pass quickly enough for me; I will not relax until you have announced your departure. My health is better—no more cough, a bit of headache and aches in my arms and legs. That may be the end of a cold or a result of the torment of knowing you to be in danger. […]

2/4/1916.

I received yesterday your letter of February 1. The attacks in our area have made a mess of the mail. I have written, as always, absolutely every day, sometimes maybe not very much depending on what was happening. How could you think that I don't want to write to you, that would be a dreadful idea and unthinkable, as you are always in my heart. […] While I was going to get the wounded last evening, I saw the colonel who has lost a lot of weight. He told me:

"So, Durosoir, we will soon make a bit of music again." I replied that it would be with the greatest pleasure. [...]

I got a new pair of pants, a lovely pair for the artillery, all lined between the legs, made for horseback riding. I couldn't get any shoes—there were none. I have plenty of underwear, my pack is terribly heavy. All civilians have been evacuated from Cappy, a good idea. It was painful to see the women and children in the midst of the shelling. During these trying times, my thoughts turn inward and toward everything I've loved; it's often very difficult. [...]

2/5/1916.

I received last night your letter from February 2. [...] You share with me the *communiqués* of January 29 and 30. But you missed the one which talks about the town of Frise falling into the hands of the Germans. Fortunately, completely by chance, Caplet's battalion had not replaced the 25th as it was supposed to. The 25th was caught and decimated. Later I will be able to explain the reasons for this tragedy. For sure, the 129th cannot be held responsible for that failure. To the contrary, it came out of it in high esteem. Pourel's battalion stopped the *Boches* who were heading for Cappy and he fought with the bayonet. All that in the midst of dreadful shelling. [...]

There have been a great many errors made in our sector. In good conscience, we cannot be blamed for them. The high command kept saying that an attack where we were was impossible! The *Boches* decided to prove the opposite and, without the 129th and a few colonial companies who got themselves butchered, they would have gotten past. Those are the facts, and I am not telling you everything. Later I will explain in detail. I think that, at this time, the *Boches* are attacking out of desperation, hoping to gain an advantage they can use to open peace talks. They are certainly much mistaken and only manage to exhaust themselves more. [...]

Tuesday, February 8, 1916, noon.

I received this morning your letter from February 5. The *communiqués* have never said much, and the German capture of Frise has not been mentioned. They don't talk about the mistakes of those incompetents that we have as leaders! I find it extraordinary that, when it comes to any action with a bit of importance, the commanders are not up to the task. We give all those men enough money so they will do their duty! If they are incapable, whether by laziness or stupidity, they should be hanged! If they feared for their lives, they would get the job done willingly or by force. (It seems to me however that we should be smart enough to replace those who are good for nothing.). It is the ordinary men, the poor soldiers, who are sacrificed for the faults of their leaders. (I don't dare say betrayed, but these mistakes are repeated frequently enough that one is over-come by a terrible sadness in the face of all that is happening). When necessary, the sacrifice of human life, despite the horrible thought of it, is understandable. But for the repeated errors of the government to lead not only to the deaths of thousands of people but to a catastrophe from which we may never recover, that is something totally incomprehensible. A superior officer must be made to real-ize that a serious error on his part will be severely punished and that he will be taken to task for accepting a position which he was not going to be able to fill when he could have left it for someone with greater intelligence or more energy and courage. If there was iron discipline, many would give more thought and certainly do their job or let someone else fill their position. [...] The beginning of the war was terrible but I am truly fearful that the end will be atrocious. The Germans will do everything possible, use extraordinarily destructive offensive and defensive tactics, and especially hang on! Will we succeed? So many agoniz-ing questions! [...]

2/6/1916.

I received last night your letter from February 3. There is nothing new in our sector other than the daily bombing and the talk of an attack soon. An attack on our part, that is. You talk about the senior officers as though they were eagles. Alas, with all their superior intelligence, what mediocrity and out-of-date con-cepts. In the face of what is happening, the generals should have modernized their ideas a bit. Such a lot of effort and often, unfortunately, totally useless! One cannot remake himself, especially at 60 years of age, the average age of our supreme leaders. They continue on their hobbyhorse and the *poilu* pays with his life for the faults of those doddery old men. There is my unembellished conclu-sion after 18 months of war. [...]

When I left Ch... the bombing had mostly spared that little town; only a few shells had hit around there. In the past few days that has completely changed. Apparently, Ch... was hit with a lot of incendiary bombs and is in a piteous state. [...] As for pianos, there are none left in C... they are all in little pieces. [...] I've passed the cello to the mayor of Ch...; it was saved from destruction by my having borrowed it. The home of the people who loaned it to me is totally demolished and they were evacuated to Amiens.

Your income needs to be 5000 francs for you to have tax imposed. As of now, you haven't earned that much. [...] It is true that the question of money is becoming painful, at least for the middle classes who don't receive any state support. [...]

I received this morning your letter from Sunday February 6 and very much hope that today you have a fixed date for your departure. You talk of an offensive (on your part). I think it will be made with the fresh troops that replace you and not with your exhausted and decimated forces. If not, everything is lost and we have to assume that the leaders are looking for another failure accompanied by painful and useless sacrifices! Any sensible person knows that to launch an effective and useful offensive, the leaders should use troops that are fresh and ready and not soldiers weakened by two months in the swampy trenches and worn down by fatigue and the superhuman effort they have just made! [...]

2/7/1916.

I received yesterday your letter of February 4. The musicians right now are carrying the wounded, those from our regiment and those of the other regiments involved in the attacks in our sector, so there is a good deal of work. I spent most of the night carrying the stretcher and am exhausted. That's why I'm writing less; I'm going to rest. We will likely be moving again tonight. [...] You can well imagine how happy I was to get back to my provisions; in moments like this it is not possible to pay attention to cooking. [...]

2/8/1916.

I received yesterday your letter of February 5; I can't write much more. We marched all night to transport the wounded; then, having been relieved, we set off at 3:30 a.m. and arrived about 9 a.m. at our first stopping point. I think we are going to rest for 48 hours then set off for Ailly-sur-Noye or Chaussoy, where we were three months ago. Excuse me for not writing more but I am very tired. [...]

2/10/1916.

I received yesterday your letter of February 7. I could not write yesterday; right after lunch the colonel asked for us and we talked for more than 2 hours. After that I had to go rehearse with Caplet and Lemoine the program we wanted to play that very evening, despite having also played the night before. All that made the afternoon pass very quickly and the time for mail collection was long past when I had a free minute. I am quite badly situated here but fortunately we are supposed to leave for our rest tomorrow or the next day at the latest. [...]

If I go to the United States after the war, I will not want a manager. I will just go there myself with good recommendations and, if necessary, stay for two or three years. There is a lot of money to be earned. I still am not able to write very much as I am pestered on all sides. But I do have the advantage; I am "Monsieur Durosoir," and in the music regiment they leave me alone and give me complete independence. [...]

2/11/1916.

I received yesterday your letter from February 8. Our weather right now is abominable. It is cold and rainy. And more, we are very badly housed. While we await to be relieved, we are in a little village behind C.... piled one on the other. This will not last long; any time now we are to be taken to the rear. Everyone is worn out. Now that the fever of battle has abated, we are left with an over-whelming fatigue. [...] You overlooked the *communiqué* that spoke of the loss of Frise. I read it in *Le Petit Parisien*. I'm going to explain a bit what happened.

We had a battalion in Frise, another near Dampierre, and between them, to give the soldiers some rest, there was a battalion of territorials. I don't want to tell you their number, but it was mostly made up of guys from the Midi. The *Boches*, who certainly knew what to expect, attacked their sector. The pigs, instead of resisting even a bit, either fled as fast as possible leaving behind their arms or surrendered. The result was that our regiment was cut in two. Frise is at the bottom of a steep cliff with the canal on the other side. Thanks to the cow-ardice of the territorials, it took the *Boches* no time at all to get to the top of the cliff, behind our comrades, who were trapped like rats; there was nothing they could do. But that's not all: the *Boches*, having tasted victory, turned to the left, as they had done to the right. They had already encircled the 1st battalion and the colonel. That's where the Pourel battalion, having raced from Chuignes, threw itself at the *Boches*. The bayonet mêlée was terrible but we got the best of them, in the sense that the *Boches* didn't capture the 1st battalion. But, alas, they took several lines of trenches. Naturally, a number of other regiments arrived, but not until the next day. I know that, at this time, everything has been taken back except Frise. It seems that Mangin took up a rifle and led his men in the attack of the trenches. They just posted a derogatory report against the swines who ran away and caused all the trouble. What a profusion of projectiles! The colonel estimates that the *Boches* launched 100,000 shells in the first two days. We paid them back with interest by seizing more than 400 cannons, many of them high caliber.

The house where I was staying, in Cappy, was razed by a shell. My violin and Dumant's were buried (he had one sent three weeks ago). We dug them out. Dumant's violin is in pieces. Mine, with the greatest of good fortune, has no damage at all. What luck! I lost my *livret militaire* in the process,[173] along with

---

[173] The *livret militaire* is an identification document carried by all persons in military service. It documents the entire military career of the individual.

the envelope with the postcards of Port Lazo and your portrait. They were on a table, all that just disappeared in smoke and rubble. All my things are intact: backpack, *musette*,[174] etc. I had just gone out not five minutes earlier, called by the doctor to take command of three teams of stretcher bearers. It's just fate! I didn't want to tell you this right away, for fear of torturing you. Now that we have been relieved, it doesn't matter. I am certainly lucky. [...]

February 12, 1916, 6:30 p.m.

I received today at 4:30 your letter from Friday February 11. [...] That letter came very quickly: the postmark is the train station at Amiens. [...] Your adventure seems a bit like the one in Courcy in May 1915. One should never group together men from the Midi. Since they always behave so badly, they should be mixed in small numbers with other soldiers to avoid possible catastrophes. The Germans, with their well-organized spy service, knew exactly what they were doing and attacked the part of the sector occupied by a territorial battalion made up mostly of men from the Midi. [...]. It is dreadful to think that the defection of those no-goods could have let the Germans pass through the front. [...]

2/12/1916.

I received yesterday your letter from February 9 and today, much faster than usual, your letter from the 10th. [...] I am probably going to buy a wonderful raincoat from an Englishman. When they get drunk, which happens often, they charge 5 or 10 francs for brand new raincoats, sturdy and lightweight which certainly cost about a hundred francs in Paris. I will do what my buddies do and take advantage of the situation. [...] Truly, the length of this war, its continuation under such abnormal conditions, is terrible and weighs on us. The suffering is worse this winter. There is no doubt that our bodies are less strong and we are overwhelmed with fatigue. There is nothing else to do but pick ourselves up and take our courage in both hands. If we don't leave tomorrow, I will play in the church, first at the Burial Mass for a captain [...] and then at the High Mass. [...] The church of Cerisy-Gailly where we are, is quite lovely and the harmonium not bad. [...]

2/13/1916.

Today I'm writing at my usual time, that is about 1:30. I've not yet received the mail. On the other hand, yesterday I received the package with the two little bottles of rum. [...] The weather is cold, damp, foggy; we are going through the

---

[174] Purse-like bags worn over the shoulder, used to carry essentials.

worse part of winter. [...] I keep thinking how lucky I was with my instrument, as it wasn't damaged at all. The one Dumant had received which, fortunately, was worth only 100 francs, is in dreadful condition. [...]

2/14/1916.

I received yesterday your letter of February 11. We are still in the little area about 10 kilometers behind C. awaiting our departure for the rear. [...] The weather isn't really very cold, but the rain and the mud it creates make it disagreeable. We hear complaining all around as boredom is rampant. Personally, I have little to complain about. [...] I am somewhat better lodged than my comrades, obviously on straw but with heat, in a room, while they are lodged in barns or attics open to the elements which in this season is unpleasant. The food in the mess is always good, that's why at this time there is no reason for you to spend money to send me packages. [...]

2/17/1916.

I couldn't write yesterday nor the day before, the 15th. We left our camp and, after walking all day long, arrived in a little area five kilometers from Villers. We were soaked to the bones as we walked in the midst of a hailstorm. Yesterday I moved again to a neighboring area to join Caplet and Lemoine's battalion, so I am now with them. That took all day long. Today we are going to find Niverd who is with the postal station. We will ask him to join our rehearsals, as we think we will be here for two weeks. It is just a 10-kilometer round trip for him by bicycle. I'm going to mail this letter in Villers, with a stamp, and hope it will arrive more quickly. [...]

Saturday, February 19, 1916, noon.

I didn't receive a letter this morning telling me about your new place. [...] Will the quartet be able to work? [...] Take advantage of this time to get a picture of the quartet (or trio, if Niverd cannot be there), and work on getting my ring and see Chauvel about your medallion. [...] I will not write tomorrow morning as usual. I may write in the evening when I get back from the Bastien's. I already told you that Bastien was on leave starting last Friday and that I was invited for lunch with them on Sunday, February 20. [...] You are forewarned so you will not worry. [...]

I will send you some postcards of Port Lazo occasionally, so you can see the place you left two years ago on August 3. Yes, time is passing. [...] I will be 60 years old on March 2, that's soon. But nothing is important as long as you come back safe and sound.

2/19/1916.

[…] Finally, today I am seated at a good table and free to write a long letter. For the past week, with the constant changes and all the playing I managed to do, I could only barely write, just brief letters. I will back up a bit and answer your letters since the 12th. When we left C…, we headed to Cérisy-Gailly where we were only supposed to stay for 48 hours. Truthfully, the *Boche* attacks were so vicious that, as reserves for urgent situations, we stayed there 6 days. […] The order to depart arrived suddenly very late the night before last and we traveled all the next day. We, that is Pourel's battalion, are in Dreuil, six kilometers from Amiens. […] To reach the town we are in now (in the suburbs of Amiens), we had to cross that city. What an undertaking. It's the first time we have been that close to a big city. We can't go there without special permission and the roads are guarded. […]

Always, always we are moving on: this bohemian life is upsetting. Thanks to the kindness of Commander Pourel, the move for me and Caplet was quite easy. Dreuil is 28 kilometers from where we were. A vehicle took us to Villers where we got a train to Amiens, then a tramway. From there we had to go only 3 kilometers to reach Dreuil. […] The other day in Villers, Lieutenant Laine told me that General Mangin was going to have us come. We have to think, then, that if our time here will be fairly long, the division will ask for us and we will go to Saleux. […] No need to tell you, with all this going on, that I am not doing much composition. I am in the chateau with the orderlies. No one has a bed; this area is quite small and is filled with a great many troops. Many officers are sleeping on straw. We are in a large, closed room with good fresh straw, we are fine and warm. I just received a note sending me, Caplet, and Lemoine to the division headquarters. So, tomorrow another departure, for Saleux. […]

2/21/1916.

I had to interrupt my last letter. I was saying that we were affected to the division until further orders. The colonel was upset, and Commander Pourel is not at all happy, but they have to make do with what they don't like. And we will go once a week to play for Commander Pourel, and once for the colonel. […] Saleux, where we are, is a little city of 1500 inhabitants (mostly workers), an area where they make velvet. Magne, from the 36th, is also *en subsistance* at the division. We will make our meals together. We are *au prêt franc* which means that in place of food we receive an indemnity of 1,70 which added to our daily pay of 25 centimes makes 1,95 a day. Thus, with Caplet, Lemoine, Magne and me, we have daily income (salary and indemnity) of 10,40 francs, which is not bad. We found a good place to eat in the home of a vegetable merchant who has a large dining room where we rehearse. She will cook for us and, in exchange, we feed her. We all found nearby rooms with good beds, a true joy. I am staying with a weaver who works at home, good people who have a son in the army (class of 1914) and two little girls of 10 and 13. [...] Last night the *Boches* bombed Amiens with Zeppelins or airplanes, it's not clear, but there are wounded and dead. We watched the cannons firing on those bastards who come to kill women and children. [...]

2/22/1916.

Because of the move, I've not yet received your letters, but I hope you have received mine; to be sure they get to you, I've put stamps on them. [...] I slept last night on a wonderful feather bed. What a great feeling to take my clothes off! I am with really good people, M. and Mme Jeron. They have a son of the class of 1914 who is in Salonica and was at the Dardanelles. They treat me like one of their own. [...] Niverd is better, but he still has swollen fingers, so we have thought about Maréchal, the cellist who is in the 274th. That regiment is now part of our division so it is simple. Lieutenant Laine just wrote a note putting him *en subsistance* to the division, like us. That way we will be able to make a lot of music easily. Perhaps, if Maréchal agrees, he could be transferred to the 129th which would solve the problem for good. [...] So, dear Maman, you can see that we are definitely here and hoping this lasts for a long time. We are completely free, our own masters. We've agreed with Lieutenant Laine that we will go to the colonel's and to Commander Pourel's so they can hear us. We will be transported by automobile, which will be practical and comfortable. [...]

2/23/1916.

[...] The weather is really awful; it snows from time to time. I am very fortunate, in this miserable weather, to be well lodged and sheltered. [...] We are playing today at 5:00, for General Mangin. An English general, unknown to us but who commands the neighboring sector, will be there. He will obviously come with all his staff. That may be for us the dawn of a more extended relationship. [...] Maréchal, who is a good friend of Niverd, arrives today. We will probably start work immediately on the Grieg Quartet and Beethoven's 10th.[175] I hope that within a few days they will both be ready. [...]

2/24/1916.

I received last evening your letters from February 18 and 19. I'm going to answer some of your questions. I am still part of the music regiment, my pay and clothes come from them. But in reality, I do very little with them, and never take part in their performances. It is unbelievable, I am completely independ-

---

[175] Edvard Grieg (1843-1907), String quartet in G minor, Op. 27; Beethoven, String quartet Number 10 in E-flat major, Op. 74.

ent and no one thinks about me. [...] Today we are going to have a picture of the quartet taken, with the young Maréchal (23 years old) as cellist. He arrived yesterday from the 274th where he is the chief doctor's cyclist. Like us, he is *en subsistance* here and very happy to make music; based on what he says, he was less well off in his regiment. We are very fortunate. [...]

2/25/1916.

I received last night your letter from the 22. I am replying immediately to what you say about my raincoat. This piece of clothing which, given the weather, I am glad to have bought, is a cape like the one I have at home. It's quite large so my violin is well protected under it. It buttons almost to the bottom and has two slits on the sides for arm holes. It is very comfortable and practical and not heavy. The inside is rubberized; the outside is a water-repellent, khaki-colored fabric. For 15 francs it was a terrific buy.

It's been snowing nonstop for 24 hours; this is very unfortunate weather given the floods and the current state of the Seine. [...] Maybe this weather will stop the *Boche* attack on Verdun? The cannon fire has also been non-stop here for the last 24 hours. Maybe they are trying to create a diversion that will keep us here. This German offensive in the middle of the winter must be costing them dearly. They are almost finished, that is evident, and are hoping to gain an advantage to be able to end the war on their terms. It's a trap, I think. They will lose everything they are hoping for and will not pierce through our lines. [...]

I'm not worried about my *livret militaire*. I declared the loss with the sergeant major of the section. I am just like many others who have lost theirs; it's not very important. Our rest at the division should be quite long; however, activity elsewhere can always shorten it. [...] We will take advantage of this wonderful moment. Today we will go to General Mangin's where we will again play Schumann (it has been requested).[176] I am playing the Franck Sonata with Magne, Wisniewski's *Déluge* and *Les Airs Russes*. Maréchal, who has been with us for two days, will play the Beethoven Sonata. He has a lovely sound but thinner than Niverd; he has less experience but his technique is much more advanced; Niverd has not practiced at all for some time. We may be able to have Maréchal transferred to the 129th. We are going to try. I think we will go play for Colonel Valzi on Monday. [...] Since yesterday, we are rehearsing in a salon with a very good piano; this is in a cotton thread factory, at the home of the manager (a lovely man who has put himself totally at our disposition). We are much better off here than at the home of the vegetable merchant and much less bothered. What is more, we have a piano. We will go to the colonel's or to Lieutenant Valzi, certainly by auto. [...]

---

[176] Schumann, String quartet in A minor.

I didn't receive any news this morning. [...] The German attack in the Meuse, with the objective of taking Verdun, must have required transporting a great number of wounded in all directions and the line in the north, as the others, must be feeling the effects. That is not counting the probably constant movement of munitions, cannons, and men. I'm sure you are reading the newspapers and know what is happening. I am constantly afraid that the Germans will break through the front somewhere. The Russians need to go on the offensive to relieve us a bit and oblige the Germans to pull back some men from our front. [...]

Great quantities of snow have fallen since this morning, a fine, light snow that is sticking. [...] We have to fear flooding. The Seine is very high and with the melting snow, as it is probably snowing everywhere, we can expect that new scourge! That's all we needed to add to our disasters. [...]

2/26/1916.

I received yesterday your letter of February 23. [...] Because of the snow, my good Mme Jeron every day coats my shoes in pig fat, which makes them soft and waterproof. [...]

From 3:30 this afternoon until 6:30, we are rehearsing Grieg. Then supper and we go back to work until 11:00. You can see, we are not wasting our time. [...]

2/28/1916.

Do not worry, dear Maman, we were put on alert for a departure to Verdun but then the counter order arrived. We departed anyway, everyone on foot. [...] We are in Loeuilly and leaving for Franscatel without knowing where we are headed. [...]

2/29/1916.

I am going to try to tell you a bit about some of the adventures of these past days. Last Saturday, while we were in Saleux, there was a rumor in the afternoon that the division would be leaving for the Meuse. The rumor was confirmed by the division and our regiment had to go to Saleux to leave at 6 p.m. Sunday. We had no other option. No need to say that no one was happy, especially to be taken directly into battle at Verdun. But there was nothing to be done. Then, at 3 a.m. we received a counter order. Sunday morning we received an order to set out at noon for Loeuilly, about 12 kilometers away. Ever since, we've been on the road. On Sunday, Lieutenant Laine told us: "we do not know where we are going, so I prefer to keep you *en subsistance* with the division for now rather than sending you back to your regiments; I cannot take charge of transporting your boxes and instruments, figure out something for that yourselves. Later we'll settle your expenses." And he added: "I hope you prefer this solution to returning to your regiments."

Truly, there is no possible comparison. We have met units on the move. It is dreadful, in this weather, to see those poor souls walk 20 to 25 kilometers in the snow or frozen mud. What is worse, the billets are not ready and they sleep wherever they can. The 129th is wandering around us but we don't know where it is; we are still following the division which is usually alone in a small town with the division ambulances and the mail service.

So, in Saleux, we rented a car that took us to Loeuilly where we had the good fortune to find a bed and to have dinner with some good people, whom we obviously paid. On Monday morning we set off for Francastel in a different vehicle, which we had great difficulty finding, where we ate and slept; that was a good distance away (28 kilometers).

We are now in the Oise rather than the Somme. We had supper with a farm wife who gave us an empty room to sleep in; we had as much straw as we wanted and were very well off. We left early this morning to take the train at 6:30 for Noyers-les-Martin, with all our affairs. We checked everything (not my violin, of course) at the station and walked to Montreuil-sur-Brèche where I am now and where the division is located. We are eating at the home of a farm wife and have lots of eggs. [...]

Unfortunately, this is not the end; we leave again tomorrow. The orders haven't yet arrived so I can't tell you where we will be going. All this vagabonding is less fun in this weather than it might be in a different season. We spend the time laughing as much as possible. [...]

Pierrot has started work on your ring; with everything that is going, all the changes, he must not be able to work on it very often. He has the medal in silver of the crying child; as soon as I see him, I will ask him to send it to you. [...]

Maréchal is a young man, 23 years old, straightforward and kind and a good musician; he has a lovely sound and fine technique. He will certainly play more than Niverd who had no time to practice. [...] He has no objection to transferring to the 129th. [...] He doesn't have a real cello. He had one made to measure: neck, fingerboard, and bridge. The result is rough, but what is amazing—the instrument has a lovely, intense sound, quite strange. Obviously, it has not the value of a real cello but it is far from being a terrible instrument.[177] [...] Cunault

---

[177] Maréchal's cello is on display at the Musée de la Musique in Paris. Two territorial soldiers, who had been carpenters before the war, made it from pieces of a German ammunition box and christened it the *"Poilu."* The carpenters were both killed in the Somme a few months after finishing it. Durosoir, *Deux Musiciens,* 250.

should be interested to see Maréchal's instrument. He is hoping to bring it back
to Paris where he will have some success if he plays it a few times in public. […]

I think right now that the attack on Verdun is a total failure, and in any case,
the *Boches* will not take Verdun. […]

Saturday, March 4, 1916.

Last night, I received your two letters, from Wednesday March 1 and Thursday March 2. […] I think Maréchal must be rather pleased with his new position.
What do Lemoine "the thinker" and Caplet "the comedian" have to say? You
tell me that Caplet has a good sense of humor; he should write his memoirs.
When you met him in Chaussoy, little did he dream that he would be the violist in a quartet or a quintet; that he would become one of the violins not of the
king, because there aren't any left in France, but one of the general's violins.
They should call you the "general's violins," or the "general's musicians" as
there is also a pianist. […]

3/1/1916.

I've not received the mail yet today. We moved, as planned, very early this
morning, 5:00 a.m. The quintet took a car to the train station at Noyers where
we took the baggage train. Right now, we are in a little area called Saint-Rémy-
en-l'Eau on the line to Paris. But it's just the same story, we leave again tomorrow.
We wander like bohemians. […]

3/2/1916.

[…] I leave today again with the other members of the quintet. […] We have
travel orders for 5 so it costs nothing. […] Last night we played from 7 to 8 at
the general's lodgings in a chateau, a magnificent property belonging to the
Marquis de Capellis. The general had invited the marquise and her 4 daughters.
In a fabulous room decorated with beautiful Beauvais tapestries, we played the
Adagio and *Finale* of Schumann's 1st Quartet, I played the Bach *Air on a G String*
accompanied by the three other instruments,[178] Magne played a Chopin prelude,[179] Maréchal *Le Cygne* by Saint-Saëns, and I the Fauré *Berceuse*, a lovely light,
impromptu program. […] Mangin was pleased. […]

3/4/1916.

We arrived between 2 and 3 a.m. at Gournay-sur-Aronde. I couldn't write
yesterday as my friends and I spent the day looking for lodgings and a place to

[178] Orchestral Suite in D major, BWV 1068.
[179] Frédéric Chopin (1810-1849).

eat. It was at first difficult but I managed [...] to find a very pretty room, very comfortable, at the home of the postmistress, and an excellent place to eat at the home of a Parisian clothing merchant. We expect to be here for a while so we are getting down to serious work. [...]

3/5/1916.

I received yesterday your letter from March 2. [...] You ask me what Caplet did to deserve the *Croix de Guerre*.[180] My God, it's very simple: he is friends with his doctor for whom he has played music and he asked him if he couldn't get it for him. The doctor, feeling obliged to C... could not really refuse; he used the attack of the 28ᵗʰ for the citation. C... just moved from one battery to another with his kit to give first aid to the wounded. Of course, there was a lot of bombing but it was the same for everyone; we too had to go get the wounded and do everything needed to help all the regiment's services. You can't use the excuse that there are bombs falling to let those in the front lines die of hunger or run out of ammunition; that's simply our duty. [...] The *Croix de Guerre*, which should be awarded only in certain rare cases, has been awarded to men who have never seen combat and sometimes to cowards who hid at the moment of danger. It's lost all its value; one sees it often on the chests of ass lickers. [...]

Here at the division they call us "the general's musicians." [...] Our Grieg Quartet is finally polished; it is quite difficult. [...] We work all afternoon and evening at the home of the parish priest who has very obligingly given us his dining room for our rehearsals. Without his help, we would have had great difficulty finding a place to eat and some rooms. Thanks to him, we have all we could wish for, so today we will play a little Mass for him. [...]

Lemoine is still our chief cook and he does it very well. We are able to eat quite acceptably. In all these areas we find butchers, bakers, eggs, milk, and here in Gournay there is a large watercress shop and we can eat as much as we want, which is wonderful. I receive 2,15 francs a day. Our daily expenses are about 3,50 francs a day so that is obviously not enough. We are 5, so that makes about 17 F. Food is fairly expensive: yesterday we bought beans at 1,10/pound, leeks 1,10/pound, a leg of lamb 1,80/pound (not expensive). We are much better nourished than in the regiment and the independence we enjoy is priceless. [...]

3/6/1916.

I received last night your letter from March 3. [...] We played yesterday at 5 p.m. for the general. He is in a charming chateau. On the other hand, the chatelaine is fearfully ugly and laughingly stupid. She has a troop of daughters, from

---

[180] A military decoration created in 1915, given to individuals or units who distinguish themselves with heroic acts.

15 to 23 years old, who share all the mother's qualities; they cackled like turkeys. We could have died laughing and had great difficulty staying serious, especially Maréchal, who is young. [...] We all had the giggles, from the general on down to the lowest of his assistants. We will not bother to go again to this honorable lady's chateau. There is a governess who is also a piece of work; she wanted us to use the servants' stairs and the discussion between her and Caplet took on heroically comical proportions. It would take 20 pages to describe the many events of yesterday. At any rate, Maréchal, Caplet and I played Beethoven's 1st String Trio,[181] [...] then I played the Fauré *Berceuse*, Magne the Andante from the "Appassionata"[182] and we closed with the Grieg Quartet which lasts three quarters of an hour. The effect was tremendous; if passes were not suspended right now, the general would have given us 24 hours to go to Paris. [...]

3/7/1916.

I received last evening your letter from March 4. [...] I believe that, unless there are unexpected developments, we will be here a fairly long time. Our division is charged with earth-moving; we will stay with the division as long as that is what they are doing. [...]

Maréchal is delighted to be making music and to have escaped from a difficult situation. As for Caplet and Lemoine, they are, like me, satisfied and not complaining, ready to laugh at the quirks and absurdities of the people around us. There is much to amuse us in the life we are leading; we are surrounded by human comedy. [...]

My dear *minou*, you have turned another page, that of your 60 years. I only barely thought about it, I admit, in the midst of all this moving. [...]

Friday, March 10, 1916.

[...] I never thanked you for the two pretty little violets and the primroses, which bloomed through the snow and you thought to pick for me! These modest little flowers gave me extreme pleasure: I found them in one of your letters that came yesterday. They are to celebrate my birthday which you had forgotten in the course of the difficulties of all your rapid changes of position. Alas, I am getting older and would like to be even older if that meant all these calamities were over. [...]

---

[181] Beethoven, String trio in E-flat major, Op. 3.
[182] Beethoven, Piano Sonata No. 23, Op. 57.

3/9/1916.

I received last night your letter of March 6. I will answer your questions: yes, my room at the postmistress's house costs me nothing. Lieutenant Laine gave us all housing tickets. [...] My room is lovely and opens out to the south. And the postmistress is very nice, she would bend over backwards to please me. She is from Lassigny, an area that has been severely bombed, and has taken in her parents. As for the milliner, she is a person of a certain age, and my goodness, although not as good a cook as the person in Saleux, who was a real chef, she does very well. In Saleux we ate more sweet things. We had but to ask: crêpes, beignets, puddings, anything, it was a continuous array of delicacies. Here the menu is simpler. [...]

Monday, March 13, 1916, 3:00 p.m.

I received this morning your letter from Friday, March 10. The voluminous correspondence that I have from you is perhaps not due to the pleasure you find in telling me what you are doing, what is happening to you, etc. (since I have to pull the words one by one out of you) but to the duty you recognize has to be done daily in order to give me the peace I need. I have no one else but you in this world, and have done so much for you, rightly or wrongly (you can criticize me severely), and live alone between these four walls, it is natural that I wait impatiently not for a sorry little card with four lines. I say that because of these two cards I received one after the other. They prompted me to say that, with my robust appetite, I could devour four pages. I recognize that you don't always have time to write much depending on circumstances, so you need the cards for those times. [...]

3/13/1916.

I received last night your letter of March 10. [...] In the morning I go to our *popote* very nearby, where I eat some good chocolate. Lunch and dinner are usually meat, vegetable, cheese, jam or dessert. From 5 to 7 the general offers us tea, chocolate, or port with cookies. Yesterday, Sunday, we played for him the Leclair Sonata for violin and cello; it is wonderful.[183] [...] Maréchal played the Boëllmann Sonata,[184] I played the Bach *Chaconne*, and we ended with the Schumann 1st. [...]

---

[183] Jean-Marie Leclair (1697-1764), Violin Sonata in D major, Op. 9, No. 3.
[184] Léon Boëllman (1862-1897), Sonata for cello and piano in A minor, Op. 40.

3/14/1916.

I received yesterday your letter of March 11. [...] We played last night for the colonel, in a village 11 kilometers away from here. We traveled in a carriage that belongs to a telephone operator at the division. We had an excellent horse and arrived in an hour and a half. [...] They were, I have to say, not at all generous; they gave us a bad cup of tea. When you realize that the colonel earns 1000 francs a month and the group of officers who eat with him together earn at least 4000 francs a month, I can't help but find them unusually stingy. [...]

3/15/1916.

I received last night your letter of March 12. [...] Verdun is still the *Boche* goal and so much the better. To swallow such a large parcel, assuming that they manage to take it, they will have to sacrifice at least 600,000 men. At this time, the *Boche* losses are more than 200,000 and they have not been able to take the third defensive line. One has to wonder what they will have left to oppose a Russian offensive in a few months. The Russians will put 3 or 4 million men in uniform and then what will the Germans do? That is what makes us all believe that this is the last year of the war. [...]

3/16/1916.

I received yesterday your letter of March 13. If I didn't take true pleasure in writing you about four pages every day and giving you so many details, you can be sure I would not do it. I could name many who, without being bad sons or bad husbands, write at most two or three times a week. [...]

The big news in the division is that General Mangin just had a son (what a guy!) and he's asked for leave for 3 days. I don't yet know whether he got it. If so, he should have left last night. We'll find out today: if he's not here, we won't have a concert. [...]

Saturday, March 18, 1916, 1:00 p.m.

I received this morning your letter of March 16 in which you announce the sensational news, at least for General Mangin, the birth of a son! It is important that, with the thousands lost, new lives begin. Poor France needs children. One cannot but be frightened at the thought of the overall lack of men at the end of this war: no more male arms to work the ground, no workers or artisans to engage in their crafts or work in factories! How many teachers, in the arts and the sciences, will have disappeared from this earth, no longer able to form young people. All that is very sad. For now, all we can do is hang on, repel the beast of prey who, no matter what, seems ready to devour us. It is our annihilation that he wants and has been preparing for 40 years. So many more human lives will be sacrificed. The ground of France is flooded with the blood of its children and also that of those wolves and tigers corrupted by carnage. I can't help but think of the horrible battles taking place day and night; some fight to save their country, others to subjugate and reduce us to nothing. The person who gets out of this horrendous turmoil will be able to give thanks to God. Let us, therefore, hope that 1916 will see the end of this catastrophe. […]

3/17/1916.

I received yesterday your letter from March 14 and the money order for 150 francs sent the 15th. […] General Mangin does not seem about to invite the general of our Army corps. Maybe he is afraid that, if someone higher up heard us, they would do what he did, that is, make off with us. It is true that we are now a true ensemble, there cannot be many others on the front. If it was known, we might not stay long with General Mangin. […]

Tuesday, March 21, 1916, 4 p.m.

[…] My new cleaning lady is a woman who has six children, 3 girls and 3 boys. The three girls are married, the oldest son in 34, the next is 16 and the youngest is 13. She is very serious and has cleaned houses for more than 20 years: I need to add that she works 4 hours here, 3 hours there because she always wants to have lunch at home. Her two younger boys take their meals with her. She doesn't want them eating elsewhere; she thinks the food in restaurants is expensive and not very healthy. She does her cooking in the evening and has only to reheat it at noon. This arrangement is very hard on her, but she thinks that to properly raise her children, she needs to have them home, and she is right. She is very hard-working but, in ordinary times, this would not work for me. I need someone all day long. For now, it is an arrangement that I have to make do with and it is really adequate. […]

I still have some coal in the cellar, especially little *noisettes*.[185] I didn't light my kitchen stove very often so I didn't use very much. Anthracite is selling for 136 francs per 1000 kilos; that's what Mme Bastien told me when she came to see me. […] I will need to arrange to buy some for next winter; I expect the price will go up even more. I'll see about that when I receive some money in April. […]

---

[185] Hazelnut-sized bits of leftover coal.

3/18/1916.

I received last night your letter of March 15. [...] Yesterday afternoon, we worked on the Dupont Quintet,[186] mostly on the last part which is very difficult. This famous quintet is starting to make musical sense and in two or three days we will have perfected it. Caplet finally wrote to order the Debussy Quartet;[187] he expects it to arrive Monday or Tuesday at the latest. [...]

Last evening we worked on the Beethoven 7th,[188] but it is not progressing as well as the Dupont. It is difficult in a different way, always in the upper register with tricky runs, nearly constant pianissimo nuances with sudden contrasts and much calm. This quartet requires total mastery on the part of the player; it shows us all how much we have lost in terms of precision in the fast passages.

My technique is a mess. It is only now, because we are playing more, that I notice it. I definitely need to work a lot on it: precision in jumps, agility, and intonation. I will need several months of slow, serious work. What I play seems to be fine if one doesn't listen too closely. For now, during this war, it doesn't bother me; in regular times I would be ashamed to play this way. [...]

3/19/1916.

I received yesterday your two letters from the 16th and today the one from the 17th. [...] We learned yesterday morning that Colonel Viennot, our brigade general, who is in charge of the division while Mangin is on leave, wanted to hear us that very evening. Magne and Maréchal left at 11 a.m. in a car which, with the driver, only holds 3 people. The auto came back to get us and we were at the colonel's by 8:30 p.m. Magne left early because he wanted to see the piano, which is an old one—an Ignaz Pleyel, very lovely despite its age. He had it tuned in the afternoon by a professional tuner from the music regiment. [...] Colonel Viennot received us very well: he had invited the colonel and commander of a regiment of *Zouaves* who are in the sector. Those men were delighted. When we arrived, we were immediately treated to coffee and Bénédictine, and during the evening Moët and Chandon champagne was offered several times. [...] The auto that took us there could not take us back, so we returned in a vehicle pulled by a horse sent by the division. Result: we arrived back at 3 a.m. It was Sunday but you can well understand that we did not play for Mass that morning [...]

Do not put place names in your letters; they could be opened and that would cause me problems. It is always forbidden to say where we are, but few people follow that rule to the letter. However, occasionally someone gets caught. It is better to be careful. [...]

---

[186] Gabriel Dupont (1878-1914), *Poème* for Piano Quintet in C Minor.
[187] Claude Debussy (1862-1918), String quartet in G minor, L. 91, Op. 10.
[188] Beethoven, String quartet, Op. 59, No. 1.

3/20/1916.

I have very little to add this morning, only that Lieutenant Laine killed two foxes in the park at the chateau and he is giving us part of the rear of one of them. Prepared like jugged hare, one might mistake it for the real thing. The taste is a bit stronger but, when it is a young fox, as in this case, only slightly. [...]

3/21/1916.

I didn't yet receive a letter today; I hope you are well. [...] I did however receive 3 packages. [...] At night it is freezing cold, we have had 7 or 8 degrees below zero, it's a harsh reminder of winter which we are no longer used to. Fortunately, the days are nicer, even quite hot, which means we are very cold at night and hot during the day. We already hear the birds singing in the woods, the blackbird in the morning and the nightingale at night. Spring will be here soon, today according to the calendar, not the temperature, and already the trees have little green shoots everywhere. After having suffered through the cold in the trenches, the heat will also be hard. We will be dreadfully thirsty. There is still no water and no one thinks about giving us any. Things are still quiet; however last night, about 6 p.m., there was quite a violent artillery duel. But we are so used to this type of show that we don't worry a bit about it; it would have to fall on top of us for us to pay any attention.

Thursday, March 23, 1916, 10:00 a.m.

I received this morning your letter from March 21. [...] I have to light my lamp today: the weather is very gray, and I can't see anything as I scratch out these words. It's a bit chilly. [...] I am bound to live very economically; I don't want to say: "I need money," but, in fact, "I need money." [...]

3/22/1916.

I received yesterday your two letters from March 19. I expect you will have a visit from M. Guyot about the terms for October and January for the Foyer du Soldat. That establishment is not at all like businesses affected by the war. None of the owners have been mobilized and, what is more, it serves a military purpose. We have been very generous with them, first by skipping a term, then reducing by 10 percent the rent increase. I do not see why those gentlemen should not pay the two terms already passed. You should go see M. Guyot about that, in the course of the month of April. You can explain that, since this year they are not paying rent, you are obviously free to rent the space and they would have to move out next January. [...]

Caplet returned from Amiens; he brought with him the Debussy Quartet which we read through this evening. It is not as hard as the Beethoven 7th, although Caplet declares the subtleties not easy to grasp. He exaggerates everything that relates to Debussy. For sure, like everything else, the quartet requires much work, but there is no comparison; normal instrumentalists will play Debussy if they are good. For the 7th, one can fall on his face; if the instrumentalists are not outstanding, it's pretty awful. We are the proof; we've had 5 rehearsals and it seems worse than at the beginning. We've even decided to perfect the Debussy before the Beethoven. That will give it a rest and it has to be better when we come back to it. You know the 7th; it is unusual. I had never heard it.. I think it's the most difficult of all. We were brave to take on that piece which delights in showing all our faults.

Magne comes back Thursday evening; we have a concert on Friday. We will play the C major Mozart,[189] and Sunday we will present the Dupont. To get the Dupont into shape quickly, we had three rehearsals without piano; we get the notes, rhythms, intonations all set. It's harder than the Debussy in terms of notes. It is less subtle, much more percussive. [...]

3/23/1916.

I received yesterday your letters from March 20 and 21. I got back last night very late because we were at the colonel's place. [...] There we made some important connections. We dined with Adjutant Mans and his liaison and, my goodness, we dined very well: soup, saucisson, steak, beans, salad, jam, cheese and cakes, white and red wine, coffee, cigars, all of the best quality. As you see, these gentlemen take care of themselves very nicely and take very good care of us. The adjutant saw to it that I got a pair of shoes. So now I have a lovely pair in soft leather with laces. I think I will get a lot of use out of them and be able to save my own shoes. Lemoine got a pair also. Caplet asked for a pair of pants but they didn't have his size. All those men are bored stiff (at 100 francs an hour)! [...]

You talk about buying things; I never buy anything. No, actually I bought some soap three days ago for 0,60 francs, and it's not bad soap. You might send me a package with soap, but it would cost 27 sous to send it. Either you spend money, or I do, it's all the same as our money comes from the same source. [...] When I ask for it, you can send a package using the free transport and then you could send some soap. [...]

At first, the Debussy did not seem difficult; it moves along quite easily. From the point of view of the instrument, it is obvious he is not a violinist. The writing is awkward. It's odd how, when the composer doesn't know the instrument,

---

[189] Mozart composed three quartets in C major: K157, K170, K 465.

the double stops are badly written, awkwardly placed and produce little or no resonance.

Caplet is, essentially, a strange fellow, very nice but with his own ideas. When you rub him the wrong way, he easily becomes brusque. With that character and disposition, he seems to be on bad terms with all the contemporary composers. That's why he never orders any of their music. Actually, he seems not to want to buy anything; in that case I can understand better, but I'm not going to be the one to buy the music. And darn it all, our audience is not generous; they never think of paying us anything at all. [...]

3/24/1916.

I received yesterday your letter of March 21. [...] Last night we worked on Debussy's Quartet; it's not difficult, just a little bit in the last section. Nothing compared with the 7th which is one long series of daredevil passages. Debussy's Quartet is not bad but as an enduring masterpiece, one that touches the emotions of the listener, as Caplet would have you believe, it falls short. Caplet is very close to Debussy. He orchestrated some of his piano pieces, the entire *Children's Corner* suite,[190] and doesn't see anyone near his equal among modern composers. [...] According to Caplet, a composer is not modern unless he thinks like Debussy; he places him above Bach in musical importance. That is a huge exaggeration. There is no discussion possible on this topic; I've avoided it for a long time. I keep my ideas and judgment to myself, realizing that I could be wrong. [...]

Magne's mother in Cherbourg has the largest stock of music and pianos in the department of the Manche. What is more, Magne is a professor at the Conservatory in Caen; he continues to receive his professor salary which is not to be scoffed at in times like this. He earns 50 francs a month from that institution. As for Maréchal, it seems he comes from a well-off family and his mother often sends him money. Lemoine, our chief cook, manages our budget as he is the one who pays for everything. He keeps his accounts and every 10 days we settle up. [...]

Sunday, March 26, 1916, 11:00 a.m.

I received this morning your letter from March 24 [...] You can't really say much about Debussy's music because you have never heard it or played it until now. That's why it is very useful to be working on the quartet. It may not be technically difficult for the violin but probably has something very subtle. [...] Does his music resemble Fauré's which also is filled with moving, very polished harmony? As for Debussy, the future will tell us whether his name will be

---

[190] *The Childrens' Corner*, L 113, is a six-movement suite for solo piano, published in 1908. André Caplet did an orchestration of it which was played and published in 1911.

remembered. One should never praise oneself. I seem to remember having read, quite a while ago in *Le Monde Musical*, an article in which Debussy was critical of Beethoven and placed himself above him. My memory is not precise enough to confirm what I'm saying, but it was something of that nature. He has above all written for piano and theater and his fans especially say good things about that. One has to listen and try to judge without preconceived ideas. [...]

3/25/1916.

I couldn't write yesterday as I again spent the day with a lieutenant from among us as observer from a haystack. Yesterday we bombed La Ville-aux-Bois with our 155s; it was alarming to see entire houses explode with one shot and to see the ground from the German trenches fly up to 20 meters in the air. What is more, toward evening, we launched 12 bombs of cheddite, an English explosive that is quite extraordinary. These bombs contain 2300 kilos of explosive and we fire them ourselves, a hundred or so meters, with new and quite small weapons; the effect is amazing, the detonation is huge and the displaced air current knocks a man more than 30 meters away to the ground. The *Boches* weren't laughing! I was watching all that with binoculars, and the lieutenant called constantly to correct the firing based on what we could see. We got out of our haystack just in time; about ten minutes after we left, it went up in flames after a shell fell on it.

I am not surprised that you find me wild looking, no one here takes me for a lamb and all these events have hardened me. I exude strength and energy, I have a lot of courage, nothing frightens me, that's why the lieutenant likes my company during difficult missions. He is well aware that, no matter what happens, I will not abandon him. I am becoming a nasty person and when I see heads and body parts of all these swine flying, as we did yesterday, you can be sure that I am screaming into the telephone "send more." We arrived at Concevreux at 12:30 last night and are at rest for six days. [...]

Monday, March 27, 1916,

I received this morning your letter of Saturday March 25. [...] I went to the notary last Saturday to see whether, by chance, something had been added to my account. Of course, as I expected, those gentlemen had paid nothing. Since they paid a year in advance, they don't care. They must think they've paid enough and are waiting for the end of the war to see how things turn out (or at least they are waiting until there are only six months left to discuss whether they want to stay or leave). I can do nothing and I will not go see M. Guyot. [...] They have to come to me if they want to keep the foyer. It is quite uncomfortable for me not to receive the payment; it is only Mme Boissard and M. Laville who are supporting me. That's very little. That's why I'm asking you to write to Mme Duez;

I've written at least 4 times since the beginning of January without any response. Don't neglect her; we may need her again. [...]

3/27/1916.

We played last night for General Mangin with considerable success. There were a lot of people there, I mean civilians. The only military people were Mangin and his commandant. But Mme Perrot had invited lots of others. [...] The concert could not have gone better; the Dupont was striking in its clarity and execution. We printed six programs which we are going to have the general sign, then we will all sign. I will send mine to you. [...]

Today, we are going to rejoin our regiments, the 129th is moving. The entire corps is leaving. [...] We don't know where, but I don't think we should have any illusions. [...].

Last night at dinner, after the concert, we had champagne (at least that's what they called it) that Caplet had gotten. It was both in memory of this past month of constant togetherness and to seal our friendship. We drank out of the same cup which we then broke and threw into the lake at the chateau, in Slavic fashion. That added some character! It was 9:30 at night, the stars were reflected in the lake and the evening was divinely beautiful. The general told us that when we come back, we'll find the same conditions. Until then, we will rejoin our comrades. I have a privileged situation, and can manage. Lemoine and Caplet [...] are in the trenches and the contrast will be rather hard. If we are going into the Verdun region, we have to expect a train trip of 24 hours in cattle cars; that lacks a bit in comfort. We will, however, have spent 35 or 36 days at the division headquarters under magnificent conditions. [...]

3/29/1916.

A word in passing. I am dead tired. We left yesterday at 9 a.m. and today arrived about 8 p.m. We passed Noisy-le-Sec last night, in front of the Cunaults' home, but it was night. We leave tomorrow morning, 20 kilometers on foot, for a town that makes redcurrant jam, you know, the little jars that are so good. In the end, we don't know where we are headed but we are pleased to turn our backs on Verdun. I am sending the program that Mangin signed. You will be pleased. [...]

3/31/1916.

[...] I couldn't write yesterday; we moved and arrived at our destination (30 kilometers away) very late and very tired. I am now in the Meuse. Unfortunately, we are located just next to an auto pool and they could take us at any moment to Verdun or elsewhere. We are expecting it and waiting patiently. It'll be God's will. Once we are engaged in battle, which will certainly happen, we will only see action for 4 or 5 days at most, after which we will be relieved. Fortunately, the weather is absolutely gorgeous and this is a lovely area. The cannon booms non-stop, night and day, although we are at least 40 kilometers from the front. Don't torment yourself, dear *minou*, have faith in my star. [...]

Monday, April 3, 1916, 3:30 p.m.

I received your little note from March 31. [...] You are not very far from Verdun and with automobiles that trip must not take long. [...]

I found the three violets from the Meuse in your letter, they are very fragrant. Nature is following its rhythm. Spring is reborn, and the flowers of the fruit trees, like the flowers of the forest and the fields, are opening and filling the air with their perfume. [...] Your violets gave me great pleasure: they will join the other flowers you've sent me already from different places and make a floral collection of the different parts of France you've passed through. Alas, it is rather painful to look at those souvenirs, they evoke so much sorrow and misery. [...]

4/1/1916.

Musician in the 129th Infantry. I just received your letters of March 26, 27, and 28. I don't remember whether I told you that I had lunch with General Mangin. Full of enthusiasm after Sunday's concert, he decided to keep us a bit longer. He invited me and Caplet. Alas, during lunch, the phone call came that we were to leave for Compiègne the next morning, so they took us back that afternoon. At lunch, Mangin showed himself cordial and charming.

Tomorrow we expect to leave, according to the rumors, for a sector in Verdun, next to the Oie or the Poivre.[191] But as of now there are no orders. In any case, we will only stay a short time; one only stays 5 days in that kind of area. For two days now, I've played for evening services. Martel, who is with us, asked me to and I'm quite willing to do it. The church, which is really quite large, was packed with people. That is the mystical fervor of faith in the face of danger. [...] We all realize that this is a serious moment. I've already seen everything, so let's be confident and remember I am much better situated than many. I am playing a lot of Bach for solo violin. [...]

Thursday, April 6, 1916.

[...] I read on the first page of *L'Information*: "In front of Verdun, the successes of our counterattacks" followed by a long spiel which I cannot reproduce in my

---

[191] *Oie* (goose) and *Poivre* (pepper) are names of two hills on the right bank of the river Meuse overlooking Verdun.

letter. The names of Douaumont and the village of Vaux recur all the time, then they say that, starting yesterday, that is the 4th to 5th of April, "the Germans moving from the east to the west launched a huge attack from the western slopes of the plateau against our front lines. The waves of the assault, mowed down by a wall of return fire, were forced to pull back in disarray to the north of the village in the direction of the woods of Chauffour. There our artillery continued to decimate them as they tried to regroup." This ends with "from the continual battles one gets the impression that we are the ones dominating our adversary." [...]

4/2/1916.

I received today your letters from March 29 and 30. I have a few minutes of quiet: I played this morning for the 9:00 Mass and for the 10:30 Mass. [...] The music was loaned to me by an artilleryman who plays a bit of violin. My music is still in its case, well-secured in the colonel's car. I didn't want to undo everything given our current uncertain situation. Today they are saying we may leave Monday at about 3:00 p.m., but those are just rumors. There is still no official order. As to our destination, there seems to be no doubt, it will be one of the places in the sector of Verdun and we will only be there 5 days. [...]

I'm going to answer some of the comments in your recent letters. No, Fauré's music has no resemblance at all to Debussy's. Fauré is more melodic, with musical lines that are intertwined. Debussy proceeds by little bits, like the strokes of a modern painter's brush. [...]

4/3/1916.

Still in good health, hope to write more tomorrow. Lots of work.

4/6/1916.

[...]. Impossible to write today, the work has been overwhelming, countless injured to carry day and night, superhuman fatigue, filled with the horror I'm living. I'm in good health. Hugs, Lucien.

Friday, April 7, 1916, 11:30 a.m.

[...] I see in the official *communiqué* of Thursday, April 6: "in the area of Verdun, after the relative calm of the afternoon, the enemy was very active later in the day and during the night. West of the Meuse there was a violent bombing in the area of Avocourt and Béthincourt, followed by a series of attacks with a large number of forces on the two principal advanced parts of the front. On our right, all the attempts by the enemy against the village of Béthincourt were fought off by our fire. At the same time, the enemy made a desperate attempt in the center of the village of Haucourt. After repeated failures and much bloody sacrifice, the Germans fled during the night." [...] "To the east of the Meuse, two enemy attacks against our positions north of the Woods of Caillette had no result other than serious losses for the Germans." [...]

Saturday, April 8, 1916, 10:30 a.m.

I received this morning your postcard from April 3. [...] I thank you for those few lines, however brief, with the news I was waiting for. [...] The Germans started the attack on Verdun a month and a half ago. As at Neuville, that action will last many months with little periods of calm for resupply of men and ammunition. What a tragedy! Men cannot be replaced like cannons and bombs. It takes 20 years to make one capable of handling a rifle or managing any sort of weapon. And all that just to kill others. [...]

4/7/1916.

I'm in good health, though very tired as the work is exhausting. I think we will not stay long in this hell. Kisses, Lucien.

4/10/1916.

[...] I write a bit more today: I've come with five comrades to a suburb of Verdun to catch 24 hours of some sort of rest. Our fatigue is enormous; we walk day and night over very difficult terrain. I believe we will be relieved in the next two or three days at the latest, at least that's the latest rumor. We have to hope. [...] For now, I can't give you any details. We are totally worn out and steeped in horror. [...] During our trip, my violin with my case of music was in the colonel's vehicle. As for Verdun, the *Boches* can knock each other out. Their strike is now spoiled and they could put the whole population of Germany against our defense without much result. [...]. I'm going to bed, I need to rest, I'll be back on the line tonight. [...]

4/11/1916:

Still in good health and even better, less tired. [...]

4/14/1916.

[...] We are finally relieved from that dreadful area. We left yesterday from the redoubt at Douaumont where our central post is located and, after marching 35 kilometers through a terrible storm and driving rain, we arrived in the area where we will billet. We are only to be here briefly. We have been waiting for three days for the colonel who stayed behind; the regiment colonel in charge of the move was ill. In three days, we will leave by car, where to I don't know. But getting out of this hell, that's what counts. We left 1100 of our men on the ground. Poumier, an old buddy, was seriously wounded. I'm the one who carried him out.

There have been terrible mistakes made at Verdun. There are no fallback trenches, as there are everywhere else, and the men fight in the open. There are no passageways, we climb into bomb craters. What is really terrible there, in addition to the incredible shelling, is the state of the terrain—it's nothing but one big hole, one big area of overturned earth. You go down into a hole, then have to climb up and out of that one to go down into the next, with the injured on your back. Just imagine, one has to be an acrobat to manage with an injured man on his back. The roads in the rear are so badly damaged by burning roadblocks that often we cannot get past and so we stay there for easily two or three days with nothing to eat except *singe*,[192] and nothing to drink except the water we find in the shell craters at night. It's a good thing we can't see it, we wouldn't drink it. And we are still burning with eagerness.

The music regiment has been lucky. We have had only one person injured and one killed, which is not much given the danger we run. So, praise God, here I am, again out of one of the most dangerous places. [...] Excuse me for not writing more, but I'm going to sleep. I think I could easily stay in bed for 48 hours, that's how exhausted I am. [...]

4/15/1916.

[...] I received yesterday two packages with a can of chicken, chocolate, 4 apples, and today, before your letter of April 11, two cans of vegetables from Appert and some chocolate candies. We expect to leave tomorrow in vehicles and get away from this area. The *poilus* have had it up to here. Where we are (15 kilometers from Verdun) there is nothing to buy: no wine, no coffee, nothing at all—it is miserable. When I think that the newspapers are writing that the army at Verdun lacks for nothing, what nerve! We have just enough to not die of hunger. The men are treated worse than the animals. [...] We didn't attack like the 129th, but we withstood seven *Boche* attacks and caused them great losses. I was with the colonel and the central command in the redoubt of Douaumont. What fell on us and around us is unimaginable! The nine days spent in that area will be among the most strongly felt of the war but I wouldn't want to relive all that. One's nerves are easily shattered. This countryside is abominable, it rains almost all the time. I'm going back to bed. Lemoine and Caplet have survived; Caplet

---

[192] Canned corned beef.

has a slight sprain, but it's nothing. And even if I don't sleep, my body is resting or trying to rest. When will I be able to go back to Port Lazo? [...]

4/16/1916.

I received today your letters from April 11 and 12. I have, indeed, received all my packages for which I thank you. We may be leaving tomorrow but there is nothing official yet. I just ran into the colonel who wants me to play for him this evening. It is quite a nuisance: I am, obviously, very tired, my legs are like rubber, and I will have to go get my violin from his vehicle. Those guys have no idea! But I'll talk with Caplet about what we can possibly do; I do not want to unpack my music. We are not really settled here, we are camping in a very basic, and quite disgusting, way. We will make an effort, but what a bother. My fingers are rough and stiff from carrying wounded men on stretchers; that certainly does not loosen up my joints. I'll do what I can. [...] I do not have much time— instead of resting I have to retrieve my violin. [...]

Tuesday, April 11, 1916.

[...] I read that "from the 7th to 9th of April a fierce battle took place not only on the Béthincourt bulge but mostly along 12 to 14 kilometers of front from Avocourt to the Meuse. At the price of abandoning the ruins of the village of Béthincourt, we again yesterday showed ourselves to be the masters of the maneuver. The day of Sunday April 9 will be talked about as one of those which showed the great skill of the leaders in the annals of the battle for Verdun." Then, the *communiqué* of April 10 says that: "to the west of the Meuse the heavy bombardment continued throughout the night, particularly directed at Hill 304, etc." I won't transcribe the rest except for the conclusion: "It is confirmed that April 9, around Verdun, marks the first large enemy offensive extending along a front of more than 20 kilometers. The bodies strewn in front of our lines serve as witness to the losses of our adversaries, who didn't gain much advantage thanks to the efforts of our troops." [...] The Germans continue to advance, slowly. If the Germans suffer serious losses, the *communiqués* are silent about our losses. True, that would not do much good and would add a bit to the anguish the public already feels. [...]

Wednesday, April 12, 1916, 4 p.m.

I received this morning your card from Thursday April 6. [...] I thank you heartily for these few lines which do me good; even more because it has to be a very difficult task to write even that much in the midst of such challenges and desolation. [...] You must be totally exhausted, my dear child. Do you have any news of your comrades? [...]

Between April 17 and 24 Lucien received a special permission to go home. The reason for this is not known.

4/25/1916.

A very tiring trip in a packed train. It left at 3:45, arrived in Bar-le-Duc at 1 a.m. I spent the rest of the night in the waiting room unable to lie down. Set off again about 10:30 a.m. in the direction of Neufchâteau (near Toul) to rejoin the regiment which is in Stainville. I am writing from the station that serves that place, Joigny en Barrois. [...] I believe I can get to Stainville (15 kilometers from here) if I travel in the mail truck. The weather is magnificent, very hot. I am not too depressed. I traveled with guys from the 20th corps, all furious with the *Boches*. They are talking all about the Russians, letting their imaginations go wild. [...]

Tuesday, April 26, 1916, 11 a.m.

My dear child, of course I've not received news from you since you left. The weather is magnificent, even a bit too hot which leads to more fatigue. You hadn't recovered, we have to admit it, and high temperatures do not help one regain strength. [...] You must, immediately, look into your request to become a secretary or to stay with Sergeant Leduc as an assistant. After 18 months non-stop at the front, after having taken part in 5 serious, dangerous missions, you cannot continue making the same physical effort. Your strength wanes despite all your good will. You are the oldest in the regiment, after Silèges; it is normal that you cannot hold up like the 25 to 30 year old guys. You are not pretending, just stating a fact. You are at risk of tuberculosis; if you continue to wear yourself out, you will be three-quarters dead before they realize you cannot continue to serve. Given that you have had the good or bad fortune to not have had the slightest injury which might have led to a five to six month rest in the midi, you have not the benefit of a pension. You would have no resources other than your own to care for yourself, when it may be too late.

When you are depressed, they quickly tell you to pick up your violin to entertain the officers. What do you receive for the effort? Career soldiers get double salary during the war and the hope of a higher rank. They risk little; they don't suffer much physically because they can always find a good bed and a good meal and all the rest. You have always done your duty, heroically. What more can they ask of you? [...] Don't be afraid to speak up, you can show my letter to Lieutenant Laine. I wait for your news about all this.

Same day, 4:30 p.m.

I just received your letter from Tuesday, April 25. [...] The division is at rest so General Mangin will probably ask for you. That way you will have the chance to see Lieutenant Laine. Don't wait to ask him to change you to secretary in one of his services or attach you to Sergeant Leduc. [...] I am counting on you to take care of that right away and that there will be a sensible solution. [...]

4/26/1916.

I finally arrived Tuesday at 6 p.m. by truck. [...] I am tired. I'm going to sleep. [...]

4/27/1916.

I've not received a letter yet since getting back. Magne is with us, *en subsistence.* Everyone is now here so we can get back to our music. [...] Castelnau came to see regiment just before I got back.[193] While he was congratulating Mangin and his division, he said he would be counting on us sometime soon. That means we will again take part in a nasty affair. [...] Caplet received Ravel's Trio which we will work on soon.[194] It looks complicated.

The weather is dreadfully hot which increases our fatigue. This area is simply lovely: in two weeks, when the trees have all their leaves, it will be even better. In a little bit, I am going to play for the regiment: Leclair's *Musette*, Rameau's *Tambourin* and a Paganini Caprice.[195] Darn it all, I have to play outdoors and have no idea what the sound will be like. [...]

4/28/1916.

I am feeling better and am less tired. I am replying to your letter of April 25 which I received this morning. You had never seen me immediately after a difficult period; you might have expected a significant physical let-down. It is not serious; it passes after we rest. We are in a magnificent area where the brisk air is very good for us. I beg you please do not write to Lieutenant Laine or anyone else; it would be harmful for me. This time the officers as well as the soldiers suffered significantly; the division lost many people. [...] Don't worry, I will try to get myself out of this but quietly, without drawing undue attention to myself.

We've not yet played any music together; we just changed our location again. This morning I took a piano to Colonel Viennot who is here in the same town.

---

[193] General Edouard de Castelnau (1851-1944). After commanding the 2nd Army in 1914, he became General Joffre's Chief of Staff. Durosoir, *Deux Musiciens,* 165.

[194] Trio for piano, violin, and cello in A minor.

[195] Jean-Philippe Rameau (1683-1764), *Tambourin* for violin solo. The other pieces mentioned are impossible to identify with any degree of certainty.

Niverd is tuning it today and we will start work tomorrow. I glanced at the Ravel Trio: it's very difficult and complex and appears rather subtle and dry, more a work for the brain than the heart. We'll see. Don't worry about my health; I am really much better and less tired. […]

4/29/1916.

I just received your two letters from April 26. […] The colonel is on leave right now, it's the end of the second round. Thirteen musicians are also absent, and the companies have about 40 people left. If these leaves continue like this, the second round will finish quickly. My leave was special and does not count as my third. For the 3rd round, I have number 4 in the music regiment which means that, when the system of home-leave is working normally, it won't be long until I have mine. […]

Your letters are a bit ridiculous; obviously, it's out of your affection for me that you talk like that, but, my dear kitten, everyone is in the same boat. The poor guys are tired and they still need to move when the order is given. I have little reason to complain. My situation is privileged and a good many people from the regiment (even among the officers) would be happy to change with me. Your worry comes simply from the fact that, by chance, you saw me two or three days after we got out of a very hard episode; I hadn't had time to recover. […] As I told you, that won't keep me from seeing Lieutenant Laine when he gets back and pulling a few strings to protect me a bit. I will do what I can. […]

I do not have a bed here; there are too many of us in this area to have a chance to find one. But I am in a sturdy room, with good straw and am far from being miserable. I sleep well and am much less tired. […]

4/30/1916.

I just received your letter of April 27 in which you give me a recipe for cooking the apples. […] I think we are going to play today for Commander Pourel, who, right now, has his wife with him. He is setting a terrible example, aside from the fact that I would not want to expose my wife to the rather unpleasant comments of badly brought up officers who, in the presence of a woman, can only utter swear words. […]

So far, I've not worked on music; I wanted first to rest. I'm going right this minute to get my box of music. If we are going to play tonight, we have to have some music, so I have to end my letter; if I am too late the driver will have gone off for a walk and I'll have to transport the box myself. […]

5/3/1916.

I received today your letter of April 30. I couldn't come yesterday; I spent the entire day copying the parts for violin, clarinet, etc., of the march written by Caplet for the division. We played a six-part version for Mangin, the colonel, and all their officers with great success. Now I need to copy the parts and teach them to the other musicians. [...]

I have a partial explanation for my fatigue. There is an auxiliary doctor who eats with us and is very nice. I told him about my fatigue and asked him to examine me. He had me undress and found, much to my surprise, the beginning of a hernia, certainly acquired at Verdun. For now, it's not serious but he advised me to wear a support, a bandage, in order to keep it from getting worse and to avoid some other problems. The army doesn't provide that sort of bandage so tomorrow I'll go to Bar-le-Duc to see a bandage maker. He can make one if he doesn't have what I need. Eventually I will probably need an operation to get rid of this completely. This morning I saw Doctor Goucerolle who agrees and says that 50 percent of the men in the regiment have hernias. [...] I hope you will not agonize too much by what I just wrote and will appreciate that I told you. For the moment, it might have been simpler to say nothing. [...]

I do not expect to have another leave before July and between now and then much will certainly happen. [...] I will do what I can to be in control of my situation, but one has to realize that we are all in the same boat, and even more, they are sending reinforcements who are older than I am, often with handicaps and infirmities. There is nothing more to say, those poor men give what they can, with considerable effort. It is the awful "march or die!" I am in a privileged situation; I cannot repeat that often enough. I understand and try to excuse the nasty comments that sometimes come my way from those who are envious. [...]

5/5/1916.

I received your letter of the first of May. I was not able to write yesterday because I was in Bar-le-Duc to get an excellent bandage that fits me well and is not at all difficult to wear, for 25 francs. The bandage maker said that my hernia was so small, the bandage might make it disappear. [...]

Have you read in the newspapers, *Le Matin, Journal*, etc. about the exploits of the Mangin division? [...] I know a bit more about this now. Without our division the Germans would have blown up Fort Souville and, once again, Verdun would have been in danger. Having taken the woods of La Caillette, the *Boches* were going around Fleury and marching directly to Verdun. We stopped their movement and took back the woods despite their best efforts. That is why Castelnau made the trip to compliment us; we certainly deserved it. Along with the 36th and 74th, our regiment will receive the citation of the Order of the Army. [...]

5/6/1916.

[…] Cloëz is coming this morning. I am going to benefit from his presence and Maréchal's to perfect the "Archduke" Trio and a Schumann trio.[196] […] The colonel is in a lovely house with a good piano. […] We have been reading the Ravel trio and it is, indeed, very complicated. He uses a lot of left-hand pizzicati and harmonics. When the composer is not a violinist, there are difficulties in the writing that become apparent. […]

Here's our menu from last night: carp in butter, rump steak, mashed potatoes, cheese, gingerbread and jam, wine, beer, coffee. Very carefully conceived. Chauvel just made sub-lieutenant, he was an assistant. His living situation is better, but I prefer my position to his. He's going to get himself killed one of these days. […]

5/7/1916.

I received last night your two letters from May 3. […] If you could see the regiment as it comes out of a terrible battle like Verdun, you would have the impression they were human rags. […] No one here expects to go back to Verdun. Things would have to be going very badly for that to happen, which is fortunately not the case right now. On the contrary, we think we will return to the Somme or the Oise. That is where, so we hear, the next offensive will take place. […]

We are still in Stainville and truly our rest here is magnificent; the countryside is quite lovely, and what is more, we are able to find here everything we want. […]

As for having music stands made, that is another matter. We had one, but it was destroyed and got lost during our travels. […] I use one of my boxes, and my comrades use bound volumes they find in the houses where we play. […]

5/8/1916.

I received yesterday your letter of May 4. […] Do not spend money on packages right now as I don't need anything. […] Niverd came last evening for dinner and afterwards we gave the people in the area a little serenade. For that, I picked up the cymbals, Caplet played the drum, Lemoine the bugle, Niverd the bass, etc. In short, we had great fun. We sang words written to the tune of the division march, totally stupid words, which added to the charm. […]

---

[196] Beethoven, Piano trio in B-flat major, Op. 97. It is impossible to identify which of Schumann's three piano trios Lucien is referencing.

5/9/1916.

Yesterday I received your letter of May 5. [...] We gave a concert for General Mangin, at the lodgings of Colonel Viennot. The general had invited Colonel Valzi and some other officers. We played the Beethoven Trio in D, opus 70, Number 1, then Maréchal played Boëllman's *Symphonic Variations*,[197] Cloëz played the Franck Prelude, chorale and fugue, and I played the "Kreutzer" Sonata. [...] The next time we play for the general it will be at Colonel Valzi's place where there is a much better piano. [...]

5/10/1916.

[...] Lemoine comes back from leave today. He had some trouble while in Rouen. We received a note saying he was under arrest for 4 days for having walked around the streets with a khaki rubber coat over his uniform. Everyone here had a good laugh! Those guys in the rear are priceless! Lemoine would not have shouted, that's for sure, but he must have told the guy that he was going to punch him in the jaw. I can see it from here. [...]

5/11/1916.

I received yesterday your letter of May 7. [...] We do have showers; I wonder what gave you the idea that we did not. I have profited from them twice and it's wonderful; they are well set up. It would not be wise to take cold baths; for that we have to wait for July. [...]

5/13/1916.

I received yesterday your two letters from May 9. You are still worrying about my hernia. It is nothing. [...] I spoke to Lieutenant Laine. There is nothing to be done about changing my position, but in the regiment itself I can arrange to do as little physical work as possible. Stop nagging the way you have in your recent letters. It is a bit annoying, especially when one sees everywhere so many people with illnesses or real infirmities who are obliged, all the same, to walk. [...] Baths are not possible; like all my friends, I take a shower about once a week, just to get clean. [...]

5/16/1916

Yesterday, I received four letters, one from May 11, two from May 12, and one from May 13. I am first going to resolve the question of my hernia, so you know why, for now, I'm staying put. You say that General Mangin could give me

---

[197] Boëllman, *Variations symphoniques*, Op. 23, for cello and orchestra.

a month off; you don't know the military. Things have to been done by the rules, that is, I would be evacuated by the medical service. But the Verdun area is filled with wounded, so I would have no chance of staying in this area. In order to return to my regiment I would have to stay near here. If I were evacuated to the interior of the country, I could go very far away, Auvergne, Bretagne, etc. That wouldn't displease me but, unfortunately, I would be sent back to a garrison as a simple soldier in no matter what regiment. Even General Mangin would not have the power to bring me back here. That is something serious to think about and worth reflection. My situation here is not as exhausting as that of the ordinary soldier, and that is why I hesitate. The decision could affect my destiny. I am thinking about all that; my condition is not serious and I am taking care of it. [...]

It appears that we will be sent back to Verdun. [...] It's just a matter of days, a week maximum, unless something changes, which one always has to expect in the military. [...] I have not yet gotten any new clothing; we will certainly not need them before our next trip to Verdun. If we go there to mount an attack, we will stay only 4 or 5 days at most. As to my health, I can only reply that I am completely fine. As for the hernia, it doesn't cause any pain at all and I've gotten used to the truss. [...]

I am glad you got your supply of coal. Lemoine says the price will go up dramatically next winter. You did well to buy it now. [...]

Friday, May 19, 1916, 11:30.

I received last evening your letter from May 16. [...] Suzanne is quite well; uncle Alphonse looks healthy. I waited a bit until he returned from his regular evening walk so I could see him. While we waited, Suzanne gave me a cup of tea with toast and jam. [...] Ferdinand has not been well; his health has always been delicate, but he is better. [...] Everyone insisted I say hello to you. I left there about 5 p.m. and came home. [...] The métro was packed, especially after the Concorde stop. Impossible to find a seat. [...]

Write from time to time to Madame Duez to ask about her health because she was very ill during the winter and still was not in very good health when we were there. We may need her help. I will go see her one of these days, now that the weather is warm and she can receive me in her garden (nature's salon). [...]

5/17/1916.

I received your May 14 letter this morning. [...]. I couldn't write this morning so I missed today's mail. Caplet was rehearsing his march and the bands from the 36th and 74th came at 8 a.m. to join us. At Caplet's request, I directed the drums and trumpets on the right. The entire group is split into two parts which reply to each other. [...]

We will be going back to Verdun in 2 or 3 days, that is now absolutely sure. We will be attacking a fort that is in German hands. Our stay there will be short, 4 or 5 days at most; in those situations, the men in the battle wear out rapidly. [...] Obviously, no one is happy but it is necessary. [...]

5/18/1916.

I am writing this morning very early; I got up at 5:30. I have to put my music case and my violin in the car as they leave at 7 a.m. Part of the regiment left this morning, including the colonel. We won't leave until tomorrow morning and will for sure be at the front tomorrow night. [...] I will be staying with the chief and the assistant chief this time and will not be carrying stretchers, that is agreed upon. Moreover, the trumpet players and horns will be stretcher bearers this time; the percussion did it last time. That increases the number significantly. [...] If you buy the May 13 edition of *L'Illustration*, you will see General Castelnau complimenting the officers of the 129th in Stainville. [...]

I have to cut this short; they just came to get me to move again the piano we took to Colonel Viennot's. I will be supervising the team transporting it. It is the last task of a stay that was truly restful in an exceptionally lovely area, among friendly and welcoming inhabitants. It will seem very strange to return to Verdun and the countryside destroyed by this tempest. My goodness, Brittany must be lovely. [...]

5/20/1916.

Obviously, I didn't receive any letters today or yesterday. [...] We left Stainville yesterday morning, about 8 a.m., and we climbed out of the cars at 1 a.m. near Douaumont, a little place in the suburbs of Verdun. Our trip was dreadful, with terrible heat and dust. We rested until 5:00 then went another 6 kilometers to get to V. where we slept in barracks. It is only tonight that the music regiment goes to the trenches. I am staying here where, with two or three comrades, I will watch over the instruments and the bags of our comrades. I will not tire myself; I will not have much to do, and even more, I don't run much danger. The bombing is frightening, night and day, it's a constant rumbling. We must be preparing to attack the Douaumont Fort with an extraordinary artillery strike. May it please God that this effort succeed and not cost us too many lives. According to what they are saying, we will be relieved during the night from Tuesday into Wednesday, so our time here will not be very long. It is good that you can't imagine the noise and the movement. There is a hint of fantasy about all this, it's like dreaming. And such a lot of dust! We all look like thieves; we are unbelievably filthy. […]

5/23/1916.

I received your letters of May 16, 17, and 18 but haven't written for three days as I have been very busy. As I told you, I stayed at the barracks outside of Verdun, but there was a lot to do. I helped the quartermaster with writing and distributions. We have just lived through some dreadfully agonizing hours. The attack on the Douaumont Fort took place yesterday. It was preceded by a frightening bombing, the likes of which I don't think I've ever heard. The fort was taken by the 129th and I believe that the redoubt of Douaumont has also been taken and we are now near the town of D. This is a huge success for Mangin and his division; unfortunately, our losses are enormous. The regiment has at least 1500 men unable to fight, a lot of dead officers. I still only have vague estimates. Caplet was buried twice under cave-ins, but nothing serious happened to him. He only has some bruises and will be back on his feet in a few days. Lemoine, it seems, was badly wounded, though this hasn't been confirmed. Chauvel, recently promoted to second lieutenant, was wounded, I don't have any news of my friends. The regiment will be relieved this evening and I will know more. The *Boches*, in revenge (their losses were horrible—we were walking on bodies and, in the fort, bodies were piled one on the other) drenched Verdun last night with bombs. About midnight, a hundred or so bombs started to fall on our barracks, setting one ablaze. Seeing that, the *Boches* doubled their effort. We had to move out in the dead of night. We moved to a place farther back, next to a canal and that is where we are awaiting the regiment tonight. I am writing to you in the open, seated on the bank, after a sleepless night filled with tragi-comedic adventures.

Mangin's observation post was hit but he was not hurt; however, Captain Bouteville lost an arm and two others were slightly injured. You cannot imagine the relentlessness of the battle and the horror of the totally unimaginable scene. The regiment is thus relieved this evening and the rumor running around is that we will leave on the 27th for the Oise or the Somme where we will have a long, well-earned rest. Mangin apparently asked for 3 months; he will probably get 2 which will be really beautiful. The *poilus* were truly heroic. Apparently Mangin, usually so stoic, cried as he watched the 129th throw itself at the attack on the fort. Captain Brichoux was the one who reached the top of the fort. People will surely talk about this victory. Fort Douaumont was lost at the very beginning and had never been retaken, even by the 20th Corps. The whole effort was led magnificently and I think Mangin will receive his third star. I believe that Magne, Cloëz, and Maréchal got out of it unhurt. I'm still worried about their fate as it was really quite awful. I'm concerned about what will happen to poor Lemoine,

I have no information and don't know what sort of injury he had. There were two drummers killed and three other musicians wounded, we don't yet know their names. For sure I escaped from a really dreadful dangerous situation. [...]

I am right now with Caplet who came to see me: he looks very tired and is all bent over, but with rest, he'll be alright. He ended up with a hernia also; later we will probably try to have our surgeries at the same time. We still have no news of Lemoine. I just learned terrible news: Corporal Descusse, our former corporal of the stretcher bearers and a friend, an admirable man, brave and good, was killed as he was transporting a wounded soldier. I am sad; everyone liked him. [...]

5/24/1916.

I received your letter of May 20 today. We left Verdun this morning for D., a few kilometers away and tomorrow morning the cars will take us on to S. where we will rest for a week before being sent to another area—this time the nightmare at the Meuse is over. The blow we gave the *Boches* was very hard for them, but also for us. [...] Barthe has shrapnel in his kidneys and in his arm. Three musicians were seriously wounded. Our regiment suffered huge losses. Our division conducted itself astoundingly well; people will talk about this for a long time. The enthusiasm of the *poilus* was beyond belief. [...]

5/25/1916.

I am not telling you much today other than that we have been relieved and that we are in St. I will probably leave tomorrow night (Saturday), or Sunday on pass; I will try to get a week. So, see you soon. I have much to tell you, so much has happened in the past week. Our division was very brave, in particular the 129th, I'll tell you all about it. [...]

Lucien was on home leave from the end of May until early June.

6/7/1916.

I did not arrive in Bar until 6 a.m. There was so much troop movement that the civilian train was four hours late. Instead of waiting in the station in Bar, I waited in the train which was certainly better. I took the post vehicle at 6:30 and at 7:30 I was in Stainville. [...] I have bad news to tell you: Mangin is leaving us. He's been named Commander of the 11th Army Corps and earned his third star. That was to be expected after the events at Douaumont. He's not taking any of his officers with him, they are all upset! [...] He is on leave and will come back here first so we will see him before his departure. [...] The other news is that we will be back in the trenches about the 12th, south of Les Éparges. It is, apparently, a relatively quiet area. [...]

6/8/1916.

Here I am settled into my normal life. Maréchal just arrived this morning, he took the train on Wednesday, so it took him a day longer. Magne will no doubt arrive in the morning; he was to leave last evening at 8. As for Lemoine, we expect him today or tomorrow; the trip from Grasse takes at least 38 to 48 hours. [...] Les Éparges is apparently in the middle of woods, much like La Ville-aux-Bois. We will not have a billet in the towns; in the middle of the forest there are chalet-like *gourbis*. That will be nice for the summer. There will be nothing to do; the territorials hold the sector which is supposed to be very quiet. So much the better; it will be a rest cure.

The *Boches* will probably take the Fort of Vaux, according to the *communiqués*. They still won't have Verdun; after that fort there are Tavannes and Souville. To take those new positions, they will have to lose a good number of men; I doubt they will be able to do that, especially if the Russian attack takes place. [...]

Cloëz left on pass yesterday. He escaped death in a truly miraculous way: he had just left his first-aid station, two to three minutes before a 305-shell landed on the station. The doctor, the nurses, everyone there was killed. He had a stroke of luck: it's about the same as happened to me at Cappy. [...]

6/9/1916.

Obviously, I have not received a letter from Vincennes. [...] We are going to try, right now, to have Maréchal transferred to the 129th. If the general who replaces Mangin does not like music, we might find it difficult to make that happen. [...] Should we stay here another week, we are going to organize a public concert. That's the least we can do. Yesterday, with Maréchal and Caplet, I played two Beethoven string trios. Those works are exquisitely lovely and not often played. None of the three of us knew a single note. [...]

They tell us that the sector we will be going to is very calm; there are masses of troops collecting in the Somme and the Oise where, I believe, the next offensive will take place. What makes us believe we will not take part in that is the fact that we are receiving many fewer reinforcements. [...] That seems to indicate that they are no longer counting on us to make an attack. What is more, Mangin is no longer here. We can't help but be happy about that; the constant hard battles were becoming too much. [...]

6/10/1916.

I have not yet received a letter, maybe today. […] Lemoine returned yesterday evening. We immediately resumed our work; last night we reviewed Beethoven's 10th.[198] We are planning an event next Tuesday and Wednesday, two days because the space can only hold 150 people. We will play the Beethoven 10th, the Dupont Quintet, and I will play the Franck Sonata—a lovely program. We will invite the officers from the 36th; a lot of musicians and friends from the regiments of our division will come. So here we are working hard; that will draw attention to us and right now, it is in our interest to show ourselves. The colonel yesterday expressed concern that we could be sent to the 11th corps. If Mangin could find us a way to join the army corps, it would be a great advantage for us and our risks would be greatly reduced. We will see about that when he comes to say goodbye.

Maréchal brought back a sonata for cello by Debussy which has just been published.[199] It is really lovely, fine and delicate, especially the first part (there are three parts). It is really a fantasy; it doesn't follow sonata form but call it what you will, it is none the less exquisite. […]

6/11/1916.

I received yesterday your letter of the 7th and today the one from June 8. […] Caplet, Lemoine, Maréchal and I played this morning at the church. I played the Bach *Air on the G String* accompanied by the others and closed with an Allegro from a Handel sonata.[200] Maréchal played a prayer by Boëllmann, a transcription of his *Suite Gothique* for organ.[201] Lafont sang Franck's *Panis*. We have to play again Tuesday morning for a funeral service for the regiment's dead. […]

The new general, de Roigt de Bourdeville, has arrived. We will soon learn more of his tastes and his character. […]

Wednesday, June 7, 1916, 2 p.m.

[…] I made it home fine but I had to look a bit for the line to the Bastille. With all the métro lines one can take at the Gare de l'Est, there is a labyrinth of corridors. There were a lot of people; no matter the time of day there are always large crowds there. The house seems sad; now that you are coming home fairly often, it always feels like you are here to stay. […]

[198] String quartet No. 10 in E-flat major, Op. 74.
[199] Debussy, Sonata for cello and piano, CD 144.
[200] Also known as *Air for G String* or *Celebrated Air*, this is August Wilhelmj's 1871 arrangement of the second movement of Johann Sebastian Bach's Orchestral Suite No. 3 in D major, BWV 1068.
[201] Boëllman, *Suite Gothique* for organ, Op. 25.

Thursday, June 8, 1916, 3 p.m.

[…] This nasty weather as well as the Russian offensive will probably quiet down the activity at Verdun. However, the Fort of Vaux must be in German hands. An article in *Le Matin* says: "The Germans claim to have taken the Fort of Vaux. The indescribable violence of the bombings made it impossible yesterday to have any communication with its heroic defenders," followed by a long diatribe of explanations. From that one has to deduce that the fort has fallen to the Germans. […]

Two years of interruption are terrible for your career; we may need to change plans and look at the future very differently. What a difficult, painful question to think about! Our first wish is the end of the war without anything bad happening to you. That is all we can desire right now, but all those uncertainties are very hard on me. […]

Friday, June 9, 1916, 12:30 p.m.

I still have not had any news. You could have mailed a note with a stamp from Bar-le-Duc. You aren't in much of a hurry to write! […] The Germans now have control of the Fort of Vaux and I fear greatly that soon Verdun will be in their power. It seems we are doing everything possible to make it easy for them. If we had held Fort Douaumont, that strategic position might have stopped their advance. To kill so many unfortunate men with no benefit is ignoble and shameful. Certainly nothing was done to protect Verdun. What good is the high command if it doesn't know what is going on? Isn't it his job to see everything, to predict everything and to take necessary precautions? […]

6/12/1916.

[…] Our concert next week is at 8:30 p.m. We will be lit by lamps which the automobile drivers will loan us. The room we will play in is in the Town Hall and usually used as a first-aid post; it can hold between 120 and 150 people. […]

They are saying that our stay in this sector will be prolonged. […] So much the better, as we are fine here. There is always time to go back into action. I have faith in the Russian offensive which is taking on enormous proportions. The *Boches* will be forced to help the Austrians and pay less attention to us at Verdun. It is sure, however, that we, with the English army, will keep them busy. In that case, I don't know that they will have sufficient forces to throw at the Russians. The end of the war, in these conditions, may be expected this year. […]

Thursday, June 15, 1916, 9:30 a.m.

I received last evening your letter from June 12. [...] I am writing early because I have a lot of sewing to do and want to make some progress. Yesterday afternoon I started the repair of a flannel shirt and hope to finish it today. Time passes quickly when I am busy taking care of things. I don't have to do a lot of cooking, but I need to have something to eat so I prepare a few things. All that takes quite a long time. [...]

In this weather, my strawberries are not ripening ; still I ate 4 or 5 one evening. They are not very red, because of too little sun. The slugs are eating them. [...]

6/14/1916.

[...] General Mangin came yesterday. We started the day with a funeral service for the regiment. [...] Right after the Mass, we gathered in the division's gardens where the music regiments of the 129th, the 74th, and the 36th came together to rehearse Caplet's march. The march was played after the lunch in the general's honor. [...]

We still have no details about our new general. They say that he has commanded the sector of Bordeaux since the start of the war. If that is true, our division will not be doing very much; this general must be an old good-for-nothing as they say in the military.[202] They would not give a chief like that to the 5th division if they intended to use it in dangerous places. [...]

Friday, June 16, 1916, 2 p.m.

I didn't receive a letter last evening nor this morning. [...] As it wasn't raining last night, I went to check on the strawberries. I picked 15 but had to throw away a few of the nicest ones. The slugs had devoured them. They make a hole in the outer part and enter, stay for a while and eat the heart. I even found two slugs in the same strawberry. Of course, they pick the red, ripe berries in order to enjoy themselves. Do you find strawberries at S...? I read in *L'Information* that the troops will receive 50 cl of wine a day per soldier and a lot of fresh vegetables. [...]

---

[202] General Henri de Roig-Bourdeville. Contrary to Lucien's expectation, he was about the same age as Mangin and brought a sense of proportion to the battles in Les Éparges. He understood how little harm his artillery fire could do to the Germans. He also realized that the French did not possess enough mines to have an effect. As to raids, in order to overwhelm the well-organized German trenches, a raid would only succeed if accomplished quickly. He once said: "At the moment, our situation is so precarious that a violent reaction on the part of the enemy could be fatal." Roig-Bourdeville in Smith, *Between Mutiny and Obedience*, 160-161.

Saturday, June 17, 1916, 3 p.m.

[…] Madame Bastien came to see me yesterday with young André. She has rented a small place in Fontainbleau for the nice season. She will settle in there on the 24ᵗʰ of this month. She invited me to come dine with her tomorrow, to eat the beautiful white rooster you saw, which had wounded the hand of its mistress. Nasty beasts end up that way, in the pot. […]

Sunday, June 18, 1916, 9 a.m.

I received last evening your letter from June 15 which I am answering this morning […] so I am not too late arriving at Madame Bastien's. […] We will probably dine early, because of the time change. In Montreuil there is no more gas once the clock strikes 8:00 in the evening. I have no interest in going to bed at 11 p.m., nor do those women who have to work the next day; and Madame Bastien has to prepare for her move. Of course, she has to take linens, even sheets, cooking pots, a whole pile of things. […]

6/16/1916.

I haven't received mail today yet. […] It is likely today that we will move a piano to where the postmen are. They are very friendly and have offered us their dining room so we can rehearse comfortably, unbothered, without all these annoying people. […]

6/17/1916.

I am writing early today. We are going to rehearse at 9:30 a.m. because Cloëz is going to check in with his regiment later. […] Yesterday they read us Joffre's proclamation thanking the army of Verdun and saying that, thanks to them, a number of other offensives have been prepared. Some say that the offensive where we are has started. […]

6/19/1916.

I received yesterday your letter of June 16. We had yet another particularly busy day yesterday. […] At 1:30 all four of us climbed into a vehicle […] and by 2:00 were in Dannemarie. […] We got back to Stainville about 8:30 p.m. after some amusing adventures: our horse suddenly refused to go forward. We had to get down and push the vehicle. We laughed like youngsters; it was a nice ray of sunshine. Finally, after some blows from a stick, our animal decided to move again and we made a nice entrance in Stainville. Everyone was outdoors at that time of day and there were laughs from all sides. Ah! Our life is not dull; there is always the unpredictable. […]

We are now called Mangin's orchestra: it's quite amusing but our situation does seem to be accepted. Everyone asks for us. Even if it is not to the tastes of the new general, I think he will accept the situation. We are providing delight to too many people for it to be otherwise. We've not yet seen the general; he left on leave right after he arrived. [...]

The warm weather is back and I remember sadly how, two years ago, we were settling in at Port Lazo. Watch over your strawberries and fight the slugs for them; it would be stupid not to get to eat them. We have here large quantities of wild strawberries, fragrant and tasty; we just need to go pick them. For that we employ two signalers who, for 20 sous each, go out each morning at 4 and come back at 10 with 3 to 4 kilos of those delicious fruits. [...]

I just learned that we will leave for service near Les Éparges about the 24th. I am writing to ask you to send a few packages of foodstuffs. You could buy the June 10 edition of L'Illustration which is about us. You will see Mangin looking at Douaumont and the big back of Lieutenant Laine, plus some admirable pictures taken from an airplane during the attack. [...]

Sunday, June 25, 1916, 2 p.m.

Naturally I didn't receive any news this morning. You must be just barely settled in your new sector. And mines are exploding for your arrival! [...]

I imagine that your officers will explore your new sector in order to be familiar with it and not leave room to make stupid mistakes. For all of you, it is more dangerous to be always camped somewhere along the front. You must be very careful and observe the ground carefully. It is probably mined. I saw a picture of your woods which they say is no more than 40 meters away from the Germans. [...]

Monsieur Alan came to see me Friday and found me feeling poorly. I must have gotten chilled at Madame Bastien's last Sunday; we spent a long time in her yard and the weather was chilly. We ate at 8:30 p.m.; her rooster took forever to cook. She had put it on too late despite the advice of her mother. I got back to Vincennes at 11 p.m. [...]

6/21/1916.

We are a bit keyed up because we have a concert this evening and the 3rd battalion leaves tomorrow Thursday. I will leave with the colonel. [...] Friday morning. We are traveling, I believe, by car: we have 60 kilometers to cover to get to Les Éparges. We will be quite near Rupt-en-Woëvre. [...] From everything they tell us, we will be in a particularly calm sector, defended up to now by territorials. I believe we will also be in the woods; there is nothing wrong with that in the summer. All the little towns have been evacuated and we will be living a bit like wild men, never seeing a civilian face. And as there are no people in the villages, there is no possibility of finding food. There is a total absence of any commerce. That is why I asked you to send me some provisions. Go at it modestly, however, and once you have sent 5 or 6 packages, wait for a letter with more details or requests. [...]

It is obvious that, if the war lasts a long time, Caplet will do everything he can to become a sous-lieutenant, to have more money and comfort. But I think now that the war will end rapidly; that is to say that we will be home by next January first. In those circumstances, ambition seems useless. Peace and quiet here and getting home in good shape, that is all I want. [...]

6/24/1916.

Today is Saturday; I did not write yesterday nor the day before. Here is why. Our concert took place Wednesday evening with the greatest success. The sublime Franck Quintet was particularly well received. After the concert, we had a little supper and got to bed quite late. The 3rd battalion was to leave with the trucks that very morning. We had to look all over for our music, pack the cases, and find someone to transport them. [...] With all that coming and going and the packing and organizing, I could not write that day. On Friday morning we set off at 6 a.m. and arrived near Dugny, a place with unpleasant memories. We could easily see Verdun and the shells landing on the ridges. This was all quite exhausting; it was dreadfully hot, and we had to cover another 15 kilometers to get to a farm two kilometers from Rupt-en-Woëvre. The lines are 3 kilometers in front of us. We are in the middle of the woods and this sector is quite calm, barely a cannon shot from time to time. [...]

As we passed other towns, during our 15-kilometer march, we left Magne, Maréchal, and Cloëz with their respective regiments. According to rumors, we will be here about a month and a half, then go for rest, maybe in Stainville, and the other division of our corps will come here for a month and a half. That would get us nicely to October. Things will certainly happen between now and then. Today there is even talk of sending the music regiment back to an area 6 kilometers to the rear, because this area is so calm. [...] The Lyon son was enchanted by our concerts. He said he will be going home soon on leave and would see whether he had, at home, a piano that could be taken apart (into five pieces), made expressly for the colonies. If so, he would bring it back for us. [...]

I would ask you to send, if possible, some fruit, some lemons, and some sugar. I tasted a product yesterday sold by Potin, African lemonade, the essence of lemon. I've never tasted anything so perfect; it was like drinking the juice of a real lemon. [...]

6/25/1916.

I received yesterday your two letters of June 21 and 22. We, the band, are billeted on a farm, where we each have a bed constructed by soldiers: it consists of a metal trellis with feet. [...] We sleep well on it and are quite happy with our little room. We may manage to play a bit of music; it is quite calm here. The countryside is quite hilly with lots of woods; all in all, the Woevre is lovely. It is a wet area with a lot of water—springs everywhere with lovely fresh water.

I just saw Rolland, who was in the trenches. It seems they are very well constructed, with arbors, benches, tables because of being in the forest. [...] It is quite the restful sector and curious to find barely 20 kilometers from Verdun, the scene of indescribable horror. [...]

Starting tomorrow, for as long as we are here, I will eat [...] at the same place as Caplet. That means I will lack for nothing. Send only what I asked for yesterday. So there, you know all about where I am sleeping and eating. [...]

Monday, June 26, 1916.

I've not received any news since Wednesday June 21 when you announced your departure for the 23rd. [...] The German attack on Verdun continues, they are in Fleury. Verdun will be taken soon. The effect on the morale will be terrible. The English are not budging; we should probably be cooperating with them but are we prepared, do we have enough heavy artillery? [...]

Today I sent 3 registered packages by mail: 6 hard-boiled eggs in a little wooden box with some salt, 12 peaches in a box, and a little glass bottle with a red Bordeaux, Brivezac. I think they will arrive in one piece and that this shipment will please you.

I am feeling better, less fever. I wonder where and how I caught this; it is not the grippe. My whole body hurts and it's as though I'm about to have cramps in the hands, the legs, or even the neck, very strange. [...] I am impatient for news from you. [...]

Thursday, June 29, 1916, 3 p.m.

I received this morning your letter from Sunday, June 25. [...] You needed Caplet to come and make things happen. You are truly a bit simple. A bed, for example, the first thing to take care of. I tell you, and I sing it in all keys, they would have to bring you one for you to accept it. Enough! Now that you have a bed and reasonable food (though you don't tell me what it consists of), I hope you will think about the residents of the woods, who could be eaten, and about the inhabitants of the brooks and streams, which are abundant where you are. You should find river trout, crayfish; think about all that to vary your menus. [...]

I did not receive a letter yesterday. [...] You will have seen in the newspaper that they are fighting in Fleury. I am sure that the redoubt where our post was located is now in the hands of the *Boches*. They are slowly advancing, but at what a cost! [...] For the past 48 hours we hear the roar of the cannon over near Verdun; things must be heating up. When I remember that, two years ago, we had just arrived in Port Lazo and were settling into that pretty house, our life was peaceful, and we couldn't imagine the catastrophe that was coming. One can wonder whether all these events are not just a nightmare from which one will someday awaken. We are just one little atom among all those millions of men who, all over Europe, are caught in this, all because of the desire and ambition of a very small number of individuals. All this will seem so vain and out of proportion to historians who will later study this gigantic conflict. [...]

6/28/1916.

[...] It is possible that with all the activity that is starting the mail will work less well, so do not worry if you don't receive any letters for a few days. I will, of course, write daily as always. [...] If home leave continues to be given as it is now, I may be home for my third time in the course of July. [...]

Friday, June 30, 1916, 3 p.m.

I received your letter of June 28 put in the mail in Paris by a person on leave, and this morning your letter of the 25th. Those two letters tell me about the packages you've received and the beauty of where you are. France is such a beautiful country; it has been the envy of many foreigners, and at the same time soiled, invaded, and ruined by them. [...]

6/29/1916.

I received this evening your June 25th letter. [...] I am distressed to know you are not feeling good; you catch colds very easily. It is about time for you to get back to the salt air. [...] I don't see why you should not go back to Brittany for a month or two. [...]

6/30/1916.

I received today your letter from June 26. [...] I am worried by what you tell me about your health. Where could you have gotten that? You should have taken some aspirin to reduce your fever but if you continue to feel ill, do not hesitate to see the doctor. [...]

I received your letter from June 27. […]. We may be playing music very shortly; a lot of the officers in this sector are bored. The enemy doesn't take up any of their time because there is very little activity. They don't know what to do with their ten fingers.

A couple of the musicians started a protest against me; they wanted me to take part in their chores. […] As soon as I got word of that, I spoke up sharply, threatening to speak to the colonel. Everything settled down immediately. […] The famous "chore" they were bothered about is taking soup to the telephone operators. They leave at 8 p.m. and are back by 11. […] Aside from that they do nothing. […]

I received my violin today. It is in good condition and I am going to start serious work on my technique until further orders; I have the time and the calm necessary. […] Do not get the idea that the English are incapable; to the contrary, they are going to accomplish astounding things. According to knowledgeable people who have seen them, their army is superb and their weapons absolutely overpowering. When they finally start moving, we can have confidence that they will be ready. […]

7/3/1916.

I received today your letter of June 29 and at the same time two packages: the one with the prunes was in good shape, the six peaches in the other were all damaged and partly crushed. It is in part your fault; sugar boxes are not very strong. You have to remember that these packages are handled roughly so fruit has to be packed especially carefully. […]

7/6/1916.

Yesterday, I received your letter of July 2. I still haven't received the package with solid alcohol and the jam. I have little hope for that shipment. Today I was in Génicourt. […] I had lunch with Cloëz but I didn't play any music. The piano Cloëz was counting on had not yet been moved from the awful room it is in to a more appropriate location. […] Commander Lambrigot and Lieutenant Laine were on leave so I couldn't see them. However, the paymaster was especially nice. He promised that, for my next leave, he would provide transportation as far as Souilly. One can't be nicer than that. […] The music regiment hasn't played a note since we've been in this sector. […]

I practice violin at least three hours a day, although I am frequently interrupted. […] I am working on the first movement of the Beethoven concerto which gives me enormous pleasure.[203] It is very difficult and hard to play in tune. [...]

I've already told you that our meals consist of roast beef or beef stew, rarely some mutton, new potatoes and cabbage. When we have peas or green beans, which is not often, they are canned. And there is nothing in the woods except strawberries. [...]

Lucien was again home on leave, probably for the usual seven days.

7/19/1916.

My trip was fine; I arrived last night about 8:30 at the farm. [...] I found Caplet in good health. He has not yet seen the new general either, nor the brigadier who is replacing Viennot. It is annoying for us that all our leaders left us; we are totally ignorant about what the new ones will be like. The good comrades around us are already making predictions. I am sure that, if the new chiefs do not like music, the nastiness will surface. Yes, the colonel is still here, but if he also had to leave, I would have to go back to the music regiment and there would quickly be chores to do. I would much prefer, for many reasons, that the war not last more than another six months.

I do not know whether we will try to make a bit of music; we are all spread out. Maréchal is 8 kilometers away and Lemoine is in Génicourt. To bring us together requires orders from the division. One of these days I will go to Génicourt to see Lemoine and also Laine and see what can be arranged. We need to be cautious; we don't know what sort of situation we are stepping into. If it is favorable, you can be sure we will take advantage of it, and the nastiness will be squelched. [...]

7/21/1916.

I don't know whether I will receive a letter today, I hope so. [...] Caplet saw the division officers. The general opinion is that, for now, there is nothing to be done, we are on service. Later, when we are at rest, everyone expects we will have the freedom to give concerts as we have done, and I think we will play for the general. [...] I just saw Maréchal; he is on service right next to us and took advantage of it to come say hello. His cello is getting warped; he just added a second sound post to support the top. It's amusing; despite all that it continues to have a decent sound. [...]

---

[203] Violin Concerto in D major, Op. 61.

Friday, July 21, 1916, 11 a.m.

I still have no news this morning. It seems a little long. You should have arrived in your sector the afternoon or evening of the 18th. You could have mailed a little word from the station in Bar-Le-Duc. I don't think you had to go to another area to find your regiment; you would have been alerted by a comrade. No matter, it's just I have no news and am starting to worry. I read in *L'Information* of the 21st that "A German plane brought down by one of ours crashed near Grémilly, near Verdun." I looked on the map but couldn't find it. I do not know if it was near you, or if, by chance, on your trip back you found yourself witness to that event. […]

Saturday, July 22, 1916, 11:30.

Still no news this morning. What could have kept you from sending some word with a stamp to let me know sooner that you arrived safely? I see that German planes bombed Lunéville and Baccarat the 17, 18, and 19 of July. That's not near you. And Grémilly […] is north of Verdun; I saw it on a little map in *Le Matin*. So I am reassured (more or less) in that respect. […]

7/22/1916.

As expected, I received last night your letter from July 18. […] We still have strawberries in our woods. We are starting to see wild raspberries. There are loads of hazelnuts, but they are not yet ripe. There are rumors circulating about a departure at the end of the month. The division knows nothing about that, so there is nothing official. […] In the past few days, they have installed magnificent new showers, just 100 meters from us. They function from 7 a.m. to 7 p.m. That is very convenient and enjoyable. If one wants to take a cold shower, he needs to go around 6:30 before the water heater is lit to allow warm or hot showers. […]

Tuesday, July 25, 1916, 12:30 p.m.

I received this morning your letter from July 22. […] The cleaning lady, whom I had only briefly and whom you met here, is no longer coming. She found another position much better for her which she took without delay. You left Monday night the 17th; the next day I waited in vain for her. She came Wednesday evening to tell me that I should no longer count on her. On Thursday, I met Mathilde on the rue du Moulin and asked her whether she cleaned houses and would come to my house three afternoons a week. She accepted and started work yesterday. […] I am very happy to have her and think she will stay. […]

7/23/1916.

I received last night your letter from July 19. [...] I met the commander of the 36th, Commander R. who just had his head chewed off for I don't know what mistake, and who, while waiting to be taken to face a board of inquiry, is at Rupt. He talked at length, first about his problem, and then of the pleasure he got from one of our recent concerts. He was one of our faithfuls. If he has to leave, I will miss him. [...]

There is a new wrinkle in all these changes. We will have a new chief of the music regiment; we saw this appointment in a newspaper from Le Havre. His name is Rippe. This is surely a huge inconvenience; I don't know whether he will go along with the modest role I play with the musique of the 129th. I will obviously ask for the colonel's support, but we cannot forget that neither Mangin nor Viennot are there and we know nothing of their successors' ideas. [...]

I hear serious people saying, not just rumors, that we will be in this sector at least until the end of August, another 5 weeks. So much the better; we'd like to stay here even longer. Over time this life is weighing heavily on us. [...]

7/24/1916.

I received yesterday your letter from July 21. [...] I saw Maréchal just a few minutes ago; he was passing by on his scooter. I had seen Magne who spends his days putting points on round posts, how interesting! He is being annoyed by his music regiment also; they are making him pay for his prior absence. It seems that Cloëz is in the same situation. We have to figure out whether, between us, we can fix that. [...]

Maréchal heard from Cloëz that Mangin had asked to have us transferred to the 11th corps and the army refused his request. I didn't know that although I am not surprised because I knew Mangin was very interested in us. But I knew also that, unfortunately, everyone hates him. His intelligence and the frankness with which he expresses himself must have displeased many people. [...] The colonel who replaced Viennot as brigadier doesn't seem very good; he is very "military" and only cares about what the rules say. [...]

7/25/1916.

I received yesterday your letter from July 21. [...] The news that Caplet brought back from the division is not very good. Our new general does not like music; he doesn't give a damn about it. Recently he heard *Werther* at the Opéra-Comique and declared it boring. The only music he appreciates is something like *La Belle Hélène*.[204] [...]. As long as he allows us to get together during our rest! As for the

---

[204] *Werther,* Jules Massenet (1842-1912); *La Belle Hélène,* Jacques Offenbach, (1819-1880)

new brigadier, he is even worse, I think. He doesn't like music or musicians. He is a military man; he sees the rule book and nothing else. And more, the commanding general of the army corps is always on our backs, annoying us with unimportant details. [...] Apparently Mangin's corps is not far away; Caplet is going to write to him, and perhaps try to see him and explain our situation. If he could get us away from this, that would be a worthy service. [...]

Our brigade general, who stays near us, got the idea that we weren't doing much, so he ordered us to play a concert every Sunday in Rupt. The 36th will give a concert every Thursday. This is the first time the music regiment has had to play when on service. What is odd is that there are no longer any civilians in Rupt and at most one or two territorial companies. The area is bombed from time to time, unpredictably. It would be interesting if they started shelling right in the middle of a concert. Those are the ideas of military men. [...]

7/26/1916.

I received yesterday your letter of July 22. [...] There are a number of air battles here. No day goes by without the anti-aircraft batteries going into action, or there are battles between planes with machine guns. It's very interesting to watch. The day before yesterday, we saw a *Boche* brought down in flames by the anti-aircraft batteries. [...]

You should keep M. Alan's eggs; it is not the quantity of food here that is the problem. We have huge pieces of meat that, in this weather, becomes inedible. I eat as little of it as possible. For fresh vegetables, that is easy: potatoes, cabbage, rarely carrots, sometimes dried beans. Sometimes, in the place of meat, some salted pork from America which is nothing special. I find that we are less well fed now than 6 or 8 months ago. What is missing, aside from fresh fruits and vegetables, is variety. [...]

I am reworking the Bach Sonata in A minor;[205] it is so rich and delicious. I really need to work methodically on my bowing and my fingers. I figure that it will take me six months of work to rebuild my accuracy and confidence. I would greatly love to start that work tomorrow! [...]

7/28/1916.

I sent you this morning a brief note that will arrive quickly; a person leaving on pass is taking it to Paris. [...] As for the piano which is coming to Bar-le-Duc, and may already be there, Caplet and I have given it much thought. Although the colonel knows very well that we are receiving a piano, we will not, for now, move it. [...] Our brigadier general or the division general will decide soon whether we are accepted, which seems quite possible. In that case we can have

---

[205] J. S. Bach, Violin sonata in A minor, BWV 1003.

the piano brought to the regiment. Right now, caution is still the rule. [...] For now, we have to play dead with our instruments. Lyon, who is on service in this sector, is coming to see us today, apparently to discuss that subject. That Lyon is a daring fellow. He has a beautiful Arabian greyhound and enjoys making him jump over his cane, and over the trenches, which the greyhound does with unimaginable grace and flexibility. He is totally bored here: he has the bad luck to be in a battery with a totally stupid leader, so the time seems very long. He asked to be transferred to an anti-aircraft battery. Right now, he is in the 11th artillery regiment. He is quite special—his intelligence simmers and burns. [...]

As for how long we will be on service in this sector, no one knows. The colonel yesterday told us to expect to be relieved on August 10. But that evening we learned more definitive news: that we are here for an undetermined length of time. [...]

It is hard to realize that the best years of our lives are being spent in this dangerous, stupid, pointless existence. Caplet has been here a month and could do some work, but he does nothing. The mind is elsewhere and no ideas come, we become stupid. We pounce like crazy men on the newspapers, always hoping for the news that never comes, that of the end of the war. [...]

7/29/1916.

I received yesterday your letter of July 25. [...] Today I had Magne and Maréchal for lunch; with Caplet we went into the woods and all four of us lunched on the grass. Clearly, we used a lot of our own provisions. [...] Lyon came to see us; we talked at length about the piano that is coming. We hope to put it on our farm. He may go see Colonel Montbrisant, our new brigadier. He does not think he is such a devil as he appears. We will have to wait for more news from him. [...]

7/30/1916.

I am writing a bit late today because I had lunch with Rolland, Vessot and Pierrot. I saw my letter openers. None is finished, but I pushed Pierrot and in a few days they may all be finished. I also managed to get a *Boche* button, which means he will be able to start your ring without delay. [...]

Thursday, August 3, 1916, noon.

I received yesterday your letter from July 30. I am delighted that you spent a nice day with your old buddies Rolland, Vessot, and Pierrot. When you see them again, please thank them for all their wishes for me. I think that, at least for Pierrot, you will not wait long to see him again. That is the only way to get him working on the letter openers you want. [...] German buttons must be subject to a lot of speculative buying by jewelers in Paris. They must have soldiers providing them. *Le Matin* is filled with nothing but ads for them. […]

8/1/1916.

Musician 129th Infantry. I received yesterday your letter of July 28. […] Yesterday at 5 p.m. I was at Commander Rouge's, in Rupt. He had invited the artillery officers of the 84th and 11th. You have to admit that is a start; if we go back for evenings of that sort, the news will spread and there will be more people. […] The commander kept us for dinner. Here is the menu. You will see that, for an area that has been ravaged, it is quite acceptable—tapioca soup, pot-au-feu with cabbage, carrots, turnips in abundance, cassoulet, new carrots in butter, cheese, jam, cookies, red and white wine, coffee, Bénédictine. […] Magne is going to try to go there every day, or at least every other day, to practice the piano. We were very lucky to have been able to find a decent piano, Lyon's should be arriving soon. […]

8/2/1916.

I received yesterday your two letters from July 29. […] It is getting hotter and hotter every day and becoming almost intolerable. I don't know what it is like in Paris but here, despite our woods, we are suffocating. The climate in these areas with a lot of clay is terrible; there is either too much dust or mud up to our knees, really charming! […]

8/3/1916.

Yesterday I received your letter from July 30. […] I will soon have the ring I'm having made for you; as soon as I had the *Boche* button, I went to find a guy who is part of the percussion section and does lovely work. He got right to it. […] I had news yesterday from Cloëz who is in the woods at Ranzières; he too is the butt of all sort of annoying jokes. […]

This morning marks two years since I left Port Lazo. It's an anniversary that I, like many others, didn't expect to mark more than once. May God's will be that I, still in good health, not see a third anniversary in these conditions. This war is so very extraordinary, it is so different from what war was like in the past that it is still difficult to predict its duration. Everyone is begging, with all our hearts, for it to end, but, alas, that doesn't change anything. Time is passing and the hostilities continue, month after month. What a life! And we are wasting our best years! At least, right now, we are not those who have the most to complain about. But one starts to believe that we appeared on this earth too soon or not soon enough. Surely it would be preferable to be either 16 or 50 years old. […]

8/4/1916.

I received last evening your letter of July 31. [...] For 48 hours, the cannon has rumbled terribly from the direction of Verdun. They just told us that Fleury has been retaken and that, in 2 days, we took 1700 prisoners. The goals of the attacks we are making now are to retake territory and widen the zone around Verdun, which parenthetically is very necessary, but also, as much as possible, to keep the *Boches* and their weapons away from this stronghold. It's no secret for anyone that, currently, the *Boches* have brought huge numbers of men and artillery into the Somme. It is possible that, as a diversion from there, we will attack the *Boches* on a third front, all to stop them from constantly shuttling back and forth their reserves. For sure, all these battles are wearing them down; unfortunately, we also have losses, which is quite sad when we think of the slaughter of all those French men over the past two years. The *Boches*, at all times, show proof of incredible resilience and in no way give the impression of a people who pull back, as we'd like to be able to say. To the contrary, they fight with fury, and that's no small credit when you think of everything that is falling on their heads. That is what makes us believe that the war cannot last for many months; in such struggles, fighting men melt away like snow in the sun. No matter, the *Boches* were strong in terms of intelligence, organization, and preparation for war.

You can rest easy; I drink responsibly as I know that abuse can be bad. Right now, I am trying not to eat meat, all the more because three out of five times, it arrives in terrible condition. It's incredible to admit what lack of foresight and what ineptitude there is in the distribution. The army is spending a crazy amount of money for all those provisions and the *poilu* gets spoiled meat; most often it has to be thrown out. What a waste of money! And then he starves, because there are not many vegetables either. There is a lot of bitter complaining right now. Refrigerated cars should be able to reach our kitchens, but things don't work that way. There are two or three transfers in the heat, with the dust, flies, and the sun. The result is to be expected. It's beyond the pale that this is the best they can do after two years at war. There is nothing more to say. [...] Caplet is, at this moment, making the piano reduction of his march as a gift for Mangin. That will be an excuse to go see him. [...]

Your ring will be very lovely and very well made. They are often made from a *Boche* button with the outer circle cut away. At least it is a souvenir; Rolland got the button at Douaumont. [...]

Tuesday, August 8, 1916, 10 a.m.

I am writing early this morning because; as soon as I finish my correspondence, I will have lunch then go to Villemomble. [...] On my way back from Villemomble, I will probably buy some jam like that I've already sent. It is made by the fruit merchant on the rue du Midi next to the charcutier I use. I may be mistaken, but this fruit merchant seems to have once been a cook. That jam is nothing like the commercial ones. It is, however, very expensive—the price of a small pot varies from between 1,10 and 1,30. That does not mean you should not enjoy it. Do eat it, but don't share it often. […]

My ring should be finished soon. That is much faster than with Pierrot. If you had made that decision long ago I would have it already. I would have preferred to have the crying child at the center of the ring. But you could ask Cloëz to get a little gold medal with the crying child, send it to me, and I could wear it around my neck on the fine gold chain which I received from the gardener association for my first communion. It was tradition to give children of members of the association a gold chain for their first communion. I am very happy that the button for my ring was picked up by Rolland, a precious souvenir. Thank your friend. […]

8/5/1916.

I received yesterday your letter of August 1. […] Tomorrow Lieutenant Lyon is coming for dinner with us. Caplet invited him. Magne and Maréchal are coming also; we will all be together. My friend Franchet, a former comrade from the squad, now cook of the 3rd, will prepare the dinner using our resources. We will discuss the famous piano. […]

Caplet went to Génicourt yesterday to use the piano for a piece he is trying to write, and, I think, for his own personal affairs, as you say so often. Suddenly, about 4 p.m., Captain Heron, who commands our section, came to find me; he had just had a phone call from Lieutenant Bernard, who is still at the brigade. He asked that Caplet and I come play some music for Colonel de Montbrisant. I had to send a bicycle to alert Caplet and ask him to bring back some music. Totally by chance, he saw Maréchal in Génicourt […] and informed him about the plan; he asked him to request permission from his colonel to come back to the brigade. […] That is how it happened that we all worked together at the brigade for 8 and a half hours. Colonel de Montbrisant welcomed us warmly; he is a polite man who says he likes music. He prefers light music, or at least music that is easy to understand. But he understands perfectly that we get together to play as an ensemble for the benefit of the regiments. He finds it very good for morale. […] It is a ray of sunlight in a period that up to now has been fairly somber. That was enough; for now, the nastiness of others has stopped. […]

8/6/1916.

I received yesterday your letter from August 2 and 6 packages. […] Tonight is our dinner with Lyon. Here is our menu: lobster with salad, hard boiled eggs and mayonnaise, green beans, rice nicely arranged with strawberry jam and peaches, then cheese, wild strawberries with condensed milk and some honey cake that Magne got from the *curé* in Rupt (he is the only civilian left in this little town), some ordinary wine and two bottles of better wine and coffee. That is, for sure, a menu that is more than acceptable; not many could manage it. [...] We will also have flowers on the table, simple wildflowers but there are some very lovely ones: mauve, white, and pink snap dragons, and others whose names I don't know. [...]

8/7/1916.

Yesterday I received your letter from the 3rd of August and a package with 4 lemons and the *Mercure de France*. The ring I had made for you is ready; Dehuysser, who will be on leave soon, will bring it to you, that's the safest way. [...]

8/8/1916.

I received yesterday your letter of August 4 and three packages. [...] The chief of the music regiment arrived; I saw him this morning; he is a distinguished little man who seems quite sensitive but a bit bossy. [...] He does not seem to be in very good health and I doubt he will be with us long. In any case, he greeted me nicely. I explained that I hadn't played the cymbals for 8 months (Jacquet had told him the same thing), he had no objection. [...] He looks to be about 30 to 32 years old, not at all unpleasant, and seems to possess a certain amount of culture. His arrival may muzzle the musicians a bit. [...]

Last night the cannon rumbled terribly from the direction of Verdun. [...] We may try to retake the fort of Vaux, but all this fighting is destroying a great many lives. I think, however, that we are on the eve of some decisive events; major attacks will soon be launched on our front, on the Russian front, and on the front in Salonica. The *Boches* will be squeezed from all sides. They won't be able to move their troops everywhere, a game at which they have excelled up to now. [...]

8/9/1916.

I received yesterday your letter of August 5. As I told you, I had my case brought to me; it is now in Captain Heron's lodgings, where I can lay my hand on it easily. Caplet [...] is going to Génicourt tomorrow to make arrangements to transport Lyon's piano; we have official word that it has arrived in Bar-le-Duc. [...] There seems to be a rumor running around that we will be here for a long time. All I can say is: so be it! Nowhere else could we be so well off, at least for the summer. In the fall and winter, the mud must be frightful, but my goodness, Cappy, this past winter, was no better. And here at least nothing changes, we are really safe and calm.

8/10/1916.

I received yesterday your letter of August 6. [...] The third package contained a box of cocoa and a *Mercure de France*. I thank you for sending that. I also received *L'Illustration*. Those editions are particularly interesting; the trenches in the Somme with all those holes made by our artillery are impressive. [...] As for the *Mercure*, it is an especially serious publication. I am only just finishing the last one; it is filled with background articles which can't be read as easily as a novel. [...] It is a good gymnastic exercise for the brain to read a magazine like that. [...]

You could send me some Vaseline. In this hot weather, the leather of my shoes quickly absorbs all I give it and I run out quickly. Maybe you could put it in a little pot tightly sealed, as it is not an easy product to ship in this heat. [...]

Tuesday, August 15, 1916, 2:30 p.m.

I received yesterday afternoon your letter from August 11. [...] I also received [...] a remarkable little photograph showing you after your dinner with Lieutenant Lyon. It looks like you are having refreshments in a magnificent garden on a beautiful summer evening. Everyone's eyes are fixed on you. The dog is the only one looking at the camera; it's a curiosity for him. He is a splendid animal.[206] [...]

Wednesday, August 16, 1916, 3:30 p.m.

I received this morning your letter from August 12. [...] Very often I run two errands in the morning, as today for example. I have lunch, I write, I take my thionhydrol between the two major meals. Sometimes Mathilde comes in the morning and sometimes in the afternoon.. [...]

8/13/1916.

I received yesterday your letter of August 9. [...] The violinist I met while in Stainville is in the 74th regiment, not ours; his name is Mayer. [...]

Thursday, August 17, 1916, 12:30 p.m.

I received yesterday afternoon your letter from August 13. [...] My health is good in spite of the heat these past 3 weeks. I follow my treatment, not to the letter because I would never manage to do all that is written on the prescription. The doctoresse told me to do what seemed best to me. Let's see: warm foot

---

[206] Find this "remarkable little photograph" in this book's gallery.

baths, cold sponge baths, big warm bath at 37 degrees. That seems a lot of water for rheumatism. I must be sensible and not too extravagant. [...]

8/15/1916.

I received yesterday your letter of August 11 and today the one from the 12th. [...] I did not write yesterday because I spent the entire afternoon picking up Maréchal's cello, which was in the Raugières forest. Maréchal came today by bicycle, an easy trip because he did not have to carry an instrument. In the morning we worked on the Mozart Clarinet Quintet, the larghetto.[207] Duchamp is the clarinetist; he is a professional who has only been with us a few months. His brother is one of our musicians. He was a territorial and asked to come to us. It may not be possible to switch from active service to the territorials, but it is quite easy to move from the territorials to the active service. No one will stop you from trying to get your face smashed in. [...] That rehearsal took us up to lunchtime. I left right after lunch to get Maréchal's cello.[208] [...]

Mass today was at 11 a.m., rather late but that time suited everyone except our colonel, who had documents and reports to sign. [...] The colonel who commands the brigade was there with his staff, as well as the colonel of the 108th territorial. Plus, there were a good number of regimental officers and officers of the battalion who are at rest right now with the colonel. [...] Rolland came down also to hear our Mass. Martel served at the Mass which was said by an officer of the 108th who is a priest. There was a very good attendance and we met with great success. The officers of the 108th invited us for a drink today at 5:30. We also have Vespers tonight at 8 p.m. Magne came to hear us and had lunch with us. Lieutenant Lyon, who is taking a course in Ancemont, came by car. I have rarely seen such an audience, especially in the open air. [...]

I am going to answer some of your questions from August 10, 11, and 12. Yes, the green beans we ate with Lieutenant Lyon as part of our famous dinner were fresh; the cyclist of the 3rd company brought them back. [...] The *curé* of Rupt who, with the mayor, is the only person left here, has a few beehives. What is called honey cake is natural honey on the comb. It can be eaten just like that and is delicious; you just have to spit out the wax which gets stuck to your teeth. You thought it was some sort of recipe. The heroes of old didn't bother with that; they offered simply what their bees produced.

You now know that our Mass was in the open air. No piano or harmonium. Our little orchestra was made up of Jacquet (flute) and me (for the vocal line), 2 clarinets, Caplet on the viola, a bass saxophone, and Maréchal on cello. The ensemble was not bad; we accompanied the plainchant. [...]

---

[207] Mozart, Clarinet quintet in A major, K 581.
[208] For more about Maréchal, see Sylvette Milliot, "So, who was Maréchal?," *Soundpost*, December 1992.

I am not haunted by the obsession that the people around me are envious, nasty, and jealous, but it is true, they are. The day they can do something to hurt me, they will. I've known for some time that the music regiment is a bad environment; that is why, not being able to predict what things would be like, I was hesitant to join. […]

[…] August 15 was a total success.[209] The commandant from the 108th, as I told you, had invited us for an aperitif at 5:30. He had also invited Captain Heron and the officers of the 129th who were there. For the aperitif we had several bottles of Graves and little Palmers cookies. […]

The commandant raised a toast to the 129th and all the officers who represented it. He also thanked the musicians who lent their talents for their comrades of the 108th. […] Martel, who stayed for lunch, was part of the party; he never misses an occasion to drink or eat. That evening, at 8, we played for Solemn Vespers. […] That reminded me of August 15 last year when I was on leave for the first time; the same day two years ago, we had organized for the 23rd a celebration at Gonneville—Mass in the morning and in the afternoon in the courtyard of the chateau of the marquise, I don't remember her name. Three years ago, for August 15, we were in Erquy. That seems very far away. Let us hope that August 15 next year we will be together, at the seacoast, and this hell of a war will be over. […]

I received yesterday your letter of August 13 and today the one from August 14. […]

A big event in our *popote*. For some time, the food has not been very good, everyone was complaining about it, no one was happy, so Captain Heron decided to put me in charge. I am now promoted to chief cook. I am the one who will buy the food. That will be easier and here is why: three weeks ago, the battalion founded a cooperative. The person in charge is Dardelle, a comrade I know well. He did not find much to buy in Bar-le-Duc so he got permission to go to Paris to replenish the food. Every five days he comes back with a big load: the last time he bought 5000 francs worth of merchandise. In two days, everything was sold. If I give him the list of what I want, he will bring it back. Thus, I beg you, do not send me any more packages; save your money, at least for now. […] I hope not to spend more than 1 franc 50 a day per person. There are 11 of us, so that makes 16,50 every day. We can make serious improvements in the regular food with that sum. I would like you to send me a catalog from Potin to see what

---

[209] The Ascension of Mary.

they have that might be useful. [...] Wine is not included in the 1,50; anyone who wants a bottle of good wine will pay a supplement. [...]

Monday, August 21, 1916, 3 p.m.

I received this morning your letter from August 17. [...] I am halfway pleased that you were chosen chief kitchen man, that is, in charge of buying your food. With essentials so expensive that is a difficult task. The amount of 1,50 a day, per person, seems very skimpy. You should not be forced to contribute from your own pocket to supplement your little daily budget. [...]

8/18/1916.

Today I received your August 15 letter. [...] Today I also received a pair of blue velvet pants and a nice shirt, which makes three, and a pair of blue gaiters; I also received two lovely pair of wool socks. [...] Today I went to buy a lot of provisions for our *popote*: green beans, peas, tomatoes and three melons. I also got a 4.5 kilo case of grapes and 4 kilos of peaches, then some butter, condensed milk. Next time I will pass the order to Dardelle directly. [...]

8/20/1916.

I received yesterday your letter of August 16. [...] Yesterday I received my three letter openers. I had not yet made the package, so I will do it today and can send them with your ring and some other things I want to send back. [...] I will write to Mme Duez for her feast day and, my dear kitten, I send tender wishes to you for yours, as well as some little flowers from our woods. [...]

8/22/1916.

I received yesterday your August 18 letter. [...] Yesterday afternoon, we assembled the piano that Caplet brought back. That was no small task; we spent almost 4 hours, but finally, it is all put together and ready though, obviously, it needs to be tuned. It is a little one but with not bad sound. It is very clever: it fits in four large cases. To transport it is not easy; I predict numerous difficulties in the future. But we aren't there yet. [...]

Friday, August 25, 1916.

I received yesterday morning your letter from August 21 and at 4 p.m. the one from the 22 as well as my ring, the three letter-openers, the little glass bottle, and the box for the ring. They all arrived for my name day, and I thank you very much, they pleased me. [...]

Sunday, August 27, 1916, 2:30 p.m.

I didn't receive any news from you last evening, nor today. [...] I went to see Mme Duez yesterday; I took her the 6 months of interest we owe her. The interest is thus paid in advance until February. I've already told her that I would probably not be able to pay back the money she loaned me. I did not stay for dinner with her; I had told her I would not stay in the note I sent to wish her *bonne fête*. She did not try to keep me; she was expecting a visit from her young cousin who had been in Salonica and is now on convalescent leave in Paris. He arrived with another young man, in civilian clothes, just as I was leaving. I preferred not to find myself with them and Mme Duez for dinner. I would have bothered them, would have spent a not very interesting evening, and gotten home late for no good reason. I will go some other Saturday and, if she wants me to stay for dinner, I will accept in order not seem to flout her invitation.

When I arrived, I found one of her friends who had come to wish her *bonne fête*. She had brought a box of chocolates and a little rose bush. We chatted in the garden. After that woman left, I accompanied Mme Duez to the second floor to see her petrol stove. Even though she bought it quite a while ago, she has never used it (she wants to exchange it for a smaller one). As she doesn't have any gas in her house, she uses charcoal in the morning in the kitchen to make her breakfast. In a bad season, she makes breakfast in her bedroom so she doesn't get too cold in her kitchen. For her other meals, she has them brought from elsewhere. [...] If there are people who are too fond of luxury and comfort and spend more than they have in order to satisfy their sumptuous tastes, that is not Mme Duez. [...]

8/24/1916.

I received yesterday your August 20 letter. [...] Please send me soon a bit of *savon de Marseille* so I can wash my linens.[210] We still are not receiving any, or so little it doesn't help. When there was no water, we received soap; now that we have plenty of water, they don't give us any soap. That is again the beautiful logic of the French army! It is why many officers end up saying "we'll take them in spite of our generals!" By that they mean that the generals make almost all possible stupid mistakes and cause us to lose this game. Honor to the smart, clever *poilu*! Shame on the stupid, careless generals. [...]

Monday, August 28, 1916, 3:30 p.m.

I received this morning your letter from August 24. I am writing a bit late because Mathilde left a bit later than usual. [...] I went to the post office about

---

[210] *Savon de Marseille* is a type of soap made with vegetable oil, especially olive oil. It dates back to 1370.

10 a.m. to send two boxes of fruit that I wanted to send as quickly as possible, I warned Mathilde that I would be gone for a half-hour. When I returned, she had just had an altercation with her older daughter who is a maid in Vincennes and had just quit her job. I must explain that Mathilde has a 21-year-old daughter and had a son who would have been 25 years old. He died last year at Meurthe-en-Moselle. Those two children were raised mostly by her mother in Limousin. The daughter has a nasty personality and can never keep a job for long. She came to make a scene; fortunately, I did not witness it. None of those family quarrels have anything to do with me. [...]

8/25/1916.

I received yesterday your two letters from August 21. [...]. Dardelle is going to bring back some live chickens and rabbits. That will provide some variety; no two ways about it, the food right now is very ordinary. I feel sorry for those who do not receive supplements. One of the cooks comes with me to buy our food; he brings a wheelbarrow to bring back the supplies. The cooperative is about 800 meters from our farm. We have a good basement to keep our provisions in; we hang them on a metal trellis because of rats. [...]

Yesterday Caplet received 12 Debussy études for piano. As he and I were studying them, me seated next to him, seven shells landed less than 50 meters from our farm. No one was hurt and nothing destroyed. There was a moment of shock as nothing ever happens here. Just a little incident. [...]

8/26/1916.

Yesterday, I received your August 22 letter. [...] Our piano is legendary; it is all they are talking about in the regiment and the battalion officers at rest come see it. It's quite funny; one would think they were coming to see a prehistoric animal. [...]

8/28/1916.

I haven't received your letter yet today. [...] Last night we had a terrible storm with buckets of water. I do not ever remember seeing so much rainfall in such a short amount of time. [...] We didn't get any sleep as we needed to take steps to prevent flooding. We were among the most fortunate; there was relatively little rain in our little room. We put the piano in the barracks where we eat and where Captain Heron sleeps. Fortunately, last night, seeing the terrible weather, we had the smart idea to cover it with a tent. Otherwise, it would have been flooded. [...] We had also contemplated putting the piano up on planks, but it was saved anyway. This accident obliges us to make a different plan. We have located an empty attic with a pretty good room, a little space that can be easily fixed up. That attic, which is pretty waterproof, will be just what we need. It is quite large; once our piano is moved, it will be well protected. We will be able to work on music there without disturbing anyone else. I will also put my music case in that attic. There is also a stove that can provide some heat if we are here during the winter. [...]

Wednesday, August 30, 1916, 5 p.m.

I didn't receive a letter today but I might at 7:00. [...] Your famous piano which everyone is examining seems to me a strange beast, is it a grand piano? You say it takes 4 cases to pack it. When it is time to move it, that will be a true "aria" and if one of the cases happened to go missing you would be stuck. You need a vehicle just for it. [...]

Friday, September 1, 1916, 9:30 a.m.

I just received your letters of August 27 and 28. I will get busy looking for a wick for your *bougie Pigeon*. I think you will be satisfied by the things you ordered from the food co-op and that your meals will be varied and substantial. Despite all that, I warn you not to give up everything else for food. You are not doing very much which requires physical effort, so take it easy. [...]

Every two weeks, when I send you the *Mercure de France*, I will include some pots of jam, and some cocoa, according to your needs. Be sure to tell me ahead of time what you'd prefer. You are the only one who knows about your personal supplies and what is missing. Don't wait until the last minute (as is your so praise-worthy habit).

Second letter, same day, 1:00 p.m.

I am writing again today because there is much I forgot to tell you. For the *Mercure de France*, you need to send it back to me. That gives you a good excuse not to loan it to others. You can tell them the truth, that your mother sent it to you without reading it so you would have it first but she wants it back as soon as possible. The issues come out on the first and 15th of the month and cost 1,50. It is worth the price and, because of its literary interest, deserves to be saved. I always meant to tell you to send it back, but I thought that would occur to you also. After the war, the collection will sell for a lot of money. It would not be smart to damage or lose the issues I send you. Try to not get them dirty or let them deteriorate. [...]

There are some works by Corelli for two violins, viola and bass, the cello could take that part. I could send you a volume containing those pieces. You'd only need to copy out the separate parts. That would be the occasion for you to become acquainted with some of those works. Bowing in Corelli is difficult.

That would be an excellent exercise. I am very happy that you are polishing Bach's Sonata in A for solo violin. That is very useful work and a good use of your time. The fugue is splendid: it needs to be played with a broad, calm, well-placed motion. The ending has amazing breadth, it is a Michelangelo-like fresco. The last page of that fugue must be played more and more broadly, more and more nobly. As a musician, Bach was a great painter—one needs to understand and be able to interpret him. The first movement, Grave, with its intimate, religious feeling, is not easy. In the Andante, the melody has a delicate charm, flowing, gliding with great freedom in the bow. The final movement, the Allegro, is unusual, with a very pronounced rhythm. Bach indicates the "pianos" and the "fortes" intentionally. Doesn't Caplet know his music? What does he have to say about it? Maybe he never studied much Bach. […]

8/30/1916.

[…] Yesterday I went to the cooperative and made my purchases: for 132 francs, I bought 8 beautiful cauliflowers at 1,20 each; 6 bunches of celery; 10 kilos of green beans, artichokes, tomatoes; magnificent pears for 1,90 a kilo; beautiful grapes (black and white); bananas, and apples. […] We are working to transform our attic into a music room. We will put the piano there and will be much more independent than where we have been. […]

Sunday, September 3, 1916, 4 p.m.

[…] I received yesterday afternoon your letter from August 30. […] I did a purge today and I feel better. My stomach was a bit heavy and I had some swelling. The heat we had in August fatigued my stomach and intestines, so it was smart of me. I am feeling quite well, but I stopped for now taking thionhydrol. I thought it was causing my stomach swelling these past 10 days. I remember a few years ago that calcium phosphate powder mixed in water from Pougues,[211] ordered by Doctor Bretonville had the same effect but not to the same degree. I could be wrong, but I prefer stopping for now. Mme Bohm only ordered one bottle; she wanted to see what effect it had. I will write to tell her that I will come see her early in October. […]

8/31/1916.

I received yesterday your letter of August 27 as well as two packages, one with 4 pears, the other with black grapes. Both packages were badly damaged; they had been crushed, and the grapes were turning to wine and the pears were

---

[211] Pougues-les-Eaux is a town in the Nièvre. The water from the spring was first commercialized during the reign of Louis XIV.

mush. Listen to me when I tell you something. I do not need any fruit. At this time, I find everything I want at the cooperative. [...] You are spending a considerable amount of money and rather pointlessly. I am sure that the two packages cost you more than 5 francs. I have all I need and more. Aside from condensed milk and cocoa from time to time, there is nothing else you need to send me except *L'Illustration* and the *Mercure*. [...]

Monday, September 4, 1916, 11:30.

I received this morning your letter from August 31. [...] That was the last time I will send fruit because I know now that you are the one doing the shopping and you can get all the fruits and vegetables you want. [...] I don't need to spend that money. You have everything you need. [...] I also see that Caplet is in the habit of taking leave and coming back late to profit more from the freedom; of course, it's because of women. He knows his march can be played without him. [...]

Recently the *communiqués* are talking about Apremont, Saint-Mihiel, and Bois-le-Prêtre. The Germans must be planning to attack those areas. And it was not just by chance that bombs hit your farm; the Germans want to destroy men and they must have looked for you. [...]

9/1/1916.

I received yesterday your letter of August 28. [...] This morning the division general visited us; he came to see the lodgings and the stables of the supply carriages. He's a big, gangling, unpretentious fellow, with a friendly and agreeable look. But he puts on airs and I would not have a lot of confidence in how smart he would be in the face of danger. His comments don't show him to be very bright, far from it. The rumor is that we won't be here very long. We will be considered a worn-down unit, out of service, at least for a certain length of time. That would be wonderful news for us. Pray it is true. We would spend winter hidden away, far from the world, in our slippers. The *poilus* all agree; and if the war could end by spring, that would be perfect. These are totally self-centered thoughts. [...]

Tuesday, September 5, 1916, 3 p.m.

I received yesterday afternoon your letter from September 1. Mathilde's son was killed in April 1915, he was 24 years old. His grandmother raised him. [...] That poor old woman, who must be 80 years old, doesn't know about the death of her grandson. They tell her that they have no news, that he must be a prisoner. Mathilde doesn't know whether he died in battle; his comrades wrote to tell her they had buried him in a little village named Fleury in Meurthe-et-Moselle. She thinks he was killed by a bullet in the head as he looked over the top of a trench. She really couldn't explain what had happened. But it is certain that he is dead. [...]

Mme Boissard came last week to tell me that the gutter above the kitchen must have a hole in it because water was pouring along the wall behind the toilets and damaging the wall. I went to Durand who sent a workman. The gutter was filled with dirt. The workman took out a huge bucket full. The chimney sweep comes next week to clean the chimney in the kitchen and in the dining room. I owe him for last year; I will have to pay him. I also need to pay the sewer charge for 1915. So I will need to spend a bit of money. I will have to pay attention to my funds. I will also buy several 50-kilo sacks of wood. A few logs put on the fire at night keep burning and give enough heat and I can save on coal. [...]

9/2/1916.

I received yesterday your letter of 29 August and two packages. [...] I received the 100 francs you sent and cashed it yesterday. I needed it for my daily expenses. I can only repeat that you should suspend the shipment of packages—no more fruit, less jam (only two jars every two weeks). Send a package with two cans of condensed milk. That milk from Normandy is truly delicious. If you have never tasted it, you should, just out of curiosity. Gueroult tells me that, in Normandy, all children are brought up on this milk from the time they start drinking from the bottle. With this milk they never have colic. It is certainly better than milk from Switzerland or elsewhere. [...]

As for the shells, none have fallen since the other day. Those were from a tank and pretty powerful. Our farm is not a target; for sure, the *Boches* know about it because it is on the maps, but they have never struck it. Maybe they think it unoccupied. But no matter; after the 8 shells of the other day, the musicians have started making a bomb shelter, which will be 5 meters below ground with supports. It is well under way and in a few days will be finished. The territorials also are getting to work and building a trench shelter; on the farm there was no protection. We are at least 4 kilometers from the front lines and in a low-lying area. [...]

Home leave is being granted on a regular basis and, if this continues, my turn should come toward the end of October. [...]

9/3/1916.

Yesterday I received your letter from August 30. [...] Lyon's piano is not a grand piano, what are you thinking, for heaven's sake? It is an upright and small, made to be exported. Still it has a nice sound and is easy to play. When we move, it will take 4 hours to take it apart and pack it; obviously, we don't want the cases to get lost. Each one will be in a different vehicle. If we put them all together, we would need a vehicle just for us and we are not in that sort of position right now. […]

9/5/1916.

I didn't receive a letter yesterday, but I received two packages. […] I finally managed to get the piano moved, no small task, even with some very strong men. They do not know how to handle furniture of that sort and so they use more effort than necessary. But now the piano is sheltered, with the commander of the 109th, where it will at least be safe from rain. That is essential in this bloody region where it rains all the time. I just received two letters from you which I will read later. […]

Saturday, September 9, 1916, 9:30 a.m.

I received yesterday your letter from September 5. […] Your letters are peppered with as many language mistakes as flowers in the fields—the daisies, buttercups, poppies etc. that decorate the prairies and brighten them up with their strong colors. That is shocking from a young man of your education and intelligence. You need to review your grammar, especially the verbs. […]

9/6/1916.

I received yesterday your letter from September 2. […] This morning I composed a bass part for saxophone, for a *cantique de Jeanne d'Arc* that only had two parts.[212] We will now accompany the song with three parts. I also wrote to ask Niverd to come tune the piano, and to M. Labeyrie, the paymaster, to give him permission to come. I hope that, in just a few days, our piano will be in good shape. It is in a good location and will not be damaged. […] My box of music was transported with the piano and is now safe from bad weather. […]

Sunday, September 10, 1916, 1 p.m.

I received yesterday your letter from September 6. […] You could easily compose something for your violin, but you don't want to bother. You have the time right now. That would be good for you, force you to work a bit. If you wait until you know all the elements of composition to write a piece, you will end up 80 years old and unknown. […]

---

[212] Jeanne d'Arc's significance as a French heroine grew during the war, and this era saw many pieces written in her honor.

9/7/1916.

I received yesterday your letter of September 3. [...] For more than 3 weeks, we have had no potatoes. It's rather extraordinary that the supply officers don't make more effort to meet the needs of the troops. We have nothing but beans or awful lentils, always the same thing. I found a way to buy some in Lehm, an area not far from Souilly. A cavalry man who came to see a friend in the 129th told me about them. I sent a vehicle and we now have 100 kilos which cost 30 francs: not cheap but we really cannot manage without potatoes, they are such an essential vegetable. [...]

Monday, September 11, 1916, 11 a.m.

I received this morning your letter from September 7. [...] There are not many potatoes here right now. [...] Monsieur Bouchard says it is because of the harvest. Everyone is busy harvesting and threshing the wheat; they forget to ship potatoes (shortage of manpower). It seems to me they could use prisoners both for the harvest and for gathering potatoes, in order to be able to provide enough tubers for civilians and soldiers. We are just as badly organized for practical things as in the past. We lack sensible, intelligent leaders. [...]

9/9/1916.

I had no time to write yesterday. [...] The day before I got a mosquito bite on my right hand which formed a lump. I had to put a damp dressing on it. Yesterday it bothered me when I played. Today it is much more inflamed. The doctor says it will take several days. We have had a number of these bites in the regiment. I tell you this because the bandage on my right hand makes it more difficult to write and my handwriting is not very good. [...]

9/10/1916.

I received yesterday your letters of September 6 and 7. [...] My hand is much better. With the moist dressing, it formed a little abscess which ruptured. The relief was immediate; just a few more days of treatments and it will be nothing. I do not really know what bit me; I did not notice anything at all. [...]

I am not in the least becoming depraved, but a pretty little blonde is just what I need, unless she was a hot brunette, I don't care. I think that those totally natural, healthy functions need to be used like all the others and to restrain them too much is wrong. We are exposed to explosions and other shocks to the senses. I hope to pay a bit more attention to that subject, my overall health will be better and I will be less nervous. [...]

Wednesday, September 13, 1916, 4:30 p.m.

I received this afternoon your letter from September 10. […] Monsieur Alan was in Meaux last Sunday and came to see me on Monday to bring me news of Josephine. She is still in Meaux with her youngest daughter, who is my godchild. I gave Monsieur Alan her address so he could check on her. With the things that took place in Meaux during the Battle of the Marne, I thought she might have disappeared. She is 77 years old and doing as well as one can at that age. […]

9/11/1916.

I received your letter from September 7 yesterday. […] A decision was announced this morning that made everyone groan. It seems that the high command thinks passes for leave are given too quickly, so they will slow down the wheel. The result is that the 4th round of passes won't be until December 1. That means I can hardly expect to have a leave until sometime in January of next year. That is the most recent news, unfortunately true. I don't know what the colonel will think when he gets back. We all think he will protest as vigorously as possible; the poor *poilus* have nothing but that pleasure to help them be patient. If they are only given leave every 7 or 8 months, that will not give them much heart! And everything will suffer. Those who decide all those things have no idea of what the *poilu* is going through, nor his state of mind after 24 months of war. The officers, who are relatively comfortable, who receive good monthly stipends and don't suffer physically, don't realize that the poor *poilu* awaits his leave with feverish impatience. That is the only reason he accepts everything else. I feel the big chiefs are taking advantage and that will come back to haunt them. […]

Friday, September 15, 1916, 11 a.m.

I received yesterday afternoon your letter of September 11. […] When one is young, one should not only work but also know how to prepare for old age, I tell you all that because I find that you are becoming lazy. You pass hours in the evening in not very serious conversations. It would be better for you to do a bit of counterpoint with help from Caplet. He can give you some advice which you would probably find useful. When you were in the trenches, it was impossible for you to think about doing that but, in your current location, you should enjoy getting back to that. […]

9/12/1916.

Yesterday I received your letters from September 8 and 9. […] I had thought that I would work on fugues and counterpoint with Caplet, but I realized that his ideas on those forms are narrow and conservative. I prefer to hold off, ready to get back to work a bit later with tireless energy. I am determined to do it. I will start by reworking 4-part counterpoint, imitative and free, then retrograde, and I will restudy fugues. I will work 3 to 4 hours a day. And I will certainly compose. It is not that I am lacking ideas, but I realize too well that I have not mastered the form. After several months of exercises along with study of music theory, I will start to compose in order to use the forms more freely and I will produce, I am convinced, some mature works. [...]

Cloëz thinks that there is a good chance we can get together and make music if we stay here for the winter. He says that the officers are getting bored, and we provide a distraction too important for them to abandon us. [...] The musicians mounted a direct attack against me yesterday. They complained that they do too many chores and that I don't help with any of them. The chief rebuffed them nicely: he explained to the delegation that I was there on higher authority and that they were not to bother me, that, in fact, as far as the music regiment was concerned, I did not exist. You should have seen the faces of those musicians when they heard his categorical answer which ends completely all their maneuvers. The chief was very forceful. [...] Since yesterday, the few musicians I have seen have given me the nicest smiles. [...]

My hand is much better. I always practice violin for an hour or so. Then I chat and I read. Caplet also has a *bougie Pigeon* which gives us two of them. It is sufficient light, gentle, and doesn't flicker so it doesn't hurt the eyes. I do not read novels. Caplet receives a good number of books from the French-American committee but no novels. Right now, I am reading about the life of Walt Whitman, an American poet who died 10 years ago. [...]

We are trying to get Magne out of the mess he is in; he is overworked, and I never see him. They are taking revenge for the privileges he had early on. But I think that Laine will be able to get him transferred to the division as telephone operator. [...]

9/13/1916.

I did not receive a letter yesterday and once again it seems the postal service is not always regular. [...] I don't know whether you understand that our area, quite nice in a good season, becomes very sad in bad weather. The sense of isolation is especially strong, and it takes a lot of willpower to avoid being depressed. I am not talking about me with my privileged position; for my friends it is very hard. [...]

Sunday, September 17, 1916, 12:30 p.m.

I received yesterday afternoon your letter from September 13. [...] The weather has been nice these past few days [...] but the nasty season will be upon us very soon and if you stay where you are, as you expect, the time will be very sad. That is why, every way you can, you should practice violin and organize concerts at the same time as you dig into counterpoint. [...]

9/14/1916.

I received yesterday your letter from September 10. [...] For our Mass I had to turn to two saxophones—a baritone saxophone for the bass and for which I wrote the bass part for the song of Jeanne d'Arc, and an alto saxophone. The saxophones work pretty well in terms of timbre, giving a sound a bit like the organ. [...] Thus, for our Mass, Jacquet played the top part on flute, then me on violin, then Dehuysser on alto saxophone, Duchamp on clarinet, Quinnaud playing Caplet's viola, and a baritone saxophone for bass because Maréchal was on leave.

I needed to change the orchestration a bit. The sound was quite good, a real success. Caplet has worked on Bach fugues, but not as a violinist, so he is not very familiar with the solo violin sonatas. And his temperament is not much suited to Bach; Caplet is subtle, like Debussy. He is not Debussy's student but he has been strongly influenced by him. [...] I found the piano *études* interesting; they are very difficult, demanding much work. Caplet couldn't play them; he would stumble through them. Debussy's style is very much his own, not at all modern in the sense of Tournemire. Sometimes, amidst all the strangeness a hint of an early music sound breaks through. It is enormously delicate and subtle. [...]

9/15/1916.

I received yesterday your two letters from September 11. [...] Contrary to what you say, compared with my comrades, I am not the least clever, far from it: my situation is clear, perfectly defined and I do absolutely nothing military. I am certainly the one of our group who has the fewest military obligations. To change what I am doing would be a huge mistake, and I will not risk it. The entire group would have to go with Mangin, be attached to him and I might still have less independence. [...] If you were to see one day Vessot, Rolland or others of my comrades, you should ask them what they think of my situation. They will all tell you that my position, unique in the regiment, astonishes them. I must not complain. With the concerts we will be giving, this position and situation will be guaranteed by the general, so all is for the best. You cannot even imagine how much care I had to use to undo all the nastiness and machinations I was subjected to. I had to be quite the diplomat! [...]

9/17/1916.

I received yesterday your letter from September 13. [...] Cloëz just alerted us to a note from Central Headquarters that this winter, concerts, plays, and other distractions are to be given to the *poilus* to bolster their courage and morale. [...]

9/18/1916.

I received yesterday your letter from September 14. [...] My mastery of Bach is absolute. I no longer have difficulty with the sonatas. After the war, I will certainly want to get back to my idea of playing all the Bach sonatas in two concerts. They will be mature and ready. It is something that few violinists can do. [...]

9/19/1916.

I left the farm yesterday morning for Génicourt. Having left at 11 a.m. with the ambulance, I arrived about noon. I had lunch with Cloëz and one of his friends, a professional contrabass player. I rehearsed the Saint-Saëns *Rondo* and worked on music for an hour. During that time, M. Labeyrie, the paymaster, arrived and insisted that I play some music that evening. So, instead of leaving with the vehicle at 6:30, I stayed in Génicourt. After dinner, we got organized to play some music. I read the second Saint-Saëns trio, which I didn't know.[213] It is quite difficult, has a nice sound and the public likes it. However, it is rather shallow music and a bit old-fashioned. I also played some Bach and a few other pieces. We got to bed very late. This morning, I was at the division. There was no vehicle leaving for our farm, so I stayed here for lunch and will leave about 12:30 or 1 with the mail officer. [...] I slept at Cloëz's first-aid station, in an excellent bed that usually is that of a doctor right now serving elsewhere. I was nice and warm and slept very well. It rained heavily last night and those poor guys in the trenches can't have spent such a pleasant night. [...]

We are going to take advantage of a note from Joffre requesting we make music. That note, from August 28, is almost a month old. The division general doesn't like music at all. But we will try to make something happen. [...] I think we will succeed, all the more because an oppressive boredom is starting to settle on everyone. [...] It is with some emotion that here, from the heights of Génicourt, I watch the Meuse flowing. Once across that river, it is Souilly, Bar-le-Duc, and Paris. One day the time will come when we can return to our homes in peace. [...]

---

[213] Saint-Saëns, Piano trio No. 2 in E minor, Op. 92.

Thursday, September 21, 1916, 3 p.m.

I received yesterday your letter from September 18, and in the evening the one from September 17. […] This morning I went to look at sleeping bags at the Louvre. Nothing but a few pieces of junk from last year. At the Belle Jardinière I found two styles I liked. One is canvas, lined with goatskin, for sleeping indoors, at a price of 69 francs. The other is lined with wool fleece, the outside rubber, beautiful quality, for 79 francs. Tell me which you prefer in a stamped letter so I can get it quickly. […]

Second letter, same day, 7:30 p.m.

I received this afternoon your letter from the 19th. […] So General Joffre put out a note on August 28 requiring distractions for the soldiers, but your division general doesn't pay much attention. He may not like music very much; still, he should carry out the orders he receives and certainly realize that his men need entertainment and encouragement to face another winter of suffering. It is not very generous nor humane on his part. The higher the rank of an officer, the more he should be a father, a support, a comfort to his men. […]

It must be pretty cold in your room if the ceiling has holes in it. No wonder you feel the cold and humidity. If the room cannot be repaired, you should do what Caplet did, move. […] Your sleeping bag must be damp and very dirty. […] You should have had it washed when the weather was hot. On the same subject, I think you didn't get your jacket washed either. A cloth garment, with lining, should not be washed in the nasty season; it would take two weeks to dry and all you need is to wear damp clothes! […]

Friday, September 22, 1916, 1:30 p.m.

[…] I sent you this morning in the mail two registered packages: a can of condensed milk and a can of sardines, a box of biscuits I had in the house, and Bach's *St. Matthew Passion*.[214] I had meant to send that for a long time. You will find some arias for solo violin accompanied by various instruments, one for cello, and the really lovely one for contralto accompanied by first and second violin and organ. (Could the bass replace the organ?). I don't know whether the alto voice could be replaced by an instrument. That way either Caplet or you could play it (with some work you might be able to play viola for that). No matter how, the violin accompaniment is by itself very expressive. There you have a program for future concerts, and some wonderful pieces for the Mass of Toussaint and the Dead. Play those pieces on a concert to get them in your fingers and make their beauty come alive. That way they will be all set for the first days

[214] BWV 244.

of November. [...] I hesitated to send the *Passion*; you already have so much music from here. Now that you have different instruments available, you should be able to do something good. [...] I thought of the viola for the aria because you will not find the voice you need, and then, one cannot sing in German! [...]

I sent you a letter from Josephine's daughter, my goddaughter. She invites me to come to Meaux some Sunday. I will first thank her, then I need to find out whether I need a "safe conduct pass" and the train times. Once I know, I will warn them if I decide to come see them, especially Josephine who is elderly. [...]

Saturday, September 23, 1916.

Since the letter you sent from Génicourt, on the 19th, I've had no news. [...] I hope to have a letter this afternoon. This morning the weather is lovely, the sun is shining brightly and its rays are warm, which feels good. Autumn started a 9:00; we have to hope that it will be dry and that we will still enjoy a bit of warmth in October. I wish it, especially for all of you. [...]

9/23/1916.

[...] An interesting thing happened as a result of General Joffre's note from August 28 calling for the organization of celebrations, concerts, etc. to entertain the men. As a result of that note, the Army Corps asked for a list from the divisions and our names were provided. Captain Liberos told us about this and said we might well be asked to play soon in Ambly where the officer training takes place. [...]

The weather today is nice, but the air is cool, almost cold. Inside my tent cloth, which is buttoned to make a sack, there is straw which makes a mattress on the metal frame. I put my sleeping bag on that, climb in after taking off my pants, and put on my sweater from Brittany. Then I put the blanket over it and under me. Then over my feet I put my jacket, and higher up my *capote*, and over everything, my oilcloth. That way, I am nice and warm. When I have a warmer sleeping bag, I'll be able to withstand colder temperatures. [...]

9/24/1916.

I received yesterday your letter of September 20. [...] Today is an anniversary: last year on this same day, we were in the trenches in Neuville, on the eve of the famous offensive of September 25 which was so deadly for us. Here we are, a year older and this terrible war continues; despite undeniable victories over the *Boches*, nothing leads us to see the end of this dreadful thing. [...]

There is a lot of repositioning right now in our sector. A division on our left, which was holding Les Éparges, has moved out and was not replaced. We have all stretched out a bit to fill the void. Since this area is the worst spot in the sector, as much for the muddy ground as for the land mine war that goes on endlessly, they have decided that each regiment in the division will take a turn here. The details of these changes are not yet worked out, but the result is that we will not stay here, safe and quiet, on our farm. As for staying in this sector, there is not much doubt that we will be here until next March. [...]

9/25/1916.

I just received your letters from September 21 [...] and am answering immediately with regard to the sleeping bag. I need the cloth one with the goat skin lining. I never sleep on the ground, and if I did, I have the means to keep out the damp, with my oilcloth which is in very good condition and the waterproof canvas I just received. For now, I have buttoned the canvas, forming a sack which, filled with straw, serves as a mattress. The sleeping bag lined with goat skin is perfect for me; I will be very cozy. [...]

Thursday, September 28, 1916, 6 p.m.

I received this afternoon your letter from September 25. I am writing a bit late today because this morning I went to the Belle Jardinière to buy your sleeping bag and this afternoon Mathilde came to make up the 4 hours she owed me. Monsieur Alan will come tomorrow and take the package to the rue de Palestro. So tomorrow I will send you a canvas sleeping bag with a goatskin lining. [...]

9/26/1916.

I received yesterday your letter of September 22. The important news from yesterday is this: we received a note from Lemoine that there is going to be a concert in Ambly on October 4 and we need to provide an hour of light, entertaining music, and send the program back with the courier. We answered immediately with the following program: we will play Gustave Charpentier's *Napoli*,[215] then Bizet's *Adagietto* and Boccherini's *Menuet*.[216] I will play *Méditations de Thaïs* and *Airs Bohémiens* with two Brahms dances in between.[217] Then Maréchal will play *Prière* and Popper's *Tarantelle*;[218] we will end with Caplet's March for the 5th Division. Cloëz will provide all the music.

We had just sent our reply when another message arrived from Lemoine stating that the Army Corps was authorizing us to get together twice a week in Génicourt for rehearsals. So here we are, once again together to make music!

[215] Gustave Charpentier (1860-1956).
[216] Georges Bizet (1838-1875) from *L'Arlésienne*, Suite No. 1.
[217] Massenet, Symphonic intermezzo from the opera *Thaïs*; Pablo de Sarasate. Brahms *Hungarian Dances* (1879).
[218] Boëllman, *Prière à Notre Dame,* from *Suite Gothique;* David Popper (1843-1913).

No need to tell you with what joy we received this news. We told Maréchal, who happened to be passing by on his bicycle, and he immediately went to tell Magne. They were like two crazy young boys. I can understand that; their situations are much worse than ours. If this message doesn't completely free them from service, it does show that the division, and even the army corps, is interested in them. The result was that those around them immediately muted their nastiness. […] It is a bit thanks to me that all this happened. When we were last in Génicourt, we had a meeting to decide what to do. I proposed exactly what has just happened. Caplet decided to go along with us, but he favored moving more gradually. […]

Here is a copy of the note: "The soldiers whose names follow: Caplet sergeant, Durosoir soldier are chosen to participate in the musical events that will take place in Ambly, in the courtyard of the company commanders. All means should be put at their disposition for the travel necessary for their rehearsals. As a result, until further orders, they will come together under the direction of Sergeant Caplet Tuesday and Friday of every week." The text is absolutely delicious and I hope to send the note to you as a souvenir. […]

Monday, October 2, 1916, 2 p.m.

I received this morning your letter of September 28. You've received all your shipments. I think you will find the butter I sent very good. You should also have the money order. The sleeping bag is on its way; you will probably have it tomorrow. The horrible weather is back; it's been raining since noon and is not at all warm. […]

In your current situation, you can't do much but remain calm and try to get out of all of this healthy and in one piece. […] But do start thinking about yourself and imitate your friends; think about yourself, you are your best adviser and your best friend. […] I would like for you to always have confidence in me, my dear little *chami*,[219] I do so want to see you where you should be and I would do anything to save you problems. You talk too much; you open yourself too much to your friends. They are careful to do the opposite. Copy them and keep quiet. […]

10/1/1916.

I didn't receive a letter yesterday. I hope you are in good health and that is not why I didn't receive the usual news. As for us, we have some news. Suddenly, in the middle of yesterday afternoon, we received the order to move to Mouilly. This morning, very early, everyone left for this village, no more than 1500 meters away. I stayed at our farm with Duthiou, a sergeant in charge of

[219] A term of endearment, possibly related to camel (*chameau*).

equipment. I will leave for Génicourt tomorrow morning, Monday, with all my stuff. As we have to rehearse on Tuesday and have a concert on Thursday, and another rehearsal Friday, I have no scruples about staying all week in Génicourt. [...] The regiment is billeted at Rupt, where it will stay for several days before going to Éparges. They will be much better there than in Mouilly which has been totally destroyed by bombs. [...]

I will try, if possible, to get leave after the concert on the 5th of October. The pretext (which is true) is that my violin is coming unglued and needs to be repaired. In fact, after the damp weather we've had recently, the top is partly unglued causing a decrease in sonority. My pretext is thus totally reasonable and I will try to profit from it. [...]

Yesterday, as soon as we learned about the decision to move, we called the division for a car and transported the piano and my case of music to Génicourt. [...] A rumor is running around that we will soon be part of an army group which Mangin will lead. Obviously for us, personally, that would be advantageous. The *poilus* don't want it, which I understand. [...]

Tuesday, October 3, 1916, 10 a.m.

I didn't receive a letter yesterday; you must be busy. [...] Come on, my dear little *chami*, get over the nastiness you see around you. As you say yourself, let your art be a breath of fresh air and purification for you. Confide all your feelings and thoughts to your art, so it will be a reflection of your soul. My *mimi*, tell your old mother what they did to you. Be careful in what you say, even with your friends; they don't always say what they think. Do they make fun of you? [...]

Intrigue was not part of how I raised you because I also knew nothing about it and I hate that sort of behavior. I am all honesty and sincerity. My parents also knew nothing about it—all the families of the market gardeners were a bit like shepherds in the Bible, they married their children very young among themselves (even first cousins). They all shared the same type of honesty, the same financial situation (never very high). They never tried to cheat on others. I never saw around me the evil thoughts, lies, jealousy that are found in other parts of society. [...] I always tried to point out to you those things, to make you wary of those who would try to put you down. It was my duty. You should understand that and start paying close attention to the people around you before you speak without thinking. Words are silver and silence is golden. [...]

10/2/1916.

[...] You must have read in the papers that everyone is supposed to get three leaves a year of 7 days each. Truth is that, in the regiments, a lot of men only had leave every 7 or 8 months. It's really not enough. Everyone is worn out by the length of the war; they have to do something for the *poilu*, at least look like they are paying attention to him. One has to expect, after the war, some strange revelations and violent objections which will be oddly bitter for many leaders. […]

10/3/1916.

I received this afternoon your two letters of 29 and 30 September which the quartermaster brought me. […] Here in Génicourt we will take every meal at the kitchen of the division secretaries, that is, our portions of meat and vegetables. We just need to buy some things to supplement that, a fairly small personal expense. And we all add from our personal provisions. […]

The Army Corps vehicles will come pick us up on Thursday at 6:30 to take us to Ambly. It's quite chic. I don't dress very warmly for the rehearsals. For more than a year now, I've not had a cold or sore throat: this life in the open air is totally good for one's health. […]

10/4/1916.

I received today your letter of September 30 and I sent you 3 *Mercure* and the aluminum bottle that contained rum. I've given instructions to have my sleeping bag sent to me when it arrives. I am rather shocked by the weight; 5 kilos are a lot for a soldier. I will try to put it in my music case when I need to move. […]

10/8/1916.

I haven't written as I was hoping to leave on permission; I am probably not going to get the leave. Tomorrow I will go back to Génicourt and will see Commander Lambrigot with Caplet, but you should not count on it.

There is no question that this is all the fruit of the jealousies that surround me. All I can do now is maybe send my instrument with another soldier on leave. The clarinetist Duchamp is supposed to have leave soon. Or I will wait until I have leave myself, probably not before the middle of December. […]

Wednesday, October 11, 1916, 4:30 p.m.

I finally received a letter dated October 9. I was starting to worry. How is it that you didn't write after October 4? What were you doing? […] I don't think you were locked up somewhere; you could have scribbled some news for me with your pencil. […] You told me you would be coming on leave, so I didn't know what to think. […] I haven't sent any packages for several days, thinking you would be coming to Vincennes. I am thus going to wait until you explain everything that happened during that time. […]

Second letter, same day, 7 p.m.

I am writing again because I received this afternoon your letter from October 10. [...] I see that you are in Rupt, and that the 25 musicians went to Les Éparges with the regiment, so they must need them. There are not enough Red Cross stretcher bearers. If the mud in Les Éparges is so terrible, what would it be like if it was raining? Right now, the weather is nice and rather warm. [...]

Friday, October 13, 1916, 11 a.m.

I received yesterday afternoon your letter from October 10. [...] Don't send your violin with a soldier on leave. If you come home on regular leave in November, you will bring your violin for the visit and can have the work done and take it back repaired. [...] Two advantages: the pleasure of being home for a few days and an easy way to get the violin repaired without wasting time. [...]

10/11/1916.

I didn't receive a letter yesterday; that is easy to understand because I had told you I would come home on leave soon. You were waiting for me so did not write. We are supposed to give a concert on Thursday for a battalion of the 36th which is here on rest. We should have an answer by 10 a.m. this morning from Commander Ménager of the 36th. The issue is the hall. If a house in which the troops are staying can be cleared out, the concert will happen; if not, then it will not happen. We have orders to build a theater like the one in Ambly, but it will not be ready for 10 days or so. We envisage, therefore, that we may be able to give two or three concerts a week.

We will have work to do. Forestier, a student of Widor,[220] came to see us yesterday. Artilleryman, he is part of a group attached to the 6th Division. He is also an excellent musician with an amazing memory. He plays piano and accompanies a great many pieces from memory. We worked on some Schumann. We worked again on the first trio, which we have already played, and read through the 2nd and 3rd which are both fascinating in various ways. Schumann's works, especially those with unexpected flights of fantasy, are always heartfelt and tender. The next time, we will work seriously on his 2nd trio. Those difficult works, which demand serious attention, are rarely played. But what beautiful music! [...]

10/13/1916.

Yesterday I received your two letters from October 8 and 9. We set off yesterday at noon for Rupt, after a quick lunch. The concert, at 2:00 p.m., was in a not very resonant but vast barn. Many of the *poilus* from the 36th were there. The

---

[220] Charles-Marie Widor (1844-1937).

colonel also. An ammunition truck transported us there (we also took the piano), waited for us and brought us back—we were back by 6:00 p.m. The concert was not bad: the music regiment of the 36th lent a hand. We interspersed singers, actors, and monologues in our program which was very successful. In the near future we will give another for the 74th, and in a few days, when our regiment is here, we will also take part in a concert. And we will give a special chamber music concert; so we are seeing things evolve quite nicely. [...].

10/14/1916.

I did not receive any letters yesterday. [...] The good news for us, just today, is that we will be assigned, *en subsistence*, to the division. You have to agree that good things come to those who wait. What is best is that we didn't ask for anything. It is the division that realized the inconvenience of having to shuffle us back and forth. With this change all our difficulties evaporate. [...] We will avoid all the coming and going in the mud which is the lot of our poor comrades, and which, in a region like this, will make life this winter particularly hard. [...] We owe this to General Lebrun who heard us play in Ambly and seemed quite satisfied. [...]

10/17/1916.

[...] Something happened to me, fortunately not of great importance; I lost my wallet. At 11 p.m. last night I went to the WC and this morning I realized that my wallet was no longer in the outer pocket of my jacket. This morning I retraced my path and didn't find it; maybe someone found and took it to his company office. Today I'll file a report and will go to the various company offices to see whether it was left with any of them. Fortunately, there was no money. I'm not in the habit of putting money in it; I put my money in a silk money holder or in my other money holder. So the wallet only contained your two letters from yesterday, a letter from Bastien, and some unimportant papers. [...]

10/18/1916.

I got my wallet back. It had been picked up by someone and left in the office of another company. I had barely mailed your letter yesterday than they brought it to me. [...] Yesterday I received your two letters from the 13th and two packages. [...] Try to get rid of the idea that I don't play my cards well. I am not always able to control people or events [...] but when I have the opportunity to make a move for myself, rarely do I not succeed at getting what I want. [...]

The music regiment posted in Les Éparges is serving as relay runners for the injured, or making tea for the companies, or taking soup to the central post of advanced units. In short, the music regiment in Éparges had work that was not so easy, given the mud and the weather in this damned countryside.

At this moment, in the *sapes*, we sink in up to our waists, and if our comrades didn't help, it would be very hard to get out. This winter we have to expect some of them to get stuck in the mud. In the ravine of F, there are, apparently, 30,000 men, French and German, whose bodies sleep, stuck in the mud, it's frightening. Civilians know nothing of all these horrors. In certain spots we see the bayonets sticking up, the *poilu* is underneath, still grasping his rifle in his clenched hands. We haven't been very fortunate; for a year we got out of all sorts of dreadful situations and they put us in a relatively quiet area! But Les Éparges shouldn't be described as "quiet:" the living conditions are terrible. [...]

10/27/1916.

I received yesterday your letter of October 23. We rehearsed the "Archduke" trio yesterday. [...] Colonel Dumesnil, commander of the 43rd artillery, has invited us to the division for an evening party he hopes to hold soon. It appears that he likes music very much and plays the cello a bit. He is very "military" and was not making any music up to now, apparently in order not to set a bad example. Now that he sees that, on orders from higher up, music is "à la mode," he wants to take advantage of it and asks for us. [...]

10/28/1916.

I received yesterday your two letters from the 24th and two packages. [...] We have a date set for the first rehearsal of the quartet, tomorrow, Sunday, at 8:30 p.m. We will have to rush back from Sommedieue where we are playing in the afternoon. And we play tomorrow morning for Mass. [...] As you see, we are always working on something; meanwhile the months go by. [...] Cloëz and I are starting to work on Beethoven's C Minor Sonata to give him a break from the Fauré which is getting on his nerves.[221] I had not played it in a long time; how very lovely and sad it is! [...]

Monday, October 30, 1916, 6 p.m.

I received this afternoon your letter of October 28. [...] You ask me sometimes whether Mathilde is doing what I need. [...] She works in the morning for another lady and, when she comes to me, she is often tired from her morning's work. She has aged and no longer has the same strength. I work with her on the afternoons she allots me so that all the cleaning gets pretty well done, that is, in

---

[221] Fauré, Sonata for violin and piano, Op. 13.

the dining room and the bedrooms. I never clean the stairs, the entryway, or the kitchen. I am still very happy to have found her, she's a good, honest person. [...]

10/29/1916.

I received yesterday your letter from the 25th as well as a package with a can of Amieux sardines, two little cans of Alsatian pâté, and a can of salmon. Send less chocolate than you did in the past, a box every three weeks is plenty. That, with some unsweetened condensed milk, makes an excellent snack; or, when we have rice, we make chocolate rice which is also very nice. We find in the co-op everything you could send and for less than you pay. What they do not have are the Amieux sardines. You could also send from time-to-time jam and some butter, as much as a pound—a pound every Saturday or Sunday, especially in the colder weather. [...]

11/1/1916.

[...] The 36th and the 129th are now both in Les Éparges, that is to say that they alternate a week on service and a week of rest. The colonel has agreed that we will give two chamber music concerts during the week of rest. So we have our work cut out for us. [...]

11/3/1916.

This morning's mail is late, it is 9:30 and it has not yet arrived. Since the recent problems in Verdun, there is a bit of difficulty with the distribution of letters and packages. [...] I saw Rolland yesterday. He gave me a *Boche* button recently taken from one of our prisoners. I am going to have a ring made for me modeled on the one that Lyon made. There is a fellow in the battery who makes that model beautifully. By my next leave, I will have a lovely ring made from a button from a German captured in Les Éparges. The Lyon ring, which is quite lovely, is only suitable for men. [...]

Monday, November 6, 1916, 7 p.m.

I am writing today to talk about myself; you scold me for not doing that often enough. I always start my letters with important things, and there is always so much to tell you that I get to the bottom of the last page and put off until the next day more personal things. You keep asking me whether I've gone to see Madame Bohm. No, because I am feeling fine and have no intention of taking any medication. However, I do want to go see her to thank her and find out how much I owe her. The three afternoons when Mathilde is here keep me very busy; I do not have much time left to sew. In the morning I shop and prepare lunch.

Nothing extraordinary as cooking goes, but I still need to do it and then clean up. I don't want to do any sewing in the evening by lamplight to keep from tiring my eyes. Night comes early, the day goes by without having time to do very much. [...]

11/4/1916.

I did not receive a letter yesterday; maybe you did not write. [...] Maréchal left this morning on a 48-hour leave to bring back a cello. His *"poilu"* (we call it by that name because it is in light wood, made by a carpenter) doesn't make a sound. The top is very warped; he needs to hold it together with string. He is going to bring back his prize cello, a Caressa. [...] Our next concert will be in Ambly, November 9, and Maréchal will be there for that one. All this work does not happen without an element of fatigue; that is when we notice our lack of practice. My violin is getting worse and worse, it is time for me to have a leave. [...]

11/8/1916.

I received yesterday your two letters from November 3 and 4. As to the concert programs, I can only send you those that exist. Up to now, it is only at Sommedieue that programs were created. For sure, the way the programs are done doesn't give the public much information. When we go on stage, there is a guy who is the stage manager. He announces, for example, *Airs Bohémiens* by Sarasate, violin solo by Monsieur Durosoir. That way the public is sufficiently informed and we can change the program. [...]

There are almost no civilians in Génicourt, aside from the mayor, his wife, his daughter, and two other women. I know no one. Génicourt is very small, maybe 150 residents normally. As for postcards, they disappeared a long time ago. [...]

11/9/1916.

I received yesterday your letter of November 4, and four packages. [...] The weather is dreadful, but it's not very cold. The humidity is awful, I really pity all the guys who are in mud the likes of which you cannot imagine. The artillery horses come back from resupply covered in mud from their heads to their feet. They sink into it above their bellies, so you can just envision men in such conditions. Our regiments are dwindling seriously, a great many men are evacuated. By the end of the winter, the 129th will not be worth much at all. Those who remain will be totally worn out. It is not possible to imagine the mud at Les Éparges, and along with all that, the *Boches* detonate mines about once a week, it's all a lot of fun! [...]

11/10/1916.

I received yesterday your letter of November 5 and today, earlier than usual, your two letters from November 6. [...] Yesterday we played for the 36th; the hall was not really ready, not in terms of lighting and other things. It was total improvisation from start to finish. Maréchal had not yet returned (he only arrived at 5 p.m.), so Niverd played cello. [...] Maréchal arrived exhausted by his trip; his cello caused a lot of difficulties. He took his *poilu* to Cunault who was very interested in that instrument. He will repair it. We will probably see it during my next leave. [...]

11/11/1916.

Today I did not receive a letter. [...] Yesterday Deschamps, an old comrade from the trenches, came to see me. Even with all their faults, it is a pleasure to see again those who have been spared. We remember so many tragic events. Deschamps had transferred to the motorcycle unit [...]. He realized we were here after he heard talk of the concert we gave, the day before yesterday, at Ambly. We talked a long time about shared memories. [...]

11/14/1916.

Yesterday I received your letter from November 10 and two packages. I have to admit yesterday was a particularly busy day: we rehearsed at 10 a.m., left at 2:30 for Rupt, spent the afternoon rehearsing, and the concert was at 8:30. The colonel was lovely and invited me to dinner, explaining he could not invite all three of us because there was not enough food. What a charming man he is! Dinner consisted of a soup of pureed peas with croutons, braised beef with carrots, roast chicken and salad, cheese, apples and bananas and egg custard. During that time, Maréchal and Cloëz were stuffing themselves at my former kitchen where there was an excellent dinner all prepared. [...]

11/16/1916.

I was not able to write yesterday because I was busy, up to the last minute, with the inauguration of the theater. I received your letters of November 12 and 13. [...] Before I leave, I will send you some clothes, even dirty things, otherwise I will have too much to carry. [...]

Lucien again had leave, apparently about two weeks long, based on the letters.

12/3/1916.

I took the 8:30 train to Revigny. There I found a train leaving for Souilly that did not leave until 3:15. I didn't get to Souilly until 10:30 a.m.: I got off in the new station, 1 km from the town. I set off in the direction of the town; there was no vehicle at that station in the middle of the fields going toward Génicourt. Fortunately, as soon as I arrived in the town, I found a truck going to Ambly which took me to within 200 meters of Génicourt. I arrived at noon. Magne, Maréchal, and Delmas were just sitting down to eat. They greeted me and my goose and my chicken with cries of joy. We drank the red wine I had in my bidon and in the evening a bottle of Sauternes. [...] I found my pack and all my stuff. It is very nice here, but very cold. It freezes every night, to 4 or 5 below zero. [...]

12/4/1916.

I've not yet received a letter, maybe tomorrow, but that seems still a bit too soon. [...] The weather is dreadful, not only cold but lots of snow. [...]

12/5/1916.

I've not yet received a letter. [...] It's now pretty sure that we will be here until February. That is nice for us; it is not the same for the *poilus*—their life is dreadful. It snows all the time; hardly ever do we have a clear day. The snow covers the ground and Génicourt, because of the traffic, is an indescribable mushy mess, so I leave my boots hanging on a nail and wear my other shoes with covers that the government gave me. [...]

Sunday, December 3, 1916, 6 p.m.

I will not mail this letter until tomorrow morning. I do not want to go out this evening because of my cold which is at its worst stage. [...] I went out twice this morning to buy butter and cheese so I could send a package to you. You didn't have any of those things in your rucksack. [...] You need to eat well with the cold weather we are having and do not go to bed too late. You will be much better off in your warm sleeping bag than scratching away on the violin until 11 p.m. [...] In a room without heat, it must be frigid when you get in bed and it must take hours to warm up. I hope you have the intelligence to drink something hot during your rehearsals. [...]

Monday, December 4, 1916, 5 p.m.

I am writing a bit late, first because Mathilde is here and she keeps me busy, then because I wasted a lot of time uselessly today. The water was shut off on Saturday, December 2 in the afternoon and all Sunday morning. I had planned to cook up what was left of the goose with some cabbage and various vegetables. Without water I could not wash the vegetables properly. I put all that off until this morning, hoping finally to have a decent lunch. At 9 a.m. this morning the water was shut off again. I had barely started peeling the vegetables. I couldn't cook anything without water. [...] I had to send Mathilde to Monsieur Bouchard for a few buckets of water in order to clean up a bit. That is not at all funny. I fear I may be without water for a few days. So everything was delayed and forced me to do my letter writing a bit late. [...]

This piercing cold freezes one to the bones. It looks like it might snow. [...]

Tomorrow is your birthday. Maybe you saved the white Bordeaux you took with you. You will drink it with your friends to celebrate. If Lieutenant Lyon happened to come see you, he will have chosen a good moment. At any rate, the days go by, the years go by and the years add up without any big change. All of that is so sad one soon will stop talking about it. We need to find new words to convey this tragedy. We have run out of ways to groan, or at least ways to talk about it. [...]

12/7/1916.

I didn't receive a letter today, but I did receive a package. [...] Caplet also just got back from leave. He has a strange sort of stove in his room. He lit it last night and went to bed. During the night, for an unknown reason, the air intake suddenly stopped and Caplet was almost asphyxiated. He found himself on the floor in the middle of the night and had a lot of difficulty opening the window. This morning they came for us very early, Cloëz and me. He ached everywhere, was vomiting, and had a terrible headache—all the symptoms of carbon monoxide poisoning. He was very lucky to be able to get his window open. So today we took care of him and investigated the problem with the stove. We will get over the emotion, but accidents like that are really stupid. We are going to get to work on the "Archduke" and on Chausson's Quartet with piano,[222] obviously without Caplet. Sunday we will go to Sommedieue and play for Mass in the morning. [...]

Saturday, December 9, 1916, 5 p.m.

I received at 4:00 your letter from December 7. [...] Caplet was almost asphyxiated? One never lights a fire before going to bed. You light the fire during the day to be able to watch it and get the room warm, and in the evening, you extinguish it and carefully close all the vents. Most or all of the fuel is used

---

[222] Ernest Chausson (1855-1899). This is probably his *Concert* for violin, piano, and string quartet, D major.

up; there is no danger of asphyxiation. [...] There is no excuse for going to sleep with unburned coal in a stove. [...]

12/8/1916.

[...] This year, even the division officers have great difficulty finding enough for heat; you can imagine that they don't give a thought to us in such conditions! Fortunately, these past years we've gotten used to not having a fire. We can warm up from time to time at the first-aid post, with old planks, an old beam, with all sorts of things we've pulled out of the ruined homes. We are not being kind to this area! [...]

12/10/1916.

[...] We just played for Mass; I am writing this in a hurry. It is 10 a.m. and at 11:45 we leave by car with our piano for Sommedieue. I just wanted to tell you that we will be 6 for the *Réveillon* because Caplet will be with us.[223] And if Nelly Martyl comes to sing,[224] Caplet insists that she celebrate with us despite the competition from some of the officers. I would like you to send me a rather large foie gras, or 2 medium-sized ones. Magne is in charge of the wine: he asked his mother for 6 bottles of Champagne. As for Caplet, he is getting a pineapple. So please send me one or two particularly well-chosen packages. [...]

12/11/1916.

I received yesterday your letter from December 6 and several packages. [...] We have a lot of work to do on all this music, enough for at least 6 to 8 months. Unfortunately, the war will last longer than that. We get the feeling that the people behind the lines are starting to care about all this. They finally understand the reality of this horrible war and the sacrifices that will be needed if we want to get out of this honorably. They certainly did not have a clue up to now. Suddenly they see the situation and they are all in a tizzy, it is a staggering blow. We have known the suffering and horror for a long time now. One is beginning to finally understand the prodigious acts of heroism of the humble French people who do not flinch under the torrent of fire poured on them while everyone else against whom Germany has turned its immense power has let themselves be crushed. The proof is the incompetent Romanians who pull back and flee

---

[223] Christmas Eve.

[224] Nelly Martyl was a star of the Opéra-Comique by the time she was 20 years old, singing the works of Bizet and Offenbach. When war broke out, she signed up as nurse and gave recitals to boost the morale of the troops. She won the *Croix de Guerre* and was promoted to sergeant. After the war, she cared for French prisoners coming home from Germany, and later created a foundation against hereditary illnesses.

like hares: why didn't they do as we did at Verdun? And they were certainly not subjected to the concentration of fire power we saw there. [...] We all hope that soon the English will absorb more of the sacrifices if we want to see this war shortened. [...]

12/12/1916.

[...] We are starting to be very busy working with the *beuglards* we want to use during the Christmas Mass.[225] Those guys, musicians maybe or not at all, have no sense of meter. We need to sing the Mass in two parts, so we've got a lot more to do. We didn't need this annoyance, Caplet started it all to please the division. [...]

Yesterday I went to see Commander Lapere, who is in charge of the engineers; I wanted him to make available a place where we could rehearse with our singers but also give concerts. It is absolutely impossible in the theater: it is too cold and cannot be heated properly. We went to look at an unused building and agreed that, with a bit of work, we would have a very proper place where we could bring together about 100 people. That is exactly what we need. The commander was very nice and promised to arrange to have it quickly fixed up. [...]

12/15/1916.

I received yesterday, in addition to Cunault's letter, your three letters from December 9, 10, and 11. [...] Everyone at the division is half-crazed because Nelly is coming. We will burn 600 kilos of wood to try to heat the theater, with no success; we'll only increase the breezes. They first need to block up all the holes in the roof and there are a lot.

Commander Lambrigot will go to Bar by car to fetch her. He cannot contain himself. How wild these men are, like starved dogs, it's quite funny. It seems Nelly, who is very bright, excels at making fun of them. She is the wife of Scott,[226] the painter; you have surely seen his drawings in *L'Illustration*. He is rich, and they own a grand house near l'Étoile. She thus is well positioned to not give a damn about others and she shows it. She is quite right to take pleasure in all that; those are the very best occasions. [...]

Monday, December 18, 1916, 2 p.m.

I received this morning your letter from December 13 and the one from December 15. [...] So the much talked about concert on the 16th with Nelly Martyl took place. All the officers were in turmoil; it is rather comical. You'd

---

[225] Bellowers, singers who make more noise than music.
[226] Georges Scott (1873-1943), French war correspondent and illustrator.

think they had never seen a woman and that it was a revelation to them. Your personal success must have been overshadowed. [...]

12/17/1916.

Yesterday I received your letter from December 13. I could not write yesterday because of all the things we had to do. [...] I think that, for Christmas, Caplet will receive some lobster and mayonnaise, a chicken, a pineapple, other fruits, a whole lot of good things. I will not eat any oysters. I have never eaten them. Nelly wore her nursing uniform for the concert; it is decorated with a special hospital medallion. That is how she is able to travel around behind the front lines. [...]

12/18/1916.

[...] You should not despair about the situation. If the Germans have proposed a peace, it is first of all to cause division among us, and because the situation at home is dreadful, according to their newspapers. They should be interested in discussing peace. [...] Even though the continuation of the war is a terrible idea, I think that it will produce good results for us and the Germans know it. That is why they are working on ending it now. All that does not mean that we haven't made enormous errors. With a bit of follow through and will-power, all should have been over by now. [...]

Wednesday, December 20, 1916, 6 p.m.

I received at 4 p.m. your letter from December 18. [...] I don't think it was the singer's place to participate in your concert. When one joins a regiment of nurses, one must realize that everything else has to be forgotten, that one's duty is to what is happening. It is pointless to come to the rear to sing in that sort of concert. I would have understood her participating in a big charity event organized to benefit some hospital. I would not say that to everyone, but I tell you what I think. There must be a good many wounded in the hospitals, especially around Bar-le-Duc. Despite the *communiqué* which says our losses were light in this last offensive, there must be many dead and wounded and there are probably not enough nurses and doctors. It is sad to think about the publicity around what she did. So many people are using the war as a way to get attention. [...]

12/20/1916.

[...] We had an unpleasant surprise in Rupt. Because of the cold, the colonel decided that our concert would not take place in the little hall which has room for 150 people, but rather at his place, for him and the people around him. That is not the same and we were not at all happy; most of the officers with him don't like music and that prevented over 100 friends from hearing an excellent concert. We were quite upset and played with little heart. All the friends who were waiting for us were furious and I completely understand them. […] Tomorrow our little hall in Génicourt will be finished and we will be able to arrange musical evenings right here. […]

12/24/1916.

I received yesterday your letter from December 20. […] Since last night, the cannon is booming frightfully, not only over Verdun, but all over the front. Could the Germans want to attack? We know nothing about it yet. […]

12/27/1916.

I've not written for two days, which is very rare for me, but when I tell you about my life for the past two days, you won't be surprised. During the day, Sunday, we rehearsed for the last time. After dinner, while waiting for time for Mass, we amused ourselves by drawing in pencil our silhouettes on the wall of our emergency station then coloring them in with black. We passed the time until 11 p.m. Then we went to the church which was packed beyond belief. The luminary was lovely, lit with 10 acetylene lights. Nelly Martyl was not able to come. We have since learned that she stayed at her hospital where she had arranged for a Christmas tree for the wounded. […]

For our celebration, we were 15 together at the table. We had put new cloths, made for wrapping up the straw mattresses, on the tables of our first aid post; they looked like tablecloths. In the center shone a Christmas tree that Caplet had received in a crate. We lit the candles; it was very gay. Caplet, who draws caricatures nicely, as you can see, wrote out the menu with my image. I am famous in the division for my *tenue de poilu.*[227] We are making 20 copies for friends; you will receive one which will amuse you. Our *Réveillon* started out wonderfully; the guests brought bottles of wine and other things, so nothing was lacking. We had to put some of them to bed. […] We watched dawn come up and at 9 a.m. were at Mass. To say our playing was brilliant would be a lie, but we managed.

Then at 1 p.m. there was a presentation in the theater. Martyl was supposed to come sing. Because of a broken-down vehicle, she did not arrive until 6:30 p.m. The concert was over. We decided to give a short one that very evening, at 9 p.m. Martyl sang and met with great success. […] It was after midnight when I got to bed. […]

In the afternoon, Cloëz and I went to place a crown on the tomb of Feliers, a contrabass player, a close friend of Cloëz. […] With some emotion I saw Ver-

---

[227] *Poilu* outfit.

dun again; shells were still falling on the Pavi section. It is heart-wrenching to see the countless resting places all over the place, where so many poor fellows sleep their final rest. And they have tombs; there are even more who have never had one. We got back about 6 p.m., had dinner with Caplet. I went to bed about 10 p.m. [...]

12/30/1916.

I received yesterday your letter of December 26. [...] The pharmacy of the first-aid station is not as well stocked as you imagine. For two months now it has only received half of what was requested. That results in medication shortages. [...]

12/31/1916.

[...] This morning I bought a chicken for Boussagol;[228] he has been on artillery duty for the past 48 hours and wants to be able to celebrate the Saint-Sylvestre in style. I paid 11,50 for it; the co-op had 150 of them all lined up. The cost for Christmas day was more than 1400 francs; it's unbelievable how much we spend here. I met the general in the street; I was holding my chicken by the neck. That made him laugh and he asked how much it had cost. He found the price a bit steep, he seemed to know what he was talking about. [...]

---

[228] Louis Delmas-Boussagol became a contrabass teacher at the Conservatoire de Paris after the war. Durosoir, *Deux Musiciens*, 174.

1917

The beginning of 1917 was horrible for Lucien. His good friend, Henri Martel, the unit chaplain, was killed. The danger and stupidity of the war were suddenly, tragically, and personally, brought home to Lucien. Overall, though, for the French, the first few months were generally very calm, to be followed by the offensive everyone had been hoping for, led by General Nivelle.

General Nivelle, who replaced Joffre as Commander-in-Chief in December 1916, had directed the victorious offensives at Verdun. He had great faith in his offensive strategy which had worked at Verdun. In early spring of 1917, he planned to launch a major French offensive near the River Aisne while the British pinned down the German reserves with a separate offensive at Arras. Nivelle's plan was for two French armies to break through the German lines before a third came through the breach, all under cover of a massive artillery bombardment.[229]

The initial well-planned attack worked but attempts to capitalize on the initial success totally failed. Nivelle's success relied on the element of surprise, but the Germans had gotten word of the attack and were ready. The battle lasted nearly a month, not the forty-eight hours Nivelle had predicted, and the cost in French lives was enormous. 30,000 Frenchmen were killed in one week, with 100,000 wounded and 4000 missing.[230] The offensive cost Nivelle his command.

After yet another costly and essentially failed offensive, the morale of the *poilus* was terrible. Years of watching friends be killed, risking the same, wading in mud, and eating horrible food were proof of what Lucien states over and over, that the leaders had no idea what they were doing or what they were asking.

One of the battalions in Lucien's division participated in the mutinies that marked the spring and summer of 1917.[231] Starting on May 28, in the 1st battal-

---

[229] Hart, *The Great War*, 329.

[230] Hart, *The Great War*, 341.

[231] These are the "serious events" Lucien refers to in his letter of June 30, 1917.

ion of the 129th RI, the mutiny lasted more than a week, up to June 5-7, when the 5th DI was ordered into the front lines. Here is a description by Lieutenant Colonel Brenot, 74th RI, of the events in his regiment:

> Battalion commander Schaeffer spoke directly to about three hundred assembled men, "calling on their best sentiments, showing them the cowardice of their conduct, the grave consequences to which they were exposing themselves, the crime they were committing against the Patrie, and advising them to be on time for the assembly for the departure to the sector." Schaeffer was greeted with the unanimous cry: "*Nous ne monterons pas aux tranchées!*"[232]

While all this was happening, the United States declared war on Germany on April 6. All of President Wilson's efforts to remain neutral and to be the broker of peace failed after repeated German aggressions against the American Navy. America's situation was in some ways similar to that of Great Britain at the beginning of the war: both were great naval powers but had very small armies. This was even more true of the United States. Once war was declared, Wilson called up the entire National Guard and introduced the draft, a system of conscription that would ultimately register some 24 million men. Of these, 2.8 million were called up for service. They required everything from housing to munitions to training to experienced generals, and they were needed urgently in Europe. The American 1st Division arrived in June 1917 and the American Expeditionary Force was established on July 5, 1917, under the command of General John. J. Pershing.[233] But the important contribution of men and material had to wait until 1918.

The second half of 1917 marked four long, hard, costly years of war with nothing much changed. The struggle to save Verdun, and the failed Nivelle offensive resulted, for the French, in more mutinies and further loss of morale. The French needed to recover from all of this in terms of men, material, leadership, and morale. Lucien and his division remained in the sector of the Chemin des Dames where they fought to maintain their advantage. The war was starting to take its toll on Parisians in terms of out-of-control inflation. A strike by clothing workers resulted in the government agreeing to a 1 franc a day increase in pay and a five-day work week as well as rules against the employment of foreign workers, advantages that were soon granted to other sectors of the economy.

It was now the turn of the British to take the major role in the fighting. With their eyes on the English Channel, they turned their attention to the German positions in Flanders and around Ypres. The first step was to dislodge the Germans from the high ground of the Messines ridge. The combined power of nine

---

[232] We will not go to the trenches. Smith, *Between Mutiny and Obedience*, 185.
[233] John Joseph Pershing, 1860-1948.

assault divisions and a reserve force of three, over 2000 guns, seventy-two tanks, and huge mines proved enough to accomplish all the proposed objectives, at the cost of almost twenty-five thousand casualties.[234] The third battle of Ypres, which involved some French forces, was more difficult and in the end neither the Germans nor the British had achieved much but to kill and maim over 40,000 men each. Still, Hart comments that the British had become the real danger to the Germans; up to then the danger had come from the French.

The first American shell was fired in October 1917. The Russian Revolution of 1917 removed the threat to Germany from the east; an armistice between Germany and Russia was signed on December 15.

---

[234] Hart, *The Great War,* 349-351.

The Letters

I received your letter of December 28, and two packages, one with condensed milk, figs, the other with cocoa and two little cans from chez B. [...] This is the first day of a year which, I really believe, will see the end of our misery. True, the same words were heard in 1916 and we know what came of that. But one can always hope, and this catastrophe cannot last forever. Whatever happens, let's pray that what I told you a few days ago proves true and that this year will find us finally reunited. [...]

This year is starting out very wet, lots of wind and heavy rain; drier weather would help us a lot. Starting tomorrow, we will begin work on our program for the 7th. Commander Vézinet, the stupid old man who refused my leave, has just been named lieutenant colonel in I don't know what regiment; he is leaving us, good riddance. Captain Auberge, who is replacing him, is a lovely man whom we know well and who loves music. This change increases our chances with the commander of this regiment. [...]

1/2/1917.

I received yesterday your letter from December 27 and two packages, one with an electric battery, the other with a piece of gruyère, half a camembert, and *des gaufrettes sultanes* which, my gosh, were really good.[235] [...]

Our hall is almost ready; we took the piano there last night and today we will start work on the Franck Quintet. [...] There is no doubt that no one in the division headquarters likes music; what protects us here is the memory of Mangin. From what they say, he is to take over the command of an attack force and will certainly ask for us. He would be quite unhappy to learn that we had not been used when the opportunity was there. That thought is certainly what is protecting our status. Everyone pretended to be interested in music because Mangin liked it. [...] It is quite sad to see an ensemble like ours almost neglected because the superior officers care nothing for music. [...]

Would you please copy and send the entries about César Franck and Chausson from Riemann;[236] we will use that as the basis for a little lecture we may give for those who come hear us play. [...] We are still waiting for an answer from Paris; really it is Caplet who is waiting because he is the one who wrote to Dalimier. I don't know what that will produce.

---

[235] These are cookies that resemble small, flat waffles.
[236] *Musiklexicon*, a music encyclopedia founded by Hugo Riemann in 1882.

Thursday, January 4, 1917, 8 p.m.

I received today at 4 your letter from January 2, and my letter of the 27th which I'd asked for. [...] It is not a bad idea to introduce to the public the composer whose work you are playing. That will be fairly easy for you, you can always put together a few words. Which one of you will speak? I hope it will be you. I've not made the effort to copy all that information for someone else to profit, making himself more noticed by the audience. [...]

1/3/1917.

I received yesterday your two letters, from December 29 and 30, as well as the two packages you announced. [...] Last night we worked on the Franck Quintet and looked at Dupont's *Poème*. The Franck is sublime, really very moving. [...] The sound in the hall is neither good nor bad, just a bit dull. With 50 people in the room, that will change. [...]

Friday, January 5, 4:30 p.m.

I just received your letter from Wednesday, January 3. [...] There is a lot of talk in the newspapers right now that Switzerland has been violated. Are the Germans spreading this intentionally? Couldn't it be a trick to surprise the English and take Calais? We don't know what to think. For sure there are huge movements of troops. We have to expect you to move. [...]

I went to see Mme Tavernier on Wednesday because she had some fabric of mine she'd not returned. I asked her to make me a bag and a little purse. The bag is to replace the one I take every day for shopping and the purse is for when I go out; my leather bag is starting to look old. [...] I took her a piece of blue silk so she can make me a sort of bonnet like the one made in Port Lazo which I wear every day. [...]

1/4/1917.

Yesterday I received your letter from December 31, but not the packages you list. They will probably arrive today. Right now there is so much mail that a bit of delay is no surprise. [...] Yesterday afternoon we rehearsed the Franck Quintet; we had a bit of an audience. When people heard the harmonies, they came into the hall. Among them was Commander Auberge [...] and also, for a short while, Colonel Valzi who had come to Génicourt to preside over a court martial. He came in to relax a bit with some music. He has aged significantly. The quintet is wonderful; the more we play it the more we like it. [...]

Saturday, January 6, 1917, 7 p.m.

I received at 4 your letter from January 4. [...] The loan from Madame Duez is due to be paid February 1. Will we pay her back or renew? I would have liked to discuss all these questions with you face to face. Stay well, little cat. [...]

1/5/1917.

I received your letter of December 31, and one package. [...] We were not able to rehearse last night because the division decided to show a movie to the 129th before it leaves for the trenches. So they moved the piano to the cinema theater; during the movie, a pianist, either Magne or Cloëz, played all sorts of musical jokes. It's not really much fun. We only have one piano so we could not rehearse. [...]

Sunday, January 7, 1917, 9 p.m.

I am writing a few lines this evening to tell you about my visit with Mme Bastien. When I arrived, about 4 p.m., all the guests were still lunching. Lunch started at 2 p.m. I was a bit annoyed but truly how could I imagine that, at 4 p.m., I would find that they hadn't even had coffee? Fortunately, several other people arrived for a visit right after me and found themselves in the same situation. Everyone left the table and after a half-hour of conversation, tea and coffee were served along with *galettes des rois*.[237] Bastien looks quite well; his face looks nothing like what I saw the last time. He had been in Verdun and the suffering and horror were still evident in his face. [...]

1/6/1917.

I received your letter of January 2 and a good number of letters and cards you are sending me. I am profoundly sad. Yesterday while our unit was being relieved, Martel was killed. There was a lot of activity all day long; shells rained down everywhere in this sector, some even close to Génicourt. This news is very painful; Martel was part of a group of comrades, along with Descusse, Rolland, Vessot, Pierrot, with great fondness for each other. We had been through so much together and knew each other very well. He was charming, gay, a true *poilu*, not at all like a priest, and everyone who had a chance to know him liked him. He was killed by a bomb that fell next to the ambulance he was in. His thigh was cut in half, and he died in several minutes. [...] We need to remember those we've lost with reverence. At that moment we were in the middle of a rehearsal—such is life! We will rehearse again tonight. [...]

---

[237] King cake, made for Epiphany.

1/7/1917.

I received yesterday your letter from January 3. [...] We have more details about Martel's death, a loss that has affected us deeply as he was loved by everyone. The ambulance was arriving in Les Éparges when there was a burst of fire from 77mm guns along the road. One of the shells struck the front of the vehicle. Martel, seated next to the driver, had a leg totally pulverized (it was never even found). He will be buried today; the ceremony will be in Rupt at 2 p.m. and he will be buried in a cemetery we created for our dead, very close to the farm at Amblonville. There are at least 150 from the 129th buried there; he will be with his buddies. It is very likely, though not certain, that his sister and parents will bring him back home after the war. [...]

Second letter, same day, 12:30 p.m.

Next week, when the 129th will be at rest, we will play for the funeral service in Rupt when the colonel and as many *poilus* as possible can be there. This death is stupid when one thinks of all the dangers we've lived through for the 27 months he was with the regiment; to be killed stupidly, to no purpose, what a sad business! There he rests, with so many others these past two years, entered into eternity. With Schratz, Descusse, these are very dear friends who are disappearing. At this moment, we are totally disgusted by this war; but then the sense of duty takes over and life goes on. It's sad. [...]

Monday, January 8, 1917, 5:30 p.m.

I received this morning your letter from January 5 and this afternoon the one from the 6th. The news of the death of your friend Martel saddens me profoundly; one cannot help having tears in one's eyes at the thought of all those broken lives and all those that will be broken until the war ends. [...]

Tuesday, January 9, 1917, 5:30 p.m.

I received yesterday your letter from January 7. Your poor friend's death was sudden—such a stupid death. [...] Many men will be saddened by his loss. Wasn't it he who was the source of comfort for most, reinforcing the courage of some and raising the spirits of others? His mission was noble and God should have permitted him to live. [...]

1/8/1917.

I did not receive any letters except the one with the articles on César Franck, Debussy, and Chausson. Thank you for those notes; we can add to them but the basics are there and that is essential. [...]

Poor Martel was buried yesterday at 2:00. I was extremely sad not to be able to go to his service. He is buried very near our farm in Amblonville in the midst of his comrades of the 129th. [...]

1/9/1917.

I received yesterday your letters from January 4 and 5 and two packages. [...] We worked a bit on the Beethoven 9th Quartet last night.[238] [...] It is a bit cold, but clear and transparent like Mozart, with many more high passages, totally exposed, every false note is noticed. [...] Caplet likes modern music; that is good for me also because I will probably never play many quartets and might at some point need to play a modern work. It is in my interest to know as many as possible. [...] You can say what you will about the modern composers, there are not many who compare well with the Beethoven violin sonatas and quartets. I do not like Debussy's music very much. There are some charming, sensual passages but the general impression is of something that doesn't hold together. [...]

If we give some short talks about the composers, I will be the one speaking. Caplet can barely put two words together; he falls all over himself. It's rather curious for someone like him. I'm sending a new caricature. The "do, do, do" refers to the Dupont which ends with three uts in different octaves and are difficult to play rapidly. Several days ago, at the end of a rehearsal, I was practicing that exercise very fast over and over while Cloëz improvised a waltz in C major. It was so funny everyone was overcome with laughter. Caplet came up with the caricature yesterday. [...]

Thursday, January 11, 1917, 5:30 p.m.

I received this morning your letter of January 9 and my letters up to January 5; and the caricature with "do, do, do, c'est moi Do...rosoir." Caplet was really on form when he did that. He hadn't showed that talent until now, had he? [...]

Yes, the music of the modern composers is much easier for a violinist to play than that of the older composers who treat the violin like the voice and constantly make the instrument sing. The musical line is charming; the sonority always pure. Haydn, Mozart, Beethoven (I leave out Bach) played violin, they would never have written a note that would have been harsh on the violin. The modern composers, for the most part, have never played a string instrument; they do not know how to make those instruments ring. [...] One might say that modern music for violin has only one goal—noise. That is why working on the music of the old masters is so valuable; there are so many different difficulties for the bow that the artist who pays attention benefits by truly mastering his instru-

---

[238] Beethoven, String quartet in C major, Op. 59, No. 3.

ment. In a modern work, one can be brilliant without much effort. For Mozart or Beethoven every detail has to be perfect. [...]

1/10/1917.

I received today two of your letters, the second from the 6th and the one from the 7th. [...] I am writing a bit late today and have to rush to catch the mail. I left early this morning with a car and driver to go get the Pleyel which Lyon had with him. I only got back at 1:00 and needed to eat. [...] The woods were magnificent with the snow that covers everything. Lyon is very isolated but his *gourbi* is comfortable and nothing to complain about. He's arranged with his commander to come for dinner tomorrow night and stay for the concert. He is thrilled; he is a straightforward, charming man. [...]

Friday, January 12, 1917, 3:30 in the afternoon.

[...] I sent you 6 top strings with some foie gras, a nose protector you sent back last winter, two pairs of shoelaces, one in leather, the other in cloth. I forgot to mention those articles. The sad news of the death of your friend Martel so upset me that I was stunned for a few days. [...]

Saturday, January 13, 1917, 3 p.m.

[...] I read in *L'Information* that a Zeppelin was seen in Fontainebleau Thursday and could not continue its route. It was probably headed for Paris. Yesterday, M. Alan asked me whether I had heard the alert at 7 p.m. on Thursday. [...] This morning, when I took some thyme and laurel to Mme Boissard, she asked me the same thing. I heard absolutely nothing, it's very strange. I've not suddenly gone deaf, fortunately for me. I must have been totally engrossed in my letter writing. I know I wrote to you that evening. According to M. Alan, we are no longer warned by bugles but by automobile horns. I did not know that. There are a lot of cars passing that make an infernal noise; I must have been no more attentive than usual, so I was not upset. They shouldn't bother to warn people because it changes nothing. Many people who are deathly afraid would not wake up. Wasn't it last year, around January 22, that a Zeppelin did so much damage? I like to think we are capable of stopping such attacks and that we could pay them back in kind.

The 129th must be at rest now. Will you have a Funeral Mass for the soul of Martel? [...]

1/12/1917.

I received yesterday your letter from January 8ᵗʰ and two packages. [...] I couldn't write yesterday because I was busy all day. [...] Lyon arrived by 6:30 and we sat down to eat. We had some steaks provided by the division which we cooked for ourselves with buttered potatoes. Then cheese, fruit, apples, truffles. Three liters of white wine complemented our ordinary red, so we set off for the concert in excellent humor. The hall was packed. The evening was a success beyond our greatest expectations. We played the two quintets just the way we hoped. Nelly Martyl sang Chausson's song, *Le Colibri* and Franck's *Mariage des Roses*,[239] and obviously she was very well received. She sings with great intelligence. The evening was a true triumph. [...]

Sunday, January 14, 1917, 1 p.m.

[...] Last evening about 5 p.m., Monsieur Guyot came to see me. He came out of politeness to thank me for my note at the end of December thanking him for the money he sent to the notary. At the same time, I added my best wishes for him and his family for the New Year. He asked for news of you and would be happy to see you when you come home. A lot of young soldiers spend time at the foyer. The foyer reminds them a bit of family life; it is wonderfully quiet. They have, at their disposition, paper for writing letters, books to amuse them or to learn from, a safe haven where they can warm up without having to pay to go into some sort of wine bar where they would find all sorts of unhealthy opportunities. He invited me to come to the foyer some evening to see for myself these interesting get-togethers. Of course, I will not go unless someone comes to the house and insists. [...]

1/13/1917.

[...] The weather is abominable with a lot of snow. I think about the Seine which is rising rapidly: if only we are not subjected to a serious flood! This is really not the right time for that. After the flood of 1910 there were a lot of good words pronounced but nothing was done to protect Paris and the suburbs against a similar scourge. Sorry to say, we are a people of big talkers. [...]

1/14/1917.

Yesterday I received your letter of January 10, and two packages. [...] You tell me that your money is getting low. I do not understand why you send so many packages—a huge expense just for shipping. You send an average of at least 50 a month; shipping for those packages comes to at least 60 to 65 francs (two francs

---

[239] *Le Colibri*, Op. 2, no. 7 and *Le Mariage des Roses*, FWV 80, CFF 183 (1871).

a day), a useless expense as you get nothing for it. It would be better for me to spend more money here to buy what I need at the co-op. Even if I spend 3 or 4 francs a day, it would still be less than for all the packages you send me. The cost of the contents of each package comes to at least 4 francs. For 50 packages plus shipping that makes 260 francs a month, at a very minimum. So even if I spend 150 francs a month, we would still be saving a lot of money, which is important at a time like this. I think that it would be good to change the system. Do not send any more packages, or no more than one or two a week. I will wait for your answer to this before changing the way I do things. Please tell me what you think. Myself, I think this is a waste and what really hurts is seeing all the money lost in shipping. [...] Give some thought to the packages and send me your answer. [...]

Maréchal will probably bring back a quartet by Fauré,[240] and Florent Schmitt's Quintet,[241] and maybe a Trio by Lekeu.[242] We will have a lot to chew on. We still have Schumann's Quintet, Debussy's Quartet, Frank's Quartet, the Ravel Trio, the d'Indy with clarinet.[243] Then there is Schumann's Third which I'd like to know.[244] In short, considerable work, not counting the sonatas.

1/15/1917.

I received yesterday your letter from January 15 and a package with a large piece of ham, a can with two little potatoes, and two packages of little filled cookies. This package arrived just at the right moment, we were to sit down for lunch with Mans, Taconet, Gracieux, Cavanagh and the auxiliary doctor of the 3rd battalion. [...]

Wednesday, January 17, 1917, 2 p.m.

I have some free time so I am writing today before the 4:00 mail. I've asked you several times now whether you had received any news from Madame Duez. Is she so sick that she is doing nothing? Maybe she is angry that I don't go see her very often. The trip from Vincennes to Boulogne is long and, in such damp, cold weather, I risk getting very ill. And it is not at her place that one can warm up. [...] Her home has so little heat it is laughable, and she would never offer something hot to drink which might help keep me from catching cold. [...]

---

[240] Fauré composed two piano quartets: No. 1 in C minor, Op. 15 and No. 2 in G minor.
[241] Florent Schmitt (1870-1958), Piano quintet in B minor, Op. 51.
[242] Lekeu, Trio for piano, violin and cello, in C Minor.
[243] Vincent d'Indy (1851-1931), Trio for piano, clarinet (or violin) and cello, Op. 29.
[244] This may be Schumann's Piano trio No. 3 in G minor.

1/16/1917.

I received yesterday three letters, one from January 9, and two from the 12th. [...] The service for Martel will take place in Rupt tomorrow morning. Cloëz, Magne, Lafont and I are going. [...] We will probably stay in Rupt to lunch with my old friends from the mess there. The *curé* in Rupt will lend an excellent harmonium; the one in the church is terrible. There will also be a service in Génicourt for the 129th battalion on Thursday or Friday and one for the *poilus* on Thursday. [...]

I saw yesterday, with relief, that the Seine is going down. [...] Here we have ice and fog, and right now it is snowing. Our woods are mostly covered in snow, at least 30 centimeters, and it is truly lovely. [...]

1/17/1917.

I received today your letter of the 13th. I am writing this evening because tomorrow we leave early in the morning for Rupt and we will get back too late to send mail. [...] It snowed today all day long and is still snowing; the snow is very deep. [...]

I saw in the papers that there was an alert in Paris about a Zeppelin, but I think it was either a false alarm or nothing happened. In any case, we shouldn't make a big deal of it. You can easily calculate your risk. There is so much space around you, it would be total chance for a projectile to hit your house. And if that is to be your fate, nothing you might do would change anything. You certainly know that; if I was in my bed, I would not leave it. All the more because the Zeppelins do not launch thousands of projectiles, twenty or so at most. So the chance of an accident is minimal and there is no reason to worry yourself. Here projectiles fall by the thousands. [...]

Friday, January 19, 1917, 5 p.m.

I did not receive a letter today. You must not have written on Wednesday as you left early for Rupt to play for Martel's funeral service. [...]

Is the area of Les Éparges going to see some activity? I read in the Wednesday's official *communique* that on January 14 "in Les Éparges, thanks to the explosion of a mine, the Germans launched an offensive that was repulsed after some serious man-to-man fighting. In the Apremont forest there was also a little German offensive." [...]

1/18/1917.

I received yesterday your letter from January 14. We left for Rupt very early this morning. A car from the 129th was supposed to be at the division at 7:30, but

at 10 minutes to 8 there was still absolutely nothing. By chance, at the last minute, an ambulance vehicle was leaving for Rupt. We got in, all the faster because
it was very cold outside and snow was making the roads difficult. At 9:10 we got
off in Rupt. [...] We went directly to see the *curé* to make plans to transport his
harmonium to the church. The old codger no longer wanted to loan it because
of the weather. I was so insistent that he finally gave in. We quickly got together
a team of drummers and musicians who carried it to the church. The *curé* followed along behind to see whether we were taking all the necessary precautions.
It was truly ridiculous. The *curé*'s home is disgustingly dirty; there is, of course,
no one to do his housekeeping, and he, himself, never cleans, that's for sure. [...]

The service for Martel was one of overall reverence; the division chaplain said
a few words, all really very well done. I played Bonporti's *Lamentevole* and some
Bach Chorales;[245] Lafont sang Stradella's *Pie Jesu*. After the ceremony we took
the harmonium back to the *curé* and went to lunch with our buddies. [...]

The weather was beautiful, cold and dry so we walked back. We were home by
5 p.m. Today we have a service for the *poilus*. [...] Tomorrow there is a service
for Martel in Génicourt so the *poilus* from the 3rd battalion can also be there. [...]

1/19/1917.

I received your two letters from January 15 and 16. [...] What I told you about
the packages makes sense. You should not send me anymore; with the co-op here
I can buy anything I want. They now sell fresh butter and fruit. I do love getting
packages from you, but when I think of what they cost you, I think that we could
manage our money much more sensibly. [...]

1/21/1917.

I received yesterday three letters and two packages. [...] When I wrote to you
about stopping the packages for now, it is not that I am not pleased to receive
them. For sure, I truly appreciate the care and attention you bring to making
each package. Your affections are present, if I can say it this way, in every little
thing wrapped with such care. But you are still paying an exorbitant amount.
[...]

1/22/1917.

I received this morning your letter from January 17 as well as two packages.
[...] There is no reason to send these packages by registered mail. It is no real
guarantee, and you spend, I think, an extra 5 or 6 sous per package. And what

---

[245] Francesco Bonporti (1672-1749), Invention in C Minor, Op. 10, No. 6:1.

is more, a regular package always arrives a day sooner than one that is registered. [...]

Take care of yourself. For your aches, you should try Gilbert's tisanes; I believe they are very helpful for rheumatism. [...]

1/23/1917.

I received your letter from January 19 yesterday and two packages. [...] It is extremely cold and the temperature drops rapidly, last night to 10 degrees below zero—that is seriously cold weather. It's been a long time since there have been temperatures that low. Aside from that, the weather is splendid. [...] The sun shines brightly but is not very warm.

This region is seeing more action. It was the 36th that suffered the mine explosion and the *Boche* attack. There were two men killed and 15 wounded; we are occupying the crater caused by the mine blast. There is also more bombing from time to time. [...]

We will need to pay close attention to the question of rents; I see in the newspapers that those who can pay are going to be obliged to do so. They won't be able to take advantage of the moratorium much longer. That's desirable. To manage all of this, I think that we should hire a businessman and give him a certain percentage of what he is able to get for us. That would probably be the best solution. [...]

Friday, January 26, 1917, 5:30 p.m.

I received yesterday your letter from January 23. It is exceptionally cold and that makes me worry about you. I'm not only worried about you, I wonder how the men in the trenches are doing. Of course, this weather lowers the water in the Seine and calms the fears of a flood, but it is awful for the soldiers, they will just suffer more. [...]

1/24/1917.

I received yesterday your letter from January 20 and two packages. [...] Today I am writing much later than usual; it is 2:00 and mail has not yet arrived. This is because of the intense cold which, along with the snow, makes the roads almost unpassable. Last night, in Génicourt, the temperature was 14 degrees below zero and in the house in the woods, not far from here, 19 degrees below zero. In such freezing weather, any movement is nearly stopped or, at least, much slowed down. There is no need to tell you that it is dreadfully hard to do anything at all as the cold is the master of everything. We don't have the means to counter such intense cold. I never take my gloves off and am writing now with them on. The little bit of wood we had for our little room was burned a long time ago, and obviously they don't give us more; right now everyone is hunting for anything that will burn. We've decided to buy some from central headquarters or the adjutant general quarters. There they are selling 100kg of wood for 9,5 francs for the use of the officers. That is very expensive, but we will be very happy to get it; an officer is going to sign for it as though it is for his use. Without him, we would have to do without. We will buy 300kg, but with this cold that will not last long. It's been many years since the weather has been this cold. [...]

For several days now, the *Boches* have launched a number of attacks and we've had serious losses. Behind us there is important troop movement, and we see a good number of regiments passing by on the road. I think they fear a *Boche* attack in our area and are urgently bringing reinforcements; our division is so worn down that it wouldn't hold out long against an attack. [...] There is still talk of our moving in the first week of February, but there has been no positive information and nothing official. It is snowing today and the wind is so cold that it's almost impossible to be outside. [...]

1/26/1917.

I received your letters from January 21 and 22. [...] I did not write yesterday; in the morning I had a rehearsal with singers preparing songs with violin accompaniment. That took much more of the morning than I expected. The concert was at 1:30. It was so cold I could not play. My fingers were totally stiff and refused to do anything. And I think I caught a cold, despite taking all possible precautions. It was just too cold and there were too many drafts, so this morning I got up at 11. [...]

1/29/1917.

I received yesterday your letter from January 25 and two packages [...] Our weather is still very cold: the thermometer hovers always around 15 degrees below zero. The *poilus* are suffering dreadfully. Our regiment has been sorely tested this time; it leaves the trenches tonight; in a week we lost 250 men, killed, injured, or evacuated due to frozen feet. [...]

According to rumors which I have reason to believe true, based on their source, it appears we will be here for at least another two months, maybe more. We are not part of the offensive so this is a blessing. We will just need to defend against any eventual offensive that might happen. We are taking extraordinary precautions, even against tanks; it is likely the *Boches* have some. [...]

I have absolutely no need for more money; I spend very little and still have at least 140 francs. [...] I am not cold at all. Here is how I organize things: I put the fur sleeping bag on the mattress, I wrap my feet with the cloth sleeping bag, then wrap up in my blanket, over which I put my oil cloth, my *capote* and my jacket and then wrap everything up in my rubber raincoat. You can well imagine that I am not cold. Once I lie down, I put on my nose protector and it is "good night everyone." My paper jacket is still in good condition, and I certainly use it right now. So no, I am fine and do not suffer from the cold at night. During the day I stay less warm because I have to move about and the air is biting and our heating is unpredictable. But the boys on the lines are the ones to feel sorry for. [...]

There is a rumor running around that there will be no more passes after February 1. That would be the sign that the offensive is near. It also keeps rumors from the front from reaching the back and possibly reaching the *Boches*. There seems to be a huge amount of hope placed on this offensive. It's the same each time, and I am beginning to no longer have much faith. I know that we will use unbelievable amounts of equipment, much more than ever before, but the *Boches* must surely have predicted that. I do not doubt that we will cause them serious losses, but without moving forward. We have put so much faith in our successive offensives that we need to be careful about our expectations. [...]

Our paymaster loaned me a book called *Le Feu*,[246] written by Henri Barbusse, whom I know. I went to meet him at Éditions Lafitte, Champs Élysées. That book, which is about the Artois and describes in detail life in the trenches, is a marvel. Please buy it, for yourself, to read, and to keep. I haven't read anything by him except about this war. It seems that he is unleashing tremendous hatred, because he is telling the persons in the rear and others what is happening. And it is not written for the elite; he uses the language and characters from the trenches, very natural and singularly moving. [...]

Wednesday, January 31, 1917, 5:30 p.m.

I received at 4 p.m. your letter from the 29th, my letter of January 25 and three little pictures—two from the church in Génicourt and one from the church in Les Éparges, at least what remains of it. [...]

From the details you give me, I gather that you are well-covered at night. You really need that with these temperatures. Today a bit of snow fell, or rather sleet; it is so cold that it cannot snow. [...] Sadly, I think this cold weather will continue and one can't help thinking constantly about the extraordinary suffering this causes the soldiers.

Things are starting to get active and something big may happen soon? Really, the Germans will be using tanks against you? What an abomination! It is dreadful to use machines like that. [...] Maybe the monsters will spout fire. What we know for sure is that they leap over the trenches. The English used that machine, not enough of them, in the Battle of the Somme. That only served to reveal to

---

[246] Henri Barbusse (1873-1935), *Le Feu* won the Prix Goncourt. It appeared first as a serial in a daily paper then in book form, published by Flammarion at the end of November 1916.

the Germans a new means of attack. Now we are the ones who will suffer the consequences. Who knows what one will invent to destroy men, as fast as possible and as many as possible. [...]

Mme Duez wrote, I will send you her card tomorrow. She is very sweet and asks for no more than to give me another year to pay the loan she gave us. [...]

1/30/1917.

I received yesterday your letter from January 26. [...] This morning there is a rumor circulating that we will be leaving between the 5th and 8th of February and based on some indications, I rather believe this time it is serious. I would certainly prefer to stay here another month or two; but we haven't much to complain about. Things have been quiet for 7 months. It's been very long since we had such a long period of calm. When we leave, it will be for rest and everyone is hoping for a month. That would take us to the middle of March before we are sent back into the fight. [...]

It seems to be colder and colder. Last night the thermometer in Génicourt reached 18 degrees below zero, which has to mean that, in some places like the plateaus, it is 20 degrees below zero. [...]

I am going to send back to you all the sonatas you sent me. If we resume our mobile life, we will never be able to look at all that. And I need to put my goatskin sleeping bag, my boots, and my pants in my music box. It's a lot and there is not much space. I will take care of those packages tomorrow.

I just received the mail. There are no letters from you [...] but there was a package that appears to be clothing. If so, I will send it back to you; on the verge of departure, now is not the time to add to my already considerable load. If there is a shirt, I will stuff that into my pack. [...]

If your income was more than 3000 francs, you need to declare that for income tax.[247] I do not think you earned that much in 1916. Next year, 1917, you will earn more than that. If you see Pierron, talk to him a bit about your tenant in Boulogne. Perhaps he knows a businessman who, if necessary, would help us. I believe that, with all these regulations, it would be to our advantage not to have to manage of all those affairs ourselves. [...]

Thursday, February 1, 1917, 7:30 p.m.

I received your January 30 letter at 4:00. I'm writing a bit late and will mail my letter tomorrow. I was busy with the plumber who came to take care of the faucet that turns off the water. He took it apart, lubricated it, put in a new washer and some sealant. Now it works very well. This evening before bed I will turn

---

[247] An earlier letter states 5000 francs; this may be a misreading of Lucien's writing in the transcription or some confusion on his part.

the water off. That way I will not worry. It is a little task to be done morning and night, to make sure there is no water in the pipe coming up to the first floor that could freeze. It snowed this morning; with the frozen ground and the sleet from yesterday, one slides when trying to walk. It is very hard for the horses. [...]

1/31/1917.

I received today your letter from January 18 and three packages, including one by registered mail. [...] I am sending back to you this morning a dirty flannel shirt, a dirty pair of socks, and a dirty handkerchief. If we are leaving here in a few days, I do not have time to get those things washed and I prefer sending them back to you. Do not send me any shirts: I have plenty with the one I have. You are really trying to overload me like a burro but I won't let you do it. I only need the essential, that is absolutely all. [...]

2/1/1917.

I received today your two letters, from January 27 and 29. I also received a package with bars of chocolate. Yesterday I received two packages. [...] I have more news which doesn't make me very happy. Colonel Valzi is leaving; he's been promoted to colonel in the headquarters of the 2nd Army. He will be replaced by a commander from the infantry who has been promoted to lieutenant-colonel. This change doesn't please me at all; the colonel, in addition to being a music lover, is the best of men. I was on familiar footing with him in a way that will be difficult to achieve with his replacement, no matter what he's like. [...] We saw the colonel this morning and gave him a photo of our group which pleased him enormously. [...] Commander Auberge, who has replaced him, is very nice and is crazy about music. That is a bit of luck in the midst of misfortune. [...]

I also received your money order for 100 francs which I will cash immediately. I have absolutely no need for this money; you haven't changed. [...]

I am truly pleased that Pierrot has gotten out of this mess. It is terrible to have to stay in the trenches and put up with such suffering for years. Certainly, if those who are running this war had to live our lives, all this would have ended a long time ago. What is really amazing is that the *poilus* take it all without mutiny. They are gentle, heroic guys with enormous devotion which is not appreciated in the rear where, despite everything, one has no idea of our living conditions. [...]

2/2/1917.

I received today your letter from January 30 as well as two packages I've not yet opened. My head cold, which was never very bad thanks to intensive treatment (inhalation of gomenol),[248] went away very quickly. It is still very cold and we can't get away from it. Up to a certain point one can get used to it. [...]

I cashed the 100-franc money order this very morning. I went to the post office where everyone knows me. Being a bachelor during this war is certainly a blessing in terms of state of mind. I see the torment of those who have wives and children; I am glad not to share their anguish. [...]

Sunday, February 4, 1917, 6 p.m.

Today is Sunday so I didn't receive any mail. I hope that means two letters tomorrow. [...] It is still very cold; it froze last night at 14 degrees below zero. [...]

Mathilde is leaving tonight for home: her 80-year-old mother is ill so she will be gone at least 3 weeks. I will not do much cleaning; it is so cold that it is impossible to shake anything out on the balcony. [...] Mathilde's husband has agreed to come every other day to bring up some coal. [...]

2/3/1917.

Last evening, I opened the two packages I received and saw that they contained 4 oranges, 24 truffles as well as some cough drops for my cold. I thank you very much. You should not send fruit in this weather. The oranges arrived frozen, which is a shame. With these temperatures, we need good, solid food, not fruit. This morning it is even colder: the thermometer in Génicourt went down to 22 below zero. It seems it was 25 below in some parts of the sector. This temperature is extraordinary in our country. Fortunately, there is no wind, or it would be intolerable. For sure, we will remember the winter of 1917. If we have to move in this weather, it will not be fun. [...] We are burning everything we can put our hands on. All the wood in our house not essential to the solidity of the structure ends up in the fireplace. It would be funny if it were not so very sad. No matter. The Parisians who don't have any coal must be starting to recognize the pain of the war. [...] As long as it was only the soldiers living through this; those in the rear noticed nothing. It is very easy to accept the anguish of others; two or three words of compassion suffice and then one can enjoy a warm bed, a good table, and a good fire without guilt. What does it matter if others are suffering and dying! So, it is almost with joy that the *poilus* learn that the teeth of civilians are starting to chatter a bit. They all say: "Finally!" Civilians still don't have much to complain about. To have to cut back on good food or luxuries is still not significant compared to what the *poilus* are living through. [...]

---

[248] Gomenol (Malaleuca viridiflora) is an evergreen with pointed leaves and spiky long yellow flowers, used as an antiseptic.

2/4/1917.

I received yesterday your letter from January 31 as well as two packages with figs and gruyère and 9 little potatoes. I think the poor little things got rather cold. Magne, for his part, received a huge package by rail with a 5-kilo pot of orange marmalade, dates, tobacco, and another with 12 andouillettes de Cherbourg, a delightful specialty. We grill them wrapped in greased paper. I made a grill from the tin can cover; that does the trick. [...]

The cold is becoming almost intolerable; last night it was 22 below zero. This is the climate in Russia and obviously our installations are nothing like in Russia. There is nothing we can do in such weather, no work, no rehearsals. It's totally idiotic.

We shouldn't be afraid of the tanks, that's what all the *poilus* think. For sure, the *Boches* will have them, but many fewer than we and the English have. It seems that we now we have super tanks designed to fight and destroy other tanks. The character of the war is changing and will be even more fierce. There is nothing much more to say. As with all the tools of war we've seen, we will figure out a way to save ourselves from these also. [...] Our departure seems to have been put off; we may not leave until the 10th or 12th. I prefer that; one has to hope that, as time goes on, it will be less cold. A move in these temperatures is not at all funny. [...]

It doesn't matter if Mme Duez consults with her businessman, what counts is that she renew the loan for a year. I fear only one thing, that a year may not be long enough. We will worry about that later. You should have received two years of interest from Breton. You now need to think about a new investment, which shouldn't be difficult in this period. [...] We should be able to make a good investment right now, in terms of the interest rate and the security. It just takes a little work. I'm counting on you. [...]

Apparently, Colonel Valzi departed in disgrace. He was punished, so it seems, for the loss of about 60 men during the last attack in Les Éparges. None of that was his fault, but he is being held responsible. He was too nice. When you have someone like that, the people who complain loudest always win out. [...]

Tuesday, February 6, 1917, 7 p.m.

I received at 4 p.m. your February 4 letter and last evening the one from the 3rd. [...] At this time you have unwillingly stopped working on music. You need to do physical exercise, to move, because the cold is so severe that as soon as you stop moving, your extremities freeze. Monday it went down to 17 minus zero, this morning I think it was only 12 below. The sun was lovely from noon to 2. I took advantage of that to open the window of the toilet room and your room and mine; I hadn't opened anything for two or three days. One has to hope that the weather warms up but it certainly doesn't look likely. [...]

Friday, February 9, 1917, 6:30 p.m.

I didn't receive a letter today; maybe one will come at 7:30. [...] We had a hard freeze last night. And yesterday there was a strong east wind that made the cold more painful. This harsh weather is lasting a long time which is unfortunate from any point of view. [...]

Speaking of the cold and of the fire I have to burn in the kitchen and dining room, here is what I do. When I get back from shopping, I clean out the stove in the kitchen and set the fire which I light right away so I can heat up the leftovers for lunch; I set the fire in the dining room but do not light it; I eat in the kitchen. After lunch I clean up and let the fire go out, usually about 2:30. Then I light the fire in the dining room; that way I don't waste coal and I have hot water when I need it. I am a bit more tired and hurt a bit more, but I am being very careful. I do very little housework. I live like a gypsy, just like Mme Duez. If she could hear me! [...]

2/5/1917.

I received your letter from February 1 and two packages—one with a bottle of rum and some apples, the other with a pot of apple jelly. I thank you very much. However, fruit in this weather is not very useful, we don't want to have diarrhea. [...]

What you say about my pack makes me laugh. Of course, my things (my box of music and my violin) will be transported. As for Azor,[249] it is always on my wonderful shoulders. I beg you to believe that, were you to put it on your back for an instant, you would quickly put it back on mine. It is useless for me to have three changes of underwear, I never use more than two. [...]

Cloëz came back very sad last night. It seems his wife's father was killed in a munition accident in Bourges, in a factory where he worked. It must be true; otherwise, he's putting on a good act. [...]

Fortunately, the wind has died down; otherwise it would be very difficult to keep going. [...] A good number of men fall and sometimes get hurt. We have to be careful. The area around Génicourt is very mountainous and the roads turn into wonderful slippery slides. I believe we are going to have this freezing weather for the entire lunar month, that will take us to about February 20. It's been a very long time since we've had such a difficult year: I think we need to go back to the year you were ill in Boulogne, when I was making so many fires, that must have been 1893.

2/6/1917.

I received today your two letters from February 2 and 3 and two packages which I've not yet opened. [...] The 129th, which is at rest in Génicourt, leaves

---

[249] His backpack.

tomorrow, the 7th. The two other battalions will leave, I think, on the 8th. Then, that evening, the 36th, the 274th, and the 74th will be relieved. We will be the last to leave, probably not before the 10th. It seems that we are going near Gondrécourt, south of Ligny in Barois, in the direction of Neufchâteau, much to the south of Bar-le-Duc. [...]

The loss of the colonel, although regrettable, will not have the same importance for me as it would have a year ago. They are now used to seeing us around the division and find things for us to do, which makes us hope this will continue for a long time.. [...] The new colonel won't be that bad; all those around him are good people and only want to be nice to us. [...] Commander Vaginet, who was nasty, has left and his replacement, Commander Auberge, is the nicest of men and loves music. [...] I am not worried. And then, this war may end sooner than we think. I believe the intervention of the United States, and quite likely other neutral countries, will help. [...]

2/8/1917.

I received today your letter from February 5 and two packages, yesterday I received three. [...] The cars leave tomorrow; today we are turning in all our packages. As for me, I may not leave until the 10th or the 11th. In that case we will spend a day in Bar-le-Duc and then go on to our destination, Abainville near Gondrécourt. In any case we need to be there for the evening of the 12th at the latest.

Our tour will start without delay; that has been set for a month now, 5 days per billeting site. There are 30 of us in all to set up the theater and the piano. It is quite an undertaking. There will be three large vehicles to transport us and all our things—it's all very odd, what a strange war! In addition to the music regiment shows, we will play some sonatas and trios. Caplet, of course, with the demands of the pigeon coop, is not part of all this. He says he is going to try to have us play for the Army Corps, at least he thinks he can do that. It would certainly not be a bad idea. So our life is going to be busy.

The cold is less severe; we still have heavy freezes, but at least it is not 20 below, thus much more bearable. [...] In my pack I have a change of underwear, my new gaiters, socks, handkerchiefs, etc., plus my boots and a pair of pants. That is all I could get in, using all my cleverness. I am carrying with me, with a strap, my goatskin sleeping bag, my cloth sleeping bag, my blanket, my oil cloth, my raincoat, that is, another 10 kilos. Plus I will have my two *musettes* and they will not be empty, you can bet on that. Then my canteen; I will have more than enough on my back. [...]

2/9/1917.

Today I did not receive a letter, and no packages. Things are getting a bit disorganized as everyone clears out. [...] From what we know, our general is not very interested in fighting and we don't think he, unlike his predecessor, will volunteer us for such dreadful tasks. His lack of ambition works to the favor of the *poilus*. They have had it up to here and the spirit of our regiment does not resemble what it was. I do not believe that, in serious combat, our division could fight brilliantly right now. I think the higher command understands the situation. Our division has been completely worn out. The time in Les Éparges, marked by some success but horribly difficult, served to wipe out what good was left. [...]

2/10/1917.

I did not receive any mail yesterday and today the mail has not yet arrived. [...] The area we are going to, Abainville, has 500 inhabitants and hasn't seen any troops for a year. We are hoping to be comfortable there. We will ask to have a pied à terre for 4, so we can occasionally leave the tour behind, not sleep under the stars, and have a place to leave some of our things so we don't have to drag everything with us. [...]

2/12/1917.

I couldn't write yesterday because of our move; I will tell you a bit about the day. [...] By noon we were in Bar. At the Hotel du Commerce, for 4 francs, I found a nice room, with heat, where I could clean up. I got a haircut, etc. After that we went to find Nelly Martyl in her hospital. She received us very nicely; since she was free in the evening, we agreed to make a bit of music at the home of Prienski, the piano merchant in Bar. [...] He loaned me a violin, what a dud! I managed to play the "Kreutzer" Sonata with Cloëz, Nelly sang a beautiful *Requiem* by Fauré which I did not know. [...] Except for the family of the merchant and the surgeon from Martyl's hospital, we were the only ones there. The surgeon is a passionate music lover and wants us to play a concert at the hospital for the wounded. Martyl will work on that and ask our general for his authorization. Obviously, this project is very interesting for us and could have good consequences. Martyl has a lot of work at the hospital: she is on duty every third night. She is up every day at 6 a.m. and her day finishes at 4 p.m. When she is going to sing somewhere, which she does quite often, she can do it after 5 p.m. Even if she doesn't return until 1 or 2 a.m., she still goes back to work at the normal time the next day. We saw a lot of people at the hospital, wounded, personnel, and heard nothing but praise for her devotion. [...]

2/13/1917.

Here we are in Abainville and this instant I received two packages and two letters. [...] We have been lucky enough to find ourselves among people well off and very nice who gave us a small room for 4, with nice straw. We made ourselves a splendid bed on which we slept very well. We spend the day in the kitchen, which is huge and well-heated by an enormous stove. In this home there is the grandfather, grandmother, their daughter, and their 8-year-old granddaughter. The little girl's father is in Verdun, with the engineers. We are with good, friendly people. They have agreed to hold our place because tomorrow morning we leave for Gondrécourt. [...] We hope to be back here very shortly. [...]

The cold weather, which had abated a bit for a day or two, has come back with a vengeance. The wind today is absolutely frigid. We are very happy to find ourselves in this nice, warm room. I received Mme Tavernier's letter that you sent; I understand her torment at the departure of her son. But the artillery is still better than the infantry. So now we have the class of 1917 swallowed up by this horrendous octopus. We have some of them here and already everyone is complaining about them. Those poor children have little resistance and are often cowards. They didn't think war would be like this. [...]

Thursday, February 15, 1917.

I've no news since your February 12 letter from Bar-le-Duc. I don't know where you are or what you are doing. [...] I've had a cold for 2 days; I had hoped to escape but it was not possible. The inhalations I do and the care I take make me feel a bit better but do not make it go away, it has to run its course. I wanted to write to Cunault this evening but, as I am a bit tired, I prefer to finish this letter and go to bed. All the more because I have to do an inhalation and take my lemon drink, then I need to boil water to put in the hot water bottle that is my bed companion, and the last thing is to turn off the water in the basement. I have to go up and down stairs I don't know how many times, it all takes a good three-quarters of an hour. [...]

2/14/1917.

I received yesterday, belatedly, an envelope with some paper and a letter from Coraboeuf. That poor guy. He is an honest man who wants only to pay his debts rather than not paying, as do so many others. That loyal position raises him even higher in my estimation. Some people I know would consider his attitude stupid. [...] I feel terribly sorry for him and would so like to be in a position to help him in a substantial way. He too will have given his all to this war, in his own way and with all his force. [...]

The good old people with whom we are staying are meticulously clean, and extremely nice. They own this house, which had been used by a wine merchant and as a restaurant. They spent a lot of money and made it into quite a comfortable home. We have, for our use, a very lovely room, which is meant for weddings. We have arranged a corner for us; we have 30 centimeters of good straw, and with our blankets and sleeping bags, are quite well settled in. [...]

You haven't mentioned your reimbursement. Has it not happened? You should pay some attention to placing this money which would mean additional income for you. I understand that you were not able to go out to deal with this in the cold weather. As soon as the temperature becomes more reasonable, I think you should not wait. [...]

2/15/1917.

I received your letters from February 10 and 11. [...] I fully understand that my letters are a consolation for you, that is why I make it a duty, whenever possible, to write every day. Today, for instance, if I were a lazybones, I would not write. We are going to play in a town about 9 kilometers from here so, this morning, I went to see Lieutenant Brunet to see whether he would loan me a carriage and two horses. [...] He was very nice and I have the vehicle. We will leave in an hour, taking with us my music case and Maréchal's cello. That explains in part why I asked for a car. We need to have the music with us because we are going to be playing all over the place. A lieutenant, someone with a great fortune, asked us to go play in Gondrécourt at the home of a woman, wife of a clerk, who is very musical and has a good piano. Among those invited will be officers from the Army, civilians like the chatelaines from Abainville, very rich people with a lovely place about two kilometers from here. [...]

Yesterday I got back to practicing violin and right now, at 20 minutes to 1, I am going to grab my instrument to work on the Wieniavski *Mazurka* and the prelude to *Déluge* which I will be playing soon, works that are very effective with the public.

Saturday, February 17, 1917, 7:30 p.m.

I received at 4 p.m. your February 15 letter. [...] The profession of a soldier is a school for laziness and little by little you are sliding down that slope. You shouldn't write to me out of duty but because you need to talk to me; otherwise it is useless to write these letters with no interesting information, and more, you often don't answer all my questions, they are completely unimportant to you, you ignore them. [...]

Sunday, February 18, 1917, 6 p.m.

I didn't receive a letter today but that is no different from other Sundays. It's the mailman's day of rest and for me total solitude. I catch up on Monday by reading two. Tomorrow I hope to learn that you are settled at the division and that work on quartets, quintets, trios, virtuosic solos will be the order of the day. [...]

I received yesterday two letters, one from the 8th which is very late, and the other from the 12th. [...] Yesterday we were in Toureilles; a car took us there at 1 p.m. and we were back at 5, a very practical system. Nothing is happening today: the theater is moving to Gondrécourt where we have a show tomorrow. We will go there on foot as it is at most 2 kilometers away. I think that the tour will then head for Houdelaincourt which is also very near where we are now. Then, fairly soon, there will probably be some requests that get us out of this undertaking completely. I'm not worrying about that at all. [...]

Those who are involved in this tour, the actors, are filthy like pigs. They are billeted wherever there was room, poorly fed, have terrible sleeping conditions, and what is more, they have a good deal of work. They all have to help set up and take down the theater. [...] It is fortunate we were able to get out of that part. [...]

Tuesday, February 20, 1917, 6:30 p.m.

I received this morning your letter from Saturday, February 17 and at 4 the one from Sunday 18. [...] I see you are busy with church services and concerts. Don't get angry, my kitten, and tell me I don't appreciate your daily letter. What gives it value is the trouble you go to so I have one every day. [...]

2/18/1917.

I received yesterday your letter from February 14 and 2 packages. [...] I just got out of Mass, it is 11:30 and I'm writing hastily because we leave at about 1 for Gondrécourt where we rehearse at 2. Caplet will not come; he came back from Nancy with a bad cold and it's better he not come. All the more because there is a damp fog and it is thawing so there is a lot of mud. [...]

The Abainville church is quite lovely and very large, with quite a good harmonium. The sound in the tribune is mushy, but apparently the effect in the church is fine.

I sent my package of music from Génicourt. I gave it to a driver going to Bar. Because he was in a hurry, he took it to a place that arranges shipments. The important thing is that you receive it because it contains music worth a lot of money. [...] I didn't keep the Mozart because I already am dragging around too many pieces we don't play and may never play. Our work is always done quickly and not regularly. For us to work properly, Mangin would need to still be with us. Then we would have offered two concerts a week and would have had to work on new programs. I look back on what we did at Gournay-sur-Aronde, what we would have done had he stayed with us. It's yet another reason to miss him. […]

2/19/1917.

I received yesterday your letter from February 15 and no package. I am not pleased to learn that you again have a cold. […] I am shocked that you have not received any letters since the one I sent from Bar. I write every day. […]

We played yesterday at 3:30 in the home of an important brewer in Gondrecourt, a rich man with a lovely home and beautiful rooms with a wonderful Érard upright. It's odd that we don't find grand pianos very often. They gave us slippers; with the thaw that has turned the roads into mud holes, our shoes were far from clean and the mistress's beautiful oriental carpets would certainly have been damaged. We put on the slippers in a side room and made our entry into the salon that way: it was quite comical. There we found the owner, his wife, the grandmother, a charming teacher, and 5 children (4 girls and a son). There were also a number of officers, including the governor general of the 3rd Corps who has the rank of brigadier general. A worldly man, fairly well on in years, he seems to like music. We talked a bit and he left quite happy. I think he will try to organize concerts in Gondrecourt for officers from several army corps. […] After the departure of the principal officers, the daughters served a lovely tea with cake. […] The owner offered us champagne […] and then led us to our cars. […]

2/20/1917.

I did not receive a letter yesterday but did receive a package with two packages of sultanes, and a quarter pound of butter. Thank you for that. I hope your grippe is not getting worse: at night when you go to bed, put some gomenol oil in your nostrils, it is excellent. And during the day do three inhalations of gomenol and drink hot liquids. If you follow that treatment, you will get better very quickly, without a doubt. Do that simple and effective treatment. If your throat is sore, gargle three times a day with two tablets of potassium chloride dissolved in hot water. There is nothing better. The soldiers all use these treatments, even for acute bronchitis. […]

I just saw Lieutenant Bernard from the administrative service; he has asked Commander Lambrigot to allow us to play Thursday for the Salmons, the chatelains of Abainville, and then to discuss some events to be organized in Gondrécourt for the Army Corps. We will have more news about this soon. […]

Yesterday, in Gondrécourt, I saw Pierrot. He came to have coffee with us. He is very happy with his situation as a driver where he has very little to do. He said there was no possible comparison with the poor guys in the trenches. […]

Unfortunately, I could not write today before the mail because we left for Houdelaincourt at 1:30. Lieutenant Bernard's request to Commander Lambrigot for our participation did not please Captain Liberos, who is in direct command of us, because it would free us a bit from his clutches. So he asked to see us. As in all situations which pose some risk for us, I took the floor. The conclusion of the discussion was that we would only play one concert a day, the one in the afternoon, even on days when there are two concerts. And we will be transported by car. That way our evenings will be free and we will have two days a week without a concert. That suits all of us. The discussion was quite heated at times. Fortunately, I have some authority when I speak and that was effective. In the end, Captain Liberos was courteous and friendly; all he asks is that requests for us to play be addressed to him (I don't see a problem with that) and that there be some concerts for the *poilus* also. [...]

I received some fruit sauce, a can of apricots, some figs, and some sugar. You overdo it with the last, which is so hard to get. I ask you to send me a little bit, and not only do you send me quite a lot, but then you send me even more. I fill a can; once the can is full, the rest is a bother. That is why I asked you to send me only a little; my supply of sugar is sacred to me, I use it very rarely. When I ask you for a small quantity of something, moderate your response! [...]

If I write to you every day, it is not because it is my duty, it is because you are dear to me. It would have to be for that reason; there are many days when, if I did not know how you wait for my letters, how much of a comfort for you they are, I would not write, that is for sure. When there is not a letter from me every day, it is because it was impossible to write. [...]

Sunday, February 25, 1917, 5 p.m.

As it is Sunday, I've not received a letter today. Tomorrow I will have two as payback. [...]

They are now giving us ration cards for sugar. I went the Écoles de l'Ouest on Boulevard Aubert for mine; that is where they are distributing them in our area. It is time to stop the hoarding which has been going on for some time; some people have 50 kilos of sugar or more. So rationing is starting; we will surely have it for bread and meat. It is forbidden to sell cookies and cakes on Tuesdays and Thursdays. There is a tax on butter; it is sold for about 4 francs but since the tax the butter merchants rarely have any to sell. They find they don't earn enough money; they have the public captive in the sense that the quality is mediocre and the quantity is minuscule. The bakers as of today are only selling day-old bread to get people to eat less. All that is not so bad, but some people are really angry. Gas is getting scarce. I need to buy a couple of bottles. [...]

Today I have barely time to write. We played for the 10:00 a.m. Mass and it is 11:30 now. At 1:00 we leave by car for Bonnet and will be back about 5:00. This evening, at 9 p.m., we have a concert at a café. [...]

2/26/1917.

I received yesterday your letter of February 22 and two packages. [...] Take care of your health. I am going to send you today Mme Duez's letter. Obviously that nice old lady exaggerates a lot, but I do think you worry too much and that is not good for your health. Realize that whether you worry or not, none of that will change what is going to happen. If I am meant to be left here, I will be left here, and the opposite also. Don't make a big deal of it. If I do come back, which I certainly hope to, you need to be in good health. [...]

3/1/1917.

I am writing this morning earlier than usual, before the mail. [...] Yesterday at a theatrical production, there was a bad event. The theater troop arrived in Delouze, where a battalion of the 129th is billeted, the second under Mangin's command. Either Delauney, the lieutenant who directs the group, made a blunder, or he presented himself badly—no matter, he was greeted like a dog in a game of skittles. What's more, the entire troop was greeted in the same manner. The quarters they were given were shit-holes, pigsties. Commander Mangin had Delauney brought before him, told him that he didn't need these concerts, and finally, in the course of the discussion, put him under arrest for a week. We were supposed to be part of the concert in Delouze. As the concert is not going to happen, we won't be going there this afternoon. [...]

Last night we gave the concert in Houdelaincourt for the 74th with the colonel present. [...] It took place in a large hall in a café in front of an audience of at least 200 people, including some civilians. Our piano had been brought from Gondrécourt to Houdelaincourt thanks to the efforts of the Army Corps. It is rather beaten up by all these moves. It is not good for it to be all the time in barns and cold breezes. Today, thanks to Colonel Bruneau, from the 74th, it will get back to the touring troop in Baudonvilliers. [...]

3/4/1917.

I did not have time to write in Bar. [...] Here is a summary of what took place. [...]

We left Friday morning on the 9:15 train to Gondrécourt. We arrived in Bar at 10:30. The doctor who was waiting for us took us directly to lunch in the doctors' mess. At 2 p.m. we were with Martyl in the hospital, rehearsing in her room. Her sister Georgette, a singer also, was there. She's at the Conservatory and received a second prize last year. She is very nice and a very good musician. Martyl served us tea and excellent little cakes and splendid cream puffs. At 5:30 we moved to the room in the hospital where the concert was to take place. In that quite large room were about 30 wounded in beds and another 150 on benches or chairs. In addition, there were at least 100 guests: doctors, nurses, civilians. [...] There was a piano. I played the Recitative, Fantasy and Finale of the Franck Sonata; then a Beethoven Trio, then Fauré's *Berceuse* and two mazurkas by Wieniawski. Maréchal played Fauré's *Élégie*. The two sisters sang some 18th-century-style duets, very charming. Martyl ended with *La Lorraine*. We had considerable success; it was the nicest concert I've given so far. The head doctor thanked us publicly. Then, after endless handshakes with the wounded, we had champagne with the doctor-in-chief. Finally, we had dinner with the two sisters. By 9:00 we were at the home of the piano merchant where we played for Martyl and some music-loving doctors. I played the Franck Sonata and as an ensemble we played the Chausson Quartet. Then we all escorted Caplet to the station as he was going on leave. By the time we all separated, after warm thanks and the promise to see each other soon, it was 1 a.m.

The next day, Saturday, I spent most of the morning in bed, then had a quiet lunch with Magne. Martyl came to invite us to tea. We chatted for a long time. She immediately asked me to agree that we (all of us) would get together to make music after the war. I don't need to tell you that I am thrilled. I could make a lot of contacts that way. She is really charming and a good friend.

We took the train at 4:42 and were in Abainville at 7 p.m. This morning we played for Mass and at 2 p.m. I played at Baudonvillers. The division is on maneuvers for the next 3 days. We are going to take advantage of the pause to bring the piano here. [...]

3/5/1917.

I received yesterday your letter from March 1 and a package with a Camembert, half a pound of butter, and a can of sardines. [...] I learned yesterday something touching, which increases my admiration of Colonel Valzi. Before he left, he made a point of passing us to his successor and recommending us to him. It is a thoughtful act from a good heart and we will be sure to thank him. In fact, the new colonel does not like music. When he was speaking with Jacquet, the director of the music regiment, Jacquet replied that, in addition to the regular musicians there, he had Durosoir. The new colonel replied: "Oh, oui, Durosoir, I know he is at the division and his situation will not change," so Colonel Valzi's recommendation was not in vain. [...]

I just saw Lemoine who is back from a pass and he didn't bring very good news. According to him and connections he has with officials in Rouen, we should expect the war to continue, very likely through next winter. That does not surprise me at all. My opinion is that we will only beat the Germans through exhaustion, and that will take a long time. [...]

3/6/1917.

Yesterday I did not receive any mail because of the division move. [...] I had a long talk with M. Labeyrie about the future after the war. He doesn't think it will be rosy, far from it, and he predicts years of misery and deprivation. We have to expect that life will certainly be harder after the war than it is now. We also have to fear revolts from the *poilus* who have been subjected to such iron discipline that, once they are free, they will surely react. [...] We are trapped in a terrible chain of events from which we cannot escape. Governments will have to come to their senses, set aside their pride, and consider the practical side of the situation. Until then, the *poilu* suffers and dies. The awakening will be that much worse because the sleep has been so long. [...]

3/8/1917.

I received yesterday your letters from March 3 and 4 and a package with 6 tangerines and half a pound of butter. [...] I will be on home leave very soon. [...]

Lucien had his first leave of 1917 during this period.

3/26/1917.

My trip went well although I was considerably delayed. In fact, we didn't get to Nancy until 10:30 and not to our destination until 2 p.m. I traveled with Magne whom I ran into at the Gare de l'Est. [...] I found everyone impatient for my return and with good reason because we had a concert to play that evening. It had already been announced and they were getting quite anxious. No one expected us to be gone so long. But we managed to get there before the concert so everything was fine. [...]

3/27/1917.

We played again last night in a show for the *poilus*, a show that took place at 5:30 p.m. in a magnificent hall that usually serves as a movie theater. It's the first time in this war that I've played in a concert hall, this one has about 800 seats and is lighted by electricity—finally, a return to civilization. The acoustics were excellent. In addition to the soldiers, there were a number of civilians. [...]

We are leaving here tonight, apparently for rest. We will assemble with other army corps to create a pursuit army. [...] It is quite likely that I will not be able to write tomorrow. If I can send a postcard, I will. [...]

Sunday, March 25, 1917, 6 p.m., new time.[250]

I expect you had a good trip with your friend Magne and you both arrived in good health. Another leave finished. It was, once again, quite painful for me. I was not able to enjoy going out with you. I didn't even have the pleasure of coming to your departure as I usually do and taking leave of you at the last possible minute. It is a difficult burden; we have to resign ourselves and accept all the suffering God gives us, knowing that there are others even more unfortunate. [...]

I hope that you will have more confidence and open your heart more in your next letters. What's the point of being alive if my child treats me like a stranger? And is even wary of me? All my advice is always for your happiness and well-being, that is the only purpose. So, in everything you do, don't let yourself be used by others (man or woman), guard jealously your moral and physical independence. Do not bother yourself about what others may say about you, and stay on the straight path. Stay the way you are, with all your faults and all your good qualities. [...] Be frank in what you write about what you are doing, that is the greatest blessing I could wish for. [...]

Tuesday, March 27, 1917, 2 p.m.

[...] I hope you are eating properly and with a good appetite. If you continue to let yourself be overcome by an unhealthy dreaming and 1830's romanticism, you will become a skeleton, and could say goodbye to the exceptionally good health you have enjoyed so far. The air of Vincennes was good for you, and your mother's cooking gave you again the joy of being alive. You drank and ate like old times; continue the same way and leave behind the lethargy and despair which are not consistent with your gay, carefree nature. You should think of nothing other than getting out of that dreary abyss. [...] You must reply to me about all this and not avoid anything. Candor is a quality you don't display very often. That is unfortunate, for you and for me, as there are some misunderstandings coming between us. [...]

---

[250] Daylight savings time.

Sunday, April 1, 1917, 4:30 p.m.

I received this morning your March 30 letter, sent with a stamp. You see, the civilian mail is working very well and that way I receive your news very quickly. [...] You seem to be quite far from the front; I found on the map where you are right now. [...] In their retreat the Germans poisoned the wells and springs; you mustn't drink the water and I don't know how you will manage to prepare meals. [...]

3/31/1917.

We did not receive any mail yesterday. That means that today, Saturday, it's been almost 8 days since I've had any news. [...] I wrote to Mme Duez so she wouldn't feel neglected, and apologized that I couldn't get back to see her again. I think I put together a nice little letter which will make her very happy. [...]

I am very well lodged in an excellent room. I had a good deal of luck; very few people (other than officers) have rooms. [...] We have orders to get rid of everything useless and only keep a change of underwear and the barest minimum. I even think we will be leaving behind our jackets and only keeping a sweater and our *capote*. They are really thinking of pursuit and want everyone as unencumbered as possible, no doubt to be able to run better. Please God that they are not again deluding themselves. It appears that the forces going into action are of an unimaginable scale and the *Boches* cannot possibly resist. We pray that is true and that this nightmare ends this year. Let's keep hope in our hearts, but not feed on illusions which are followed by disappointment that makes it all more bitter. [...]

Wednesday, April 4, 1917, 2 p.m.

I received last evening your letter of March 31. [...] I just interrupted my letter. A cleaning lady just arrived, sent by the butter merchant on the rue du Midi; I had asked for someone over a week ago. This is a young woman with two children and already a job in the morning. She will come 4 afternoons a week, Monday, Tuesday, Wednesday, and Friday. She keeps the other two afternoons to do her laundry and her own housecleaning and organizing. That will be enough for me, especially since she is young. She will start next Monday. [...]

4/1/1917.

Today I received mail from you for the first time since my return, your letters from February 25, 26, 27, and 28 [...] I am actually writing this letter on March 31, it is 9 p.m., I am alone in my room and no one will disturb me. Tomorrow morning Mass is at 9:30 and I am afraid I will not be able to write all day long because of all the tasks that will fall to me. Our laundry truck has not yet arrived; it is bringing Maréchal's cello and the box of music. We are not worried about it in the long run, but we are supposed to play a concert tomorrow night. [...]

I have no doubt, my dear old kitten, that this leave, in some ways, was very painful for you. We have never been apart and, despite all we can write, we are so dear to each other! For me, there is no question that souls like ours, so close to each other, will never be separated. And I spend really so little time with you each year, it is no surprise that it is a terrible sacrifice for you not to be able to come with me. I do not distrust you, my dear old *minou*, but I am always afraid that you will take badly what I tell you. Quite frankly, you seem a bit jealous of any affection I may have for women. I do not want to make you suffer. I know well that there are people in this world who just want to catch, or to try to catch, others, but we must not make such generalizations. They negate all that is good or beautiful in the world. I do not want to hide from you the fact that I have some feelings for Mlle Muller. [...] Why, at a time like this when we have so little joy, should I try to forget such a sweet memory? That young woman, to whom I promised nothing, has my address and may write from time to time. So far, I've received nothing. I will send her letters back to her, and promise to tell you about it each time. I cannot say more, nor give you more proof of trust. I never talk to anyone about my intimate feelings. Those things are between me and God. [...]

4/2/1917.

Yesterday's mail has not arrived, it must have gone in some other direction and will arrive one of these days. I received this morning your letter from March 30. [...] Yesterday afternoon Caplet and I rehearsed and, in the evening, we played in a small hall that is part of the American installation. There were about 100 people including three American women and a few officers and friends. [...] It was a small, intimate concert. The very friendly Americans offered us café au lait with little cakes, and cigarettes for those who smoke. In short, a delightful little event.

I think we will stay here a bit longer than was predicted. We are reserve troops; the events for which we are in reserve will certainly take place but, right now, nothing is happening. I am so comfortably lodged that I would only be happier if our stay here were to be prolonged. I am sure I will not find such comfort anywhere else. [...]

Thursday, April 5, 1917, 5 p.m.

I just received your April 1 letter, and the one from April 2. [...] Thank you for the trust you are showing me, it may be the first time. It makes me happy and sad at the same time. I was very troubled during your leave; I saw that my poor big son, so naïve and simple, was being influenced by dreams that could be very costly in the future. Why keep up a correspondence with that young woman? It will make her believe in a future that will probably never come true. [...]

I already told you that a touch of madness has come over you when you talk about burying yourself in some provincial town. What would come of all those years devoted to interpreting the works of the great masters to end up as a teacher in any old place where your talent would sink to nothing after a few years. And you had that idea because a somewhat nice young woman turned your head? [...]

4/3/1917.

I received this morning delayed mail, that is your letter from March 29 and a package. [...] Don't send more packages; I don't need them and what is more, when we are on the move and especially if we move forward, we are not sure that anything will reach us. When they arrive, everything except canned food will be spoiled. The packages themselves may be lost. If we move forward, we will go a week or more without receiving mail. Fortunately, you will receive mine; there are always empty vehicles to take letters to the rear. [...] Nothing is happening despite the huge number of troops which push services to the limit.

Our music and Maréchal's cello are in the laundry truck, which has still not arrived. It must have broken down and the people driving it, aware that they are not needed, are in no hurry. [...]

Saturday, April 7, 1917, 2:30 p.m.

I didn't receive any news yesterday and none so far. [...] This morning I sent you in the mail a package: 250 grams of butter, a Camembert, 250 grams of Gruyère and some tissue paper. There is not much to chew on, but enjoy everything I send you. I spend a lot of time on fruitless errands. Getting supplies is hard work and I think that will get worse. [...]

I need to refute one of your arguments to which I've not yet responded. You write: "I think you are a bit jealous of my affections for women." That thought appears to me base and nasty. (It is nasty of you to even say it to me.) No, you are not a very good psychologist. It is revolting to me when I see that, in the presence of women (as happened in Abainville), you disappear entirely; in a word, your faculties are destroyed to the extent that you can no longer make sane judgments about what is happening around you. You are overcome by a numbing idleness, exquisite pleasure that puts in front of your eyes a thick veil and takes away all energy and manliness. [...] I am profoundly sad to realize that I was unable to pass on to my son my energetic virility, qualities which I have in abundance and that a good many men would envy if they were aware of them (do you understand the nuance?). Rebellion is strong in me. I would wish you strength of soul and I find only sentimentality and whining. You have great qualities, my beloved child and, at the same time, such childish ideas about the world that one might think you no longer live on this earth.

As I've said already, I suffered greatly during your last leave and I am still pained. I found you so changed this time, physically and morally. The open gaiety which was always your gift has left you; you seem weary at heart. Up until now, you have no reason to complain; destiny has protected you. I realize that these years of dreadful warfare and suffering and deprivation about which we, civilians, have absolutely no conception are affecting your mind and changing your nature, but seeing that was hard for me. You were so on edge and inclined toward unexplained melancholy that I suffered even more. There is one fact that can explain this. The refugee family in Abainville had such influence on you during your brief time there, by their tears about the present situation, a situation that is true for thousands and thousands of others, that you adopted their way of thinking. [...] These lines will probably annoy you. But I beg you to read them attentively, not so you can follow my advice if you don't choose to, but so you can reflect on them and write your thoughts. [...]

I think you will cling to your art, which should be of great comfort to you; you will cling to it even more because of your past and not repudiate it as you seemed intent on doing while here in Vincennes. That is still another great distress, the thought of such abandonment just at the point where your talent, ripe and full, gives your brain the means to interpret the works of great masters. That is another folly that besieges you. [...]

Sunday, Easter, April 8, 1917, 5 p.m.

I received yesterday afternoon your letter of April 3. [...] Come on, my dear child, may your courage not weaken and your faith in the future rest strong. I would so like to be at your side to spur you on, a flick of the whip here and there, and the wonderful thoroughbred you were, would take up again the route to fight to the end. Promise me not to weaken and not to write to that woman in Abainville who is the cause of your depression. [...]

4/4/1917.

I did not receive a letter yesterday, but I don't think that is because of your health. In any case, I hope to have a reassuring letter today. [...] Today is an anniversary—one year ago we were attacking the Douaumont redoubt and were about to experience a harsh test of endurance. May God keep our men from finding themselves again in such a place! [...]

4/5/1917.

[...] This morning the weather is somewhat nicer; although it snowed quite a bit last night, the snow is not sticking. The result is a dreadful *bouilli*.[251] [...]

For this evening's concert, I will play Dvořák's *Humoresque* and Wieniawski's *Obertass* which fortunately are well received.[252] Caplet will accompany me, playing from memory (our music has not yet arrived). I'd have preferred to play something else, but we have to make do. Here is our menu from today: steak, beans, jam, cheese. This evening pot-au-feu with cabbage, carrots, celery, and potatoes. A very healthy dinner. All the actors from the theater troop are here and are very badly housed; they all look at me jealously. I try not to notice. [...]

4/6/1917.

Headquarters of the Division SP 93.[253] You will write me from now on at the address at the beginning of this letter. As you can see, there is no division number. That is for the best; in case we move forward, no one should know where the division is located. Since yesterday, our fate is settled. When there are serious actions, I become secretary to the division, which means I stay with them and work with them. Caplet becomes chief of the pigeon keepers. When the troops are advancing, we get their latest news by carrier pigeon. As for Magne and Maréchal, they are serving as bicycle messengers between the division and the 9th and 10th brigades. Thus, we find ourselves in the service of the division. As for me, I have the best position, as secretary, which doesn't require any physical effort. [...]

There couldn't be a better solution for us: no need to tell you that the theater troop envies us. When their rest is over, they return to the division garrison from where they can each be sent to the regiments as reinforcement. I hope that doesn't happen to them as some of them are nice, friendly men. [...]

Yesterday a stretcher bearer from the 129th who had come to see the chief doctor gave me two pictures from Rolland which are dear to me—the portrait of Martel, taken several days before his death in Trottoir, a section of Les Éparges, and the picture of his grave. The nearer tomb is Varin's, the ambulance driver killed with him. These pictures, which I received at 3 p.m., brought back so many memories that I needed all my willpower to be able to play the 5:00 concert. We, the musicians, are the ones who created the cemetery at Amblonville where 500 of our fellow soldiers, along with Henri, lie. He was a noble, remarkable person. We talked often about the problems of the soul and the infinite to which he found answers in his religious faith, but still he was open to discussing

---

[251] A sort of porridge; boiled flour and liquid.

[252] Antonin Dvořák (1841-1904), *Humoresque*, G-flat major, Op. 101, No. 7; Wieniawski, Mazurka for violin and piano, Op. 19, No. 1.

[253] SP, headquarters for preparation.

them philosophically, outside his Catholic beliefs. […] We think often of him and know he would have been happy to finish this war with his 129th. That good fortune was not granted to him. […]

I still have no news from Abainville and I cannot say that makes me happy. However, I am changing, and, with time, this subject will be put to rest. […]

Second letter, same day.

This is the second letter I am writing today. I received about noon your letters from the 2 and 4th of April. Caplet just got back from the Corps. […] Commander Pompée, the second in command at headquarters, spoke to him about us, clearly interested in knowing where we are and that we would be safe. […] That proves that the higher ups are not uninterested in our fate.

They are forbidding all personal baggage. We can only keep one blanket, one change of underwear. Baggage needs to be reduced to the bare minimum. Lemoine has sent his violin to Paris with someone going on leave; he, like Caplet, will go get it once this adventure is over. That's for the best. I will ask M. Labeyrie to transport my violin in the postal vehicles. He will certainly not refuse. We are supposed to go the American women tomorrow at 5:00 to play some music, in the evening we will go to M. Labeyrie's home to play the Franck Sonata and probably the Bach G minor Sonata. […]

Wednesday, April 11, 1917, 2:30 p.m.

I received this morning your letter dated Holy Friday, April 6. […] The time in Abainville, however brief, was for you lazy and pleasure-filled; it deprived you of all will except to let yourself yield to temptation. I had suspected that and was already feeling the pain, I don't know how, before you came home on leave. Your letters showed your mind not free and that something abnormal was going on. It is a new burden for me; we two do not need to cause each other pain over a stranger. […]

4/7/1917.

As I told you, I received yesterday your letters from April 2 and 4. […] We finally have news about the laundry truck. I saw the driver this morning. The vehicles are 30 kilometers away from here, still broken down. As for our things, everything is safe and we should not worry. Right now, it is just as well that those vehicles keep our things which we can find later. […]

We play today in a theater belonging to the American women; this theater is for the crippled. There is a coterie of crippled soldiers here, some two hundred of all sorts. […]

If we go on pursuit, we will be sleeping in a tent in the fields. I will be lucky; as I am serving as adjunct to the secretaries, and for sure I really will work with them. During the action, I will be sheltered. Here is why. Expecting this pursuit, headquarters has gotten a very large tent in which the officers attached to the general staff and their secretaries will be grouped. I do not have to worry; I will always have a roof over my head, albeit a cloth roof, but still a roof. We will spend no more than two weeks then we will have a rest time, an immediate pleasure for many of us.

Caplet did not bring back an instrument, he is having his restrung. When we are out of this quagmire, he will go get it. A 48-hour leave for Caplet is simple and totally natural. If this weather continues, we will have a sad Easter. I may try to get a new 2-liter canteen. There are some at the station for the sick or lame and I will ask the lieutenant who wants us to play for him to try to get me one. It is no small advantage in case of an advance. I would really like to leave here with 3 liters of wine, because I am sure that the farther we advance, the less we will have. [...]

Second letter, same day.

It is 2:30, mail has been distributed and I have no letter today. No mail and dreadful weather make for depression. Our cases are stuck 30 kilometers from here, with the laundry trucks. A little car left this morning to get Maréchal's cello and the food for the postmen. Magne went with that car; he will open our music case and bring back a bit of music so we can play a little concert today at 5 p.m. [...]

4/9/1917.

[...] I just received your letter from April 7 [...] Dear *minou*, your reproaches are not justified. I have written a lot to you since I've been in Crézancy, often twice a day. I would ignore all other correspondence to send you, as you say, a "bone" to chew on. You make me laugh when you talk about your bone showing up under the door. You may be alone, my dear *minou*, but you are not a *minou* without any letters. You can't say that; it is false. [...]

I protest, formally, when you claim that I lose all control of my faculties in the presence of a woman and cannot make any judgments. And that I have no energy, nor vision. It is a total error. You seem to say that love does not exist; or, if it does, the man who feels it becomes immediately feeble, without any energy. I think you are gravely mistaken; far from snuffing out energy, love profoundly stimulates one's energies. [...] My spirit is as strong as anyone around me; I am not subject to sentimentality, as you put it. I do not have the mind of a child, rather one of a poet who has lived more in the heavens than on earth. That is a bit your fault, but it would be wrong for me to complain. During this war, I have been forced back down to earth and when I see a pretty woman after all the horrible things I've seen, my poetic soul awakes. Why scold me for that? Why use such bitter, disappointed language? Illusions help one be happy. It is only old people who have no dreams, and I do not yet have white hair. [...] I have no intention of giving up my art, far from it. If I said something like that at Vincennes, it was when I was angry or upset. Don't believe a word of it. I intend to work hard to regain my form. But to push away all human affection, that seems to me not necessary or desirable. I am not a music monk. [...]

We will soon have a lot more to distract us. In my position, the risk is very limited and you should not worry. But there is no doubt that I will have a lot of work. Apparently, I am to be a sound watchman, I will listen for explosions that get closer or for the noise of a motor. It's important for the artillery's settings. [...]

4/10/1917.

We are leaving tomorrow morning, it's now decided, and from this moment we will be going back into a more active phase. Not that we will again be in battle, but we will be closer to the battle lines. As of tomorrow morning, I am at the disposition of Sergeant Madeline, the chief of the secretaries, and from then on until new orders I will be sharing their fate in terms of sleeping arrangements and food. I won't be too uncomfortable and have nothing really to complain about. During the moves, my pack goes in the truck with the archives; we have only our *musettes* to carry. Frequently the secretaries travel in vehicles, although at times they walk. [...]

I did not receive any mail today; that saddens me because, once we start moving, we will not receive letters. [...] Caplet put my violin in a large case which will easily hold it and in which it will be sheltered. It will be in a vehicle belonging to the co-op and will be as safe as a package can be under the circumstances we will be facing.

The weather is absolutely dreadful today; it has snowed hard five or six times. So, my dear *minou*, it is very unlikely that I will be able to write tomorrow, unless I arrive early enough to use civilian mail. [...]

Sunday, April 15, 1917, 2:30 p.m.

[...] I read in *L'Information* that in the Aisne region "two enemy strikes failed under our fire." Are you in the battle? Of course, I don't know. I pray God to make you forget those untimely distractions and give you a clear mind to manage the current situation. Being a sound watchman must be difficult and tiring, requiring constant attention. [...]

Monday, April 16, 1917, 6:30 p.m.

I received this morning a second letter from April 10 as well as the picture of Martel's tomb, taken by Dumant. The picture, if I may say so, is very well done, a lovely perspective with the view of tombs scattered amid the greenery and the trees. It is a peaceful final resting place.

I am writing late today because my cleaning lady was here. She comes Monday, Tuesday, Wednesday, and Friday from 1 to 4. That is not much time. She has to hurry to do a proper cleaning in 3 hours. She can't give me more time as she needs to be free to get her son at school at 4 p.m. He is 4 years old, just a child, and she also has a very young daughter whom she takes to daycare so she can work. She picks her up at 6; she's a very proper young woman. Her husband is from Brittany, his name is Le Huéron. He was doing his military service at the beginning of the war and spent a year in the trenches but fell ill. After his convalescence, he became part of a health service. He has just been sent back to the infantry. Right now, he is in an area near Reims; he doesn't know how to read or write, so one of his comrades writes to his wife. [...] Henriette, that is her name, is worried, especially as one of her husband's brothers was killed at the end of March in the latest battles in the Somme or Aisne. There are 12 in her husband's family, orphaned very young. They needed to go into service jobs; that is why they never learned to read or write, it's sad. There are a good many unfortunate people in this life and, when they have the courage, they manage to make their way all the same. [...]

Your destiny has been easier. The war, for you as for so many others, is a harsh ordeal which you are getting through, scratching up your knees. But so far you are safe and healthy and you need to thank God for sparing you. We must pray that He be willing to leave you here, in my tender arms, so that after the war, to thank Him, you can once again be the artist you were, enthusiastic and confident in your star. Why turn your back on the past, the past where your art occupied all your attention, for some misplaced illusions, some crazy chimera in which one makes his own misfortune by not seeing things for what they are. Such follies are understandable in a young man. Look into your heart and, if you are honest, you will realize that you may be tired of living in this hell (which is natural) and that you were mistaken about your feelings, that an aberration of your senses was the cause of all the sadness. If this struggle cleanses your soul and returns the calm and clear-sightedness to your life, let's thank the heavens and bless your suffering. [...]

As for my life, it is quite mundane despite my hoping it to be other. I spend my time running here and there to find butter or fuel or canned goods of some kind. [...]

Dramatic news this morning, then a very funny spectacle—everyone in the street shouting at the top of their voices. The reason: a counter order, we are not leaving. I myself had all my stuff on my back on my way to the division when I heard the news. If the departure is put off for several days, then it's only a bit annoying. But if we have to leave tonight or tomorrow, then it's a real pain, getting everything organized again. But that is military life, plans change frequently. What is funny is that in many cases, there had been touching goodbyes, sometimes with drink, between people and their landlords, those who were not well-lodged and had argued with their landlords, as well as those in better situations. It's good comedy when they end up back where they started. [...]

The doctors at the station for the sick had all said goodbye to us and wished us good luck. The American women filled Maréchal and Magne's pockets with a lot of English cigarettes. [...]

I am not renouncing my art, far from it, but I will require a long rest and time in different surroundings to find the joy again. As for the serious reading I've been doing, I don't mind that it changes me; it is an evolution toward a greater ideal and more noble goals. If the soul suffers at times in indefinable ways, or in ways difficult to explain, it's from a need for beauty and perfection it has not yet found. The poet sleeps in the musician and the poet is a dreamer. But the dreamer, when in contact with reality, suffers, suffers often and closes in on himself. I am not going crazy, for sure, my ideas have never been clearer, nor my vision of how to conduct myself in so very many situations sharper. The physical and, more, the psychological suffering of such a long and difficult war only increase in me, and in many others, the need for affection. I am painfully aware of the solitude of my existence. Unlike in my earlier life, I do not have the enormous work to keep me busy and sustain me. It is understandable. I realize it is not an excuse to do stupid things; relax, I will not do anything stupid. I will not write to that young woman; so far, she has not written to me, I find her reserve excessive. But no matter, the fact is that she has not written to me, and I, suppressing my desire, will not write to her. I am revealing the bottom of my heart to you, and I can say, for sure, this is the first time I talk about this sort of thing. [...]

I arrived here about 2 p.m. After getting up at 5:45 a.m., we covered about 16 kilometers, and we are nearing places we were at this same time in 1915. Here we are again on an adventure; in a few days, we may well be on the front line. I walked with the secretaries, that is, without my sack which was in the division truck. The walk was not terribly hard. However, the condition of the roads is horrendous, nothing but swamps everywhere. The cause is the enormous amount of equipment, horses, men, all of which, for two months, have passed over the roads in this area. It is astonishing and impressive to see all this—a huge group of people on the march, and with them, monstrous machines. What a sight! It is interesting from many points of view to see all that, I doubt that I will regret having seen it. [...]

4/13/1917.

Today everything is calm. The division will leave tomorrow to advance 15 or 20 kilometers. I slept quite well. I was in a large attic with at least 60 men from different services of the division. We received some straw and, good heavens, our beds were not bad. [...] We are housed in the servants' quarters of the chateau. The chateau itself is destroyed; the general and officers are in the out-buildings. Compared with the men out in the field, we are pretty well off. This poor area is disgusting, a true pig pen. The troops are squeezed into an area of 217 inhabitants so they are lodged in the foulest of conditions and this is only the beginning; it will be something else in a few days! [...]

Here we are living the life of bohemians which will probably last three to four weeks, if not more. Fortunately, we are entering a good season. The new moon is the 21st, I hope it will again bring us nice weather. Last night, the cannon fire was fierce, and we hear the never-ending rattling of the artillery. [...]

Music is, for now, on the back-burner and probably will be for a good while. Our lives are a series of images and the unpredictable; our minds are busy if only in finding solutions to necessities. Just to find a bundle of straw or a bit of fresh bread, we often need to use as much intelligence as to wrap up a serious business deal. We are returning a bit to the wild life and our thoughts get buried in it. We are the beast who walks, sleeps, and eats. Nothing more. I was rather tired yesterday. We are no longer accustomed to these movements on foot, none of us are. That will come back quickly. [...]

Tuesday, April 17, 1917, 8 p.m.

[...] I received this afternoon your letters from the 12th and 13th. So, you are on your way again. [...] Mme Tavernier stopped in today. She didn't say much about André who must be in supplies. She spoke vaguely about worn-out horses, that André was tired of being always on horseback, that he was riding his second horse, and that they made the horses walk until they died. [...]

4/14/1917.

We did not leave this morning; there was a counter order last evening. I think it will be for tomorrow morning. [...] The move of about 20 kilometers will bring us a bit closer to the front. [...]

I barely have any time to write; at this moment I am adjoint to the sergeant orderly from 8 a.m. to 8 p.m. There are so many orders to carry and people to be kept informed that I have not much time. I have nothing much to tell you other than I saw Dumont who is very depressed. Caplet, chief pigeon keeper, received 10 pigeons. He is very funny with those animals: he calls "*petit, petit*" and the pigeons come peck at him. [...]

I note that my letters are arriving with quite a delay. I have no time to write more; this poor letter has been interrupted many times. Goodbye.

4/15/1917.

It is 7 a.m. We are just arriving after having walked 25 kilometers. My feet are like liver pâté. We leave again tomorrow morning about 7 a.m. and we are going either in the region of Mme Marion, or to the place where we took the picture of me with my beard, or to the region of M. Colas, the clerk in Boulogne. In any case, three days from now, we'll be in the mêlée. Just do not worry, it does no good. I am a fatalist. [...]

4/16/1917.

This morning, as we were walking, they brought me your letter from April 13. After arriving last night at 7 p.m., there was no possibility of sleep. The division worked all night. There were orders that needed to go everywhere, in short, no way to close an eye, even for a minute. We left again at 4 a.m. in the morning. We didn't arrive until about 11 a.m. because of all the blockages on the road; we are now near the area where we were at rest the winter of 1914-1915. At this moment, everyone is on alert. For food, *singe*, chocolate, biscuits, that is the food of the good old days. [...]

4/17/1917.

[...] Last evening, about 6 p.m., we were ordered to retreat; 20 minutes later we were on the way, moving back 6 kilometers. Fortunately, the division settled in the town hall and classrooms, which are generally clean. We spread ourselves out on the floor and fell asleep, putting our blanket and *capote* over us. That is life in all its rudimentary essence. Since we are part of an army in reserve, and are still in reserve, they can move us around all along the front, wherever they think they will need extra men. [...]

I received this evening your letters of April 14 and 15. [...] As I expected, we have received the order to depart, to the rear where the army is. [...] It seems the plans have changed. The offensive, although having some success, was not going as well as predicted on paper, so we are making a move to the right. As an army in reserve, we can wander about for a long time without being used.

We will no doubt leave again tomorrow. I received a package which I've not yet opened. The cannon fire is dreadful this evening, a total roar. I do not have time to reply to all you tell me; I have to go to bed. We are walking huge distances daily, in terrible weather and over roads destroyed beyond description. [...]

I have still not received a letter from Abainville. I do not understand your saying that I hurt you deeply; love is a normal, strong feeling. There is nothing to get all upset about. I will have more to say about all you write, but I don't have the time, and this is not the moment. It is not the time to talk about life when death hovers all around us and so many are dying; this offensive will certainly be very costly. The Germans defend themselves with the energy of despair. [...]

4/18/1917.

We have arrived! I left this morning with the secretaries; we walked 25 kilometers. We are back at the place where we spent three days. I think we leave again tomorrow, and I don't know whether that will be for the place where we spent 15 days and I had a bed, which I hope to find again. Since this morning, we have had snow falling on our backs without stopping; we are, as one might say, quite chilly. With three friends from the general staff, I stopped in an area where a good guy made us onion soup, a 15-egg omelet with lard, then cheese and jam, and coffee with rum. That wonderful lunch gave us the courage and strength to finish the trip which, given the weather and the state of the roads, was exhausting. We do not know what all this movement means. What is certain is that they are wearing out men, horses, and equipment. A few more days of this life, in this weather, and no one will be able to do anything useful. Lots of horses are dropping dead. [...] I am wiped out. I am going to eat, go find a woman I can buy a stick of wood from, dry my *capote* and go to bed. [...]

Saturday, April 21, 1917, 9 p.m.

[...] They are leading you forward then back to the rear quite often; you walk kilometers and kilometers playing this game and must be very tired. I don't know that this offensive will be successful. I suspect that, as usual, we will be forced to stop and that thousands of men will be killed to gain a few kilometers. The Germans are so well-fortified that it will be impossible to break through their line. We will never finish this with weapons.

I saw Jean Alan today; he has been on leave for 2 days. [...] He says the Germans do not lack for bullets, bombs, etc. They always fight back. It is a lack of food that could get thorny for them. He says that men are good for nothing when they are starving. If that happened, the war would be over.

Madame Armengaud stopped in with Mlle Andrée at about 4, Jean was still there. I had served him a bit of wine with a cookie, but he stayed for tea with them. They chatted while I made the tea and prepared all the other things. Apparently, when you had dinner with the Armengauds, you told some funny stories that made everyone laugh. Mlle Andrée asked me whether I knew those stories. I know none of them. What I do know is that, during your leave, you were not at all funny and, even though I was ill, I had to boost your morale. You were a different person when you left. The air in Vincennes did you a lot of good. True, it was your mood that was sick whereas with me it was the body.

4/19/1917.

The mail is working; I'm much better today, my health is good. I will write this evening.[254]

Second letter, same day.

I received this morning your letter from the 16th, but not the one from the 15th. [...] So far, we have not received the order to depart tomorrow. I think that we were obliged to stop the troop movement because of general exhaustion of the men and the animals. One cannot march barely eating and sleeping in the midst of terrible weather without suffering the consequences. [...]

What you say is totally contradictory. The life of an artist is one of dreams and illusions, that is the basis of his art. He does not know real life; generally, that is what people reproach artists for. I do not regret my destiny, in civilian life or in the military, as I've been very lucky, at least up to now. I do not renounce my art, far from it, and I am certain that when I am able to return to serious work, my enthusiasm will be just as it was. And why do you believe that one cannot reconcile one's art with human love? Thank heaven, there are many artists, among the greatest, for whom natural affections played a big role. You seem to conceive of the artist as a monk who should take a vow of celibacy and chastity. On that you go too far; that it is not true. These ideas, you say, are only understandable from young men. However, Berlioz, Massenet and so many others were wild up to their final days. I still have not received anything from Abainville and that must make you happy. You must believe that young woman has an unusual sense of what is proper. Let's drop this subject, as you yourself have said. [...]

Tuesday, April 24, 1917, 4:30 p.m.

[...] I had hoped to have news from you at 4 because, in the card from April 19, you promised to write that evening. Did something keep you from writing? I want to know where you are and whether you can sleep a bit better than you have up to now. If you can take off your shoes, you would be able to change

---

[254] This was a picture postcard rather than a letter.

socks and that would warm your toes. You say you are well, and I really want to believe you, but I have difficulty imagining that it's true with the kilometers you have covered with your feet in snow or freezing water. Quite a few men will end up with bronchitis. I believe you are not one of them, but I am fearful. If you've gotten back to Crézancy, you should do everything possible to get back your room and your bed, that will help to recover from the fatigue. [...]

My cleaning lady's young son is sick; she had to take him to the doctor today. He has a high fever. Still she came yesterday and today, only working for 2 hours each day. I hope he won't get worse, first for her and for him and then for me; in this young woman I've found a very clean, correct person. [...]

Wednesday, April 25, 1917, 6 p.m.

I received this afternoon your letter from the 19th and the one from the 20th. [...] I really wish you would go to the rear, in Crézancy or somewhere else where you could find a bed.

This offensive has definitely not produced what we had hoped (it's always the same thing). Behind their front lines, the Germans have very strong positions with large numbers of machine guns—so guess the result. It is sad to think of all those humans cut down, eliminated and for what? An advance of a few kilometers. The Germans can hole up in their shelters, they always have more behind them while the French are hit with everything that human ingenuity has invented to destroy one's fellow man. [...]

You are always deforming my thoughts when I write about them even though I express them clearly. When an artist experiences an emotion or a feeling, no matter what, he must always put it to the service of his art. [...] I am not demanding that you to write a masterpiece. Your study of composition has not been long enough. But it seems to me that this fleeting romance should encourage you to write a little poem for the violin. I call it a "poem," a short inspiration. You speak of wings, my poor child, but what I reproach you for is that, in the company of a woman, your wings are clipped (speaking of the artist), you fall to the ground, you can do nothing. You deserve a prize for the mistakes you would like to make in tying yourself down, stupidly, thoughtlessly. [...]

Your words are bitter for me when you say I must take pleasure in the silence from that woman. How could you think that I could find joy in the disappointment of the one I cherish the most in this world? It is really nasty of you, my great big child; I hope that you will forget a person not worthy of you. [...] If you do not want to remain single, you must look for someone in your own world. [...]

4/22/1917.

I received yesterday your letter from April 19 and two packages with a half-pound of butter, some tuna, a can of foie gras, sardines, etc., and some tissue paper. I am grateful for these things, but please do not increase the number. I don't need more and, by myself, it is difficult to eat everything. As I am the assistant orderly, I usually eat alone in the general's kitchen which is next to the door so I can see everyone who arrives. [...]

It seems we will be in this spot for a month; that is not very funny because we are really in the middle of nowhere. But this is better than having to go on to get beaten down. I think our offensive has failed, that the *Boches* have unfortunately shown us that they are still here. It was wise to cut our losses when it was obvious that the results were not what were hoped for. [...]

I am eating like all the others now, with the rolling kitchens. That means coffee at 7 a.m., slop (usually beef with beans or potatoes) at 11, soup at night. Along with that, 2 quarter liters of wine and half a loaf of bread. That is the standard, daily fare. Fortunately, the person in charge is a food professional, serious, clean, and does quite a good job. The big thing in this area is to pick dandelion greens. They are everywhere right now, and we can easily make a simple salad. [...]

Our life here will be mind-numbing; we no longer have music. Aside from me, we have no instruments. And I do not see any place where I could work. I might call this "homesickness." I admit that right now I am disgusted by everything, even myself, and by life. The cold ugly weather adds to that feeling; it certainly doesn't brighten my mood, far from it. This life of sudden exhaustion alternating with prolonged laziness, nothing could be more depressing! I will get over this, I have to. [...]

4/25/1917.

I just this instant received your letter of April 23. I also received a package with 250 grams of butter, a Camembert, and two little cans of tuna. [...] I got my violin out of Caplet's case and will soon start to practice a bit. To do that, I can use Commander Lambrigot's room. I asked him and he very nicely agreed. That will be a powerful tool against boredom. [...]

In terms of coming home safe, I think I will, but destiny will decide. Whether I seek out or flee danger will change nothing. Like Orientals, I am a fatalist and like them, I do not worry. That is why my hair is still black and my color good, while others are turning gray with worry and anguish. [...]

4/26/1917.

I received today your letter from the 24th. [...] Tomorrow, Friday, there will be a party at the chateau, on one of the lawns that surround it. There will be a soccer competition between the teams from different regiments. We will also be able to reunite the division's three music regiments to play Caplet's march. Then there will be concerts all over the place. [...]

Roland is coming for lunch. We will make something good; we may be able to get some rabbit. We are in Fresnes, not far from Château-Thierry, but the country is really ugly, there are no civilians, or very few, and no resources. I got through the fatigue of these past days very well; I'm a tough old guy, like leather, and for sure the great-grandson of Napoleon's grenadiers.[255] [...]

4/27/1917.

I received this morning your letter from April 25. [...] We thought for a while we would move farther to the rear, but we don't seem to be budging from here. As long as we stay in this sad area, naked to the core, there is no possibility of a room with a bed. Fortunately, the weather is now nice, though the nights are still cold.

They are trying hard right now to explain our offensive; it is likely that sometime soon they will again try something. It seems completely clear that the desired objectives were not attained. There were quite a number of wounded. [...]

My dear *minou*, you talk to me about composing, but first one has to be safe, have a place completely to himself, and then completely clear out one's head. The brain is quite dazed and numbed by this senseless life we have been leading for three years. Caplet doesn't manage to write even a few notes and God knows his facility with the pen. He writes music more easily than prose. [...]

According to you, I am nothing but a turkey, the laughing stock of all my friends, etc. I am society's clown. That is completely not true, I am not like that at all. First, I give no one the honor of being my confidant; secondly, anyone who wanted to make fun of me would have to deal with me. As for the silence from the person in question, I'd prefer not to say anything. I am well aware that, should I want to marry, after the war I will find 100 young women for one. [...]

Thursday, April 26, 1917, 11:30 a.m.

[...] I am writing to you this morning; I don't have a cleaning lady today and I did a purge for the second time. I can't go out to run errands so I am free to take care of my correspondence. [...]

My cleaning lady's little boy is a bit better, at least that's what she said yesterday. She is still coming but is in a rush and only stays for 2 hours. That's not enough for a proper cleaning but sufficient to keep me from wearing myself out. I have to be content with a "that'll do." My life is nothing if not simple; I am always at home. [...] I spend my time on boring, easy tasks (not always as easy as one might think). That has always been my lot, to stay home and devote myself

---

[255] Lucien's great-grandfather was a pontoon captain in Napoleon's Grande Armée; he participated in the retreat in Bérésina and received the Saint Helena medal.

to my family. How many frivolous women prefer to run around and ignore their homes. A devoted wife, frugal and well-organized, is the exception. [...]

Monday, April 30, 1917, 4:30 p.m.

I received this morning a whole avalanche of letters. [...] I am so happy to read what you write. I thank you for your regular and loving correspondence and urge you to continue opening your heart to me. What would my life be if my beloved child did not make me a part of his joys and his anguish and didn't ask me for the consoling balm that only mothers know how to rub on heartaches, the same way they can perceive the blackness of people and try to help the loved one protect himself from life's dangers and disappointments. [...]

Remember you are the great-grandson of one of Napoléon's grenadiers, think of your brave ancestors who were such good, strong people; by their determined hard work they built up an inheritance from which you have benefited. It gave you the independence to become the artist you are. It is your duty, and an important one, to protect it. I always believed we would act as one to manage it. Haven't we always worked that way for your art, your future? Your tastes were mine and mine yours, even for material things. [...] I raised you simply, honorably, with such pure aspirations that you cannot stray from the current. That is one of the principal things I wanted to talk to you about. I hope that we will discuss all these questions face-to-face and that we'll be stunned by the clarity that results. [...] So, my dear, my beloved child, my unicorn, do not accuse me of spitefulness. (I wonder why you do so, when to the contrary, I am very sad to see you hurting.) [...] I am sending you in a separate envelope a word from Léontine; think always of the pain of that mother who lost her child, nothing compares with that. [...]

4/28/1917.

I didn't receive any mail today. [...] Yesterday a sergeant of the army theaters arrived, the same position that was offered to Caplet. We now know what it amounts to. It is totally exasperating. That guy is in charge of one of the mobile theaters; he has nothing but a big truck in which he stores all his pieces of wood. He arrives at a base and is welcomed in many different ways. Most of the officers send him packing; others, who are nicer, let him mount his show. He is alone. He asks the corps or the division for people to help set up the theater in a hangar or a barn and auditions *poilus* (singers or actors) to put on the show. He adds nothing to what already exists. [...]

I am fine, but still depressed. I'm fighting it and making some progress. I do not mean that my heart is not suffering, but that will pass. [...]

4/29/1917.

Today I received your letters from April 26 and 27. […] We avoided the storm this time. There are certainly so many people crushed by grief and suffering that our hardships seem minor. I realize that and don't complain. […]

As for how my day went, I wrote, I practiced violin for an hour and a half. That is all I can do. Generally, in the evening I play a game of chess, or at least I play for an hour or so. I read for a bit and go to bed at 10:30. I get up at 7:30. Right now I am reading *Les Forces Tumultueuses* by Verhaeren,[256] powerful, excellent, but a bit uneven. Not to read, that would be a fate worse than death. One only lives through the mind. […]

Tuesday, May 1, 1917, 5 p.m.

I just this morning received your letters from April 27 and 28. […] We've agreed that I will send you only one package a week. […] My cleaning lady's son is much better; he's gone back to school but only in the afternoon; he is still very weak. […]

5/1/1917.

I received today your letter from the 29th and the package with a half-pound of butter, a half of a Camembert, and another cheese. […] My dear *minou*, again you haven't received your daily bone. It makes me very sad that you don't receive my letters regularly. I write letters, long and not so long, every day; this orderly job takes a lot of time. […]

Now the public is aware that the offensive didn't work as hoped. Are our leaders dreaming? I don't think so; one has to believe they can't be complete idiots. I think that they made a concession to the public who, in total ignorance, found it strange that there was no offensive. However, it simply makes sense to say that, if the *Boches* have to be defeated by starvation and deprivation, why not wait for that to happen, with our arms ready. Swamp them with bombs, which our artillery throws at them nonstop, not only to kill their infantrymen but to disrupt their resupply. But for the love of God, our infantry should not throw itself into deadly assaults which have no meaning, only to retake 1 or 2 or even 6 kilometers! The cost of that ground is too high, and we do not have the means (the men) to play that little game; we've played it much too long already. That is a very straightforward way of thinking. The *poilu* will hang in there another year or 18 months if necessary, as long as he knows the *Boches* will succumb. But he is sick and tired of launching offensives for which they promise miracles and which, in the end, lead to nothing. What enormous losses! One has to be crazy

---

[256]   Émile Verhaeren (1855-1916), Belgian poet and art critic.

to believe that, in our current state, we will get to the border. If the Germans resisted, we would have to kill 2 million men and still the result would not be assured. [...]

5/2/1917.

Today the mail is late and I've not received anything. [...] Caplet left to take a course on keeping pigeons; he should be back tomorrow. The weather is lovely—a change from the long and hard winter we went through. I practice violin daily, about an hour and a half. I'm doing nothing but scales and technique to get in shape, I can't do more than that. Rumors circulate that we will be here until May 20. I hate that; completely isolated, I can do nothing and music is postponed indefinitely. [...]

This monotonous life drags on; I admit I've never been so often bored as right now. There is nothing for distraction. I cannot practice all the time. And the job of the orderly is trying: I have to be here but there is not much to do. It's not very demanding work. My thoughts go elsewhere and depression sets in.

There is a lot of discussion in the papers about our recent offensive, a lot of stupid comments by those who are supposed to have authority. A good number of those dandies from headquarters should spend a month in the trenches with the *poilus*; in those unhealthy places they would change their way of thinking. Everyone wants to see this war end, but I firmly believe that we are in this for some time. The *poilus* need to be able to speak up; in the current system they are strangled. [...]

Friday, May 4, 1917, 4:30 p.m.

I didn't receive any news at 4:00. [...] You never explained what "serving as an orderly" means. You carry orders for a senior officer, is that it? [...] You should have time to write, work on violin, and all sorts of other things since you are replaced by someone else after 12 hours. You don't explain that very well. You could think to jot down a few musical ideas and phrases if you find the time too long. That would serve you in the future and would be a souvenir. You are quite lazy. You are not bothered by the composition demon. [...]

5/3/1917.

I received this morning your letters from April 30 and May 1. [...] As for the outright lecture you are giving me about Mlle Muller, I will answer thus: that young woman was sweet, shy, charming. It is possible that her mother, much stricter, prevented her from writing. [...] Time and the lack of stimulation kill a passion, especially with the violent, colorful life we are leading. I will forget this adventure, or it will fade away. I may, in the future, regret it. Life will carry me

359

on: will it bring me peace and happiness? I don't know and cannot worry about it. Satisfying bodily needs is not everything in life. I have no desire to, as you put it, waste the ancestral goods. I don't need that, and I know that with my violin, moving to another country, I will easily earn a good life. [...]

I have seen so many comrades fall that I am forced to become a bit stoic. Yesterday was their turn, tomorrow may be mine. [...]

Saturday, May 5, 1917, 4 p.m.

I received this morning your letter from May 3. [...] Your letter is a bit crazy: you say your mind is solid but I think there is a hole in it! If you come back to your senses after the war, it will only be half bad but I fear that those who manage to get out of this will come back with their heads all messed up. [...] Your head has been on backwards since that affair in Abainville, you don't think of anything else. [...]

I've asked my coal merchant for some wood and I think she will deliver it next Monday. I also asked for some coal, which she will bring as well. That would please me because starting in June we will have ration cards for coal. If I can get my supply for winter now, I will not have to worry about that. I am also getting a supply of gas because I fear there will be a shortage. [...]

Write me a long letter, my dear child, and try not to be sad. [...]

5/4/1917.

I have not yet received mail today. It is late. We have had several very hot days; yesterday it was like July. The first hot days are tiring. Fortunately, we have water in this area; there are a number of little rivers everywhere and that makes washing easy. [...]

Second letter, same day.

I just this minute received the mail. I got your letter from May 2 and another letter with the card from young Tavernier. He is starting to become acquainted with military life in wartime and notes that it is not only not very much fun, but that civilians have no conception of what it is like. And he is lucky to be in the artillery. Even with what he writes, he cannot imagine life in the infantry. One has to have lived through it to talk about it. [...]

5/5/1917.

I received yesterday a package of underwear that I've not opened yet. I thought that this morning I'd put on lighter underwear, but the weather was cloudy and chillier, so I put off the change for a day or two. I will send you what

I am wearing, that is to say, my dirty underwear. Today I received your letter from May 3. [...]

Second letter, same day.

I had to cut short my letter; mail was going out. For you to receive it without delay, I had to finish it abruptly. The unpredictable weather of this morning has changed and become really lovely. It is suddenly very hot. [...]

Tomorrow, Sunday, Dumant will come for lunch with us. I invited him two days ago; we will try to put on a sumptuous meal. I made a crêpe batter and tonight, after dinner, I will make crêpes, we will eat them tomorrow with jam. [...]

From now on, at general headquarters, there will be a group of *poilus*, real ones, from the trenches, second class *poilus*, intelligent *poilus*, who reason, think, and reflect. The officers in charge should seek their advice often. [...] Unfortunately, one has to realize that the army and administration in France are made up of the most mediocre men, this is proven. Honor to the *poilus*, brave, intelligent, heroic, who have done all the work and sadly have not found, in their leaders, what is necessary to profit from their admirable qualities. Without them, without their persistence, the *Boches* would have been victorious long ago. That is the truth. Obviously, not everyone likes to hear it and for the moment I don't think it can be published. There will be a lot to say about all this; I think volumes will be written which will shock their readers. [...]

Monday, May 7, 1917, 11:30 a.m.

I received this morning your letter from May 5. [...] When I tell you to be joyful and to push away the dark butterflies that may be flying around you, I am speaking allegorically. I don't see you jumping and singing for joy because the sun came up and the bushes are covered with flowers, certainly not. By that I mean that the dark, sad winter that is working so hard to give place to the flowers of spring should bring you hope and consolation. This slave existence, which has lasted so long and to which there seems to be no end, is not designed to delight you and makes you immune to the beauty of nature. [...]

5/7/1917.

Yesterday I received your letter from May 4 but, unfortunately, I could not write. There were many changes in billeting sites in the division and I spent the entire morning sending out orders and answering the telephone. Mail goes out at 1 p.m.

We had a wonderful lunch yesterday; I had invited Dumant and Brenner had invited one of his friends, so there were 8 of us at table. Here is the menu:

coquilles St. Jacques, beef tongue with spicy sauce, sorrel in butter, lobster salad with mayonnaise and dandelions, crêpes with jam, brie, cookies, white wine from Bordeaux, cheap reds, and champagne, so a truly fine menu. In Paris a meal like that would have cost at least 15 francs a person. For dinner, there was tapioca, cold veal, lettuce salad with eggs, and chocolate mousse. We are taking good care of ourselves, as you can see. There is nothing else to do here. [...]

I have not yet put on my summer underthings; the weather is still pretty cold with lovely days but chilly nights. You should have listened to me and only sent underwear when I ask. But you will never change. The job of orderly is to be in the outer room of the officers' work room, to receive the officers coming to headquarters, to answer the phone and provide the information requested, to go find cyclists to take orders to their recipients, all sorts of things like that. It is not very difficult, but it keeps you busy, with constant interruptions. I cannot write a letter without having to start again at least ten times. And more, one has to be alert, to be sensible, and not make any errors. A dummy could not be an orderly. When I practice violin, I have to ask a friend, a cyclist, to take my place for an hour or two. Otherwise I could not get away. I have the day shift, 8:30 a.m. to 8:30 p.m. [...]

We finally captured the Craonne plateau. I hope we will be able to keep it. It is a position that cost us dearly and is very important. One has to expect that the *Boches* will respond violently. [...]

Second letter, same day.

I have a bit more time today; I'll use it to send another short note. The mail arrived rather late today; I received your letter from May 5 and a package. [...]

I am pleased that you have received some rent money. [...] I am also happy to know that you will have firewood and coal; let's hope you do because, if ration cards are instituted, it may be a big deal to get some. If you can have your supply for next winter, praise God. Yes, all this is expensive, but in view of what is happening, it is necessary. That is why, given my comfortable situation, packages are no longer necessary; one a week is more than enough.

Tuesday, May 8, 1917, 4 p.m.

My dear child, my letter was interrupted by a visit from Bastien who is on leave since May 5 and Mme Bastien and Mlle Jeanne. They didn't stay long; they seemed a bit rushed. Probably they were going to have dinner in Paris. Bastien looks very well; he's even put on some weight. He must be quite calm in the Parrot Forest. He brought me a little sprig of flowers; I don't really know why. [...]

Thursday, May 10, 1917, 7 p.m.

Today I went to see the Cunaults as I told you I would. I brought two little rose bushes for Mme Cunault to put on Coco's grave (I knew that would please her). I must admit that I was a bit shocked to find, in their yard, a grave like that of a person. It is fine to love an animal and even bury it in one's garden, but without a special marker. That is none of my business, but I find it a bit extravagant. [...]

5/8/1917.

Naturally this early in the morning mail has not yet arrived. The weather is crazy; there is a windstorm and it is going to rain. And that is what we had for part of the night. The temperatures are getting cold again; I am waiting to change out of my winter underwear. [...]

Yesterday, the mayor of R., M. Valin, captain in the 43rd artillery, came to the division; he brought 500 francs to be used in the best way possible to entertain the men. Because we are at the beginning of nice weather, the decision was made to spend 300 francs to buy soccer balls, and 200 for a tennis net and equipment. That will be just more to carry with us. [...]

Friday, May 11, 1917, 4 p.m.

I didn't receive a letter today; I hope for news this evening. [...] Right now, Cunault is not working on anything; his workshop is closed, the new violins are drying in the attic. He put a new roof on his chicken house, arranged his garden and planted peas, beans, chicory, and lettuce. In short, he is a gardener; working outdoors is good for him. He sold the violin he paid 1200 francs for at the ham fair to Daniel Herman who will probably be able to sell it for twice as much; he's trafficking in violins, but still he's a good client for Cunault. The violin didn't hang around very long; once repaired and adjusted, it was sold. Cunault is very lucky; that is quite a good sum of money that fell from the sky. [...] With it he paid 300 francs for 1000kg of anthracite for the stove in his dining room. His tenant who is a cashier for Breton had the coal delivered. He told me all that quite frankly. Speaking of coal, I saw my coal merchant this morning; she promised to deliver my wood next week, without fail, and also promised me some coal. [...] If there are ration cards starting in June, I wonder what the conditions will be for dividing up the supply. [...]

5/9/1917.

Madame M. got here very late last evening; she arrived at night purpose so her arrival would not be noticed. The commander went to the chateau with a car to get her, and the car took her back this morning at 5 a.m. I was not able to see her or to speak with her. Dinner lasted until after 11 p.m., and obviously I was not going to wait in the corridor until midnight, which might have displeased the commander. I needed to be cautious.

The funny part (as everything has a comic side) is that she was supposed to come the day before. Obviously, dinner was all prepared for that day. In general, the officers here are stingy. They want to eat well but don't want to spend anything, so they were quite annoyed and decided to keep most of the meal for the next night. That is how hot chicken was served cold the next day. There were little cream puffs which were kept for the next day, also a mocha cake. No matter that the pastry was no longer fresh; they had put out a certain amount of money and were not about to do it a second time. How stingy, how miserly, to entertain a lovely woman who traveled 300 kilometers to see them! [...] Since I am now living amid all the people of the division, I am more aware of the character of all the superiors, and have to conclude that, with the exception of one artillery captain who has great scientific training, all the others have mediocre minds and piteous moral values. [...]

Second letter, same day.

[...] I have already said that one can't just decide to be happy. When I am trying to drown my sorrows, I say stupid things. That may be the moment when, deep down, I am the saddest. We distract ourselves by eating and drinking like pigs; we end up keeping ourselves busy with nothing but what we eat. It's a bit like the man who finds oblivion in the bottom of his glass. One must fight against this deplorable, coarse materialism. From what I can see, only time can help one forget and bring consolation in all these matters.

Work is, of course, a diversion, but we do not have the means here to benefit from that. Ask anyone here, from the least to the grandest, all are suffering from the blues, a bit more or a bit less. That is why so many are paying attention to their souls, to destiny. The least intelligent, with the least education, make do with religious beliefs from their youth and do everything their religion demands from them. So much the better for them because they find, with little effort, consolation and some source of peace. The same is not true for those who are more reflective and tortured by doubt. It may make sense to look for earthly pleasure, a distraction from the suffering of the soul, suffering that is not well-defined and which one has difficulty expressing. [...] I prefer not acting like so many others who get drunk and head for the brothel whenever possible. Things like that do not help one forget and are demeaning; they lower you in the eyes of others and in your own opinion. [...]

Saturday, May 12, 1917, 4:30 p.m.

[...] I received your second letter from the 9th and the two from the 10th and the one from the 11th. I didn't realize what a terrible storm there was in Paris last

Thursday. I was in Villemomble waiting for the tram in the station; the lightning bolts followed one another without interruption, the thunder rumbled and there was heavy rain. I was lucky that the worst of the storm passed while I waited for the tram; it was only raining a little bit when I reached Vincennes. [...]

5/11/1917.

Apparently yesterday there was a terrible storm in Paris. Here we saw lightening in the distance but had no storm. During the evening, it started to rain and part of the night it rained quite hard. This morning there is a magnificent sun shining, promising us a very hot day. [...]

5/12/1917.

Today the heat is suffocating and ever since this morning there isn't a breath of air. Our departure is near. They are talking about maybe even tomorrow morning, but I think it will not be until Monday. I do not think I will have the chance to be stationed closer to home. [...]

5/13/1917.

Here we are, moving in terrible heat. We left this morning at 7 a.m., fortunately for us, thanks to the good will of the commander, in Red Cross vehicles. This move is supposed to last three days, and we will have transportation all that time. We have to be grateful. [...]

Sunday, May 13, 1917, 11 a.m.

I cut yesterday's letter short. When M. Alan comes, he stays a long time and keeps me from writing or sewing. [...] This morning I picked some lilacs; I gave a bouquet to Mme Boissard who will put it tomorrow on her son's grave. [...] I also gave one to the milk lady. Although I do not drink milk daily, I do take some from time to time. I don't want to go to the shop in the morning and stand in line for a half-hour or so to get milk (that has happened three or four times). So I stay home and here's how I get my milk: when I have peels from potatoes or other vegetables, bread crusts, I take them to the milk lady who is fattening a pig. I take her also my milk pot and pick it up later. That way I get my milk without being pushed around or standing on one leg in the store. This life is really quite idiotic: I spend a lot of time not doing very much and need always to think of ways to combine tasks. [...]

Mme Hérault, the wife of our mason, died and was buried last Wednesday. I did not go to her funeral. I did learn that their last son, who had received a good education and had taken the first exams to be a surgeon before the war, died 6 months ago from pleurisy he caught at the beginning of the war, during the Battle of the Marne where he was caring for the wounded. [...] His death hastened that of his mother who had been ill for some time. Directly or indirectly this war is messing up people's lives. [...]

Wednesday, May 16, 1917, 3 p.m.

[...] I received this morning your letter of Sunday, May 13, with a stamp. The letter had been opened on the side and resealed with a special tape on which were the words "military postal inspection." So your letter had been read; had it contained the names of places and other details, they would probably have been covered with ink. At least I think that is what would have happened. [...]

I don't know what's going on with the telephone. It kept ringing, so I picked it up and repeatedly said "hello." I heard "hello, what do you want?" [...]

5/15/1917.

I write just a brief word; I could not write yesterday. Finally, today, we've arrived at our destination and will be a bit calmer. I received yesterday and today a lot of mail. I will write this evening or tomorrow; I need to clean up and sleep. I have a room, that is the most important thing. Today I received the package which must contain butter and tea. I have no time. We are setting up the office in a lovely chateau; it's always "Durosoir, here, Durosoir there." [...]

5/16/1917, 11 a.m.

I received your letter from May 12 a little while ago. The mail goes out at 2 p.m.; I barely have time to write today because we have a show soon. Monsieur Falot,[257] of *La Pie Qui Chante*, just arrived. He will present a number of songs from his repertory; we have to intersperse a bit of music. I'm going to have to unpack my instrument and practice. For a month there has been none of that.

We don't know what we will be doing; it all depends on how long we stay in Nogent-l'Artaud. We are in the chateau and the garden is spectacular, especially now that everything is in flower. [...] We have found a good place to eat at the home of a woman who makes corsets. We will organize nice little meals. This is a tiny city and there are resources, although quite expensive. I am staying with an elderly couple who work in the local corset factory. They are honest people with a nice 25-year-old daughter and 3 sons. Their daughter's fiancé was killed. [...]

In about a week, I hope to have a 24 to 48-hour leave. [...]

---

[257] Charles Fallot (1874-1939) was a French singer and actor. With Paul Marinier he founded the Cabaret *La Pie Qui Chante* (the singing magpie).

Lucien was home for a few days mid-month.

Monday, May 28, 1917, 3 p.m.

[...] I hope that you played for Pentecost at the church in Nogent-l'Artaud with success. You could send me a postcard of the church and one of the chateau where the secretaries are staying. The weather is very nice today; the oppressive heat of yesterday has given way to a more bearable temperature. It must have been very hot for Caplet when he directed his march. Write him a note to thank him for getting us places at the Trocadéro last Thursday. And tell him that you hope he will finish his piece for violin which you will be happy to play at the Conservatory next June 17. [...] Mathilde came back yesterday; she brought me this morning half a pound of butter from her cow and 4 eggs. I had not yet had lunch so I dined on three fresh eggs from her chickens with very creamy Limousin butter. [...]

5/26/1917.

I am only writing a bit; there has been a change: we leave tomorrow morning, and by car. That is important; it means that we are going to relieve others in an area where there is fighting. [...]

5/28/1917.

We moved yesterday, in a hurry, and after covering 60 kilometers in a vehicle, we landed very near the town where Cézanne once lived. Our departure happened with great haste; one might think that, given the way we were rushing, there was some urgency. We will be stationed for 3 to 4 days here. There must certainly have been some threat to this part of the front or we would not have come so quickly. This area is perched on a height, very pretty with many remains of large ramparts, a keep, and a fortified castle, but it is very small. I managed to turn up a nice, clean room with clean straw where the three of us will sleep. [...]

5/29/1917.

Naturally I've not received anything since my arrival. All our moving around must be the explanation. Yesterday we changed billeting site and we've been moved about 4 kilometers away. All this because at Berry-le-Sec, the officers found themselves a bit crowded. [...]

5/30/1917.

I received today your letter from May 27. We are not at the front; some serious, very serious events have just taken place, about which I cannot say more. […]

5/31/1917.

I received this morning your letter from May 29. We are not in the action and are not likely to be for some time yet. I cannot explain any more. Right now, our letters must be subjected to heavy censorship, if they get through at all. Later I'll be able to tell you about it; I do not think I will ever be able to write about it, it is too dangerous. What I can say is that right now I have considerable work and barely time to write. […]

Thursday, May 31, 1917, 7:30 p.m.

[…] I just received your two letters from May 29 and one from the 30th, as well as the menu from the 26th. […] What is going on? Your puzzling letter worries me, the one from the 30th in which you talk about serious events that just happened, probably not good for us. I worry about you being mixed up in what is happening, then for our country which, despite all the efforts of its defenders, could fall under the German yoke after so many months of battle and so much suffering. The *communiqués* haven't said anything, or not much, for several days. They do say that there is a lively artillery battle south of Saint-Quentin and not much in Champagne or the Meuse. How sad all that is! […]

6/1/1917.

Division Headquarters. I did not receive a letter today. This morning there was a large meeting of the generals. They needed to review recent events and discuss what tactics to use in the future. Nothing came of their deliberations. […]

I am waiting for Caplet to return; I expect to see him this evening. I will then know whether the June 17 date for our concert is still good. That will tell me when to plan my leave. I don't want my regular leave to coincide with the special permission, I'd gain nothing that way.

It is horribly hot, fortunately the division is settled on a quite lovely property with a lovely park and shade that is much appreciated right now. We are eating just fine, even better than fine. But these days there is so much to do that our meals have been a bit neglected. During all this, my music has been left at Nogent-l'Artaud and my violin is in a vehicle belonging to the co-op 5 kilometers away. Caplet's boxes which contain my accompaniments are in a wagon which has not yet arrived. No point in telling you that we have not worked on music. [...]

6/2/1917.

I cannot talk about what has happened. Not only is it forbidden, but censorship is very severe right now. I don't want to risk anything; it's not the moment. What is sure is that we did not move to the battle lines and the planned attack didn't take place. All sorts of rumors are circulating right now: they say that things are not going very well in Paris, that there are street fights. I cannot really tell what truth there is in these rumors, which can be badly exaggerated.[258] I am in a good position to know how much the *poilus* can deform what is happening and what they hear. But, in the end, what is happening here and in Paris proves that there is enormous lassitude and a wish to be finished with this war. It would be quite unfortunate, and disastrous, to have to act under public pressure. I hope that those in command and the government understand the danger and will ask our allies for more soldiers, which right now is more important than equipment. The poor *poilu* who, for almost three years, has endured the most dreadful moral and physical suffering, has had enough. He can give no more. To ask more would be to exceed human strength and risk great misfortune. I have not much hope that the higher command understands the problem; they have spent so little time with the *poilu* and have treated him too much like a tool to be used. What wrongs in a country like ours! In the end, very few understand human nature. Thus, the gulf widens between the commanders and the *poilu* and that situation could become worrisome quite soon, if some serious efforts are asked of our guys. You have to read between the lines now. [...]

Monday, June 4, 1917, 3 p.m.

[...] I received this morning your letters from June 1 and 2. [...] The strikes are settling down and I don't believe there has been any serious fighting in Paris. For sure the leaders were almost all from elsewhere, supported by the Germans who want to sow disorder among us and will do anything possible to break our morale to see the end of France, France which has defended itself valiantly but, having lost almost all men between the ages of 25 and 35, is beginning to ask for mercy. Germany would like to make things happen more quickly so the United States will not have time to help with men and equipment. [...]

---

[258] What Lucien was hearing was true: a first wave of strikes hit Paris in January 1917 and a second, led by women, started May 14, 1917.

6/3/1917.

I received this morning your two letters of May 30 and June 1. Yesterday Magne went to Berzy to pick up my violin and the package of music that was in the co-op vehicle; this morning we went to play in a church 2 kilometers away where General Lebrun was attending the 8:30 Mass. Then we came back to Septmonts to play for the 10:00 Mass. [...]

Magne heard from Caplet who will not come back until the 7th; the ministry extended his leave. [...] It appears we will stay here for about 20 days before changing sector. Would that we could have stayed in the Marne valley where we were so well off! [...]

Don't worry about my mask; it is in good condition. It's a very important item and the *poilu* never forgets what it is for. I am still assistant orderly and have no lack of work, at least right now. The events of recent days created a lot of work. I have some rum and everything I need, no point in sending anything at all. [...]

6/4/1917.

I just received your letter from June 2. [...] In a little while, I should be able to give you some explanations; however, I prefer talking about it rather than writing. It is certain that we will be going into the battle zone shortly, maybe in two days. Fortunately, that area seems quite quiet; the *poilus* are not all fired up to fight. I think that our stay there will not be long. [...]

Count on me to be careful; what is more, I've never been in a better situation in the face of danger. I hope in any case to be able to come home soon, for a concert or an extra leave. [...]

Tuesday, June 5, 1917, 2:30 p.m.

I received two letters yesterday so I am writing today without waiting for the mail. The weather is very warm and I'm comforted to know that, for now, you are in an area where there is a good deal of shade. [...] I am quite afraid that the repeated attacks by the Germans in your sector may send you to the front lines. [...] I read in the papers that there are still some partial strikes, but I think all that is ending. Many people are demanding an allowance to compensate for high costs. Everyone is hoarding, grabbing canned goods, gas, etc., so the prices of everything rise accordingly. People are buying so much that the merchants, faced with the demand, raise their prices day after day. [...]

6/5/1917.

Today I received your letter from June 3. We are going into the battle zone tomorrow, for an unknown length of time; I think no more than 2 weeks. [...]

I am not depressed right now. Compared with many others, danger does not bother me; in fact, I feel more useful then than at other times. [...]

6/6/1917.

We are going back to the front. Magne, who is leaving on pass, will bring this note to Paris as he passes through on his way to Cherbourg. I am well and will be well sheltered; I will write in more detail. [...]

6/7/1917.

Yesterday I received your letter from June 4. We made our change of location by vehicle so it was not very difficult. However, it was terribly hot and this area of Soissons is extraordinarily dusty, a white, fine dust, very disagreeable. We have another move to make before we arrive in the battle zone. I do not know whether everything will happen as planned; things are still happening that could change everything; we will see. [...]

6/9/1917.

Thank you for your letters of 5, 6, and 7 June. I couldn't write yesterday because of our move. Right now, I haven't a minute to myself. But things will settle down now that I'm settled in a charming house in a little village, with civilians who have stayed here. An old couple, very nice. [...]

The area I'm in is bombed from time to time, but less than previously; there is no great danger as long as one is cautious. I do not know how long I will be here, maybe three weeks. Caplet has some news; it's about going to Turin, in Italy, to play his march with the musicians of the division. We might be able to also give a concert of French music. If this happens, it will be at the end of June. Caplet might bring Rose Féart to sing some songs.[259] If only that plan can become reality! I would bring you to Turin; for those who come with us the trip might be free or half-price. But I will have time to talk to you about that. [...]

It is extremely hot here, fortunately we have water, and there is also the canal and the Aisne. [...]

6/10/1917.

I didn't receive a letter yesterday; I am now well settled in. The house we are in is quite nice, with a shady courtyard for our meals and free time. I am sleeping in a room on the second floor on a bed. [...]

---

[259] Rosalie Gautier, known as Rose Féart (1878-1957), opera singer.

Up to now I've not had a minute to myself; you can't imagine what is involved in feeding 11 or 12 men when you want to give them something other than meat and dried beans. Naturally the few merchants in the area charge exorbitant prices and even more, one has to join the crowd. As soon as they manage to get hold of something to sell, there are 10 people fighting for it. That means I have to be clever and not waste my time. I've gotten acquainted with a few locals and I try to get eggs and some lettuce from them. In about 10 days, there may be strawberries and new potatoes, but right now it is not easy. I don't get much without bartering. I buy wine from the supply offices for 70 centimes a liter, I ask for a bit more than I need and sometimes I sell it to the locals at cost. That way they keep some eggs for me; I am becoming a businessman. [...]

Here, at the canal, a few coal barges have been sunk. We drag the canal and pull out some coal. However, I got a voucher from the division to get 100 kilos from the supply unit. You can't imagine the number of things I needed to do and the people I needed to see for such a simple thing. But now I have the voucher and I will get the coal tomorrow morning. Then I will go pay for it; I have to go someplace else to pay. If everything is done this way in the French Army, I understand how those with good ideas get discouraged. It is not easy to be in charge of food in such conditions. No need to tell you that I frequently ask the others for funds. I cannot avoid expenses which amount to, on average, 25 francs a day. With the difficulty I am having, I understand how much effort is needed to properly feed friends. No point in saying that music, for now, is put off for however long. It would not be very smart to call attention to our presence; someone could tell us to eat with everyone else at the mess. [...]

6/11/1917.

I did not receive a letter yesterday. This morning, there was a fairly large shipment of vegetables and I bought artichokes, cauliflower, asparagus, peas, radishes, leeks, oranges, really quite a good selection. I have enough now for at least three days. [...]

My gas mask is in very good condition. That is something very important and we check it often. However, this area is getting quieter and quieter; the attacks by the English in the North are probably responsible. So much the better for us. [...] I got my violin this morning and will be able to practice a bit. Caplet, who is here with me and also comfortably settled, is working on his piece for solo violin. He should be able to give it to me soon, at least I hope so. [...]

6/12/1917.

I received your letter from June 9 yesterday. [...] We are to the right of Cerny; our zone is relatively quiet at least compared with the one next to us which has seen a lot of activity. So for now, it is calm here, much better than Verdun which they had warned us might be our location. […] Caplet is working hard on his piece for violin; he has already changed the entire prelude. It will be very interesting and also very difficult to play.

Rumor has it that we may be in this sector for two months. That would really be a long time; however, I am well settled in, hardly to be pitied, and in a good situation to watch that time go by. […]

6/13/1917.

I received yesterday your letter from June 10. […] I ran into Meyer, the driver of one of the Red Cross vehicles. I was thrilled to see him; in order to get to the rear on the day I go on leave those cars will be very helpful. I just sent you the picture of Fresnes because I only just received it. I always send on what I receive for two reasons: first the pictures would get damaged if I keep them, and then, I know you will be happy to have them. […]

Friday, June 15, 1917, 9 a.m.

[…] I received a little bit ago your letter from June 13. […] I am happy that your sector is relatively calm. But I read in *L'Information* the *communiqué* from June 14, 4 p.m.: "the enemy launched short, ferocious bombing in the region of Braye, north of Craonne, to the north-west of Reims on the left bank of the Meuse near Cumières." I hope that you didn't suffer from that.

Don't reply so nastily. […] You know I always speak my mind; the same is not true for you, you know. Why deform my words and cause me pain? I suffer enough from your absence and the dangers you face. I must have struck a nerve. So you get your back up rather that acknowledging your faults. Be fair and judge me reasonably. If you find me unpleasant, then don't write, it's very simple. […]

6/14/1917.

Yesterday I received your letters from June 11 and 12, and just this minute the one from June 13. […] I think I will be able to leave around the 20th. I am studying a map for a way to get to the rear; here we are far from everything. […]

I just saw Caplet; he passed by in a car with another pigeon keeper on the way to the division command post. Sadly this will interrupt his composing. […]

Saturday, June 16, 1917, 10 a.m.

[…] I received at 8:30 your letter from June 14 […]. Magne came to see me yesterday afternoon […] He told me a bit more about the events you spoke

about. They are regrettable and must have coincided with the strikes in Paris.
[...]

6/15/1917.

I haven't yet received a letter today, maybe the mail is late. For two days now we have had illustrious visitors. General Franchet d'Espèrey, commander of all the armies of the North came to see us, as well as General Pétain. Needless to say, these visits created a lot of rumors and conclusions that are as likely to be wrong as right. I will tell you when I'm there on leave what I think of all that. In a letter, the most basic prudence stops me from expressing my thoughts, especially right now. [...]

6/16/1917.

I did not receive any letters yesterday. On the other hand I did have a letter from young Alan, a letter that arrived very late and had been opened by the military authority. Fortunately, Jean didn't say anything much. At this time it is wise to be cautious. [...]

The plan is for me to go on the afternoon of the 19th to get my leave permission which will be dated the 21st. I will come back to Bourg with the telephone operators about 9:30 or 10 at night. I will then set off for Fismes, about 10 kilometers away where I will take a train on the 20th about 6:00 a.m. I should be in Paris about noon. That way I gain almost a whole day. And walking 10 kilometers at night, not rushing, is nothing much. If I left at 11:00 on the 20th, I would not get to Vincennes until about 2 a.m. the 21st. That is a big difference to me, so I don't hesitate. So very soon I will show up in Vincennes for 10 days or so. [...]

6/18/1917.

I am sure I will have my leave the evening of the 19th into the 20th, but I do not know exactly what time. For two days the bombing has been quite heavy and the telephone operators, who usually go to the front at 8 a.m., left last night at 1 a.m. in the morning and didn't get back until 5. If that happens during the night of the 19th, I will not be able to get the early train. [...]

Lucien was on home leave for the remainder of June.

Sunday, July 1, 1917.

[…] You are off again for the unknown. […] Think of me and don't be unpleasant or unjust. […]

Monday, July 2, 1917, 5:30 p.m.

[…] I sent this morning a registered package—it's the music you copied. I hope you can quickly find a time to use it. During your absence, I hope Caplet managed to arrange something that allows you to get back to playing together. I fear, however, that the recurrent German attacks near you make all hope of making music impossible. North of Verdun, the Germans are showing themselves; they would like to have some results before the Americans add their support. That is very worrying. […]

I paid the coal lady this morning; she promised again to bring me a bit of coal from time to time but I don't know whether she'll be able to keep that promise. […] Stay well and be very careful. If only you are not sent to Verdun! […]

Tuesday, July 3, 1917, 5:30 p.m.

Still no news from you. […] Mathilde's husband will come several times to split my wood, starting July 14 because he doesn't work that day. I hope to have my wood stacked by the end of the month; that will reassure me. Remember to have your jacket repaired by the woman you are staying with; she must be happy with the slippers you brought her, do they fit? […]

Wednesday, July 4, 1917, 11 a.m.

[…] I have here Dumant's letter. It is very unfortunate that that young man was caught up in that awful business and I understand your pain. His father must be very sad! One has to hope that they will realize that not all those men participated to the same extent and that some will be given permission to go see their families. If that happens, you could ask Dumant to come to Vincennes, with advance warning. […]

7/2/1917.

General staff of the Division. So, I left yesterday on the 9:26 train. I learned later that there was also one at 10:30 but because they are afraid the soldiers on leave will arrive late, no one talks about that train. So in brief, I arrived in Villers, the control station, at 12:15 and took another train at 3:15 for Fismes. Naturally, I had lunch during the three-hour wait. I arrived in Fismes at 6:15 and found, right next to the station, a truck taking persons on leave to Bourg.

That meant that, thanks to the extra care they are taking of us, I was back at my destination by 7:30 p.m. [...]

I asked again, with insistence, for my shoes. They have not yet arrived. We still know nothing about how long we will be here. I think that, unless something unexpected happens, it will be two months, as they said originally. [...]

7/3/1917.

Of course, I've not yet received a letter. [...] Now that I know where they are, I am going to write to some of my friends in the 129th, including Rolland and Vessot. That is the least I can do. Life here continues to be monotonous. We are settling down. I can hear artillery fire and airplanes continue their tasks almost daily. There is still no plan for us to leave this area, but there are always rumors: some say we will leave in 6 days, others in 2 weeks. None of them have any serious basis or precision. [...]

Second letter, same day.

I am writing this evening because things are calmer. It is hot, I cannot sleep, and the cannon fire is terrible, so I am writing to you. That will not stop me from writing tomorrow. [...]

I saw Caplet today when he came to the sector to exchange pigeons. He did not go get the case of music or the cello, first because the Army Corps had moved [...] and then because so many men have been killed recently it doesn't seem the right time to work on music. For the moment we just have to wait. [...]

A *Boche* plane came over about 3 a.m., dropped three bombs, two harmless, a third which unfortunately fell on the road near the bridge just as 3 engineers were passing; one was killed and the other two injured. It was an unfortunate coincidence. Then a French plane chased the *Boche* away. [...]

Thursday, July 5, 1917, 1 p.m.

[...] I received this morning your letter of the 3rd. [...] I read in the official *communiqué* of the 4th: "at the end of the day yesterday that the Germans attempted a strong offensive that lasted all night against our positions north of Jouy. Special attack forces focused principally to the east of the Froidemont farm and to the west and south of Cerny." etc. The fighting must have been intense Tuesday night. You say that enemy planes appear daily. And we don't have any to stop them. That makes me very anxious. I'd like to see you out of that dangerous spot, you've been there long enough. [...]

7/4/1917.

Our night was interrupted by a bombing that was not very heavy but important because of how long it lasted. First, about midnight, 22 shells were fired at 50-second intervals, then, at about 1:30 a.m., about 30 the same way. Our night and our sleep were not calm. There was no important damage; only one person killed and one injured, which is not much. [...]

I received today your letter of July 2. Yes, the weather is lovely, hot, but bearable. Today has been quite calm except for a *Boche* plane which dropped a few bombs near the bridge. Fortunately, they served no purpose, many fell in the water. The artillery fire has calmed down but not completely. If the Russians manage to continue what they have started, the *Boches* are in for some difficult days, that is for sure. They will need to pull back some of the forces they have amassed against us to fight the Russians. [...]

It is possible that coal will not be as hard to get as it was last winter. Not only are our mines working at a greatly increased pace; England is using American ships to send a lot. [...]

Le Bienvenu is coming tomorrow afternoon. He is going on leave. He will have dinner with us and leave at night. Still no new rumors about our departure, we know nothing. All that makes one think we will be here for all of July. [...]

7/5/1917.

I just did my shopping and bought what I needed; I have a moment and take advantage of it to send a quick word. Last night was very calm, no shells or bombs; and the sector this morning is calmer than usual. [...] We are waiting for Le Bienvenu and will prepare a nice little meal. I am starting again to try to get some coal. I hope to succeed more quickly than the last time. De Varenne, the chief of the auto unit, says that we will probably be relieved between the 20th to 25th of July. That would make 45 days for us in this area. [...]

[...] We had a really classy dinner this evening. There were 9 of us. Le Bienvenu came to this sector because he is supposed to go on leave tomorrow morning. Unfortunately, he cannot leave until Labbé, another secretary, returns from leave. Everyone expected him this evening and so far he's not shown up. So tomorrow morning poor Le Bienvenu will go back to his sector to wait for him. It is annoying and stupid. Jubel is also going on leave. Still, here's what we had for dinner: an omelet with herbs, ham with a russian salad, new potatoes, cheese, chocolate pudding, oranges and redcurrants, with white and red wine (Saint Émilion) and champagne (Moët and Chandon).

7/6/1917.

The night was quiet, at least for us. Some *Boche* planes made it to the rear to drop some turds; we heard the explosions in the distance. As they were returning those planes had to contend with our three-seaters around 2 a.m., I heard machine guns in the air. Our three-seater has 5 machine guns in turrets with two men; they can fire at the entire horizon. Except for their eyes, they are completely protected. It's a very destructive piece of equipment, and dangerous, for airplanes and for those on the ground. [...]

I did not receive a letter today, but did receive a package with tissue paper, soap, and a battery. Yesterday I bought a battery for 0,85. No problem. I put the battery you sent in my sack, well protected from dampness, and will have it when I need it. [...]

There is lot of commotion in our sector right now. Bourg is quiet; by that I mean that it hasn't been bombed, but the cannon, once again, roars dreadfully. The *Boches* are desperately focused on Chemin des Dames; they would like to take back from us important observation posts—so far they've not succeeded. [...]

7/7/1917.

Caplet left this morning, after spending the day and night here. He told me that he might call on us for a concert, maybe in Paris or elsewhere, not at the front. What is stopping him, and he is right, is the fact that this would really not be the moment for that. We are in a very tough area; too many men are falling for us to go play music while our comrades are being killed. [...]

7/8/1917.

Today I received your letter from July 5. [...] Please do not worry about me; I am one of the luckiest, and more, I am careful. We will get out of this place one of these days. [...]

Second letter, same day.

I received today your letter from July 6. Today was totally calm; however, this evening all the sectors seem to be boiling over and the artillery is firing nonstop. The *Boches* must be going to attack. Up to now, our town has not been hit at all. But I think we will be hit around midnight. That is the usual time; one could say the *Boches* have taken a pledge not to let anyone sleep. The last *Boche* attack was, for them, a real failure; our losses were minimal. A division just next to us, however, lost a lot of men. All that is chance. But it is true that the *Boches* were willing to make huge sacrifices for absolutely nothing. [...]

7/9/1917.

Last night the sector was terrible, a crazy amount of bombing. During the night, a great number of vehicles arrived, pouring out infantrymen who went directly into battle. The arrival of those reinforcements is proof that the attacks were fierce; the cannon fire left no doubt as to what was happening. The *Boches* had other things to occupy their attention than dumping bombs on us; they dropped only four bombs on the bridges. We have three bridges here, in a row, that over 700 to 800 meters cross two canals and the Aisne. Given the expanse of the target, their shots have to be less concentrated than for only one bridge. That favors us, reducing the danger considerably. With all that racket last night, I don't need to tell you that sleep fled far from our eyelids. [...]

Second letter, same day.

Today I received your letter of July 7. It was much quieter today but this evening, at the time I write this, the artillery is starting up. No bombs fell on us today; for the past two or three days it has been stormy and overcast so the planes have had to leave us alone. [...]

Friday, July 6, 1917, 1 p.m.

[...] I understand, my dear child, how you could not have slept a wink during the night of July 3 to 4. According to the report in *L'Information*, the Germans attacked an area of 20 kilometers near you with huge numbers of troops. "This operation, one of the largest and most powerful we have seen from the enemy in a long time, was a total failure. Near Cerny and on the California plateau, where there have been repeated *Boche* attacks for the past two weeks, the waves of assault were almost totally annihilated by our fire." I hope this article is true, but the French losses have to have been just as great. I hope the bombing will diminish and that the little place you occupy will be less exposed to bombs and to airplanes. The danger is even greater because the house you are staying in is near a bridge! I so wish you would be relieved. For sure, with all these events, you cannot think about music. Your music case and Maréchal's cello are still in Nogent-l'Artaud and safe? [...]

Wednesday, July 11, 1917, 2 p.m.

Today I received your letter from July 8. [...] M. Alan was telling me that American soldiers had arrived at the front. I don't know what truth there is in that, but will those soldiers fight? The French have great need of replacements, but we do not know under what terms those soldiers have come. [...]

Second letter, same day, 7 p.m.

I just received your letters from July 9 and 10. [...] Thank you for the pretty little flower I found in the first letter. It made me very happy; the color is somber and the stem stiff, like a capillary, a souvenir from a place that has been heavily bombed. I make a wish that calm return and that you get out of that dreadful spot soon. Obviously, it is easier for them to keep you there than to bring in others. [...]

7/11/1917.

Our night was far from quiet. We had three successive bombings of about 20 shells each time. About ten fell in this area. Very fortunately, no one was hurt; two horses were killed and two injured. We will be eating horse meat, that is the morality of the times. The *poilu* always manages. [...]

I received today your letters from July 9 and 10. [...] Caplet came while I was off buying food; I did not see him. He brought my violin and what music he had. Every three days he exchanges his pigeons and every day he works on their training—letting them fly 2 or 3 kilometers from the pigeon loft. He says he is very busy. Starting tomorrow morning I will be able to work a bit on technique. [...]

7/12/1917.

I did not receive any letters today, just an envelope with a clipping from *L'Information*. The speech by Painlevé which took up all of one side of the clipping is remarkable.[260] Unfortunately, his words are addressed to people with culture. And the *poilus*, as a group, are not very cultured. His words, adapted and with commentary, might, at one time, have been good for them. Right now, I fear they would have no effect at all on those bitter, tired men. The *poilu*, a simple person, tells himself only one thing: that all those lovely thoughts about him are written only because they fear him, because he is stronger, not because they are interested in him. With his good sense, he thinks that, if people like someone, they don't wait three years to worry about their suffering and more, they take steps to help them. If the government is speeding up the American effort, that is because they know what will work. [...]

I received a letter from Lieutenant Poumier, the young engineer whom I met in Cappy and at whose place I played. The letter followed me for at least 15 days. He saw that the 129th was in his sector and figured I was not far away. He didn't know everything that has happened, only that I had moved to the division

---

[260] Paul Painlevé (1863-1933) was a mathematician and politician. Named War Minister in March 1917, he was faced with mutinies and failed offensives at Chemin des Dames in April 1917. He was replaced by Georges Clemenceau.

office and he thought I must be in the area. I answered him right away, sending quite a long letter with some of the details of how our life has been. I told him we had played some music over the winter, and what we had played. He will surely reply. He is a charming young man and passionate about music. [...]

7/13/1917.

The night was quite calm except for 5 bombs dropped about 10:15, nothing after that. [...] Pétain sent out a flier yesterday about the food for the troops; you can believe it is truly good news. I don't know whether it will be applied, but it is imperative and promises the *poilu* a major improvement in his meals. [...]

I received yesterday four letters, one from the 11th, two from the 12th, and one with a letter from Mme Armengaud. It seems to me that she is not embarrassed to have talked about sugar over dinner, but that doesn't mean I can send any, especially not that much. In any case, I would not take the risk of sending some, even if only 100 grams; that could be very costly to me. When I come home on leave, that is different; with some planning, I can bring, in one or two packages, a kilo or two. I will surely do it, first for us. It will be easy, as I know the date of my departure a few days early. But I cannot ship any. [...]

I received a letter from Vessot; apparently the sanctions were quite harsh.[261] I am troubled for him; if the battalion is disbanded, what will happen to him? To be sent back to a company after three years of war is rather hard. I hope that, in his case as in others, his bright, clever mind will manage to find a way out. I am less worried for Rolland, as he is a corporal stretcher bearer, almost a career post, and even if changed, he will probably have the same situation. I admit that to have their futures settled would make me very happy. I too am not about to forget the year I passed with them, in the mud of La Ville-aux-Bois, and the horrors of Neuville and Souchez. Those memories cannot be erased. [...]

Second letter, same day.

Today continues calm; in the evening there is always a bit of activity, but compared with what usually happens, tonight is nothing. [...]

I read today that the law about rents will be voted on and the moratorium will probably be suspended as of October to allow application of the new law. We will have to watch all that closely; it will surely change the current state of affairs with our tenant. You should consult the young woman bailiff that M. Moisy recommended and put her in charge of our interests. I don't want to get involved at all with those people in Boulogne. [...]

News of our departure is getting a bit more specific, one week to wait. Rumors go so far as having us at rest around Paris. I don't see the future as quite so rosy.

---

[261] His friend, Césarine Vessot, was in one of the battalions that mutinied.

All I want is to be able to move my body around somewhere other than on the Chemin des Dames. That is a sensible wish.

7/14/1917.

Morning. Last night was terrible. Starting at 10:45 all sectors successively burst into flames until there was one continuous line of fire. We shared in the party between 11:30 p.m. and 3 a.m. About fifty bombs fell on the village and the immediate surroundings. No need to say we did not sleep. We couldn't rest a bit until almost morning. It's probably our national holiday that earned us this renewal of *Boche* rage.

While I am writing this, there are frightening thunderous sounds from the direction of the Froidemont farm. That still will not keep us from having a nice lunch. The weather is very heavy, very covered, and we will certainly have rain. This morning I bought some lovely fresh cabbages which we will cook with the ham we got. Lismon cooks his ham in a broth with onions, thyme, bay leaves, pepper, for at least an hour and a quarter; forty-five minutes before it is done, he adds the cabbage to cook, and before serving, he adds a chunk of butter. [...]

Second letter, same day.

[...] I saw Pierrot today; he drove some officers to the sector and was awaiting them in our village. He's just back from leave. His wife and children are all well. He received a letter from Théo, a stretcher bearer friend, who gave him these details: in the 1st battalion four men were shot, four sentenced to forced labor, 14 to public works, and 41 to disciplinary punishments. As for the battalion it will be dispersed: some will leave for Indochina, others for Salonika. [...] I was very lucky to be at the division headquarters. I have to say that luck, in all these events, has been on my side. It's quite amazing to see how it continues. [...]

Thanks to a friend, I think I've found a guy to make my three rings. It seems that he does magnificent work. As for lighters and other junk like that, please don't think any more about it. I do not spend my money that way. For Mother Duez I will send flowers and she will be happy.

We should leave between the 20th and 25th; they are speaking more openly now about that. Today it is atrociously hot, although cloudy. We are cooking in our juice. [...]

7/15/1917.

Evening. There was a lot of activity today, although this evening seems generally to be calmer. All the ground lost to the *Boches* yesterday was taken back. I received your letter from July 13. [...]

Lismon is the one who made the tarts. He works quickly; he is very clever. We made two: one rhubarb, the other frangipane and gooseberry jam. They were both very good. Today for lunch we had saucisson and butter; roast beef with onion purée, new potatoes, cheese; this evening potatoes and eggs in white sauce, green beans, gooseberries with sugar.

You will have to put in the next package a sky-blue armband with the numbers in white metal 274. I now belong to that regiment and I have to wear their numbers. [...]

Tuesday, July 17, 1917, 9 a.m.

I received this morning your letters from the 14th and 15th. [...] When you were talking about the feast days for Lemoine and for Madeline, I thought about your friend Martel whose name was Henri. Did that occur to you? The poor boy, had he lived maybe the guys in his regiment would have behaved differently. [...]

7/16/1917.

Morning. The night was quiet, at least in our village. [...] It seems that I do nothing, but it takes all day. I get up about 7:30, breakfast on a bit of hot chocolate or café au lait, then get cleaned up and dressed. Suddenly it is 9:00, when I go make my purchases. Not only do I go to merchants, I especially go to civilians who have gardens in the hopes of finding lettuce, vegetables or fruit. That wastes a lot of time; one day this person doesn't have something, the next day someone else doesn't have it. Going from one to the other takes a long time, especially as those folks don't try very hard to serve you. When I get back, I have to help Lismon peel vegetables. That doesn't seem like much, but with 10 to 12 people to feed, it's a lot of work. I go for water, I bottle the wine, in short, I help Lismon who does the actual cooking. Mme Carne helps us, but we don't have too many hands. Then I always write in the morning. After lunch I take my mail to be sent, pick up letters which I read, and papers. I practice violin for an hour and suddenly it's time to get more provisions, to get food from the mess and take care of supper. It is 9:00 in the evening by the time all is finished. We spend a bit of time outdoors, relaxing and enjoying the fresh air. I go up to my room about 10:00. I take care of my mail, read a bit and am in bed regularly by midnight. There you have it, my life, certainly centered on material things. I am always thinking about food but someone has to take charge of that. My comrades are very appreciative of the way we manage. It is a humble life with easy, boring work, all embellished with shells that fall around us from time to time. [...]

7/17/1917.

Morning. Last night passed without incident. [...] It appears that we are headed to Fère-en-Tardenois or somewhere near that town for our rest. Apparently, it is not very pretty. We will never find a place prettier than the Marne valley. But where we are is not important. We cannot expect this rest to be long, maybe 2 to 3 weeks. Then we will move into another sector. [...]

Second letter, same day.

Evening. I received today your letter of July 15. [...] Today, thanks to the chief of the music regiment of the 74th, right now in charge of a clothing store to dress up soldiers going on leave, I received a lovely pair of satin pants, a shirt, gaiters, and a pair of shoes. [...] Once I am in Fère, [...] I will try to practice two hours a day, even though circumstances do not lend themselves to music. Not forgetting that our general not only does not like music, he hates it. [...]

Thursday, July 19, 1917, 2:30 p.m.

I received last night your letters from the 16th and the 17th. [...] Right now, your relief is all that matters. I hope you will use your time to your advantage, that is, in playing music. You always lend a deaf ear when I scold you for not writing some sort of piece for your instrument. Others, who may have less instruction than you, have given it a try. Even if the work was not perfect, you could have created something quite acceptable. That would have been a precious memory for you. But you have too much pride and are afraid of the criticism of Caplet or others. [...]

7/19/1917.

We moved today; I left this morning at 8:30 in an ambulance car and we were in Fère at 11:00. It's a pretty little town where we will find everything we need. Lismon and I found a wonderful kitchen in the home of a painting contractor, and I also found a splendid room with an excellent bed. We will have a great rest; let's hope that it is long and that we can play some music. [...]

Friday, July 20, 1917, 1 p.m.

No news last evening nor this morning. I read in the 4 p.m. *communiqué* of July 19: "Violent fighting between the artillery of both sides along the entire front, especially violent between the Somme and the Aisne, near Vauclère and Craonne and on the right bank of the Meuse." Your silence worries me a bit. The Germans show no signs of letting up or stopping their bombing in the

Aisne. That little area you are in, or have just left, I prefer the latter hypothesis, will end up no longer existing. I hold out hope for a letter at 4 p.m. [...]

I went this morning to the notary. Laville paid but not Mme Boissard. M. Chevallier was busy in his office with clients and it would have been an hour before he was free, I left without getting the money Laville paid. I will go back early next week. After I mail this letter, I will go a bit farther, to Mme Boissard's, to say hello. She will probably tell me, at least I hope so, that she will go see the notary. I stopped in at the coal merchant yesterday morning; she promised to deliver 5 to 6 sacks of coal during the first days of next week. [...]

Saturday, July 21, 1917, 3:30 p.m.

I received last night your letters from July 17 and 19, nothing from the 18ᵗʰ. There you are, settled, in la Fère-en-Tardenois. You need some calm; it will seem nice to no longer hear the bombing and especially to not fear the bombs. I hope the planes will not come find you. If Fère is a pretty little town, you will probably play in church on Sunday and maybe you will meet some amateur, or even professional, musicians who would be happy to organize a concert or something. In any case, make sure to work on your instrument several hours a day—a bit of careful technique, and some Bach, and some detached note work for the bow. [...]

This morning I went into Paris, I needed a new corset to replace the one I wear every day which is worn out, coming apart, and gives no support. Since I left at 10 a.m., I figured there would be all the free seats I could want in the tram and the métro, etc., but no, a mob of people in the tram, the métro packed in both directions. I think there were fewer people moving around during peacetime than now. [...]

7/21/1917.

I couldn't find time to write yesterday; I spent all day getting the kitchen set up and buying what I needed. In the train station, two army corps and the supply officers have set up place to sell certain goods, like wine for 0,70, fine wine at reasonable prices, oil, vinegar. [...]

I have a charming room and a good bed, in the home of a woman who has two daughters who are seamstresses, and three sons serving the country: one is a prisoner in Germany, one has been wounded 3 times. [...]

Maréchal left last evening for Nogent-l'Artaud to get his cello and my music case. If I cannot take it with me, I will leave it here. This is a very convenient area. Caplet has not yet been relieved; apparently the division that replaced us does not have a chief pigeon keeper, so he had to wait. It is only a matter of hours until he is relieved; today our division took steps to make that happen.

Tomorrow I will go see the *curé* about playing for Sunday Mass. There is a large organ in the church which is quite lovely. We are hoping to be able to make some music here. There have to be some resources, i.e., a piano. There are 2500 inhabitants in this cute little town, which is clean compared with the factory town of Villers-Bretonneux. […] I am paying 1 franc a day for the room I am renting; rent here has gone up a lot so that is not very bad. […]

7/23/1917.

Today I received your letter of July 20 and a card from Rolland, on leave; I am envious. He doesn't say much, he's not one for words. Yesterday we played for Mass, and Caplet, who came back late Saturday night, improvised a prelude and music for communion. Amazingly, the bassoonist Bourdeau, the son of the well-known choirmaster, was in the church. When he heard the improvisations and what we played, he came up to the organ to see who it was. He found us, recognized Maréchal and Caplet. We had a long talk with him and his captain. Bourdeau drives a vehicle at a large air base for the Army and is in this area. The captain, second in charge of this large unit, immediately invited us to come play for them. Bourdeau came to get us at 2:00. Those pilots don't refuse themselves anything. They are camped in the midst of the fields, but they have planted gardens and parks, built barracks that are almost luxurious, the atmosphere is very special. Several women from the Red Cross were there, brought in from various places. Very simply, we were able to breathe the air of civilization. Even more, those people seemed to really like music, which is a change from our officers. The piano they have is not very good; we mentioned ours, which is in Lunéville. The captain decided to send one of his men this morning to bring it back. We will have the piano tomorrow night. If we want to practice in their large living room, they are offering to send a car every day to transport us. They could not be nicer. What is even better, they want to organize a concert for next Sunday, and bring from Paris a certain Madame Chenal or Cheval and another chick, as they say. Those pilots are priceless. This could be a real connection for us; it is not impossible that we could transfer to an aviation group. […]

Sunday, July 22, 1917, 2 p.m.

[…] Here is what I read in the 2 p.m. *communiqué* of July 21: "Along the Aisne front, the night saw especially hard action north of Braye-en-Laonnois near Cerny, Hurtebise, and Craonne. In a number of places, violent bombing was followed by attacks. Southeast of Cerny the forceful enemy attack led to a savage battle. Twice the Germans penetrated our forward trenches along a 250-meter front, but twice a strong counterattack pushed them all the way back. Southwest of Cerny a German attempt also failed despite their use of flame-throwers.

South of Ailles, our grenadiers totally broke two successive attacks, etc." If the *communiqué* gives so many details, one has to conclude that the fighting was very intense and that we have to have had huge losses and a certain number of men taken prisoner. [...]

7/24/1917.

I received your letter of July 21. Of course, my bed is a normal bed, with sheets, blankets, etc. [...] Today we started to deconstruct Ravel's trio. It's a terribly complex work and will take a long time to perfect. It's very interesting, but more an intellectual work than one of feelings and passion. The brain plays a bigger role than the heart. It is really very difficult. [...]

You write that there are a lot of people in the métro; since there are no longer any buses, that is the only transportation available. And you are no longer used to going out, so it is no surprise that you were a bit shocked. [...]

7/25/1917.

I received your letter of July 22. We should not celebrate too soon; we were on the point of being sent back into the sector where, for a time, things were heating up again. The 6th Division was sent in; they had been at rest for a good 10 days. Fortunately for us, we just got here; still, we have to realize that we came very close. We saw a lot of troops pass by in trucks, reinforcements arriving suddenly. [...]

7/26/1917.

I received your letter of 23 July and a letter from Vessot that I'm sending to you. You will see that my old friends are in a terrible situation. Fortunately, Césarine is very clever and I'm sure he will figure something out. Yesterday we went to the aviation unit to play for them. They came and collected us in a car. We go back today and there will be a big reception with the colonel or the commander of that group of reservists. He apparently likes music. Lemoine is coming with us. [...] Our piano has arrived so we will rehearse there. It will be tuned today. [...] I located a violin for Lemoine; it is not very good but doesn't sound that bad. [...]

Commander Lambrigot is leaving; this had been planned for months and was delayed probably because of the events you know about. Fortunately, Captain Bouteville will become Chief of Staff. He's a man we know well, a good fellow, and the only person in the division who cares at all about music. [...]

7/27/1917.

Today I received your letters from July 24 and 25. I also received the letter with a twig of honeysuckle, which pleased me greatly and for which I thank you heartily. […]

We have been very lucky to come upon the officers we needed and who make everything much simpler. Bourdeau, in addition to winning a bassoon prize, is an excellent musician, pianist and organist. He is music director at Saint-Philippe-du-Roule. […] It is agreed that we all will join the aviation group or none of us, we do not want to be separated. That is quite natural; we have some power because we can play quartets and quintets, something very rare. […]

Absolutely nothing unusual is bothering me; it's just that we are all a bit excited about the idea of joining the aviation group. […] My dear *minou*, how you torment yourself! True, if I enter an aviation group, I will see a lot more ladies and nurses than where I am; the pilots have the talent to attract women. Do not think that this is more dangerous. Nothing is more dangerous than the infantry with no prestige and no glory. One suffers and dies in obscurity, in the mud, heroically but without notice or relief. For the gentlemen pilots it is a different story. I will not lose my virtue unless I really want to, and I am not at that point. […]

7/30/1917.

I couldn't write yesterday because we didn't get back until three o'clock in the morning and we had to play for Mass at 10. […] We had gone to play in Vauxtin, where there is an important aviation center. We dined very well with the officers, including the ace Durand who has already brought down 8 or 9 *Boche* planes. We gave a famously light program, some little pieces, the inevitable Haydn Trio, also an arrangement for string quartet of *L'Arlésienne* and Grieg's *La Mort d'Ase*.[262]

The pilots certainly do take it easy, no doubt about it. No matter what hardships they endure, they return to comfort and even luxury—that is, a good meal, a good room, and rest. The foot soldier is far from all of that. We are little by little becoming acquainted with people who organize musical events. Mlle Mici (?), a 30-year-old woman, student of d'Indy and the Schola, who lives in the area is introducing us to all the homes where people like music. […] We met a retired notary, M. Fonte, who has a good Érard upright which we are welcome to use, as well as music stands and a lovely room. He also has a beautiful piano-forte, square, from 1830-1840. […]

---

[262] Haydn wrote forty-five piano trios. *La Mort d'Ase* is an excerpt from Grieg's *Peer Gynt Suite*.

Wednesday, August 1, 1917, 9 a.m.

I received last evening a 4-page letter from July 30 which made me very happy; I was wondering whether you were on the move. [...]

I am sending you in a special envelope a Bengal rose from the garden; it has kept all its fragrance because it was pressed fresh in a book. It will be, for you, a part of the house and of your home. I also sent a poppy and I have to explain why. A few little sprigs of poppy from who knows where grew in one of the little gardens in front of the house. [...]

8/1/1917.

Headquarters of Division SP 93. I receive yesterday your letter from July 29. We are starting a new month and you will receive this letter on the anniversary of my departure, three years ago. It is extraordinary to think about that. Three years of life gone and nothing yet points to an end of this situation. In fact, we are no closer to the end than we were three years ago. [...]

We are very involved with our rehearsals. With Magne, I am polishing the Fauré Sonata, which is going well and will be appreciated. We expect Caplet tomorrow morning and, after a good rehearsal, the Beethoven 10th will be fine also. There is every reason to expect the concert tomorrow night for General Maistre to be successful and it could produce some good results. Magne has found two homes with very good pianos—a brand new Érard [...] and a good Gaveau. [...]

8/2/1917.

I received yesterday your two letters from July 30. Today is the dreadful anniversary of the departure of so many people, many of whom were leaving forever. In looking back, one can't help but shudder at all that has happened. Fate and the gods have kept me in one piece, while so many others have been left behind.

[...] My thoughts today go back to Brittany, and I can see my departure as if it were yesterday. But dwelling on the past serves no purpose, certainly right now, when duty obliges us to look at the future. [...]

Friday, August 3, 1917, 8 a.m.

[...] Today, three years ago, you left Port Lazo and nothing yet promises an end to all this calamity. France and its people are sure to be totally destroyed because our government and military leaders persist in a struggle from which I believe there is no way out. It's natural that the English force us to keep fighting because they want to get out of this impasse at all costs, otherwise it would be the end of their domination of the high seas and by that, their end. So we are trapped in a slag heap we cannot get out of. It's a terrible problem and our politicians will be able to say they led France to the lowest depths by their incompetence, their vice, and their lack of conscience. For them a sack of gold has replaced the word "nation." Material pleasures have won over the noble ideals that should be foremost for all well balanced and well brought up people. [...]

Saturday, August 4, 1917, 9 a.m.

[...] I received last evening your letter of the 2nd. [...] You didn't leave on August 2, it was the 3rd. Remember, André Tavernier had come on Saturday August 1 for his first lesson and Maria came running with the news about the declaration of war. We didn't hear the bugle because we were far from Plouézec and the wind did not carry the sound to us. The regulations for you were that you had to leave on the 3rd day with two days-worth of food. You checked at the town hall in Plouézec and left Monday morning, August 3. I seem to recall that you needed to be in Paimpol at 6 a.m., or at Plouézec, I don't really remember. What I do know is that this long-lasting memory is very painful! God has willed that you still be with us, and unhurt up to now. Let's pray that He continue to protect you. [...]

8/3/1917.

I received yesterday your letter of July 31. [...] We are not rehearsing today; we all got to bed very late last night and are rather tired. [...] Today's big news is that General Pétain is coming to visit us. Everyone is all in a tither. I have to tell you that I don't much like this sort of honor; I've often noticed that, after visits like this, they lead us straight out to fall on our faces. They ask us very nicely: "Little fellow, little fellow, how do you want to be eaten?" [...]

Second letter, same day.

I have more time to write now; all the details of tomorrow's concert are set. [...] They are beginning to tell the *poilus* that the Americans will replace them, but they also add that it will be at least a year before they have enough men here to do that. It's really just brain-washing. For the Americans to have between 200,000 and 700,000 men on the front will already require a huge effort. And what would that add? A single German class is 500,000 men; we French have at least 3 million at the front. To really replace us, they would have to bring several million men, which is not impossible but would take many years. What is more, our newest classes are quite awful; all those young men are in no hurry to be smashed to bits, unlike their older counterparts. [...]

So, quite frankly I see no solution unless both sides make concessions, and the Germans are less inclined to do that now than ever. [...] We may well be talking about 1920 or 1925. No one can say. But then there are the voices of the *poilus*, and I fear they will make themselves heard in a way that the rear will go deaf. [...]

8/5/1917.

I barely have time to write today; we are playing this morning for 10:00 Mass. [...] No news yet about our departure. There is much talk of going back to the Chemin des Dames, but more to the right than last time, that is toward Huertebise. It's no better, to the contrary. [...]

8/6/1917.

I received today your letters from August 4 and a card from Vessot, who is on leave, telling me he passed his chauffeur's test. All the better for him that he gets a better spot for himself, he deserves it after three years on active duty in the trenches. [...]

8/8/1917.

We spent yesterday with the aviation unit, but I did get your letter from August 5th before leaving. We had lunch with the captain, the doctor in charge of a nearby hospital train, and two nurses from the train. [...]

We were able to play some music after lunch. Then, as three pilots from a neighboring squadron had come with their planes, the ladies wanted to go up in them, which they did. Then it was our turn, and Magne, Maréchal, and I, we all took a turn in an airplane, at least 15 minutes. In my case, I went up to 800 meters, flying over la Fère. We were in an AR, a biplane, one engine, speed of 160 kilometers an hour. The feeling of being in this machine is absolutely delicious. You are flying without feeling it, only a bit in the turns do you feel a bit of movement. Coming down you feel hardly anything, ten times less than in an elevator. You sit in an armchair in a fuselage that looks a bit like a comfortable canoe. It's amazing how one sees the countryside underneath and at a distance. I understand now why one needs to hide as soon as a plane is spotted; the slightest movement on a road or in town is easily seen. There are no words to describe the feeling of ease and pleasure one gets from this sort of travel. One feels completely safe. [...] I passed at least 3 times over the bell tower in Arcy, and had the impression that I could catch it. In the turns, when one of the wings dips down, you see everything at an angle. It's strange. My friends and I are delighted with our excursion. [...]

Second letter, same day

[...] This morning I met Commander Lapeyre, of the engineer division. He spoke enthusiastically about our performance and especially of the Beethoven

Quartet, the 10th, which is magnificent. What amuses me is that, at the beginning, Caplet declared that he was not impressed by that quartet, now he finds it one of the most beautiful.[263] [...]

Saturday, August 11, 1917, 9 a.m.

[...] I'm sending this morning several articles from *L'Information* that will interest you. You will see that the Japanese may be going to intervene—they might have provided their support two years ago as some papers were suggesting. The Chinese also seem to want to go to war against Germany. Soon the entire world will be in the fray which doesn't point to an end anytime soon. All those people want to be at the feeding trough when peace comes in order to get a piece of something. How horrible! And all those poor fellows are dying for all that greed.

I am haunted by a wish that there would be a huge cataclysm (since France is already lost) which would upset the line that divides the water in Europe and would drown that same Europe in floods without end. Emperors, monarchs, conquerors, all those evil bandits, along with all the people of course, would disappear. [...] It would be the end of ends! [...]

Sunday, August 12, 1917, 9 a.m.

[...] Monsieur Alan came yesterday afternoon; he told me some sad news, the death of his son Clément. He was grievously wounded on August 3 and died of his injuries while being transported out. He had been in the unit for some time and was hoping to come home soon on leave. I think Jean mentioned to you in a recent letter that he was trying to find a way to be with his brother. [...]

Second letter, same day, 8 p.m.

Of course, I didn't receive any news today because it is Sunday, so I will be able to read your words tomorrow morning. Tomorrow afternoon, I have to go to the school, to turn in a questionnaire about a coal ration card. I was given the

---

[263] This may be a description of the concert: "The concert took place in the courtyard of the elementary school. A stage had been set up with a primitive decoration. Choice of program: Beethoven's "tenth quartet" (sic), César Franck's "Sonata for piano and violin," the *Poème* by my great and poignant Gabriel Dupont. An unusual, colorful public. [...] The first measures of the Beethoven quartet rise amid the attentive silence and the deep contemplation of the listeners. Perfect, impassioned execution by the soldiers, true artists, a bit encumbered by their slightly tight, faded, and worn-out uniforms. Sergeant André Caplet [...] covered the viola part not very skillfully. We quickly forget the long arms squeezed into too-short sleeves of the fascinating violinist. Phrases filled with tenderness and calm grow, mix with others, lose themselves and then find themselves again. An immense wave of sweetness drowned the souls. Eyes brighten at the splendorous glimpse of dawn, a vision of better times to come." [...] Henry Malherbe, *La Flamme au poing*, (Albin Michel: Paris, 1917), cited by Streletski, "Entre fatalité et choix;" *La Chaîne de Création*, 33.

questionnaire yesterday when I went to renew my sugar card. I would be wise to get the coal card because my coal merchant still has not brought my order. [...]

From all points of view, it is regrettable that you have not composed a piece based on the war for your instrument. There is still time; a piece like that doesn't need to be brilliant, just a lovely melody and technically difficult but with effect. You know your instrument well enough to draw out all the possibilities, in terms of sonority, double stops, harmonics, varied bow strokes. Nothing would work better in America, and elsewhere, than performing a work composed at the front. [...]

8/10/1917.

[...] Today we went for coffee with the pilots; there we saw the Marquise de Chabannes and played a bit of music. If we are still here on Sunday, we will give a new concert for the Foyer du Soldat. It will consist of the first three movements of the Debussy Quartet, the *Chaconne*, one movement of a Grieg Sonata for cello, and the Andante and last movement of Chausson's Piano Quartet. We do not expect to have enough time to prepare the end of the Debussy which is very difficult. We rehearse tonight and will see then. [...]

8/11/1917.

I received yesterday your letter of August 9 and am sending you the program for tomorrow's concert. [...] It is now sure that we are leaving. Our regiments start moving tomorrow. We are the last to leave, on August 15. For that holiday, we will go back into the field, a bit more to the right than last time, near Hurtebise. It is not a great location. They say we may be there for a month. The last time we were here we got a good taste of the Chemin des Dames. [...]

8/13/1917.

Today I received your letters from the 10th and 11th. [...] Our concert yesterday took place; to say it met with great success would not be accurate. The reaction was one of astonishment—the Chausson Quartet and especially Debussy's left the audience dazed. We are pushing things a bit with these people who have never, or rarely heard music. That concert created a sort of revolution; you can't imagine the passionate discussions we are causing. In the middle of the program, the *Chaconne* fell like a ton of bricks on the heads of our unfortunate victims not knowing what to think. Everyone was astounded. Caplet, who never smiles, was overjoyed. We must not overdo concerts like that; we will not convert anyone, just the opposite. The problem is that Caplet is furious; he only wants to work on his choice of modern composers; for the classics, he's happy to criticize and doesn't want to work on them.

Tomorrow night at 11:00 we will leave; we have to pass over a ridge in sight of the enemy, so we need to move at night. […]

8/14/1917.

We are in the midst of all the preparations for our move tonight. Today was market day in Fère and we took advantage of it to buy all sorts of fruits and veg- etables that we will take with us into the field. […] There is a lot of fruit right now; we bought beautiful peaches this morning for 2,40 a kilo; plums for 0,70 a kilo. […]

8/15/1917.

We arrived this morning at 4:00 and are settled in Hanotaux's house.[264] Our kitchen is set up in the library of the house; we enjoy not only a beautiful room but also a splendid view. This town has only one side. It is perched on the side of a hill, like an amphitheater. We have a superb panorama in front of us. Hano- taux picked the spot well. It's a strange town: much less exposed, no comparison with Bourg which has been totally destroyed. So here we are and we should have a comfortable stay. […]

8/16/1917.

We had dreadful stormy weather today. […]. The roads are totally soaked. We were barely settled when the *Boches* let loose a fierce attack: they were not only repelled, but the 274th counterattacked, took some prisoners, and a good bit of territory. […]

Saturday, August 18, 1917, 10 a.m.

I received last night your letter from August 14 and this morning the ones from the 15th and the 16th. […] In *L'Information* today they talk about the Ger- man attack of August 16. That attack was to be predicted because I've noticed that the Germans seem well-informed and always attack when a unit is being relieved. "Yesterday, that is August 16 at night fall, after heavy bombing, the enemy launched a strong attack along a 2-kilometer front between the Vauclère mill and the California plateau. Violent and repeated attacks on positions we recently took back east of Cerny suffered the same bloody defeat. It is confirmed that the German losses were particularly heavy from 13 to 15 August near the Craonne plateau."

---

[264] Gabriel Hanotaux (1853-1944) was a French statesman and historian. During his long career, he was elected member of the Académie Française in 1897 and served as France's delegate to the League of Nations.

[…] I forgot to tell you we had an alert last night. […] I had heard the planes, probably reconnaissance planes; everything ended about 5 a.m. I don't know whether anything happened in Paris; today's papers were printed yesterday so don't say anything. I'll know more tomorrow. […]

8/18/1917.

I am writing early this morning, before the mail comes. […] The Americans seem to be making a serious effort. Let us hope that, by next May, they will be able to take over the major part of our job. […]

Contrary to what they were saying a few days ago, I believe we will be here for 2 to 3 weeks. We are not badly lodged, better than in Bourg, and definitely safer. We enjoy a superb view. In front of us, to the left, is Mézy. Beaurieux, on the other side of the Aisne, is hidden from us by a sort of spur. From that prominence, we easily see Concevreux and the Chateau of Roucy. […]

Second letter, same day.

I just received your letters from August 15 and 16. […] Hurtebise is, in fact, a farm and is not mentioned on the postcards you have. We are the ones occupying Ailles: this area is terrible, but we shouldn't let that bother us. I find we are much better off than in Bourg. General Lebrun just arrived and he shouts a lot: the best thing to do, in that case, is not to show oneself when you don't have to. […]

You are a nasty darling to call me naughty and mean; I will bite you and give you a good whipping as punishment during my next leave. […]

As to our lodging, it could not be better, it's a dream. No comparison with Bourg. The only inconvenience is we are a bit shaken by the artillery's 240 guns which are only about 200 meters away. The vibration, night and day, is massive and disturbs our calm. We put up with it, but it's not easy. The eardrums of the men who fire those guns must be in a dreadful state. […]

8/19/1917.

I received today your letter from August 17. […] A good many of the people who came to my concerts and saw my success and the society surrounding me believe I must have powerful connections that I could have used to get me out of the war. As you know, their reasoning is wrong on two points. First, despite appearances, I do not have any powerful connections; and two, I never looked for a way out. And truly, at this time, I do not regret what I've done, nor how I've done it. On the contrary, at times my conscience tells me that I could be fighting the enemy in a more useful way. We should all pick up a grenade and throw it at the pigs. [...]

8/20/1917.

I am writing to you early this morning; our corps was relieved yesterday and there is a rumor afoot that we will soon join them. [...] Last night, about 5 p.m., we were treated to a rather impressive show. A *Boche* plane with a very clever and daring pilot, whom no one had seen as he was very high up above the clouds, took advantage of a moment when very few of our planes were in the air. Like a cloudburst, he suddenly appeared above a *saucisse* and shot it up point blank, in less time than it takes to write this. He inflicted the same on a second and a third *saucisse* several kilometers away. The pilots use incendiary bombs, so the *saucisses* very rapidly caught fire, and in about two minutes, under our shocked eyes, the three collapsed in flames. You should have seen how the observers jumped out into the air with their parachutes. According to what we heard that evening, the six observers landed safe and sound. After this exploit, the *Boche* plane quickly went back behind his lines. He ran across two French planes which, based on what we hear, attacked him halfheartedly. He escaped from their attack beautifully, doing loops and hops worthy of an acrobat and left us all stupefied by his daring and his prowess. As soon as he was gone, 25 French planes appeared in the sky. About time! [...]

Friday, August 24, 1917, 9:30 a.m.

I have no news since August 20 letter. [...] I read in *L'Information* from Friday the 14th: "The night before last, very strong attacks were launched on at least 6 of our positions at the Chemin des Dames. They all failed. Very violent artillery fire continues in that region. On the 23rd of August the German artillery was very active north of the Aisne, notably in the region of Braye-Hurtebise." I am not without worry in that regard because you must have been heavily bombed. [...]

Saturday, August 25, 1917, 10 a.m.

I received yesterday at 4 p.m. your letters from August 21 and 22. [...] You cannot find in Hanotaux's house a volume left behind by chance? As everywhere else, they have to have helped themselves. If you find even one, send it to me. When you are home on your next leave, we could give it to him. That would be a way to make his acquaintance and to talk to him about his house. [...]

Second letter, same day, 8 p.m.

[…] Mathilde's husband finished sawing up the wood that we got when you were home last. Today, to finish, he broke up some wicker baskets with worn-out bottoms to make kindling. On Friday my coal merchant sent 6 sacks of anthracite and 6 sacks of wood; next week she will send 4 more sacks of anthracite. With the coal ration card and what I have in the cellar, I will get through the winter without worry. […]

8/24/1917.

I received today your letter from the 22ⁿᵈ. I also received the leaflet on Caplet which is quite amusing. All those variations in his life do not surprise me in the least. He is, basically, very versatile and changes ideas abruptly. He can be burning with enthusiasm and, suddenly, he drops everything—he will come back to it later or maybe never. That is why he has, in a way, not written anything. Too bad, because he certainly has a dream-like, poetic way of working. His talents, as I know them, are Debussy-like, with a bit of originality. One can only regret his laziness and casualness. I really would like for him to finish my piece,[265] but to bring it up is the best way to make him put it aside. So I take care not to ask about it. […]

8/26/1917.

I just this minute received your letter of the 24ᵗʰ· […] Don't worry about me. Where I am in this village, there is not much danger. The noise of our big artillery guns is more annoying than the rare bombs that fall around here. As the crow flies, we are about 5 kilometers from the front lines; and more important, this village is tucked into a cliff which protects it from bombing or, at least, would make it very difficult. The attack we were going to launch has been put off for reasons we don't know, but I think it will take place and we will not be relieved before then. […]

8/27/1917.

For 24 hours we have had a dreadful wind and pouring rain; this morning it seems to be clearing up. Yesterday there was great excitement in the division. About 2 p.m., eight bombs landed. One especially badly placed, fell on the corner of the dining room of Hanotaux's house. The officers' office is right next to there and everyone was there, the general and other officers of the general staff. By great luck, no one was hit, but the house is half fallen in. We are in a build-

---

[265] Caplet never finished his piece for solo violin, although some portions remain in the Bibliothèque Nationale de France.

ing about 20 meters away, across a lovely courtyard, so we felt nothing. But on the other side of the building are the servants' quarters where the vehicles were kept. Two of them were badly damaged, and De Varenne, the chief of the vehicle personnel, was seriously injured and died last evening in the ambulance. [...]

Tuesday, August 28, 1917, 8:30 p.m.

[...] The famous library which you use as a dining room is separated from the house by 20 meters. Probably Hanotaux used it as a refuge where he could have quiet in order to work, far from the brouhaha in the rest of the house. This time there is something good about an annex; usually I detest them as part of country houses. I praise heaven that you and your friends found refuge there. Maréchal is very lucky to go on leave at this time. Things are much better in Paris than in the Aisne. [...]

8/28/1917.

This morning I am writing before the mail arrives. We are having a terrible windstorm which, along with the rain that fell all day long, combined to prevent the planned attack. I think now that it will not happen, or at least we will not be part of it. We are being relieved in three or four days. [...]

Once again, we are to pick up the walking stick and travel over the rocky roads. This bohemian life is, in the end, haunting. But the true bohemian from the plains of Hungary travels with his house trailer; however humble it may be, it's still a home. We, however, are continuously obliged to find a new place to stay. [...]

Wednesday, August 29, 1917, 4:30 p.m.

[...] You must have been bombed again the night of the 27th. The *communiqué* announces attacks, an intense artillery battle in a number of places. The Germans launched attacks all along the Chemin des Dames front. I do not know where you have found refuge or what your life is like since the 25th. The *communiqué* admits that our losses were heavy but says that the German losses were just as bad if not worse. When they write things like that it means that there was serious loss of life. [...]

8/29/1917.

Today I received two letters from August 26 and 27. I am happy to learn that your coal merchant finally gave you some coal and has promised to give you more. Based on your coal card, what quantity will be distributed monthly? If you managed to buy 500 kilos of anthracite, with what you had left, you should have about 800 kilos of coal and 1500 kilos of wood. Your kitchen stove should be able to use wood. You should try, so you can save the coal for the coldest weather. […]

8/31/1917.

I am writing early this morning. I've not yet received the mail. Yesterday was a turbulent day. About a dozen shells fell nearby. Fortunately, everyone was alert this time; no one was injured. But the orderlies and secretaries are not very brave. They may never have seen a battle; they certainly lack guts. Only Le Bienvenu comes off well and shows himself honorably. I don't much like to see that; it is irritating to be surrounded by cowards. It could be a serious problem in case of real danger. […]

Monday, September 3, 1917, 5:30 p.m.

I received at 4 p.m. your letters from the 30th and 31st. […] I read in the *communiqué* of September 1 that "along the Aisne front, after a brief preparation by the artillery, we attacked the enemy positions northwest of Hurtebise. Violent counterattacks were broken by our fire." […]

9/2/1917.

General Staff of Division SP 93. I have had so much to do these past two days that I could not find the time to write, even a short note. So here is the story of those days. A while ago we heard that we were going to have to leave Parnan on the morning of the 31st to spend the day at Longueval, sleep there and the next morning take the train for Fismes. Because it was very calm, the general cut out the intermediary step and decided that we would head directly to Fismes at 1 a.m. Only (there is always an "only") he had forgotten that orders had been issued for the famous attack to be launched the evening of the 31st. So the artillery preparation started on the 30th. I don't need to say that the *Boches*, when they saw all that was coming down on their heads, figured out immediately there was going to be an attack. So they reacted as best they could, and their best in this situation meant that they crushed Parnan with bombs. About 11:30 p.m., big shells started falling on the town and, in particular, in our area. […]

When the general saw that, he was sorry we had not left at 8 a.m. for Longueval. It was calm again by 3 a.m. so, quick, the orders, quick everyone load the vehicles, quick everyone hurry, get moving. We forgot half of our stuff. In the end, despite being dangerous, it was quite comical. We were on the way about 4:30, barely out on the open ground and the shells started whistling again. You should have seen the stampede, it was hilarious. I finally got, safely, to Longueval with

Le Bienvenu. […] I will long remember our flight from Parnan, it was worse than the flight out of Egypt.

In Longueval, we managed to eat at the home of a good woman but there were so many of us that we all slept on the same floor. […] We had the good luck, in the end, to go to Fismes in trucks. To recover from all the excitement, we wanted to have a good lunch. We found a welcoming house, and here is the menu: omelet, roast beef, beans with butter, salad, cheese and black grapes, 4 bottles of Mercury, two bottles of Champagne.

We set off at 2:00, gay and contented, happy to be alive and able to look around us. About 9:30 at night we got to the town of which for a long time has been said: "The Germans are still in N…" We realized, as we crossed the city in small groups, me with Le Bienvenu, a guy about my age and whom I like a lot, that this little city is intact. We had another 6 kilometers to go, so we took our time. Finally, happy and content, we arrived about 11:30, worn out, at the Chateau of Porquéricourt which is way out in the country, 800 meters from the town of that name. The superb building is not destroyed but totally emptied of furniture. Once more we lay down on the parquet floor (we make do) and sang at the top of our voices: "if the company had used some oil, we could see well in the wagons (bis) but…! the company didn't use any oil so we didn't see well in the wagons" and it all repeats. This morning we got moving early, for two reasons: we are very stiff and we needed to find food. After a good bit of discussion, we are on good terms with the concierge of the chateau, who has two charming angels (one of them slept with a German and has a little *Boche*, with red hair and porcelain eyes, but that doesn't matter!) […] There you have our two days. […]

9/7/1917.

I did not receive a letter today. […] Lemoine just alerted me that Captain Bouteville wants some music this evening. This is because Madame Denaux and her daughter, absent from the chateau since May, are coming back from Paris tonight. The general, who found the chateau empty, will receive them. He is suddenly going to find himself guest of these two women; they are the owners. Niverd, who is always ready for such circumstances, will come tune the piano. I have very little music with me, and especially not much ensemble music. Fortunately Lemoine will bring the Franck and Fauré Sonatas. […]

Monday, September 10, 1917, 3 p.m.

I received this morning your letter from the 7th. […] You practice, you read, you meditate. So that your meditation not be sterile, my dear child, I want you to compose a piece for your instrument, at least put on paper some ideas, some melodies that you must have in your head and will be a living symbol of your current life. [...]

9/8/1917.

I received today your two letters from September 6. [...] We did not play last night at the chateau; the two women were quite tired so we will play on Sunday. [...]

9/12/1917.

I received today your letters from September 9 and 10. Life goes on here in a rather monotone way without any major daily events. [...] We are supposed to leave Sunday morning for Guiscard where we will spend 3 days, and on the morning of the 19th, we will be in the active sector. [...]

It is totally expected that we provide food to our concierge and her two girls. When they pulled out of this area at the end of last February, the *Boches* took her husband, who was 50 years old. Since then the poor people have had no news of their husband and father. [...]

9/13/1917.

I received today your letter of September 11. [...] Grimoin, who was the pigeon keeper for the division, is leaving. He's from the class of 1895 and was able to get himself called back to a factory in Paris, as a carpenter. That's his profession. I may be the one who takes his place as pigeon keeper because I am not doing anything useful here. [...]

Certainly, money is disappearing quickly with the current prices for basic foodstuffs. That is no surprise. And the Americans will make the cost of living go even higher; they spend without counting. Their pay is so good they can do that. An ordinary soldier gets 5 francs a day, and we get 0,35. A regimental physician gets 3000 francs a month. In conditions like that, they throw money out the windows. [...]

9/14/1917.

I did not receive a letter, that is rather unusual. Something happened today that I'm going to share with you, although it may not be a good idea. Captain B, Chief of the General Staff since the departure of Commander Lambrigot, asked to see Caplet. He told him he had received a good number of anonymous letters about the quartet, saying that we were doing nothing at the division. He said he would have to take some action, send Maréchal and Magne back to their regiments and me to the division garrison with the request that they give me a job. Caplet was stupefied. [...]

I talked with Le Bienvenu about this; he said that Captain B. had been crazy for some time now and that for sure the general, even though he doesn't like music, was not in agreement. In short, he thinks there is nothing to worry about. [...]

9/17/1917.

Division Garrison, 5th Division 20th Company 274 Infantry Division. Things happened so fast that I did not have time to write. The nastiness has finally gotten its wish. Since this morning, I am here, at the division garrison, and Magne and Maréchal will have today joined the 74th and the 274th where I do not believe they will find anything to do. And all of this for no apparent reason. [...] We will still see each other. [...] We are supposed to play again tomorrow night at headquarters, and they will come for us. You can imagine that my friends are indignant about this sneaky, cowardly action against us. I really cannot tell you more because I fear my letters are being watched right now. [...]

9/19/1917.

I can finally give you more explanation for these feverish few days that have passed so quickly. It was last Friday that Caplet heard of the general's decision. There is no point in talking more about what happened, all brought about by the deep dislike and jealousy shared by the musicians in the band and the general. He had the impression that, no matter where we were, we were at rest; we were too much in demand and treated too well. The general took advantage of the absence of Commander Lambrigot, who has a lot of authority, to send me to the division garrison and poor Magne and Maréchal back to their regiments. Captain B himself told me that he would watch out for me and would expressly see the colonel at the garrison about the job I was to do. He did come see Colonel Guedon, a very nice man who greeted me very well, likes music, plays the piano quite well and had heard me in the past in Laval. I asked to be assistant to the supplies lieutenant who took me on as cyclist, without a bicycle, which is funny—so I have nothing to do.

Sunday morning Lieutenant Bourquin, head of an automobile unit which also polices the roads, came for us. This lieutenant, who is crazy about music, was responsible for our playing for the Army; he was a blessing for us and continues to be, he is great at working things out. We played in the afternoon of the 13th for an ambulance unit, a concert organized by Corporal Taillant, a friend of the lieutenant and also very clever. It was a great success. [...] We made the acquaintance of Captain Pallain, the son of the governor of the Bank of France, someone also very powerful in this army. [...]

When I got to the division garrison, the colonel welcomed me warmly. I went off to meet my fellow comrades in supplies, some of whom are old friends from the 129th. I spent the day with them, dined with them, and shared their sleeping quarters. The next morning, we set off for a village near Ham where we will stay when the division is on service. [...] I arrived at 10 a.m. in Noyon, went immediately to find Lieutenant Bourquin and Caplet. We got to work. [...] We presented a program as follows: the Andante and Finale from Boëllman's Sonata; a Chopin Prélude, the Svendsen *Romance*, Wieniawski's *Mazurka*, the Andante and Finale from Chausson's Piano Quartet, Saint-Saëns' *Rondo*, two waltzes for two violins, piano and cello that Caplet composed for Commander Pourel. The success surpassed our expectations. There were at least 50 officers, including a number of generals. That will help for the future. [...]

Obviously, here, in the garrison, the officers noticed all that, so the lieutenant in charge of lodgings offered me a little room where I am very comfortable. [...] Lieutenant Bourquin promised that he was almost sure that he would have the pleasure of having us in the TM 105 transport unit,[266] the unit charged with transporting everything from place to place in 10 days or so. That would be easiest in my case because I am 2nd class and a territorial. It will be a bit more difficult for Caplet who is sergeant; and even more so for Magne and Maréchal who are of the classes of 1910 and 1912. But we'll get there. Today Magne and Maréchal had to rejoin the 74th and the 274th respectively.

We were very lucky to have met Lieutenant Bourquin. Here's how it happened. You will agree with me that when danger gets close to me, destiny comes up with something to save me. Magne went by bicycle one day to Noyon, with two or three friends. He celebrated a bit too much. At 10 p.m. he heard someone playing piano through an open window of a house. He went to the window, saw a young woman and an older lady, declared that he was a pianist and asked whether he could come in and play the piano. They were a bit shocked. The lieutenant was nearby and saw a group near the window and asked what they wanted. He told Magne that it was too late that evening and set up a meeting the next day. So Magne played the piano, enchanted the lieutenant, told him about us; the lieutenant came with a car to get us and I played, Maréchal played, and that started the ball rolling. Providence at this moment gave us a fine perch which we really needed. [...]

9/20/1917.

So here I am, settled at the garrison. We are in a charming little town which fortunately has not been too badly damaged by the *Boche*. We are exactly 6 kilometers northwest of Ham. [...]

Things seem to be heating up at the division. All the young secretaries are being sent away. The changes have to be made by November 15. That will be a really big change: Lismon himself, class of 1905, will leave. Out of all the secre-

---

[266] TM, *transport du materiel.*

taries, only Le Bienvenu, who is class of 1898 like me, will stay. I may be called back to the division to do some sort of job. Once the clean-out is finished, they will turn to the territorials, and I am one of them. But I hope that, before then, I will be out of here, definitively. I cannot easily be moved to the rear as, on my papers, I am a violinist and they will never ask for musicians, rather workers in steel, iron, wood, engines, etc. It is not possible for me to leave. But have confidence all the same, I will manage something.

As to money, up to now, we should not be worried. We have not suffered tremendously from the war. If it becomes necessary, so you don't have to go without, which would be stupid, we will take some money from the treasury bonds. [...]

I don't understand why you talk to me the way you do. I have the deepest love for you; if it is not particularly obvious from the outside, it is still very deep. I can assure you that, if you were not there waiting for me, I would be in the front lines looking for a fight. [...]

Saturday, September 22, 1917, 12:30.

I still have no news from you. I hope that it is a change of position, in your favor, that is keeping you from writing. [...] My coal merchant did not deliver the 4 extra sacks of anthracite she had promised. I'm not upset by that because that would have taken all my money, even though I need heat. I had seen recently that wood was available at the town hall; I bought 500kg of sawed wood of a size that will fit in my kitchen stove if need be. The price was 13,20 for 100kg. I will have to pay 5 francs for transport which will make 71 francs. The wood will be delivered next Wednesday at 6 p.m. With the wood and the anthracite that I still have in the basement, I will not have to worry this winter. [...]

9/21/1917.

Today I received no mail. [...] The news of my friends is not good. At the division, all the secretaries have been sent elsewhere. Only Le Bienvenu, because of his age, is still there. The orderly sergeants, Pleindoux and Lemoine, will not be spared. It is a complete reshuffling and quite brutal. Magne, whom I saw yesterday, has today a spot in the division garrison. I was quite lucky to get him a job as secretary to the doctor of the division. That will keep him out of the company, which is a big step.

I was quite fortunate. On the 17th I played in an officer dining room, and the doctor was there. He likes music and we had a long conversation. When I heard that Magne was coming here, I went to try to get him a spot in the Red Cross and was lucky to be successful. So far there is no decision for Maréchal, who is still cyclist to the division. [...]

9/22/1917.

I received today your two letters from September 20. In principle, the division garrison is a place where troops stay until they are needed as reinforcement in areas occupied by the regiment. There are ways to manage to stay put for quite a while, but one day or another the departure has to happen. I have some friends who have been here for a year. I was recommended for this spot, I have all sorts of support, but I remember how cavalierly we were sent off and I will do my best to get away from here. […]

9/23/1917.

I did not receive anything today, Sunday. […] The weather is really splendid, though the nights are starting to be cool. I am fortunate to be well-housed and don't feel the cold at all. It must be beautiful in Brittany during this quiet time. I imagine the milky blue sea and the loveliness spread over everything. All that is so very far away, will we ever see it again? Ah, this horrible, long war, what a scourge! Fortunately, I am still in excellent health and endowed with a serene outlook, somewhat haughty, like Prometheus chained, nothing can affect his spirit. […]

9/24/1917.

I received this morning your letter of September 22. I am happy to announce that Magne, thanks to my intervention, has just been named secretary for the doctor major of the division. […]

I am shocked that you say you don't receive any letters; I write quite copiously every day. You accuse me of not caring, you are terribly mistaken. It is just that, when I'm doing everything I can to get out of a bad situation, I don't waste my time writing about uncertainties. […]

Lieutenant Bourquin told Magne that he will come see us before Saturday. He realizes that it is important for officers to come visit us. Here, the colonel and all the officers are totally considerate. It's quite amusing to think that I, a simple soldier, 2nd class, thanks to my bow and the magic of my talent, can make so many jealous, hostile people bow to our wishes. My violin keeps them in check. […]

9/26/1917.

I just got back; Lieutenant Primoire did not really understand what was taking place. The automobile group in question was having an outdoor celebration, sack races, jousts, etc. […] There was obviously no place for me at that festival. The lieutenant in charge of the event was very sorry for my trouble, he made all sorts of excuses and promised to arrange something in the future, more like a theater show. I had a nice car ride and could see that the town where the automobile group is stationed has been totally destroyed. [...]

I am attached to the supplies garrison as cyclist, a position that did not exist and was created for me. I will even learn how to ride a bicycle, which is not very hard. [...]

9/27/1917.

I received today your letter of September 25. That was the anniversary of our offensive two years ago, where I lost a good friend from the 23rd territorial. [...]

Yesterday an order was issued sending the class of 1897 immediately to the rear, so the class of 1898, which is mine, is now the oldest left at the front. [...]

9/28/1917.

Today I received your letter from September 26. [...] As I told you, I would do the impossible to get away from here; I no longer have any confidence in the people in charge who, after all we have done, got rid of us in such a disgusting way. [...] I will never accept that my life depends on the good or bad will of the officers I know, who are so second-rate. I am putting up with my fate for now, but as soon as I can, I will leave joyfully. [...]

9/29/1917.

I received today your letter of September 27. [...] Magne and I will go on leave about the same time, around the 10th. We may examine carefully what we can do to get into the TM 105. His future mother-in-law, who is powerful and has a lot of family, may be able to help us out. [...]

10/2/1917.

I received today your two letters of September 30. [...] Once the bicycle ordered arrives it would be ridiculous not to be able to ride it; and if I don't, the news will spread around, and I will have to leave the supplies garrison. Riding a bicycle will serve me well. Why didn't I go to Noyon to get my music? Because I would have had to walk 12 kilometers to Ham. By bicycle, that would be nothing. But here I am, stupidly stuck in place because I have no means of getting around, I can't expect them to send a car for me all the time. It is stupid on my part not to be able to ride one of those things; I have often bitterly regretted not being able to ride and have missed out on some important events because of it. The past two days I've taken lessons from Cavanagh and, in a week, I will be able to ride like everyone else. It is not that hard and is surely much less tiring than walking. [...]

10/3/1917.

I received this morning your letter of October 1. [...] I will probably try to leave on Tuesday the 9th on the 10:30 p.m. train. [...] That way I will arrive in Vincennes around 6:30 a.m. On Sunday, despite Magne's absence, I will play in church in the morning, accompanied by Sergeant Lefevre, a fine amateur who is secretary in the colonel's office. [...] I am rereading Sophocles and after I've finished one of his plays, I reread a play by Aeschylus. I prefer the latter. He is much more a poet, his charming comparisons are delightful, but he also has his share of grandeur, all very beautiful.

10/4/1917.

I received today Cunault's card and two letters, one from the first and one from the 2nd of October. [...] I forgot to tell you I had received the clippings from *L'Information*. I saw the little paragraph about the ministerial decision to give 2 francs a day to the *poilus* on pass. That decision is only fair. The officers and the non-commissioned officers certainly get their pay, being on pass doesn't change anything. I believe that the government should give the men on pass what it spends for their food, that is 2,54 francs a day. Just because you get three meager leaves a year, you have to starve during that time which is supposed to be for relaxation. Not everyone has drawers full of money and it is sad to think that these *poilus* have to work during their leave in order to eat. This tiny allowance, however overdue, is not a favor, far from it. [...]

I see in the papers that they plan to reduce the sugar allowance to 500 grams a month and give out cards for bread. With poor harvests and the carelessness that is everywhere, it is all waste and need. [...] Here, for example, there are a lot of apples; do you think anyone picks them? Not at all. Two-thirds of the production rots under the trees. When the DD was in Libermont,[267] the men cut the rye the *Boches* had planted, and which the growers said was magnificent. So the men harvested it, but it stayed there and spoiled because there were no orders to do anything with it. It is the same for everything. Here at the DD men play dumb, when everyone should be at work in the fields. When you see all this, then you read all the articles in the papers, you shrug your shoulders; action would serve better than words. I feel sorry for the intelligent people who want to take charge of all this mess. [...]

Lucien had home leave for the next two weeks.

---

[267] *Dépot de la Division.*

I've not had a minute to myself since I left home. [...] We got to Ham about 5:00. We immediately joined the bursar Martel who was organizing the concert. We rehearsed the Brahms Dances, and a few other little pieces with piano accompaniment. We slept at the Hôtel de France in rooms reserved by the bursar. Yesterday, Sunday, after the concert in which Nelly Martyl sang (parenthetically, she was very nice to me, and told me she had written to me), we went back to Noyon where there was a concert at 8:30. [...]

10/24/1917.

I am in a hurry to write to you today and will give you all the details of recent days. We gave a concert Sunday afternoon in Ham with the greatest success. [...] This time General Humbert was there, and he quite appreciated our concert. [...] The officers were all extremely nice, offered us supper, and Captain Pallain begged us to stay for breakfast the next day, and invited us for lunch also. I slept in a wonderful room with an excellent bed. The next day, after lunch, Captain Pallain told us he was determined to put us out of harm's way. He is going to put Maréchal and Magne in the wireless unit; Caplet as pigeon keeper, and I will probably go to the TM 105. All that will happen very soon. The captain had some derogatory comments about our division, which I cannot repeat. But he told me that he considered us the country's heritage which, at all costs needed to be kept safe. [...]

10/25/1917.

I received this morning your letter of the 22nd. [...] Colonel Guedon received us as friends, shaking hands almost enthusiastically. Never has anyone paid so much attention to us since our departure from the division. I think the general must find us a big nuisance; he doesn't understand all the esteem the higher ups have for us. When I think that Captain P told the general that we were a French treasure and because of that they needed to watch over us! I would have loved to see his face when he heard those words. [...]

10/26/1917.

I am sending this letter with someone going on leave so it reaches you more quickly. Today I've received no mail. Magne and I left Offoy and arrived at the division about 3:30 and set immediately to getting settled. We are staying in rooms set aside for cyclists where there are extra beds. [...]

Today we started to work on *La Croix Douloureuse* by Père Lacordaire,[268] which Caplet set to music. It is a very lovely thing with quite profound feeling; when I know it better, I will tell you what I think. In any case it is a sophisticated work tending toward the modern. I do not know what our audience will think of it. It will be sung by a guy with a lovely bass voice whom Caplet is teaching. He knows very little about music but he has good musical sense and comes to us with great good will which is worth a lot. We will probably add 3 other pieces, also by Caplet: *Notre Père, Je vous salue Marie, Je crois en Dieu*, all in French, with a little prelude. It's quite a lot of work. Taillardat, a tenor in the 6th Division, will come work on those pieces. I think we will give the concert again in Noyon, with Martyl as soloist. […]

Magne and Maréchal are asking to take a course in wireless which would take place near Noyon. Captain P is supporting this request. It is the first maneuver to get us all out of here and I hope it will be a question of just a few days now. I stay well out of the way and make no effort to chat nor to socialize with the officers. After all they've done, there is no reason to be nice to them. And we will not play for them, even if they ask us. We will find some excuse. […]

Sunday, October 21, 1917, 5 p.m.

I am writing a bit late but I did a lot of cleaning up. I put your room back in order in case you can come tomorrow as you hoped. The weather today is simply magnificent, a splendid sky, a perfect day to air out both our bedrooms. I also cleaned mine and having done that, set to my correspondence. I have nothing new to tell you; my grippe seems to be mostly gone but not completely. […]

10/27/1917.

I received today your letter of the 24th. There are turbulent events about us. You will understand. […] Two days ago, an officer from the Army, sent by those who are in charge of us, came to have the "two young ones" make a request,[269] as was agreed. It worked its way up the hierarchy to the division. The effect was like a bomb: General Lebrun, once alerted, came yesterday, furious, and demanded immediately to see Caplet and asked him why we wanted to leave the division. Caplet explained the injustice done to us, especially to me. Lebrun told him that he does not want us to leave. He gave orders to put me with the pigeon keepers, with Caplet. All that is just fine but doesn't please me. […] General Lebrun was breathing fire. Will he go so far as to ask the Army to keep us here? I don't know. But we can boast that we have made people talk about us. […]

---

[268] Henri Lacordaire (1802-1861). Caplet composed *La Croix Douloureuse* during the war for his fellow soldiers.
[269] Magne and Maréchal.

I will keep you informed about all this. In the midst of all this commotion, we continue to work on our Mass for November 1, as though nothing was happening. Caplet's music is becoming clearer. I think it will impress our listeners, especially the *Notre Père*. It would be better, obviously, to hear those works with an orchestra to add color. The feeling is poetic if a bit monotonous. There is no denying that Caplet is a very gifted musician, unfortunately lazy. He could have written so much. [...]

10/28/1917.

I just received your letter from the 25th. I am astounded that you haven't received a letter because I write absolutely every day, no matter what is happening. I sent a letter with someone going on leave, you must have that one. Caplet has a very bad cold. I'm actually quite worried about him; it seems to be turning into bronchitis. I make grogs for him using my rum because we can't find any here. This morning General Lebrun called Caplet. We told him he was in the field; he will call back at 10 a.m. It has to be about the request made by the two young ones. [...]

Wednesday, October 31, 1917, 4 p.m.

I received this morning your letter from October 28 and the one from the 29th with a stamp. [...] So Caplet has a cold? You are taking care of him, making him grogs. That is very charitable of you but you will have nothing left when you need it. He goes on leave very often; he should bring some back. You are always the one giving him things and you get no credit. [...]

10/30/1917.

I received today your letter of 27 October, and I am very hurt by what it says: not only do I send you a letter every day, but even more, these past few days I gave two to men going on leave so they would reach you faster. It has to suffice when I assure you that I am not corresponding with any other person. I have no intention of imitating the people around me. They do what they like, and I do the same. As for saying that they are of bad character, you go a bit far. I have not at all lost my desire to work; on the contrary, it becomes painful at times. Unfortunately, the conditions of daily life here make all continuity impossible. For example, there is no place to practice. We rehearse in the chapel where it is beastly cold. There is not a free spot for individual practice. [...] You are creating specters and then suffering because of them; it's very hard on me to know that you are tormenting yourself with things that aren't real. [...]

11/2/1917.

Posted to the division. I didn't have time to write yesterday. Here's a bit of detail about the day. As I told you, I slept in a good bed. About 8:30 we were at the church in Ham, and Mass took place according to the planned program. I played the Bach *aria* accompanied by strings. In the afternoon, we played a concert at the theater in Ham organized by the sub-orderly. [...] Then, about 5:00 we set off by auto and about 6:00 we were in front of the place where Captain Pallain is staying. We dined with all the men who make up the 2nd and 3rd army office, and with Nelly Martyl. After dinner, we rehearsed with her a hymn to those who died last February which I don't like very much. We went to bed about midnight. [...] This morning at 9:00 we were in the Cathedral, which is beautiful and has lovely acoustics. The service was superb. [...]

11/6/1917.

I received today your second letter of the 3rd, a letter from the 4th, and a package with a bottle of rum and a light undershirt. I thank you for this shipment, but I still have at least two-thirds left of the rum I have. [...]

Something completely unbelievable happened yesterday. [...] Captain Liberos, running into Caplet in the course of the afternoon, said to him: "Caplet, come play for us this evening. You can let the commander hear your pieces that were so successful in Ham." I was disgusted when Caplet recounted this conversation and this request. So there you have it, those people who kicked us out like beggars have taken us back because they were forced to. So last night we played in the dining room of the chateau where there is a baby grand Pleyel, unfortunately badly maintained. They treated us like friends, and we parted with the fond hope of seeing each other again. I have to say it was truly laughable. The division personnel who have followed with growing interest the events surrounding us for the past month couldn't believe their eyes. [...]

11/7/1917.

I just this minute received your letter of November 5. I am shocked that you are not receiving my mail; in spite of moving around, I do what I can in the midst of this bohemian life to find the time for your daily letter, and it is not always easy, believe me. [...]

11/8/1917.

[...] We are working on two new Brahms dances for which Caplet is making parts for viola, cello, and bass. The public loves those dances. Caplet hates Brahms. In fact, he likes very little other than Debussy, Ravel, and himself.

I am writing this morning very early, before mail time, because we are leaving about 11:30 and the morning will be filled with rehearsal. We are performing the final Trio from the First Act of *Faust*,[270] with Taillardat, Cosson, and Martyl, accompanied by piano, violin and cello. Just imagine the effect that will have. […]

11/10/1917.

[…] The theater for the ambulance company in Driant is a shack. The stage is quite well arranged; they made a pit in front of it big enough for a dozen musicians. When we arrived, it was dark, the electricity was not turned on. And there Caplet, not seeing the pit, fell into it. He squashed two stands and a stool and kicked Maréchal's cello which happened to be there. He didn't do much harm to himself, but his foot cracked the back of the cello. Fortunately, it's on the side, near a corner, about 15 centimeters. In that spot, it will not bother the sound, but the instrument will have to go back to Paris to be repaired without delay. Despite all those events, we started the concert and met with great success. The Trio from *Faust* with Martyl was a triumph. […]

11/12/1917.

When I got back this morning, I found your two letters from the 9th, and one from the 10th. […] With respect to my job as pigeon keeper, I am going to learn the details.

There is a concert on the 17th, in Paris, where Caplet's works will be played—he wants to be there. He will be away for 4 days including travel, and, of course, he is leaving on the sly. I will therefore replace him for those 4 days. He is obviously counting on me. He will give me written instructions; I will have to do the repositioning of the pigeons. […]

11/13/1917.

I received today your second letter from November 10 and the one from the 11th. […] I am still lodged with the cyclists, in a little room with a fireplace and only two of us. […] At first, I was in a room where we were 5. After tomorrow evening, when Caplet leaves, I will lodge at the T85.[271] I'll be in what they call a pigeon loft, a vehicle with pigeons, a large, double thick tent where Caplet and two men who take care of the birds sleep, and a hut that serves as office for Caplet. So tomorrow I will go sleep under the tent for a few days. It is pretty

---

[270] Charles Gounod (1818-1893).
[271] The pigeon units were identified by T plus a number.

comfortable; there are three cots, and one doesn't get cold with the protection of the double thick tent. [...]

Thursday, November 15, 1917, 2 p.m.

[...] So there you are in the company of pigeons? I don't know whether they coo or cry. They are probably trained to make as little noise as possible. [...]

Friday, November 16, 1917, 2:30 p.m.

[...] I received this morning your letter from the 13th. [...] You will be living in a tent for a few days to help out Caplet. I don't like that very much. It won't be for long, then we will see whether Caplet will keep his promise to ask General Lebrun to take both of you. [...]

I have always shared, in a very clear way, my most intimate thoughts so you know where you stand. Frankness is an important quality: cultivate it. It is like a rare flower to be picked and held close to your heart to give you the power to contemplate it often. Speaking of flowers, I sent today a delicate little Bengal rose which bloomed again just for you. [...]

11/14/1917.

I received today your letter from November 12 and also a letter from Vessot, in response to mine, in which he announces his nomination to the automobile corps. I am very happy for him; three years at the front, in the trenches and on the battlements is really hard. [...]

This is a moment of great rest, here at the T85 the pigeons do nothing. They stuff themselves with food; they almost die of hunger while they are in the trenches. That is done on purpose, so they are eager to get back to the roost where they are well taken care of. There are 100 pigeons in a pigeon coop. You see, it's quite a big group. It is interesting; the creatures are very pretty. We use a hunting rifle to shoot the kestrels and sparrowhawks who gather around the pigeon coop looking for prey. [...] Out here, in the fields, the pigeon keepers catch rabbits and partridges, which supplement their food. The men taking care of the pigeons are almost all from the North, where pigeon keeping is common. [...]

November 17, 1917, 9:30 p.m.

[...] I have to tell you: this morning I received an invitation with the program for the recital in which some of Caplet's works were played. Thus, he did not forget to send me the invitation, which is very nice of him, giving me the pleasure of hearing some real music. I very much like his *3 Prières* and *La Croix*

413

Douloureuse as well as *Le Vieux Coffret* and *Solitude*. Caplet's music is poetic and fine; he's a true artist and I would be delighted if he could finish the solo for violin he was working on.

The little hall where the recital took place is small and doesn't have a special room for the artists, so they were mixed in among all the others. I was able to see Caplet surrounded by people. I left my seat in order to thank him. [...] He took a while to recognize me, then came to talk to me. [...] He spoke about you and said that, after all that has happened, you would be with him and the pigeons. [...] May God watch over you; stay well, and a long letter please? [...]

11/15/1917.

I received today your second letter from the 12th and the one from the 13th. [...] I've been at the front now for three years without a single evacuation. That is something of a record; few of my friends can say the same. Being evacuated for a slight wound or an illness might be considered something like rest. Two or three months in the rear would be very nice; right now, a sprain which would help me avoid the hardships of winter would be welcome. Being constantly in mud, cold, and lacking any sort of comfort ends up becoming very hard to take. One doesn't really get used to it, despite what Mme Duez says. [...]

11/17/1917.

I received this morning your second letter of November 14 and one from the 15th. [...] It is very foggy right now, which makes it hard for our pigeons to work; in such weather we can't let them out for fear that many would get lost. We exchange the pigeons in the trenches every two days, on the even days. Right now, a good many have colds; their feet are too often wet when they are in the trenches. We put tincture of iodine in their throats. It's totally comical; they roll their funny eyes. [...]

Our pigeons do coo, but very sweetly, if I can put it that way. They are well-trained and are much more intelligent than I would have thought. The good fellow who cares for them here at T85 is from Lille, a great fan and owner of pigeons during peacetime. The animals are sacred to him and woe to anyone who touches them. He knows them all very well, their good points and their bad. He gives them names and it is funny to see the pigeons sort of answering roll call. They are all very tame. When the entire coop takes flight and circles around us, it is quite a lovely sight. [...]

Our quiet sector is slowly becoming more active and if that continues it will become a pretty bad place to be. There are rumors of a departure on the 24th, but nothing certain has come down. [...]

November 19, 1917, 2:30 p.m.

[…] I received this morning your letters from November 16 and 17. […] I see you are interested in the pretty little creatures you have charge of in Caplet's absence. Papa Marie was fond of homing pigeons and took care of them when he was younger. He had all sorts: some gray with a white collar, some with a big beak and red bumps like turkeys, all the colors of the rainbow—I remember them well. […]

Send me Caplet's military address so I can congratulate him on the concert. There are still no lights on the streets in Paris but I was in an area we had lived in so I wasn't lost. […]

11/18/1917.

[…] My pretty little grasshopper was at the concert; she was there to hear Caplet's songs, *Les Prières* and *La Croix Douloureuse*. I know all about that because today, after lunch, about 2 p.m., at my T85, I saw Caplet who had just arrived. He told me had seen someone from the rue du Moulin. I immediately realized he had been true to his promise and had sent you an invitation. […] He seems very satisfied by his trip. I know the songs you heard, based on poems by Rémy de Gourmont. Of course, I've never heard them sung. I am delighted you heard all that so you can tell me what impression his music makes on you. […]

Tuesday, November 20, 1917, 5 p.m.

[…] No news yet; I hope this evening to have the pleasure of your chicken scratches. […] Try to get two shirts and a pair of socks. All that is very expensive. Mathilde is knitting a pair of socks for you. I had to buy four 50 g balls of wool, not of the best quality, for 1,60. There, you see how much a pair of socks cost. Find a little ring or aluminum heart to thank her; she won't let me pay her for her time. […] There is every reason to think that there will not be enough coal and the ration cards will be good for nothing. What a life! […]

11/20/1917.

I received today your long letter from the 17th and one from the 18th. […]. Don't worry about after the war, for sure I will work on composition. In terms of the violin, I won't need anyone to push me, I will push myself, but for that I will not stay in France. America will be there, and it offers enormous possibilities. It would be stupid not to look to the future. […]

Thursday, November 22, 1917, 3:30 p.m.

[…] I received this morning your letter from the 20th. […] I sent you the program from the November 17th concert. Woolett had put on the program one of his songs, some little piano pieces, and his Prélude, Fugue and Finale. He is learned and well taught; one might reproach him for his music being a bit too scientific—meticulous and reasoned. He seems to be a thoughtful artist who loves what he does.

After the war there will be much to do in America and an artist of your talent should be able to do well. What is more, you must. That is why you should have worked with Caplet during this war, if for no other reason than to force your brain to think, reflect, search. That would have been a relaxing cerebral exercise, just like gymnastics for the body. […] Don't show so much pride with me; admit that I am right to tell you these things. […] My love for you knows no limits and I would like to see you the happiest person on earth, the greatest artist in the world, the most passionate about his music, reaping the rewards of all your hard work. That is what I wish, and you should not wish for less. So you must do everything possible to get yourself in your rightful place. Be nicer and don't get so angry. […]

Friday, November 23, 1917.

To keep and meditate on: Horace, Book 1, Letter 18. To counsel you if you ever need a counselor:

"Flee the one who asks questions, for he talks too much and open ears do not retain faithfully what they are told; and words, once let out, are in the air forever."

11/21/1917.

I received today your two letters of November 19. […] Carrier pigeons are interesting; I did not know that Papa Marie kept pigeons when younger. The pigeons have two enemies: hawks and falcons. We need to be constantly vigilant to keep them away. I stay with my pigeons because I'm in the pigeon keeper service, that is my job. There are three of us, me, Caplet, and a sergeant. When Caplet and I are away, Niel gets stuck with all the work. Two other men are attached to each pigeon station, to care for and train the animals. […]

We are here to put the pigeons to work, relieve them from the trenches, put on the tubes, and make sure that the messages reach the DI as quickly as possible. When all is quiet, there is almost no pigeon service. We become important when there is danger; we hold in our hands the fate of many comrades. The pigeons are used in the front lines when other forms of communication are impossible:

broken telephone lines, barriers on the route that block runners. At the most tragic moment, the pigeon is there, carrying news and requests for help. [...]

The *Croix Douloureuse* is the piece of Caplet's I like best. You keep talking about working but it is absolutely impossible. Once I find a quiet corner, I am quickly surrounded by guys arguing or playing cards with loud shouts. Nine times out of ten there is no table. Very often I write on a plank on my knees. In Amblonville, in our tiny room, Père Bernard and I went out of our way to let Caplet work a bit. That is where he started work on his three pieces and his *Croix Douloureuse*. He worked a bit more this winter in Génicourt because, as director of the theater, he was able to get a little room, that is, someplace calm. He finished them; then with the excuse of his trip to Algeria, he was able to shut himself up for a month at his home in Le Havre. That's where he polished them and two little songs. There you have the result of two years of work. It's not much, and Caplet was always privileged to have place to work and able, with a variety of pretexts, to go on leave, which let him work a bit.

It was only when I was with the division, where I had a little room and quiet, that I could work a bit. I did manage to practice violin there which I'd never been able to do before. I had dreams of working on counterpoint, but unfortunately that didn't last. It is not in a tent, with my two other pigeon keepers, that I can work on anything at all.

It's been a week since I opened my violin case; I have no place at the division to practice if I had the time. The chapel is a glacial tomb; after 15 minutes one is chilled to the bone. You think we can do as we please; no, that is not exactly the case. [...]

You are quite wrong in thinking me lazy; you don't understand that, in order to write to you every day as I am doing, my hands freeze and I am blown by the winds. For sure, if I were in a room with a fire, or a heated office, with two or three hours of work a day, like many of those fine gentlemen messieurs, then I could practice. Unfortunately, that is not my case. More often than not my feet are in water and mud rather than in front of the fire. There is a price to everything. Those fine guys in the offices always have colds, and I am in excellent health. [...]

Second letter, same day.

[...] A friend just back from Ham told me that we may be here until the middle of December. Apparently huge numbers of French troops are passing through Ham on the way to the North, to reinforce the English whose effort there seems to have been remarkably successful. [...]

11/22/1917.

I received today three letters, two with only clippings from the newspapers, the third a letter from November 20. [...] This has been a very busy day. Early this morning, at 6:30, I went to Noyon by auto to get Maréchal's cello. Once I got back to Auroir, we immediately rehearsed the Brahms Dances and two extracts from the ballet *Coppelia*.[272] I was with Mayer on violin, Niverd on cello, Delmas on contrabass, Couliboeuf on clarinet, and a flutist. Caplet was at the piano—it was a little orchestra. [...] The English general was very enthusiastic. He asked the general to let us come to his place. The success with all those Englishmen was such that the general came to thank us. It's a bit funny.

Lieutenant Brunet, who is a bit crazy, sometimes says very funny things. So he told me, "So, Durosoir, you will have seen some really funny things during the war!" And it is absolutely true. [...]

Lucien was able to make a short trip home between the dates of these letters.

11/27/1917.

Of course, I don't have a letter yet today. Last night, I moved out of my tent. One of the men who care for the pigeons came back 48 hours early from leave. He wanted his spot back, the one I was occupying. I willingly gave it to him, and, with his help, I carried my things to a little room in the chateau where Lemoine sleeps: there was an empty bed. [...]

11/28/1917.

As expected, I have not received a letter. I should have one tomorrow. Last night we had quite an adventure. A *Boche* plane, lost in the fog, landed 400 meters from the division. An officer from the plane, who didn't know whether he had landed in France or behind the German lines, came to get information. Obviously, recognized immediately as German, he was captured along with his comrade who was watching over the plane. [...] The aviation unit came to get the German plane which was brand new. [...] The cannon is roaring from the direction of the English troops. [...]

This morning the T85 moved; it's heading toward the rear. [...] That may signal a new departure, truly no one knows anything. Because of the move, I worked quite hard this morning. I helped Caplet move his shack which was next to the pigeon loft. It is a thing that can be taken apart and isn't good for much.

---

[272] Léo Delibes (1836-1891), choreographed by Arthur Saint-Léon (1821-1870).

The rain comes in and as soon as the weather is cold, it is unbearable. It's only good in nice weather. [...]

11/30/1917.

I received this morning your letter from the 28th, and yesterday those from the 26th and 27th. I could not write yesterday because of all the flurry around the concert for the English. [...] Now I will tell you about it. We played some dances by Brahms, then I played *Les Airs Bohémiens* and *Obertass*. Jouatte, a singer in the 6th Division who came to replace Taillardat who is on leave, sang two songs. He has a very nice voice.

We arrived at the English division about 3 p.m., went to look at the hall—very nicely set up. Then we had tea with butter, pâté de foie, jam, celery, in short, English style but excellent (parenthetically, their bread is delicious). It was a long concert; we took a break in the middle. Aside from us, there was a professional troop of artists and clowns, one of whom dressed as a woman and sang soprano perfectly. Those artists do nothing but perform, they are very good and make a very cohesive group. It's obvious that they work hard. That lasted until 8:30. We then had supper with cold meat, hard sausage, jam, cookies, tea and beer. We returned by car, totally charmed by the wonderful reception and the courtesy of the English officers. That division is leaving in the morning for a more active area and we lose excellent neighbors. [...]

12/3/1917.

I received this morning your letter of December 1. I also received the newspaper articles and the bouquet of flowers which I will keep, and for which I thank you. Alas, yes, I am now 39 years old, and the war doesn't look at all like it wants to end. It is frightening to hear the cannon fire in the English sector. Apparently, the battle is fierce, and the ground is piled with cadavers. We get news from the English liaison. The *Boches* brought Von Bulow's army back from Italy and a good number of divisions from the Russian front. All of that will not result in the success they are hoping for. [...]

12/5/1917.

I received this morning your letter from the 3rd. [...] It has been very cold for a few days, that reminds us of Génicourt. You could send me by train, registered of course, my goatskin sleeping bag. This is the time when I will appreciate all its warmth and softness. I still cannot bleach my underthings; that is why I send them to you. With the cold we've had for the past few days, I can no longer work on music. I don't have a heated room and it was 8 below zero—I can't do anything. This afternoon I think I will go to the room of a captain who is in charge of agriculture in this sector. He lives in a barracks; his room is heated by a little stove. He rather likes music and he gave me permission this morning to go practice there for an hour or two. I'm going to take advantage of it, but I fear he will be there, and I'll spend my time playing for him, which is not at all what I need to do.

For several days, I've gone to bed very early; first it is very cold and then the lighting is poor. I still have my *bougie Pigeon* and the fuel costs me nothing, but it is freezing cold and I don't manage to read in bed. I get up about 7 a.m., clean up, then have my coffee with bread and butter. About 8 o'clock I go get my mail and Caplet's, then I go see him about the pigeons. During the morning, I will swap the pigeons or go to one of the pigeon lofts to do what is needed. In addition to that, I go to Forestte to purchase food for the kitchen; I come back to the kitchen where I give the cook some advice and sometimes some help, and we eat at noon. Then it is WC time, then my time to write until 3:30. I practice violin until 6:00, at least right now. I go back to see whether Caplet has received any orders for the pigeon service. I return to the kitchen. While watching over dinner, I read the papers and a bit of Horace, at table at 7:00, finish at 8:15. I make a hygiene stop, I go up to my little room. I organize my things, make my bed, and at 9:00 p.m., I am in bed. That is the routine of life when nothing unexpected happens to upset the calm. But it is rare to have three days in a row without the unexpected. Yesterday, taking advantage of clear weather, the *Boche* planes bombed the billeting sites. Ham, in particular, received 35 bombs. There were few victims, fortunately. The nice weather always brings out this type of unwanted bird. [...]

12/6/1917.

I didn't receive any letter. I only received an envelope with two steel chanterelles.[273] Caplet went to Noyon today. [...] During the day I will thus stay in his little room so I can respond to anything to do with the pigeon coop. I will take advantage of that to keep warm with his fire, using his wood without any compunction. In fact, he told me not to worry about it. [...]

The division officers are now going to ask for music. They want to hear us from time to time, so they say. They are now courting us and are afraid to see us leave. They do not realize the support we have and how enormous was their error. [...]

The *Boche* planes wander around and drop bombs everywhere in this region. Up to now, from what I hear, no significant damage. But hearing all those dirty birds buzzing around during the night, dropping their turds, gets on the nerves. [...]

---

[273] The violin's top string.

12/7/1917.

I received today your two letters from December 4 and 5. […] Time passes, and we still see no solution; the *Boches* are always getting the advantage. The armistice has been concluded on the Russian front. If the Romanians do not do the same thing, they will be crushed fairly soon. The English are having a very hard time right now, as the *Boches* react with formidable effort. They have retaken Marcoing and since the start of the counter offensive have taken 9000 English prisoners and 138 cannons. […] In all that, there is nothing to celebrate, and the future is gloomy. With all the forces brought back from Russia, the *Boches* will pounce on us and make life hard for us. There are new massacres on the horizon! It's very sad, as the heroic *poilu* is going to pay for the countless mistakes since the start of the war. […]

12/8/1917.

I received today your letter of December 6 and I am writing quite late; I was particularly bothered. Last night Captain Libéros asked for me and told me: "Madame Pavie, the owner of the chateau, just arrived from Paris. The general invited her for tomorrow and he is asking you to play some music after lunch. So please alert Caplet." You get the picture. I told him immediately that Caplet was out in the field, probably with the 74th music regiment working on the orchestration of his *Croix Douloureuse* for military band. Fine, I left him. Two hours later, the captain asked for me again and told me that they called the 74th and Caplet was not there, so where is he? "If he was not at the 74th, he is probably at the 5th, or with an officer who invited him, or maybe he went to Ham to see General Lebrun to settle on a date for his *Croix Douloureuse* to be played." Hearing all that, the captain answered: "Really, all that is quite a nuisance; we cannot reach him and the general wants very much to give a concert for this lady." I replied: "Rather than run after Caplet, without any assurance of finding him, how about calling the 5th and asking for Maréchal?" The captain caught the ball on a bounce and said: "It's agreed." So Maréchal arrived this morning.

One could say that Caplet put me through a rough quarter of an hour. All's well that ends well. That they should suspect something is none of my business. I answered with assurance and calm and the situation was saved. When Maréchal arrived this morning, we immediately started to rehearse. That fellow is a good musician but never has time to practice (he is nurse in the 5th) and is quite rusty. […]

12/9/1917.

I received today your letter of December 7. […] Mme Pavie, the chatelaine, who is a pretty woman, talked with me yesterday after a little concert. She finds her chateau in poor shape. I replied that one only had to look around a bit in this area to see that she is lucky the chateau is still standing. The furniture has more or less disappeared but, really, by comparison, she has nothing to complain about. She also told me, and I had a good laugh, that it was tremendous to still be so agile. I almost said what was on the tip of my tongue, "at your service, Madame" but that was too much like a soldier. [...]

12/10/1917.

I received today your two letters from December 7 and 8. [...] True, territorials are sometimes (rarely) called to join the auto brigade, even not knowing how to drive. I only saw that once this year, last July. But the Central Command will never let me put my name on a list; they want to keep me here. I was assured again these past days of all the good will possible. This turn of event is easy to understand. The general staff, including the general, have measured the extent of the error that was committed. They have realized that those in high places want us to stay with the division but also want them to leave us alone. Never have I been the object of so much attention. For sure, nowhere else could I be more independent and have so little to do. [...]

12/11/1917.

I received today your two letters of December 8 and 9. [...] Caplet got back last night quite late; he took his time. He had lunch in Noyon with Lieutenant Bourquin who asked him to go see the archbishop to arrange a religious concert on December 23 at the Cathedral. On the program will be *Les Prières* and *Croix Douloureuse*. [...]

12/12/1917.

I received today your letter from December 10. [...] I am totally fine here and would only change places if I could go directly to the 105. Here I am very free, as free as one can be as part of an army at the front. [...] A lot of people who never paid any attention to us have said, since our return, "Durosoir must be a celebrity and must know very powerful people to have been able to come back to the division that way." So now it is "Mister Durosoir," and tips of the hat in all directions. [...]

12/14/1917.

I received today your second letter from the 11th and the one from the 12th. We still have no answer from our singers. Nevertheless, even if Caplet doesn't have an answer tomorrow, he will go to Paris. He absolutely has to work with Vieuille, who is supposed to sing *Croix Douloureuse*. And I need to stay here to rehearse the strings. So it is Caplet who will bring back my instruments. You have to take them to the address he will give me. He apologizes that he cannot come to the house to get them, but he has too much to do. [...]

You should probably send, in the double box, the Guarnerius and the Guadagnini. Add the box of rosin in the drawer of my nightstand. And for bow, you will send my Lupot. It's the one I prefer: you will recognize it by the large frog and the case covered with mother-of-pearl. [...] In addition to the Lupot, send a Lamy.[274] You should also ask for three G strings wound by Serdet. Ask him not to use the new system which he used for the last ones. [...] I didn't like it very much, the strings seemed to roll. [...]

Caplet will take them to Noyon. Except when I am using them, they will stay in Captain Pallain's room. We will tell the public about the instruments on which we are playing, it is good publicity. I will bring them back home. I don't know whether that will be on Christmas or the next day. We may be kept here by the Army for Midnight Mass or the *Réveillon*; in any case I won't be any later. I am delighted to let my instruments be heard in these conditions, in a beautiful cathedral with such lovely sound. [...]

Second letter, same day.

I sent the letter I just wrote with someone going on leave, you will have it soon. [...] Caplet says he will not have enough time during his brief stay in Paris to take care of my instruments. Since he doesn't want to bring them, or leave them with a third person, and I have to stay here because of the pigeons and rehearsals, here's what he proposes. He will send Mayer on the evening of the 20th; Mayer will arrive in Paris at 10:00. He will go to Vincennes on the 21st, get the instruments, and get take the 8 a.m. train on the 22, at the same time as Caplet. Mayer will thus show up at your door. You will easily recognize him; he is in the picture with Captain Faillant at the aviation unit. [...]

Caplet is in quite a state with all the organization. I think he will soon go to Noyon as there are many things to put in place. We will be 14 to house and feed. And that does not count the artists coming from Paris. [...]

Monday, December 17, 1917, 2:30 p.m.

[...] I received this morning your letter from the 14th. This morning I went to see Serdet. The tramways were working! I have to explain why I write it that way. An enormous amount of snow fell last night; it is sticking on the grass but in the roads, with the footsteps of the animals and people, it makes a dread-

---

[274] Lupot and Lamy were very valuable French bows; Serdet, a friend of Lucien, made his violin strings using a secret technique.

ful cold muck. I had Serdet wind four G strings. [...] I explained to him what you wanted, that is, metal wound with the gut without any other material. He thought the weather was not very good for winding strings, but I told him I couldn't wait for a nice, sunny day. [...]

12/15/1917.

I received today your letter or December 13 and three packages, the third being my sleeping bag which I was very happy to get, not because it is very cold right now but because I feared that, with the Christmas season, it would take a long time to arrive. [...]

No one is helping us move this project along. This morning Caplet asked Commander B. for a pass for Niverd to go get a cello and viola. The commander did not go along with the plan, saying that since it was the Army in charge of the concert, the Army needed to give the pass, that all this was against the rules. It's the same for Mayer and Delmar, figure out yourself how to get them here. Caplet couldn't believe his ears! He came back to see me, to talk about all that, he was deeply vexed. I think this may hasten our departure; Caplet told me: "Ah! If they treat us this way, we should just leave." [...]

12/16/1917.

I didn't receive a letter today. [...] I slept last night in my magnificent sleeping bag, it's truly wonderful—a really comfortable way to sleep in winter. The cold weather seems to be coming back but it's bearable, and, so far, we are lucky not to have much water around us.

With the help of an English interpreter, we managed recently to buy about 10 kilos of jam and a variety of marmalades. It is 1,10 francs for a pot of 500 grams, and it's first quality. [...] The English canteens are better supplied than ours and the prices are very reasonable. The French troops in liaison with the English are forbidden to buy from them. [...]

Wednesday, December 19, 1917, 6:30 p.m.

[...] I received this morning your letter from December 16th. [...] I'm writing a bit later this evening because I went to the Town Hall to pay 77 francs for the 350kg of anthracite I was allowed for December, then I went to the rue de l'Église (the storage place) to arrange for them to deliver it. I received the notice about all that the day before yesterday. They brought it at 4:30 so I now have the anthracite for November and December in the basement. I paid 0,50 a bag for the delivery and another 0,50 to take it down to the basement. That is normal for everyone. It is very cold; if you have had as much snow as here in Vincennes, Caplet's shack must look pretty miserable. [...]

12/17/1917.

I received yesterday your two letters of December 14 and 15 and also a letter from Cunault. Because of the bad weather and the accumulation of snow (in some places up to 10 centimeters), communications are difficult and today no mail reached us. Caplet returned last evening and gave me these details: the concert in Noyon is postponed until Sunday December 30. We are supposed to play in the church in Ham for General Lebrun on Sunday the 23. Or he may come with some people from the central bank in Noyon on Christmas Day. Nothing is very definite. But for the 30th in Noyon, we will have all the singers. […]

12/21/1917.

I am writing in Caplet's little room, next to a stove that heats well. […] It is possible that I will be the one who comes to get my instruments, leaving Wednesday, the day after Christmas. […]

12/25/1917.

I cannot go for my violins. Our pigeon keeper Caplet once more has to go to Paris to help everyone rehear, and I have to stay here in his absence, so Mayer will come on Thursday in the afternoon for my instruments. […]

12/26/1917.

I received this morning your two letters of December 22 and 23. […] We played for Midnight Mass in the Chapel in Auroir and afterwards went to the *Réveillon*: turkey with truffles, pâté de foie gras in pastry, foie gras, champagne, everything was delicious; in fact, this exceptional meal was truly splendid. […] In bed at 4 a.m., up at 7, we left for Ham in a truck. We had a hot chocolate at General Lebrun's mess and at 9 a.m. we were playing for Mass. Then we all had lunch at a mess hall newly created for the officers in which General Lebrun had reserved a room with a table with flowers, seven places set, and a nice fire. […]

12/27/1917.

I did not receive a letter this morning. […] My morning was very busy with the pigeons; unfortunately, our sector is heating up and the *Boches* are bombing us heavily. I have to be ready for the pigeons to come back with messages. […]

Tomorrow morning a car will come for me; passing through Ham we will pick up Paray, the organist. I should arrive in Noyon about 11 a.m. to be there when Mayer arrives with my instruments. A number of officers from the division as well as from the 5th artillery division expect to come to the concert. General Lebrun, of course, is supposed to come. We will be 8 violinists in this lovely city of Noyon. [...] That is becoming a serious orchestra.

Today Mayer should be at our place to get my instruments. He was as happy as a king, that good Mayer; he is very pleased to be able to play on a really good instrument. I completely understand. [...]

Second letter, same day.

I chat a bit more with you; I am right now at the STDI, which is where all the maps, projects, and work plans are made for the sector.[275] It is far and away the most interesting office in the division. The room is lovely; it is nice inside with a decent stove that spreads a nice warmth. I found a desk free, pen and ink, and this lovely paper which I really appreciate. It is a joy to write on good paper. I can't ask for anything more. I come here regularly now to do my correspondence. [...]

I think that at this moment Mayer must be with you, telling you all about our adventures. He must also be playing the violins and trying the bows you are showing him. [...] We no longer hear anything about being relieved, and I think we are here until the end of January. [...]

Lucien had a few days of home leave at the end of the year.

---

[275] *Section topographique de Division d'Infanterie*; the map section.

1918

The year 1918 started badly for the Allies: the Germans began the year with what would turn out to be a six-month stretch of bombings of Paris, from the air then from cannons. The British and the French had differing opinions on where to put their energy. Each army was commanded by its own generals, making combined efforts difficult. The French wanted to protect Paris at all costs; the British wanted to keep the Germans from reaching the English Channel. Both armies needed the other to ensure success. Neither side expected the war to end before 1919.

On March 21, the Germans decided their fate by launching an attack on the British at the Somme River. The German offensive of March and April, followed by another starting in May against the French, restored the war of movement and unleashed the events that would bring about their defeat and end the war before the end of 1918.

Over the next few months, the Germans came within reach of Paris, took back the hard-won Chemin des Dames, almost took the important city of Amiens, and nearly pushed the British into the sea at Dunkirk. But they overreached: they were far from home and the supply line was weak; they were mostly fighting in the open, having left their well-constructed bunkers far behind; and they underestimated the determination of the fighting forces of all three countries.

Still, the Allies were far from assured victory. In June of 1918, the *New York Tribune* concluded an article on changing strategies with this statement: "The worst is far from over in the campaign of 1918."[276]

Two major developments changed the course of action and put the Germans in a defensive position, stopping them then pushing them out of France. First, on March 28, General Ferdinand Foch was given command of the allied forces on the Western Front, providing for the first time a unified approach to deploying

---

[276] Frank H. Simonds, "Warfare is Now in Transitional Stage—Allies Must Modify Tactics," *New York Tribune*, June 9, 1918, p. 3.

forces; and second, the American forces arrived in huge numbers, with massive amounts of impressive military equipment and a lot of courage and energy.

Lucien's description of the last months of the war captures the rest of the story well. His division took part in three attacks: the second Battle of the Marne from July 18 to 26, the push toward the Hindenburg Line between August 26 and September 18, and, with the Belgian Army in Flanders, the pursuit of the retreating Germans between October 14 and November 11.[277]

---

[277] Smith, *Between Mutiny and Obedience*, 231-232.

The Letters

I had an easy trip back. I arrived in Ham at 8 a.m. and found a truck that dropped me in Frute about 8:45. I found Caplet, who had arrived the day before, busy with the pigeons. [...]

1/3/1918.

We have some news from Magne and Maréchal, a short phone call telling us that things had worked out well for them. That must mean that Colonel Brenot received our young friends well and assigned them either to the TSF regiment or to the music regiment.[278] In either case, they are pretty sure to be safe. [...]

This evening we have movies at the division and Caplet and I are going to make some music to accompany them. We could not very easily have escaped doing that job. These films are usually perfectly stupid. The Army provides them, with the projector and projectionists. I myself find cinema annoying. True, that equipment could serve useful, instructive purposes but, far from using it for that, they seem to want to film idiocies. [...]

This morning I moved the T85 and the T220; they are returning to the rear. These are the first signs of our departure. At 8 a.m. I took 4 horses to get the dovecotes from the fields and move them to the road where tractors picked them up and transported them to near Noyon. Moves of this type are quite an adventure. Taking down tents in this cold is no easy feat. We need to use a spade to get the stakes holding the lines out of the ground, and it takes up to 5 minutes just for one. But, finally, everything got done without problem and we were finished by 11:00. Tomorrow it will be the T49 who will, also, head for the rear so only the T17 is on active duty. They are talking about our leaving here on January 12. [...]

I will probably head out for Noyon tomorrow morning. As it happens, the Buick, the car belonging to the laundry unit, needs to go there tomorrow and I will take advantage of the opportunity. [...] I have to pick up Niverd's cello which the engineers took to Ham. In Noyon, I will repack my music case carefully; I also have to bring back 4 music stands. [...] Thus, I will be on the road some of tomorrow. The weather is still cold, but in small doses it is bearable. I think I've found a way to get a bit of sugar for when I come home on leave. I can't go into details but I think I can get two or three kilos. [...]

---

[278] *Télégraphe sans fil,* wireless.

1/4/1918.

I received today your letter of January 1. […] Last night there was a cinema show at the division. Caplet played the piano during the particularly stupid films. And worse, watching a movie show fatigues the eyes. The image shakes constantly and the eyes get very tired. I think that someone who watches movies often must quickly find his vision changed. […]

This morning I was in Noyon to get my music case. I left in M. Jouvente's Buick about 9 a.m. […] I saw Lieutenant Bourquin who is very sad to see us leave. I promised to send him one of my signed portraits; just between us, he certainly deserves it, he has been very devoted and helpful. Then I repacked my case which is stuffed full. I had to take out my old shoes and will send them to you. Those shoes saw Verdun and for that reason we should keep them. I then headed back, still in the Buick. […] I was back about 12:45; the car is very fast. My lunch was waiting for me and after the trip in the open air I had a good appetite. […]

The bad news about last month is now finalized. The monthly expense was not abnormal, not more than 5,30 francs a day. But the *Réveillon* added 65 francs a person (8 of us shared the expense), so the month came to 213 francs. I received 90 francs in salary and subsistence pay, meaning that 123 francs will have to come out of my pocket for December. That is a lot. Of course, this is an exception. After I pay everything, I will have 70 francs left. That is enough for now because I don't have to spend any more until the end of the month. We usually spend about 150 to 160 francs a month. […]

1/5/1918.

It is 11 a.m. and I just received your letter from the 3rd. I also just saw Caplet; we are leaving for Noyon at 2 p.m. General Humbert is asking us to play a concert tomorrow. […] I'll have to open my case to get the music we need. Magne and Mayer have arrived; Maréchal is on leave. We will take Niverd with us. Our life is a true kaleidoscope. It seems that this time the Army will house us and feed us. […]

1/7/1918.

I am writing quickly so you receive a letter. I am leaving Noyon soon and will write in more detail this evening. Everything happened magnificently, and there are new, important things in store for us. I do have one piece of bad news: Magne broke his leg, a fracture of the fibula, fortunately a clean break, but he will be laid up for three months at least. He slipped on the ice. […]

Second letter, same day.

I am just back from Noyon and want to write immediately. I found here your two letters of January 4 and 5. [...] To start with, General Lebrun told Caplet yesterday that he would take Magne and Maréchal as radiomen for the Corps, and that Caplet and I, because of a new organization of the pigeon unit, would also move to the Corps. This will take place as soon as we are at rest. It was not General Lebrun who had this idea; Commander Naudet, Chief of the 3rd Battalion of the Army, came to see the general, a personal friend, and told him this was the wish of the General Staff and General Humbert. [...] Magne's stupid accident lessens our joy. Nothing is official and the division knows nothing about this. Lieutenant Bourquin cannot contain his delight. He is happy to see us out of that hornet's nest. [...]

1/8/1918.

I received this morning your letter of January 6. [...] We are leaving on the 12th and apparently going near Nogent-l'Artaud, if not to that town itself. [...] As far as I know, we will be going for a long rest, at least 40 days. That will take us almost to March 1. [...]

Second letter, same day.

I write to chat a bit with you. I am in Caplet's little room, with a good fire and, despite the bitter cold, I am pretty comfortable. There was a big snowfall today and the temperature, which yesterday had moderated, has dropped again. [...]

Captain Libéros asked to see Caplet; I went in his place. He wanted us to give him the names of all the musicians, singers, actors we know of in the entire division, in order to have a troop that can move from billeting site to billeting site to entertain our comrades during the next rest. I said nothing, but I hope we will be with the Corps by then and thus able to avoid all that nuisance. We will certainly play music but under Caplet's direction. [...] Knowing what I know, it was with a certain pleasure that I listened as he laid out his plans. I said to myself: "go on, my friend." He will learn soon, I like to think, about our new plans and realize that he has to do without us. Le Bienvenu, who is aware of what is happening for us, told me: "I am very sad to lose such a good comrade, but there is no doubt that it is better for you to get away from here." [...]

Lieutenant Bourquin was quite emotional yesterday as he said goodbye to us. His TM is leaving for an unknown destination. He could just as easily be sent to Alsace as to Italy. He has done so many good things for us and has been a true friend. We will never forget him. [...]

1/9/1918.

I received this morning your letter from January 7. You don't need to send paper and envelopes so often. [...] Pay attention to writing paper and envelopes. If you happen to go to Paris, to the Louvre or to a good stationery store, buy a good amount of suitable paper and a few hundred envelopes. The paper crisis threatens us seriously and it is quite possible that it will soon be very difficult to find writing paper in the rear. We have to be prepared. If the war lasts long, which seems to be the case, many things will become hard to find.

I am saving your postcard and the flowers, and I hold on to the wish to celebrate at home in 1919. Alas, I am not very hopeful. Caplet seems a bit depressed. He had to spend two whole days copying music. Then the trip back here in this snow and cold must have chilled him to his soul. [...]

1/13/1918.

I received today your letter of the 11th, and also a letter from Maréchal and a letter from Magne. From what he says, it is not clear that he has a fracture; he is more bored than happy. [...]

It is very likely that we will not be called to the Corps until we are at rest. I'm not worried; it was the general who called Caplet to tell him that. He is very proud and will not go back on his word. But I will not rejoice until it is all said and done. [...] Our life right now, or better, my life, as I am the only one of us here, is straightforward. My time is spent on material things; Lismon and I think only of ways to put together delicious menus. And we succeed quite well. That is all I have to tell you for now. [...]

1/14/1918.

I received today your two letters from the 11th and 12th. Nothing new for now. Our departure is announced for the morning of the 16th. The train leaves at 2 p.m. and we expect to be in transit for 24 hours. We are going to the middle of dusty Champagne, near the Mailly camp. We may be charged with training the American army. That army grows constantly, and the newcomers need instruction. It seems natural for each division to instruct an American division. [...]

1/15/1918.

I received today your letter of January 13. [...] General Lebrun has been on pass for several days. It is only after he returns that we will move to the Corps. We must not be in a hurry. You can well believe that, in Caplet's absence, I am ignoring Captain L and his distractions. I use the absence of our venerable leader, as Magne would say, as an excuse. You think I am timid: that is an error, but I break windows in a totally different way than Caplet who always acts on the sly. After what has happened to me, I am not eager to make waves. I do just what is asked, and no more. […]

1/18/1918.

We are settled in Saint-Ouen, in an area bordering camp Mailly, not very far from Chalons-sur-Marne. […] The trip was quite difficult, 30 hours by train then 14 kilometers on foot, in frightful mud, the mud of the Marne which sticks like cement. […] I was lucky to find a tiny room with a good bed, really good luck as this town is tiny (300 inhabitants) and packed with soldiers. […] The *poilus* are for the most part in barracks and camps; for them this rest is very pitiful. They find that no one cares at all about them. After 4 months isolated in a destroyed region, bringing them to this dump for rest is nasty and insensitive. […]

Tomorrow Mayer and I are going to Chalons-sur-Marne to try to rent a piano. I don't know whether we will succeed. If I have time, I will try to see Mme Pineau who, I believe, still lives in the same house. A car will take us to Sompuis and from there it is 30 minutes by train to Chalons.

1/20/1918.

I am writing this morning, not very early—it is already 11 o'clock. I've not been out of my room yet; I just finished washing up. Yesterday was very tiring and unproductive. Mayer and I left very early; we both got up at 4:30 a.m. The horse wagon picked us up at 5:15 and took us 12 kilometers to Sompuis where we caught a train at 8:49. […] We were in Vitry-le-François at 9:30. We had an hour and a half to wait, so we went into town to see whether we could find a piano. Impossible. We found nothing at the two piano shops. We left at 11:00 for Chalons. We were delayed because of major flooding and did not arrive until almost noon. We rushed to see Mama Touprit, nothing! And nothing at the other shop either. In desperation, I went to see Papa Huet, thinking maybe he could direct me to an individual who would loan a piano. I did not find him. I found his wife who recognized me and sent me to a person on the Suippes road, beyond the caserns of the 106th. We rushed there; it was right next to where Vigneron lives but I did not have time to see him. That lady didn't want to rent her piano. It was 1:00. I told Mayer it was lunchtime. We ate lunch in a restaurant very near La Haute-Mère-Dieu, then we had a bit of time.[279] The next and only train to take us back was at 3:41.

I had a free hour and went to see Mme Pineau, who now lives on the rue des Juifs, in a house less grand than the previous one, but still quite nice. I found her

---

[279] Well-known hotel in Chalons.

alone with her mother; Mlle Isabelle was out taking care of the wounded. She was very happy to see me and said she thinks often of us, and of your loneliness. And she spoke, of course, of her son Jean who was reported missing in 1915 in Mesnil, in Champagne, and of whom she has no further news. Alas, I know what that means, but these poor women cling to hope. Jean graduated from St. Cyr in 1914. Gillet, the priest, had told me he had been killed. Mme Pineau said that life was not very gay for three women alone; she also lost her father, which I easily believe. She said that she had not been able to make any music for over a year, but for the past 6 months she and her daughter had started again. She was frankly touched by my visit. […] I think that Libéros will send me back to that town soon to get costumes for the theater. Maybe I can take my violin; I think that my playing a sonata with her daughter would give her immense pleasure. I admit I am curious to see that young woman who must be at least 25 years old; as a child, she was so sweet and adorable.

We arrived in Sompuis at 6:00 and there, the nastiest part, we gave ourselves the gift of 11 kilometers on foot. We did that in 2 hours, which is good, and by 8:30, we were eating in the mess. After dinner, I saw Captain Libéros and we arranged to have a piano tonight. Levieuse, the chief of the automobiles, has a chateau 32 kilometers from here and will loan his piano. They left this morning to get it. With all that business, it was almost 11 when I got to bed. […]

1/21/1918.

I just received your letter of January 18. […] Maréchal is heartbroken by everything he saw in Paris. Huge numbers of young musicians are hanging around in the capital and they find reason to complain. What we could tell them! Maréchal tells me that the concert […] on Saturday, during which they played Caplet's *Mélodies* and *Les Prières* with Rose Féart was a huge success. Caplet doesn't stop appearing everywhere, which is all the more amusing as he really is at the front. […]

1/27/1918.

I received this morning your letter of the 23, and 2 from the 25th. It seems to me that, right now, you have a nasty mindset. […]

Second letter, same day.

I'm writing again because there is a lot I didn't tell you in my earlier letter. Our concert yesterday evening in the theater of the camp of the 74th was the scene of all sorts of incidents. Maréchal didn't arrive back from Paris with his cello and Caplet's viola until almost 6 p.m. He had said he would be there about 1 p.m., so we sent a car to Sompuis to get him and all his things. The car, not finding anyone, came back empty. So Maréchal arrived by bicycle, and we had to send a car to go get the instruments. As a result, ten minutes before the start, the instruments had not yet arrived; everyone was worried. What is more, Caplet was exhausted.

Today there was an open air celebration in the camp (fortunately the weather was favorable). The general had asked Caplet to direct his Marche Héroique with the three regiment bands. It was hard to say no. But the musicians from the 5th and the 224th did not know a single note. He has worked very hard for two days to get to a result that he says will at best be mediocre. [...]

1/29/1918.

I received today your letters from January 27 and 3 top strings. [...] You are totally laughable with what you demand. "You must have a pianist." A pianist, like in the restaurants! You might just as well tell us we need a bassoonist or a harpist. They could send us one specially, by plane, it could also bring the piano, that would be very convenient. When Magne gets back, we will all be happy for lots of reasons, partly to take the pressure off Caplet and also because with Caplet we cannot play any modern sonatas, except for Franck and Lekeu. He manages because of his musicianship. Today we are rehearsing the program for the artillery. We will also read a number of fantasias that Delmas brought back to see what we can use. They are well-known, successful, people hum the melodies, the music speaks to them. It is much harder than you can imagine to come up with successful programs; we have to base them on pieces that have had some success because our public here is not nearly as cultured as those who love concerts. To make sure that everything stays calm, people have to like our concerts. The day they don't like them, we'll be sent packing without another thought. [...] We have to be content with a good concert from time to time, like the lovely one in Noyon. Out of 600 listeners, 550 found the fantasia on *Samson* pretty hard to listen to and would have preferred a tango or some refrains from *The Merry Widow*.[280] [...]

Friday, February 1, 1918, 4 p.m.

My dear son, I received this morning your letter from January 29. [...] I haven't told you about everything I had to go through to borrow a bit of money. I went first to the bank then to a notary to ask M. Chevalier for a notarized signature. He was surprised and said that we needed a loan document. I went back to the bank. There they told me to go to the town hall to get the notarized signature. At the town hall, I asked to talk to M. Guyot and was taken to see his

---

[280] "*Grande Fantasie*" from *Samson et Dalila*, Camille Saint-Saëns, Op. 47; *The Merry Widow*, Franz Lehar (1870-1948).

brother. He signed as witness to my signature on a blank piece of paper. One of his colleagues provided the second signature. Thanks to him, I did not lose too much time. I went back to the bank where, after a few formalities, they gave me the amount I asked for. I can withdraw funds up to a certain amount without any interest. […]

1/31/1918.

I received yesterday your letter from January 29. I was quite worried when I learned from a *Boche communiqué* that they had dropped 14,000 kilos of bombs on Paris. I hope that our area has been spared in this catastrophe. Unfortunately, we have to expect this sort of thing this year. We need thus to take precautions. I will try, if possible, to bring you a mask; you never know whether they will drop gas bombs. […] Of course, the censured newspapers have said very little about these happenings. I admit that I am waiting impatiently for your letters. […]

I am staying with some old people, rough farmers; my little room faces directly toward the south. It is cold; there is no fireplace, nor any other way to make a fire. True, if there were such a thing, I would have nothing to burn in it. You can imagine how easy it is to work in these conditions! No, serious work will have to wait until I get out of this hardship.

Sunday, February 3, 1918, 3 p.m.

I received this morning your letter from the 31st. […] You found out about the air raid on Paris and suburbs the night of the 30th very quickly. There wasn't much about it in the newspapers, is that on purpose? M. Alan told me that they were aiming for the gas meters in the Cours de Vincennes that are almost in front of the two stations at the end of the métro. The bombs collapsed the neighboring sidewalks and completely wiped out the release valves. The gas, set on fire by the bombs, shot out of the ground like torches.

I don't know why there was so much destruction and so many dead and injured at la Tourelle. M. Alan said that they were hoping to hit the ammunition factory and, when that was not possible, they dropped their bombs just anywhere. […] The warehouses in Pantin and St. Denis which contained food stuff were targeted and caught fire. The firefighters worked for hours to put it out. That fire lit up a part of Paris and made things easier for the German planes. […] It was the north and north-east part of Paris and the suburbs that suffered the most. That is the route they use to reach Paris. There will be more of such events. It is difficult to stop them. On a clear night, the planes fly very high and aren't noticed. The hospital in the Faubourg St. Antoine was hit. […]

2/2/1918.

Our entire day yesterday was devoted to work. [...] We are playing this evening for Colonel Brenot in the camp at Saint Ouen. Tomorrow morning, Mass for our DI: at 10:30 a car from the 103rd heavy artillery will come for us because the captain of the group we are playing for invited us for lunch. That evening at 9:00 we play for a concert the division is offering to an English general. [...]

They are beginning to talk about the damages in Paris from the *Boche* bombing. It appears some of that happened not far from us. I admit I'd like to have a letter from you to reassure me. I think you must not have been too afraid. We will talk more about that during my leave; there is not much in terms of shelter in our place. [...]

It is bitter cold and working in an unheated space is very difficult: we have a combustible crisis. There is not the tiniest piece of wood to be found. [...]

Monday, February 4, 1918, 2:30 p.m.

I received this morning your letter from February 2. [...] You have now received my letters about the air raid. The best for me during an alert is to go down to my dining room. I have no other place to go. These shows serve no purpose other than to bring grief to those who lose loved ones. There is plenty of evil and destruction to regret without adding new crimes, but the Germans find all means of terrorizing us. [...]

2/3/1918.

I received your letter from January 31. I am happy to see that, once again, we came out of the bombing unscathed. I was quite fearful; I knew that the bombing was not far from us. Apparently, a bomb fell in the Cours de Vincennes, on the gas meters. Fortunately, it fell in the courtyard and not on a gas reservoir or there would have been a terrible explosion and fire. The Parisians will remember the night of January 30 to 31, 1918. [...]

Second letter, same day.

I am taking advantage of a free minute to write a short note. I received today your letter of February 1. [...] We played for Mass this morning. We left at 10:30 for Dampierre where we found the officers from the 103rd, who were very friendly. Excellent lunch. After lunch we went to the Chateau of Dampierre where the concert took place. The officer commanding the group was well informed; instead of giving a concert for the *poilus*, he arranged for it to be for officers and certain guests. The Chateau of Dampierre is a sumptuous feudal castle. The current owner, M. Bourrie, was there. He is married to a Russian.

[…] The chateau has a music room laid out strangely. With reproductions on the walls of Japanese drawings by Boucher, it has the feeling of a large aviary. In any case, the room has good acoustics, and even better, a first-rate Steinway grand piano. […] We immediately changed our program. Delmas left by car to get the music we needed. In addition to *Airs Bohémiens*, I played the Lekeu Sonata. With the piano, that worked well. […]

You don't say anything about the raid. That must mean there is less talk of it in Paris than here. Feelings are still intense here. It is agonizing to know one's family is exposed to such stupid and useless accidents. […]

Tuesday, February 5, 1918, 4 p.m.

I received this morning your letter from February 3. […] During the night of January 30, I realized how great the danger was but I had to accept what might happen to me. I cannot imagine this war lasting much longer. No one can suffer more than we have already. On their side the Germans (the civilians) cannot be doing very well. I think it would be better to make peace. They talk a lot about that in the newspapers. I think that those in the upper echelon of government must be seriously discussing that possibility and that the meeting of the allies was called as much to talk about peace as a military and economic truce.

I'm going to write to Léontine to find out how she is and to learn whether the planes did a lot of damage in Boulogne. M. Alan was telling me that the Berraut factories had been targeted; I know they are in Billancourt and that it is only their offices that are located across from Léontine. […]

2/6/1918.

[…] I see that the planes came really close to us; I thought as much without any real information. Fortunately, the torpedo that fell near the Prévoyance did not go off; they cause more damage than the bombs. They said last night that some shit fell on the train station in Vincennes. You must know the details. We must expect these sorts of things to happen again. That is why it is important, in case of alert, to take the required precautions. They are not great but better than nothing. […]

2/7/1918.

I just this minute received your letter from February 5. […] As to the length of the war, don't delude yourself, it will last a long time. Each time I am home, I tell you the same thing. Nothing has changed that can make us hope for a quick end. The Germans are amassing troops all over the place. They were, of course, slowed down a bit by the strikes in their mines and factories, and by the flooding.

That is why there has not been an offensive, but I don't know that this state of calm will last much longer. [...]

We will see [...] whether the general will speak to us about his plans for us. We are no longer part of the 3rd Army Corps, and I don't know whether we will go back to them. That means the support we had in that Army is not very helpful. In any case, the DI is very proud of us. The series of concerts we just gave made us very popular and they want us everywhere. [...]

2/9/1918.

I received this morning your letter of February 7 with the article from *L'Information*. The article by Chéradame is particularly interesting.[281] For sure our leaders have never seen clearly. At Verdun, where the breakthrough never happened, the Germans prevented us from sending soldiers to places where they would have been victorious. Those in charge of this nation, civilian and military, seem to have been chosen from among the incapable and short-sighted. When you realize that there are still some who believe in a breakthrough. It's crazy! The *poilus* have said it for a long time now. The result would be halfway; there would eventually be a moment when, because of the problem of transporting so much material or because of the enemy reorganizing and pushing back, we would have to stop and start over. The *Boches*, no more than we, will be able to get decisive results on the battlefield. [...] Unfortunately, our leaders still believe in Napoleonic ideas. Everything has changed since then. [...]

You have seen that the American army took over the sector south of Saint-Mihiel, in the area of Commercy, Void, and Gondrécourt. That should free up two French divisions. It is reasonable to expect that they will rapidly expand their front. But what will these forces be able to do against the *Boches*? That's what the future will tell us. It seems that these troops have much better equipment, but their courage is unknown. And having perfect equipment doesn't help much when faced with the depressing effect of the aerial bombs and the shells. The men also need to have hearts of bronze. Very few civilians understand what that requires. [...]

2/9/1918.

I am writing this evening; tomorrow morning we leave for Arcis very early. [...] These days, there is a note saying that it is illegal to have numbers in metal, they have to be in wool for the soldiers, and embroidered for the non-coms and the officers. I wonder what difference that makes. It seems that the military profession has a mind to cause annoyances. Who are we bothering in this instance?

---

[281] André Chéradame (1871-1948) was a French journalist who saw German politics as entirely devoted to world domination.

So, for now, I've taken the numbers off my uniform as the rule is effective immediately. […]

2/11/1918.

I just returned from Arcis and found your letter of February 9. […] Our concert was a great success, at least that is what different people told us. General Lebrun was there but we did not see him; by that I mean that none of us spoke to him, not even Caplet. I remain persuaded that Caplet will not make a single step toward leaving here where he has total freedom. As for the general, he is no longer associated with the 3rd Army; he seems to be taking his previous promise lightly. I also saw Pierrot there. He introduced me to the wife of a friend in the 129th, Lallemand, who was part of our stretcher group and very close to Henri. […] That young woman, the niece of the *curé* of Arcis, is living with him during the war. That means I also met the *curé* who welcomed Pierrot and me warmly and gave us a bottle of local wine which was very good. The young woman was happy to meet me. She kept saying: "Oh, Monsieur Durosoir, I have heard so much about you for so long, it seems to me that I am not meeting you for the first time." […]

2/15/1918.

Yesterday, we were with […] in Arcis; we gave two concerts, one in the afternoon and one in the evening, and with great success. We were well received by the officers who invited us to join their meal. […] The division is supposed to leave between the 16th and 23rd to work on defense, in the middle of Champagne wine country near Cumières. The division should be at Boursault, in the chateau one can see on the hill. That wouldn't be bad. They are saying we will leave three stages. […] You can bet that, the night before the departure, I will set my sails for Paris. So my leave should happen soon. […]

It is good that they are taking measures to hide the lights; apparently Paris was quite lit up the night of the raid, especially the factories. That event reminded us that we are at war, and it is wise to take precautions. It takes very little effort and the planes no longer have any landmarks to guide their firing. I think there was a lot of damage in Vincennes; Gross Papp heard that it was the town that suffered the most. He got to Paris during the night of the 30th into the 31st in the middle of the bombing. He was able to see how stupid the people were, not realizing the extent of the danger. He saw more than 100 people take refuge under the glass awning of *Le Petit Journal* and thinking themselves safe. One shouldn't treat bombs lightly, especially torpedoes, and if there is shelter nearby, they should go there. I think that lesson served a purpose. […]

Lucien was correct; it was his turn for a period of home leave.

Saturday, March 2, 1918.

I received your letter from February 19. [...] The weather is abominable, snow nonstop since you left. [...] I am sorry you couldn't stay in Vincennes today for the anniversary of my birth. [...]

3/3/1918.

What adventures for the past two days! I left Sunday at 12:30 from Épernay and arrived in Suippes about 4 p.m. The station is 2 kilometers from our town which, importantly, is not much destroyed. [...] Here we have a stationary dovecote, not trailers and tents. Our dovecote is in a lovely villa in town. We have a splendid installation, really comfortable, which will make a lot of people jealous. We've never been so well off. The pigeon keepers from the other division are leaving today and I'll settle in immediately. If we stay for a while, this will be a period of comfort. The DI we are relieving was here for five months. We are 8 kilometers as the crow flies from the front lines. [...]

Sunday, March 3, 1918.

I hope you arrived without too much delay and not too many problems because of the snow and the cold which graced your departure. [...] I see in *L'Information* that the Germans have attacked all over the place, but especially at the Chemin des Dames, in Champagne, on the right bank of the Meuse, and in Cambrai. [...]

3/5/1918.

I received today your letters of the 2nd and 3rd. I note with pleasure that your cold is better. As for mine, having returned to life in the open air, I can say it is completely gone. [...] We have a little villa just for us. There are three who care for the pigeon plus Caplet, Niel, and me. From every aspect, it's a good deal. We are one kilometer from the train station, and it takes 40 minutes to get to Chalons. It couldn't be better. [...]

3/6/1918.

I received this morning a large envelope with *L'Information* from the 3rd. [...] This morning, a *Boche* plane brought down one of our *saucisse*. I saw it fall in flames, and the observer float down with his parachute. I think he was able to land safely. The *Boches* do this sort of thing often and it is no longer lucky to be an observer in a balloon. [...]

I am sending you an invitation for the concert of the SMI on the 8th.[282] It was sent to Caplet. The concert is at 3 p.m.: it's a good time of day, and a superb, interesting program. The Debussy Piano and Violin Sonata, played by Yvonne Astruc and Madame Fourgeaud-Groulez, Florent Schmitt's *Ombres*,[283] some piano pieces by Loyonnet,[284] a Quintet for strings and harp of Inghelbrecht;[285] and five melodies by Caplet. A magnificent program. Moreover, you will get to hear the Debussy Sonata. I'll be interested in your impressions. Please send them to me as I will be working on that piece with Caplet. [...]

3/7/1918.

I didn't receive a letter today. [...] While I'm thinking about it, I need you to send me a metal mute, you know what I mean—I lost mine. [...]

I hope you will receive the ticket in time and that you will be able to get to the Salle Gaveau. Since you are sending a package, could you include a few fine tuners, and an inflatable rubber pillow? Caplet has had one for a year and quite likes it.

We are quite well off here. In addition to our co-op, there are army trucks run by the Damoy company selling really good products. If this area stays calm, I will be able to work and to read a bit; as time goes by, I will ask you for some books. [...]

Our house has two rooms and a kitchen on the ground floor; same for the second floor. The third floor is set up as a pigeon coop. The three who care for the pigeons are on the second floor with Niel. I sleep on the ground floor in the same room as Caplet. The other room serves as a washroom and kitchen. It stays cold as it faces north. There is a rather large garden with benches, outhouse, wash basin, all the necessities. We have a pump in the kitchen and a stone sink. The army chose a good-sized house to set up the pigeons. The men who care for them have been here for two years; some people have been really lucky. [...]

Friday, March 8, 1918. 10:30 a.m.

I received this morning your 2nd letter from the 5th, and a whole shipload of other letters. And, I forgot, the invitation for the concert of the SMI this

[282] *Société musicale indépendante* was founded in 1910 by a number of Fauré's composition students, led by Maurice Ravel. Caplet was one of the fifteen directors. Roger Nichols, *The Harlequin Years: Music in Paris, 1917-1929*, (University of California Press, 2002), 48.

[283] Schmitt, Op. 64.

[284] Paul Loyonnet (1889-1988).

[285] Désiré Émile Inghelbrecht (1880-1965), Quintet for Harp and Strings in C minor, 1917 or 1918.

afternoon. Unfortunately, I will not be able to go. My cold, which had seemed initially not very serious although it was very violent, has gotten quite bad or at least it's moved to the bronchi (which has happened in similar cases). It would be very imprudent of me to go out in spite of my regret to miss the pleasure and joy of a sort I sorely need. [...] For someone for whom the life of the mind is everything, being deprived of the pleasure of hearing music pains me greatly. But I should not complain, rather put up with my sorrows with great patience, because destiny, up to now, has quite happily protected you. I should think only of that and thank heaven, despite all my little hardships and disappointments. Nevertheless, I would have taken great pleasure in hearing such a lovely program. Thank Caplet for me and share with him the sincere admiration for his songs I'd have loved to have heard. [...]

Saturday, March 9, 1918, 1:30 p.m.

[...] Last night, we had a visit by the German planes, from 9 p.m. to midnight. I know nothing more, but I think there was damage in Paris. I think there were serious battles between German planes and French planes—the noise was unbelievable. [...] I saw in *L'Information* a few days ago that the civilian hospital in Reims had been burned by the planes. [...]

3/8/1918.

The mail hasn't yet arrived. [...] Quite by accident, Caplet saw General Lebrun yesterday, who talked with him for several minutes. He told him that General Gouraud, the Chief of the 4th Army, which we are now part of, really likes music. That is good news; now we need to find out what sort of music he likes. [...]

3/9/1918.

I received yesterday, quite late, your letter from March 6. [...] Caplet and I had dinner with the ambulance group. We ate quite well, and the company was rather enjoyable. After dinner, we played Beethoven's Sonata in F and a whole bunch of other pieces, including *L'Abeille*, Veracini's Minuet and Gigue,[286] things that we don't usually play. Everyone was pleased and Bord invited us back for the 18th, hoping that Maréchal will be able to join us.

I am going to start studying English regularly every day. [...]

3/10/1918.

I received this morning your two letters from March 7 and 8. Paris again received a visit from the airplanes the night of March 8 to 9th. Right now that is

---

[286] Francesco Maria Veracini (1690-1786). Violin Sonata in E minor, Op. 2, No. 8.

all we know. The government should realize that there are 700,000 to 800,000 men at the front from Paris and suburbs. They have the right to be informed, rather than passing two or three anguishing days waiting. It is fine that the papers do not publish any news, but it would not be impossible to get information to the armies. I heard vague rumors from a man back from pass that the area around Saint Lazare and the Madeleine were hit, also Aubervilliers and Le Bourget. Give me some details as quickly as possible. [...]

The weather is absolutely splendid, our pigeons are cooing in the coop and the first buds are appearing. If this continues, we will soon see the first leaves. [...]

Tuesday, March 12, 1918, 4:30 p.m.

[...] The weather is lovely, the sun is even too warm, but the air is still cool. [...] The Germans are taking advantage of the nice weather and clear nights. Last night we had again a visit from them, from 10 p.m. to midnight. That is becoming rather routine; since I don't sleep much those nights, my nerves suffer. A bomb fell in front of the building with the tabac, at the corner of the rue de Paris and the Place Bérault, where the post box is. No one was killed and no one injured. However, all the windows of that building and those next to it were broken. I heard a German plane pass over our house then a huge explosion. I think the Germans are hoping that, with actions like that, we will ask quickly for peace. All that is very sad; there are more and more ruins and deaths. [...]

Wednesday, March 13, 1918, 4 p.m.

[...] I received this morning your letters from March 10th and 11th. You must have received my letter with the news of the raids in Paris on the 8th. You probably also know they came back on the 11th. I have no information on what happened in Paris during the first one, because there is nothing in the papers and I have no one to tell me. But I believe that the second caused damage and that there were victims in Paris. If what *L'Information* says about the planes is true, one has to believe that, even if some did no damage, the result was still terrible. We should find a way to keep so many planes from arriving in and around Paris, but that must be very difficult. [...] Mayer must have witnessed the last raid; I don't know where he lives. M. Alan, who came to visit yesterday, said that in the rue Geoffroy-Marie where the luthier Deraus lives, a 6-story building was destroyed by a bomb or some other sort of explosive device. The basement had been chosen as a shelter. [...]

3/11/1918.

Just because I was so eager for your news this morning, I received nothing from you. I hope that Vincennes and around us in particular was spared but, really, I know nothing. The papers obviously have not published where the bombs fell, nor the names of the killed and injured. That leaves us in total ignorance. [...]

Mayer passed by here on his way home on leave. He took with him for you one of my little bags with about 3 pounds of sugar lumps. That is all I was able to buy from Maurice; he bought 20 kilos from a grocer in Épernay who was forced to close his store. [...]. Mayer will bring the bag to Vincennes. He will keep a kilo for himself, or rather, for his mother. [...]

I accompanied Mayer as far as the station in Suippes, which is 1500 meters from here. That station received about ten *Boche* bombs yesterday. Fortunately, they fell far enough away that there were no victims and no damage. This area is not bombed often, but when the *Boches* start shooting, it's always in this direction. It is not very dangerous. We have a wonderful bomb shelter in the dovecote, and to get there we do not need to leave the house. We take the stairs to the basement and from there pass into the shelter. The engineers did this work, and it is very carefully done. [...] At this moment, it is 11:30, I hear bombs from planes landing several kilometers from here, no doubt on the billets. Up to now, Suippes has been mostly spared and, at the first bomb, we head for our shelter. [...]

3/12/1918.

[...] For three days now I've had no letter from you. If I hadn't received the box this morning, sent on the 10th, I would be really worried. You choose the day after a raid on Paris to stop writing! [...]

Caplet at this moment is engrossed in work, and has begun a Sonata for Piano, Soprano, and Violoncello. The singer does not sing words, but is treated exactly as an instrument, and articulates the gestures either on vowels or on consonants, giving the impression of bow strokes. This will be deemed crazy or bizarre by many, but there's no reason why one should not make use of the timbre of the human voice as if it were an instrument. The snag in all this is that one would need a singer with a very lovely voice, a well-developed vocal mechanism, and also great musicality. This is asking a lot and makes such a work difficult to perform. Caplet has chosen the cello to contrast with the soprano and to give a greater range of sonorities. It will be interesting to hear a work of this type. He calls it a sonata, but I think that this will have a very unconventional form. [...]

Thursday, March 14, 1918, 4:30 p.m.

[...] I received this morning your letter from the 12th. [...] Mayer came this morning about 10; he brought me your cloth bag. I thanked him and offered him some muscatel and cookies. He drank very reasonably. [...] He arrived in Paris on Sunday night the 10th and was there for the raid on the 11th. There was damage on the Boulevard Voltaire near the rue Bréguet where he lives. [...]

3/13/1918.

I just received your two letters from March 11 and 12. This morning was the 4th day without a letter. I admit that I was starting to be really worried. The strange thing is that you do not mention the raid and you don't seem the least concerned about it, while here, that is all we think about. The one two nights ago must have been terrible. People coming back from leave talk of serious damage, though we have no way to assess what their allegations are based on. [...]

For the raids, I've already told you, no need to get out of bed. With the bombs the *Boches* are using, it's senseless to believe that a floor or two will provide protection. On the night of the 8th to the 9th, they used bombs with a delay. One of those, from what someone back from leave told us, fell on a 7-story building, went down through all floors and exploded in the basement. The house was, obviously, destroyed from top to bottom. Worse, the basement of that building had been designated a shelter and was crowded with people. [...]

Friday, March 15, 1918, 3 p.m.

[...] I am an hour late with my letter writing because I, like everyone else, had quite a scare. About 2 p.m. there was a huge explosion. They say it was an ammunition factory that exploded, or at least a boiler, either at Bagnolet or Aubervilliers, it's not clear. I was just going from the dining room to the kitchen; I saw from the window on the stairway an enormous flame and felt the rue du Moulin tremble. I thought it was a bomb from a plane. But there was no alert; it must have been an explosion caused by accident or sabotage. We have to hope there were not too many victims. [...]

3/14/1918.

I received this morning, with much delay, your letter from March 9, and also the one from the 12th. I see that the bombs fell very near us; the tobacco store on the rue de Paris is barely 50 meters in a straight line from us. What is important is that they do not fall on our house. That is why the best chance of escaping danger is staying home. Hundreds of bombs could fall without anything serious happening to our house. Let us hope that the foggy weather which is returning will stop the raids for now. Here, our sector is quiet; there are very few wounded, one or two a day. I was much more worried for you than for me. [...]

I think that you didn't have any windows broken. To protect them from a nearby explosion, you should open them. That is not really possible in bad weather, but once it gets nicer, it is possible. You could also glue strips of paper in a cross which supports the glass. I tell you that because window glass must be extremely expensive or, maybe, not even available right now.

The accident in the métro was dreadful.[287] Frightened men smothered women and children. That's why it is wise not to go out. I am afraid the planes will start coming during the day—more dangerous for them. We are doing it so there is no reason why they won't try the same thing. During the day, they can use machine guns. [...]

Debussy has not yet composed his 6 sonatas. He began by publishing the first, which is the one for cello and piano, while announcing the 5 others. The 2nd is for alto flute and harp, the 3rd for violin and piano. Caplet says the 4th is in progress although it is not going quickly because Debussy is very ill. I am thus going to get to know this Sonata for Violin and Piano; this should be an interesting task with Caplet who perfectly knows the composer's intentions.

For three days, starting this morning, we have 16 artillerymen with us for training in pigeon keeping. They are probably going to expand the use of pigeons to the artillery. Up to now, they have not had use of this sort of communication. [...]

Saturday, March 16, 1918, 4 p.m.

[...] The explosion I told you about was in Saint Denis. There are still no details in *L'Information* but it was an accident and not sabotage. It must have been quite awful; there are thousands of windows broken all over Paris. [...]

3/15/1918.

I am writing this morning early; mail has not yet arrived. [...] Considerable infantry and artillery reinforcements are arriving non-stop in this region. The higher ups must believe the *Boche* attack will happen soon. We await it with confidence; here our positions are especially strong and the sector very well organized. [...]

3/16/1918.

[...] The writing of Debussy's sonata is fine and clear. He very often uses perfect chords, but he adds developments that are very foreign to the chords. There is a twittering in the background: the bird sings, he may vary his song, but the grass remains green. This work builds on that idea. [...]

---

[287] The Bolivar métro station, in the 19th arrondissement in the north of Paris, was a bomb shelter. During a bombing on the night of March 11, 1918, frightened people rushed to get to safety. The doors eventually gave way under the pressure of so many people, and in the stampede to get down the stairs to safety, many people were trampled.

3/17/1918.

[...] The Debussy sonata is difficult and requires a light and ethereal execution. I am going to study it carefully with Caplet before continuing to work on it. The fingering and even the bowing in a work like that cannot be fixed without thorough study and comprehension of its structure. [...]

3/18/1918.

It is now 11 a.m. and the mail is not here yet. [...] I just finished relieving one of our posts. I left with an auto about 7:30 and took all my birds to the agreed-upon location. There was a bit of activity in the sector, and around Trou Bricot, several bombs landed not from our vehicle. Fortunately, we were moving quite fast, and they were small caliber bombs. This region is really sad and desolate, to a degree I cannot describe. There has been so much fighting in this squalid Champagne—the offensive of September 25, Perthes, Souain, Trou Bricot. In short, the countryside is so ravaged that the tortured earth gives off the impression of unprecedented sadness. What is more, there are large cemeteries everywhere and isolated graves, and at any moment one can read on these poor crosses "two unknown, no name, etc." All that, under the full sun, creates a mournful image. The area of Saint-Quentin, although completely destroyed, didn't appear quite so sad. This earth turned inside out, the white chalk brought up to the surface, there is no name for such an upheaval. The exchange of the pigeons happens rapidly and of course we don't stay long at any post. [...]

Wednesday, March 20, 1918, 11 a.m.

[...] Mme Duez wrote but did not mention the money order I sent for 25 francs. Right now, she is staying with a midwife [...] who is treating her for a flu she caught. I will send you that note so you have her current address. I like to think she will be able to go back to her home. [...]

Second letter, same day, 8:30 p.m.

[...] A mass of people are leaving Paris. [...] Those people who are leaving cannot be taking more than the travel bag they have with them on the train. They will have to buy linens and clothing where they go, thus will have to spend money. I think they need to stand in line all day to get tickets which don't let them leave until 2 weeks later. [...]

3/19/1918.

I am writing before receiving mail. [...] We are taking many precautions against poison gas attacks; we will receive new gas masks, similar in shape to the ones the *Boches* use. Apparently, according to the doctors, this one is much improved. Its price is much higher, an average of 25 to 30 francs. [...]

3/21/1918.

I received this morning your two letters from the 18th and 19th. [...] In the past 24 hours, things here have really heated up. Is this just the *Boches* sounding us out or the prelude to a general attack? I don't know, but in any case, the cannon is roaring like in the good old days. This morning I changed the pigeons and was lucky to do it during a quiet moment, but all the roads I used showed the effects of the bombing during the night. I was able to take care of seven of the 8 DI posts. The firing around the 8th was such that I couldn't consider passing through it. If it gets a bit calmer, my comrade Niel will take the pigeons tomorrow by bicycle.

Right now it is 1:00 and the cannon is booming horribly. The *Boches* just launched several bombs on Suippes itself, no longer just on the train station. There was not much damage. This morning, between the Wacquyes farm and Souain, I saw Delmas spring up from the ground. [...] I didn't know he was in this especially bad location. He didn't expect to see me and told me not to stay long, it was really dangerous. I was aware of that and only stayed long enough to do what I had to do. If these attacks continue, the DI will go to its command post which is outside this region. In that case, Niel will go with them and I will stay alone at the dovecote with the sergeant. [...]

You can understand that, with all these events that keep us breathless, music has been replaced by a different sort of music. [...]

Saturday, March 23, 1918, 12:30 p.m.

[...] Last night, at 8:30, we had a false alert which lasted an hour and a half. Not knowing what to take and quite upset with waiting, I heard the all-clear at 10 p.m. With all these upsetting events, I don't sleep well and life becomes quite depressing. Especially because this morning, at 8:30, there was another alert and the all-clear has not yet been given. You can hear the cannon from time to time and there are planes buzzing overhead occasionally. Maybe it is just to make sure people are not in the streets. [...] I heard right now a loud boom from a cannon.

I got up a little late this morning and just as I was about to have breakfast, the alert sounded. I closed all the shutters and lowered the shades. I just ate my breakfast with two eggs and a petit suisse that I bought yesterday.[288] I was planning to go to the schools to get my food ration card: they are giving them out today, tomorrow, and Monday. [...]

---

[288] Similar to a yogurt.

Finally, the all-clear was given at 4:30 p.m. [...] M. Bouchard, from whom I bought a few things, told me that a German plane had dropped a bomb on the Gare de l'Est and killed several people, including some men on leave. I don't know anything about that but, in fact, German planes managed to come during the day. The tramways were not working and that must be true for the other forms of transportation. It is not any fun to find oneself in Paris, in such circumstances [...]

3/22/1918.

I am writing this morning before the mail arrives. This sector was perfectly quiet last night; I think that the important effort the *Boches* made, and which was for them a complete failure, will not have any follow-up right now. Yesterday they launched 70 shells at Suippes and the train station, fortunately not in the area where the DI is. Last night *Boche* planes roamed overhead and dropped at least 40 pieces of shit. Fortunately, our courtyard was spared. [...] In any case, our pigeon coop has a very solid, well-constructed shelter. [...]

Captain Libéros, who was in the field yesterday, received a mild exposure to gas. He has conjunctivitis, as the new gas attacks the eyes. One must not hesitate to quickly put on the mask as soon as a bomb lands nearby and doesn't explode. The gas bombs are special that way; they explode only a little and it seems to be a failed explosion. That is a mistake; it is a gas bomb and one has to immediately put on the mask. [...]

Sunday, Palm Sunday, March 24, 1918, 3 p.m.

[...] Saturday night at 8:30 there was another alert which lasted until 10 p.m. The cannon fire was much closer to Vincennes but I know nothing about what happened; I ended up going to bed at 11, hoping the all-clear would sound several times to be assured all was calm. But at 6:30 this morning, that is, Palm Sunday, I heard a cannon. I got dressed and immediately the siren sounded in warning. The alert is still in effect although the tramways are working again. [...] The Germans are trying to cause chaos everywhere. [...]

3/23/1918.

Here are a few pretty violets that grew in our garden. They are very fragrant. I'm sending them to you as a souvenir of Suippes. [...]

I received this minute your second letter from the 20th. [...] Yesterday a number of bombs fell in different parts of our little town; an unfortunate 105 drifted down on a neighboring little house that was housing some Italian soldiers here to work on farms. No one was injured. These days the *Boches* are using a lot of gas bombs, as are we. That is what gave us at least 300 evacuees. With the injured or killed, in all the regiments there are no more than 50 men left. [...]

You can imagine that, because of the intermittent bombing these past two days, we had to always be on alert. Our work suffers, and so does the Debussy Sonata. [...]

3/24/1918.

I am just back from the field where I made the pigeon exchange very calmly. [...] I do not think they are holding up mail because of the aerial bombing, but I do know that this morning I received only one letter, from the 21st, and logically I should have received one from the 22nd. They should not take more than 2 days to reach me. [...]

Chalons was bombed recently and apparently there were quite a number of victims. Up until now, that city had mostly been spared. Last January I noticed that none of the buildings showed any evidence of bombing. You remember, when you cross the Marne, there is a traffic circle in a little square. It seems that one bomb fell on one of the houses in the square and totally destroyed it. The Hôtel d'Angleterre which is near Notre-Dame was also hit. Madame Pineau must have been very scared because the rue des Juifs is near the traffic circle. There is much talk about the *Boche* attack on the English. We only know what the *Boches* write in their *communiqués* and that is not to be trusted because they try to undermine our confidence. [...]

Tuesday, March 26, 1918, 2:30 p.m.

[...] I told you that yesterday there was another alert at 6:30 a.m. I saw in *L'Information* that the all-clear sounded at 11:30 but not in Vincennes, so we were all day without knowing anything. I think the town is a bit overwhelmed with all that. In any case, the people are starting to have had enough of constantly rushing into basements. Lots of people are catching colds. The cool temperatures and the dampness of the basements are not good for some, especially when they have to stay there for a long time. Still, for most of them, it is comforting to believe themselves safe. [...]

3/25/1918.

The news that Paris was bombed by long-range cannons is unbelievable. One cannot help but think of it as a tale by Jules Verne. [...] The exodus of Parisians will grow. Apparently, a bomb fell on the Place de la République near the monument, and also at the Gares du Nord and de l'Est, and in Montrouge. This kind of bombing, unless it becomes more intensive, is less dangerous than torpedoes or aerial bombing. [...]

Ham has fallen back to the Germans. I cannot think about Annois, Ham, Offoy—all those areas certainly devastated to which civilians had started to return and where life was resuming—without feeling sad. [...]

The *Boches* attacked with almost 1 million men; one can say that all the artillery in Europe is now concentrated on our front. [...] A lot of men will still be killed. I think the Americans will now be used. Apparently, there are 100,000 in the sector, mixed in with our men. Those who have seen them speak of them with praise. [...]

3/26/1918.

I did not receive a letter this morning. [...] There is fear of an attack near us, and they are taking precautions. I'm going to try and send my case of music back to Paris. Monsieur Jouvent, from the laundry group, is leaving for Paris tomorrow. I am hoping to give it to him. If I can, he will leave it at the Gare de l'Est and send you the receipt. You will have to go for it. Take the métro to the train station to get it and a taxi home. [...] I admit that I will be much happier after I send my case. [...]

3/27/1918.

Because of the current situation, we've had no mail for 3 days. Based on what I know, I think the situation is serious and that we are going to have to make a huge effort to stop the *Boches* who must be planning to attack Amiens to cut the French army off from the English. I don't know whether they will succeed but they are throwing a million men at that goal, obviously an enormous effort. [...]

This morning I carried out my pigeon relief with no problem; at the fifth one, two shells came to say hello, that was the only incident during the trip. Days are passing, there is a certain anguish at this moment because of the terrible battle in this area. [...]

Second letter, same day.

I finally received news, your two letters from the 23rd, and one from the 24th. I see that the cannons are not aiming at Vincennes; that reassures me a bit. [...] I think all the alarms are getting you a bit too worked up. Unless you could get to the vaulted basement of a 5 or 6 story building, going from the first floor to the ground floor provides no protection. It would make no difference if you were on the first floor, or the ground floor should a bomb or shell fall on the house. So I'd suggest you not take any specific precautions, go about your day normally. Sure, you could close the blinds. But stay in your bed, where you are comfortable; you'd end up catching a cold or bronchitis and wearing yourself out. [...] Do what I do when there is danger I can do nothing about—think about something else. Think of us in the middle of all this filth (chemical and other). [...] If fate would have it that a bomb falls on our house, nothing will stop it so let's not make ourselves ill over the remote chance that something like that might happen. [...]

3/28/1918.

I just this minute received your letter from March 25. [...] We also received the newspapers and note the strong German advance. It seems now to be at a standstill. It is the French forces that are meeting this German advance. It is sad to note that the Germans have won every time we were not there. No one else would have hung on at Verdun. Ah! We have sad allies. The English never wanted to take orders from the French, probably out of pride. The result is that those men, well equipped, are not worthy of their equipment. Fortunately, the Americans are willing for us to teach then and they accept our guidance, with much better results.

Apparently, the cannons firing on Paris are aiming at the Gares de l'Est and du Nord, the Boulevard Saint Michel, Luxembourg, and of course the suburbs of Pantin and Aubervilliers. It seems the shells do not do much damage. Up to now, they have all exploded, so we cannot study the form or construction of the shells, which would be interesting. [...]

Noyon is again in the hands of the *Boches*. I fear that, this time, the cathedral has not been spared damage. Our December 30 concert is becoming part of history. The poor archbishop must be heartsick. [...]

3/29/1918.

I am writing this morning before receiving any news. [...] I am seated at a table next to a fireplace with a nice warm wood fire. Ah! I have to admit that we have never had such lodgings. [...]

Based on the most recent news, the *Boches* have taken Montdidier. That is really sad because up to now that town had been spared. We all hope that this advance is just about finished. From what they are saying, I think that, due to the pressure of the current situation, the command has finally been unified. They say that Maréchal Haig keeps command of the English army, Pétain command of the French army, and Major General Foch has command of all. If that is the case, we are sure not to relive events like these. [...] I do not believe that the *Boches* will succeed in their goal of cutting the French army from the English, of pushing the English into the sea and turning on us. That move has failed, but they have gained a good deal of territory and this decision alone will not push them out of France. [...]

Second letter, same day.

I received this minute your two letters of March 25 and 26, as well as the announcement of the death of poor little Lili Boulanger, 24 years old.[289] I knew about her distressing illness from Caplet, who is in frequent contact with her sister, Nadia, and that there was little hope of saving her. [...]

We are receiving very few letters right now. The service is surely a bit confused. I really don't know whether the Amiens-Paris train line is still running; it could be caught under the German shelling. Oh! How sad all these events are! [...]

3/30/1918.

I am writing this morning before the mail. [...] Our sector is completely quiet; we have the impression the *Boches* have withdrawn some men and artillery to send as reinforcements to the North. [...]

Sergeant Pici came back from leave yesterday. He told us that a lot of people are leaving Paris. The provinces must be overrun and in a good many areas it must be hard to find a place to stay. I'm very curious to see what Paris looks like right now. People are creating shelters with table, sideboard, armchairs and trying to arrange for some heat. Follow my advice and stay calmly in bed when you have nighttime alerts, it's infinitely wiser for your health. Don't get upset, keep calm, that's what you have to do. In the midst of danger, if you can get your body to stay calm, you will withstand the hardships. In the case of a true alert, your head will be clear which nine times out of ten is what gets one out of difficulty. [...]

When Caplet returns, if events permit, we will be able to work with good results on the Debussy Sonata. Speaking of Debussy, it seems he has just died. Maréchal, whom I saw yesterday, was the one to give me that news. It was expected; Debussy was gravely ill with an intestinal illness; I think it was colorectal cancer—a terrible, painful illness. He had been bed-bound for six months and had written practically nothing. I think he leaves his 4th sonata unfinished. One of the most original of modern musicians is gone. Caplet had the good fortune to be in Paris; perhaps he was present at the last moments of his friend. They were very close. His violin sonata is his last work. He was not 60 years old I think. [...]

---

[289] Lili Boulanger (1893-1918) was a child prodigy born into a family of musicians. She was in ill health from the age of 2 but composed up until her death at age 24.

3/31/1918.

I just received your letter of March 28 and am astonished that you do not mention my box of music, nor the letter with the receipt. Monsieur Jouvent took the letter and posted it with a stamp in Paris. I hope to have news tomorrow. If the receipt is lost, it will be very difficult to get the case.

The battle underway will be one of the deadliest; we cannot fall under the domination of those savages. The *Boches* have had enough; they want to be finished with this and have attacked with all the forces they have been able to assemble in hopes of destroying us before the buildup and intervention of a strong American army. […] They will not succeed; we can go head-to-head with them. Our equipment now is up to the demands of the battle. The *Boches* can bury millions of men if they want, they will not take much territory. […]

4/1/1918.

I am writing this morning before mail arrives. […] A new note arrived for Lemoine which assigns him as chemist for the air unit, in Paris, rue Choiseul I believe. We forwarded the note to him in his new group. He must be in seventh heaven; from now on, he will be based in Paris and home every evening. He can just coo with his young wife. […]

Another new month! A year ago we were in Crézancy, two years ago we were in Rancourt (near Revigny and ready to go up to Verdun), and three years ago we were in La Ville-aux-Bois. All that seems so far away and fades into a past that seems like a story. […]

You say you can only get 200 grams of bread; is that enough for you? I know that you will get a pound of sugar in April. Tell me more about all those things. […]

4/2/1918.

Today's mail has not yet arrived. Nothing new to tell. The sector is still very quiet. […] I saw in the papers yesterday that there is terrible fighting in Moreuil. We have stayed in control of that little town. When I was in Ailly-sur-Noye, I played in Moreuil on November 1, 1915. It was then the seat of the Army Corps commanded by General Hache. They came to get Rolland and me. There was quite a decent organ in the church, which was quite pretty. A priest I didn't know and have not seen since then gave a remarkable sermon. That little town is 12 kilometers from Ailly-sur-Noye, where the Amiens-Paris train line passes. The *Boches* are fighting to gain control of that very important line. That would not cut us off from the English but would impose a long detour. And they want to take the line that provides our supplies, Paris-Gisors-Dieppe. I think now they are too late; the *poilus* are there, and they will not get past them. From what the papers say English units are mixed with French. That is a good system. Not only can we lead by example, but it arouses their pride. Fortunately for us, the American troops will be commanded by French officers and certainly blended into our units. […]

Second letter, same day.

I just received your three letters, from March 27, 29, and 30. I see that my case made it to Vincennes without any problems, I am very happy. Give a nice tip to M. Alan and thank him heartily for me; he had to struggle to transport it. My case weighs 60 kilos.

I learned about the incident in the church in the papers. I was a bit puzzled as the people listed were from all over Paris. They had all come to a church to hear a concert. The papers described an old church, I thought of Saint-Gervais or Saint-Germain-des-Près.[290] It's very sad but one should be less afraid of bombing as it is not as dangerous as airplanes. Those people who fear an invasion are true imbeciles; it is insulting for the *poilus* who for three and a half years have held the *Boches* back. […]

4/4/1918.

The mail hasn't arrived, but Caplet has. […] He got to Paris just a few hours after the death of Debussy. He is the one who was in charge of all the details, had his funeral mask made, pictures, and a drawing. He was very happy, if one can use the word "happy," to be there for all the final details. He sat watch over Debussy's body for two days. […]

4/5/1918.

I received today your letter of April 3. I am shocked that you aren't receiving my letters. […] Last evening Caplet and I played the Debussy Sonata. What I mean is that, while I was playing, Caplet was following the piano part and making all the gestures, exactly as though he was playing. We hope one of these days to go get the piano […] and start our work. […]

Our pigeon service is growing. From now on we have 3 posts per regiment. […] Right now, 26 men from a regiment stationed here and in the surrounding area are taking courses at our pigeon station. I'm the one who serves as the serious, learned professor. […]

---

[290] On March 29, 1918, Good Friday, a shell from "Big Bertha," an enormous German gun seventry miles from Paris, fell on Saint-Gervais-Saint-Protais, a church in the 4th arrondissement built between 1494 and 1657, killing around 88 people. Fierro, *Histoire de Paris Illustrée*, 167.

I am writing before the mail; it arrives very late right now. That is why I received yesterday your two letters of April 4 and 5 in the afternoon. I note that you are not receiving my letters; alas, you are not alone. Niverd was saying yesterday that his wife was complaining that she hadn't received anything from him for a week, and he writes nearly every day. [...]

Yesterday we managed to get the piano which was in a house occupied by AD5.[291] After a lot of red tape, we received the authorization to bring it to the pigeon station. Then we needed to figure out how to transport it. Niverd and a team from the laundry service were tremendously helpful. In short, by 5:00 the piano was in place at the pigeon station.

Caplet and I started working on the Debussy Sonata last night. It will go quickly; when Caplet interprets Debussy, there are no missteps. The music is strange, original, but with smooth and particularly delicious harmonies. It requires a nimble and light execution, intelligent, and it is not easy to give this sort of delivery. There is much individual work to be done. We will be able to work in peace now that we have the piano. Our house is quite isolated in the middle of the fields, and people don't pay us much attention. Our pigeon exchange is tomorrow morning; Niel will do it. We take turns; that means each of us every 9 days. That is not very much. [...]

4/10/1918.

[...] Caplet has set about working seriously on his Sonata for Violoncello, Piano, and Soprano. At this moment he is totally occupied with this piece and has dropped everything else he was working on. His only distraction is working with me on Debussy's Sonata. It seems to be going less well than it was, but this is understandable. As we struggle to perfect it, we become more and more exacting. [...]

4/12/1918.

[...] Monsieur d'Estrinteaux [...] came yesterday to hear the Sonata. He was totally astonished. He is an excellent music lover, but he knew nothing by Debussy. He was stunned by what he heard. It is obvious that one doesn't immediately appreciate music like Debussy's. It is disconcerting, giving the impression of an exotic flower, strange and monstrous, with a morbid scent. There is all of that in this music, as well as an exquisite flavor, a rare feeling of equilibrium, and above all it is very French, light and frothy like sparkling wine. It delights and, at the same time, tortures the nerves a little. [...]

---

[291] Fifth Artillery Division.

4/13/1918.

[...] Maréchal came to see us yesterday, and we seized the occasion to play Debussy's Sonata for him—it is going quite well now and produces its effect; the first unmistakable impression is that of a slap to the face. One is gently suffocated, but quickly recovers from this surprise and then begins to taste the strange flavor of this music. [...]

Caplet was greatly surprised with Cool's observations.[292] He leaves perfectly bad passages uncorrected, and by contrast he criticizes excellent things. I must say that Caplet, from what I've observed, understands counterpoint differently from me. He approaches it musically, and not precisely by what is allowed or prohibited. Because of his musical perspective, he allows things that the rules prohibit [...] as long as the result is lovely music. The contrary absolutely annoys him. Certainly this is more aimed at producing something musical. Basically, if one wants to compose, it is not for the pleasure of writing counterpoint but rather to arrive at making music. Caplet, from what I've observed, never strains himself with writing counterpoint or fugues. He is happy that I am re-studying all that—for he will himself profit by reviewing and considering modern ways to use the techniques. [...]

4/15/1918.

I received yesterday your two letters of April 10 and 11. [...] The weather, alas, is not good; we have rain, wind, basically terrible weather. We can't help but think of those who, in muddy Flanders, are fighting fiercely. [...]

Second letter, same day.

I am writing again this evening as I may go to Chalons tomorrow. [...] The weather is atrocious, cold rain and biting wind. You can believe I appreciate my lodgings and thank heaven and the god of fortune. Our sector has been a bit active for two days; one of our regiments made a fortunate move recently. I think that made the *Boches* quite unhappy; they are showing their anger by increasing the artillery fire. [...]

4/16/1918.

I am writing this morning before the mail arrives. I hope today to have more luck than yesterday and receive some letters. [...] The weather is cold and gray and reminds us of last year at the same time; it was the day of the offensive. We were at Romain, behind Ventelay, and the cannon boomed furiously. It was for

---

[292] Louise sent some of Lucien's counterpoint exercises that had been corrected by Eugène Cools.

us a failure as well as the cause of considerable suffering. I will remember for a long time that week of moving through the snow, without food, and with very difficult stretches, the starry night for lodging. Fortunately for us, so far this year is not subjecting us that sort of ordeal. But many other men at this time have to be experiencing hardships like that. [...]

4/17/1918.

I received your letters of the 11th and the 12th. [...] I spent today working on counterpoint. Petit, the trumpet player chez Colonne came with Monsieur Coppet: both of them are starting to learn counterpoint and brought their first attempts. That means that our pigeon station is changing into a counterpoint classroom. [...]

Second letter, same day.

[...] Caplet and I just sightread the sonatas by Vierne and Neymarck.[293] It is hard to enjoy these works after that of Debussy. Vierne's sonata is full of formulas, of old-fashioned ideas, and of details that Caplet rightly describes as impoverished. Even though it has all these defects, we will work it up—for it also contains superficial qualities that will assure a certain success before the common public that surrounds us. It will take us very little time to prepare a work like this. As for Neymarck's sonata, it is unspeakable rubbish without any value. We conscientiously read through all of the movements to see if there might be, in one or another, an interesting passage—giving some indication of future promise. But nothing! It is horrible, appalling triteness. What a shame that such rubbish is not printed on toilet paper. He is a young, little rich man who has paid handsomely to have his musical rantings published. I won't bother sending this rubbish back to you; it is not worth the price of postage. The last page was blank: I tore it off, cut it in half, and I will use it for stationery. It is on one of these halves that I am now writing to you. The remainder is unfortunately unus-able for this purpose, so it will serve to light my fire—that is all that it's good for.

Upon receiving this letter, you must send me two other sonatas: that of d'Indy, and that of Pierné.[294] I would benefit from working on them seriously. As soon as we play through the Vierne, I will send it back to you. Maréchal came by at the end of our session; we played for him the first part of the Vierne and, upon his request, the Debussy. What light and what charm this sonata has; in comparison the others appear thick and coarse. [...]

---

[293] Louis Vierne (1870-1937), Violin Sonata in G minor, Op 23.; Jean Neymarck (1889-1913), Violin Sonata in F-sharp major.

[294] D'Indy Violin Sonata in C major, Op. 60; Gabriel Pierné (1863-1937), Sonata in D minor, Op. 36.

4/19/1918.

Yesterday I received your letter of April 15. [...] We are very lucky to be well-sheltered during this awful weather. There is a good log fire in my fireplace. I am thinking of comrades in the Nord, in the mud, with rain and big bombs falling from the sky. Our fate is to be envied. We have the Americans with us, mostly their artillery. They arrived several days ago. They give an impression of force and have an excellent spirit, and more, they have admirable equipment. [...]

4/20/1918.

I am writing today before the mail arrives. [...] Petit and Coppet are coming this afternoon to have their counterpoint efforts corrected. That means that today there will be no personal work. The Debussy Sonata is going very well, it is light and airy. As for Vierne's, the more we work on it, the more we see its lack of substance. [...] It goes on and on without saying anything. [...] How very different from Debussy's in which the musical language is subtle and refined, where there is nothing superfluous. [...] Caplet is right. Had Vierne composed this at the age of 20 or 25, one might say he showed promise. But to compose it at age 45, that means he has nothing to say.

We have increased considerably the number of pigeon stations. [...] For each exchange, we take 36 pigeons. [...] Here at the stationary post, we are training the young birds. We have fifteen who are not yet flying and need to be trained. It is very interesting. [...]

4/21/1918.

I am just back from exchanging the pigeons. I left this morning with my partner Niel. I dropped him in a spot where he could visit two or three posts: from time to time we need to visit the posts to make sure everything is all right and the pigeons are being well-managed. This exchange came off without incident. All is calm for us. In this area, we have what they call a helping hand—a patrol, rarely more than 20 men, who try to bring back a few *Boches* in order to drag out of them, if possible, some information. [...]

4/22/1918.

I think you are wrong to let yourself be influenced by all the gossip of Madame Boissard and others. [...] The people in Paris disgust me. What a lot of complaints because of a few unfortunate strikes by bombs. For sure, some fall on groups of people: they need to try to avoid large groups in certain areas as much as possible. For the others, it's God's will. It is astonishing that those people are so afraid of death. Obviously, they have not often had to face it. [...]

You are breathing unhealthy air in the rear; you live with fear or with people who only think about what they have to gain. It's dreadful! You go so far as to believe the Bank of France will not pay, that is truly crazy. It is useless to take out funds you don't need and which are earning interest. I do not understand, absolutely not at all, any of these fears. Please, do not let yourself be won over by arguments of the stupid, cowardly people around you. I understand better than anyone the agitation the detonations you hear can cause. [...] Try to be like me who is never afraid and who, in all circumstances, stays courageous and lucid. Don't pay attention if the people around you flee; they are truly imbeciles. Certainly, in Vincennes, you have no particular reason to be afraid. And especially stop saying that the *Boches* are going to wipe us out, knowing how hard the *poilus* have fought. When one thinks about all their spirit, it is almost blasphemous to talk like that. [...]

4/24/1918.

Still no mail. [...] Last night our sector was quite active, a lot of firing. The Americans have very large caliber (320) batteries which, for the past few days, have been very busy. Those 320s are not little pieces. They must weigh at least 250 kilos each. [...]

Mayer came to see us yesterday and returned to the frontline last night. Upon his request we played for him Debussy's Sonata, which continues to get better, and which is truly beautiful and of an indescribable charm. In comparison, the other sonatas have difficulty competing! We have read through d'Indy's, which is quite difficult to perfect. It is without a doubt superior to the Vierne but compared to the Debussy—how pedantic and academic it appears, without any freshness or originality. It is constructed of 1st theme, 2nd theme, all of which combine perfectly. But one knows in advance what is going to happen, and there is neither freshness nor spontaneity. He is a man who knows his trade, even too well, for it is totally evident. Debussy also knows his trade admirably, but nowhere is it obvious. To the contrary, the unexpected troubles you and charms you; the balance, even though it is new, is admirable. D'Indy's Sonata seems cold, ossified, stillborn, opaque and heavy. This is not French; Caplet rightly called it "*boche,*" it is a turn of mind that comes out of Leipzig. Debussy is truly an admirable master; with him the heart is warm, always with the subtlest sophistication, and always of the greatest nobility. We are going to work seriously and perfect with great care the d'Indy; in order to truly evaluate a work critically one must first work on it seriously. That is the least we can do. [...]

4/26/1918.

I received today your second letter from the 23rd. [...] I get up at 7:15 except when I make the pigeon exchange; on those days, every 9 days, I get up at 6 a.m. I wash up, and every two days I shave. In general, I go for coffee and toast and butter about 8:15. When I get back, I chat a bit with Caplet who goes to bed very late and generally gets up about 8:30. It is then mail time and time to work on counterpoint until 11:00. From 11 to 12:30 I practice violin, technique. About 2 p.m., after lunch, Caplet corrects my work, then I go back to my room. I write a letter, and do an hour of counterpoint, and then practice violin for an hour and a half. At 5:00, sonata rehearsals with Caplet. Dinner about 7:30; about 9:00 an hour of counterpoint, a bit of reading; fifteen minutes of conversation with Caplet and it is bedtime. [...]

4/27/1918.

Still no mail. Today I'm sending the picture of our pigeon station that M. d'Estintreaux took. [...] The big tree that fans out in front of the house is a chestnut tree in full flower. The little river is the Suippes. [...]

Poor Villers-Bretonneux must be in a sorry state. I think with a heavy heart of all those good people who had to leave rapidly. Mme Delacour's precious birds must have been asphyxiated and her beautiful house has to be in ruins. There were also important tapestries, machines, material, everything is destroyed. It's truly awful.

The *Boches* really want to take Amiens, but I don't believe they will. Unfortunately, the cathedral will most likely suffer the same fate as the one in Reims. [...]

5/1/1918.

Of course, there is no mail yet. [...] When our battalions come back for rest, they do communication exercises. Every two or three days we give the battalion 9 pigeons and they send them back with training messages. We are really in the business of raising pigeons here. In this little house, there are three pigeon roosts [...] One of them has right now 50 young ones. A one-day old pigeon is ugly, covered with a kind of fuzz and a beak that seems huge compared with the body. After a week, the fuzz starts to fall off and tiny little feathers start to grow. After 3 months, we can start training the pigeons to go to the trenches. The training takes 15 days. [...]

In a fixed pigeon station like this one, we do not lose very many; the pigeons, born here, come back home easily. The pigeon is very useful and it's a real business to run a pigeon station. [...]

5/1/1918.

I just this minute received your letter of April 29. I am replying immediately to explain the policeman. Don't worry. Here is what must have happened. When the 129th had all those adventures, which you know about, at the beginning of June last year, I was sent to the division. In order for them to keep me, as the 129th was leaving the division, they transferred me to the 274th. Probably the notification of that transfer was not sent to the 129th, so I am still on their list. Recently they must have been reviewing the list and realized that I was not there and asked the *gendarmerie* for more information. You gave them the wrong information: since the end of October I am no longer assigned to the 274th. That is when I was again transferred. The 274th was dissolved and the division wanted to keep me, so I was transferred again, this time to the 74th. [...] You just need to tell them that I belong to the 74th Infantry (CHR), 5th Division, SP93.[295] This little incident is proof of the state of the paperwork here. [...]

I note that Madame Duez just died. Contrary to what we expected she died before her sister, who is older, so her sister will be her heir. [...]

5/3/1918.

Finally, beautiful weather, slightly cool, but a beautiful azure sky. What a lovely temperature and what lovely light! This most seedy countryside is bathed with splendid luminosity.

In their most recent attacks, the *Boches* suffered a terrible failure and enormous losses. They cannot possibly continue such costly and unsuccessful attacks. The effect of the unified command is evident; reserves are sent where they are needed. If all our forces had been under unified command in 1915, the war would be over. The English would not have had to make the sacrifices they did, or at least the results would have been different. [...]

5/7/1918.

[...] Everyone here is getting busy; all available land is plowed and planted with vegetables. If we are still here in two months, we will have lettuce and greens and vegetables in profusion. [...]

5/8/1918.

I received yesterday only your brief note of May 4, with a money order for 100 francs. [...] For sure, Villers-Bretonneux is nothing but ruins. I have so often thought of those poor workers who lodged me so well and always feared that one day they would pay dearly. Those poor people have left, Lord only knows

---

[295] CHR, *compagnie hors rang*, regimental company that consists of administration, logistics and command. SP, preparation service.

how, and with what. I once saw the departure of residents. It was in Cappy, and I will never forget it: women and children in tears, holding poor bundles, piled into all sorts of vehicles, under bombs, not just one or two as in Paris, but hundreds and in a little village. It was distressing and heart-wrenching. [...]

5/11/1918.

[...] I received today your second letter from the 8th and one from the 9th. [...] You shouldn't be so prudish; remember our old ancestor, Rabelais, very French, who called things what they are. Three or four scantily clothed women would not annoy me at all. It's much less dangerous than a 210 shell. I think that the joys of the flesh can be good at certain times, and they don't diminish one's artistic ideal. Moderation, moderation, that is what is needed, and that is rare. Just like with counterpoint: in principle, nothing is forbidden but one has to use techniques with moderation. [...]

5/12/1918.

Of course, mail has not arrived. The weather is dreadful. In our sector the American infantry is arriving. Two regiments are coming through here. The focus is on combining troops. It is basically the best way to quickly make use of the foreign troops. I think the Americans have made a huge effort in the past two months to send in troops, an average of 100,000 per month. Everywhere the guys on leave have been, there have been some Americans, it's quite simple. We have to hope that the moment will come when we see them at the front. In any case, we have a lot more confidence in their worth and the way they will be used than in the English. One has to admit that the latter fell short of our expectations. [...] Fortunately, an energetic man like Clemenceau is in charge now—the last crisis would have been fatal for us. [...] I am sending you a tiny branch of white lilacs. We have a bush near the river, it's small and doesn't have many flowers. We have a hawthorn bush which will bloom soon. I'll send some as soon as it does. [...]

5/13/1918.

[...] Caplet is going to the Noblette camp, 15 kilometers away, to take a class on gas. That will be the 16th and 17th. A note came out last night on that subject, also naming me chief of the pigeon unit during that time. Everyone at the mess wanted to toast to that, but I vigorously refused, all the more because the wines we have are not very good. [...]

5/14/1918.

I hope to have mail today. […] Yesterday an official listener came and we played the first movement and the Scherzo from the d'Indy Sonata. Those are the two movements I prefer; the Scherzo is the best part. There is a background of hail in that sonata, created on purpose to mimic combat. It sustains a principal that can be debated. It is closer to German music whereas Debussy, so very French, relates directly to the music of the 18th century. There is a world of difference between the two composers, and it is not surprising that they hated each other. Without hesitation, I am for Debussy, the charmer, who evokes powerful irony, the wind on wet leaves, the smells of the earth, thousands of little things. That music is thrilling. D'Indy's music protests; it is cold and calculating. D'Indy is connected to the past, Debussy opens the way to the future, bright and transparent. […]

5/18/1918.

This morning the heat continues. […] Right now, we are so happy and calm that we have no need to try to move or give concerts all over the place. We very wisely play dead. The time will come when we will need to come out from this shadow. Much to the displeasure of Maréchal, Caplet has no interest in making any effort to give concerts of any sort. […]

The class on poison gas which Caplet took, as head of the unit, was not very useful according to him. He did not learn anything we don't already know. Oh yes, they are giving the chemical components of the various gases being used. That's not much help to us and for most of the people in the class completely incomprehensible. We know the reagents. One has to put black camphor soap on sexual organs, the anus, the armpits, in short, all the warm, damp areas. Clothes impregnated with these gases have to be disinfected and not touched except with hands protected by rubber gloves. They give us oilcloth capes, as the gas slides off without penetrating. In short, this is technology about which civilians haven't the slightest idea. But Caplet didn't learn anything new! […]

5/19/1918.

[…] The heat is awful. […] Apparently, because of a shortage of raw material we will not have lightweight pants. Last year I had a pair of shiny blue pants which were very useful and also a pair of white pants. We cannot count on anything like that this year, so I would like you to send me a pair of my coarse cotton slacks. I have one or two pairs that I used for fencing. […]

5/20/1918.

I did not receive a letter today, but there was a flat package which contained the poems of Ronsard, a lovely little volume, charming in many ways. [...]

5/21/1918.

[...] I just finished the class I was teaching on pigeon keeping. My good *poilus* left happy. They will come back soon to visit the pigeon station and that will be the end for them. There will be another group on the 23rd and 24th, pigeon keepers from the regiments who are coming for more advanced training. [...]

General L asked for Caplet yesterday. [...] He asked whether we were all together, if we were working on music; learning that there was nothing like that happening, that our instruments were in the rear, he shared his displeasure with our general who got all twisted up in explanations. It's truly laughable. Caplet is going to try to use this to get Maréchal here as radioman for the Corps. [...]

Second letter, same day.

Today I received your letter of May 18 and one from the 19th. [...] I hope there will be strawberries on our strawberry bushes..If promises about leaves are kept, I have a very good chance to be home at the end of June. [...]

After November 1, I will be a territorial reservist. But obviously, as anyone with a situation like mine, I will make a request to stay where I am. Otherwise I could be sent to a territorial regiment and become once again a 2nd class soldier, obliged to break up stones on the roads, or other such unpleasant tasks. You amuse me when you say I could come to the rear. To be mobilized into civilian life, one usually has to be a big shot or to have a career important for national defense, and even with that, it doesn't always work. One is a soldier until age 48. When he was younger, Balembois worked in the silk mills. I think it was the Louvre store that asked to have him come back to Chalais-Meudon where they need skilled silk workers for airships. [...]

5/22/1918.

Yesterday we received a note from General Pétain about all sorts of possibilities in case of a *Boche* offensive, including the suppression of leaves. We have, unfortunately, to expect that, one day, the *Boches* will attack again. [...]

5/24/1918.

I just this minute received your letter talking about a shell that fell on the corner of the building. It happens occasionally that unexploded shells fall back down. The great luck for you is that it did not explode when it landed. I don't quite understand where it fell; it must have just caught a corner of the house. […] I hope you were not too scared. The shell must have been from one of our anti-aircraft batteries. It fell intact. You will find it on the ground. That is the only thing it could be. […]

To come home on a special 4-day pass, I would have to receive a telegram telling me that you are very ill. The worst part is that, for some time now, the police stations are making inquiries to verify that the person in question is truly sick. There certainly have been abuses. In the case of cheating, the punishment is very harsh. You can imagine that I am not going to put myself in that situation. […]

5/25/1918.

I received today your letter of May 24. […] The general told Caplet today that it was impossible for him to bring Maréchal to the Corps […] but he told Caplet that we had to reestablish the quartet and make music. He called Boubou, our Chief of General Staff and gave him the order. […] Here is what we are going to try to do: take Desormes as violist; Caplet, as pianist, can accompany works with piano and voice. It is agreed that we will no longer play for the *poilus*, we will only play chamber music. I am going to try to come to Vincennes for at least two days to get some quartets, we will make a little box for the music. […] Desormes is an excellent violist from the Opera. […]

5/28/1918.

I received today your letter of May 23. […] From what I can tell you are barely getting any sleep. It was very nice of Madame Peyrot to offer you good shelter nearby. I can understand getting out of bed to go to a safe shelter, but to just go into the dining room seems totally useless to me. I hope the electric company will quickly repair the wires so you are not deprived of good light for long. […]

Lucien had a very short home leave between May 29 and 31.

5/31/1918.

I just this moment arrived after a very tiring journey. Yesterday the train didn't leave until 11 a.m. At first, the station master didn't know whether there would be a train. We arrived this morning, finally, at 9 a.m. We went via Coulommiers, Fère, etc. The main line was reserved for military transportation. What a lot of people and goods in movement! One needs to see that to believe that the *Boches* will not get very far. Where will Foch engage the battle? […]

6/1/1918.

Obviously at this moment mail is halted. I don't know when this letter will reach you. For sure, we are on the eve of significant events. Our sector is still relatively quiet. Reims which, in these circumstances is a pivotal location, has not fallen. As long as that location holds, we will not budge. What will be our role in the battle which is certainly going to happen? Will it be passive? We can't know, but it is wise to believe we will need to do something. Thus we, like the man in the Scripture, will need to gird our loins and draw on our moral strength and willpower. As I was telling Caplet this morning, I am ready for the fight. I can only say one thing, the morale of our troops is extraordinary, and one has to hope the same for our allies. You are more up-to-date than I am about what is happening, as you have the newspapers. Here we only have *communiqués*. What I can say is that no one is worried. We expect Mayer and Maréchal back today with their instruments. It is not worth pointing out that this is a strange moment they have chosen. […]

Second letter, same day.

[…] We know next to nothing. Lots of rumors are running around. What is pretty much certain is that the *Boches* reached the Marne and that the Paris-Châlons line is completely cut. Mayer and Maréchal arrived this morning, bringing with them the things you know about. They were bombed by planes last night in the train station of Épernay but they finally managed to get here without incident and relatively quickly. Both of them were quite tired. In truth we don't know where all these events are leading. The *Boche* advance is worrisome, and we need to figure out what is going on as fast as possible. I hope that's already been done. That should tell you how impatiently we wait for the *communiqués*; for sure we don't receive any newspapers. The sector here is quite calm. We think we are noticing movement in the sectors just in front of us. We believe the *Boches* are slipping in reserves as far as Reims to support their offensive. We will no doubt do the same. That is why the infantry divisions already in the field will probably stay there, unless of course there is general movement. So, for now, it is all unknown. […]

Again, good luck smiled on me. I was able to bring you the food thing we talked about, which is significant, and I got to see you. God only knows when we will see each other again with all these events. I heard tell that we were going to really throw the Americans into the battle as, at this moment, there is no reason to spare anything. […]

I am sending a very pretty little flower from the garden: I don't know what it is. I also do not know when these letters will reach you. […]

6/2/1918.

It seems there will be mail today. This would have been the third day with nothing. […] Our sector is relatively quiet but we hear the cannon booming around Reims. They say, but then what don't they say, that Mangin is leading the attack army. In any case, the *Boches* have put almost 2 million men against us, in the hope that this time they can break us and turn their attention to other enemies with less resistance. I believe that once again they will not succeed. They have already made huge advances and we have to hope we can retake some of that and push them out of the Marne region. It is at times like this that we see the moral worth of those around us. […]

6/3/1918.

[…] I received this morning a letter from Pierrot which I am sending you. It will show you that my former comrades in the Red Cross of the 129th were not very lucky. We are forced to admit that when one is healthy, my God, all the other things are nothing. For sure, in all that, compared with my former comrades, my fate is certainly enviable. I am sure that my violin truly saved my life. […]

The *Boches* seem to have been stopped and we have to hope that they will be pushed back a bit farther and the Marne valley freed of them.[296] […]

Since this morning there has been talk of some changes in our division. I don't know whether we will change our pigeon location. We will never find anything better, just the opposite. In this area, except for our fixed pigeon station, there are only trailers and little wooden shacks for houses. We are not bad off here, but it is not our usual palace. We cannot be too greedy; tomorrow will make 3 months that we've been here. Lots of others have been in much more misery, so complaints would be misplaced […]

Second letter, same day.

I received your letter of May 30. […] Our soldiers are, of course, being killed, but right now 100,000 *Boche* bodies are fertilizing the fields from the Chemin des Dames to Château-Thierry! It is frightening how much this is costing them and it is hard to see what good can come of such sacrifices. They hoped to end

---

[296] The Germans attacked on the Aisne, where the allies did not expect them, advancing within fifty-six miles of Paris. Ludendorf, the German general, added new troops that were stopped by Foch's reservists. Taylor, *The First World War,* 228.

this; they were certainly mistaken. The French are too strong; we will come back from this challenge with the same willpower that right now is giving the *poilu* the strength to make a supreme effort. [...] We think that Mangin is in Reims, the guard dog who already defended Verdun. [...]

6/4/1918.

Tomorrow I will be 39 ½ years old, headed for 40. That is a turning point for men. Generally, it is when one settles down or pulls things together. I do not need to pull things together; I have never let them come apart. What is sadder is that I am getting old and have not been able, or barely able, to realize my dreams. [...]

Mayer is quite ill; he has a fever and a pain in his side. We do not know what is wrong. [...]

6/5/1918.

[...] Mayer is still very ill; he has a high fever and we do not know what it is. The doctors here do not mess around. Once a fever reaches a certain degree, they don't bother trying to find out what is wrong; they evacuate you. It's a simple solution but does not give the doctor the observational skills he should have. We are going to ask one of the doctors from the ambulance unit to examine Mayer and tell us what he thinks. Unlike a *poilu* in the field, Mayer does not want to be evacuated, he will gain nothing by it. [...]

Vincennes. Friday, June 7, 1918, 5 p.m.

I have just received at 4 o'clock your 2nd letter dated Tuesday, June 4, that of Wednesday, June 5, and my letter of June 1. [...] At the moment we are a little upset, I mean everyone, because we are afraid of the German advance on Paris. Many factories moved to the provinces and the workers and their families have followed. The employees received their June salaries in advance so as not to have too much money in the coffers if, by chance, the Germans were to arrive in Paris. [...]

At 2 o'clock I went to the police station to get a safe conduct in case I decided to go to Brittany (they are only good for 15 days). If you don't leave during those 2 weeks, you need to get another. I do not really plan to leave; however, if the bombing were to increase, I think it would be prudent to move away. [...] What bothers me about all of this is that I cannot solve the rent issue if I am not here. [...] If the situation becomes too bad, I might have to leave hastily. I say all this, not to torment you, but to keep you informed of what is happening. [...]

Saturday, June 8, 1918, 1:30 pm.

[...] I received this morning your 2nd letter dated Wednesday, June 5 (birthday of your 39 years and a half). I am pleased to see that, so far, you have yet to leave the dovecote. How long will it last? No one knows. [...] You do well to work on the Bach for the bowing [...] and on counterpoint. [...] That makes me very happy. [...]

I am thinking of leaving for Plouézec Tuesday morning, June 11. [...] If the Germans succeeded again in an advance, it could be very serious; they could force the inhabitants of Vincennes to leave. It would be prudent to leave before that happens in order to avoid a hasty departure that only allows only one small package! [...]

6/6/1918.

I hope to have mail today; yesterday we received newspapers. I read the *communiqué* of last night. It notes a retreat by the *Boches* in several regions. In any case, it seems they are stopped; and their active forces are melting away rapidly. They say the *Boches* sent 55 infantry divisions against us. That makes 600,000 to 700,000 men. [...]

Mayer is still sick. He has the flu, like the epidemic that was all over Spain and now is in France. [...]

6/7/1918.

This morning I am writing very early. Our pigeon exchange has been moved to an hour earlier. In this new area, we are more easily seen. It is in our interest to move very early, when a light haze still covers the ground. [...]

If Foch and Pétain are not mounting a strong counter offensive at this time, they must know that the *Boches* still have strong forces; we will undertake a new offensive in a month or two. If they actually did it now, we might win, but the opposite is also possible. If we use all our reserves now for an unsuccessful counter offensive, what would we have left for autumn—the English in whom we have little confidence or the Americans whose military capability is not yet known? I understand the worry of the leadership. [...]

Sunday, June 9, 1918, 1:30 p.m.

I received this morning your letters dated June 6 and 7 and your counterpoint sheet. [...] I had told you in my previous letters that I might go to Brittany; I probably won't. That decision is too important; it takes me farther away from you and I would not be able to send you things you might need. And then, I think it better to stay at home with my routine and minimal expenses. I sent Jean

Alan yesterday to the Gare Montparnasse to find out about train times and baggage allowance (50 kilos in all). [...] There are three trains per day (Paris-Brest), one at 7:30 a.m. with a restaurant car and 2 in the evening. All the provinces must be crowded with evacuees and people who have left Paris, and everything (rooms, meals) must be overpriced. Since I could not rent a house, I would have to take a pension from someone, which would be very expensive. [...] I think it is better to stay in Vincennes despite the frequent aircraft raids (we've had nothing for 2 nights.) [...]

6/8/1918.

I hope to have mail this morning. Nothing new to tell you. [...] Our pigeon station is selling our lettuce incredibly fast; you might say we don't even give it time to grow. The longing for edible greens is enormous. [...]

Mayer is still sick; in the morning his fever is 39 and in the evening 40; no other symptoms. The doctor doesn't know what it could be other than a strange illness. We could use some rain. All the roads are covered with dust beyond imagination; fortunately our house is set back pretty far and the road that runs past here is not a major road. [...]

Second letter, same day.

I received today your letter of June 5, the day I was 39 ½. Just think, 4 years ago we were talking about leaving for Brittany around the 20th. How long ago that seems! But we must have hope that we will see happier times. They will be all the happier in having made us wait for them. It is certainly true that many leaders in the rear are well set up in restful, productive careers; the longer this goes on the truer it becomes. They forget too often that war is not lucrative for everyone; what is more, for most, this career, if you want to call it that, is filled with suffering and danger. For some leaders, their present situation is the climax of their lives, the crowning of their existence. It takes a thunderbolt like we just experienced to remind them that there is more to what they do than stopping at payroll at the end of the month and busying themselves with bureaucracy. Responding with lucidity, clairvoyance, and quick decisions is not what they are accustomed to doing. All those men in charge are too old; they were raised with ideas that this war has proven wrong, and my God, they have a hard time changing if they even try. When they encounter younger leaders with more modern ideas, all those old profiteering popes jump on them, if they don't do worse. And the *poilu* is there to redeem their faults! Happy are those who suffer, as they will see God, says the scripture. I hope so. But I also hope that these leaders will not see God and that they will suffer for millions of years to redeem their stupidity and pride. [...]

Monday, June 10, 1918, 2:30 p.m.

[…] I received your second letter from June 7 and that of June 8. […] If the Germans advance, Vincennes could be cut off from the front and I would no longer receive your news. If I were in Brittany or elsewhere I could always correspond with you. […] I think it would be wise to make up my mind. You never give me your opinion about it? You never breathe a word about all this; yet you must have an opinion for or against? I will probably have Mathilde's husband buy my ticket to Paimpol tomorrow; he could carry my trunk to the station. The trains are always full in advance so the departure may be as much as 5 days after buying the ticket. I'm very tormented but, if I have a ticket, I will have to leave! It's painful for me: it seems to me that I'm moving away from you forever. […]

6/9/1916.

Mayer came back this morning to the ambulance unit. […] He has pleurisy. He must have gotten chilled in a *sape*. True, for a long time he'd been complaining of a pain in his chest. This morning they drained his chest; that explains his persistent fever. […] He was greeted by the ambulance unit as a friend; they gave him an officer's room, a nurse comes to read to him, in short, they are caring for him like a chicken they would like someday to roast. […]

I read in the papers about the last air raid over Paris; it appears there were a few victims. The creation of a fortified camp, which is pompously announced in the papers, seems to us quite ridiculous. The *poilus* at the front are the defense of Paris; nothing else is needed. The Americans seem to be very capable, which gives us great hope. […]

Second letter, same day.

I received today your letter from June 6. […] I went to see Mayer; this morning they drained his chest and took out almost a quarter liter of serous fluid. He is much more comfortable after this procedure, his fever is falling, and I do believe he will be up and about in a week and will not need to be evacuated to the rear.

The closest the *Boches* are to Paris is 80 kilometers; but they have to set up their guns (like Bertha) pretty far from their lines, so we have to figure 100 kilometers. For the moment they have no interest in bringing those guns any closer. An immediate offensive would be very costly for the French troops, that is why it has not happened. […]

Tuesday, June 11, 1918, 1:30 p.m.

I received this morning your second letter from June 8 and the one from Sunday, June 9. [...] I decided to have Mathilde's husband buy for me a second class ticket to Paimpol. It is the Paris-Brest train that passes to Saint Brieuc and Guingamp. I have to get off at Guingamp for the little train to Paimpol. From there I will go to Plouézec, I do not know how. [...] I'm waiting until tonight to find out when I'll leave. [...] I will write to Maria as soon as I have my ticket. [...] All this is very worrisome because I do not know exactly what I am doing. Alas! What an ordeal! Had you received my letters faster I would have known your opinion. [...]

6/10/1918.

I received today your letter from June 7. [...] I completely understand that Paris is upset by the unexpected advance of the *Boches*. While I can praise the precautions being taken and tell you that you would be better off in Brittany than in Vincennes, I do not believe there is any reason to panic. The *Boches* will not be there tomorrow. If you leave, you should take with you sugar and winter clothes. You don't really know when you will come back, so you should be prepared. It would be wise to take a bit of money; get 2000 extra francs from the bank. That will make 4000 for you to use and leaves 10,000 in the bank. Life in Brittany is not expensive. Of course, we have to hope that all these events will subside quickly and that you will easily come back to Vincennes. Or that I, if I have a home leave, can check on the state of our house and the other buildings. [...] You can thoughtfully and calmly prepare your departure; in fact, I think a ticket is only good for 8 to 10 days after it is purchased. Work on all those details and don't worry; one has to be philosophical and try to see the big picture. It is easy to be frightened, but we should not throw in the sponge; the *Boches* haven't reached the end of their difficulty. [...] Thank you for the lovely roses you sent. [...]

Wednesday, June 12, 1918, 2 p.m.

I received this morning your second letter from June 9 and the one from June 10. [...] Naturally I will go to Plouézec where they know me. I will take your violins—the Guarnerius and the Guadagnini. [...] I will leave tomorrow morning early to take the train from Paris-Brest which leaves at 7:30 a.m. and arrives in Guingamp at 6:30 in the evening. If there is no delay, I will get the small train that goes to Paimpol and arrives at 8:20 in the evening. I will sleep in Paimpol and leave the next morning, that is to say on Friday, June 14, for Plouézec by the bus which serves the post office. Just yesterday I received a letter from Maria asking for our news. I replied that I was coming to Plouézec and asked her to pick me up in Paimpol. [...]

6/11/1918.

I received today your letter of June 8, the one in which you say you will probably leave on the 11th though you do not confirm that. [...] When you leave, it would be best to take all our valuables, and my instruments. [...] The offensive north of Compiègne, although it seems well contained, is nonetheless dangerous. But all we can do is see what happens. Here, we are still calm and safe, although all that could change in a minute. You will have nothing to fear in Brittany; our naval forces would make a landing impossible. [...]

I do not believe at all that Paris will be taken, and I do not think that would end the war. The Americans have not entered this war to see it end badly for us or for them. [...]

6/13/1918.

This time we have a plan: in a few days we will gather and head for new shores, certainly less peaceful. It will be at least two weeks before we enter into any action. We cannot complain; we have been here for three and a half months, and Lord knows a lot has happened during that time. [...]

Everything is set for our departure, but we have no official orders yet. I think it's just a matter of a few days. Yesterday I got my hair cut so I won't be bothered by all the moving around and the dust. Captain Zeirer thinks this is the *Boches'* supreme effort. He says the Americans are pouring in 200,000 men a month. That will soon break the gridlock. [...]

Plouézec, Friday, June 14, 1918, midday.

[...] Here I am in Plouézec; I'm sleeping at Maria's house tonight and I think I'll arrange to stay here. [...] At Maria's I will always have her service at my disposal, despite the fact that she works. [...]

6/14/1918.

Most likely I will leave tomorrow for La Cheppe, very near the place where some time ago I dined with the pilots and the concert was interrupted because one of them had been killed. [...]

It is summer, it will do you good to be where the air is healthy. I hope that events will let you easily come back at the end of October. As for us, we are packing our things. That will not take very long; we soldiers have quite a lot of things, but they still fit into a small space. [...]

As soon as I know the date of your departure, I will write to you in care of Maria so there will be the least possible interruption in my correspondence. You will give me your address. I hope that, with Maria's help, you will be able to find an acceptable place and that you will profit greatly from this time in Brittany. You should not be so hard on yourself, and you should not listen to all the alarmists around you. Right now, our resistance is so great that the *Boches* will not long be able to continue their attack. They would lose millions of men to get as far as Paris. The shock of the Chemin des Dames was a dreadful surprise, but one should not conclude that the entire French army was rotten, that the *Boches* only needed to show up and they would be in Paris a week later. [...]

6/15/1918.

Today I am writing a little later than usual; we leave tonight and we had to pack everything and straighten up. I just went to check on what vehicle we will put our things in, as they have reduced transportation by 50 percent and it is getting difficult to find room for our things. We called General L about our instruments. He said we should take them to Troyes where the Corps has a supply garrison which will be guarded. So Maréchal left this morning to take the instruments, some music and a few packages. He will be away at least 45 hours.

I just this minute received your letter of the 12th, in which you say you will leave on the 13th. [...] I am afraid that Maria may not receive your letter in time and not be able to pick you up in Paimpol. You should have sent a telegram. In any case, I hope that in a few days you will be settled comfortably, rested and in good air. You are terribly discouraged and that is not good. [...]

The growing size of the American army, young and valiant men, combined with our younger soldiers, will create a crack army which will absolutely wipe out our adversaries. All that doesn't make for a short war; I think that we still have two years to go! Next year we will start to push them back and, in 1920, we will see the crushing defeat. [...]

Sunday, June 16, 1918, 7 a.m.

[...] Maria tells me that Évreux was bombed. [...] I believe that Normandy will not be spared: half of France will receive bombs and shells, it is an almost general devastation. I do not know if I did well to leave Vincennes. However, I believe that the situation is serious, and I feared that I would not hear from you again. Compiègne is, I believe, under threat; if this city fell to the power of the Germans as well as the railway line, what would happen? [...]

Sunday, June 16, 1918, 1:30.

I received your second letter from June 11, your two letters of the 12th, and the one from the 13th (the day of my departure) and, the most important, the very funny caricature of you by Caplet! [...]

I have already told you that I am staying with Maria, first because I know her and then there is no room anywhere. Mme Pierre, in Port Lazo, is living in her kitchen because she has rented her two rooms on the second floor and her dining room. Otherwise, people who have extra rooms save them for family members. [...] I did not come to Plouézec for a comfortable vacation. [...] I do not think that there is any danger on the Breton coast, at least not much! For now, the tranquility that we enjoy in here is almost disconcerting. [...] I see that you have been able to do some more counterpoint. [...]

Tuesday, June 18, 1918, 1:30.

[...] I have brought with me more than the necessary amount of money. [...] I have to pay a monthly rent for the room I occupy at Maria's; for food, either I advance the funds every day as I have done until now or Maria asks for a fixed price (it is about the same). Everything is more expensive than before, despite the fact that there is a big difference with Paris. [...]

Wednesday, June 19, 1918, 9 a.m.

I am writing to you in the morning because the only mail departure is at noon (official time).[297] Maria keeps the time of the church, that is, the old hour; all the peasants are like that, they do not comply with the laws. I relied on that time so, without knowing, I was putting my letters in the box too late.

Maria no longer runs her business as she used to but she still has a few responsibilities—she writes for many people whose relatives are at the front. She does this mainly on Saturdays and Sundays, days when people from other villages need to come to Plouézec.

I attach to my letter a wild daisy and some gorse flowers that we picked on our way back from Port Lazo last Sunday. Plouézec does not yet have rationing for bread; it was discussed two weeks ago but has not been implemented. They do have tickets for sugar and gasoline; since I brought my sugar cards, I can add to what Maria gets. [...]

6/18/1918.

Alas, we are nowhere near Paris. We spent 30 hours on the train, a particularly tiring journey and ended up in an area I know well. [...] We are settled in

---

[297] The law creating winter time and summer time in France was proposed in 1916 and became official in 1917.

a lovely chateau with an admirable garden and we could wish for nothing more than to stay here. [...] Of course, no letter today. I know nothing of your departure from Vincennes. [...]

Thursday, June 20, 1918, 2 p.m.

I have not heard from you today. I know you are in Noisy-le-Sec, so I was hoping you could send me a word; you may have done it, but belatedly, and I will have to wait until tomorrow to have the pleasure of reading you. [...]

Friday, June 21, 1918, 2 p.m.

I did not receive any news today (or yesterday); since the mail comes only once a day, I must give up all hope of reading you. If you stayed in Noisy-le-Sec, it seems to me that you would have had time to write a few lines; I don't know. Have you been busy or too preoccupied to do so? Finally, I hope to hear from you tomorrow with news of your situation and of the correspondence you have received from me. [...]

Saturday, June 22, 1918, 2 p.m.

My dear child, no news yet! [...]

Sunday, June 23, 1918, 2 p.m.

I have not yet heard from you today; I'm starting to worry! It is not possible that you are in Noisy-le-Sec, otherwise you would have written! The station there must be heavily bombed by planes because of all the troop movements. I fear for you in that sense. There may be a delay in the delivery of mail from the front, because I see just now in the copy of *L'Information* I have just received the following: "The postal service of the armies which until now had been very satisfactory has been experiencing considerable delays in mail delivery." [...] I hope that this is why I have no news. Nevertheless, I am tormented. [...]

I think that tomorrow I will hear from you and that I will know what has become of you. It is very painful for me to remain without news. [...]

6/19/1918.

[...] We are still in our beautiful chateau, but the rumor circulating has us leaving tomorrow morning to go to the front. This area for now is very calm. There was no letter yesterday. Because of our move, I will not have any mail for a week. [...]

6/20/1918.

I received yesterday a pile of letters but not one with news of your trip. We moved today to a post in the 2nd line. [...] The *Boche* advance is now ended. [...] Their losses were unbelievable around Montdidier and Noyon. Mangin distinguished himself. He is the one who lead the counterattack that protected Compiègne and stopped the Germans. [...]

Plouézec, Monday, June 24, 1918, 2 p.m.

[...] I finally received news today in the 1 p.m. mail. I have your letters dated Wednesday 19, Thursday 20 and Friday 21 June. The last letter I received was dated June 16, so I'm missing 2 letters, if you wrote and 17 and June 18. I do not know where you are because it is likely that the letters with that information are the ones that I did not receive. [...]

It has not been warm in Brittany; the wind is very cool and very strong, sometimes even icy. Yesterday, Sunday, June 23, the temperature was warmer, the sky was blue, and the sun deigned to show its nose. I went to Port Lazo with Maria who felt she had worked enough during the week and wanted to take a walk. Her job is difficult but, like all the people in the countryside, she runs hither and yon, doing 10 laps for 1, to arrive at the end of the day without much to show for it.

We went to the beach in Port Lazo. We took two pieces of toast and butter in a string bag as a snack. We ate them sitting on the kelp (dry) and pebbles watching the sea rise (high tide being at 5:10). I rediscovered a little of the beauty of the landscape of yesteryear, but the current circumstances are so sad that nothing is pleasing. I would rejoice in your presence but we should not think about it at the moment, despite the fact that the permissions have resumed. [...]

I haven't yet told you about my trip. I did tell you that Mathilde and her husband accompanied me to the Montparnasse station with all my packages. Despite my request to Mathilde's husband to buy me a second-class ticket with a reserved seat, (48,80 frs, it has increased!) he did not, so I could not find a single seat. I travelled 3rd class to Rennes, fortunately in good conditions because the cars for Rennes were not full and I was in one of those cars. I naturally had to get off in Rennes to change to a compartment going as far as Brest. I found a seat in second-class as far as Guingamp; but it was annoying to be forced to get off the train with all the baggage I had. However, I found a man who carried everything for me. In third class, I was very calmly installed with a Breton woman and her three children going with her to the country and who also got off in Guingamp. [...]

The 7:30 train from Paris-Brest included a restaurant car; I had lunch there at 12:30 (5 fr. lunch without wine). It was nothing special, and it was a day without meat! I ate nothing in Vincennes in the morning before leaving and in Guingamp, when I arrived at the hotel where I slept, I took nothing but a cup of linden tea before going to bed, so the expense was not too great. In Guingamp, the room cost me 2,50; 0,50 for the car in the evening and morning and 1 fr for a café au lait and bread and butter taken in my room. [...]

6/22/1918.

I just received your two cards from Guingamp. You still haven't given me any details of your trip. [...] For now, our area is quiet; we are 11 kilometers from the most advanced portion of the front line. [...]

6/23/1918.

Still no news from Maréchal who is not yet back from Troyes. We expected to be heading back into the maelstrom or a new catastrophe, that is why the instruments and music were sent to Troyes. Had we imagined the current calm, I would have kept my violin and the others the same. It's really Caplet who insisted that I send my instrument with the others; I wanted to keep it. It would have been good, yesterday, when Commander Bouteville asked Caplet to play at Mass. Caplet told him that there had been orders to send all the instruments to Troyes. The commander replied: "What, Durosoir didn't keep his violin?"

That leads me to believe that one day soon we will go for the instruments. [...] We are in a difficult situation. People here put up with us rather than like us, so at times, they act in bad faith. [...]

For two days we have had a fierce wind and the nights are almost cold. Fortunately, we are well-lodged. I share a room on the 3rd floor with 4 secretaries who, obviously, are never there during the day. [...]

Second letter, same day.

No news from you today. [...] I still do not know what Army we belong to; I think it is the 1st. In case of attack, it appears we are under the orders of an Australian army corps. I do not know whether that is true; for now it's all a big muddle. It would seem the Americans managed to bring 250,000 men in May. That is huge. We have to expect that, before autumn, the American forces will relieve us significantly, either by taking over sectors, or by responding to *Boche* attacks if they continue. [...]

6/24/1918.

I hope to have news from you today. Nothing new to announce. [...] Yesterday a comrade had news from the 129th. They were involved in the battle of Montdidier and Noyon and conducted themselves laudably. Captain Abbé whom I knew as a junior lieutenant—a good man—was killed along with other officers

I knew. [...]. It seems the regiment suffered great losses. I'm going to write to Rolland to try and get news of former comrades. We have been very lucky for a long time now. Our mess is well set up and we continue a quite comfortable existence. Yesterday we managed to buy 27 eggs for 0,35 each, not expensive for this area, and some butter at 4 francs a pound. [...]

Second letter, same day.

I received today your letter from June 20, the one from 2:00 p.m. [...] The newspapers do not say much about this, but the news is not bad. First food is a terrible problem in Austria. And the offensive against Italy is a total failure. We hear that things are not going well for the Austrians. If that's the case, the *Boches* will need to send some troops to help Austria. They would have to take them from our front because they are obliged to leave in Russia the few troops that are there. If they have to send reinforcements, that would be 15 or 20 divisions. The result would be stagnation along our front or an attack by our troops. [...]

6/25/1918.

I received today your letter of June 21. [...] The weather you are having is similar to what we have here, a strong wind and very little rain. I still have my good old wool blanket which is nice and warm, two foot covers from the regiment, a piece of tent cloth, and my oilcloth. Maybe next winter I'll try to get a new blanket. Some members of our mess are sick with this epidemic, and I had to take care of our purchases. I spent more than two hours finding 5 kilos of peas, 5 pounds of new potatoes, and a bunch of new onions. [...]

Friday, June 28, 1918. 2 p.m.

I have just received your letter dated June 25. [...]. I made crêpes again today, a dozen. We had some left for tonight; that's all we ate, with curd that served as cream cheese. I also bought a pound of strawberries (0,70); they are not very ripe because it is not very hot, although for 3 or 4 days the weather has been improving. [...] In the morning, so far, I have café au lait with bread and butter. There is no chocolate in Plouézec; [...] I did not bring any sugar or chocolate, fearing that my trunk would exceed the official weight, and yet it did not weigh 50 kilos. [...]

6/27/1918.

[...] I just had quite a surprise. Lieutenant Bourquin made the request to move me to the Army Park as motorcyclist. It's a pretext; I can barely ride a bicycle. Once there, he would arrange to bring me to the TM 105. I admit this was totally unexpected and that I had nothing to do with this request. But the request will reach the DI; there will be quite a reaction. He said they could not oppose it as I was needed as a specialist. The funniest part would be if they asked me to ride a moto. So that is where things are for now. Caplet knows about it, but I've not had a chance to talk to him. [...] Boubou must suspect something; he said to the messenger this morning, "I hope you are not thinking of taking them from us." [...] The hardest part will certainly be when Boubou asks for me, and says, "you are a motorcyclist?" I will reply that I used to ride, more than 10 years ago, but that in two weeks I'd be back at it. For sure, I will not get on a motorcycle, but with Bourquin I will learn to drive a car which is not difficult and could be very useful. In this request, they insisted on the fact that I was very tired. I will obviously tell him that I have a lot of aches and pains. So, if this works, I may join the automobile unit on the sly. [...]

Second letter, same day.

I received today your two letters from June 22 and 23. I am very sorry to learn that you are not receiving mine; I write every day. However, you should not worry as you do; the mail can be held up to avoid indiscretions during the change of sector. You realize that, if we were engaged in something like the last offensive, you could easily go 2 or 3 weeks without mail. You need therefore to be patient when you don't receive any letters, especially when it's a delay I can do nothing about. [...]

We were again lucky in leaving our last place just before the offensive at Reims. You can well believe that our sector at Suippes received a lot of blasts. Once again, luck was on our side. [...]

6/28/1918.

I didn't receive any mail today. I talked with Caplet about this request for my mutation to the auto service which should soon arrive at the division. Caplet said that it would be much better in terms of safety and to work on music. He says that, if it is successful, he will do everything he can to get Maréchal moved for good to a safe place and, once that is accomplished, he would set off for quieter, nicer regions. It's a real plot and everything depends on my success. [...]

The chateau where we are is an ugly house, but has a very lovely large park which makes our stay nicer, all that rich greenery. We easily find peas and potatoes, so we don't lack anything. [...]

Planes fly over our heads often, but they pay no attention to us. We have quite a good number of airplanes and daily we see squadrons of 15 or 20 heading toward the *Boches*. [...]

Monday, July 1, 1918, 9 a.m.

I am writing this morning without waiting for the mail. [...] Yesterday we took a walk as far as Port Lazo; we walked along the beach but since high tide was at 9 p.m. we couldn't enjoy the waves coming in. We came back by the old road, the one that starts at the well you used to get fresh water from and goes up hill. Along the way I picked two fat stalks of thistle that I put on the mantle in my bedroom. It's a good decoration: the folks who saw us bringing them back had a good laugh. [...]

I am not at all unhappy that you are learning to drive, it can be very useful. [...] You will probably have special clothes and goggles? Your vision is not very good so be careful. I hope you will not ride a motorcycle—it's too dangerous. I also hope that you will spend your time on music and that the automobile will just be an accessory. [...]

Tuesday, July 2, 1918, 8 a.m.

I received nothing from you yesterday; I hope that your silence is caused by the fortunate move you told me about and not to an increase in action around you which is what the *communiqués* from the past few days suggest. [...] I didn't tell you about our meal yesterday: we had a shrimp omelet (I used some milk in place of one egg) then some sautéed beef (the meat left over from the pot-au-feu). [...]

I received yesterday a few lines from M. Alan telling me about the air raid on the 28th. There was another one on the 29th. I think the Germans will soon launch a serious offensive. I think the war might end this year. We want that so much that we make ourselves believe in illusions and take hope for reality. You might come to Brittany soon for 15 days unless events turn serious and all leaves are canceled. [...]

6/29/1918.

Mail has not yet arrived today. [...] The weather is very heavy, but not a drop of rain. The few wells in the area are drying up, it's a problem in this area. The countryside is pretty, very wooded, and also very hilly which makes walking difficult. [...]

The drone of the planes over our heads is quite extraordinary. They come by the hundreds. The huge development of aviation will certainly contribute to the end of this war. I don't know whether you can imagine the extent of fear a fighter feels with, in addition to all the other dangers, those machines over his head, shooting and bombing without pity. The hardiest of nerves give way quickly; it is a danger against which one is powerless. [...]

6/30/1918.

I hope to have news from you this morning. For me, nothing has changed. The artillery has been more active for two days. Maréchal arrived yesterday afternoon after more than two days of travel, totally exhausted. He left his cello and our instruments in a storage place and of course got a receipt. [...]

You read in the papers that the law on rents will go into effect on July 15. Arbitration commissions will be set up and there will be a few changes because so many people have left. As a result, if we cannot make arrangements ourselves with our tenants and they cannot pay us, the state will guarantee to pay us 50 percent of the rents. Just for the tenant in Boulogne, that will be 4 years in October, 4 times 4800 makes 19200, half of which is 9600. That is the sum the state will pay for the Boulogne tenant. [...]

Wednesday, July 3, 1918, 8 a.m.

I am not waiting for the mail to write although I'm quite eager to know whether your change has happened. I hope that the letter I will receive today gives me all the details and confirms the good news. That would be a new life for you, and new contacts. Remember to keep to yourself so you conserve the independence you need as an artist. [...]

Second letter, same day, 2 p.m.

[...] If you manage to transfer to central headquarters with work to do there, that means you can't be sent to the front. That seems to me to be a good change. [...] I keep forgetting to tell you that I am sleeping on the second floor at Maria's, in the big room, where there are two beds. I sleep in one; the other, which is very old, has no springs and looks really dirty. If you come home on leave, you could sleep in my bed and I would have the other cleaned so I could use it for 12 days or so. [...]

For water here, there is a well not far from Maria's. A nice old man performs the job of water carrier for those willing to pay him. Every two days he brings two buckets and more if necessary. If you come on leave, you will need a new jacket and new pants to be properly dressed to go out. You should bring with you, for travel and indoors, an old jacket and pants. [...]

7/1/1918.

I received yesterday the note that transfers me to the automobile service. I will most likely leave tomorrow for Gournay-en-Bray, an auto instruction center between Rouen and Dieppe. I will probably not stay there long; Lieutenant B. will ask for me. They pulled this off very nicely. I've not yet talked to an officer, but I have seen the secretaries and I can state that there is total astonishment. Fortunately, Boubou left on pass yesterday. [...]

7/2/1918.

I received this morning your letter of June 29. [...] Regarding my transfer to the auto service, I think the entire thing has been sunk. The general does not want me to leave; he must have involved himself in this affair and personally called the Army. I can affirm that the note I received counts for nothing. This is all annoying; it proves I will never be able to leave the DI. These men will always do everything possible to prevent my escape. It's all the odder because they do not like music, or not very much! It must be their pride that makes them want to keep us, to be able to say that the division has famous musicians. [...]

True, I am fine here; very little is required of me. But elsewhere I would be able to work regularly, because of the fixed schedules at the TM. That is impossible here. I can work for a month, and then things change, and I don't touch an instrument for months. The whole plan is a failure. For it to be successful, my transfer would have to come from the War Minister or Central Headquarters. Other than that, I will never be able to leave, except in case of evacuation for illness or injury and I certainly don't want that. [...]

The division got all excited about my business: will he leave, won't he leave? For 24 hours that has been the theme of all conversations. Tongues got a good work-out. And with all of that, I gain nothing by all that chatter. B will be quite disappointed; he thought things well underway. [...]

7/3/1918.

Nothing new; my transfer has certainly and definitively been buried. [...]

Saturday, July 6, 1918, 2 p.m.

[...] So you are staying at the division. I hope you will be able to get hold of your violin and that you will not let yourself be separated from it again. [...] It was tactless on your part, as an instrumentalist, to let go of the instrument that has paved the way for you. How can you please those who want to hear you if you don't have your instrument? [...]

7/4/1918.

The weather is cloudy and quite cool. The cannon last night was horribly loud in the direction of Villers-Bretonneux; it's been a long time since we've heard such loud booming. Maybe it was to celebrate the American birthday that there was such a serenade at 3 a.m.

Maréchal has lost quite a bit of weight and is not at all well. He went to see the doctor who gave him 8 injections of *cacodylate de soude* to boost him up a bit.[298] When the doctor heard that he was leaving soon on pass, he told him: "You should go to a hospital for a month of rest and a diet of milk and fatty foods." I think that this torment for Maréchal is the result of being sent back to the regiment where he is in more danger than at the division and has less comfort. [...]

Second letter, same day.

I received today your letter from July 1. [...] The intense bombardment last night was the Australians, who took Hamel, northeast of Villers-Bretonneux, and 1000 prisoners. We are having a lot of success right now in small, focused battles. [...]

Don't have any illusions about the end of the war; it is not at all near. Next year will see horrible battles with, fortunately, at least 2 million Americans fighting, making about 3 million men.

When I come to Brittany, it will be for, at a minimum, 10 days; the trip will be long. [...]

Plouézec, Sunday, July 7, 1918, 1 p.m.

[...] Maria says that her cousin is not like his wily old father. He is hard-working, tough as a rock, and you would never think he is 72-years old (a former captain of a cod-fishing boat, I think). He still has a boat and a sailor with whom he goes fishing for mackerel. Mackerel is selling for a very good price; that old man earns an average of 20 francs a day. There is some good in this war.

You've not left the front for 4 years now, even for a minute. Territorial, you have always been part of the fighting. I don't see how anyone could oppose your return to the territorial reserves in October, given your age and your service. [...]

7/5/1918.

I did not receive any news from you this morning, but I did get a card from Dumand who is in the hospital in Nantes. Since January this year, the poor fellow has done nothing but hang out in hospitals and he was a healthy young man. That proves that, after 4 years of such ordeals, someone in the ranks, or even in a music regiment, has had enough and no longer has the strength to withstand the ravages of a war like this. He was a good friend; I wish him a complete recovery. His father must by very worried. [...]

---

[298] Cacodylic acid.

7/6/1918.

I hope to have your news today. [...] If nothing unusual happens to stop the granting of leaves, mine will be from the 20th to 30th of this month. I'm not saying that too loudly because an offensive would totally interrupt all permissions. Nothing new for us, but as General Headquarter reserves, we could be on the road in a few hours. Our situation is totally unstable; we could just as easily be here for a month. [...]

Plouézec, Tuesday, July 9, 1918, 7 a.m.

Yesterday [...] Maria got rid of the old mattress from the wooden bed in my room. We will put on a clean mattress and a coverlet filled with oat husks and the bed will be ready for me to sleep in. I have the pleasure to have a lot of fleas because this room is very dusty. Maria scrubbed it once, but I think she needs to do it again. Those beasts choose me over others; I'm flattered but they are a great nuisance. I hope to get rid of them for good. [...]

Maria talks often about *bouillie* so I asked her to fix some.[299] She is not very skilled in that art because what I ate was like glue. I may not have enjoyed it very much, but it gave me something to laugh about. To make it, you have to use a long stick (broom handle) to stir the flour and milk to keep from leaning too far into the hearth—your face would be directly over the fire for 20 minutes. It takes a long time to cook. I have to admit, I didn't much want Maria to use her broom handle which, even after getting the good cleaning it needed, still was not to my taste. For dinner, Maria filled her bowl with buttermilk into which she put the mush and ate it licking her lips. It's a bit like food for piglets; in fact, they do give it to pigs to fatten them up. [...]

7/7/1918.

I received today your letters of July 4 and 5, a letter from Lemoine, and a particularly friendly letter from Lieutenant Bourquin. He has not lost all hope. I also have an idea which I will tell you more about in a few days when I have the information I need. [...] Militarily speaking, men are slaves; without question we are like objects to those gentlemen and they will not allow someone to make a decision about a subordinate without their permission. [...]

Yes, about the sugar, you were a twit; you could easily have carried a kilo or two in your handbag. You know well what a precious commodity it is and how hard it is to find. [...]

I would not have had to worry about food if I was with Lieutenant Bourquin. You have only to read what he has written to realize I would not have needed

---

[299] Literally, something boiled. In this case it was flour and milk boiled together for a long time.

anything there. I already am fine; and there I might have gotten a bit too fat. Maybe that is why blind fate left me here. I believe so strongly in destiny. I certainly have not done anything to help chance. And still I have been spared and have passed through all the dangers. Do not worry; enjoy the clean air and quiet life. The unknown is all around me, watching over me and inspiring me with the tranquility I enjoy.

You still have not answered my question, that is, whether Mlle Hames is nice. It would certainly not be unpleasant during my leave to see a pretty face. It's relaxing; I much prefer it to Boubou. [...]

Second letter, same day.

There is something new for us: they have just completed the plan for our embarkation, all the orders have been given, we only need the final phone call to send us on our way. I expect that in the next 48 hours we will again be on a train. Where we are to go is known only by the General Headquarters. This morning Maréchal left on leave, it was his turn. During this leave, at home in Dijon, he will try to get himself hospitalized, and after a month in the hospital, get himself sent to a convalescent hospital for another month. During that time, he will do everything he can to be transferred to the auxiliary. [...]

The three of us talked until 1 a.m. this morning; we have a plan laid out. Caplet says that, if it succeeds, he himself will make sure that the two of us get out of here. Boubou has no idea what is up. Maybe we will manage to get out of the grips of these people who cling to us no matter what. [...]

It seems we have a new poison gas bomb, absolutely terrible and used only recently. [...]

Thursday, July 11, 1918, 2 p.m.

[...] I didn't write this morning. Maria was busy with writing letters for the women who receive mail from their sons or husbands. During that time, I took charge of lunch so we would not eat late. For lunch we had a 6-egg omelet with a bit of milk for volume and shrimp in butter. There was no way to have any fish because of the high wind and rain yesterday morning. High tide right now is in the morning and late in the evening. Tomorrow I'll make crêpes and a salad. If there is any fish, I'll buy some for supper, but I mustn't count on it. Fish are either scarce in Plouézec or the fish merchants take them straight to Kérity where they can sell them for more money. [...]

7/8/1918.

It is extremely hot and not a drop of rain. So far, we have no departure order. [...] If I manage to leave on pass at the end of the month, I hope to bring a bit of sugar so that I can eat strawberries, gooseberries, etc. with sugar during my time there. [...]

The weather is such that a swim in the sea would be the ultimate pleasure. I dream of doing that several times in Plouézec. [...]

7/9/1918.

I hope to have news from you today. For us nothing has changed; we still are waiting for the final orders. [...] A lot of soldiers have the flu, so I am help-ing the sergeant orderly a few hours a day. I am the person who admits people and introduces them: a lot of English and Australian officers come here. When everyone is back on their feet, in a few days, I will leave this job. [...]

I hope you will not wait until the last minute to arrange a bed for me. I have absolutely no idea what time I will be arriving in Guingamp; from what you say, there are only two trains each day, morning and evening. [...] There must be chickens and rabbits for sale in Plouézec; we will eat all that and also fish. Maybe you can get hold of a lobster. We will try, if possible, to go to Lézardrieux by car to see the countryside and what it has to offer. We will treat this time like a holiday. [...]

Friday, July 12, 1918, 8 a.m.

I am writing this morning before the mail. Maria went to get butter and eggs and her wonderful buttermilk so we can have crêpes.

For sure, 50 years ago, the Bretons must not have eaten much better than their animals. Even now, in the interior, dirt and basic food must be the rule. On the coast, things are cleaned up a bit because the seacoast attracts tourists. The women who work for foreigners (that's what they call them) find good food there which has produced a healthy change. In spite of all that, when they are in their thatched cottages, they resort to what is natural, and filth becomes the mistress. Maria, who is not really dirty, lets herself go and would use a lot of dirty things if I were not here. My presence and her pride make her seem a bit sophisticated but, underneath, she is the same as all the others. If you come on leave, you must play at being demanding. That will push Maria more and she will do herself proud. I don't let her fall back on her careless ways; even here in the country I want to maintain a certain amount of cleanliness. People have the habit of throwing things on the ground, of spitting on the ground; Maria doesn't do that, either by restraint or good taste. When you are here, you must demand cleanliness and not find that everything is fine just because in your life as a sol-dier you are used to filth. [...]

7/11/1918.

The reaction to my vaccination is waning. I slept well last night and this morning I have only a little discomfort in my shoulder. In all, I was not very sick. Some comrades have fever for three days. That must be due to the general state of health and also to the strict fast on the day of the vaccination. A good many *poilus*, despite their instructions, eat and drink normally rather than fasting.

There is still no news of our departure; I'm beginning to think we will be here a long time. Not far from here the Australians held a horse race and invited the general and the officers of the infantry division. Those English are astonishing. They organize in the rear remarkable festivities—races, tennis, hockey, football, in short, all the popular sports, all well set up, very comfortable. They are not very worried. [...]

The *Boches* seem to be taking a long time to stage an attack; I truly wonder whether they will do it. [...] While we wait, the Americans are arriving, delivering 10,000 men a day, not a small matter. The battle conditions have to change quite soon; the influx of those reinforcements and of enormous quantities of military equipment will upset the balance. And the Americans don't seem inclined to dawdle. They want to get into action immediately. [...]

7/12/1918.

I received mail today much earlier than usual, [...] namely your two letters of the 9th and 10th. I am totally fine now; the fever brought on by the vaccination is gone. I absolutely cannot say when I will arrive in Guingamp; I'm taking a train of men on pass leaving from Achères and I've not the slightest idea of when it will leave or when it will arrive in Guingamp. There, obviously, I can only take the morning train or the evening train. If I arrive on the evening train, don't worry, I'll walk. I will try to give you some idea of when I will arrive. We should not broadcast this too much; I fear all leaves will be stopped very soon. [...]

Tuesday, July 16, 1918, 2 p.m.

[...] I see that the recent air raids hit Boulogne and there were victims and damage. [...] In Plouézec bread has been hard to find since yesterday. The only baker in the area may still have flour, but those in surrounding towns do not and everyone rushes to Plouézec and we stand in line at the bakery, often for an hour, to get some bread. [...]

7/14/1918.

Yesterday I didn't receive a letter. Lieutenant Bourquin brought me back quickly and at 11 a.m. I was at the DI. It was an exhausting day of packing things up; we got into the trucks about 8 p.m. and arrived at 3 a.m. in a very lovely countryside where we are all gathering. We are 50 kilometers from Paris. But it seems that tomorrow we are leaving by train in the direction of X. […]

I am putting a stamp on this letter as obviously the military post is not working. I hope that you will receive this letter without too much delay. We were able to buy lovely peaches at 0,50 each and also radishes. We found a good place to eat at the home of a fine woman with two children; Caplet and I have a room there. If we were to stay here, we would be comfortable. We are in Neuilly-Hartel, near Beaumont. […]

Second letter, same day.

I'm sending this letter the normal way. […] The rumor is that we are not leaving tomorrow but may stay here three or four days. In all of that we gain time; passes have still not been interrupted. […]

I forgot to tell you that, leaving Crèvecoeur by car, we almost ran over a tall thin soldier. We stopped; I was amazed to see it was Deschamps, an old friend from the trenches. […] We only had a few minutes to talk, but I will write to him soon. Chance meetings like that are truly bizarre. […]

Wednesday, July 17, 1918, 9 a.m.

[…] Everything is getting expensive here; we are following the example of Paimpol where everyone is staying (there are no rooms for rent here). In Plouézec, it is mostly children who are swelling the population. Those good Breton women (I say "good" ironically) rushed to take the 50 to 100 francs a month offered for each child, taking as many as possible. Some have 3 or 4; they will quickly get tired of this because it is not always easy to have charge of children who are not your own. They need to know how to do what is needed and take care of them, feed them well. In Brittany, bread with butter is the main food. Still, it is important to provide a safe place for children of refugees and those who are leaving Paris because of the bombing. […]

7/15/1918.

There had been a counter order that we would not be moving on. Just this instant they announced that we leave this evening at 7:00. Things could still change between now and then. […] So far, the *communiqués* do not talk of anything, and all seems calm. There is furious cannon fire in some areas, but nothing has really started. Passes have still not been interrupted, but, honestly, I expect it to happen. I will be really lucky if I leave in 10 days. […]

Second letter, same day.

I received today your second letter from July 12. [...] We received this morning word from Maréchal. In Dijon, he saw the chief doctor who listened to his chest and said he had one damaged lung. He will be in the hospital tomorrow, July 16. Once there, it's up to him to do what he can to be transferred to the auxiliary. [...]

7/16/1918.

I received today your two letters from July 13 and 14. We are going through a very exhausting time with all these movements that will, inevitably, someday put us in the middle of everything. In brief, we left yesterday about 8 p.m. and we got out of the trucks at 9:30 a.m.: that makes 13 ½ hours of travel by truck. We climbed out of those boxes all stiff and exhausted. [...]

We are in a very little village in the midst of a superb forest. At least we have plenty of water. This morning, when I arrived, I was able to really clean up, shave, etc., which did me a lot of good.

There is some news that I've been expecting but won't please you at all, it's the interruption of all leave permissions as of today. Of course, it's normal as the offensive has just started again. They couldn't do anything else. This offensive seems to be a big defeat for the *Boches*. In about 10 days their losses will be so great that they will have to stop. I hope that the permissions for leave will return and that I will be able to come at the beginning of August. [...]

Friday, July 19, 1918, 5 p.m.

I received a bit late your letters from July 15 and 16. I am delighted to have news from you and to know you are well; I am very afraid, however, that you are in the midst of the fighting! I see that General Mangin pushed back the Germans I don't know how many kilometers near Villers-Cotterêts and that his counter offensive, made without any fanfare or artillery preparation, truly surprised the Germans! So much the better! That general continues to distinguish himself by actions marked with great intelligence. But you live in his orbit and that becomes dangerous. [...]

7/17/1918.

I received no letters this morning; the mail is beginning to be held up. Apparently, during this offensive, you will receive no letters or, if any, with significant delay. This is to avoid any indiscretions. It is sad that it comes to that because of some people who cannot hold their tongue. [...]

The important step is crossing the Marne; the *Boches* have been partly pushed back and it doesn't seem possible for them to hold on to what they have left on the south side of the river for long. The Americans are participating in this action at the Marne, and they have acted admirably. [...]

The big Berthas have been firing again on Paris; we don't know how many shells have landed. Last night, *Boche* squadrons were heading to Paris, and here the firing was terrible. There was certainly a raid in Paris. [...]

7/18/1918.

I am going to try to make sure this letter reaches you. By the ordinary route, you might not have news for a week.

I've covered more than 20 kilometers since leaving this morning at 4 a.m. I went as far as the general's command post and came back to a little place where I am in a fine position. This is where the first echelon of the first group is—I am part of that battle formation. No point in telling you about the operations. I mustn't. You should know only that they are incredible, that we have every reason to be confident, and that they could have huge results. Tonight, I will sleep in a good bed, with a mattress, and I hope to sleep well as today was exhausting. [...]

I saw quite a few *Boche* prisoners pass by, they looked really terrible, about half of them were very scrawny. They seemed happy to have been captured. I hope to get this letter to you quickly, if I can give it to a willing driver. [...]

Tuesday, July 23, 1918, 2 p.m.

I just received in the 1:30 mail your letter from July 20. I am happy to have news from you; given the recent events, I feared you would not be able to write. I see that you have pushed the Germans back and made a big advance. You must be very dusty, maybe muddy, in rags, and exhausted. But the results of your counteroffensive seem so real, so tangible that joy overcomes everything and makes you forget your physical misery. [...]

7/21/1918.

[...] This time we are in the thick of things. We are dirty, dusty, in rags, and really tired, but our faces are bright and there is great enthusiasm. The *Boches* are clearing out at full speed under tremendous shelling. The number of prisoners is growing rapidly. The DI is constantly moving, so I go kilometers with my liaison pigeons. But no one is thinking about fatigue. [...] There are a considerable number of *Boche* bodies. Up to now, especially in light of the progress, the DI has not lost too many men. We've taken back at least 15 kilometers of territory. You cannot imagine the traffic on the roads in the forest, it's indescribable. Finally,

General Foch has made a good move and again, the *poilus* with the Americans are the ones who are winning. Our guys are magnificent. This is field warfare, no more trenches. [...] The *poilus* worn down by all these years of war are quite simply amazing. The American officers with us never get tired of praising them, saying that to see soldiers as energetic and as hardy is astounding. Everyone, no matter the branch of service he belongs to, is making a serious effort.

I don't know whether this letter will arrive quickly. In any case, I sent today a pre-written card to say that I am fine. [...]

7/21/1918.

Am fine. I received a letter from you recently. L.D.[300]

7/22/1918.

Today I received your letter of the 18th and the 17th. Mme Roch's butter, given the current circumstances and difficulty getting food, served me very well: it was wrapped in a damp, salted cloth then in strong tinfoil, which insured the transport and conservation. [...]

It's an honor to be with Mangin and to have been part of these historical moments; we have been at the heart of this entire offensive and have played an important part. The DI has lost a lot of men and will need to go for rest and to rebuild itself, so our role will be reduced. Two or three days from now I hope that will be a done deal. [...]

I learned just this minute that Desormes, the violist from the 43rd, our friend, was very seriously wounded and has a perforated lung. I hope he'll survive. He is 26 or 27 years old. [...] The new colonel of the 74th was wounded and evacuated. The attack is still getting stronger, and we continue to advance. This is getting harder as the *Boches* are rapidly bring in important numbers of troops. [...]

Sunday, July 28, 1918, 2 p.m.

[...] I read in *L'Information* that General Mangin's army is facing significant German reinforcements that make your advance very difficult if not impossible. [...] Where you are there are 15 extra German divisions. I read in *L'Information* that "to better protect the rear of its right flank, between the armies of von Hutier and von Bohn, the enemy inserted a third army commanded by von Eben against General Mangin. That brings the number of German divisions between Soissons, Marne, and Reims to 40 or 45; there were 25 or 30 on July 17." [...]

---

[300] This was an official card, on which soldiers were instructed to omit any useless information.

7/23/1918.

I received today your letter from July 19. [...] The response of the *Boches* is now quite strong and we are no longer taking back much territory. To the contrary they shell us—there's one now. I just saw Caplet; he is very tired. The pigeon station is about 40 kilometers from the front line right now and he spends part of his time on the road, transporting the PV. I hope that soon we will be relieved; we really need it. Our weather is very hot, and you would not believe the dust. We all look like little doggies who have run a long race; our tongues are hanging out. As for me, I can't complain. I am still with the first group because there is no pigeon station at the command post. I do a little bit of everything. [...] Feeding the guys on the front line also takes up my time. We are dirty like pigs; you cannot imagine how Plouézec and bathing makes me dream. [...]

7/25/1918.

I received today your letter from July 21. [...] I think they tell the *poilus* that letters will be delayed simply to keep them from writing; that way, there will be fewer letters and the postal service will have less work. [...]

In Brittany, the war is far away; the only indication is the absence of men. Since most of the men are sailors and frequently absent for months, even years, even that doesn't change things very much. [...]

7/27/1918.

I received today a letter from Suzanne who is in Trégastel with Denise. She writes like a baby, my poor god-daughter. What she writes about the bomb that fell on Mme Duez's house is delightful. Fortunately, Mme Duez is no longer alive. [...]

Our weather since yesterday is really awful. [...] I am lodged on the edge of a little village, with a friend, in a sort of cellar into which we dragged the mattresses we found lying around, so, in fact, I have a pretty decent place to sleep given the circumstances. As for food, we have enough; we have no scruples about taking from the gardens, mostly potatoes and lettuce. [...]

I hope to be able to leave here around August 6; I should soon be able to give you more information. [...] Yes, the soldiers' postcard is very brief, but think of the people fighting who cannot write letters; it at least sends word to their loved ones, that is a lot. [...]

7/28/1918.

I didn't receive any letters today. Our units have started being relieved, and we believe the DI will be relieved tomorrow. Since Cercy, we are the ones who have taken Billy-sur-Ourcq, Oulchy-la-Ville, and Oulchy-le-Château. This is a huge success for our DI and the losses, although quite high, include a large number of slightly wounded who will have recuperated in less than two months; and the advance continues. I think that within a month the *Boches* will be pushed back to the region of Craonne and Chemin des Dames. This offensive will end for them in an unexpected way, with losses in soldiers and equipment beyond all predictions. [...]

7/30/1918.

I received your letter of July 25, but because we were leaving, I could not write. [...] We left last evening and once again spent the night in a truck—there's nothing funny in that. We are on the banks of the Oise. It seems that we will leave for an unknown destination in 2 days, but I don't know whether that rumor will turn out to be true. [...].

7/31/1918.

I just received your letter from July 28. [...] The *Boches* right now are pulling themselves together; it will be some time yet before we chase them out of France, that task is for 1919. We mustn't have too many illusions. Once again, this war is changing shape and tanks are beginning to have considerable importance. The small ones are quite funny looking, and each infantry company will have, in the near future, one of their own. Those remarkable machines save large numbers of human lives and they are starting to be used everywhere. It's the only way to fight against nests of machine guns. I'll explain all that while on leave. [...]

8/1/1918.

[...] I expect to leave on the 5th, in the evening, and arrive on the 7th in Paimpol. The only thing that would keep me from leaving is a departure of the DI. [...] As for sugar, I will bring some; and for cocoa, don't worry. [...]

8/2/1918.

I received today your letters of July 30 and 31. [...] Today is 4 years since the mobilization and the end does not logically seem on the horizon. They will call on the class of 1920 in October in order for that class to be ready for action in the spring of 1919. [...]

8/3/1918.

I did not receive a letter this morning; it is Saturday. I will not write tomorrow because I will surely leave Monday evening and by the 7th I will be in Paimpol. [...]

We have just made a good advance and are entering Soissons. We will certainly get to Fismes and the banks of the Vesle. The *Boches* will surely fight back at the Aisne; their positions at Craonne and the Chemin des Dames are formidable. [...]

We are having rain and storms. I will come without my *capote* but with my rubber raincoat which will be very useful. Oh, the day I paid 10 francs for that raincoat! I was certainly not robbed, and I have to say it has been tremendously useful. I have two packs of tobacco, which we can give to Maria's uncle. [...]

I will be happy to see you in a few days; it is 4 years day for day since I left from Plouézec. Who could have imagined such a thing! The *Boches* did not expect to unleash the entire world—especially not against them. If they had been able to read the future, they would have stayed peacefully at home. They have been led astray by their immense pride. [...]

Saturday, August 3, 2 p.m.

I received in the 1:30 mail a card from M. and Mme Delaune announcing the glorious loss of their son Roger Delaune, cadet in the 205th infantry regiment, who died for France on June 11, 1918, at age 32. [...]

Lucien joined his mother in Brittany for the next two weeks.

8/18/1918.

I was very late arriving in Paris. [...] I was furious, and tired. In the train from Paimpol, I met M. Torty who has been a photographer in Paimpol for 23 years. You must have noticed the man on the platform with the raucous voice. Aside from that, he is very nice and funny. He begged me to come see him if I come back to the area, and told me he would indicate good places to eat trout. He was taking his son back to Paris and profiting from the trip to run some errands. He took me to an excellent hotel in Guingamp where, with him, I dined very well. The train was packed; fortunately, in Rennes they added some cars and thanks to M. Torty, who knows all the train workers, we reserved a compartment in one of the new cars. We were four in the compartment all the way to Paris.

After cleaning up, I went to Avenue Mozart, to the home of Caplet's brother. He had just gone out, but his lovely wife, in her dressing gown, greeted me very warmly. I can well understand why Caplet is wary of her; she is unbelievably curious, asked me tons of questions. In order not to answer, I played dumb. She must have told herself I was a goose or a font of discretion. Then it was late; I went for lunch about 1:00 at Scossa's. A huge crowd; Paris is full of people right now. [...]

I had a devil of a time finding a taxi for the Gare du Nord. Finally, all my tasks finished, it was 6:00 and I found a patio where a Dubonnet with lemon was particularly refreshing. I am sending this letter from there. I take the train at 10:50; the American canteen will greet me with open arms and a lovely Yankee girl will serve me, with a hand I hope to be white and with the food my body needs. [...]

8/20/1918.

We are jinxed: our DI had to leave Saturday night. I think they are in the midst of what just happened between Carlepont and Soissons. At 1 a.m., in Orry-la-Ville, they made me wait until 5 a.m. for a train leaving for the area of Beauvais. That is where the rallying point is and where I am right now. I am forced to wait here, with a lot of others, until they can put together a detachment to find the DI. If they have gone into the tempest that is raging, I hope it will take a few days to find them. By then it will be time for a long rest. [...]

8/21/1918.

I am still at the rallying point; we were supposed to leave last night and were awakened about 3 a.m. But just as we were ready to leave, there was a counterorder and now our departure is set for 6 p.m. tonight. [...]

We are fed here by a mobile kitchen and, by golly, not bad at all. The cooks try really hard; and there are two well-stocked cooperatives. All the *poilus* prefer being here than in the midst of the fighting. As for me, I really don't care about that; I'd prefer to find my unit and my friends. [...]

Saturday, August 24, 1918, 3 p.m.

I received in the 1:30 mail your card from the 21st. [...] I am enclosing some clippings from *L'Information* on the intimate health of the soldiers; you will see the warnings and care the Americans give their men. One has to praise them. It is so easy to catch a disease! I am talking about these matters because it seems you pay more and more attention to women. [...] That upsets me. You who used to be very protective of your body, you should continue with that same practice, for your own good. [...]

8/23/1918.

What adventures these past few days! I took the train in Hermes, near Beauvais, and arrived in Le Bourget at 3 a.m. with a detachment of 500 *poilus*. We spent the day, in the midst of dreadful heat, in a barracks with guards at all the doors, as though we were criminals. Finally, at 9 p.m., we got on a resupply train which didn't leave until midnight. I got off this morning in Longpont, very near

Ciry where fortunately I found a vehicle to take me to the division which was 18 kilometers away. […] I found here a good many letters: I will write more tomorrow. Tonight, I'm going to go to bed and get some rest. I cleaned up and already feel better. […]

8/24/1918.

I am writing quickly this morning as the mail leaves at 10:30. […] I found a little laundry room in pretty good condition which I can make into a nice, clean room. I found here a number of letters, some of yours from the beginning of the month and also from the 18th and 19th. I will write more soon; this morning, I have to get settled and go find my things so I can change underwear. […]

I found a little piece of heather in one of your letters. Thank you. Sadly, here I will not find any flowers to send to you; the countryside is totally ruined. […]

8/24/1918.

[…] I don't know what you are complaining about when you talk about uncommunicative letters. Not only do I write regularly but I tell you everything that happens. […] I didn't find Niel when I got back; he was sent back into the 5th Infantry Division after having made a scene while quite drunk. I had warned him about that. He was a good guy, but a bit of wine and a cigar made him crazy. His replacement is Asseline, a pigeon keeper from the 74th whom I've known for a long time, a fine fellow. I saw the general this morning, who seems to be nice and apologized that it took me so long to get back to the division! […]

Second letter, same day.

I received today your two letters of August 21 and 22. I also received the two packages of shrimp: they were totally spoiled, and we had to throw them away. Caplet left this morning on leave; I accompanied him to the station. […] When I got back, I learned that, for sure, we were going into the battle soon. I am probably the one who will go to the pigeon station and play Caplet's role. I hope that this time the pigeon lofts will be closer than during the last offensive. […]

It seems we will be going to the left of Soissons. We are still in General Mangin's army. Permissions for leave will again be suspended, but the announcement will likely not be put out until tomorrow. Thus, our dangerous bohemian existence continues. Don't worry. I will try to write every day. […]

8/27/1918.

I received today your last letter from August 22. […] The first echelon of the DI is leaving today. As for me, I don't leave until tomorrow with most of

499

the personnel. We are going to the Soissonais, to the same place we were at the beginning of last year, when the 36th and the 129th were struck by lunacy. It seems that this very lovely area is now just ruins. The attack we will be part of, led by our former general, is of the greatest importance. I know the objectives; if we are successful, it will make quite a story. [...].

I think often of Brittany, with its charm, freshness, and calm, and I cannot help but yearn for the freedom lost during these long years. Still, let's hope that the current fight, with its repeated attacks, will weaken the *Boches* and that, sooner than I would have believed two months ago, there will be a peace that makes up for the present hardships. Despite all the positive signs, I think that we will have at least another year of war; the *Boches* push back, and, with the energy of desperation, will push back even harder. [...]

8/28/1918.

I really don't have time to reply to all you tell me in your last letters. We are in full battle; I took out the pigeons last night. I never got to bed. In any case, the earth is my mattress and the sky my blanket! [...]

Second letter, same day.

I am a bit freer and am in a hurry to write to you. [...] The question of war and women, that is of no interest to me. I would never go with one of the chicks at the front; it's too dangerous. I want to stay healthy. Our health service is nowhere near as well organized as the one the Americans have; there would be too much risk. You can rest easy in that regard. [...] Without question, depriving a strong, healthy man like me of all contact with women is just crazy. [...]

Saturday, August 31, 1918, 3 p.m.

[...] I read in the *communiqués* that the battle is fierce and difficult and that Mangin's army, although it continues to advance, does so with great effort because the Germans are putting in significant reinforcements. They are fighting with knife and bayonet. [...]

8/30/1918.

I received yesterday your letter of August 26. We are still in the middle of action, and it is very hard to make progress. This is a big bite to swallow. We have to cross the Aisne under *Boche* fire and building bridges or walkways in these conditions is not easy. Despite that, two of our battalions made it to the other shore, but it's difficult and communications are regularly lost. All the regiments of the DI have received citations. My regiment received the *fourragère*.[301] During my next leave you will see me with this decoration. The cannon barrage is still furious, and our formidable artillery deafens us with its noise. Up to now, my pigeons have caused me very little difficulty, I hope that continues. We are blessed by cooler weather, and it is not raining, so it's perfect. […]

8/31/1918.

I received yesterday your letter of the 27th. […] Our attack is making progress. We've passed the Aisne, but it was very difficult. Last night we bombed the *Boches* horribly; we are surrounded by *Boche* batteries which meant the noise was such that it was impossible to close our eyes for a second. The *Boches* responded weakly, a few shells did land near us about 1 a.m. If our troops advance, we will move forward. It seems that we cannot stay in a situation like this for more than 10 days. […]

I just interrupted my letter to go down to the basement; the 5 shells that just landed sounded very near to us. The *Boches* have good habits: they always launch the same number, five last night, five this morning, everything according to their rules. […]

9/1/1918.

I received yesterday your letter of the 28th. […] Our general was so proud of the work of the DI during the last attack that he asked Caplet if he would mind composing another march for them. Caplet accepted as he anticipates a number of favors and freedoms. He explained his plan to me: he will link the march you know to a slow, funereal movement commemorating the fallen, and add to that a new movement, all of that obviously for the three music regiments. I think he is planning to prolong his leave on the pretext that he needs calm to work. He is clever. We relieved the 129th when we arrived here and Caplet left, supposedly to visit that regiment while, in reality, he was headed to Paris. […]

Don't worry about me; my masks are in good condition and I keep my eyes open, so relax. This is hard on us and we are barely making any advances. We are up against formidable resistance and very strong positions. Mangin must not think we could take them; in these circumstances we are certainly playing the part of the sacrificed. Unfortunately for us, this is what is necessary. I do not believe that our relief can wait much longer; our losses are becoming significant and then there is the fatigue. Crossing an important river with cliffs on the other side is no ordinary task. In that situation, tanks are of no help. And everywhere, the *Boche* resistance is strong. […]

---

[301] A military award in the form of a braided cord.

9/2/1918.

I received yesterday your letter from August 29 and one with pictures of Port Lazo, some really lovely ones I didn't know. That gave me real pleasure. I also saw several articles in *L'Information* on the role of intellectuals during the war. Nothing was ever done for them and certainly their skills were not put to good use. Those who had no interest in becoming an officer, or who did not have the right skills (that doesn't mean they weren't very intelligent) were left as serfs and mostly unemployed. It is an absurd injustice. [...]

We still know nothing about being relieved. I don't think we will stay more than 5 or 6 days, despite the obvious fact that they are wearing down the fighting units to threads. This year, 1918, will be marked with a cross: yes, we do see deliverance, but it would be an illusion to think the end is near. We know what this year is costing us. I don't believe we could continue more than a few months like this; I am forced to admit that next year, the Americans will almost totally replace us. [...]

Yes, my leave in Brittany left me with wonderful memories. You should go see Mme Pierre soon to see whether she will rent her house to you from April 15 to October 15; I am much in favor of the idea that you stay for a long time next year. [...]

Wednesday, September 3, 1918, 2 p.m.

I just received, in the 1:30 mail, your letters from the 1st and 2nd. I am glad to have news from you; I expect things are very difficult for you right now. The Germans are using everything possible to stop your advance. [...]

9/3/1918.

I received your letter of August 30. [...] Nothing new here, except our regiments are in battle and, in these conditions, this cannot go on much longer. You can be confident: all precautions are taken when we enter a village in ruins. The DI only goes into villages that our troops have already passed through; there should really be no nasty surprises. [...]

9/4/1918.

Today I did the exchange of my pigeons, so I just got back to the DI and found the mail had arrived earlier than usual. Yesterday I didn't have a letter, but today I have the one from the 31st, and those from September 1 and 2. [...]

Caplet didn't seem to want to go on leave early in August. He wanted his septet. As soon as I got back, he stopped talking about the septet which I brought for him and got very enthusiastic about a poem by Henriette Charasson and wanted to leave as soon as possible. [...] Did he suspect that we were going into another maelstrom? Maybe. He was in the first one and wanted to avoid the second. [...] To compose music, one needs great technique plus quiet. When I see what he scratches out, erases, it's unbelievable. He proceeds by trial and error and resorts to the piano. [...] For me, up to now I've worked to be a virtuoso, not a composer. I will compose, that is certain, but I know that I need a lot of work. That will not keep me from trying to write a few little compositions, songs or short pieces for violin, once I am home. [...]

9/5/1918.

Today the mail has not yet arrived. Nothing has changed. Things are going much better, and our troops are advancing. Even the DI may move, not today, but maybe tomorrow. Our losses are not that great; I think that is why they are leaving us on the front longer. [...]

Yesterday I saw Captain Zeirer who said: "So, we are not making any more music?" I answered: "Right now there is a different sort of music, but the time will come when sweeter music will reclaim its rights." When Caplet is back, I will ask about the instruments and will certainly go get them in Troyes once we are at rest. [...] I will leave both Maréchal's cello and Caplet's viola in Paris; I will bring back only Mayer's violin, mine, and the music. That will be a huge task, but I will be able to have my violin again. No matter what they tell me, I will never let go of it again. [...]

9/6/1918.

I received yesterday your letter of September 2. The *Boches* are fast pulling out of here, and yesterday an echelon from the first group moved up. This time I was part of it. I crossed the Aisne on a bridge of boats and here I am in a totally destroyed town. I spent the night with some comrades seated on boxes. This morning we will try to find some place among all these ruins to settle into. [...]

9/7/1918.

There is excitement everywhere. The *Boches*, under widespread pressure, are still pulling back. They are under relentless, non-stop artillery fire the likes of which you cannot imagine. Under this barrage, once out in the open, things become terrible. [...].

I received your letter of the 3rd. [...] Right now I can only write what is most important and even then, I have to want to write to manage to do it. Everyone is enthusiastic, though very, very tired. Our army is like an entire people on the march. You cannot imagine the immense convoys and everything else that stretches out along the roads and the fields, it's absolutely fabulous. And all of that is being done easily, without obstacles, as though by people who over the past four years have become masters of their new profession. We are truly favored, this time, by continued good weather, really exceptional. If this continues, we will very shortly not only have regained the lines from before March 21 but gone beyond them. If the good weather continues until the end of October, we can allow ourselves all sorts of hope. [...]

It's official, our citation is the *fourragère*. And more, Mangin just congratulated us again and I think we will receive another citation. [...].

9/8/1918.

I received your letter from September 4 and also a card from Magne who continues to enjoy happy days. So much the better for him, it is compensation for all those in miserable conditions. There is still no talk about being relieved. To the contrary, we have orders to attack, in the direction of Laon. And oh, Mangin is pushing hard, digging in, and asking of the troops their maximum effort. When they take us out of here, we will have been completely used up and emptied like a squeezed lemon. True, from the military perspective, he is right to take advantage as much as possible of our success., but those who are in the fight have good reasons to grumble. Still, all the rationalization in the world isn't worth anything; when the wine is poured, it needs to be drunk. [...]

My letters are not, as you say, insignificant, but unfortunately, for months now, it is totally impossible to write more. Time still goes by with the absence of all work of any kind. Right now, I am in a basement, half fallen in. In front of me a huge pile of stinky manure, and a piece of a wall that shakes with every blast and will fall down at any moment! I am not the most badly lodged. I am mostly sheltered from the rain. The way we are living is outrageous. One would have to be with us to understand! [...]

9/9/1918.

I received yesterday your letter from September 5. [...] Still no news about our being relieved. Last night I even saw a colonel from one of our regiments who had come to protest against the attack orders, arguing that his men would not make the attack. What is certain is that, at this point, everywhere everyone needs to push to extremes in order to take full advantage of the *Boche* retreat. [...]

9/10/1918.

I received yesterday your letter from the 6th and today the one from September 7. [...] The rain last night was ferocious; it inundated everyone in the general headquarters. We are camping in mines and caves; in dry weather that is fine. But with the bad weather, water rushes in everywhere and it becomes unbearable. So, this morning, as soon as it was light, we went to a camp of engineers near here to get corrugated tin, asphalted cardboard, all sorts of things to block up the cracks and stop the water. Darned if everyone didn't have to help out in this task; I spent my time today playing roofer and carpenter. Now, no matter what, water will not get into my little spot. […]

I wonder whether you aren't becoming a bit crazy when you tell me to work, to compose, when you write about the love of my art in the midst of the life I'm leading. That is a cup I've not drunk from in a very long time. For sure, one of these days I hope to take up the drink, but at this time I must not think about it. In terms of expression, it takes the form of the putrid odors which reach us right now and the magic of sound is summed up in the roar of the cannon. To read your letters, I would believe myself to be at the garrison in Caen or Évreux, in a nicely closed room, with hours to spend at will. Alas, I am in mud and dust, I smell bad, I am sweaty, and I am trying to get past the dangers as best I can. I can do nothing else. That said, I am proud of myself. Goodbye.

Plouézec, Côtes du Nord, Tuesday, September 17, 1918, 2 p.m.

I just received your letter from September 10. […] I fully understand (maybe too well) your suffering. It seems to me it has lasted much too long, alas! And that, if there were any justice in this world, they could give you a job suited to your age and your service. I've said that in all sorts of ways, but nothing changes. The people at the top must not worry much about fairness, or about the soldiers' merit, age, and the length of time at the front. […]

9/12/1918.

I received today your letter of September 9. It was my day to exchange the pigeons; fortunately, all went well. The place I took my animals to has been subjected to destruction like I've never seen. […] Mangin came to the DI yesterday. He insisted forcefully that, at all costs, we had to break the lines. […]

9/14/1918.

Today I received your letter of September 11. I am distressed to know you are not well. How do you manage to get chilled, or develop indigestion? I hope it is nothing and that your little purge will be good for you.

Caplet arrived this morning, very mysterious. I had very little time to talk to him, but he will be leaving us soon. He finally accepted to go to the American Headquarters in Chaumont to direct a school for American Army band directors. He may not have the same quiet as here, but it is the way out of this place, even though he says it's only for 4 months. He doesn't want to leave until his new march is completed and performed, so he will try to stay at least a month. […] That doesn't bother me; the obscure powers that have protected me will continue their work and, with the help of my violin, I will always manage to do well.

My dear kitten, you are picking a quarrel with me about my literary responses. If you knew how little time I have right now, how hard it is to sleep with all the crap going on around us, you would understand that my brain is not in a place to write about such things. I have barely started to read Guerin, I've not opened Samain's Stories.[302] […] I am putting hope in our relief, we are very tired. They are truly drawing on the essence of human force. […]

9/16/1918.

Today I received your letter from September 13. I will answer right now about what Mme Pierre writes. Living as I do, always in the open air, often serving as moving man (here we have to load and unload carts), I do not cross my arms while my fellow soldiers work. In such conditions, I cannot keep either the complexion or the hands of a young lady. […] To put it another way, all that seems to me very childish in the midst of the period I'm living through right now, when I find myself in such a miserable place, when men all around me are falling like flies, I am not very interested in what people who get to sleep and eat say.

As for the *fourragère*, I will of course wear it, as it's awarded to the regiment. But I will not forget that this vain trinket was bought with the suffering and blood of the 25,000 comrades who, over the past 4 years, have been part of the 74th. The tears of the mothers, the wives, the children, the sisters, the fiancées have been spilled so that a certain number of individuals can be showered with distinction. The greatest number of those who will wear this *fourragère* will have had nothing to do with the feats that earned it. Those who earned it for the 74th are the dead and the wounded. Regimental citations represent a great amount of blood and grief. As happy as I am to see the enemy retreat, I cannot forget the price that we will have been obliged to pay. These honors are dismal honors indeed! True, we will grit our teeth; true, we will kick the *Boches* out, but once all that is finished, we will shed tears for the total massacre of our people and its life blood. […]

We attacked again this morning, took prisoners, and made noticeable advances, but what remains of our *poilus* is no more than a feverish, sickly shadow. Our relief cannot wait long, it is impossible to continue much longer. […].

Since yesterday the cannon fire has been frightening and planes, from one side or the other, are dropping their crud like raindrops. Where is the umbrella? In such an atmosphere, don't worry about my complexion. […].

---

[302] Léon Guérin (1807-1885), author, poet, short story writer, and naval historian; Albert Samain (1858-1900), poet and author.

Wednesday, September 18, 1918, 11 a.m.

[...] During the night of the 15th there was a new air raid over Paris that lasted quite long. Apparently there is considerable damage. They are not talking about victims, but there must have been some deaths to mourn. The Germans always take advantage of a beautiful clear night. [...]

9/17/1918.

We just got the news that we will be relieved tomorrow, the 18th. We will leave in the morning for a village 10 kilometers to the rear, and on the night of the 18th we will set off by truck. We have to hope this rest will be long; this time the DI is totally worn out. [...] Yesterday, again, the *poilus* made a successful attack, taking cannons, prisoners, and making major advances. To do all that as tired as they are, there are no words adequate to praise those poor men. One has to have lived with those guys, who are sacrificing their very being, to realize how nasty and base are the complaints of those far from danger. [...]

Thursday, September 19, 1918, 2:30 p.m.

I received today your letters from September 16 and 17. [...] My opinion of this terrible war has never changed; the French people will almost cease to exist, and more and more ruins will pile up. The American participation, although a help for us, is also proof that the war will last another 6 months or more. They will want to reap the reward for their sacrifice and France, in this perpetual agony, will all the more be destroyed, wiped away. And later, when calm has returned (everything has an end eventually) she will be prey to all sorts of foreigners who want to make a buck and take over. I wrote you some observations about your situation. If they make you angry, you are wrong. [...] If at times my health is not perfect, that is because I think constantly of the suffering you endure and the dangers you run. If I beg you to think of yourself, that is, do what you can to improve your position, it is for the best. You should not always trust chance and think that some unknown force will protect you. [...]

I read in *L'Est Eclair* about a catastrophe that just happened: a train of men on leave headed for Normandy was crushed by a freight train that was following it. [...] Many men were killed and injured. [...]

Your regiment will receive a *fourragère*. By wearing it, you honor the men who died as they, alas, cannot wear it. [...]

9/19/1918.

I am writing in haste. We are at rest; will it last? I don't know. They are talking of staying here only a little bit of time and going somewhere else. I will write

507

more tomorrow; I am very tired. I traveled all night and, once here, had to find food and a room. I was lucky to find what I needed. I'm going to clean up a bit and rest. [...]

9/20/1918.

I received today your letters from September 17 and 18. I reply immediately. Contrary to what you say, I am in a position that totally suits my class and my length of time on the front, although to tell the truth very little attention is paid to the latter. Sadly, a good number of *poilus* from the class of 1898 are still in fighting regiments. One of our good friends from that class, Sergeant Lemonnier, whom we named the King of Calvados because he owned a lot of apple trees and made quantities of eau-de-vie, was just killed. I also learned yesterday of the death of Commander Auberge, the commander of the 129th who played cello quite well. Right now, we are paying a heavy price and from everywhere comes bad news, so I am far from complaining. [...]

As for Caplet, he's not letting on, but I think he is not very eager to take the new position. [...] If Caplet leaves, I would prefer to be named corporal if that would mean I would be chief of the service; I would not at all like to have Caplet replaced by a sergeant who might really pester me. What is more, I've essentially been doing his service so that wouldn't change anything. I wrote to Lieutenant B about 3 weeks ago, so far, no response. [...]

9/21/1918.

[...] I passed an excellent night and am well rested. This afternoon I am going to see Commander Bouteville about the instruments. I expect to leave directly for Troyes then I will pass by Paris to drop off Caplet's viola and Maréchal's cello as well as some things belonging to Caplet. [...]

Caplet is working on the orchestration of his march which is almost finished. Then we will have to copy out the parts which will take time. Caplet is pushing to finish because, if he leaves, it will certainly be October 1. The march has to be performed before then. That seems doubtful to me given the time we have. We are a reserve unit, and no one knows what awaits us. We all worry that we will be involved for a third time in a bad situation. Everyone is starting to have it up to here; 24 days in the midst of attacks like we just had is truly awful for the poor *poilus*. [...]

Tuesday, September 24, 1918, 1:30 p.m.

I just received in the mail your letter from September 21. You tell me that you are leaving for Troyes on the 23rd and will come back to Paris to deliver Caplet's viola and Maréchal's cello to their respective homes. You must have an open-ended leave because you tell me it will take three days or more to do everything. I think that 5 francs a day is very little. We have no more money; we are eating into our capital. I know you don't think much about that question and what is important is to find yourself in the wonderful city of Paris. That seems a bit childish to me! [...] I am very sad to know you are in Paris, close to Vincennes, and I am not there so you can come home. [...]

9/22/1918.

I will definitely leave tomorrow for Troyes then to Paris to drop off the instruments. I will write from Troyes and send a few postcards. Caplet is nearly ill; he is working night and day on the orchestration of his march. It's a bit too much with the fatigue from all this moving about. [...]

Thursday, September 26, 1918, 1:30 p.m.

I just received your four postcards from Troyes. You arrived there in the morning.

You were very careful not to tell me you were coming to Paris; I was certainly pleased that getting your violin and music from Troyes meant there was a chance that you could practice and leave behind the dull military life. You will end up taking a 6-day leave and getting quite tired. (You never took so many days when you came to Vincennes to repair your violin when it really needed it; you cleared out quickly after a day or two!) And you will spend money as though you were rich! You will do what seems right to you, that is for sure, whether it be important or stupid. You don't pay much attention and seem quite indifferent, but if the war lasts another year, how will we manage to have enough money?

Let's turn to another topic, which may seem remote from the first one, but is relevant. You write that Caplet is rushing to finish his march because he will take up his new position as Director of Military Music on October 1. Well, you should do all you can to replace him as the sergeant in charge of pigeons. Not only do you already do his job, you will not be happy to have a new sergeant who will surely cause you a lot of trouble. I think Caplet should request that and you should also. You will be safe and will receive a salary; that is nothing to sneeze at. I don't understand you: it is fine for you to serve your country, but for you to receive nothing is pure stupidity. The pay would keep me from having to send you any money, or almost none. I receive no allocation or indemnity as many others do. You are giving of yourself [...] and you won't try to replace Caplet in order to receive his pay? You are going crazy; I don't know what you are thinking of. [...]

Finally, I am back. I left Sunday night, was in Paris about 11 p.m. I stayed in a hotel near the Gare du Nord. The next day I ran a few errands for the division officers, then took the train to Troyes. I was to have gotten the instruments but, alas, the box with the music and Caplet's things were being held by the military police. The commander there was an old brute who thought my mission orders were not correct, that I should have had a transport order, in short, all sorts of difficulties. I prevailed but it was not easy. It was 8 p.m. when the instruments were finally registered. I left the next morning and was in Paris by noon. I waited until 3 p.m. for the baggage, took them to the hotel, then went to see Maréchal's father and Caplet's brother. It was 6 p.m. when I got back to the hotel. I looked at my violin and it was all unglued. I took it immediately to Serdet who said he would return it the next day at 5 p.m. On the Rue LaFayette I bumped into Dumand, who let out cries of joy and invited me for lunch on Thursday. He is on medical leave until October 19.

On Thursday night I took the train from the Gare du Nord, arrived in Crépy-en-Valois at 12:30 a.m. Sentinels from the 74th informed me that the infantry division had left the day before for an unknown destination. I was quite concerned. I headed for a barracks nearby and spent the night. Friday morning, I came out of my shelter and met LeBailly who said he was leaving at 10, and suggested I come with him. […]

We traveled all day and about 9 p.m. were near Saint-Omer where I was lucky to find a car to take me to where the DI was. When I arrived, I found all your letters and will respond to all your objections. I think we will soon be fighting in Flanders and that is why we are here. Caplet will not go to Chaumont: from what he says that effort was not successful. It is very hard right now to leave the front. […]

Saturday, September 28, 1918, 2 p.m.

I have not received any news yesterday or today, so I don't know what to think. Are you ill? Your train didn't have an accident? […] I don't know what to believe and am very worried. I wish you good health, my dear child, and hope to receive news as quickly as possible. […]

Undated letter, 2:30 p.m.

I am completely shocked to have had no news from you since the 23rd, the day you went to Troyes. You told me, on the two picture postcards you sent, that you would leave for Paris on Wednesday morning, the 24th, and would write once you arrived. What is going on? […]

Tuesday, October 1, 1918.

I just received in the 1:30 mail your letter from September 28. That three-page letter says a lot of things that are rather confusing, and really is a mishmash. [...] I think you mostly wanted to spend money and wear yourself out, coming to Paris to get to Troyes then back to Paris. None of that was designed to help you recover from the fatigue of three weeks of fighting at the Chemin des Dames. [...] One hundred francs for a promenade like that is a bit expensive; I remind you that you are not rich enough to throw your money out the window. [...]

9/29/1918.

For sure life is never calm; we leave this morning for an area near Cassel, 22 kilometers from Saint-Omer. [...] I had found a perfect little room with a bridge keeper who operates a turning bridge on the canal. Those people, the father, the mother, the 15-year-old daughter and the 17-year-old son are so very good, so nice. They don't want any money and they have such a special manner that I took their address: Monsieur Vandenbergue, Bridge Keeper, Saint-Momelin-par-Watteau, Nord. They are people I will really miss; I am very sad to have only been here 8 hours.

I packed my violin in the general's car, suspended from the roof with a good rope to avoid bumps. Most likely we will be in the battle soon. The English took Cambrai and 10,000 prisoners. Things are moving everywhere and the *Boches* are pulling back. Under these conditions, we may not be able to have a rest. We need to pursue the *Boches* at all costs. It's an adventurous life. As long as we have nice weather, it will not be very hard, let's hope the good weather continues. My dear little kitten, for the past week my life has truly been like a movie, the countryside changing astonishingly fast. [...]

9/30/1918.

[...] I am astounded by the frankly nasty letter of the 26th. I am the first to regret my trip to Troyes for the instruments: had I realized how exhausting it was going to be, moving around, in a wind and rain storm, I would never have gone to get them. Aside from the fact that the instruments add a new impediment, there is a chance they will be damaged. The commander who sent me could not have expected this sudden departure. And I was really fortunate to immediately find the division; it would have been very challenging had I had to gallop after them with the instruments and the music. Juhel, who goes to Paris often on business, told me about the hotel near the Gare du Nord where I was comfortable. It is a proper place. It is unbelievable the hordes of women around the Gare du Nord and the Gare de l'Est. [...]

My expenses for the trip will be reimbursed. And now I have my violin and will not let go of it. I hope that the present, awful conditions will only be temporary. I really do not understand all the reproaches you make; you still treat me like a little boy of 8 rather than a man of 40. [...]

Friday, October 4, 1918.

No mail today. [...] Everything is ready for my departure October 7. I will take the 3 p.m. train from Paimpol and will change in Guingamp for the 7:30 train from Brest. I think that is the train you took. [...] I will be very happy to get home and back to my normal life. [...]

10/1/1918.

Still on the move. [...]

Saturday, October 5, 1918, 2:30 p.m.

[...] Today I received your letter from October 1, two from October 2, as well as my letters and a note from Rolland. I see he was seriously wounded; had he not been taken to surgery by ambulance, the results might have been dreadful. Now there is hope that he will be well soon. Praise God! [...] You tell me to give thanks to destiny; I do that every day. [...]

10/2/1918.

I received this evening your letter from the 29th. [...] I just received a letter from poor Rolland; I don't know how to express my sadness when I learned of his serious injury. I truly hope that what he wrote is true, that he is out of danger. Praise heaven which up to now has protected me. Rolland was under fire for four years, almost always in the front lines. [...]

You can imagine how comforting it is to see you so upset, here in the midst of all our weariness! I hope by now that you've calmed down and will resume a normal life and write nicer letters. [...] It may happen that I cannot write for a week; that is no reason to kill yourself. [...]

10/3/1918.

Here the mail comes very late, about 4 p.m. The DI is located in a convent 3 kilometers from a pretty Flemish town. This quite large convent is surrounded by a rudimentary village, fairly spread out. In a small part of the convent there are still a few nuns and about 30 orphans. The outbuildings are large, and we have been able to spread out. We were supposed to leave immediately, but we are still here after 3 days. Up to now, no orders have led us to believe that, after all the exhaustion of the rapid movements in terrible weather, we will not be able to prolong this stay. This morning, I got my violin from the general's car and practiced a bit. Darn it, my fingers are hard and stiff. But that will all come back quickly. Yesterday afternoon, I also did a bit of counterpoint. [...]

10/4/1918.

I received your letter from September 30. You are again complaining of no letters. You certainly should have had one by now; the moving of the DI has to be the reason for the delay. [...] We have to move again, about 20 kilometers forward, I think near the forest of Houthulst. [...]

I cannot send any tobacco—there is a rule that expressly forbids it. In addition to the disciplinary measures against the sender, the person receiving it might have to pay a fine of 500 to 1000 francs. [...]

For a while now we have no more jam; those I brought you are the last I have seen for sale. Everything becomes very difficult, and I think that it will be harder, this winter, to get things that up to now were easy to find. Apparently, chocolate is becoming very scarce—you should try to get some cocoa. If I can, I will bring some. Everything, like our clothing, is getting harder to find. We get nothing; it's a big effort to get a pair of pants. When the division orders 50, it receives 10. [...]

10/5/1918.

I received last night your letters of October 1 and 2. For sure, if the weather in Brittany is as nasty as here, you might as well go home. I would have loved for you to stay there for all of October, but only if the month was lovely and as warm as it can be. Up to now, there is nothing but rain and storms; I understand that staying in Plouézec is less fun and that you would be better off in Vincennes. Therefore, I'm sending this letter to Vincennes.

We were supposed to move but it has not yet happened. I think that our advance depended on the English attack and their advance; apparently the attack was not very successful, so we are staying put for now. I share a place with Caplet and my fellow pigeon keeper, a shelter built by the English out of wood with a corrugated tin roof. It is quite comfortable. We have a stove and for now we have wood, so we are pretty well off. [...]

10/6/1918.

I received yesterday your letter of October 2. [...] Amazing news just broke— the central powers are asking for an armistice and agree to discuss peace based on President Wilson's 14 Points. This has made everyone crazy with joy; but we must not have any illusions because I don't think the allies have agreed to discuss peace based on those points. They will demand that the central powers accept the armistice without any discussion. In any case, that is a good indication of the German situation. They see that they have lost and would like to stop the sacrifices that will no longer lead to victory. I wonder whether they will lower their pride enough to accept what will be very harsh conditions. [...]

In any case, things are moving very quickly and there may be a sudden change. This war has lasted so long that one has difficulty believing it could end so quickly. We are sort of stunned by such news. [...]

I went to talk to the Dean of this convent to see whether it would be a problem if I were to play for the 9:00 Mass. He replied that it was forbidden by the Pope; that I would cause a distraction and the faithful would listen to the violin and not follow the Holy Office. [...]

10/7/1918.

I received last night your letter of October 3. [...] With respect to Vessot, Caplet knows some women [...] in charge of projects to aid war victims in all sorts of ways, notably those who have lost all their furniture as is the case of Vessot. He has also written to them to recommend Vessot, who has only to go knock on the door and tell them what he wants and what sort of help he needs. [...]

Sensing the end of the war, Caplet asked me whether I would want to be part of an organization to present good modern music. I told him he could count on me. In addition to being personally interested in the project, I would meet composers and a rich, powerful public, if rather snobbish. I have never had that advantage. [...]

I think today, right now, is when you are leaving Plouézec. [...]

Tuesday, October 8, 1918, 2 p.m.

I arrived in Paris this morning at 7 a.m., the train was an hour late. Mathilde and her husband were waiting for me. I found an open carriage to hold all my baggage and the violin case but, unfortunately, I couldn't also bring the trunk. [...] The train was very crowded with many soldiers. The trip was exhausting. I took a third-class ticket; the car was very full, and I had a dreadful time finding room for all my packages. I had to put them on the floor. The violin case was leaning against my side the entire trip. An entire night stuck in one place and unable to move—it was very tiring. [...]

Second letter, same day, 7 p.m.

[...] My trip didn't start off well. To start with, in the little train from Paimpol to Guingamp, there was a woman facing me who was drunk; she never stopped talking loudly and chewing on little bits of tobacco. In Guingamp, I was in a compartment, but the door didn't close. [...] There was a broken window across from our compartment, so we traveled all night with a breeze on our faces and legs. Fortunately, the night was not terribly cold. [...]

10/8/1918.

I received yesterday your letter of October 4. I hope there was no serious accident on the line from Brest and that you could leave on the day you planned. [...]

I think we will leave here to move forward in no more than 48 hours; this time there is no doubt, we are going into another huge battle. This area is exceptionally gray and damp. [...]

Germany's proposal, or rather the proposal of the central powers, doesn't seem to be meeting with much success. It is presented in a way that one has to see a trap to divide us and make out better. But the trap is very obvious; we won't fall for it. All of this makes me sure that we will not be home until sometime next year, truly maybe another year. I don't think it will be sooner because, even if Germany no longer has the force to defeat us, they still have enough to put up a strong resistance. To break that and force her to ask for mercy may take 7 or 8 months at best. [...]

I hope you arrived this morning in Paris, not too tired, and that you found a car to take you to Vincennes with your baggage and my violins, which are the biggest inconvenience. [...]

Thursday, October 10, 1918, 7:30 p.m.

I received at 4 p.m. your letter from October 8. [...] Mathilde's husband went to the Montparnasse station to get my trunk. It took him a long time to find it. There are mountains of all sorts of baggage, stacks of trunks and boxes. You have to climb all over to find what belongs to you. [...]

10/9/1918.

I received yesterday your letter of October 5. [...] We will be in a physical situation that won't be much fun—on the plain and without (or almost without) shelter. So, it is again tents that will be our refuge. We will put them up and, good heavens, that will rejuvenate us and remind us of 1915. If only we have a fairly dry period, it won't be half-bad. [...]

By God, the *poilus* have had enough of all this; rest is almost nonexistent. The last move was very difficult: our regiments walked long distances in rain and wind. Things have settled down a bit for a week, but only for us to immediately move on, under very difficult conditions.

You say stupid things when you suggest I write twice a week. I would miss it if I didn't write every day. [...]

I received last night your two letters of October 6. [...] I don't know why you call my trip to Paris "cruel." For sure, I was wrong not to write but I had so many errands to run and was terribly tired! But "cruel?" You exaggerate! The "cruel" fact is that I now have my violin and can practice at least occasionally. What would be really cruel would be to have, like Rolland, a fractured skull, or if, like Vessot, I had tuberculosis. How you build things up!

But I want to talk to you about something very serious. It seems that the Spanish flu is quite lethal; you have to be careful. Do not go see anyone who has the flu, which is very contagious. And if you start to feel achy and very tired, you should immediately do a purge, 50 grams of salt. You also need to put mentholated Vaseline in your nostrils, and inhale gomenol. You should have the doctor come immediately. [...]

I received yesterday your two letters from October 8, this time from Vincennes. [...] Tomorrow morning we are leaving again for heart of the battle. The news going around is getting more and more extraordinary. There is talk that Wilhelm will abdicate, that Hungary and Austria are giving up. Under those conditions, it is sure that the war will not last long, that in just a few more months at least my class will be home. The younger classes will obviously still be mobilized for some time. We can finally envision liberation, which was impossible in June of this year. The comeback happened after July 15. It's really amazing. The effort of the Americans was, for sure, colossal and produced an undeniable result, although it didn't spare us from making a similar effort. Foch was sure of the result, and it is understandable that he asks the maximum effort from all of us. In short, by Christmas this year, we will have a clearer picture. [...]

My doorbell is broken so the mailman slid the mail under the door. [...] I see that Germany has accepted President Wilson's proposals; that shows that she is desperate and wants to keep us from entering her territory and doing all the evil she has done to us. Hope to God that this is the end. I ran into Mme Boissard yesterday afternoon and she said she'd been to the notary to pay last term's rent. So tomorrow I will go get that money then go to the town hall for my coal ration card; they will deliver the two monthly supplies I am entitled to. [...]

10/12/1918.

I received yesterday your letter of October 9 and today am writing in the morning—we will soon have no time: we are bundling up our things for our departure tomorrow. [...]

Few men will go to the command post, only the most needed; the command post is situated in the middle of a field with barely enough shelter for the officers. [...] So I will stay with Caplet and my fellow pigeon keeper in a village with the last group. And we just learned we will not have any pigeons until the 15th. [...]

10/14/1918.

I received yesterday, when we arrived at our new site, your letter of the 11th. [...] I am right now with Caplet and Asseline in the second lines; the installation at the command post is so dangerous and short on space that we cannot join them. We are in a camp set up about 2 kilometers from a pretty little town. The camp, in a little wood, is a model of what it should be. All in corrugated iron, the interior walls of the shelters are of wood with comfortable bunks. [...] The English and Belgians built good shelters. When you look at what the French army did to house the *poilu*, it makes one wonder about the difference with the other armies. [...]

We spent 10 days in the convent at Poperinge; the English had stayed there and we used the shelters they built. [...]

10/15/1918.

I did not receive a letter yesterday; but we did have news that shook up both Caplet and me. We received a note from the Central Headquarters sending Caplet to Chaumont as director of the technical school for military music. Caplet had given up hope of this happening; I read the letters from his friends in Paris who said definitely that there was no chance at all, that he should no longer count on it. Probably there were some new movements that he knew nothing about; the transfer order arrived yesterday about noon. This morning, after sorting all his things, I took him to a car which was to take him to Calais. It is not without sadness that we parted, after two years of life together. I cannot forget all the good times making music and the thousands of memories attached to all the places we passed through together in this miserable and picturesque life. Caplet was also very moved, although visibly he tried to control his emotion. [...]

So here I am, the last one of the old music group. Of the old group, Caplet, Lemoine, Maréchal, Magne, Cloëz, have all left. I admit I will feel a bit lonely. Of all those around me—for sure good friends—it was only with Caplet that I could talk about more serious things and to whom I felt close. Fortunately for me, I hope the war is now coming to an end and that, in a few months, we will be able, finally, to breathe freely. May God make it happen, as this ordeal is so great that even the strongest souls suffer great anguish at times. [...]

Thursday, October 17, 1918, 2:30 p.m.

I received no news from you this morning. I am anxious to know what has become of you. [...] The *communiqués* speak of good news from Flanders and the north of France, but that doesn't reassure me. I went to see Ligneul after going to the post office. I bought some things to have on hand as prevention in case the flu comes for a visit. I do hope it will deprive me of its presence, but it is better to be prepared. Pharmaceutical products have become prohibitively expensive. It took almost all of a 5-franc bill to buy a little bit of mentholated Vaseline, a bottle of liquid gomenol, a few violets and some eucalyptus lozenges. [...] Yesterday I went to the notary to withdraw the 300 francs Mme Boissard paid. [...]

10/17/1918.

I couldn't write yesterday; we moved forward about 20 kilometers. And I was bothered by the pigeons delivered during the day which I had to take to the DI during the night. When I got back to the division it was almost midnight and I'd been on the move since 5 a.m., so I was very tired. We have gotten past the zone of destruction and where we are going now, we will find ourselves in cities or towns somewhat damaged but where we will still be able to have a roof over our heads. That is already an improvement. The *Boches* are pulling out and our regiments, accompanied by cavalry or tanks, are chasing after them. Tomorrow morning we will move another 15 kilometers forward. Our general direction is toward the city of Gand; we are not very far from there. Everything is going very well, but the overall fatigue is quite bad. Still, everyone keeps going, excited by all the amazing victories. The *Boches* have turned tail without stopping. [...]

10/18/1918.

Because of our constant movement, I did not receive a letter today. We left this morning at 5:30. I traveled, quite comfortably, on the seat of a large hay wagon. There was dense fog, but at about 10 a.m. the fog lifted and the day was lovely, one of the lovely October days which, in this Flemish land, are much more muted and subdued than in France. In this country, light seems rare. There are a lot of civilians here; they have all lost their joy after living sadly under the domination of the *Boches*. Before they left, the *Boches* mined the church which collapsed. I found a little room at the home of a baker which will suit me to a tee if we stay here several days. [...]

These Belgian towns are lively and the residents very welcoming. They have really suffered greatly. The price of food is unbelievable: 35 francs for a kilo of butter and 1,25 for an egg, chocolate at 65 francs a kilo, and all is subject to increases. You can imagine that in such conditions these people are skinny. Almost all have tired eyes and faces in which one can read their suffering. It's as impressive as it could be, and I do not regret seeing this rather curious stage of the war. [...]

10/19/1918.

I received today your two letters from October 15 and 16. We are undoubtedly going to move tomorrow morning; our troops continue to advance. Right now, they are on the banks of the Lys. Today is my day to exchange the pigeons but because of all the obstacles on the road the pigeons have not yet arrived. It will be a real headache to take them to the DI with all the movement around me. One might think we were on the Boulevard des Italiens on a Sunday in peacetime. [...]

10/20/1918.

I had to stop my letter because the pigeons arrived. I tried to find a vehicle: absolutely nothing because of our move so Asseline had to help me carry them. I covered the 10 to 12 kilometers between Ardooie and Tielt on foot, with my 18 traveler pigeons, along a road, muddy beyond description, and in the midst of an unbelievable crush of all sorts of convoys. When we got to that little town, it was 9:00 at night. The *Boches* hadn't left until that morning; we found many civilians, jumping, gamboling, dancing, and who embraced us. A good number of women wanted to make off with us; it took all our good sense to resist those invitations. Needless to say, once we had turned over our pigeons, we found a good *gite* and good food, at the home of a female baker. There was none of that other stuff because we didn't want it, and we were totally beat.

The DI arrived this morning. It is Sunday, so there was a *Te Deum*. The mayor had invited the general. A photographer took a picture of the officers in front of the Command Post for *L'Illustration*. [...]

10/22/1918.

I didn't receive any letter this morning, but I did receive two packages. [...] We have finally moved solidly to the other shore of the Lys. At this moment, an attack is underway and having very good results. The *Boches* launched a bunch of 130s and 240s on our little town last night and unfortunately there were victims among the personnel of the DI. One of the big projectiles fell on the kitchen wagon and killed 7 men, all old guys who felt safe. [...]

10/23/1918.

I received just now your letters from the 19th and 20th [...] and this morning a letter from Vessot; I will answer him. We do not have to worry about him. Before leaving, Caplet showed me a letter from the woman in charge of the charitable association saying that she would be happy to do all she could for our friend from the 129th. [...]

10/24/1918.

I am writing this morning in haste; we are at rest starting this morning and we are staying where we are, in this little town. Everyone here is asking me to play for them. At the home of the mayor there is a lovely room with a grand piano that just needs tuning. Niverd is coming today to do that. Even more good luck, two days ago an auxiliary interpreter arrived—a young man of 26 named Drouin. He was in the aviation unit and wounded twice. He is a pianist, student of Philippe, and spent two years at the Conservatory.[303] [...] But I do not have any music. I will undoubtedly go to Bruges by car to try to find something like sonatas. [...]

10/25/1918.

I went to Bruges yesterday by car. What a beautiful city! I am sending you and will send for several days some postcards which you will certainly find very lovely. I found a piano merchant who sells music. He gave me 4 Beethoven sonatas and one by Mozart, edited by Schott during the war. [...] Bruges is intact except for a few intersections with bomb damage. [...] I have to get to work.

10/26/1918.

I received today your two letters from the 21st and 23rd. I also had the wonderful surprise to receive the picture of you dressed in a Breton costume. [...]

10/28/1918.

I received yesterday your two letters of October 24. [...] Unfortunately I couldn't write yesterday because we had to move. To make room for a division coming into the sector, we left our little town of Tielt for another little town, 8 kilometers to the northeast. I found a pretty bourgeois house to settle into more than comfortably. I have an excellent room and am cared for like the child of the house. [...]

---

[303] Isidor Philippe (1863-1958).

Friday, November 1, 1918, 8 p.m., All Saints' Eve.

I did not receive news from you today. There is no 4 p.m. mail so tomorrow morning I will have the pleasure of reading your words. [...]

10/31/1918.

I received just now your letter of the 27th. [...] I just rehearsed with an organist; tomorrow I am playing for 10:00 Mass. It is All Saints Day. I am playing *Le Sommeil de la Vierge* and the Bach aria;[304] the organist is not very good and has enormous difficulty accompanying me. [...]

Saturday, November 2, 1918, 1:30 p.m.

I didn't receive news this morning. Are you at the front? That is more than possible; I read a sidebar in *Le Petit Parisien*: "a 16-kilometer advance by the armies in Flanders." The Belgian *communiqué* says: "The offensive operation undertaken by the armies in Flanders continued to meet with success during the day of November 1. In the south, the British second army pushed the enemy from the Escaut. In the center, the French-American army of Belgium, having taken the bitterly defended heights between the Lys and the Escaut, pushed as far as that river along a 16-kilometer front from Nelden to Ecke. In two days they advanced between 8 and 16 kilometers and took back 19 villages." [...] Let's hope this is the end. Turkey has signed an armistice, and Austria-Hungary is asking Italy for an armistice. Hindenburg has resigned; for sure all these signs lead one to think that Germany, abandoned by all, is starting to have had enough. The newspapers say that President Wilson is coming to Paris. So, they are preparing for peace. Peace and its conditions? What can we hope for? [...] It is important to be cautious when the Germans pull out of towns and cities. They are mining some buildings—churches, town halls, train stations. [...]

11/1/1918.

This morning I am writing early. The main reason is because I am playing at the 10:00 Mass. [...] I saw Mme Baroness Van Bruggen. I am invited for lunch tomorrow and then she and I will play music. She's about 40 years old, blond, a little plump, with pretty eyes but sadly she has rosacea on her face. [...] I am painfully aware that I need a good pianist. There is no shortage of good instruments in this area, but people who play well are definitely in short supply. [...]

Events seem to be moving rapidly: Austria and Turkey are giving up. I believe, this is my personal belief, that Germany will hold on for some time. In any case,

---

[304] Massenet, *Le Dernier Sommeil de la Vierge*, for violin and piano.

they are definitely putting up bitter resistance and those who figured we'd progress as easily as through butter are much mistaken. [...]

Sunday, November 3, 1918, 1 p.m.

I receive your letters at 4 p.m. and today, being Sunday, the mail comes in the morning, so it will be a spiritually slim day. [...] Brussels will be retaken because they want to bring King Albert back to his city and return it to him. If that happens, there will be celebrations. You will probably be there. You need to be prepared to do what they want. [...] After the war, you might well find a position as professor in Belgium, for example, at the Brussels Conservatory. [...]

11/2/1918.

This morning I am writing very early because, at 9:00 there is a Mass for the dead at which I am playing the prayer from the *Trille du diable*. After that, today's the day I am going for lunch at the Chateau of Wildenburg, the home of Baron and Baroness Van Bruggen. After lunch I will play for them. [...]

11/3/1918.

Yesterday I was at the home of the Baroness Van Bruggen. They live in a lovely home in Wildenburg, 4 kilometers away from our little village. It's a Flemish-style building, large and superbly placed in the middle of vast lawns bordered by white begonias and roses creating a soft and luminous effect—very lovely. The Baroness is quite a good musician, and has studied a lot, which is obvious immediately. Her playing is not extraordinary, and she misses a lot of notes, but she is always with me and finds her place easily. And more, the musical feeling is right. We played the Beethoven C Minor and the Franck Sonata. She accompanied me for the Cools pieces, not badly at all, and I closed with the *Chaconne*. We had lunch which, although very simple, was very good: a potato omelet, ham with spinach, boiled potatoes. A large glass of water, a small glass of burgundy (excellent) and, to finish, a glass of sherry and coffee with cream, and champagne. In short, an excellent lunch, very elegant, served by a maid in white gloves etc. Overall, refined and elegant society. They are true lovers of music, both of them, and have heard a lot. They follow the Rhine festivals and the Mozart festivals in Salzburg. The Baronness told me: "I knew you well by name, but I had never heard you." [...]

These Flemish are attractive people and very wealthy, as evidenced by the countryside and the comfortable houses everywhere. It's a pretty, very pretty country, which leads you to understand the primitive Flemish painters. It is sumptuous and pleasing, a house like the Baron's is a dream. [...]

11/4/1918.

I received your letter of October 31 and also a card from Rolland. I am very happy to know he continues to improve. He was very lucky to survive such a serious injury. [...]

We have the unbelievable luck to have magnificent weather, which allows us to continue the large-scale military operations, and, at this moment, they are having great results. One must hope that, in a month, French soil will be freed; that is already a result one didn't expect six months ago. [...]

I have the feeling that Gand will fall in a matter of hours. There are large numbers of American forces here and they continue to arrive. [...]

Second letter, same day.

I received today, much earlier than usual, your letter of the 31st. [...] At this time, everything is falling apart for the enemy, and we will finally be able to reap the fruits of our long effort and painful sacrifice. It will be victory, but for brave, thoughtful men it will be with heaviness of spirit that they return home. They will not be able to stop thinking of the price paid for freedom and the way in which French men have been engulfed in this inferno. People continue to talk about our sacrifices, but numbers are not provided. When we know, there will be an enormous, painful shudder. Freedom is worth any price, but the French have paid dearly so others could live and be free. [...]

11/5/1918.

This morning the weather is abominable, a true storm with wind and rain. We are lucky to be sheltered in a nice room. Of course, my bed, which I described as "good," has sheets. The blankets are mine; the woman who is lodging us did not have enough for herself. She is a widow with an 11-year-old daughter; she owns a notions store. In her large house, there are two officers and me, making three rooms occupied; plus, she feeds a group of pilots. In any case, I am just fine here and ask only to stay until the end of the war. [...]

The Americans are arriving in huge waves, a good thing because everything might be over before they are involved. [...]

11/6/1918.

I received yesterday your letters from November 1 and 2. [...] I think that soon they will announce that Gand has been taken. Aside from the strong *Boche* resistance, advancing quickly is complicated by all the water—the Escaut river, the canals, and the flooding. You would have to see it to understand the conditions under which this fierce fight is taking place. [...]

11/7/1918.

I received yesterday your two letters of November 2 and 3. Before responding to them, I will tell you that I had lunch yesterday with the Baronness, an excellent lunch, [...] then we rehearsed a bit the Lekeu Andante, the "Kreutzer," and the *Rondo*.[305] About 3:30, Commander Bouteville, Captain Pivier, and Lieutenant Le Coconnier arrived and a bit later a Belgian general who commands the heavy artillery to our left. [...] We have agreed to play again on Saturday. We have to hurry, because we will be leaving, probably on Sunday. Of course, we are advancing. [...]

I would never take a position as professor in Belgium. [...] The Belgians pay very little and that will not change. In America, the situation is different. Still, I would prefer as much as possible to continue performing. It will take me at least 6 to 8 months of rest and careful work. Then we will see. Caplet will want me to be part of a group he hopes to create, a group of former combatants supported by a journal. That is tempting, for the struggle and also for the artistic interest it will present. I've thought a lot about the resumption of normal life; the projects we may design here will, no doubt, not be what happens. [...]

11/9/1918.

I could not write yesterday because of our movement; we left in the morning and only arrived about 12:30, in a tiny village where we had to find places to stay. [...]

We are here only for a short time; tomorrow morning we are going forward to take our combat positions. It's a matter of taking Gand, and that will again be a devil of a task. We are with the Americans, a lot of them, young and passionate. While waiting, they've attached them to the old, heroic 5th DI, which will again have a very difficult task—to cross the Escaut, in small boats under protection of a rolling barrage. In short, a difficult and delicate operation. For the moment it is no longer a matter of music, all that is in one of my large pigeon baskets where, with all sorts of clothes, my violin sleeps soundly. [...] The roads are flooded with an enormous line of artillery convoys and that explains why this is taking so long. At least we managed to eat last night, mutton chops and beans. That was the only real meal of the day. [...]

11/10/1918.

I received last night two letters, one delayed from November 4 and one from the 7th. [...] We have moved and are now in the area of the fighting. Along with Maurice, Eugene and Asseline, I managed to find lodging in the home of some

---

[305] Saine-Saëns.

peasants, with good straw, in a nice, closed room. We are lucky as we are in the midst of nowhere and a lot of officers do not have lodging. [...]

11/11/1918.

Finally, the armistice was signed this morning about 5 a.m., the news arriving by TSF that hostilities were ended as of 11:00. It is crazy to see the widespread joy here, it's like being drunk.

We attacked again last night, and sadly, there are, once again, some who left their lives there. At this moment of the end of the war, I am thinking of all the friends who fell, of the long suffering we've all gone through, and I am deeply shaken by so many sacrifices. Only the future will be able to tell, try to explain, without being able to, the amazing strength of spirit we all showed, in conditions that no man had ever known. For now, my heart is too full to say any more. It is with thankfulness that I turn to the forces that, so obviously, protected and sustained me through such dreadful ordeals. We may still be separated for a good period of time but, at least, death is no longer prowling around me. Many big hugs my dear, beloved little kitten.

Monday, November 11, 1918. 3:30 in the afternoon.

I did not hear from you this morning. I think I will have the pleasure of reading you at 4 p.m. Finally, the armistice with its conditions is accepted by the Germans. Peace will be signed. The war is therefore over in terms of hostilities. The soldiers of the oldest classes will return to their homes. [...] What did Ludendorff's resignation do at this critical time for the Germans? It simply meant that this man, knowing the situation of his country and its imminent fall, withdrew so that his already crumpled pride would not suffer a greater shame! It is said that the *poilus* will keep their helmets as a souvenir; I do not know what inscription will be engraved on them. The gun thundered at 11:15 this morning to announce the armistice to the population—not 101 cannon shots, but perhaps 25. Paris must be all decked-out. You're probably going to play more than ever. In Belgium there will certainly be parties. [...]

Wednesday, November 13, 1918, 6 p.m.

This morning I received your letter from November 11, an immortal date in the annals of history, ending this horrible, cruel war which surpasses anything that had come before in terms of barbarism, ruin, and despair. Alas, the dead number in the millions, the sick and crippled also in the millions. Those who have been in the midst of this inferno from the beginning and are getting out of it unhurt have to thank the heavens, each day of their life, to have gone through such a hell without being hit. We cannot believe it is the end of the evil; I am stunned, and my joy is sad, if those two words can be put together. There has been so much suffering we don't dare believe our loved ones are coming back. [...]

11/13/1918.

I received yesterday your letter of the 8th but could not write; we moved from Papelenkasteel, a forgotten place that is nowhere, in the canton of Nazareth. We will stay here 2 or 3 days before moving forward; without any doubt, we will go as far as the banks of the Rhine. [...]

Joy is everywhere, and on all sides; at night you see colored rockets in the sky. Using up the stocks of ammunition creates amazing fireworks. I hope you will send me *L'Information* because right now, more than ever, their articles interest me. The war thus ended on the 11th; the 14th would have marked 4 years since I arrived at the front. [...]

11/14/1918.

It is exactly 4 years ago today that I arrived at the front; that is an anniversary I will remember. I will always keep the image of my arrival in Muizon in the pouring rain. I received this morning your letter of November 11. [...] I am not telling anyone of my projects, which I keep to myself. The first thing to do is to get to work and prepare as much French music as possible. [...]

I will push Caplet to finish his work for solo violin. It might be good for me to be part of an association of modern music. [...] I will have to find places to play. We can talk about all that; unfortunately, it will take more than two weeks for me to play in public with my former brilliance. Although there is no doubt that I am more seasoned in terms of talent, my technique needs to be cleaned up and put back in shape. [...]

Saturday, November 16, 1918, 6:30 p.m.

[...] November 14 makes four years that you have been at the front. [...] I think it is finally over. Peace with all the rigorous demands will be signed by the Germans. [...]

You will definitely need to work up a repertoire of French music; French musicians will be in demand everywhere. Poland and Bohemia have always hated the Germans and will demand French artists, not to mention America, England, the whole world. To see and hear a musician who fought in the Great War will be the highlight of highlights. Impresarios will not hesitate to take advantage of the situation. [...]

On November 18, a French army will make their entry into Metz, on the 21st or the 22nd the King and Queen of Belgium will make theirs into Brussels, and on the 25th a French army will enter Strasbourg. [...]

The mail today has not yet arrived. I'm writing now because, although we don't yet have the orders, I think we will be leaving tomorrow morning. We will go 40 kilometers every other day, the *poilus* will do 20 km daily. I am not going to pack up my violin. I will take it with me as well as my music. We will be taking very little with us and a lot of things will stay here in storage. Again, I need to sort my things to see what I can take and make do with a small bundle. I don't know why they are causing us so much trouble; there are plenty of trucks. They could give each division one or two and all these complications would evaporate. One could say they are enjoying the possibility of annoying us. And they manage to think up ways to bother the *poilus* with marching, parading, exercises. That will not continue long: the *poilus* will say, "We fought the war, now all we want is to go home." [...]

Thursday, November 21, 1918, 6:30 p.m.

Since your last letter from November 16 which I received the day before yesterday, I have no news. I am quite worried because I read that the main train stations in Brussels were blown up and other explosions are feared. [...] The Germans are acting with the same baseness they showed throughout the war. I know that you were leaving for Brussels, so I am very upset not to know what has become of you. [...]

11/17/1918.

I am writing late this evening; we just arrived in a little town between Alost and Brussels. We leave again tomorrow. [...] I just received mail and in one of your letters there was a letter from Mme Tavernier and one from Mme Maréchal.

We had quite an adventure today. The truck we were in did not turn over, but two wheels ended up in the ditch; it took 3 hours of work to get it out which meant we did not get here until 4 p.m. having left at 9 a.m. [...]

I will never forget the way your dishonest tenants behaved. [...] Gevin-Cassal should respond, otherwise you take all your paperwork and go somewhere else. [...] We have to remember that you are now in the category of people who do not have 10,000 francs in income and, if the tenants do not pay, you have the right to receive from the state 50 percent of the rents. But you have to take the necessary steps and provide the paperwork. You will have to work on that. I will not be demobilized as quickly as you think. [...]

11/19/1918.

I received yesterday your two letters from November 15. [...] It seems that some *Boches* in Brussels refused to leave, and they blew up the train station and a bridge. We will have to knock some sense into those mutineers. Apparently, they are revolutionaries. You do not need to tell me to be careful. You can be sure that as long as we are in enemy territory, we seriously need to keep our eyes open and not let ourselves be tempted by solitary walks in the countryside. I will never go out unarmed. Speaking of defensive weapons (I don't have anything) I would like you to send me my hunting knife with its sheath which I can put on my belt. Do not send it yet, wait until I ask for it. [...]

We will all be going into Germany because, before the Armistice takes effect, we need to take the right bank of the Rhine and the bridgeheads on that side. The peace talks will then start and could take quite a long time. We will not demobilize before peace is signed. [...]

Friday, November 22, 1918, 5 p.m.

I received this morning your letter from November 17, and at 4 p.m. those from the 18th and 19th. [...] I am relieved to learn that you are headed for Cologne, even if it is far away. I feared that you were in Brussels. [...]

Certainly, we cannot demobilize until the peace is established, but it seems to me there are enough young soldiers to occupy Germany. The bad season we are entering is not very favorable for the constant moves you make, and it is bitterly cold for this time of year. Let's hope we don't have a winter like the one of 1916-17. [...]

11/22/1918.

I've not been able to write for two days. [...] I had to turn in all the pigeon-keeping material. And did I have a lot of difficulties! We received instructions on the 17th to take all the material to the train station in Tielt, but the person who sent the orders did not know that the division was going to be moving that day and for the next two days. [...] So, on the 20th I went to the corps to turn it all in; there they would not accept it. They sent me to the army in Ninove, another 40 kilometers on a wagon in the midst of heavy fog. In Ninove they gave me a hard time about all the other places I had been sent. Despite all the fatigue and annoyance, it became quite funny. Finally, after a huge argument with a commander of the engineers, I managed to leave all my stuff in the back of a hangar, and I'm convinced that no one will do anything with it. [...]

Tuesday, November 26, 1918.

Today at 4 p.m. I received your long letter from November 22nd. I think you exaggerate when you say you will be demobilized next April. It is terribly sad to think that our separation will last that long. I think you are mistaken. One might say you want to stay in the middle of that chaos. Sometimes I wonder whether your brain is not atrophying. It seems to me that you should want to be freed, first to get out of the quagmire you've been stuck in for over 4 years in order to work calmly, then to recognize that we are not in a very good situation. You can imagine that property owners will not fare well, far from it. They will turn to us for as much money as possible. All that looks very serious to me. We owe money, we have bills, etc. and what do we receive? You will have to make an effort to make money to get us out of this rut. It pains me to realize that you do not have any idea of the situation. [...]

11/23/1918.

We receive almost nothing because there is incredible traffic, and the roads are in dreadful condition. [...] Fifty percent of the cars have broken down. [...] Mail arrives every two days, barely, and our letters are not sent. There have been no newspapers for two weeks at least so we know nothing of what is happening. And worse, our supplies come by truck because the rails are not yet repaired. [...]

11/24/1918.

We are on the move again, but this time it was totally unexpected. Rather than move forward, we are heading toward the rear, apparently to join the 3rd Corps. [...] It seems that Corps is in Alsace, so you see what this move means. It is totally crazy, and everyone is complaining madly. [...] If we head for Alsace, that means at least two days in cattle cars—not funny in this season. And also awful, because of all these nonstop movements and the breaking down of equipment, we receive no more letters. It's been three days without any mail distribution; that becomes very sad. This life is very hard. [...]

11/25/1918.

Now it's four days without any letters. [...] We are heading backwards, into France. Every day we go about 15 or 20 kilometers. Fortunately, I am in a truck. [...]

Friday, November 29, 1918, 6:30 p.m.

This morning I received your letters from the 24th and 25th and one from M. Armengaud who is talking about resuming his lessons. You will need to earn money; we have a lot of debts. [...] I received an order to pay my taxes. As soon as I receive the rent from the houses in Vincennes, I will need to pay a prorated amount. I paid a small amount on account plus the charge for the money order. I have to fill out a sheet that indicates, year by year, what I received from the tenants. I wrote to the comptroller general to inform him of my situation, but I will not have a response for 3 months. [...]

11/28/1918.

We have arrived in Ruiselede, 8 kilometers from Tielt; we leave tomorrow for Roulers. It seems we are going to Dunkirk on foot; two days ago there was an order from General Headquarters suspending for a month all troop transport by rail to allow food to be taken to the invaded countries. From what they say, there will be rail transportation again once we arrive in Dunkirk, and from there we will head for Alsace or Lorraine. But that means another 8 to 10 days of moving. [...]

11/29/1918.

Roulers. Another leg of the trip done, this one was long. [...] This evening I am a bit tired; I'm going to down a nice hot bouillon and then go to bed. This morning I got up at 5 a.m. because we left very early, so my letter is not very long. [...]

Sunday, December 1, 1918, 5:30 p.m.

[...] December 5 is your birthday. You will be 40 years old and are still not free. Your sadness must be even worse. We are impatient for peace to be signed and hoping that normal life will be better. But what difficulties we will have with all our debts, how much will we receive? It's a nightmare that causes me much anxiety. [...]

Monday, December 2, 1918, 5 p.m.

[...] I am happy to learn that you will come home on leave for Christmas. Try to get here a few days early. That way you won't need to spend extravagantly with your friends and you won't be any worse off at home, actually you will be much more comfortable. I'm putting in my letter a Bengal rose and a white rose that bloomed just so I could send them to you for your birthday. May they bring you good fortune and us happiness. Only two bloomed, is that a sign? Accept them, my dear son, my beloved cat, so that you may return in good health, able to devote yourself to your art. [...]

11/30/1918.

I received last evening your letter of the 25th. I see that you are not receiving many of my letters. There is nothing I can say, the service is deplorable. Tomorrow we leave for Proven, near Poperinge. That will be December 1; by the 2nd we will be in France, in Cassel, and by the 3rd in Saint-Omer, at least that is what I think. We still have a way to go to get to Dunkirk; we will not be settled before the 8th or 9th. [...]

12/2/1918.

Today we will not have any mail; that was announced. Because of our movements, there was most likely no time to go get the mail. This morning we left about 8 a.m. from the Château de La Lovie, in Proven, and are now in Vermouth, a French town between Saint-Omer and Dunkirk. [...] The food is terrible; I'm not talking about us—we manage pretty well—but the *poilus* receive the bare essential. Some of the protests are beginning to be threatening. This way of living is totally stupid; we see no reason for all this annoyance. We are no longer facing the enemy and there is no reason for us to put up with this fatigue and hardship. [...]

Wednesday, December 4, 1918, 5 p.m.

[...] The first 6 months of 1919 will be very difficult, more so because nothing will start getting back to normal until the peace is signed. Life will be very hard for those of us in this mess. One no longer needs to be homeless to be miserable, we will all be in that situation. [...]

Thursday, December 5, 1918, 9 p.m.

[...] This afternoon, I went to the burial of Sassot, Mme Boissard's son-in-law. He was buried in the new cemetery in Vincennes which is so far away that we took the funeral tram to get there. I will visit Mme Boissard probably on Sunday and perhaps I'll see her daughter Suzanne at the same time. [...]

I think you are well despite the awful damp weather and the fatigue. I wish you again, today the 5th, happy birthday. I imagine you received the two roses from the garden that bloomed just for you. Very curious! May they bring you happiness and may you return to me soon, my dear son. That doesn't count your leave of 20 days. I heard that those who were awarded the *fourragère* could have an additional 5 days. [...]

12/4/1918.

I could not write because of our movement. We left for Pitgam and arrived about noon. We are surprised by how tiny this village is. It was immediately obvious that there was no place for the DI to stay here. Once the general arrived, they called the Army and, after some discussion, we left for Petite-Synthe, a large village 3 kilometers from Dunkirk. We arrived at 5 p.m., that is, in total darkness. I had the good luck to find a room with a good bed for 1,50 a day; this morning I feel well-rested and really cleaned up. We leave tomorrow for Gravelines where we are also supposed to stay for two days, then leave for Alsace. [...]

Saturday, December 7, 1918, 9 p.m.

[...] I see in the papers that the French armies will take up position in Mayence. If you go there, which is likely, please send me some postcards. That will bring back memories of our little trip from Frankfort to Mayence to hear Joachim in the Beethoven Quartets. [...]

12/7/1918.

I am writing this morning before the mail arrives; I am going to practice a bit. I am playing tomorrow for 11:00 Mass. [...] My fellow pigeon keeper, Asseline, got back from leave yesterday. He left on November 13; it took him 13 days to find us. [...]

I am going to try to leave before the 20th. It will not be easy because of the envy of everyone who would like to be home with family during Christmas and the New Year. [...]

12/8/1918.

Mail today arrived late, and I am writing without having received the usual news. [...] There is talk again of our departure, without specifying a day, and rather than the transportation they had promised, we may go on foot. This is becoming a joke, and no one is laughing. A trip like this in this season is really difficult. I don't know what the Chief of Staff is trying to accomplish, but if he thinks he is taking care of his men, he is seriously mistaken. No one can comprehend the weariness being forced upon us for no good reason. The *poilus* are saying: "When they needed us to go into battle, they managed to find transportation (trucks, cars, trains), now that they don't need us anymore, our feet are good enough." [...]

Tuesday, December 10, 1918, 5 p.m.

I received at 4 p.m. your letter from December 8. [...] I forgot to ask you whether you can bring some chocolate and coffee when you come on leave; there is a real shortage because of transportation problems. As for sugar, if you could get a little bit, please do. I am not telling you to load up like a pack animal, but some chocolate, coffee, and sugar would help me a lot. The coal merchant delivered 500 kg of wood; I was not expecting it because she always promised and never delivered. [...]

12/10/1918.

I didn't receive a letter yesterday. I hope you are in good health. The weather is still very rainy and we are lucky not to be on the roads. [...] I will see the commander today about my leave; alas, I know there are many jealous men who complain about my audacity to ask for leave before my turn.

For the moment, I am in charge of our food. [...] I bought 54 superb, live whitings. We will serve them in white wine for lunch and fried for supper. [...]

Captain Pivier proposed to take me to see Dunkirk for a day; the other day, thanks to a tramway, I spent a few hours there and realized how ugly the city is. I had no desire to spend 20 or 25 francs for no reason. One meal can cost 6 francs. At the mess, we spend 6 francs a day for all our meals. [...]

I hope that your next appointment with Gevin-Cassal will soon lead to a solution to the problems with our tenants and that it will bring in some money. [...]

Friday, December 13, 1918, 7 p.m.

I received this morning your letter from December 10. [...] Monsieur Gevin-Cassal told me that the peace would not be signed until spring. From the time the peace accord is signed, they give us another 6 months to get our affairs settled. His opinion is that we start now trying to do something, to enter into conciliation agreements by way of arbitration commissions. He realizes that owners are always the ones who have to sacrifice. Monsieur Lefèvre always urges me to try to make arrangements directly with the tenants because the arbitration commissions always favor the tenants. All these matters are complex and delicate and especially annoying for the one who has tenants. [...]

12/11/1918.

I received yesterday your letter from December 7. [...] I hear that the *Boches* are being difficult about giving back all the rolling stock (wagons and machines). [...] I think General Foch is not giving an inch in all this. [...]

12/12/1918.

I've won, and will leave right away, that is the 13th or 14th. I will then see Vincennes and we will be able to discuss all our business. [...]

Lucien's home leave lasted until just after the start of the new year.

533

1919

The Armistice, signed on November 11, 1918, ended the fighting. Not until the signing of the Treaty of Versailles, though, on June 28, 1919, was the war officially over. Lucien returned to Vincennes at the end of February of that year.

What had been gained by the four years of hostilities? What had been lost? France regained Alsace and Lorraine, lost to the Germans in 1870, but most of the northeastern part of the country was in ruins. Dozens of little towns were completely destroyed, some never to be rebuilt.

Human casualties were almost beyond comprehension. France lost about 1,400,000 men; the British Empire 1,115,000; the Italians 650,000; the Romanians 250,000; and the Americans 116,000. For the Central Powers, 2,000,000 German soldiers died, 1,500,000 Austro-Hungarians, 770,000 Turks, and 87,500 Bulgarians. The estimate of military dead worldwide is about 9,722,000. There were many more casualties than that among the wounded, some maimed and shell-shocked for life. About 950,000 civilians died from military action and up to 5,893,000 from war-related famine and disease.[306]

The Peace Treaty was drawn up almost entirely by American president Woodrow Wilson, French prime minister Georges Clemenceau, British prime minister David Lloyd George, and Italian prime minister Vittorio Orlando. The European allies wanted restitution; idealistic Wilson wanted peace.[307] The conditions were rigorous, the demands of reparations excessive in light of Germany's ruined financial state, and history tells the rest of the story.

Lucien was truly one of the luckiest: never injured or seriously ill, by and large protected from the most obvious danger, and remarkably free to be a serious musician. However, as the letters and his life after the war attest, he too was forever changed.

---

[306] Hart, *The Great War,* 469.
[307] Taylor, *The First World War,* 237-239.

The Letters

[...] I had a good trip. I arrived in Gravelines on the 5th at 8:30 a.m. It seems we will be here for the whole month, but truly no one knows anything. [...]

1/16/1919

[...] While I was on leave, our division, like all the others, received a flyer from Headquarters, signed by Pétain. It urged all the heads of the armies to organize concerts and theatrical shows to entertain the *poilus* and keep them from becoming Bolsheviks. That is laughable as an explanation. Captain Pivier, after checking with the Chief of Staff and learning I was not there, called for Delmas. He knew that he had been part of our group and asked him to organize a troop. [...] When I arrived, I found them hard at work but eagerly awaiting my return. [...] I took charge of all of that. [...]

1/19/1919

[...] At 5:00 we gave our concert for the Toris (rich arms merchants); only a few people, 20 in all, had been invited. We played the little Hadyn Trio and the Debussy Sonata, the *Chaconne,* and the "Kreutzer" Sonata. A splendid program that we played enthusiastically. It is not exaggerating to say that those present were blown away. Debussy with its strangeness, the *Chaconne* with its vast structure and rich sound amazed those people who, though they like music, had never heard anything like it. Few are those who truly love real music. For those rich, well-educated people from the provinces, great music is *Faust, Manon, Werther,* etc.[308] They can't imagine anything else, so they are startled to learn that there is music capable of moving the listener more perfectly and more completely. In short, it was an experiment which was, in a way, an eye-opener.

I hope to be demobilized at the beginning of March; I'm not hopeful that it will be any sooner. Despite what Clemenceau says, everything is moving very slowly. [...]

1/20/1919.

[...] After the war we will do just as we did. [...] My art has always been my principal concern. That will not change; I believe, quite logically, that my life

---

[308] *Manon* and *Werther* are well-known operas by Jules Massenet; *Faust* is an opera by Charles Gounod.

is lost. By that I mean creating a home and a family. I absolutely need to work; I need to re-establish my position. However fast I move, however much energy I put into my work, I know that it will be several years before I will reach that point. I will be 45 years old at that time. That is not an age at which I could accept just any sort of situation. What is more, you have suffered enough from the isolation and loneliness imposed by this war for me to subject you to even more. Besides, I have no desire be tied to a ball and chain, however golden. The question of my art is all that I will think about. It is possible that I will ask you to give me a bit more freedom than before the war when I was sort of on a leash as though I was eight years old. [...]

Acknowledgements

None of this book would have happened had it not been for the fortuitous common interest in French Baroque music of Georgie Durosoir and my husband, Louis E. Auld. So, I first should thank fate, as Lucien does throughout his letters. My gratitude to Luc Durosoir goes beyond his decision to publish some of his father's letters, to the endless hours spent transcribing Louise's letters and welcoming me into his family circle. This book takes his initial goal further than I could have imagined, and to a greater audience. Special thanks and recognition go to John Powell. A close friend of the Durosoirs and a musicologist himself, he prepared a wealth of material for a website that was never created and generously offered any part of that work for this book. I am grateful to the many people who have read the manuscript and had faith in this project, most of all Linda Laurent for her painstaking attention to musical detail and commas, to Joseph Acquisto for the letter that helped introduce this book to prospective editors, and to Louis Auld and David Steegar for continued encouragement. Finally, the people who eventually led me to Elizabeth Ford, my editor, and Blackwater Press: Leonard Smith, historian, and Charles McGuire, musicologist, both at Oberlin College; Alison Mero at Clemson University Press. And lastly to the editorial team at Blackwater Press for their enthusiasm. Finding them was truly a miracle!

Glossary

Bidon: metal can, of any size.

Boche: pejorative term for Germans, in English a "jerry."

Bougie Pigeon: gas-fueled candle, made by the Pigeon company

Brodequin: lace-up boots

Capote: greatcoat

Communiqué: press release, official government statement of events

Curé: parish priest

En subsistence: temporarily in the charge of a different regiment, for food and pay

Gourbi: shelter in the trenches, from Arabic meaning a poor one room dwelling.

Képi: soldier's cap

Mimi, minou: kitty, kitten,

Molletière: a strip of leather or cloth covering the leg from the ankle to below the knee.

Musette: canvas bag carried over the shoulder

Poilu: Literally, the hairy one, referring to the infantry soldiers in World War One

Popote: canteen, kitchen

Prêt franc: Money given to junior officers and other soldiers for living on the economy, both pocket money and for food.

Réchaud du soldat: a cooking stove. In this case, a metal support sitting on a can of solid alcohol.

Sape: a deep trench, sometimes covered but never underground, that permits movement without being seen; the trenches themselves, and the passageways leading from one to the other and to the rear, communication trench.

Saucisse: a large air-filled balloon tethered to the ground, used for observation, named after the sausage it resembled.

Works Consulted

Der Morgen Wiener Mondagblatt, 1909-1910. Durosoir family archives.

Duroselle, Jean-Baptiste. *La Grande Guerre des Français 1914-1918*. Paris: Librairie Académique Perrin, 1998.

Durosoir, Luc, *Lucien Durosoir barde et mage… un étonnement sans borne: Une rétrospective de la critique discographique*. Bélus:megep.net, undated.

Durosoir, Lucien and Maréchal, Maurice, *Deux Musiciens dans la Grande Guerre*, ed. Luc and Géorgie Durosoir. Paris: Tallandier, 2005.

Fierro, Alfred. *Histoire de Paris illustrée*. Toulouse: Le Pérégrinateur, 2010.

Hart, Peter. *The Great War: A Combat History of the First World War*. Oxford: Oxford University Press, 2013.

Kelley, Laura, "The Kreutzer Sonata: Love, Murder, and the Violin." Posted September 27, 2018, https://www.chambermusicsociety.org/about/news/the-kreutzer-sonata-love-murder-and-the-violin/

Lippa, Francis. "La Poésie inspiratrice de l'œuvre de Lucien Durosoir: Romantiques, Parnassiens, Symbolistes, Modernes." In *Lucien Durosoir: Un compositeur moderne né romantique, Actes du colloque*, ed. Lionel Pons. Albi: Éditions Multilingues Fraction 2013.

Myers, Rollo H. *Modern French Music*. Boston: Da Capo Press, 1984.

Meyer, Jacques. *Les Soldats de la Grande Guerre*. Paris: Hachette, 1996.

Nichols, Roger. *The Harlequin Years: Music in Paris, 1917-1929*. Oakland: University of California Press, 2002.

Pons, Lionel "Entretien avec Luc Durosoir." In *Lucien Durosoir: Un compositeur modern né romantique*, Albi: Editions Multilingues Fraction, 2013.

Ross, Alex. *Listen to This*. New York: Farrar, Straus and Giroux, 2010

Smith, Leonard V. *Between Mutiny and Obedience: The Case of the Fifth French Infantry Division During World War I*. Princeton: Princeton University Press, 1994.

Streletski, Gérard. "Entre Fatalité et Choix: La Vie de Lucien Durosoir," in *Mon
Violon M'a Sauvé La Vie—Destins de Musiciens dans la Grande Guerre*, ed. Georgie and Luc Durosoir. Paris: Lienart éditions, 2015.

Taylor, A. J. P. *The First World War: An Illustrated History*. London: Penguin Group, 1966.